Architecture, Ceremonial, and Power

THE TOPKAPI PALACE IN THE FIFTEENTH AND SIXTEENTH CENTURIES

گهر را سپردند بر مشتری
جهاندار ازان جام چون آفتاب
زخش گشت رخشان چو جام شراب

GÜLRU NECIPOĞLU

Architecture, Ceremonial, And Power

THE TOPKAPI PALACE IN THE FIFTEENTH AND SIXTEENTH CENTURIES

The Architectural History Foundation, Inc.
New York, New York

The MIT Press
Cambridge, Massachusetts, and London, England

Library of Congress Cataloging-in-Publication Data

Necipoğlu, Gülru.
Architecture, ceremonial, and power : The Topkapi Palace in the fifteenth and sixteenth centuries / Gülru Necipoğlu.
p. cm.
Includes bibliographical references and index.
ISBN 0-262-14050-0
1. Topkapi Palace (Istanbul, Turkey) 2. Architecture, Ottoman—Turkey—Istanbul. 3. Istanbul (Turkey)—Buildings, structures, etc. 4. Turkey—Courts and courtiers—Social life and customs.
I. Title
NA1370.N43 1991 91-12268
725′.17′0949618—dc20 CIP

Gülru Necipoğlu is John L. Loeb Associate Professor of the Humanities in the Fine Arts Department at Harvard University.

Designed by William Rueter

The Foundation gratefully acknowledges the assistance of the Samuel H. Kress Foundation in the production of this book.
Publication of this book has been aided by a grant from The Millard Meiss Publication Fund of the College Art Association of America. MM

FRONTISPIECE: Süleyman I presented with the mythical ruby cup of Jamshid on the eve of a campaign directed against the Safavids; the sultan is seated in a domed hall of the Topkapı Palace, with the third court's hanging garden and its marble pool seen in the foreground. From Arifi, *Süleymanname,* TSK, H 1517, fol. 557r.

Contents

TO MY PARENTS

If you seek wealth, go to India. If you seek learning and knowledge go to Europe.
But if you seek palatial splendour come to the Ottoman Empire.

Seventeenth-century proverb quoted in Philip Mansel, Pillars of Monarchy

Preface and Acknowledgements

This book grew out of a doctoral dissertation completed at Harvard University in 1986, and both works owe much to the generous help and support of many individuals and institutions. My very special thanks go to Oleg Grabar, whose enthusiastic guidance throughout the years, filled with many stimulating conversations, was a constant source of inspiration. His scholarship was what initially drew me into the field of Islamic art history by showing how intellectually exciting it could be. I am also grateful to James S. Ackerman, whose invaluable criticism and editorial suggestions were instrumental in transforming my dissertation into a book. It was he who perceptively urged me to merge two separate volumes, dealing with the palace in the fifteenth and sixteenth centuries respectively, into a continuous narrative. Invaluable, too, were the encouragement of Cemal Kafadar, with whom I shared ideas at every stage, and the constructive criticisms of Peter Brown, Howard Burns, Suraiya Faroqhi, Cornell Fleischer, Halil İnalcık, Norman Itzkowitz, Neil Levine, Lucette Valensi, and Irene Winter, who read and commented on all or parts of my dissertation.

I am also indebted to Şinasi Tekin, who demystified Ottoman paleography for me; Orhan Şaik Gökyay and Gönül Alpay-Tekin, who provided valuable assistance in interpreting some of the Ottoman Turkish and Persian poems; Mualla Anhegger-Eyüboğlu, for her readiness to share the observations she made as architect in charge of the restorations at the Topkapı harem; and Nurhan Atasoy, for her excellent guidance in the beginning stages of my research.

I would especially like to thank Filiz Çağman and Zeren Tanındı for providing a very warm and productive atmosphere in which to work at the Topkapı Palace Museum Library, where we exchanged many ideas and formed a lasting friendship, and to Ülkü Altındağ, at the Topkapı Palace Museum Archives, for her constant help. I appreciate the cooperation of the Topkapı Museum directorate and staff in enabling me to see various parts of the palace normally closed to the public, and in allowing me to study and publish primary sources belonging to the museum collection. I am also grateful to the directors and staff of the Prime Ministry Archives in Istanbul, the Archivio di Stato in Venice, the Istanbul University Library, the Süleymaniye Library, the Bibliothèque Nationale in Paris, the Österreichische Nationalbibliothek in Vienna, the British Museum and British Library in London, the University Library at Leiden, the Marciana and Museo Correr Libraries in Venice, as well as the Houghton Library of Harvard University, for allowing me to consult their manuscript and rare-book collections and helping me to obtain microfilms and photographs. I also appreciate Reha Günay's generosity in providing me with much-needed, high-quality photographs of the Topkapı Palace. Illustrations reproduced from published sources were photographed by John Cook, and photographs of buildings without credits are by myself.

Research and travel support were provided by grants from the Fine Arts Department at Harvard University and the Aga Khan Program for Islamic Architecture at Harvard and the Massachusetts Institute of Technology. A Mellon Fellowship at the

Society of Fellows in the Humanities at Columbia University in 1986–87 gave me the opportunity to begin transforming my dissertation into a book; it was during that year that I completely restructured my manuscript, weaving together its two separate components. The King Fahd Grand Prize for "Excellence of Research in Islamic Architecture," which was awarded to my dissertation that same year, also provided much encouragement. Finally, the Samuel H. Kress Publication Fellowship of 1989, awarded by the Architectural History Foundation, gave me the wonderful opportunity to concentrate full time on the completion of the manuscript for book publication, and allowed me substantially to increase the quantity and quality of illustrations and drawings.

The shape of the book owes much to Margaret Ševčenko's expert editorial efforts. It was she who helped me to condense the restructured manuscript into its present form. Without her collaboration I would not have attempted to rewrite my original text so extensively, formulating new interpretations in the process. The final manuscript reflects the subtle polishing and careful scrutiny of Eve Sinaiko, with whom it was a pleasure to work.

Finally, I thank my parents, Ülkü and Hikmet Necipoğlu, who kindled an interest in books and in art early in my childhood.

Gülru Necipoğlu
Harvard University, Cambridge, Mass.
1990

A Note on Transliteration, Translation, Dates, and Illustrations

Arabic and Persian words have been transliterated according to the system used in the *International Journal of Middle East Studies*. Modern Turkish orthography has been used for all Ottoman Turkish, except for direct quotations transliterated according to the system employed in the *Islam Ansiklopedisi*. Terms and titles with a direct English equivalent have been translated; those found in a standard English dictionary have been anglicized. Diacritical marks have been omitted from all Arabic, Persian, and Ottoman Turkish names appearing in the text. Names are only transliterated in the bibliography.

All quotations from primary sources were translated into English by the author, except for citations from published sources in translation, whose translators are noted in the bibliography.

The A.H. (*anno Hegirae*) dates of the Muslim calendar, with corresponding A.D. dates in parentheses, have been provided in quotations from original sources, inscriptions, and chronograms; otherwise only A.D. dates are used, without designation. Since the Islamic calendar is based on a lunar year, A.H. years do not neatly correspond to A.D. years; thus inclusive dates (e.g., 1526–27) are provided, except when the exact day or month is known.

Illustrations in the book are of two kinds: plates, at the back, and figures, interspersed throughout the text. The latter illustrate specific points made in each chapter, while the plates are cited repeatedly throughout the book and do not belong to particular chapters; thus, it seemed appropriate to organize them according to type and chronology, independent of the consecutive order of references made in the text. Therefore, a map of Istanbul is followed by photographs showing general views of the palace complex, plans and maps, panoramic views, and, finally, a multiple-image representation of a reception ceremony, showing ambassadors parading through the various courts of the palace.

Introduction

The curiosity of Westerners toward the "exotic East" has produced a colorful literature over the centuries about the Topkapı Palace in Istanbul, which served as the royal residence and the seat of Ottoman imperial administration for nearly four centuries. Although it is one of the most celebrated of all Ottoman imperial monuments, it is at the same time one of the least well understood. In the second half of the fifteenth century Sultan Mehmed II conceived its layout and had its major buildings constructed; in the sixteenth century it reached its definitive form, at the height of Ottoman power under Süleyman the Magnificent and his successors. Thereafter, for hundreds of years its basic structure remained astonishingly intact, despite continuous restoration and rebuilding, almost as if it were forbidden to tamper with its essential form. Not until the nineteenth century did the imperial message of the palace begin to lose its relevance, as the Ottoman state looked to Europe for its models and changed its traditional image. The palace was abandoned in 1853 for the neoclassical Dolmabahçe Palace.

Today the Topkapı Palace appears as a haphazard aggregate of modest buildings loosely grouped around courtyards, an agglomeration incapable of conveying imperial power, lacking as it does the monumentality, axiality, and rational geometric planning principles so characteristic of the Ottoman royal mosque complexes that we now automatically associate with power (Pls. 3–12). Why was it not conceived as a single integrated edifice of monumental dimensions? The answer is often sought in the alleged pious humility of Ottoman sultans, who are said to have preferred to concentrate their architectural patronage on magnificent religious complexes and to keep their palaces modest (see Figs. 9, 10). The problem with this answer is that the Ottoman sources do not regard the Topkapı as at all modest; on the contrary, without exception they look upon it as a symbol of imperial grandeur and a source of pride. Clearly their criteria for grandeur in palatial architecture were simply not the same as those used to assess socioreligious public buildings. What were these criteria that are no longer transparent to the modern observer?

Conspicuous consumption and exhibition of wealth were the indispensable ingredients of a high position in Ottoman society. The sixteenth-century historian Mustafa Âli writes in his book of etiquette that "neither is the sultan's palace suitable for a pauper, nor is the pauper's tiny cell becoming to the monarch of the age. The world-ruling sultan must build his palace on a site vast as a desert, so that he can show off and boast."[1] For Âli it was obvious that the sultan's palace visibly proclaimed the grandeur of the Ottoman dynasty and the "prestige of the empire."[2] The ruler was expected to live in a palace that reflected his glory, and clearly in its time the Topkapı was thought to have fulfilled that expectation, even if to the modern eye its imperial iconography is no longer apparent. Uncovering the semiotic processes through which the architecture of the Topkapı Palace was once given meaning is therefore essential to our understanding of its original significance.

Fortunately, an extraordinary wealth of both visual and literary source material makes the palace one of the most fully documented buildings in the Islamic world. Studies of Muslim palaces have in general suffered from the difficulty of correlating written and physical evidence. Few sources have been able to throw light on how the structural components of either excavated or extant palaces were used. The Umayyad "desert palaces," the Abbasid palaces in Baghdad and Samarra, the Fatimid palace in Cairo, the palatial complex of Madinat al-Zahra near Cordova, the Ghaznevid Lashkari Bazar in Afghanistan, the Seljuk palaces in Anatolia, and to a lesser extent the Ayubid-Mamluk palace in the Citadel of Cairo, the Nasrid palace of Alhambra in Granada, the palace of the Shirvanshahs in Baku, the Safavid palace in Isfahan, or the Mughal palaces in India all suffer to some degree from the same problem. The Topkapı is exceptional because both the monument and a wide variety of sources documenting its construction, its ceremonial, its institutions, and the life of its inhabitants survive.

The legendary fame of the Topkapı in the West —exemplified by its role in Mozart's opera *The Abduction from the Seraglio*—was the result of an endless stream of descriptions and illustrations by European visitors. These foreign sources are complemented by a rich array of Ottoman Turkish, Arabic, and Persian histories, poems written in praise of particular buildings, inscriptions, books of ceremonies, and miniature paintings that provide glimpses of the insider's view of the Topkapı Palace. They include fifteenth- and sixteenth-century chronicles by Kritovoulos of Imbros, Tursun Beg, Kıvami, Karamani Mehmed Pasha, İdris Bidlisi, Aşıkpaşazade, Neşri, Oruç, Ruhi Edrenevi, Kemalpaşazade, Bostan Çelebi (known as Ferdi), Lutfi Pasha, Celâlzâde, Nişancı Mehmed Pasha, Selaniki, Lokman, Mustafa Âli, and Peçevi, which provide important information on the palace and its ceremonial life. Anthologies of poems from the same period such as those of Ahmed Pasha, Tacizade Cafer Çelebi, Hamidi, Helaki, Kabuli, and Figani yield dates for individual buildings through their chronograms and provide insights about how contemporaries viewed the palace. The law codes (*kanunname*) of Mehmed II and later sultans, which are full of information on court ceremonial, can be supplemented by seventeenth-century treatises on the Ottoman court's organization such as those of Hezarfen Hüseyin, Koçi Beg, and several anonymous authors. A large number of miniature paintings in illuminated Ottoman historical manuscripts, particularly those of the *Hünername* (see Figs. 28, 35, 56), show the buildings of the palace and the ceremonies performed in them, establishing the intimate connection between the two.

The European visual sources include numerous panoramic and bird's-eye views of the palace. The earliest examples are a woodcut published in Hartmann Schedel's *Nuremberg Chronicle* in 1493 (Pl. 24); a map of Istanbul based on a lost late-fifteenth-century drawing, published in several sixteenth-century versions by Giovanni Andrea Vavassore (Pl. 23); the 1559 panoramic view of Melchior Lorichs (or Lorch), who accompanied a Habsburg embassy to Istanbul (Pls. 25a–f); several views, probably based on lost drawings by Lorichs, that Wilhelm Dilich published in 1606 (Pls. 26a–c), and many others from the late sixteenth century onward (Pls. 27–32). The most detailed depictions of the court ceremonial that went on inside the Topkapı Palace appear in two Austrian picture albums compiled by Lambert Wyts (see Figs. 29, 30, 43, 44) and Johannes Lewenklau (or Löwenklau, Loewenklau; Pls. 33a–q) in the last quarter of the sixteenth century, testifying to the fascination both the palace and its ceremony evoked in the West. These multiple, almost cinematic image sequences show how architecture acted as a stage for an elaborate ceremonial.

The European written sources for the years 1450 to 1550 are characterized by an abundance of Italian reports, thanks to the establishment of a permanent Venetian embassy in Pera (Galata), the quarter for Europeans in Istanbul. In the second half of the sixteenth century these are complemented by Austrian Habsburg, French, and English ambassadorial reports. European sources also include accounts of the palace and its institutional organization by men attached to the Ottoman court as merchants, slave pages, and dignitaries. To this category belong the *Stato del Gran Turco* of Iacopo de Campis Promontorio, a Genoese merchant who served the Ottoman court from 1430 to 1475; the *Historia Turchesca* of Giovanni Maria Angiolello of Vicenza, who was taken prisoner in the siege of Negroponte in 1470 and remained in the service of Prince Mustafa until the latter's death in 1474, and from then until Mehmed II's death in 1481 in the service of the sultan's court; and the *Cinque libri della legge, religione et vita de' Turchi* of the Genoese Giovantonio Menavino, who was presented as a slave to Bayezid II by a corsair and educated as a royal page in the sultan's palace between 1505 and 1514. From the same period is *De la Origine delli imperatori ottomani, ordini de la corte, forma del guerregiare loro, religione, rito et costumi de la natione* of Teodoro Spandugino, who came to Istanbul from Italy in the first decade of the sixteenth century to claim the property of his dead merchant brother, who had resided in Pera. He compiled information about the Ottoman court from two relatives who had converted to Islam and had become grand viziers, Hersekzade Ahmed Pasha, son of the duke of Herzegovina, and Mesih Pasha, a descendant of the imperial Byzantine Palaeologus family. Finally, *I Costumi et i modi particolari della vita de' Turchi* of Luigi Bassano da Zara is based on observations made during his long stay in Istanbul in the 1530s.

To these eyewitness accounts may be added a number of short treatises on the general organization of the Ottoman court, among them those of Benedetto Ramberti (1534), Junis Beg (1537), and Antoine Geuffroy (1542). Domenico Hierosolimitano's *Vera relatione della gran città di Costantinopoli et in particolare del Serraglio del Gran Turco,* written after he served as one of the palace's Jewish doctors between 1574 and 1593, was translated into Italian in 1611, from a lost original Hebrew text. Its Italian and French translations, published by Alfonso Chierici in 1621, Nicolò Mussi in 1671, and Sieur Lenoir in 1721, without crediting the original author, are an index of the interest the Topkapı Palace generated in Europe. Earlier, sketchy accounts give way in the seventeenth century to more systematic treatises on the palace, by then the acknowledged locus of Ottoman imperial power. The first treatise dedicated solely to the Topkapı was written in 1608 by Ottaviano Bon, the Venetian bailo in Istanbul; he was given a tour of its royal apartments by the head gardener's steward, while the court was away in Edirne on a hunting expedition. He was greatly impressed, and under its spell wrote his "Descrizione del Serraglio del Gransignore," which provides a general description both of the palace's architecture, and of its institutional system. An indication of its popular appeal is its two English versions, one by John Greaves (1653) and the other by Robert Withers (1625), and its seventeenth-century translation into French by Achille de Sancy.

Michel Baudier's *Histoire générale du Serrail, et de la Cour du Grand Seigneur, Empereur des Turcs, où se voit l'image de la grandeur Othomane, le Tableau des passions humaines, et les exemples des inconstances prosperitez de la Cour,* which was compiled in 1624 from earlier sources, including Hierosolimitano and Bon, is yet another indication of the exotic appeal the palace exerted in the West. It was a companion to Baudier's *Histoire de la cour du Roy de la Chine,* published in the same year and translated into English in 1635. Yet another French treatise about the Topkapı, Jean-Baptiste Tavernier's *Nouvelle Relation de l'Intérieure du Serrail du Grand Seigneur,* published in 1675, was an account of the author's travels, combined with information derived from two exiled treasurers of the palace, whom he had met in India. Tavernier was not impressed with the architecture of the palace, which to his eye did not compare to contemporary French palaces, so he concentrated on its functional and administrative organization.[3]

Another contemporary treatise on the palace is that by Albert Bobovi (Bobowsky or Bobrowsky, known as Ali Ufki), a Pole taken captive by the Tatars and sold to the palace, where he lived for nineteen years as a royal page specializing in music. Soon after his dismissal in 1657 he wrote the *Serai enderum cioè, Penetrale del Seraglio detto nuovo dei Gran Sgri e Re Ottomani,* which exists in Italian (1665), French (1666), and German (1667) versions.[4] He too concentrates on the functional organization of the palace, which he explains step by step, using a numbered schematic plan (Pls. 16a–b, 17). *Le Serrail des Empereurs Turcs ou Othomans,* written in the 1670s by François de La Croix, a secretary of the French Embassy in Pera, derives its information from people who lived in the palace and from the historian Hezarfen Hüseyin, who had close connections with the European community of Istanbul. Its author wanted to "rendre compte exact de ce grand Serrail qui a fait jusqu'à présent tant de bruit dans le monde." La Croix was also unimpressed by the architecture of the palace and found its institutional organization more admirable than its buildings, however fabulous their reputation.[5]

Most of the seventeenth-century French accounts of the Topkapı were written for Louis XIV and, not surprisingly, unfavorably compare the architecture of the sultan's palace with the perfectly symmetrical, monumental palaces of contemporary France. Though these authors were unable to understand the architectural language of the Ottoman palace in its own terms, they display a particular interest in the ceremonies and functions of the Grand Seraglio, which resembled a republic, with its peculiar rituals, customs, and fixed codes of behavior. Louis, fascinated with "Oriental despotism," commissioned similar reports about the palaces of Safavid Iran, Mughal India, and China, which he used to rationalize absolute monarchy in France. The Topkapı Palace, the microcosm of the "despotic" Ottoman empire, with its enslaved pages, sequestered harem, and cruel eunuchs, could be made to contrast sharply with the benign ideals of the absolute monarchies in the West.[6] The palace of the sultans, which came to represent the otherness of the East, continued to attract the curiosity of European observers during the eighteenth-century craze for *Turqueries.* A stereotyped representation of it, colored with vivid images of extravagance, decadence, and unbridled sensuality, became an almost obligatory *topos* in eighteenth- and nineteenth-century Orientalist travel literature and painting, becoming forever embedded in the Western collective memory.

There is also a rich corpus of archival documents, both Ottoman and European, on the Topkapı Palace. Complementing the *relazioni* of Venetian diplomats published by Eugenio Albèri, Nicolò Barozzi, and Guglielmo Berchet, and Marino Sanuto's *I Diarii* (1496–1533), are volumes of unpublished *dispacci* from Pera, preserved in the Venetian state archives. The reports of French diplomats published by Ernest Charrière and those of the Austrian Habsburgs published by Anton von Gévay do not exhaust the wealth of documents in the national archives of France, Austria, and England. The Ottoman archives supply imperial decrees documenting the construction, repair, and decoration of palace buildings; account books of royal expenses and of construction activities; royal donations to artisans and architects; payroll registers; inventories of palace furnishings; treasury inventories and books of ceremonies, most of which are used for the first time in this book. Although there are gaps in the documents preserved in the Topkapı and Başbakanlık archives in Istanbul, and they have not yet been fully catalogued, the wealth of information they provide is unparalleled in Islamic historical and art-historical studies. Records on the fifteenth and sixteenth centuries are relatively scarce compared to later periods, but still document the general sequence of construction and repairs reasonably well.

Earlier studies on the Topkapı Palace have not used primary sources systematically. Instead, they have taken its present form as their point of departure, and lumped together its four centuries of existence without establishing the chronology of its construction and its original layout during its formative period. In doing so, they have cited sources erratically, ignored or misinterpreted aspects of the complex, and in general drawn many false conclusions.

The earliest study on the palace by the last Ottoman official historian, Abdurrahman Şeref, appeared between 1910 and 1911 as a series of articles titled "Ṭopḳapu Sarāy-i Hümāyūnı" (the imperial palace of Topkapı). Şeref provides a general history of the buildings, recounts historical anecdotes, and records the major inscriptions. His schematic plan (Pl. 13) is one of the earliest drawings we have of the entire palace complex. It is more detailed than Antoine Ignace Melling's sketchy early-nineteenth-century plan (Pl. 14) and, unlike

Cornelius Gurlitt, an architectural historian who was granted permission in 1910 to draw a plan of only the second and third courts (Pl. 15), Şeref was able to include the harem and outer gardens.

The historian Barnette Miller was given permission to make another plan of the harem between 1916 and 1919, published in her 1931 book *Beyond the Sublime Porte,* which traces the history of the Topkapı Palace from its foundation to its abandonment as a royal palace. Miller devotes her attention to political institutions and historical episodes rather than to architecture. Her book is, she says, "a historical sketch of the palace and of a few of its institutions and activities, and not in any sense an archaeological or architectural treatise, for which the time and the opportunity are not yet ripe."[7] Despite its limited and sometimes outdated architectural information, Miller's study brought together for the first time a large number of European sources, and, with its extensive bibliography, it is still the best general introduction to the palace. Another book by the same author, *The Palace School of Muhammad the Conqueror,* deals with the Topkapı Palace as an educational institution, again with little reference to its architectural history.

N. M. Penzer's *The Harem: An Account of the Institution as It Existed in the Palace of the Turkish Sultans with a History of the Grand Seraglio from Its Foundation to the Present Time* written in the 1930s, before much of the palace had been restored, draws on the European travel literature introduced by Miller in an uncritical manner, and lacks rigorous historical method. Fanny Davis's *The Palace of Topkapı in Istanbul,* written in 1970, after the palace had been restored, updates Miller's architectural information and provides more accurate plans. However, its aim is to provide an informative tour through the present palace museum, and its descriptions of architecture and objects on display are sketchy and anecdotal.

E. H. Ayverdi was the first architectural historian to investigate the formative period of the palace, in his survey on fifteenth-century Ottoman architecture during the reign of Mehmed II, first published in 1953, and revised in 1974. Unlike the works of Miller, Penzer, and Davis, which rely primarily on European sources, Ayverdi conveniently compiles relevant passages from Ottoman chronicles and bases his remarks on the restoration of the palace in the 1940s. His failure to coordinate this information with the European sources results, however, in an incomplete picture.

S. H. Eldem's *A Survey of Turkish Kiosks and Pavilions*, published between 1969 and 1973, includes hypothetical reconstructions of kiosks in the Topkapı Palace, based on information from both European and Ottoman sources, visual and written, combined with a careful study of the archaeological remains. This crucial and truly groundbreaking work, richly illustrated with European engravings, Ottoman miniatures, old photographs, plans, cross-sections, and elevation drawings, introduces archival documents into the study of Ottoman palace architecture for the first time. Unfortunately, S. Eldem and F. Akozan's 1982 book *Topkapı Sarayı: Bir Mimari Araştırma* (The Topkapı Palace: An Architectural Study), exhibits less rigorous archaeological and textual research. Its text adapts Şeref's articles into modern Turkish, excerpts selections from Tayyarzade Atâ's nineteenth-century history of the palace school, and provides a brief survey of individual buildings. To its introductory text is appended a catalogue of plans, drawings, prints, photographs, and hypothetical reconstructions, which are insufficiently annotated with short explanations. Despite the shortcomings of the text, however, this is a very useful compendium of visual documentation. Together with Eldem's earlier survey of pavilions, it prepares the basic groundwork for the present book.

In this volume, I have tried to integrate the information contained in the Ottoman and European sources with that derived from the actual architectural remains; I have not attempted to provide an archaeologically exhaustive description of every structure in the palace, nor to present a detailed analysis of its complex institutional organization, but rather have aimed to interpret its architectural program within the specific historical context of its formative period in the fifteenth and sixteenth centuries. Surprisingly, there has been no previous attempt to trace the building history systematically, or to understand the overall imperial symbolism of the Topkapı Palace. The palace is undoubtedly a monument of major importance in the field of Islamic architectural history, particularly since it is a field dominated by the study of public religious monuments, given the scarcity of palaces that have survived abandonment or destruction by successive dynasties. For this purpose, I have used a wide range of primary sources and unpublished archival documents to reconstruct the palace complex, whose naked shell is now hardly more than a dim reminder of its original form, and to bring it back to life, insofar as that is possible without the supporting evidence of much-needed archaeological investigations. I have tried to relocate the palace complex in its original context: this consists not simply of the circumstances of its patronage but also of the complex interaction among the different cultural practices, ideologies, and socially constructed codes of recognition from whose dynamics its structure is now removed.

The palace once served as a vast stage for the enactment of a ceremonial, codified down to the smallest detail, whose symbolic language emphasized the elevated status of the sultan vis-à-vis his subjects, his dignitaries, and the representatives of foreign powers who came to his court. This rigid ceremonial, formulated by Mehmed II and elaborated by Süleyman I, emphasized the aloof nature of the sultan's relationship with the outside world and clearly distinguished the accessible from the inaccessible zones of the palace. Consisting of a series of increasingly secluded courts culminating in an inaccessible royal residence, the palace was experienced in a processional sequence through which its separate courts and seemingly disjointed architectural elements were integrated into a cumulative, coherent whole, with passage through space and time as the binding glue (Pls. 10–12). Ceremonial movement articulated and highlighted the imperial architectural iconography of the palace, adding a narrative dimension to its hierarchically ordered spaces, which drew the observer from one clearly marked ceremonial station to another.

The first two public courts, which housed various administrative functions, acted as a theatrical setting for a ceremonial in which the status hierarchies of an imperial state were dramatically acted out, both to impress foreigners and to reinforce the ideology of absolute monarchy at home. The innermost, secluded third court, divided into male and female sections, was more than a royal residence; in it, the sultan's obedient slave pages lived and were educated by tutors, under the close surveillance of eunuchs, to occupy high positions as bureaucrats in the centralized imperial government. The young slave pages and concubines, dwelling in separate dormitories in the strictly delineated male and female zones of the third court, were educated in a common court culture and eventually married off to one another to constitute the loyal ruling elite of the empire. This palace school, in which the sultan and his family also resided, was surrounded by royal gardens studded with pavilions and fountains that acted as an extension of the sultan's private realm.

Simultaneously functioning as a stage set for the representation of dynastic power, as the administrative center for a vast empire, as a palace school, and as a residence for the royal family, shrouded in a veil of secrecy, the palatial complex was a collection of workshops, armories, hospitals, stables, kitchens, bakeries, baths, audience halls, treasuries, libraries, archives, small mosques, dormitories, pavilions, sports grounds, zoological parks, pools, fountains, and gardens, housing thousands of inhabitants grouped according to the inner (private) and outer (public) services of the royal household. It carved a vast space from the city to accommodate all this, and conveyed its imperial message not through the dominating verticality of a single monument, but rather through the sheer horizontal expanse of its numerous buildings, the concrete sign of a complex institutional organization maintained by an impressive hierarchy of servants and attendants.

The palace museum as it exists today, an empty stage, is generally assumed to be the result of a gradual accretion of buildings, the whim of successive sultans over the centuries. Its early history soon reveals, however, that the basic layout remained as it was first conceived, from the very beginning, even after centuries of remodeling, be-

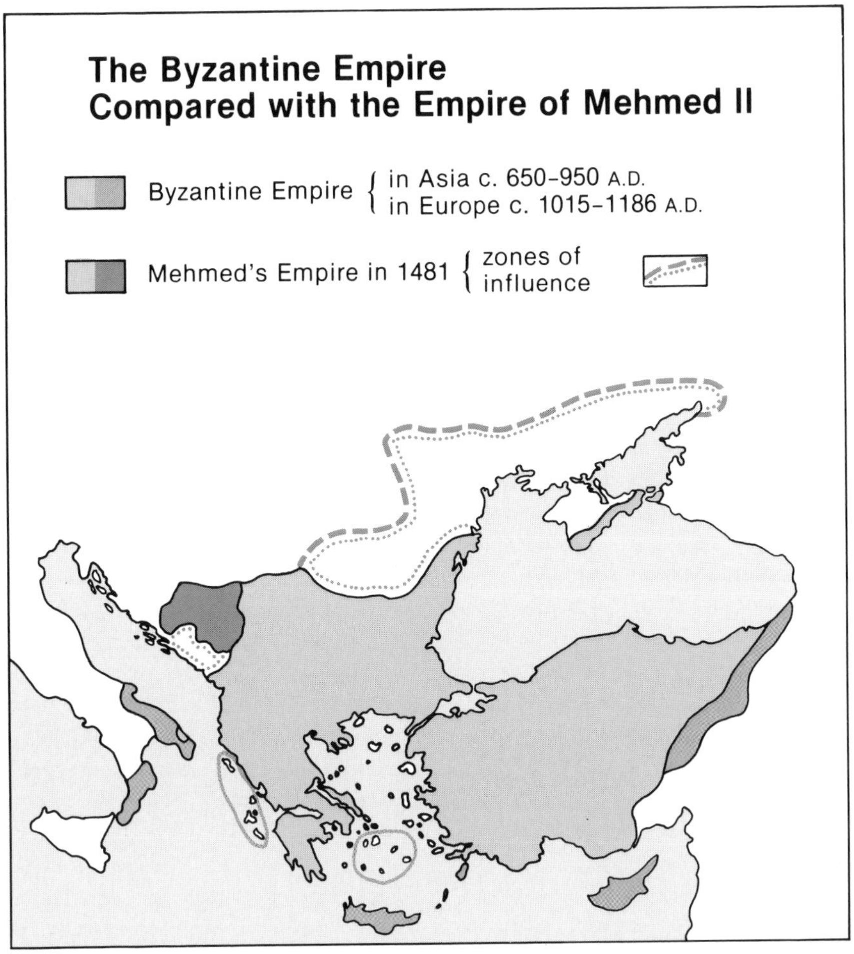

Map I Comparative map of the Byzantine Empire and the Ottoman Empire at the time of Mehmed II. Adapted from Pitcher, *A Historical Geography of the Ottoman Empire.*

cause the imperial symbolism encoded in its ceremonial and institutional organization tolerated little change. Its unchanging structural skeleton embodied an Ottoman language of imperial power. This I have analyzed by reading the complex architectural discourse of the palace in terms of how it originally functioned, how contemporaries perceived it, and how it reflected an Ottoman concept of sovereignty.

There is an interconnection between the architectonic structure of the palace, its ceremonial, and the centralized state it served; the Topkapı as a whole embodies a uniquely Ottoman imperial tradition invented in the fifteenth century and consolidated in the sixteenth. Its functionally fixed architectural skeleton and its endlessly reenacted ceremonial concretized a political structure and a concept of sovereignty which became almost synonymous with Ottoman rule itself. The palace housed and shaped a centralized system of imperial government administered by the sultan's household slaves *(kapıkulu),* a mechanism adopted to ensure autocratic central power by preventing the rise of a hereditary aristocracy challenging

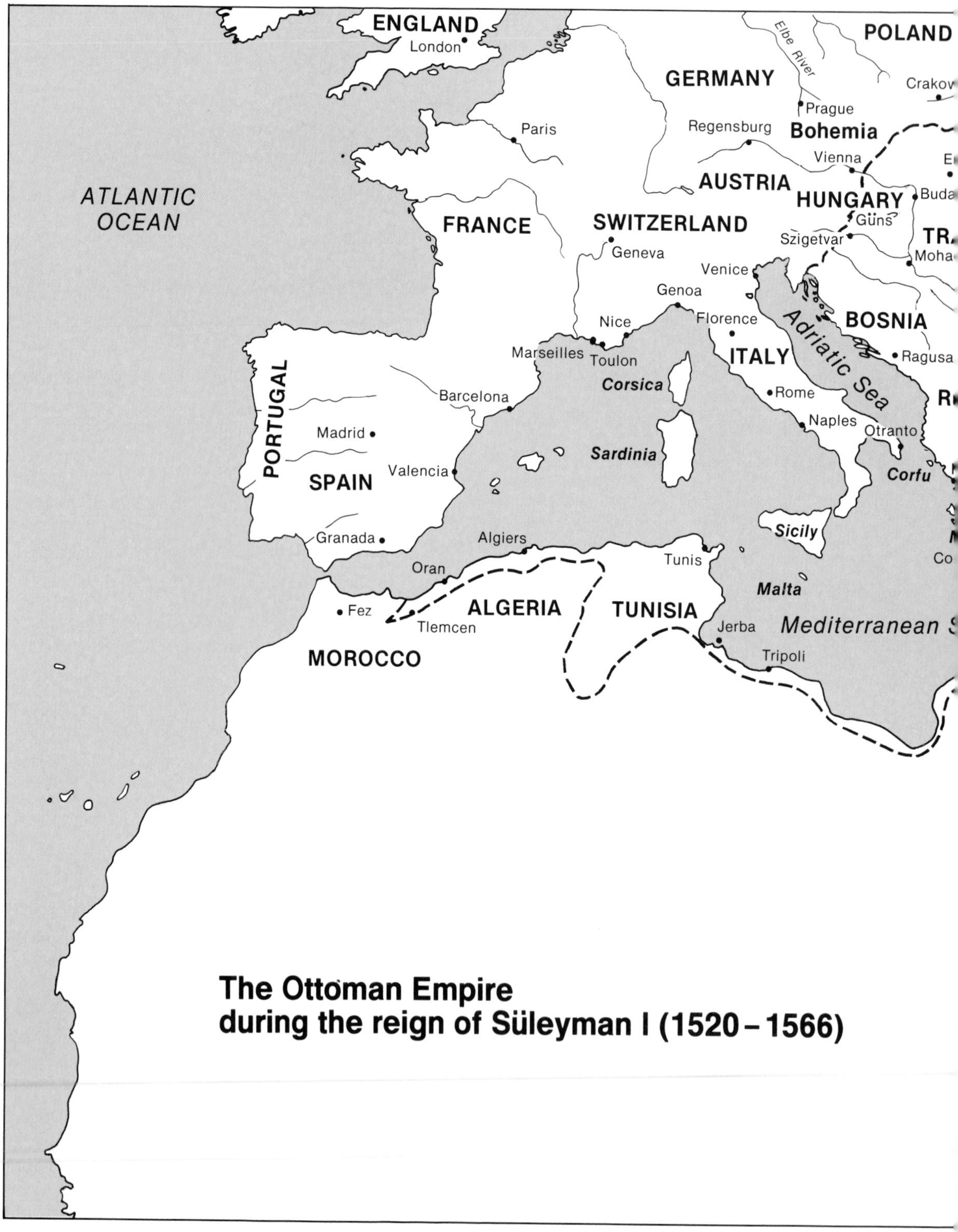

Map II The Ottoman Empire in the age of Süleyman I.

CENTRAL ASIA
Podolia
Kiev
Don River
Volga River
Dnieper River
DAVIA
IA
Azov
Azov Sea
Astrakhan
Aral Sea
Oxus River
HIA
CRIMEA
Kefe
Bucharest
Caucasus
Black Sea
TURKESTAN
Transoxiana
Edirne
İstanbul
İzmit
Bolu
İznik
GEORGIA
Caspian Sea
Shirvan
Jaxartes River
Bursa
Ankara
Amasya
Trabzon
Kars
Revan
Sivas
Erzurum
Manisa
Kütahya
Uşak
Kayseri
Çaldıran
Tabriz
Gilan
Samarkand
Bitlis
Van
Anatolia
Konya
Diyarbakir
AZERBAIJAN
Kazvin
Sultaniye
AFGHANISTAN
Aleppo
Mosul
Rhodes
SYRIA
Hama
Homs
Euphrates River
IRAQ
Herat
IRAN
Cyprus
Damascus
Baghdad
Tigris River
Isfahan
Yazd
Alexandria
Jerusalem
Cairo
Sinai
Basra
Shiraz
EGYPT
Nile River
Arabian Gulf
Hormuz
Hijaz
Medina
Arabian Sea
Mecca
ARABIA
Red Sea
SUDAN
Sanaa
YEMEN
INDIAN OCEAN
ETHIOPIA

the supremacy, legitimacy, and continuity of the Ottoman dynasty. The permanence of its architectonically and institutionally frozen deep structure resulted in the repetitive automatism of a centralized state machine.

This book both analyzes the multileveled architectural discourse of the Topkapı Palace and raises questions about the ideology of sovereignty, the meaning of court ceremonial, the interplay between architecture and ritual, gender zoning, public versus private life, and the perception of a building by contemporary audiences. In the first chapter the building program of the palace and the codification of its ceremonial are placed in the context of a historical process of empire formation, sedentarization, and centralization of power that culminated in a new imperial image and concept of state. The chronology of construction is established, the role of royal patrons, architects, and decorators (Ottoman, Arab, Persian, and Italian) in its creation discussed, and the symbolic significance of its site on the ancient Byzantine acropolis interpreted.

In subsequent chapters the aesthetic and ceremonial impact of the palace is reconstructed through a processional journey providing a step-by-step tour of its buildings. Since the complicated construction history of these buildings and their architecture has not been systematically studied before, and since there are various points of controversy in the scholarly literature, each of them is described in some detail with respect to architectural, decorative, epigraphic, functional, ritual, ideological, and symbolic considerations. It is hoped that this grand tour of the palace complex, reconstructed with the help of contemporaries (both outsiders and insiders) who either participated in its ceremonial or lived within its walls, will lead to a better understanding of its architecture as characterized by strictly delineated boundaries between public and private, exterior and interior, male and female, royal and nonroyal. The last chapter concludes with an interpretation of the imperial iconography of the Topkapı Palace within the broader context of other palatine traditions, mythical, Islamic, Turco-Mongol, Romano-Byzantine, and Italian Renaissance. These traditions are also discussed during the grand tour of the palace complex, with reference to specific buildings. In this concluding chapter the disparate themes and concepts developed throughout the book are knitted together into a synthetic account of the Topkapı Palace at the height of Ottoman power in the fifteenth and sixteenth centuries.

Architecture, Ceremonial, and Power

THE TOPKAPI PALACE IN THE FIFTEENTH AND SIXTEENTH CENTURIES

ONE

Construction of the New Palace and the Codification of Its Ceremonial

When Sultan Mehmed II made his ceremonial entry into the newly conquered city of Constantinople in 1453, one of the first places he visited was the great Cathedral of Hagia Sophia (Fig. 1). It filled him with awe. He then wandered through the nearby Great Palace of the Byzantine emperors (Fig. 2). The dilapidated state of these two great edifices led him to muse on the transitoriness of worldly power:

> The spider serves as gatekeeper in the Halls of Khosrau's dome
>
> The owl plays martial music in the palace of Afrasiyab.[1]

Although Mehmed soon had Hagia Sophia restored and converted into an imperial mosque, he neither renovated the ruins of the Great (or Sacred) Palace built by the emperor Constantine (324–27), adjacent to the Hippodrome, nor adapted for his use the fortified Blachernai Palace near the Golden Horn, to which the Byzantine rulers had moved their residence in the eleventh century. After spending less than a month in the vanquished city—long enough to arrange to have the city walls repaired during his absence—he returned to his recently completed New Palace in Edirne (Fig. 3), which was then still the Ottoman capital.[2] He had, however, already laid plans to restore the ruined city to the splendor it had boasted in the golden age of the Byzantine empire, and to make it his new capital.

When he returned the next year to Constantinople (which continued to be referred to as *Ḳosṭantiniyye* in imperial documents and coins throughout Ottoman rule, but soon came to be more popularly known as Istanbul), the sultan built a palace where a monastery had stood on the site of the fourth-century emperor Theodosius I's Forum Tauri (Pl. 1).[3] The fifteenth-century Byzantine historian Doukas tells us that when Mehmed "entered the City, he measured off an area, in the center, of approximately one mile and gave instructions for a courtyard to be marked out and for palaces to be constructed within. When the enclosure was completed, it was roofed over with lead tiles which had been removed from the monasteries which were left desolate."[4]

Kritovoulos of Imbros, another contemporary Greek historian, who dedicated his chronicle to Mehmed II, says that the sultan had a strong fortress constructed "in all haste" near the Golden Gate, where a Byzantine castle had stood (Pls. 1, 23). This is the stronghold of Yedikule. Later the same year, Mehmed returned to the city, where he also ordered the construction of a palace; he stayed there "just long enough to examine the buildings that had been constructed there, and gave orders about further work on them and on others, stipulating that it be done as quickly as possible." By 1455 the sultan "found the palace brilliantly completed, and the castle at the Golden Gate and all the walls of the city well built. He was pleased at what had been done, and rewarded the overseers of the work with money and robes of ceremony and many other things."[5]

Construction of this first palace in fact probably went on until 1458.[6] The finished group of buildings in an inner enclosure was subsequently surrounded by gardens, which were in turn enclosed by an unfortified outer wall (Figs. 4, 5). The contempo-

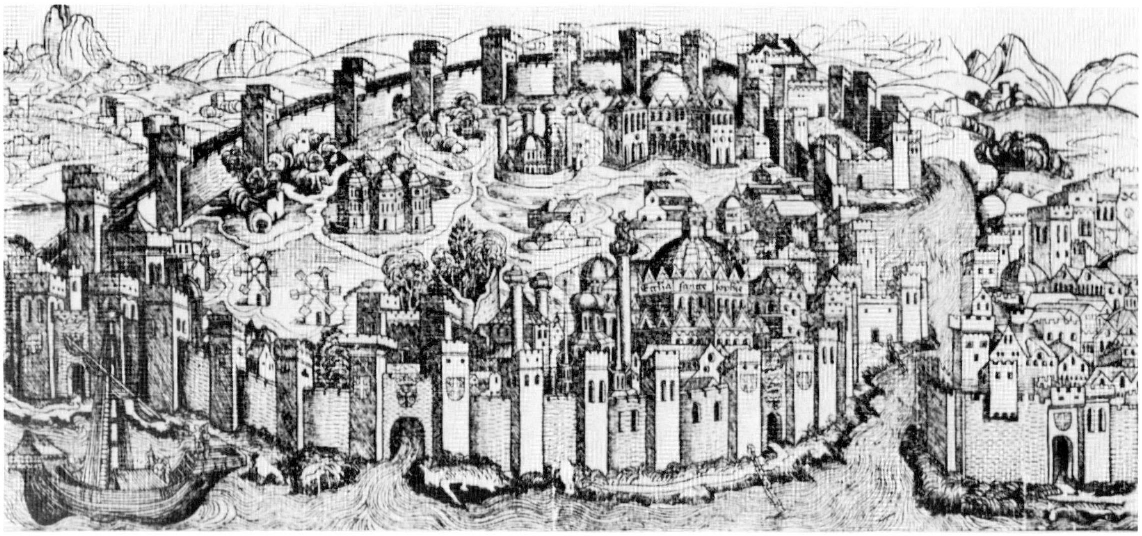

1 View of Byzantine Constantinople. From Schedel, *Liber Chronicarum*.

rary chronicler Tursun Beg tells us it had a well-protected harem, agreeable residential palaces and kiosks for the sultan and his pages, official council halls, and royal hunting preserves filled with numerous wild beasts.[7] Giovanni Maria Angiolello, who served at Mehmed II's court between 1474 and 1481, confirms the description and adds that the gardens, where animals roamed, fountains played, and birds nested in the reeds of a lake, boasted a monumental column with spiral decoration, erected by Theodosius I (modeled after those of Trajan and Marcus Aurelius in Rome) and a mile-long wall with four gates.[8] Giovantonio Menavino, who lived at the Ottoman court as a page between 1505 and 1514, counts twenty-five separate buildings, populates the garden with ostriches, peacocks, and other exotic birds, and doubles the length of the wall to two miles.[9]

Building Chronology of the New Palace and the Making of an Imperial Image

Soon after this palace was finished, Mehmed decided to build a new one. This is the one called the New Imperial Palace (*sarāy-i cedīd-i ʿāmire* or *yeñi sarāy*), or New Palace, in Ottoman sources up to the nineteenth century, and known as the Topkapı today (Pls. 1, 23, 24; Fig. 6); the palace on the Forum Tauri was then referred to as the Old Palace (*sarāy-i ʿatīḳ* or *eski sarāy*).[10] The 592,600-square-meter site Mehmed chose for this new project was the ancient acropolis of Byzantium, popularly called the *zeytunluḳ*, or "olive grove," although, despite its name, it was by that time at least partially a residential area. The sultan selected it after a consultation *(müşāvere)* with the leading engineers of the age and advisers who had traveled abroad (where they must have seen palaces of other monarchs), and after a survey was made to determine the availability of water and the cost of building there.[11]

Bidlisi, who wrote his history in the early sixteenth century, tells us that the sultan, after buying the properties he needed from Muslims and non-Muslims, ordered the grounds leveled and a series of stepped terraces built, incorporating the original retaining walls of the ancient acropolis, to counteract the steep slope that led from the hilltop to the sea. These stepped platforms are visible in the views published by Giovanni Andrea Vavassore

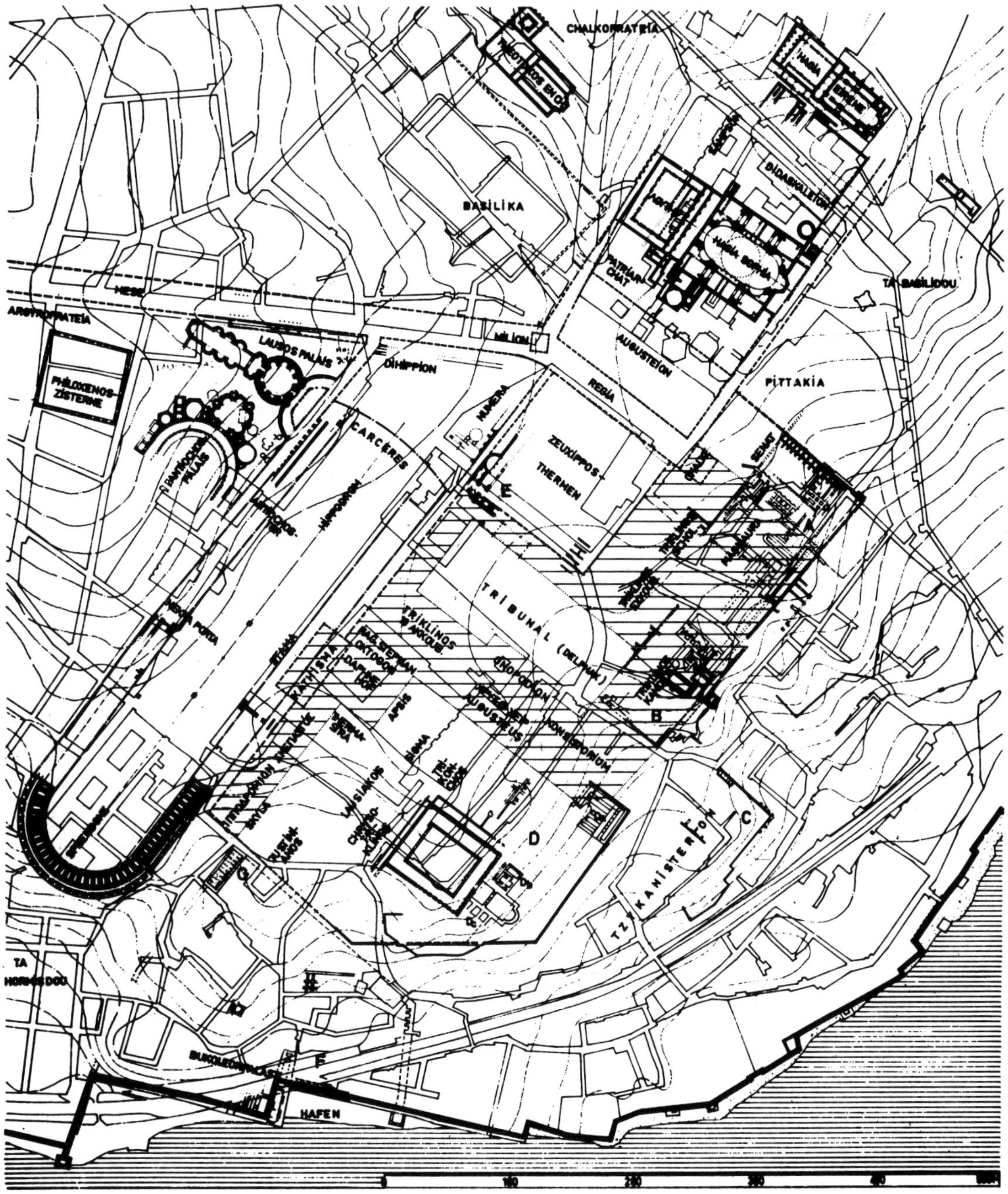

2 Reconstructed plan of the Byzantine Great Palace with the Hippodrome, Hagia Sophia, and the ceremonial avenue Mese. From Müller-Wiener, *Bildlexikon,* p. 232.

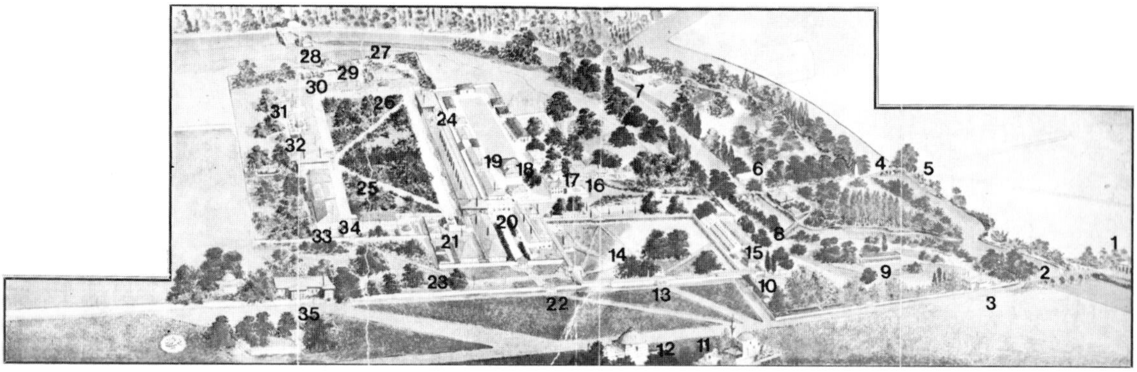

3 Plan of the Edirne Palace. From Osman, *Edirne Sarayı*, frontispiece foldout.
KEY: *1*. ‹İdiyye Kiosk; 2. bridge of Şehabettin Pasha; *3*. Kiosk Gate; *4*. bridge of Sultan Süleyman and Terazi Kiosk; *5*. Tekke Gate Avenue; *6*. Kiosk of Justice *(Adalet Kasrı)* and İftar Kiosk; *7*. Nightingale Kiosk; *8*. bridge; *9*. animal keep; *10*. dormitories of gardeners; *11*. mosque of Şehabettin Pasha; *12*. bath of Şehabettin Pasha; *13*. Imperial Gate *(Bab-i Hümayun)*; *14*. Court of Processions *(Alay Meydanı)*; *15*. imperial kitchens; *16*. Sand Kiosk; attached to a royal bath; *17*. Privy Chamber *(hasoda)*, known as the Belvedere Pavilion *(Cihannüma Kasrı)*; *18*. Inner Treasury; *19*. inner royal residence *(Enderun-i Hümayun)*; *20*. harem gate; *21*. quarters of the harem eunuchs; *22*. Gate of Halberdiers; *23*. dormitories of halberdiers; *24*. quarters of concubines; *25*. courtyard of the Queen Mother; *26*. residence of Mehmed IV; *27*. Hunting Kiosk; *28*. Kiosk of the Mill and the palace mill; *29*. Tebdil Kiosk; *30*. residence of Ahmed II; *31*. Imperial Hall *(Hünkâr Sofası)* and its bath; *32*. quarters of the Queen Mother; *33*. quarters of concubines; *34*. harem hospital; *35*. Kiosk of Processions *(Alay Köşkü)*.

and Wilhelm Dilich (Pls. 23, 26b). The main palace was built on the uppermost terrace on the brow of the hill. Here were the sultan's private quarters *(dār al-khilāfa)* and the council hall of justice *(īwān-i dīvān-i ‹adl)*, in the third and second courts respectively, of the three that ultimately comprised the palace complex, with the main gate of the whole complex facing Hagia Sophia. The inner core of the palace, along the spine of the hill, was surrounded by gardens studded with pavilions. From the hilltop, vineyards and gardens with kiosks cascaded down the slope to the seashore.[12] After the buildings and gardens had been finished, an outer wall and the monumental main Imperial Gate *(bāb-i*

4 (opposite) The Old Palace. From Giovanni Andrea Vavassore's map of Istanbul, published in Venice in 1520, based on a lost drawing from ca. 1479 (detail from Pl. 23).

5 Drawing of the Old Palace in Istanbul after it was rebuilt by Süleyman I, following a fire in 1541. From Dilich, *Eigentliche kurtze beschreibung*.

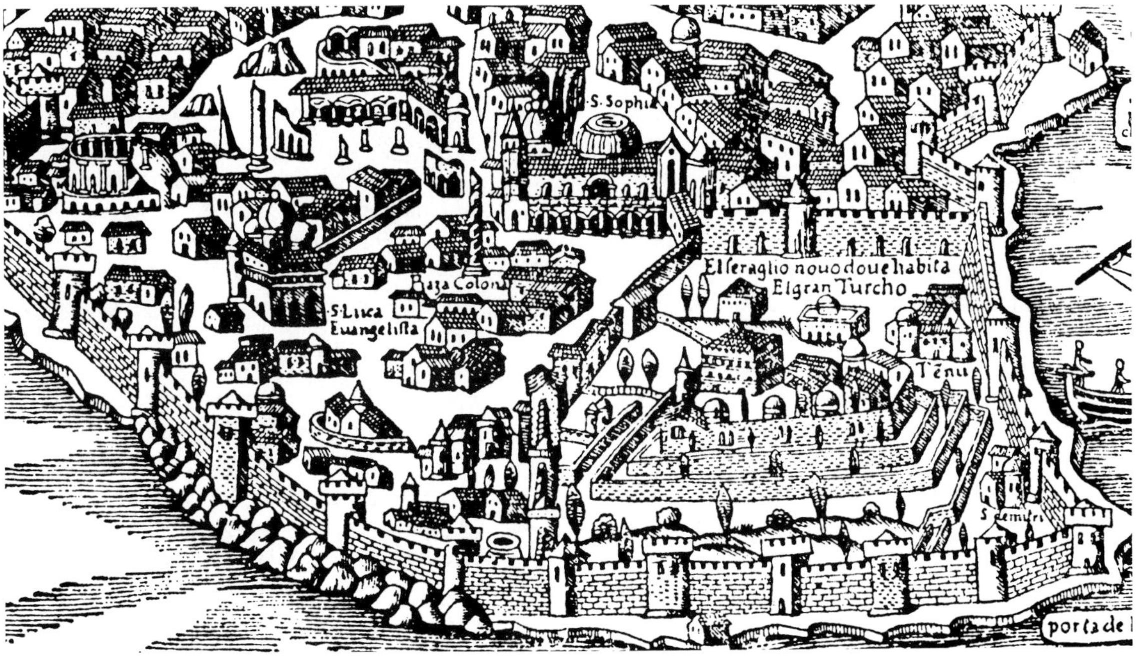

6 The New Palace, in Vavassore's Istanbul map (detail from Pl. 23).

hümāyūn) were added.[13] The gate's extant inscription and an Arabic document referring to the outer wall as the "Imperial Fortress" *(qalʿat al-sulṭāniyya)* both show that the fortress *(qalʿa)* was completed in Ramadan 883, that is, between November and December 1478 (see Fig. 22).[14]

When the outer wall was finished, an extra forecourt was formed between it and the inner core of the palace, which consisted of two courts that contained the major administrative and residential buildings of the palace. When the Genoese merchant Iacopo de Promontorio wrote about the palace in 1475, before the outer wall was added, he saw only these two courts.[15] The palatial complex gradually evolved into a processional sequence of three successive courts with three main gates, fronted by a walled hanging garden, and surrounded by an outer garden with kiosks contained in a castellated enclosure (Pls. 2a, 3, 10–12). The first two courts were reserved for the public services of the sultan's household, which regulated his relations with the outer world through governmental service buildings, offices, and an elaborate public ceremonial. The third court, lying beyond the third gate, which was the dividing line between the outer, public zone and the inner, private one, contained the residential quarters of the sultan, subdivided into male and female sections. The small fourth court of the hanging garden and the outer gardens with kiosks were extensions of this private royal domain.

It seems reasonable to accept Kritovoulos's date of 1459 as the foundation date for the whole complex, since he is our earliest source.[16] Evliya Çelebi, writing in the seventeenth century, gives the same date, 863 (1458–59), and claims to have copied it from an inscription, no longer extant, on the Imperial Gate.[17] Kritovoulos recounts that in that year the sultan decided to build an imperial mosque in the middle of the city, "which in height, beauty and size should vie with the largest and finest temples already existing there," and that he "also gave orders for the erection of a palace on the point of old Byzantium which stretches out into the sea—a palace that should outshine all and be more marvelous than the preceding palaces in looks, size, cost and gracefulness" (Pls. 1, 23).[18] These two ambitious building projects, representing the autocratic sultan's religious and royal authority, were part of his plan "to make the City in every way the best supplied and strongest city as it used to be long ago, in power, and wealth, and glory." Under the year 1460, Kritovoulos writes the following:

> When the Sultan had reached Constantinople, and had rested a bit, he gave attention to the situation in his realm and to arranging and renovating things everywhere, especially what was connected with his own palace. . . . He zealously directed operations on the buildings he was erecting on his own account—that is the mosque and the palace. He was concerned with the careful collection not simply of materials necessary for the work, but rather of those that were most expensive and most rare. He also took care to summon the very best workmen from everywhere—masons and stonecutters and carpenters and all sorts of others of experience and skill in such matters.
>
> For he was constructing great edifices which were to be worth seeing and should in every respect vie with the greatest and best of the past. For this reason he needed to give them the most careful oversight as to workmen and materials of many kinds and the best quality, and he also was concerned with the very many and great expenses and outlays. Besides, he had many overseers for these things, men who were exceptionally wise and experienced in such matters. Not only so, but he himself also made frequent inspection and watched over the work, doing everything very ambitiously and with excellent taste, altogether in the regal manner. That is how he acted about these things.[19]

This passage suggests that the first few years of work on the complex were taken up with collecting rare building materials, hiring skilled artisans, and organizing the project. This may explain why the construction dates inscribed on Mehmed's mosque complex, 867–75 (1463–70), give a somewhat later foundation date than the one given for both the mosque and palace by Kritovoulos.[20] Several sixteenth-century historians also supply a later

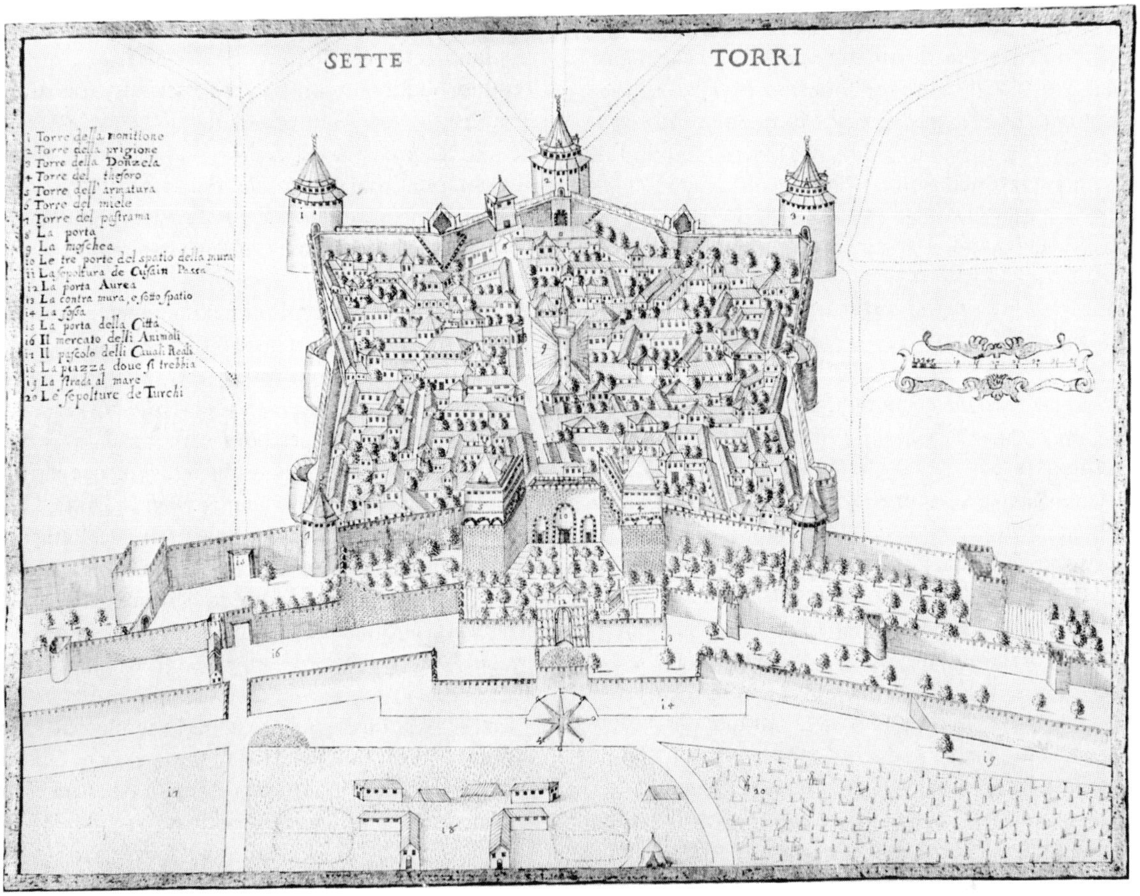

7 Francesco Scarella, drawing of the star-shaped fortress of Yedikule, 1686. MS. Vienna, Österreichische Nationalbibliothek, Cod. 8627, fol. 5r.

foundation date, around 866–67 (1462–63), for the palace.[21] Kritovoulos considers the main core already finished by 1465, but several other sources suggest that this section was actually completed in the late 1460s, including a chronogram invented by the sultan's grand vizier, Karamani Mehmed Pasha, and noted in his chronicle: "Sublime gardens and auspicious palace," which yields the year 873 (1468). Among these are Evliya Çelebi, who claims to have read the date 872 (1467–68) on the Imperial Gate (in addition to the foundation date of 863 [1458–59]), and the architectural historian Cornelius Gurlitt, who visited the Topkapı in 1910 and saw the same inscription as Evliya, bearing the date 872.[22]

The garden pavilions must have been added after the central core was finished, for Kritovoulos did not mention them in 1465. Of the kiosks cited in the sources, only the one known today as the Tiled Kiosk (Çinili Köşk) remains; it was completed in Rebi II 877 (September–October 1472), according to its Persian foundation inscription. Another kiosk, demolished in the nineteenth century, was built between 1470 and 1472, in the second grand vizierate of İshak Pasha.[23] The garden pavilions were then enclosed by an outer castellated wall, completed in 1478. The construction history of the Topkapı Palace can therefore be divided into two main stages: first, the inner core, consisting of the second and third courts, fronted by a hanging garden, was built between 1459 and 1468; second, the kiosks were erected in the outer garden, which was then surrounded by the Imperial Fortress walls in 1478. The two dates, 1468 and 1478, that Gurlitt saw on a lost inscription on the Imperial Gate must therefore correspond to the completion of these two stages of construction, and not to the foundation and inauguration dates of the palace, as some have assumed.[24]

Why build a new palace so soon after the completion of the first, magnificent construction? Although it is sometimes argued that the sultan abandoned the Old Palace because its central location precluded enlargement, this could not have been the case.[25] The Old Palace was built on a vast plot, whose flat ground would have allowed for considerable expansion. It was, in fact, the New Palace, where most of the trapezoidal complex had to be supported on terraces or subterranean vaults, that posed expansion and construction problems. To understand just how huge the grounds of the Old Palace were, one has only to remember that the sixteenth-century historian Lokman could still be astonished at its vastness even after it had been reduced by the construction of, first, Bayezid II's royal mosque complex (1501–6), then the Süleymaniye Mosque (1550–57), both of which occupied its former grounds. He said it was "still an exemplar to the people of the world."[26]

Another explanation for the new construction that has been put forth is that Mehmed, inspired by the impending naval war with Venice, which lasted from 1463 to 1478, built the New Palace as a military stronghold.[27] In view of its protracted period of construction, this seems unlikely. Speed was a characteristic of the sultan's other castle construction programs; most of them were started and finished within a year. In addition, the palace project was begun before the Venetian war broke out and the castellated outer wall was added when peace negotiations with Venice, completed in January 1479, were already under way.[28] Besides, two castles built across the Dardanelles in 1461–62 and two built earlier along the Bosphorus would have made yet another inside Istanbul superfluous. Angiolello confirms that the four castles, combined with the artillery positioned before the city walls and the Maiden Tower rising from the middle of the sea, made Istanbul so impregnable that not even a bird could pass without permission.[29] Clearly there was no need to build the New Palace as a fortress. If the sultan and his court needed a refuge, they could find it in the fortress of Yedikule, adjoining the Golden Gate, which Mehmed had built together with the undefended Old Palace (Pls. 1, 23; Fig. 7). This star-shaped fortress, designed according to new Italian theoretical concepts of ideal planning, housed the royal treasury and also included royal residential quarters for refuge in the event of attack.[30]

The late-sixteenth-century historian Âli states that the sultan's decision to build the New Palace was made largely in reaction to the gossip of Christians living in Galata (Pera), the European quarter of Istanbul, who interpreted his well-defended royal fortress of Yedikule and his Old Palace, protected by the crowded city center, as signs that he was afraid of a crusade.[31] If that was the case, then, far from being built for defense, the New Palace would have been built to advertise the sultan's fearless self-confidence, and indeed its airy belvederes and pavilions, as well as the leisurely pace of their construction, suggest something of the kind.

The palaces' ambitious building program was primarily motivated by the new imperial image of the sultan that crystallized while Constantinople was being transformed into the Ottoman capital. Unlike his ancestors, who had ruled over only a small principality, Mehmed II reigned from the Balkans to eastern Anatolia (see Map I). Through conquest he had eliminated all possible contenders both for the Byzantine throne and for rival Muslim principalities in Anatolia; this allowed him to see himself as heir to the Eastern Roman Empire and to

8 Gentile Bellini, *Portrait of Mehmed* II, 1480. London, National Gallery.

entertain grandiose ideas of world domination (Fig. 8).[32] The conquest of Constantinople had placed the Ottoman state within the European political orbit and given it new claims as the successor to the Byzantine Empire; now it set its sights on Italy. Europeans firmly believed that Mehmed intended to conquer Italy after 1453, to revive the Roman Empire, and to bring the Mediterranean basin under one rule by reuniting Constantinople with Rome. This grand ambition—culminating in Mehmed's conquest of Otranto in southern Italy in 1480, a year before his death—encouraged the sultan's receptiveness to cultural developments in contemporary Italian courts, making him one of the key figures of the Renaissance. European humanists, historians, and diplomats were well aware of his Western enthusiasms. The sophisticated French diplomat Philippe de Commynes, for example, singled him out as the grandest monarch to rule in the last century, ranking him together with Matthias Corvinus and Louis XI as one of the three wisest and most valiant sovereigns of the age.[33] At Mehmed's cosmopolitan court artists and scholars from both the East and the West found enthusiastic patronage, reflecting the sultan's catholic tastes and a world view appropriate to the universal empire he wanted to create.

Fifteenth-century chronicles attribute a vision to Osman, the founder of the dynasty, in which he saw a tree growing from his own body and covering the whole earth.[34] It did not take much imagination to interpret this vision as a sign that the House of Osman was destined to rule the world, and such a dream of universal domination seemed quite possible to achieve during Mehmed the Conqueror's reign. In his memoirs of the years from 1455 to 1463, written after his repatriation to Europe, the former Janissary Konstantin Mihailović describes how Mehmed II outlined his plan to conquer Christendom:

> The Emperor ordered a great rug to be brought as an example and to be spread out before them, and in the center he had an apple placed, and he gave them the following riddle, saying: "Can any of you pick up that apple without stepping on the rug?" And they reckoned among themselves, thinking about how that would be, and none of them could get the trick until the Emperor himself, having stepped up to the rug, took the rug in both hands and rolled it before him, proceeding behind it; and so he got the apple and put the rug back down as it had been before. And the Emperor said to the lords: "It is better to torment the *kaury* [i.e., infidel] little by little than to invade their land all at once.... " And so they all praised his speech and the Emperor's example.[35]

After 1453, the imperial-apple motif, a commonly recognized symbol of universal sovereignty, was introduced into the Ottoman ceremony of accession to the throne. After a new sultan had been girded with the sword of state, the Janissaries would shout, "Let us meet at the Golden Apple."

Here the reference had come to symbolize the hoped-for Ottoman conquest of Christendom, but its origins lay in antiquity.[36] According to legend, Alexander the Great had possessed an apple made from the gold taken as tribute from the conquered provinces, which he held in his hand as if he held the world.

Mehmed was as familiar with Alexander legends, both those in Islamic texts, such as the *Iskender-name* of Ahmedi, and the classical accounts, as he was with those of Hannibal and Caesar.[37] Arrian's life of Alexander in its Greek original is still among the books in the sultan's collection at the Topkapı Palace.[38] The humanist Lauro Quirini wrote, "He wants to become, and wants to be proclaimed, the sovereign of all the world and all the people; that is, a second Alexander. And it is for this reason that he has adopted the habit of having Arrian—who describes the deeds of Alexander very precisely—read to him every day."[39] When he tired of Alexander, two Italian courtiers, one of them a companion of the humanist Cyriacus of Ancona, took turns reading to him from Herodotus, Diogenes Laertius, Livy, Quintus Curtius, and the chronicles of the popes, the emperors, and the French kings. The Italian chronicler Giacomo Languschi, who tells us this, adds that Mehmed intended to equal Alexander's conquests, but to reverse his direction, passing from Occident to Orient to create a world empire unified by a single faith and a single ruler.[40]

Both George of Trebizond, a Greek humanist scholar, and, somewhat later, Pope Pius II tried in several letters to persuade the sultan to convert to Christianity, arguing that to unify his empire under the Christian faith would guarantee him everlasting fame, greater even than that of Alexander, Caesar, or Constantine.[41] To that end, George also proposed to write a life of Mehmed in Latin to immortalize the sultan's deeds "more than those of Alexander the Great."[42] He never wrote it, but Kritovoulos provided one in Greek a decade later. In its dedication, he says that he is recording Mehmed's deeds in Greek so that all Western nations and "Philhellenes" will know that his accomplishments are "in no way inferior to those of Alexander the Macedonian."[43]

Constantinople was certainly the ideal capital for a world empire that combined Islamic, Turco-Mongol, and Roman-Byzantine traditions of universal sovereignty. In one of his letters to the sultan, in 1466, George of Trebizond wrote, "No one doubts that you are emperor of the Romans. Whoever holds by right the center of the Empire is emperor and the center of the Roman Empire is Constantinople."[44] The sultan had a keen interest in the city's imperial past that led him to commission a group of Greek and European scholars to compile a history of its rulers and monuments. The Turkish and Persian versions of this text were based on the ninth-century *Diegesis,* a Greek copy of which still survives among the sultan's books at the Topkapı Palace.[45]

While pursuing his dream of a world empire, Mehmed II began to develop an imperial image very different from that of his predecessors. The court historian Bidlisi notes the increase in royal splendor and pomp. Although the Old Palace had certainly been capable of accommodating the growing numbers of courtiers and soldiers, it had not measured up to the sultan's increasing appetite for magnificence. Bidlisi says that the unlimited sums of gold and silver spent on the Old Palace did not add up to a straw compared with the sultan's imperial majesty.[46] Neşri tells us that he transferred his royal seat to the "olive grove" because he was dissatisfied with the Old Palace, a comment confirmed in Mehmed's *waqfiyya* (endowment deed) and in sixteenth-century histories, which point out that the New Palace also had a superior location,[47] near to two great imperial monuments, Hagia Sophia, now transformed into a royal mosque, and the Hippodrome, now used for Ottoman festivities (Pls. 1–4, 23, 24). These two neighbors it shared with the Great Palace, but the new Ottoman structures were clearly distinguished from the Byzantine ruins to stress the rule of a different dynasty (see Fig. 2). The Byzantine palace, later the site of the Sultan Ahmed Mosque, faced the Sea of Marmara; the New Palace was turned toward the Golden Horn, and its silhouette enhanced the skyline of the new Ottoman capital, as did the sultan's imperial mosque on the fourth hill, the exemplar for the mosques that would later crown the remaining hills of Istanbul. Mehmed's palace and mosque complexes, connected by a processional avenue, accentuated the distinction between the administrative and religious centers of the new imperial metropolis.

The choice of the prestigious acropolis of ancient Byzantium as a site for a palace was not without its obvious symbolic significance. One of the versions of the *Diegesis,* composed for Mehmed II in 1480, points out that the New Palace, surrounded by the Imperial Fortress, was built on the exact spot once occupied by the ancient, walled Byzantine acropolis, near which the ruins of Constantine's palace adjacent to the Hippodrome were still visible.[48] Kritovoulos was also aware that the palace had been built on the promontory of "old Byzantium which stretches out into the sea." [49] The sultan's admiration of the Acropolis of Athens, which he visited in 1458, just one year before construction was begun on the New Palace, may have helped to inspire his choice. Kritovoulos recounts how Mehmed "was eager to see the city and learn the story of it and of all its buildings, especially the Acropolis itself, and of the places where those heroes had carried on government and accomplished those things ... He saw it, and was amazed, and he praised it, and especially the Acropolis as he went up into it. And from the ruins and the remains, he reconstructed mentally the ancient buildings, being a wise man and a Philhellene and as a great king, and he conjectured how they must have been originally." [50]

Tursun and Bidlisi describe the Byzantine acropolis as a triangular site at the tip of the peninsula that jutted into the water where the Black Sea and the Mediterranean met, and commanded a view of "the two continents and the two seas." [51] Mehmed's epithet "Sultan of the Two Continents and Emperor of the Two Seas," in the foundation inscription on the Imperial Gate, shows that he was quick to use this omnivoyant, spectacular site as a metaphor for world dominion. At the time it was chosen, the Ottomans were battling with Venice for control of the Aegean Islands. To dominate the sea and open the way to the western Mediterranean, Mehmed was planning to reconquer the territories the Byzantines and the Romans had once ruled. It is therefore not surprising that the sultan named the two rows of madrasas in his mosque complex after the Black Sea and the Mediterranean, a theme that found its parallel in the siting of the New Palace, built in the same years.

A century later, the Venetian ambassador Costantino Garzoni was still remarking on the strategic and symbolic advantages of the palace's site, which "everyone acknowledges to be the most beautiful, the most convenient, and most miraculous in the world; for, standing at the edge of Europe, and close to Asia, it seems to be their key, and has a natural preeminence over both regions; and because it is situated over the strait [i.e., the Bosphorus], in such a way that it can easily prevent navigation from the Black Sea to the Mediterranean, it dominates both of these two seas." A Turkish version of the *Diegesis* written by Ilyas Efendi in 1562 further glorifies the royal connotations of the palace's site by claiming that it was once occupied by a large pleasure pavilion surrounded with gardens that had been built by the prophet-king Solomon.[52]

Role of the Patron, Architects, and Decorators in the Building Program

Mehmed II devoted particular attention to his architectural projects.[53] It was the sultan himself who established the building program of his palace. In order to fulfill the "requirements of his [Mehmed's] increased magnificence," writes Tursun Beg, "his exalted will desired the following: that he create a new palace according to his own independent invention"; the New Palace took shape under the guidance of the "architect of the sultan's own mature intellect." [54] Kemalpaşazade writes that it was designed "according to that wonderful layout and unusual manner which was inspired by the guidance of the architect of his mind." [55] We know that Mehmed himself conceived and sketched the layout of Rumeli Hisar, a castle built along the Bosphorus shortly before the siege of Constantinople,[56] so it is entirely plausible to believe him capable of designing his own palace, although to what extent remains unknown. The New Palace certainly reflects an unusual individuality of planning, which seems to have crystallized in its patron's mind, to be carried out by master builders.

It is clear from Kritovoulos's description that Mehmed supervised and "zealously" directed his palace's construction, with the help of experienced overseers.[57] His frequent bonuses to especially hard-working laborers encouraged them to complete the construction in record time.[58] The palace's chronology also supports the idea that he was directly involved with its building. The most intensive periods of construction fall in the mid 1460s and late 1470s, when Mehmed II was resting from his campaigns and devoting himself to cultural pursuits and the organization of his state.[59] In those years he gathered builders from various countries for his project.[60] Tursun says the architects and engineers came from the lands of the Arabs *(ʿarab)*, Persians *(ʿacem)*, and the Ottomans *(rūm)*. Both Tursun and Kemalpaşazade say the towers in the palace were built in the European manner *(frengī)*, suggesting that some European architects may also have been involved.[61] The sultan had already used Italian architectural innovations in his star-shaped fortress of Yedikule, so it is not unlikely that he sought Italian architectural advisers here (see Fig. 7). According to some later Russian sources, Mehmed had invited the Bolognese architect and engineer Aristotele Fioravanti to Istanbul to help build his palace before the Italian master went to Russia in 1475 to work on the Kremlin.[62] In 1480 he invited interior decorators and a master builder to come from Florence and Venice.[63] Gentile Bellini had recently arrived in Istanbul with two assistants to make portraits of Mehmed (see Fig. 8) and his courtiers, as well as drawings of antiquities such as the classical Column of Theodosius I, located in the garden of the Old Palace. However, Bellini, who had abandoned his work on the Sala del Gran Consiglio at the Doge's Palace in Venice to join the Ottoman court, is reported to have been invited

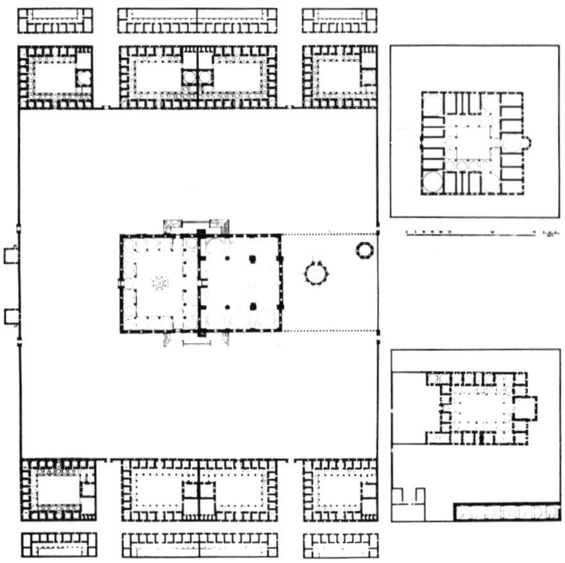

9 Plan of Mehmed II's mosque complex in Istanbul, 1463–70. From Ayverdi, *Osmanlı Mimarisinde Fatih Devri,* foldout opposite p. 368.

mainly to decorate Mehmed's New Palace with frescoes, about which no concrete information survives.[64]

Clearly Italians had a hand in the New Palace's construction and decoration. It is probably also not a coincidence that around the same time Mehmed's rival, the Hungarian king Matthias Corvinus, who reigned from 1458 to 1490, had invited artists from Italy to construct his fortified *villa suburbana* near Visegrad, with its terraced garden overlooking the Danube. In 1467 Corvinus had also invited the same Aristotele Fioravanti to Buda, and his library boasted a copy of the treatise of the Italian architect Filarete.[65] Filarete may also have been involved in the construction of Mehmed's palace, though we have no direct evidence for this. The Italian humanist Francesco Filelfo wrote on 30 July 1465, to Amirutzes, a Greek scholar attached to Mehmed's court, that Filarete was about to set out for Istanbul that summer.[66] It has been argued that the architect influenced the plan of Mehmed's royal mosque complex (1463–70), whose unprecedented symmetrical layout resembles the plan of the Ospedale

10 Aerial view of Mehmed II's mosque complex. The mosque was rebuilt after an earthquake in the eighteenth century. From *İslam Ansiklopedisi,* 1959, vol. 53, fig. 23.

Maggiore in Milan, which is included in the same architectural treatise found in Corvinus's library (Figs. 9, 10).[67] Mehmed could easily have consulted him about the palace as well. Since the Italian sources are completely silent about Filarete after 1465, it is tempting to hypothesize that he did realize his projected trip to Istanbul, where he may have stayed on.

Ottoman sources say very little about Mehmed's architects. Usta Sinan is mentioned both in an anonymous chronicle and by the historian Ruhi Edrenevi, writing at the end of the fifteenth century, as the master builder in charge of the sultan's royal mosque complex. He may also have worked on the palace until his death in 1471.[68] Ruhi says that another master builder, Usta Müslihüddin, who had built the Üç Şerefeli Mosque in Edirne (1437–47) for Murad II, also built Mehmed's New Palace on the Tunca River in Edirne and the Old Palace in Istanbul.[69] It is unlikely, however, that the sultan would have commissioned the architect whose palaces so disappointed him to build yet another one.

According to Ruhi, construction of the entire complex of the New Palace in Istanbul, including the royal residences and the Sultaniya Fortress around it, was supervised by one Murad Halife, a master builder who remained in Mehmed's service for twenty-eight years, and graduated to the status of chief court architect during the reign of his son, Bayezid II. Ruhi identifies him as the chief of Bayezid's royal architects, learned in the sciences and unequaled in his art. It was probably this otherwise unknown master mason (reported to have built several mosques and castles) who translated Mehmed's architectural fantasies into specific instructions that could be executed by the builders.[70] The result was, to borrow an expression from Filarete's architectural treatise, the true fruit of a marriage between the architect and patron, who together produced the building as their offspring. This cooperation was clearly dominated by the controlling patron, however, and his idiosyncratic taste left its stamp on the finished product.

Imperial Seclusion: The Codification of Court Ceremonial

Isolated from the crowded center of the city, surrounded by water on two sides and by high walls on the third, the New Palace was designed, among other things, to ensure imperial seclusion. According to the early-sixteenth-century historian Kemalpaşazade, the castellated walls that completed that seclusion had been constructed on the advice of Uğurlu Mehmed Mirza, an Akkoyunlu prince who had sought refuge in the Ottoman court in 1474, following an unsuccessful attempt to seize the throne of his father, Uzun Hasan. He writes, "After the construction of the above-mentioned fortified wall *[sūr]*, nothing was left incomplete in the sky-touching palace, which had reached completion. The Decree-Commanding Sultan was motivated to build it by the hint of Uğurlu Mehmed Mirza, who, during a conversation, had deemed it proper that the Imperial Palace should be separated from all the buildings around it." [71]

Bidlisi writes that Mehmed questioned the Akkoyunlu prince about the pomp and ceremony at Arab and Persian courts (i.e., the Mamluk court in Cairo, where he had stayed briefly, before coming to Istanbul, and the Akkoyunlu courts in Tabriz and Isfahan). The prince assured the sultan that none surpassed his own, which equaled Alexander's in glory, but when it came to his palace, Uğurlu Mehmed was less enthusiastic. He said that Persian monarchs had always found it both fitting and necessary to build their royal palaces outside their cities, isolated from the common herd; otherwise they would be subject to constant observation and contact, and this would soon dissipate their royal dignity. It was not suitable to have crowded neighborhoods of base people too close to the glorious palaces of the sultans. The residences of the powerful should be built on an agreeable site far removed from the common crowd; they should be kept away except on those special days reserved for administering public justice.[72]

Although this account attributes the idea of princely seclusion to Persian influence, Byzantine inspiration was not lacking. Uğurlu Mehmed had come to Istanbul far too late to have influenced the sultan's decision to build his New Palace outside the city's center — his comments seem only to have inspired the construction of the fortified outer wall. Byzantine notions of royal seclusion and the sanctity of the emperor must surely have had their impact on his choice.

Imperial seclusion no doubt also had some rationale in the security of the sultan's person, but this was clearly secondary; contemporary sources do not even mention it. Bidlisi explains that such isolation was made necessary by the sacredness of the sultan, not for his safety: this spiritual being, endowed with divine light, could not possibly dwell among ordinary mortals in the populous center of the city. It was fitting that his dwelling place be a sanctified enclosure, cleansed of impurity and resembling the heavenly realm.[73]

Royal seclusion was formalized by Mehmed II between 1477 and 1481 in a dynastic law code, or *kanunname,* which regulated Ottoman court ceremonial, listing the chief officials of the state's administrative and religious hierarchy, their ranks, salaries, promotions, and punishments, and the protocol that governed their behavior in relationship to the sultan and to one another.[74] Perhaps inspired by Byzantine books of ceremonies and the imperial codes of the Turco-Mongol khanates, this *kanunname,* issued at the very end of Mehmed's reign (when the New Palace and the imperial mosque complex were almost finished), was no doubt formulated to establish the institutional framework of these two complementary building complexes. It rigidly prescribed the hierarchical roles of dignitaries and of the secluded sultan within the palace's ceremonial, which remained essentially the same through the fifteenth and sixteenth centuries, and even in the following centuries, although changes were gradually introduced. Written in the first person, to capture the authenticity of the sultan's personal directives concerning his new vision of centralized government, the *kanunname* was the only comprehensive document of its kind to have been promulgated in Ottoman history. Its compilation marked a moment of major structural changes in the organization of the sultanate's religious and administrative apparatus, changes meant to be accommodated in Mehmed's two new building projects.

Information about Ottoman court ceremonial before the *kanunname* is sketchy. The late-fifteenth-century chronicler Aşıkpaşazade informs us that public audiences were first held in Orhan's reign (ca. 1324–60), during which members of the council, or divan, wore a special twisted turban *(burma dülbend).*[75] The sixteenth-century historian Taşköprizade Yahya puts this a bit later, in the reign of Murad I (1360–89). In public audiences Murad consulted in matters of state with viziers and religious scholars, during a ceremony which was known as the "standing divan" *(ayaḳ dīvānı),* because all the courtiers had to remain standing before the seated sultan.[76] In the reign of Bayezid I (1384–1401), the Mamluk historian Ibn Hajar al-'Asqalani recorded that a doctor sent by Sultan Barquq for Bayezid's newly founded hospital in Bursa saw the Ottoman ruler hold daily audiences, seated on a raised dais in a wide, open court, as he listened to the grievances and disputes of the people.[77] Taşköprizade similarly describes him as daily seated in audience in a "high tower" *(ʿālī burc)* of the fortified wall surrounding his palace at Bursa, to listen to his subjects' complaints.[78]

Following the defeat of Bayezid by Timur, all mention of court ceremonial vanishes from the sources for some years, a silence that can be accounted for by the dynastic crisis between 1402 and 1413. After the restoration of Ottoman rule, however, the clues begin to reappear. Historians report that Mehmed I's death in 1421 was kept secret until his successor arrived at court. His three viziers presided over the divan in front of the palace gate every day, and entered the sultan's apartment with doctors who also knew the secret. Coming out, they would inform the soldiers that the ruler was ill and needed medicine. One day the impatient soldiers, wanting to see their ruler, asked why he did not come out of the gate as usual. Those who knew that the sultan was dead resorted to a ruse: they brought the corpse out on a litter, and a hidden courtier moved the sultan's hand over his beard, using a mechanical device.[79] This incident tells us that at that time the sultan was expected to appear regularly before his troops, but that the task of administering public matters in the divan had already been transferred to the viziers.

Bertrandon de la Brocquière, an emissary from the duke of Burgundy who accompanied a Milanese ambassador to three audiences in Murad II's palace at Edirne, has left us a description of that court, dated 1433, from which it is clear that Murad no longer listened to his subjects' complaints. This duty had been taken over by the viziers, although the sultan was still expected to appear regularly in public. Brocquière says that official ceremonies were conducted in an outer administrative court built adjacent to a residential court. In the first of these three audiences, the ambassador of Milan was received by Murad II under a colonnade *(galerie)* in front of the gate of the residential court, which communicated with a large public court. Accompanied by two royal pages and a dwarf, the sultan sat with crossed legs "in the manner of tailors" on a velvet-covered dais four or five steps above the floor, with his soldiers and dignitaries lined up along the walls of the courtyard.[80] After his gifts had been paraded in the court, the ambassador was conducted to the colonnade, where the sultan greeted him standing and exchanged a few words through a Jewish interpreter. He then sat on his dais once more, while the others sat on the floor. Food was served, and drinks were available on a buffet outside the colonnade, next to which minstrels sang *chansons de gestes* praising the feats of Murad's ancestors, until the banquet began. During the banquet itself, there was no conversation, but the meal did not last long. As soon as everyone was served the servants began to clean up, since the sultan was in the habit of eating privately. After the meal, everyone rose and the ambassador left without having discussed the purpose of his embassy.[81]

Brocquière's description is remarkably well reflected in a fifteenth-century miniature from Ahmedi's *Iskendername,* which shows Bayezid I during a public audience (Fig. 11). In it the sultan is seated cross-legged on a throne under an ornate marble colonnade and is being served food. Two ambassadors are seated on a carpet under the same colonnade; the court officials are standing. There are minstrels and a buffet with drinks in the foreground, just as in Brocquière's account.

In the second audience, the Milanese ambassador was able to explain his mission only to three viziers and the governor of Rumelia, who were seated near the sultan's colonnade.[82] The third and last time the ambassador came to court, Murad II was eating all alone under the royal colonnade, while his viziers stood outside. The ambassador was made to wait near the entrance gate of the courtyard until the sultan had returned to his private apartment. Soon after, he was asked into the viziers' presence just as before, in their office near the colonnade. There he was informed that his embassy had failed.[83] About a decade later, in 1444, Cyriacus of Ancona wrote that Murad II had received him in the public court of the Edirne palace with several other Italians, "in regal splendor of a barbaric kind," surrounded by his dignitaries.[84] In 1446 the sultan granted a special audience to him and another Italian in Manisa, "in his private apartments and not in the atrium *[atrio],* where it was customary to receive ambassadors."[85]

Early in his reign Mehmed II, like his father, appeared publicly in the second administrative court-

11 Bayezid I receiving ambassadors during a banquet, with musicians in the foreground. From Ahmedi, *Iskendername* (fifteenth century). MS. Venice, Biblioteca Marciana, Cod. Nani XL (= 57), fols. 240v, 241r.

yard of his palace. According to the memoirs of the Janissary Konstantin Mihailović, the sultan twice a week presented himself to his soldiers, to reassure them that he was still alive and that they were not threatened with a usurper. It was during these public appearances that ambassadors and their gifts were received.[86] Like his father before him, Mehmed II had his viziers preside over the council and inform him privately of important matters: "The imperial council does not deliberate in the presence of the emperor," Mihailović wrote, "but far from the emperor ... and in a different room."[87]

According to Iacopo de Promontorio, a Genoese merchant who for many years served the Ottoman court, in 1475—that is, a few years before the codification of the *kanunname*—Mehmed himself was still appearing in the administrative court of the New Palace for fifteen minutes at dawn to reassure his soldiers and receive ambassadors. On these occasions the courtyard was filled with eight thousand officials wearing "vests of brocade and silk of every color and type." The sultan appeared in glory under a magnificent portico *(lobia)* in front of the gate that led into the residential court. This ceremony lasted a quarter of an hour, during which time servants offered food to the sultan on a gold tray and to those assembled on silver or copper trays, according to their rank. At the end of this banquet, at which not a word was spoken, the courtiers loudly acclaimed their ruler, extolling, praising, and glorifying his name.[88] Promontorio adds that ambassadors were made to watch this ceremony of imperial glorification, after which they were conducted, according to rank, by the viziers to the sultan's seat. After bowing and kissing his hand, they were made to sit under the royal portico until he rose to return to his private quarters. As soon as he stood he was again loudly acclaimed by the soldiers; then he sat and rose a second time to hear another acclamation, before finally entering his private apartment. After the soldiers left, the dignitaries of the imperial council ate. Only then did the viziers and the army judge *(kazasker)* listen to the cases presented, which they subsequently reported to the sultan inside the private courtyard. They then returned to the Council Hall near the royal portico to announce the sultan's decisions.[89]

This ceremonial presentation of the ruler reenacted in summary form the sultan's accession ceremony, during which his subjects expressed their recognition of his sovereignty through an even more complicated set of symbolic gestures. The sultan's appearance in public during a communal meal was an ancient custom that Aşıkpaşazade and Mihailović trace back to Osman, the founder of the dynasty, who used to distribute free food to his followers.[90] According to a common tradition, during one of these meals, Osman stood to receive the insignia of vassalage sent by the Anatolian Seljuk ruler, while a military band played. Ever since that time, it had been the custom of the House of Osman to stand up to the sound of martial music *(nevbet)* to signify his vassalage to the Seljuks and readiness for holy war *(ġazā)*, and to offer food to those gathered at court as a gesture of generosity.[91] Accepting the food was a sign of allegiance and recognition of the ruler's sovereignty—an ancient custom to which rebelling Janissaries alluded when they turned food cauldrons upside down or refused to eat food from the royal kitchens during council meetings.

In the early part of his reign, Mehmed II conformed to this ancient rite by appearing before his courtiers during communal meals, but he abolished the practice in his *kanunname*. Thenceforth he not only rejected the ancient custom of the House of Osman by refusing to eat regularly in the presence of his courtiers, but also discontinued the practice of standing to the sound of martial music, which he regarded as an unwelcome reminder of the old days of vassalage, when the Ottoman state had been a minor frontier principality. According to Âli, Mehmed was unable to tolerate this degrading ritual, and considered it pointless to stand up in homage to an Anatolian Seljuk dynasty that had ceased to exist. (Mehmed had captured the last Seljukid prince, Kiliç Arslan, in 1471.)[92] The *kanunname* in fact makes no reference whatever to any regular appearances of the sultan in public, but when it codifies the hierarchical order in which courtiers were to congratulate the sultan on the two religious holidays *(bayram)* it tells us by indirection that he would appear in the court of the council *(meydān-i dīvān)* to sit on the throne only on those two occasions.[93]

This change in procedure in the last years of Mehmed's reign coincided with the construction of the Chamber of Petitions inside the residential third court. This building, an innovation of the sultan's, was used for the presentation to him by the leading divan dignitaries of petitions regarding important state matters (Pls. 11 *[35]*, 12 *[16]*). It is mentioned in the *kanunname* as a means of further isolating the sultan from the public: "First, let there be built a Chamber of Petitions *[ʿarż odası]*. My sacred Majesty sitting behind the curtain, let my viziers and army judges and finance officers enter into my imperial presence with their petitions four times a week." By declaring that only these high-ranking dignitaries could regularly enter his presence, Mehmed made it a rare privilege to present petitions to him.[94] Ambassadors or officials who had once been received publicly at the second court were now received privately in this chamber in the third court.

Since Mehmed no longer participated in public ceremonies in the second court, he had a curtained window built, opening onto its Council Hall, and behind this he sat unseen, watching divan meetings (Pl. 11 *[25, 31]*). It is this curtain to which his *kanunname* refers. The historian Solakzade, writing in the seventeenth century, confirms that Mehmed II initiated the practice of sitting behind the curtain of a latticed window *(ḳafes)* during council meetings. He did this, Solakzade says, because once, when the sultan was presiding at a council meeting in the Old Council Hall *(eski dīvānḫāne,* known by this name after Süleyman I built a new Council Hall (Pls. 11 *[20, 25]*, 12 *[9, 12]*), sitting next to his viziers, an ill-bred man clumsily asked: "Which of you is the fortunate sovereign?" The sultan was humiliated by this impetuous remark, so the grand vizier, Gedik Ahmed Pasha, suggested that from then on he should rule from behind a curtain and leave the mundane affairs of the public council to his viziers.[95] Stories that trace the beginning of a custom to a specific event are of course suspect, but this one parallels the *kanunname* remarkably well. The coincidence is particularly striking since Gedik Ahmed Pasha was grand vizier between 1473 and 1478, just before Karamani Mehmed Pasha, under whose term of office the *kanunname* was composed (1477–81), assumed that post. Two sixteenth-century historians, Lokman and Taşköprizade, also attribute the practice of watching council proceedings from behind a curtained window to Mehmed II; they say it was instituted by the sultan to strengthen the foundations of sovereignty.[96] The window allowed justice to be controlled by a central authority in the person of the sultan, whose duty it was to protect both state and religion. It enabled the unseen but omniscient ruler to check how officials of the imperial council were performing their tasks, and whether the reports they presented at the Chamber of Petitions were accurate.

We know that the Chamber of Petitions was constructed late in Mehmed's reign, for the *kanunname* refers to it in the future tense: "Let there be built a Chamber of Petitions." The next passage, "and a Privy Chamber *[ḫāṣṣ oda]* has already been built," shows that the royal bedchamber had been constructed beforehand.[97] From this it is fair to conclude that the residential quarters of the third court were completed together with the palace's inner core in the mid-1460s, but the Chamber of Petitions was probably built around 1477–78, at the same time and for the same purpose as the outer walls, that is, to increase imperial seclusion. The fact that Mehmed's *kanunname* does not discuss in detail ceremonies related to the Chamber of Petitions also suggests the novelty of its function, which only finds extensive codification in later *kanunnames* that modify the details of Mehmed's ceremonial code.[98]

Mehmed's public Council Hall, with its curtained royal window, in the second court, and the Chamber of Petitions, his private council hall inside the third court, were the two major buildings around which the palace ceremonial outlined in the *kanunname* revolved. After a processional entrance from the Imperial Gate into the first court, ambassadors and courtiers dismounted from their horses before the second gate (Pl. 10 *[1, 21]*). Inside the second court they were received by the grand vizier and other divan officials at an elaborate banquet supplied from the neighboring royal kitchens. After this, they were presented to the sultan at the Chamber of Petitions inside the third court.

The evidence in the *kanunname* for the existence in Mehmed's time of the Chamber of Petitions and the curtained window overlooking the public Council Hall has been challenged in a study by Konrad Dilger on the development of Ottoman court ceremonial, which has become the standard work on the subject. He claims that these two buildings were first constructed by Süleyman I, not by Mehmed II, and dismisses the *kanunname* itself as a forgery intended to legitimize sixteenth-century ceremonial innovations.[99] Although there are indeed anachronistic elements in the only surviving sixteenth-century copies of Mehmed's *kanunname,* on which Dilger bases his argument, they do not prove that the whole document is a later invention. *Kanunnames* were by their very nature cumulative, and minor modifications of them were not forbidden. The anachronisms in the copies of Mehmed's *kanunname* could easily have crept in through emendations made as need arose in practice, since none of them violates the spirit of the original law. The passage about the Chamber of Petitions sets the tone for the body of legislation that has been attributed to Mehmed II since the reign of his son Bayezid II, and therefore it cannot be a forgery, especially in light of architectural evidence overlooked by Dilger, which will be discussed later. There can be no doubt that Mehmed's *kanunname* established the main outlines of Ottoman court ceremonial and centered it in the two administrative buildings that were built in his reign.[100]

The *ġāzī* (frontier warrior) ethos embodied in the ancient ceremonies of the early Ottoman period had begun to die out in Mehmed II's reign, to be replaced by a centralized bureaucratic system of government that allowed the Ottoman state to graduate from nomadic frontier principality to sedentary empire. To control the administration of the state and to rule the empire from his new capital in Istanbul, Mehmed reduced the traditional power of aristocratic families by structuring a centralized system of government through household slaves—a direction in which the Ottoman state had already been evolving. These slaves were the best and the brightest of young boys levied from the Christian subjects of the empire, selected for education in the sultan's palace as part of his household, and eventually trained to fill the highest administrative and military posts. By countering the power and potential challenge of the landed aristocracy with a bureaucratic elite, mostly of slave origins, and transforming religious scholars attached to all Ottoman madrasas (among whom those of the sultan's own mosque complex ranked the highest) into salaried employees of the centralized state, Mehmed II brought about a radical transformation in the power base of his empire. By regulating the promotion system of religious and administrative officials attached to the sultan's imperial mosque complex and to the New Palace, the *kanunname* became the main instrument of this centralization of power. It is therefore clear that the simultaneous construction of these two buildings was not accidental, but formed the cornerstone of the autocratic Ottoman regime, in which the sultan stood at the head of a ruling institution that took the form of an extended household.

During the tenure of the grand vizier Karamani Mehmed Pasha, many innovations affecting the ceremonies of sovereignty (*ā‘īn-i salṭanat*) and customs of rulership (*ḳavānīn-i emāret*) were instituted.[101] The last three years of Mehmed II's reign in particular were marked by his increasing withdrawal from the public. Foreign visitors attributed this to his affliction with gout,[102] but those years coincided with the completion of the New Palace, with innovations in court ceremonial, and with the sultan's reorganization of the administration of the state, as Aşıkpaşazade points out.[103] Appearing more and more rarely in public, Mehmed remained secluded behind the high walls of his palace, in accordance with his new imperial image. Paralleling this development in court ceremonial, the sultan began to surround himself with impressive retinues during public processions, in contrast to his habit in the early years of his reign, when he used to go to mosque from his palace in the modest company of a few young pages. Now he no longer performed his prayers on a simple carpet in the midst of people from whom he did not care to distinguish himself; his new imperial mosque featured an elevated royal tribune (*mahfil*), where he prayed separated from the rest of the congregation.[104]

The New Palace and the *kanunname* were established during a period of empire building and centralization of power which culminated in Mehmed's definition of a new self-image. With the construction of the outer wall, which screened the palace from the rest of the city, and the Chamber of Petitions, which screened the ruler from the public, the development toward greater seclusion was brought to its logical conclusion. Mehmed II possessed the autocratic power fully to implement the regulations of his *kanunname*, even when they went against established tradition. After his death, however, during the struggle for power between his sons Bayezid II and Cem, some of the law code's principles of seclusion were put to the test.[105] In the early part of his reign Bayezid II continued to receive ambassadors in the Chamber of Petitions, but reinstituted the short public banquet ceremony, in order to appease the unruly Janissaries and to ensure their support of his sovereignty. While his brother Cem was held captive in the Vatican (where he had ended up after losing the struggle for the throne), Bayezid II once more found it necessary to come out to the royal colonnade of the second court and show himself to the Janissaries. After the problem of Cem was resolved by having him poisoned, however, Bayezid no longer made regular public appearances, and his successors Selim I and Süleyman I did not present themselves in the second court, except on the two annual religious holidays.[106]

The prescriptions of Mehmed II's *kanunname,* which determined the distinctive character of Ottoman court ceremonial, were from then on firmly established. Bayezid's successors were permanently relieved of the burden of appearing regularly in public during banquets and of standing to the sound of a military band more than twice a year. The sultan's autocratic rule no longer required confirmation through regular public appearances. The two religious holidays now sufficed as a symbolic renewal of the court's promise of allegiance to their remote monarch. This constituted a radical break with the past and signaled a new imperial era.

Architectural and Ceremonial Transformations in the Sixteenth Century

Mehmed's successors preserved the original layout of the New Palace so tenaciously that the range of possible architectural transformations was severely curtailed. Throughout the sixteenth century each sultan added new structures to the palace to accommodate its growing population and to enrich the extent of its luxurious royal quarters, but the basic skeletal structure of Mehmed's extensively renovated complex was not tampered with. In the three main courts, where the relationship of one structure to another was fixed by a combination of functional and ceremonial requirements, the few new buildings that replaced the old ones over time were more monumental; the remaining majority were remodeled and redecorated according to changes in taste, but remained essentially unchanged in their functions.

Bayezid II's influence on the palace during his reign (1481–1512) was apparently insignificant, for the sources only mention his patronage of public architecture. Contemporary court historians regarded the New Palace as entirely a creation of Mehmed, which Bayezid had simply inherited soon after its completion.[107] He modified it after a major earthquake in 1509, when the damaged outer sea wall and several buildings inside the residential third court, including its royal bath, were repaired (Pl. 11 *[38]*).[108] The renovation of the damaged "wall surrounding the imperial palace and buildings inside the noble private quarters" was completed in two months.[109] Aside from these repairs Bayezid confined his architectural activities to a few small garden pavilions for the three palaces he had inherited from his father: the Edirne Palace on the Tunca River and the Old and New Palaces in Istanbul; one of these, built in the New Palace, was a shore pavilion on the waterfront facing Galata (Pl. 10 *[44]*).[110] Bayezid's successor, Selim I, spent most of his short reign (1512–20) on military campaigns, so his architectural contributions were also limited. He remodeled the Privy Chamber in the male quarters of the third court, and built a new shore pavilion at Seraglio Point at the tip of the triangular promontory (Pl. 10 *[49]*).[111]

The most extensive renovation and expansion of the New Palace was undertaken in the early part of Süleyman I's reign (1520–66), when many of the buildings were remodeled or rebuilt on a more monumental scale (Pls. 25a–f). This project coincided with the grand vizierate of İbrahim Pasha (1523–36), a time of imperial consolidation following great military victories. The empire, which in the time of Mehmed II had roughly coincided with the former territories of the Byzantine empire, was now extended both east and west to include Hungary, Azerbaijan, Mesopotamia, Egypt, the Arabian peninsula, most of North Africa, and the Black Sea (see Map II). Süleyman, who ruled over a vast empire dominating the Eastern Mediterranean basin, could now lay claim, as the protector of the holy shrines in Mecca, Medina, and Jerusalem, to the Islamic caliphate. Marking the apogee of Ottoman political and fiscal power, the reign of Süleyman the Magnificent was an era of unprecedented imperial splendor and ceremonial elaboration. Such majesty required an extensive renovation of the palace, for it was once again found to be lacking in grandeur (Figs. 12, 13).

Ibrahim Pasha oversaw the large-scale renovation of the New Palace; the chief royal architect, Alaüddin, also known as Acem Ali (or Persian Ali, since Selim I had brought him to Istanbul after conquering Tabriz in 1514), was entrusted with carrying it out. Between 1525 and 1529, he enlarged the service buildings of the first two courts, supervised the extensive remodeling of the second court, where a new Public Treasury and Council Hall adjacent to the Tower of Justice were built, and rebuilt the Chamber of Petitions in the third court (Pls. 11 *[20–24, 35]*, 12 *[9–11, 16]*). He also expanded the harem and added new pavilions to the hanging garden fronting the third court. A Persian chronogram, cited in the Divan of the poet Helaki, "He settled in the House of Felicity," yields 1528–29 as the year in which the sultan moved into his renovated palace, which resembled "the pavilion of paradise in delightfulness and the heavenly castle in strength."[112]

In 1574, at the very end of Selim II's reign (1566–74), a major fire devastated the kitchens of the second court, but did not affect the inner palace. The chief royal architect, Sinan, was entrusted with rebuilding and expanding the kitchen complex and remodeling a royal bath in the male section of the third court (Pl. 11 *[10, 38, 44, 45]*). In the early part of his reign Selim II is also known to have added some structures to the harem, which had already been expanded by his father.[113] The harem was greatly enlarged in the reign of Murad III (1574–95), who ordered the construction of a new Privy Chamber, a throne hall, and a royal bath in it, together with residential quarters and baths for its growing population (Pls. 12 *[41, 44–46]*, 27).[114] The latter also constructed several new pavilions along the seashore (Pl. 10 *[31, 44, 45]*).[115]

These successive stages of construction gave the New Palace its definitive form. By the end of the sixteenth century it had already approximated its present layout. The main ceremonial buildings founded by Mehmed II had been rebuilt or remodeled and the private royal domain had been extended outward from the constricting confines of the third court with the enlargement of the harem and the addition of new pavilions to the gardens and along the seashore. These architectural transformations not only signaled the growing political influence of women and of black eunuchs, who guarded the harem, but also a change in the way the sultans lived from the second half of the sixteenth century onward. They began to prefer a leisurely existence in their palace to the military life. In Mehmed II's time, the New Palace had functioned as a seasonal stop, where the sultan and his court could rest in between campaigns. Now it was expanded into a full-time residence inhabited by a considerably increased population. The sixteenth-century palace provided a private realm for a self-contained social organism sealed off from the world outside. The sultan withdrew into this spacious, elegant inner household.

The persistence of the original layout established by Mehmed II through a century of major renovation and the preservation of his main buildings despite changing tastes are remarkable. The palatial complex remained associated with its founder through all its architectural transformations. Chroniclers record the renovations of sixteenth-century rulers, but both the palace and the *kanunname* remained universally recognized as Mehmed II's creation. Luigi Bassano da Zara, for example, who saw the palace around 1537, after Süleyman's renovations, and John Sanderson, who was there in 1595, after Murad III's extensive construction, both still attribute it to Mehmed II.[116] By choosing not to alter the skeletal framework of Mehmed's palace radically, and to remain bound by the main outlines of its ceremonial, sixteenth-century rulers consciously brought about the consolidation of an imperial tradition that had come to represent their dynastic continuity. This policy exemplified their respect for "ancient tradition" (*ḳanūn-i ḳadīm*), which constituted the keystone of the Ottoman dynasty's claim to legitimacy.

Mehmed II, who invented this new imperial tradition, must be credited for his acute foresight and vision as the founder of a palace whose ceremonial

12 Süleyman riding in procession from the first gate (Imperial Gate) of his palace to the Friday prayer. Detail from an anonymous woodcut in nine sheets, published and engraved by Domenico de' Franceschi, ca. 1563. From Stirling-Maxwell, *Soliman the Magnificent Going to Mosque.*

heightened the uniqueness of the Ottoman dynasty for generations to come. That he intended the Topkapı to serve for posterity is revealed in the foreword of his *kanunname,* which in many ways represented a break with the past, but still openly upheld the continuity of tradition: "This *kanunname* is the tradition of my father and grandfather, and it is also my tradition. Let my honorable descendants act according to it one generation after the other."[117] However, Mehmed also envisioned the project of a universal empire which his successors would bring to completion and legitimized later changes with the following clause: "The circumstances of sovereignty have been regulated this much. From now on, let my honorable descendants strive to improve it."[118] This permission for further elaboration allowed Mehmed's successors to introduce subtle ceremonial innovations to augment their majesty as Ottoman imperial claims grew in the sixteenth century. Despite the growing pomp of the official rituals revolving around the public and private council halls, and the grandeur of the buildings that now housed them, the structure of the ceremonial prescribed in Mehmed II's *kanunname* was not radically altered.

Most of the ceremonial changes were initiated together with the extensive renovation of the palace during Süleyman I's reign, since ceremony and ar-

13 A procession of Süleyman through the Hippodrome to the Friday prayer, from a series of woodcuts by Pieter Coeck van Aelst published in 1553 at Antwerp, after drawings made in 1533. From Coeck van Aelst, *The Turks in* MDXXXIII.

chitecture were mutually dependent. Palace ceremony and protocol were increasingly elaborated together with their architectural framework. Venetian diplomats noted in 1527–28 that the augmented pomp, splendor, and architectural magnificence of Süleyman's court was unprecedented. When the Venetian ambassador Marco Minio was sent for a second mission to the New Palace in 1527, he was struck by the increase in its magnificence since his first visit in 1521: "I found the Porte excellent in order, differing from the other time I came here as ambassador.... There is a great difference between this and the other time." [119] Tommaso Contarini wrote on 8 July 1528: "In terms of pomp what it once was is not to be compared to what is here now, for everything is extremely pompous, and they have made many beautiful ornaments." [120]

Following earlier practice, ambassadors were admitted twice into the sultan's presence in the Chamber of Petitions, once upon arrival, after a public audience and banquet with the viziers at the second court, and again before departure. But earlier sultans had risen from their seat to honor the ambassadors. Süleyman I and his successors remained not only seated, but immobile. In 1521 Minio observed that Süleyman no longer rose to greet ambassadors and, during his second embassy in 1527, that he refused to speak, a silence certainly not observed by the sultan's forebears.[121]

As this practice indicates, the sultan grew increasingly arrogant in his ceremonial practice, which eventually reached a peak of haughtiness by the last quarter of the sixteenth century. Ambassadors were conducted into the royal presence like prisoners to the bar, their arms secured on either side by two gatekeepers. They were made to stand at all times, unlike their predecessors, who had been allowed to sit in front of the sultan on a lower seat. Instead of communicating with him directly, they were only allowed to catch a momentary glimpse of the idollike sultan, who had grown almost too sacred to be seen.[122] This growing haughtiness was commented on by the Venetian bailo Giovanni Moro, who observed in 1590 that the sultan's arrogant conviction of world dominion was reflected in all his affectations: in his patronizing letters to other monarchs, in his official chronicles praising Ottoman conquests to the point of vanity, in his use of mute signs instead of words, in his refusal to appear at all in public, as if mere mortals were not worthy to look upon him, in his refusal to address ambassadors, and in his sitting like a statue during audiences.[123]

Contemporary observers also noted the sultan's increasing seclusion during the second half of the sixteenth century, starting with the reign of Selim II.[124] In 1592 the Venetian ambassador Lorenzo Bernardo compared Murad III, who rarely left his sensuous palace, to Sardanapalus and wrote:

> Sultan Selim [II], father of the present Grand Signor, initiated the following opinion: That the true felicity of a king or emperor did not consist in military toils and in operations of bravery or glory, but in idleness and tranquillity, in the satisfaction of the senses, in the enjoyment of all comforts and pleasures in palaces filled with women and buffoons, and in the fulfillment of all desires for jewels, palaces, loggias, and stately constructions.
>
> In these thoughts of Sultan Selim the present sultan, Murad [III], his son, has followed, but much more so, since the former used to go out of his palace at times to hunt, as far as Edirne, but the present Grand Signor, as I said, almost never goes out.[125]

Another contemporary author, Blaise de Vigenère, likens Murad III to Narcissus contemplating his own beauty:

> Thus constantly shut up inside a walled enclosure, no matter how ample and spacious it may be, he has nobody of quality nor of wit who can entertain him, and none with whom he can familiarly chat or rejoice: since it is nothing but a seminary of boys as subdued as if in some cloister or college ... all in general poor, timid slaves, who hardly dare to look at his shadow, or at his footprints, with some eunuchs more disagreeable and decrepit than the old maid of Zeuxis.... When he has retired by himself inside his seraglio, who is the one who can admire him? For it has nobody but poor valets, stupid, and without judgment, knowledge, or apprehension. In short, all this corresponds to the example of another Narcissus, who contemplates and admires himself in a fountain.[126]

Writing at the same time, Mustafa Âli presents an insider's view of Murad III, who followed "the orientation of his ancestors by preferring isolation to mixing with people and by putting the state of hiddenness before the personal management of affairs, so as to remain an object of awe and veneration to the people." He compares the sultan in his hermetically sealed palace to a pearl hidden in an oyster shell. Referring to the sultans, he writes,

> They reside all by themselves in a palace like unique jewels in the depth of the oyster shell, and totally sever all relations with relatives and dependents. The slave girls and slave pages *[ghilmān]* that have access to their honored private quarters *[harem],* who are evidently at least three to four thousand individuals, are all strangers and the person of the monarch is like a single gem in their midst. However, they are so used to serving him and to carry out his noble orders in perfect obedience and are in their hearts so much attached to him with complete submission and affection that only the demons that served at Solomon's court—peace be upon him!—can have been command-obeying to that extent.[127]

Even in his private quarters the sultan had contact with very few people, the *kanunname* having severely restricted the number of privileged dignitaries permitted to present petitions to him. Only three favorite pages were allowed to address him in words; the others could communicate only through signs.[128] Sign language was first introduced to the palace by two mute brothers during the reign of Süleyman I. Finding this form of communication very respectful, the sultan ordered it to be used by pages attached to his Privy Chamber.[129] It is first described in the marginal notes of Melchior Lor-

14 (opposite) A ceremonial procession to the Friday mosque, showing Mehmed III leaving the first gate (Imperial Gate) of the Topkapı Palace and passing in front of Hagia Sophia with a large retinue; in the foreground are his subjects presenting written petitions. Appended to Nadiri, *Dīvān-i Nādirī,* 1572–73, TSK, H 899, fol. 4.

15 A triumphal parade of Mehmed III through the main ceremonial avenue of Istanbul, on his return from the military campaign of Eger; in the background, various spectators and the Persian ambassador are shown in observation booths. From Talikizade, *Eğri Fethi Tarihi,* ca. 1598, TSK, H 1609, fols. 68v, 69r.

ichs's panorama (1559), but it soon became so fashionable that it was considered rude even to whisper in the sultan's presence. In 1605 the French diplomat Henry de Beauvau says that this language was called "*Ixarette*" (in Turkish *işaret* means "sign") and was used in the palace as a second language. In 1608 the Venetian bailo Ottaviano Bon wrote that the sultan and his pages communicated in sign language "to observe the gravity so much professed by the Turks, and what they express with mute signs is more than what is discussed vocally; the same is done among the royal women and other ladies, for among them there are also old and young mutes; and it is a very ancient custom of the seraglio to desire and have as many mutes as can be found, particularly because the king, not being allowed to speak except for very few words to conserve his grandeur, respect and reputation, communicates in this manner." [130] By 1617 sign language had become such a compulsory attribute of royal dignity that when Sultan Mustafa refused to learn it he was criticized in the public Council Hall. Those who voiced the complaint saw it as undignified for a sultan to use the ordinary speech of Janissaries and common merchants, and agreed that he should never talk, but make people tremble by his extraordinary gravity.[131]

The principle of silence prescribed by Süleyman had almost transformed the sultan into a mute idol. What had initially been conceived as a device to enhance the monarch's dignity began to turn into a binding straitjacket. The ceremonial outlined in Mehmed's *kanunname* had originally been codified to assure his absolute power; Süleyman's innovations paradoxically robbed the sultans of the ability to exercise that immense power, as the Venetian observer Benedetto Ramberti perceptively noted in 1534. The definitive codification and consolidation of the empire's centralized bureaucratic apparatus during the reign of Süleyman the Lawgiver *(Kanuni)* allowed the sultans to retire even more radically into seclusion, since the self-perpetuating

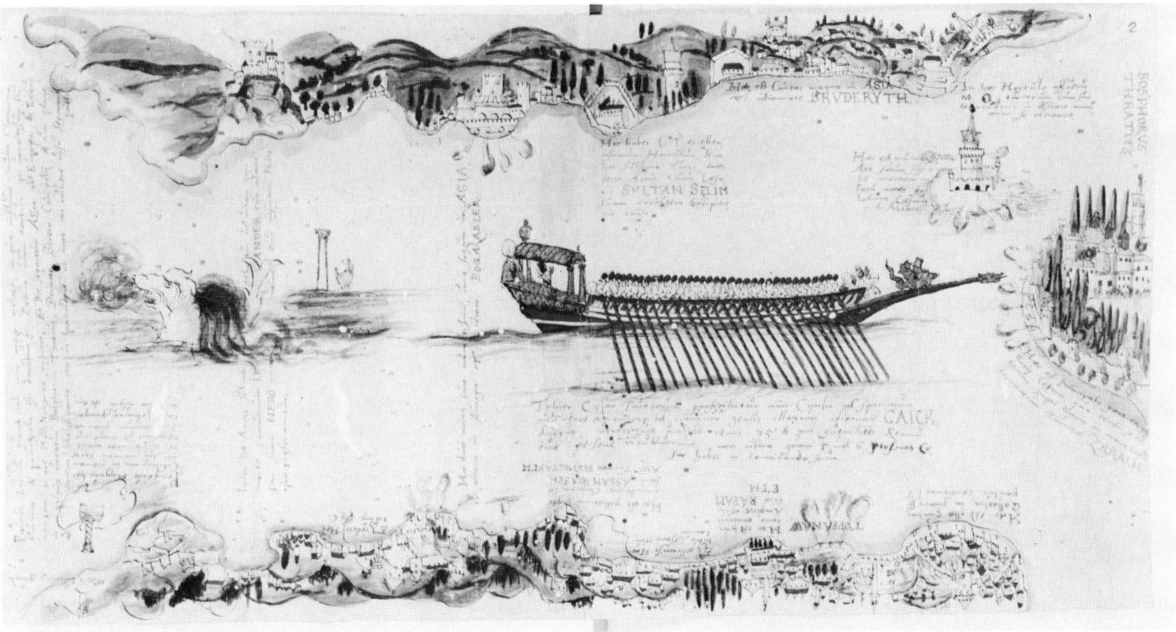

16*a (top)* Murad III in a boat ride along the Golden Horn. Lewenklau Album, MS. Vienna, Österreichische Nationalbibliothek, Cod. 8615, fol. 122.
16*b (bottom)* Murad III in a boat ride along the Bosphorus; the tip of the Topkapı Palace is seen on the right and the various royal gardens are identified on both shores. From the *Traveler's Picture Book with Scenes of Life in Istanbul in 1588,* Oxford, Bodleian Library, MS. Bodl. Or. 430, fol. 2r.

bureaucratic machine rendered government impersonal.[132] Remaining out of touch with the outer world in the regal prison of their magnificent palace, Süleyman's successors were more easily manipulated by competing power factions.

The sultan's seclusion turned stately royal processions through the city into highly charged events providing the people with a rare opportunity to give written petitions to their ruler by hand (Fig. 14). These theatrical parades to Friday mosques, the Old Palace, and to the Hippodrome, where public festivities such as the circumcision of royal princes took place, were complemented by elaborate boat processions along the Golden Horn and the Bosphorus to pavilions in various royal gardens (Figs. 15, 16a,b). Sometimes the sultan paraded with his whole court from his palace to hunt in these gardens so that ambassadors could watch his pomp from observation booths along the route.[133] To guarantee a slow and stately pace, the day before these processions the sultan's horse was suspended in the air and left without food all night.[134] Such carefully staged performances reinforced the secluded monarch's awesome magnificence. These extensions of palace ceremonial into the larger urban fabric of Istanbul were displays of imperial power that turned the iconic sultan, accompanied by thousands of richly dressed and hierarchically ordered courtiers, administrators, and slave soldiers, into a showpiece for the populace.

TWO

The Imperial Fortress and the First Court

The first court was popularly known as the Court of Processions *(alay meydanı)* because it constituted both the starting and ending point of the stately parades that linked the walled-in palace with the city outside. The city's processional thoroughfare began across from Hagia Sophia at the Imperial Gate *(bab-i hümayun)*, which was the main entrance to the first court (Pl. 10 *[1]*; Figs. 17, 18). This road was the Mese, the *via triumphalis* of the Byzantines, which came to be known as the Council Road *(divan yolu)*, from the parades of dignitaries to the council meetings at the Topkapı four times a week (Pl. 1; see Fig. 2). A sixteenth-century miniature depicts such a formal procession of Süleyman's grand vizier İbrahim Pasha to the palace, with a large retinue that included slave pages, wrestlers, and musicians (Fig. 19). The Council Road was also the route for the sultan's processions from the palace to the royal mosques on Fridays, for it was lined with imperial mosques built by and named after the successive Ottoman rulers (see Figs. 12–14). These separate imperial monuments punctuating the city's hilltops gave Istanbul its distinctive Islamic skyline. It became customary for a sultan, after his accession ceremony and on the eve of military campaigns, to visit the mausolea of his royal ancestors attached to these imperial mosques. They were linked together to form a unified statement of dynastic continuity and legitimization through such royal processions, which started from the palace, so that the sultan's role as the mediator between state and religion was stressed.

Before the castellated wall, known as the Imperial Fortress, was built to enclose the huge space that formed the first courtyard, the New Palace had had only two courts, as had the earlier palace of Mehmed II in Edirne (see Fig. 3). The relationship of one building to the other was based on the traditional order of the Ottoman imperial encampment, in which individual tents fulfilling specific functions were lined up according to a predetermined scheme, paralleled in the two-part layout of the palace. This special ordering of the imperial tents *(otāġ-i hümāyūn)* is referred to by Tursun Beg as the "Ottoman order" *(tertīb-i ‹os̱mānī)*, or the "order of the Ottoman tradition" *(‹ādet-i ‹os̱mānī tertībi)*.[1]

In 1475 Promontorio pointed to this resemblance between Mehmed's royal camp and his New Palace in Istanbul. A private, residential tent enclosure inhabited by the sultan, his pages, and eunuchs was preceded by a public enclosure where the dignitaries held council meetings.[2] The juxtaposition of two tent enclosures reflected the royal household's organization in terms of inner and outer service units grouped in two functionally distinct courts. This ordering principle, in which a strict distinction was drawn between interior *(enderun)* and exterior *(birun)*, played a guiding role in establishing the skeletal layout of the New Palace's main core. Given that the sultan's military camp and his palace shared the same semantic field as symbols of imperial power in the Ottoman ethos, the similarity is not surprising. After all, the mobile imperial tent complexes, where the sultans resided and administered their empire's affairs during military campaigns, were nothing but impermanent versions of their royal palaces, which were built with more lasting materials to mark the "seat of the imperial throne" permanently in the Ottoman capitals.

When the land wall of the Imperial Fortress, approximately two and one-half kilometers long, was joined to the Byzantine city walls that protected the sea side, this created a new forecourt appended to the palace's main core.[3] By the end of Mehmed's reign, Angiolello describes the palace as consisting of "three courts each enclosed by walls," each one entered from a double gate.[4] In the 1490s the pilgrim Arnold von Harff said it was "very large and splendid beyond measure" and had "three large squares."[5]

The Imperial Fortress, Its Gates and Belvederes

The Imperial Fortress that one encountered before entering the first court of the palace did not provide a strong defense, compared to Mehmed's other castles, which were at the forefront of the military design concepts pioneered in Italy (Pls. 3, 10; Figs. 20a–c). Following the natural terrain and adapting itself to the position of Hagia Sophia, the wall's irregular contour does not form the sharp corners useful for strategic purposes. Its relatively thin crenellated walls and towers, pierced by bull's-eye-shaped marble or brick embrasures, allow little room for maneuver. But however ineffective from a defensive point of view, the Imperial Fortress certainly gave the palace the commanding appearance of a fortified castle.

17 Malkoç Ali Pasha, the governor of Egypt, departing with his retinue from the Imperial Gate. From the *Chronicle of Ali Pasha,* MS. Istanbul, Süleymaniye Kütüphanesi, Halet Efendi 612, fol. 9v.

The failure of contemporary Ottoman sources to mention the defensive character of the Imperial Fortress suggests that it was primarily meant to be read as a statement of sovereignty and power. Tursun Beg praises its artistic design, which featured variegated square and polygonal towers built in the "Turkish" *(türkī)* and "European" *(frengī)* manner; Kemalpaşazade compares it to the heavenly castle and to the trajectory of the moon, with its twenty-eight mansions equaling the number of towers.[6] Mehmed's court poet Hamidi also stresses its heavenly and astrological associations, and sees it as a "castle of power," featuring "towers of power, conquest, and victory." A chronogram by the grand vizier Karamani Mehmed Pasha refers to it as "the castle of the palace of glory, dignity and loftiness."[7]

The fortress palace of the world-conquering ruler broadcast to the outer world an image of power. It had twenty-five quadrangular, one dodecagonal, and two octagonal towers, and was pierced by three large double gates, referred to in the sources as the Imperial Gate *(bāb-i hümāyūn),* the Iron Gate

18 A royal parade leaving the Imperial Gate. From Melling, *Voyage pittoresque de Constantinople.*

(bāb-i āhen or *demür ḳapu),* and the Gate of Stables *(āḫūr ḳapu),* also known as the Haystore Gate *(otluḳ ḳapu),* and several small ones (Pl. 10 *[1, 3, 7]*). Three polygonal belvedere towers, crowned by conical lead caps, marked the places where the wall abruptly changed its angle. These belvederes functioned as a link between the palace and its surroundings, signifying that the sultan was watching over his realm, despite his isolation behind forbidding walls (Pls. 10 *[2, 5, 6]*, 23, 24, 25e,f, 31a,b). The octagonal tower pavilion near the Iron Gate was used by the royal band *(nevbetḫāne),* which played martial music at appointed times to mark the hours for prayer and to praise the sultan.[8] The dodecagonal tower pavilion, known as the Kiosk of Processions *(alay köşkü* or *alay ḳaṣrı),* was where the sultans watched various ceremonial processions and stood to listen to the complaints of rebels during rebellions; from its windows the corpses of traitors and political criminals were thrown down, as a sign of the monarch's justice, to appease the

19 A procession of the grand vizier İbrahim Pasha, accompanied by musicians, wrestlers, and attendants, to the public council at the Topkapı Palace, TSK, A 3592, fols. 41v, 42r.

20*a*–*c* Drawings of the first court and the service areas extending along the land wall. From Fossati, *Aya Sofia Constantinople as Recently Restored by the Order of H. M. the Sultan Abdul Medjid.*

crowds gathered below.[9] According to an inscription on the windows of the kiosk, which still stands today, the original tower pavilion, "equal in height to the heavenly vault," was shortened in 1810 by Mahmud II, who brought it closer to ground level in order to hear the people's complaints more easily.[10]

The original tall tower pavilion, which appears in earlier views of the palace, is reminiscent of the "high tower" of the castle surrounding the Bursa Palace, from which Bayezid I used to listen to the complaints of his subjects, and of a tower pavilion on the fortified outer enclosure of the palace of the Anatolian Seljuk sultans in Konya, dated by an inscription to Kılıç Arslan II, but popularly attributed to his grandson, Alaeddin Keykubad.[11] The inscription on the Kiosk of Processions claims its superiority to the antiquated "*ḳaṣr*" of Keykubad.[12] Mehmed II's original tower pavilion, of which only the razed dodecagonal stone base remains, mainly functioned as a royal watchtower for surveying ambassadorial and military processions.[13] A double-folio miniature in the *Shahanshāhnāma* (king's book of kings) shows Murad III watching a Persian embassy, accompanied by an impressive escort of Ottoman dignitaries, parade past this tower, along a path in front of the Imperial Fortress, before entering the first courtyard through the Imperial Gate (Fig. 21).

The Imperial Gate repeated the theme of power in its gilt Arabic inscription, signed by the calligrapher 'Ali bin Yahya al-Sufi (Fig. 22):

By the grace of God, and by His approval, the foundations of this auspicious castle were laid, and its parts were solidly joined together to strengthen peace and tranquillity, by the command of the Sultan of the two Continents and the Emperor of the two Seas, the Shadow of God in this world and the next, the Favorite of God on the Two

21 Murad III watching the procession of the Persian ambassador İbrahim Han to the Topkapı Palace from a tower pavilion of the Imperial Fortress, the predecessor of the present Kiosk of Processions. From Lokman, *Shahanshāhnāma,* 1592, TSK, B 200, fols. 33v, 34r.

Horizons [i.e., East and West], the Monarch of the Terraqueous Orb, the Conquerer of the Castle of Constantinople, the Father of Conquest Sultan Mehmed Khan, son of Sultan Murad Khan son of Sultan Mehmed Khan, may God make eternal his empire, and exalt his residence above the most lucid stars of the firmament, in the blessed month of Ramadan of the year 883 [November and December 1478].[14]

The Koranic quotation (15:45–48) above this foundation inscription[15] implies a connection between the Imperial Gate and the gates of paradise, as well as between the royal palace and the Garden of Eden—a comparison frequently encountered in other texts:

But the God-fearing shall be amidst gardens and fountains: "Enter you then, in peace and security!" We shall strip away all rancour that is in their breasts; as brothers they shall be upon couches set face to face; no fatigue

22 Foundation inscriptions of 1478 on the Imperial Gate.

there shall smite them, neither shall they ever be driven forth from there.

These references to peace and tranquillity further argue against any notion of the Imperial Fortress as defensive in purpose. Weapons such as swords, guns, bows, and arrows, hanging on the walls of the Imperial Gate's domed vestibule, though adding to its castlelike appearance, were there only to remind the visitor that soldiers went unarmed inside the peaceful palace.[16]

The Imperial Gate, far from being the fortified bastion of an impregnable fortress, was a royal gate pavilion through which one entered the *castrum palatium*. Angiolello describes this "double gate providing access into the castle *[Castello]*," as being surmounted by a "well-designed pavilion *[Palazzo]* covered with lead."[17] The now-missing upper pavilion, which once crowned the gate's extant domed vestibule, flanked by dormitories for the gatekeepers, can be seen in two late-fifteenth-century drawings published by Vavassore and Schedel (Pls. 23, 24; Figs. 23, 24) as well as in others later on. The rectangular outer facade of the remaining white-marble ground floor has niches on either side of an arched entrance, and resembles a triumphal arch — a form appropriate to the gate's function as the main ceremonial entrance to the palace. To accommodate Hagia Sophia, the Imperial Gate had to be built off center in relation to the first courtyard. It was meaningfully positioned on the same axis with the ruins of the gatehouse of the neighboring Byzantine Great Palace, the Chalke Gate, known as the Brazen House because of the gilded-bronze tiles on its dome. The latter was a rectangular, two-story structure, with a central dome flanked by vaulted chambers, attached to the domed Church of the Savior (see Fig. 2). The Imperial Gate's position with relation to Chalke and the looming presence of Hagia Sophia, now converted into a mosque, proudly announced the end of a glorious imperial epoch and the beginning of a new one.

The plan of Mehmed's destroyed upper pavilion, which appears to have alluded to some features of the Chalke Gate, can be reconstructed from the extant ground floor (echoed upstairs) and from documents in the archives that deal with repairs. It featured an open colonnade protected by wide eaves facing the first court, behind which a central hall with a gilded dome was flanked by two subsidiary chambers. Its outer facade, which faced Hagia Sophia, was given compositional unity by means of a large window placed directly above the arched gate, flanked by three smaller, double-tiered windows. The large central window, long a feature of imperial palaces, was used for royal appearances.[18] The form of the gatehouse carried well-established imperial associations, for it was reminiscent of cer-

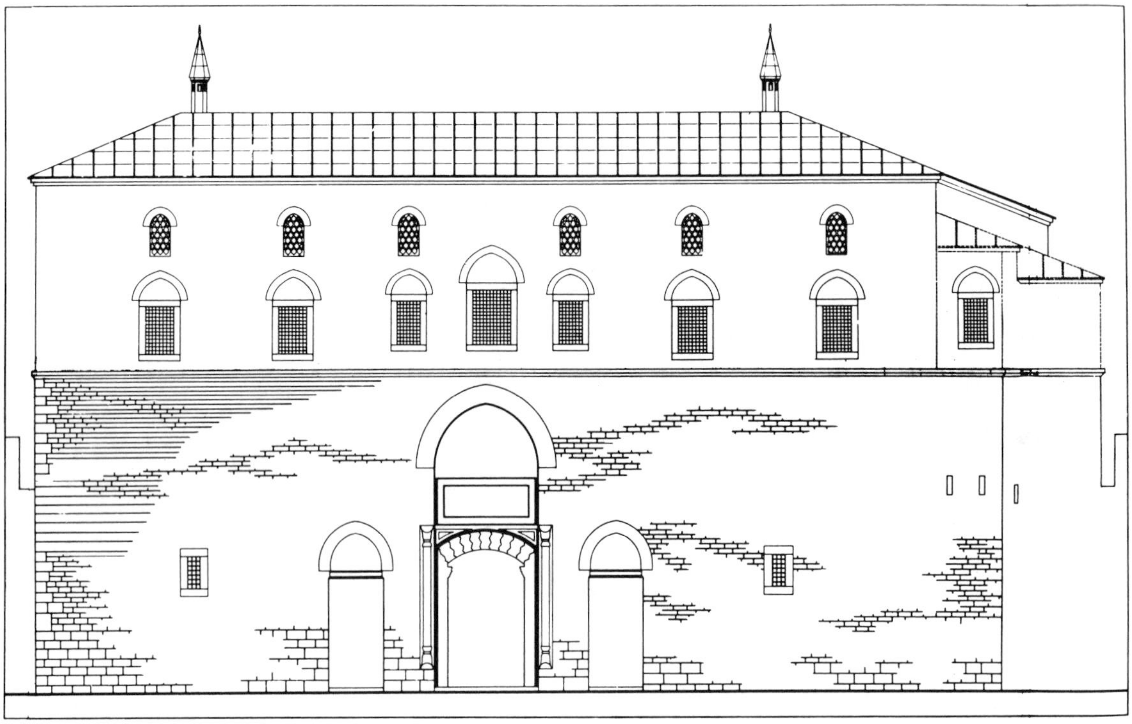

23 Drawing of a reconstruction of the Imperial Gate. From Eldem and Akozan, *Topkapı*, 1982.

emonial palace gatehouses in Abbasid Baghdad and Byzantine Constantinople, which were also crowned by royal belvederes with gold domes.

The seventeenth-century historian Hezarfen Hüseyin says this about the gate:

Having built a lofty pavilion *[kaṣr-i ʿālī]* above the Imperial Gate of the palace, Sultan Mehmed the Conqueror sometimes used to sit there, watching the Mediterranean Sea and the southern sections of the city. Afterward, the just sultans placed lattices around that pavilion in order to store in it the estates of deceased Muslims without heirs. If no legitimate inheritors showed up for seven years, they would seize these things as royal property. This was the case in the reign of the late Sultan Süleyman. Thereafter, this law was abolished. Today, an accountant sits there with his assistants, after the viziers depart from the council meeting, to collect the public taxes, which are then stored in vaults beneath the pavilion, with the help of treasurers from the Corps of Royal Tents. They also keep here the public treasure *[beytü'l-māl]* confiscated from some viziers and grandees. They transfer these collected treasures every three months to the Outer Treasury adjacent to the Council Hall [of the second court] for distribution to slave soldiers as their salary.[19]

Hezarfen's friend La Croix similarly notes that Mehmed II's original open belvedere pavilion featuring a gilded dome was closed up after being transformed into a treasury for depositing the property of Muslims without heirs.[20] References in archival documents to the repair of iron lattices that spanned its once-open colonnade facing the first court confirm this.[21] Süleyman I's grand vizier Lutfi Pasha (1539–41) claims that he was the one to initiate the practice of depositing property as a trust

28 The first court. From Lokman, *Hünername,* ca. 1584–85, TSK, H 1523, fol. 15v.

were beaten with a stick. A forbidding scene replaces this peacetime procession along the first court as one lifts a flap of paper to reveal an illustration of a different event underneath. It shows a wartime parade of victorious Ottoman soldiers along the same path connecting the first and second gates. They hold spears on which severed heads are stuck and lead chained prisoners.[36] In another Austrian album, compiled for Lambert Wyts in 1573, an ambassadorial procession to the palace is shown winding its way along a path outside the Imperial Fortress, fancifully represented with camels and palm trees (Fig. 29). Another scene takes the orderly procession through the first court, between two ranks of Ottoman officials, up to the second gate (Fig. 30).

Inside this courtyard exotic animals were occasionally also exhibited, an ancient Near Eastern royal tradition adopted by the Byzantine and Islamic courts. Süleyman's accession ceremony in 1520 featured elephants and giraffes in the first court, already filled with cavalry and a military band. According to Lokman, elephants and giraffes were also displayed in the court during feast days as a "demonstration of magnificence," lined up along the left side, beyond the Byzantine Church of St. Irene (Hagia Eirene), which had been incorporated into the first court (Pl. 10 *[10]*).[37] In 1529 Johann Hoberdanacz, an ambassador from Ferdinand I of Austria to Süleyman I, saw two elephants there, draped with precious fabrics. One year later, another Habsburg embassy encountered the same elephants and a giraffe on the left side of the first court, which was filled with cavalry soldiers.[38]

The visual impact of the first court was never primarily architectural. Its effect came from the multitude of richly clad cavalry soldiers, mounted on valuable horses with jeweled trappings, and from the exotic animals on display.[39] By itself, the first court was simply a large unpaved area with a narrow path connecting the first gate to the second.[40] Because the gates were not aligned, the path was oblique. A member of the French embassy in 1544, Jérôme Maurand, describes it as a "beautiful straight pavement, eight palms wide, made of small black and white stones forming circles and flowers";[41] it is labeled "pavement" (*ḳaldırım*) in the *Hünername* miniature (see Fig. 28).

The only exception to the simple and uniform architecture of the first court was a large octagonal kiosk built of stone on a vast raised platform and crowned by a pointed lead roof (Pl. 10 *[13]*).[42] By the end of the sixteenth century, and perhaps even earlier, it functioned as a place where an official known as the "Paper Commissioner" (*kağıd emini*) and his assistants collected petitions from plaintiffs and distributed imperial firmans to them after their cases had been settled in the second court. They

29 (opposite), 30 (above) An Austrian embassy parading in 1573 to the Topkapı Palace, and marching through the first court. Album of Lambert Wyts, 1574, MS. Vienna, Österreichische Nationalbibliothek, Cod. 3325*.

were required to sit in it on the days when the imperial council met in the second court to hear cases.[43] This very activity is depicted in the *Hünername* miniature, which shows firmans being handed out to a group of people by several officials from the octagonal kiosk, identified in the miniature as the "Tower of the Paper Commissioner" *(ḳulle-i kāğıd emīni)* (see Fig. 28).[44] In 1605 the French diplomat Beauvau describes the towerlike pavilion as "a small tower pierced with fifty to sixty windows, where the commands of the Grand Signor are distributed."[45] The Lewenklau album illustrations show the kiosk pierced with red latticed windows and packed with turbaned officials (Pls. 33f,g).

The octagonal platform on which this kiosk once stood can still be seen today to the left of the second gate. It was discovered in 1976, when the first court was being made into a parking lot. Demolished in the nineteenth century, the kiosk was called a "tower" because of its conical lead roof. It resembled the tower pavilions of the Imperial Fortress, and was probably part of Mehmed II's original building program, although the first visual evidence of it is a double-folio miniature in the *Süleymanname* produced in the 1550s (see Fig. 27). It seems originally to have functioned as a royal pavilion where the sultan appeared in front of his troops assembled in the first court before departing on a military campaign.[46] The late-sixteenth-century

Scottish traveler Fynes Moryson identifies it as the "large pulpit or open roome where the great Turke useth to shew himselfe to the Janizares to satisfie them when they make any mutiny." [47] Just as Mehmed's royal pavilion on top of the Imperial Gate was adapted to new functions in the sixteenth century, this one too apparently lost its original function with the increasing seclusion of the sultans.

Aside from this royal pavilion the buildings of the first court were entirely functional structures with red-tiled roofs; more prestigious buildings in the second and third courts had lead-covered roofs. The service buildings were constructed of cheap materials such as wood and rubble masonry that required regular maintenance. As a consequence few have survived. Each was clustered around its own small courtyard, separated from the main court by blind walls pierced with large gates.[48] Illustrations in the Austrian albums show blind walls stretching along both sides of the court, behind which the workshops were located (Pls. 33e–i; see Fig. 30). The same walls are seen on later pictures by Francesco Scarella in 1686 and Caspare Fossati in the nineteenth century (Pls. 31a,b; see Figs. 20a–c). Moryson describes them as buildings of "free stone of two stories high, with a low and almost plaine roofe tyled, and without windowes, and after the manner of building of Italy, and round about the inside, it was cast out with arches like the building of Cloisters, under which they walked drie in the greatest raine." [49]

The open sides of the first court were gradually sealed off and their views of the outer gardens lost. The court was connected to these gardens by two steep paths at the right and left sides, the gates of which were kept guarded (Pl. 10 *[12, 16]*).[50] According to the Venetian diplomat Marc'Antonio Pigafetta, the gardens were still visible from the right side of the court in 1567, and the wooden benches described by Angiolello as seats for the retinues of grandees are still mentioned in 1550 by another Venetian, Caterino Zeno.[51] But they are not visible on drawings after that date. Their disappearance again signals the expanding uses of the first court that necessitated the construction of new service buildings. Both the Lewenklau album drawings and the *Hünername* miniature (Pls. 33e–g; see Fig. 28) show a wooden portico extending along the left side beyond a fountain past the Church of St. Irene. This was the only portico in the first court available to protect the retinues and horses of grandees.[52]

In addition to the royal workshops in the first court, others were scattered in the outer gardens and outside the walled enclosure of the Imperial Fortress. Near the outer walls and in the Hippodrome area, which constituted a natural extension of the palace grounds, were additional service buildings, a menagerie, a stable, a powder magazine, an armory, an archive, and workshops for painters, tailors, tent makers, and other royal craftsmen. Those around the Hippodrome included small Byzantine churches or chapels converted by Mehmed II into an elephant house, a menagerie, and a powder magazine. St. Irene, yet another church transformed by the sultan into an armory, had, unlike the others, actually been incorporated into the first court to the left of the Imperial Gate. These converted Byzantine churches still retained their original decorations at the time of Mehmed: Angiolello writes that "all these chapels are worked in marble, and inside with mosaics, in such a manner that they are works of exquisite workmanship." [53]

St. Irene, misidentified in Schedel's *Nuremberg Chronicle* woodcut as "S. Johannes Crisostomo" (who it was popularly believed was buried there), was a storehouse for bows, arrows, cuirasses, and other armor, and it continued to serve that function throughout the history of the palace (Pls. 10 *[10]*, 24).[54] Among the weapons kept in this church, identified in the *Hünername* miniature (see Fig. 28) as the "royal armory" *(cebeẖāne-i ʿāmire)*, were those collected after the fall of Constantinople and other Ottoman conquests. They were exhibited together with various captured banners and Byzantine relics as emblems of victory.[55] The early-nineteenth-century English antiquarian Edward Daniel Clarke cites among the displays of this Ottoman military museum "weapons, shields, and military engines of the Greek emperors, exactly corresponding with those represented on the medals and bas-reliefs of the Antients, suspended as trophies of the capture of the city by the Turks."[56]

On council days, the head armorer and his assistants held office in front of the church, as the *Hünername* miniature shows (see Fig. 28).[57] In Süleyman's time its sixteen marble columns and many marble revetments were removed to decorate the Süleymaniye Mosque (ten more columns were saved from removal when the dome began to crack).[58] Gradually stripped of its decorations, by the mid sixteenth century St. Irene was a strictly utilitarian service building like every other structure in the first court.

Near the Church of St. Irene, the *Hünername* miniature (see Fig. 28) shows a pile of wooden logs and scales identified as "scales for measuring imperial wood." The accompanying text and other sixteenth-century documents refer to this area as "the courtyard of wood supplies" *(hīme-i mühimme ḥavlısı)*, or the "wood storehouse" *(anbār-i hīme)*.[59] It was capable of accommodating five hundred shiploads of wood at a time, piled up in mountains. In 1675 Tavernier described it as a building that "encloses a large court, around and in the middle of which are arranged piles of wood that are renewed each year, and there are about forty thousand cartloads of wood, each cart loaded with as much as two oxen can pull" (see Figs. 20 a,b).[60] Adjacent to it was a "stable for wood-carrying oxen" *(āḫūr-i gāvān-i hīmekeşān* or *isṭabl-i gāvān)*.[61] Novices *(acemi oğlan)* who were being trained in the first court before their entry into the Janissary corps worked in the wood storehouse and with the oxen under the command of a eunuch in charge of the first court's infirmary, the connection being that these wood-carrying novices also had the job of transporting in their carts sick pages from their dormitories in the third court to the infirmary. When one of them died in the hospital, his body was washed by the imam of a masjid located at the wood storehouse.[62] A schematic seventeenth-century plan drawn by Albert Bobovi, a royal page of Polish origin, and the Fossati brothers' nineteenth-century view both show a dormitory for these novices to the left of the Imperial Gate (Pls. 16a,b *[62]*; see Figs. 20a,b). Bobovi says that about 120 of them lived there at a time. They ran errands for the royal pages in addition to carrying wood to the kitchens and the sick pages to the infirmary and were given other menial tasks.[63] Between their dormitory and St. Irene was the open court for stacking the wood supplies of the palace.

Adjacent to the wood-storage area was the workshop where the straw mats placed under the carpets of the royal residence were manufactured.[64] Account books of Süleyman's repairs in 1527–28 refer to it as the "royal mat workshop" *(ḥaṣīrḫāne-i ḫāṣṣa)*, which had a large pool.[65] Murad III enlarged this "workshop of mat makers in the vicinity of the stable of wood-carrying oxen" in 1575–76, and in the process took over the dormitory of novices who cared for the oxen. A new dormitory was built for the displaced novices.[66] No visual record of the workshop remains, but repair documents show that it included a dormitory for the mat makers featuring the usual tile roof, the workshop itself, a pool, a fountain, latrines, a bath with marble floors, an infirmary, a masjid, and a kitchen, all organized around a porticoed courtyard.[67] Like other service complexes of the first court, it was a fully equipped, self-sufficient unit.

Near the mat makers, the wood storage, and the stables for oxen at the left side of the court was the "imperial warehouse" *(anbār-i ʿāmire* or *anbār-i ḫāṣṣa)*, used for storing building materials required for the palace from the late fifteenth century onward. The oxen stabled nearby were used to haul these materials to and from the imperial warehouse as well as to haul firewood.[68] In Süleyman's reign, the architect Sinan enlarged this imperial warehouse, reflecting the unprecedented boom in the construction industry in his time.[69] It was guarded by a "chief storekeeper" *(ser-anbārī)* and his assistants *(anbārcıyān* or *ġilmān-i anbār-i ḫāṣṣa)*. Artisans attached to its service included carpenters, stone cutters, cement layers, locksmiths, sewer diggers, blacksmiths, hydraulic engineers, glaziers, lead casters, porters, construction laborers, and painters.[70] They were, however, only a small fraction of the central organization of royal artisans that was responsible for the creation of a unified court style in Ottoman art and architecture. Others were lodged in ateliers in the outer gardens or beyond the boundaries of the palace as was, for example, the workshop of court painters, which was housed in the mosaic-decorated upper story of a church near the Hippodrome, the dark basement of which Mehmed II had converted into a menagerie. A repair document of 1527–28 mentions the "repair of the atelier of painters and of the arch above the menagerie near the Hippodrome." [71] Painter-designers employed in the first court and associated with the imperial warehouse seem to have been mainly occupied with the maintenance and repair of the palace.[72]

The warehouse was under the control of the "city commissioner" *(şehr emini),* whose job it was to oversee building activities in the capital.[73] It was located to the left of the first court, just beyond the Church of St. Irene, near the path descending to the outer gardens. Besides storage vaults for the royal construction supplies, it also had workshops where carpenters and other artisans labored without surcease to embellish the palace and keep it in good repair.[74] It was a huge building adjacent to St. Irene, which the eighteenth-century French merchant Jean-Claude Flachat describes as a "vast edifice extending along the length of the court up to the gate of the gardens," which had a fountain in front.[75]

It may well be that the monumental double-storied edifice with a fountain in front, shown just beyond St. Irene in the Lewenklau album (Pl. 33d) is this very building. Lokman certainly locates the "imperial warehouse" *(anbār-i mühimmāt)* and its "workshop of artisans" *(kārḫāne-i üstādān)* beyond the church and near the fountain seen in the *Hünername* miniature (Pls. 10 *[11],* 14, 19; see Fig. 28).[76] According to a late-sixteenth-century treatise on the Ottoman court's organization, the offices of the city commissioner in charge of royal buildings, his secretaries, and warehouse guards were inside the imperial warehouse itself.[77] The *Hünername* places the city commissioner "in one corner" of the first court, with the "office of the chief architect" *(miʿmār başınuñ nişīmeni)* "on the other side," suggesting that the Corps of Royal Architects was stationed nearby.[78] Sinan, the chief of royal architects between 1538 and 1588, is reported to have regularly visited this architect's atelier in the imperial garden; there he trained his students, who disseminated the classical style of Ottoman architecture throughout the empire. They were selected from among the novices of the first court, who were taught various crafts, including music and carpentry, in the royal workshops before beginning their military career.[79]

An early reference to the royal mint, in 1547, places it in a "workshop in the imperial garden." [80] In Süleyman's time the famed ateliers of goldsmiths, gold-thread embroiderers, and jewelers who created the masterpieces of Ottoman metalwork were dependencies of this private royal mint,[81] referred to in sixteenth-century sources as the "inner mint" *(dārü'l-żarb-i enderūnī),* as distinguished from another mint outside the palace confines near the mosque of Bayezid II, which was known as the "outer mint" *(dārü'l-żarb-i bīrūnī).*[82] The inner mint was near the Tiled Kiosk, a royal pavilion reached by a path on the left side of the first court (Pl. 10 *[11, 12],* 11 *[13]*).[83] Although it is not mentioned by name in the *Hünername,* Lokman does refer to a "council hall of finance officers near the fountain, in the vicinity of the warehouse of provisions and artisans workshops," by which he may have meant the royal mint; it probably had a financial department attached to it.[84]

In the seventeenth century this building briefly ceased to function as a royal mint, since at that time the court mainly resided in Edirne.[85] It was rebuilt when the court returned in the eighteenth century, giving rise to the misconception that it was a new institution.[86] The texts make clear that it had existed long before that time, however, and that the present building, erected in 1726–27, was located on approximately the site of the earlier building, between St. Irene and the path descending to the outer gardens. The nineteenth-century historian Şeref cites a palace tradition that locates the two on precisely the same spot.[87]

To the right of the Imperial Gate lay the hospital referred to in the *Hünername* miniature as the "chamber of patients" *(ḫastalar odası)* (see Fig. 28). According to Menavino the palace had an infirmary in Mehmed's time, but he does not say where it was.[88] The unidentified group of buildings to the right of the Imperial Gate on Vavassore's map could possibly represent it (Pl. 23). Atâ attributes its foundation to Mehmed II, but Mustafa Âli says it was built for Süleyman I.[89] Süleyman's account books of 1527–28 refer to it as the "invalid's chamber near the Imperial Gate," and mention its bath.[90]

Bird's-eye views of the first court show the infirmary as a group of buildings organized around a courtyard (Pls. 10 *[15]*, 26b,c, 31a,b; see Fig. 20c). Bobovi's schematic seventeenth-century plan shows that it was compartmentalized according to the patient's status, as were the dormitories in the third court in which the sultan's pages normally lived (Pls. 16a,b *[50–60]*).[91] Abdullah bin İbrahim Üsküdari, a seventeenth-century royal page, confirms that the hospital *(tīmārḫāne* or *ḫastalar odası)* provided a bath and separate chambers for each group of royal pages, to keep them from intermixing.[92]

The eunuch in charge of the infirmary was also in charge of the wood storehouse across from it. He sat in front of the hospital during council meetings. The *Hünername* miniature depicts a black eunuch and his assistants with one of the double-wheeled handcarts, covered with a red curtain, that were used for transporting the sick pages from their dormitories in the third court to the first (see Fig. 28). According to Bobovi and Üsküdari, pages, who were not allowed to have any contact with the outer world, would pretend to be sick and then bribe the two novices bearing them off in carts to the infirmary to move slowly through the first court, so they could talk secretly to their relatives and acquaintances. Üsküdari adds that this "cart conversation" could continue within the hospital eunuch's chamber for an extra bribe.[93] Âli criticizes Süleyman for placing the hospital in the palace's most accessible court, thus permitting sick pages contact with the outer world and contributing to their corruption. It was probably built there, far from the third court, to avoid the spread of contagious diseases. Seventeenth-century writers tell us that by their time the infirmary had become a popular recreation place, allowing royal pages to exchange messages with acquaintances, to drink smuggled wine, and to relax in its dormitories, where patients were treated with music.[94]

Beyond the infirmary, past a gate that led to the outer gardens, lay the palace bakery (Pl. 10 *[17]*). The inscription on its gate communicating with the first court says that the building of the "royal bakehouse of bread" *(furun-i nān-i ḫāṣṣ)* was completed in 1025 (1616) by the order of Sultan Ahmed I.[95] A document in the palace archives lists expenses for the "new construction of the royal and common bakeries *[furun-i ḫāṣṣ ve ḫarcī]* and their chambers" incurred in 1612–14,[96] but it is unclear whether Ahmed I founded or rebuilt them. The bakeries produced two kinds of bread, a refined loaf for the royal family and common bread for the palace employees, made from flour ground in a mill in the outer gardens along the Marmara shore. Since none of the early sources, including the *Hünername,* mention these bakeries, they appear to have been built later, thus blocking the view of the surrounding gardens. As Barnette Miller has suggested, the earlier bakery might have been attached to the palace mill in the outer gardens (Pl. 10 *[29, 30]*).[97]

In the northeast corner of the first court, just past the bakery, were the palace waterworks (Pl. 10 *[19]*). The availability of water had of course played a major role in the selection of the site for Mehmed's New Palace. He had not begun its construction until he was convinced by experts that supplying water to its site was feasible.[98] In addition to fountains and cisterns from Byzantine times, the Halkalı Channel was extended to supply water to the palace through the rehabilitated Valens Aqueduct, which had also supplied water to the Old Palace.[99] A schematic plan of the Halkalı Channel from 1748 shows how water was distributed to various sections of the palace (Pl. 19).[100] It ran from a tower at the left side of the Imperial Gate to another tower at the left side of the second gate, collecting in a distribution reservoir at the northeast corner of the second court called *gümüş* (silver) (Pl. 11 *[26]*). Smaller channels branched off to various sections of the first two courts before reaching this reservoir. An official was stationed next to it to distribute water to the third court. Tavernier writes, "A *Baltacı* [halberdier] stays there all day long to distribute water, depending on how he is ordered, and when the Grand Signor passes from one quarter to the other, the fountain of the one where he is found begins to play immediately upon a signal that is given to the *Baltacı*." [101]

Sinan's autobiography, which he is thought to have dictated to his poet friend Mustafa Sa'i, reports that the palace waterworks were enlarged by Süleyman I. It recounts that the sultan ordered the construction of a waterwheel after observing that his palace gardens were not as lush as those of his chief treasurer İskender Pasha and his daughter Mihrimah. The sultan designated the site for the waterwheel and ordered it surveyed by experts. Sinan told him that a waterwheel built there would provide water only to a limited area; if he used a higher location it would supply water to the whole garden. The sultan was allegedly outraged by this contradiction of his royal opinion, but acquiesced on condition that the architect be punished if water was not found on the proposed spot. Fortunately, a partly collapsed but excellently built masonry well from the Byzantine period was uncovered at the far right corner of the first court.[102] Sinan repaired it and built a waterwheel next to it to provide water to the outer gardens (Pl. 10 *[19]*). He also brought new supplies of water to other sections of the palace through the Kırkçeşme Channel. Four new waterwheels built by him conducted water to the imperial palace, the imperial gardens, the kitchens, and the sultan's private quarters.[103]

The waterwheel near the bakery in the first court is one of the four Sinan added. It was built near the rediscovered antique well and communicates with the second court through the Gate of the Waterwheel *(dolāb ḳapusı)*.[104] Adjacent to this gate is a reservoir to which water was pumped by a horse-operated waterwheel from the neighboring well with spiral steps. Near it was a dormitory for the men attached to the service of the "Corps of the Waterwheel," a bath, latrines, a kitchen, a masjid, a stable for the horses that turned the wheel, and a storehouse for hay.[105] These buildings no longer exist, but they can be seen grouped around a small court in Scarella's views of 1686, together with other service courts framing the right side of the first court and extending along the axis of the second court's royal kitchens (Pls. 31a,b).

The Middle Gate

This brief survey of the outer service buildings flanking both sides of the first court suggests that they acted as unobtrusive boundaries defining the limits of a vast ceremonial space. The official visitor paraded along the central path of the first court, through the noisy confusion of minor officers, servants, petitioners, and horses until he finally arrived before the second gate. At that point a respectful silence was imposed, and thereafter progressively increasing degrees of silence prevailed throughout the palace, culminating in the third court, which was as silent as a sanctuary except on rare festive occasions.

The monumental double-towered gate in the center of the high wall separating the first court from the second was the most imposing structure visible to those progressing along the ceremonial path (Pls. 10 *[21]*, 11 *[1–4]*, 12 *[1]*; Fig. 31). Beyond this imposing edifice only the sultan could ride a horse, as was also the custom at the imperial gates of Abbasid and Byzantine palaces. At the end of the ceremonial procession through the first court, all others had to dismount closer to or further from the second gate according to their relative status.[106] Unlike the relatively accessible Imperial Gate, passage through this second gate was restricted only to those with official business in the second court. The Lewenklau album illustrations and the *Hünername* miniature show the gate flanked by raised platforms that were used as horse blocks from which important personages dismounted (Pl. 33h; see Fig. 28).

Menavino provides an early description of this double-towered gate at the end of the first court, which he says is "a beautiful piazza so large that twenty thousand cavalry soldiers could stand there easily, which is walled all around, and at the end of which are two towers with a gate where everyone customarily dismounts." [107] The Nuremberg woodcut shows this gate, whose original name is unknown, with its two towers, so we know they were

31 The second gate, known as the Middle Gate. Courtesy of Reha Günay.

there by the late fifteenth century (Pl. 24). It is often erroneously assumed that they were added in the sixteenth century by Süleyman I, who had been inspired by the castles he saw during his campaigns in the Balkans. This notion has no textual evidence to support it and must have arisen from the foreign appearance of the portal, and from an inscription on its gilded iron gates that reads, "Made by Isa, son of Mehmed, in the year 931 [1524–25]," [108] an inscription that refers to the replacement of the gilt iron doors themselves during an extensive remodeling of the second court by Süleyman I, and not to the whole gate. Kemalpaşazade, who lived from the end of Mehmed II's reign through the middle of Süleyman's, attributes the construction of these "two towers in the European mode *(iki frengī burġāz)* flanking both sides of the gate" to Mehmed II. Since he refers to them in a paragraph dealing with the construction of the Imperial Fortress in 1478, they might well have been added to the rectangular core of the second gate when the outer walls were built.[109]

This gate seems to have been modeled on the Gate of St. Barbara (Cannon Gate), which was the royal seaside entrance to the palace gardens from the Byzantine city wall on the shore (Pls. 10 *[48]*, 25a, 26–32). The Gate of St. Barbara echoed the form of the Golden Gate at Yedikule. It was flanked by two octagonal marble towers and was used in the Byzantine period as a triumphal processional entrance into the acropolis. It was therefore appropriate that Mehmed's second gate, which functioned as a ceremonial entrance to the palace proper, alluded to the form of these Byzantine triumphal city gates for royal processions. Its imperial architectural iconography was further enriched by an allusion to the ceremonial of the neighboring Chalke Gate at the Byzantine Great Palace, beyond which only the emperor could ride a horse.[110] The Middle Gate's towers, on both sides of a domical vestibule, used a *palatium* motif referring back to imperial Rome. Its towered facade effectively prepared the visiting dignitary for the spectacle awaiting him inside the second court, when he had to parade past thousands of ranked soldiers to the public council hall.

Mehmed II's second gate does not seem ever to have been altered, except in its details. It was remodeled as part of a general renovation of the second court by Süleyman I's grand vizier, İbrahim Pasha. Its gilt iron gates must be the "portail doré du Serrail" commissioned by İbrahim, according to the French visitor Guillaume Postel.[111] Süleyman's royal account books from the years 1527 to 1529 record that the painted decorations of its rebuilt portico ceilings were executed by court painters, and that the dormitories and latrines for the gatekeepers' use that flanked its vestibule were also repaired (see Appendix A.1).[112] Its newly painted portico facing the second court is described by the mid-sixteenth-century French antiquarian Petrus Gyllius (Pierre Gilles): "Tis suported with ten Pillars of different Kinds of Marble; the Roof of it proudly glitters with Gold, and is beautify'd with the most rich and lively Colours of *Persian* Work." This gilded portico, featuring painted decorations of gold and azure, is also mentioned by later sixteenth-century foreign visitors.[113]

Sixteenth- and seventeenth-century sources usually refer to this gate as the "Middle Gate" *(bāb-i miyāne* or *orta ḳapu),* referring to its central position among the palace's three main gates.[114] It was also called the "Gate of Felicity" *(bābü's-sa‹āde),* as it is on an inscription in the *Hünername* miniature and in Lokman's accompanying text (see Fig. 28).[115] The eighteenth-century Armenian author İnciciyan writes that the names "Middle Gate" and "Gate of Salutation" were used interchangeably. This is confirmed by a repair inscription dated 1172 (1759), which reads, "With security and felicity, may this Middle Gate *(orta ḳapu)* be a Gate of Salutation *(bābü's-selām).*"[116] The latter name probably alludes to the ceremonial procession of grandees and ambassadors from this gate up to the public Council Hall of the second court, during which it was customary to salute courtiers lined up around the court. It may carry the distant memory of the al-Salām courtyard in the Abbasid palace of Baghdad, which courtiers, soldiers, and the viziers similarly entered in a solemn procession to take their assigned places. The Baghdad of the caliph al-Mansur was called Dār al-Salām, Abode of Peace, a name given to paradise in the Koran (6:127, 10:26), where it is described as a place of security from injury, and a place where God's angels salute those who enter it. Therefore, *babü's-selām,* which also means "Gate of Peace," appears to be a reference to the peaceful image of paradise that the official visitor would encounter on crossing the threshold into the second court. A Koranic inscription on the inner facade of the gate, facing the garden court filled with gazelles, peacocks, ostriches, fountains, and trees, does compare it to the gates opening into the Garden of Eden.[117]

In stark contrast to the peace awaiting the visitor in the second court is the outer facade of the Middle Gate, facing the first court, whose fortified appearance restates the message of imperial power proclaimed by the Imperial Fortress (see Fig. 31). Its octagonal stone towers are crowned by conical lead caps and connected by a crenellated parapet, featuring a corbeled frieze reminiscent of machicolations. These elements have been cited as evidence to support the common assumption that it was designed primarily for defensive purposes; however, they are merely decorative motifs, just as the "loopholes" are simply thin slits to admit light into the dark towers.[118] That the gate might have a defensive purpose is also contradicted by the four small, undefended service doors on the same wall, which provide access to the second court (Pl. 11 *[6, 12, 13]*). This wall separating the first court from the second is a thin curtain wall, not a defensive one.

The military appearance of the Middle Gate thus had primarily a symbolic role as an architectural statement of sovereignty and imperial power. Like the domed vestibule of the Imperial Gate, that of the Middle Gate was hung with weapons. Gyllius describes this gate as blazing with "refulgent Arms," and other contemporary observers mention the swords, shields, bows, and arrows that hung there.[119] An archival document from 1783 lists gilding expenses for twenty axes, twenty-three swords, and twenty-four shields hanging on the Middle Gate.[120] According to Lokman's text accompanying the *Hünername* miniatures, above the vestibule was a masjid for gatekeepers; its ground floor was flanked by dormitories where the gatekeepers slept.[121] The upper-story masjid no longer exists, but is clearly seen in several sixteenth-century illustrations (see Figs. 35, 101). Its incorporation into the Middle Gate may have been inspired by the presence of a chapel in the nearby Chalke Gate. The two dormitories flanking the vestibule were connected at the right to a third hall that functioned as a state prison; the Chalke Gate is also reported to have had a prison.[122] This prison is seen in the Lewenklau album illustrations under a flap of paper on which the Middle Gate's outer facade is painted (Pl. 33j). The gate's imposing military facade and the prison behind it, where high-ranking officials were executed for transgressing the law, prepared the visiting dignitary for the main themes of the second court's ceremonial: victory and royal justice. As the visitor crossed its threshold, with gatekeepers lined up along the sides, the next stage of the ceremonial began.

THREE
The Second Court: State Ceremonial and Service Buildings

After he dismounted in front of the double-towered Middle Gate and passed its threshold, the official visitor arrived under a stately portico with ten marble columns attached to the gate's inner facade (Pls. 5a,b, 11 *[1]*). Through it the second court became visible. The contrast between the gate's military outer facade and the paradisal vision of the idyllic garden court inside was striking. The gate marked a clear transition from the first court to the second one, which consisted of a completely walled-in rectangular garden, planted with trees and lawns, crisscrossed by stone paths connecting the major buildings and gates, and lined with tall cypresses. Ostriches, peacocks, songbirds, deer, and gazelles wandered on the grass, fenced in by wooden railings painted red (Figs. 32–40).[1] Golden drinking cups were suspended from the many fountains on chains.[2]

This courtyard must have been completed by around 1465, the year Kritovoulos saw its towers, vestibules, porticoes, halls, and kitchens.[3] Its masonry structures, roofed in lead, accentuated its prestige as the administrative center of the empire, especially in contrast to the first court, whose buildings were of modest materials and had cheaper red tile roofs. Angiolello, who was one of Mehmed II's courtiers, provides the most detailed early description of the second court, which allows us to visualize its original form (Pl. 24):

> Past the first court, there is another double gate, and when one enters inside, there is another court the length and width of which is like that of the first. And at the right-hand side of this second court are the kitchens of the Grand Turk, which are vaulted in construction and covered with lead. And on the left-hand side are the stables of the Grand Turk, in which the horses on which the Grand Turk rides are kept; these long stables are behind [the second court's walls], if one can peep at them, and nearby there are some fountains, which provide water for the kitchens and for the horses to drink, and all these [stables] are covered with lead and are also of vaulted construction. And a little further ahead of the court is a small tower with iron gates, which is covered with lead, and in it is kept the money of the Grand Turk consisting of the revenues that arrive daily, and when 100,000 ducats or 100 casks of money accumulate in this place, that money is carried to the above-mentioned fort [i.e., Yedikule] where the grand treasury is located. And a little further ahead are the loggia and chancery *[Loggia et Cancellaria]*, in which the viziers, or in our language the councellors, sit, and in it are all those to whom are delegated the offices of state.[4]

This description tells us that the fifteenth-century layout of the second court was not much different from its present form. Today the second court, with its kitchens, stables, Tower of Justice, Council Hall (housing the chancery), and Public Treasury, approximates the final form it took after Süleyman I's extensive remodeling project, executed between 1525 and 1529, when the basic layout established by Mehmed II was elaborated and monumentalized (Pls. 5a,b, 12 *[A]*). The second court was modeled on the traditional layout of the administrative enclave in the tent-palaces of the Ottoman sultans. According to Spandugino, the administrative tent enclosure was connected to the residential one,

32 The second court, in Süleyman I's reign, during a public council meeting; the Council Hall, with its royal window in the Tower of Justice is shown on the right. From Arifi, *Süleymanname,* ca. 1557, TSK, H 1517, fols. 37v, 38r.

where the sultan slept, by a royal gallery closed with a gate. This tent gallery was flanked by the kitchens and stables.[5] One of Mehmed II's Janissaries, Mihailović, identifies the gallery-shaped tent in front of the gate that led into the sultan's residence as a *segiwan* (i.e., *sayevan* or *sayeban,* "awning"). Coming through the gate, the sultan appeared in public under this tent-gallery, which was adjacent to the council tent of the viziers known as *danisik czaderi* (i.e., *danışık çadırı,* "council tent")."[6]

The second court of Mehmed II's New Palace translated this traditional layout into permanent architectural forms. It was almost identical in plan to the administrative court of Mehmed II's palace in Edirne, the common denominator of the two being the organizational principle of the military camp (see Fig. 3). The regularity of the second court was broken by a deviation from the perpendicular on its left, caused by a sharp drop in the terrain that required a high retaining wall. As in the first court, so in the second the two main gates are not aligned because each is centered in the wall with reference to its own court, and the two courts themselves are not the same size, due to the irregular topography of the trapezoidal hilltop.

The tree-lined path through the second court,

33 A public council meeting at the second court during Süleyman I's reign. From Lokman, *Hünername,* ca. 1587–88, TSK, H 1524, fol. 242r.

34 A public council meeting at the second court, with Süleyman I listening to complaints about the qadi of Kayseri from the Tower of Justice, holding a bow in his hand; one of the pages accompanying him carries a quiver filled with arrows. From Lokman, *Hünername,* ca. 1587–88, TSK, H 1524, fol. 237v.

connecting the second and third gates, was meant to be traversed on foot by all but the sultan. It ran diagonally from the Middle Gate to the main administrative buildings—the vizier's Council Hall, which contained the chancery, and the Public Treasury—clustered at the far left corner of the court and marked by the Tower of Justice, surmounted with a royal belvedere pavilion. The service buildings were separated from the main courtyard by curtain walls pierced by gates to allow communication among them. Since the royal stables, which formed a narrow independent court along the left side, were built on a lower platform, their long halls were not visible from the main court, as Angiolello's description indicates. By contrast, the huge kitchens, which constituted another narrow court along the right side, were given visual prominence. Their tall chimneys, rising behind the boundaries of the main court, reminded the visitor of the sultan's largesse in distributing free food to his numerous courtiers and ambassadors, following an ancient custom of the Ottoman dynasty.

35 Ceremonies in the second court. From Lokman, *Hünername,* ca. 1584–85, TSK, H 1523, fols. 18v, 19r.

Language of Architecture and Ceremonial in the Second Court

The centerpiece of the second court was the third gate, fronted by a domed canopy at the middle of a stately marble colonnade (Pls. 11 *[27]*, 12 *[13]*). Under this Mehmed II used to present himself to his courtiers during communal banquets, to loud acclaim, but following the prescriptions of his *kanunname,* by the sixteenth century sultans had ceased to appear there, except on the two religious holidays, on their accession, and in times of crisis (see Figs. 38–40). The second court was like a magnificent theater with an impressively large cast, but the principal actor very rarely appeared on stage. With a few exceptions, its ceremonial centered on the virtually absent ruler. His symbolic presence was implied by the prominence of the third gate, through which one entered the Chamber of Petitions; it was a monumental gate that expressed the supreme authority of the sultan, whose centralized state government operated from the nucleus of the second court. The administrative buildings concentrated in the left corner—that is, off the center—

36 The second court during the reception ceremony of Serdar Sinan Pasha. From Lokman, *Shahanshāhnāma,* 1592, TSK, B 200, fol. 31r.

37 The second court during the reception ceremony of an ambassador from Morocco, in the last quarter of the sixteenth century. From Lokman, *Shahanshāhnāma,* 1592, TSK, B 200, fol. 142v.

expressed the subordinate position of administrative bureaucrats in relation to the sultan, represented architecturally by the centrally placed third gate. This arrangement illustrated the Ottoman political concept of the porte *(kapı),* that is, the administration of the state and of justice in front of the sultan's gate by his extended household and administrators. The Porte, then, was both a concrete place and an abstract concept of government.[7]

The Ottomans lacked an impressive genealogy to legitimize their rule, but made up for this by their success as warriors for the Islamic faith and their record as just rulers. For the latter reason, they went further than any other Islamic dynasty in systematizing the secular, extra-Shari'a dimension of law *(kanun)* for the promulgation of a dynastic tradition of justice. Administering justice was considered the most important function of the Ottoman state; the imperial council, which was the state's supreme organ, was essentially a high court of justice. Writing during Bayezid II's reign, the historian

38 The accession ceremony of Süleyman I in the second court. From Lokman, *Hünername,* ca. 1587–88, TSK, H 1524, fols. 25v, 26r.

Bidlisi refers to the Council Hall as the "iwan of the council of justice" *(īwān-i dīvān-i* ʿadl) and says that within the large second courtyard, which he compares to paradise, the beasts of King Solomon (known for his justice) were assembled.[8] Similarly, a text from Süleyman I's reign refers to the second court as "the arena of justice" *(sāḥa-i ʿadālet)*; and Lokman calls it "the arena of the great house of justice" *(sāḥa-i dārü' l-ʿadāle-i muʿaẓẓama)*.[9] *Kanunnames* promulgated by sultans descended from the House of Osman expressed this commitment to justice.[10] It is not coincidence that the second court was founded by Mehmed II and elaborated both architecturally and ceremonially under Süleyman the Lawgiver ("Kanuni"). Both rulers were legislators to whom the most famous Ottoman *kanunnames* are attributed.

This theme of imperial justice was obvious to contemporary European visitors to the second court. Gyllius calls it the *"Forum Judiciale,"* which the Ottomans called *Divan.*[11] Justice was dispensed in the name of the sultan in the Council Hall, as he secretly watched lawsuits from a curtained window. This window announced that, though the secluded sultan might delegate his authority to dignitaries, he himself made certain that no injus-

39 A *bayram* ceremony in the second court, showing the grand vizier Osman Pasha kissing the hem of Murad III's robe. From Lokman, *Shahanshāhnāma,* 1592, TSK B 200, fols. 159v, 160r.

tice was committed against his subjects. Although invisible, his presence was always palpable. Those found guilty of perpetrating injustice in his name were imprisoned in the prison at the Middle Gate and executed in front of the Executioner's Fountain *(cellad çeşmesi)*, to the left of the gate (Pls. 33k,l; see Figs. 32, 35). The sultan, who watched these executions from his pavilion in the Tower of Justice, made his presence known by opening one of its latticed shutters while the prisoners loudly begged for forgiveness.[12]

The Council Hall's curtained royal window and the tower paradoxically signified the absent sultan's omnipresence in the administration of justice. The adjacent Public Treasury, from which his numerous slave soldiers and courtiers were paid regular wages, announced his wealth. The kitchens projected an image of his munificence. Seen as a group, these buildings exemplified the ancient Near Eastern concept of the cycle of equity, the principle according to which there could be no state without the army, no army without revenues, no revenues without prosperity, no prosperity without justice, and no justice without the state. In this way the accumulation of wealth to support the state and the administration of justice, in order to protect the sultan's subjects, was rationalized in the buildings of the second court, legitimizing the basis for Otto-

40 The accession ceremony of Ahmed I (1603) in the second court, İÜ, T 6624, fols. 1v, 2r.

man political organization.

The unimposing and loosely ordered cluster of buildings of the second court could only be perceived as a unified whole through court ceremonial. European and Ottoman sources stress equally that ceremony overshadowed the architectural framework. Completely enclosed on four sides by walls that allowed no vision of what lay beyond and uncluttered by freestanding buildings, the second court was an ideal space for focusing attention on official and administrative functions. Since architectural distractions were minimal, the observer-participant was compelled to concentrate on the ceremonial activities. In this vast theater, with its cast of thousands of slave soldiers and courtiers, the absent sultan was represented by the centrally placed third gate, the curtained window overlooking the Council Hall, and the tower pavilion (Pl. 11 *[20, 23, 27]*). The last two were the only views the secluded sultan had from his private residence into the administrative center of his empire.

The second court was visually unified by a continuous marble colonnade only after Süleyman I rebuilt its two major buildings, the Council Hall adjacent to the Tower of Justice and the Public Treasury (Pls. 11 *[20–24]*, 12 *[9–11]*). Before that, there seem to have been porticoes only in front of the two main gates and the Old Council Hall of viziers (Pl. 11 *[1, 25, 27]*). In 1503 the Venetian ambassador Andrea Gritti's secretary wrote, "They made us, that is the notables, Aurelio, and myself, sit under the portico in front of the loggia [Old Council Hall]; the attendants had to dine in the middle of the court under some trees that were there."[13] This suggests that the marble colonnade extending along the left side of the court, where later visitors were served food, had not yet been built. Before the ceremonial space of the second court was provided with a marble arcade, the plain curtain walls that separated it from the stables and kitchens seem to have served as the only backdrop for the ceremonies that were staged there.

Besides its function as a tribunal for justice and imperial administration, four days a week, the second court was used to impress ambassadors representing important monarchs with the sultan's power. A special ceremony was held for them, called the Council of Victory *(galebe divanı)*, during which all courtiers had to be present, wearing their best uniforms and lining up in orderly ranks at their assigned places.[14] During these specially staged events the second court was decorated with valuable textile hangings, precious carpets, and curtains brought out from the Public Treasury. The richness of these furnishings depended on the status of the embassy—ambassadors from countries regarded as unimportant were received without extra decorations.[15] Occasionally, wild animals and horses with jeweled trappings were also exhibited along the left side of the court, near the stables, echoing the effect of the first court.[16] In 1530 the Holy Roman Emperor Ferdinand I's ambassadors to Süleyman I, Nikolaus Jurischitsch and Joseph von Lamberg, saw ten lions and two tigers there, fettered with gold chains and roaring terribly.[17] Sometimes these Councils of Victory were scheduled to coincide with the days on which the Janissaries received their trimonthly wages from the Public Treasury, in order to display the sultan's wealth.

Every ambassador, having first dismounted as required in front of the Middle Gate, then had to walk in the same solemn procession through thousands of richly clad soldiers and courtiers to the Council Hall. At set places along the processional route he was obliged to stop and salute the various groups of courtiers in their assigned positions around the court, just as he had done during the parade through the first court. These stations were indicated by porphyry markers called "salutation stones" *(selam taşı)* (Pl. 11 *[19]*).[18] When the ambassador approached the Council Hall, the viziers came out to its portico to greet him—a custom discontinued after Süleyman's renovations as the grand vizier's haughtiness came to approximate the sultan's. Inside the Council Hall, the ambassador was granted an audience by the grand vizier, after which food was served from the imperial kitchens as a gesture of the sultan's hospitality (Figs. 41, 42). The degree of lavishness of the banquet that followed was again a reflection of the relative status of the persons being honored; lesser ambassadors were not deemed worthy to eat at the same table with viziers and were served their food outside (Fig. 43). Finally, the ambassador was conducted to the sultan's presence inside the third court.

When the imperial cavalry and foot soldiers stood in their fixed places along the court, the result was an awe-inspiring scene, described in these terms by Andrea Gritti's secretary in 1503:

> On the right side at the head of the above-mentioned court, near the entrance gate [Middle Gate], sat the Agha of Janissaries, under a portico with his *yaya başıs*, that is, lieutenants, and the Janissaries, who numbered around 3,000, stood next to one another, row upon row along the entire right all the way to the upper end, a thing certainly most beautiful and very splendid to look at. On the left side were the palace cavalry, consisting of the *sipahioğlan, ulufeci,* and *silahtar* companies and similar men of the cavalry troops, numbering about 1,500. At the head sat their leaders, the *sipahioğlan başı, silahtar başı,* and *ulufeci başı*. Nearby, in a loggia, the magnificent

41 The banquet of the Austrian ambassador Hans Ludwig von Kuefstein at the public Council Hall in 1628. From Teply, *Die kaiserliche Grossbotschaft an Sultan Murad IV*, pp. 120–21.

pashas gave audience. At the front was the gate from which one enters into the Signor's presence; under its portico, extending from one side to the other, sat the *kapıcıs*, that is, gatekeepers, and other officials of His Majesty.[19]

In his 1503 report to the Venetian Senate, Gritti himself (who later elaborated Venetian state ceremonies when he became doge in the 1520s, during Süleyman's reign) described the impact of this incredible scene: "I entered into the court, where I found on one side all the Janissaries on foot, and on the other side all the persons of high esteem, and the salaried officials of His Majesty, who stood with such great silence and with such a beautiful order that it was a marvelous thing not believable to one who has not seen it with his own eyes." His contemporary, Spandugino, describes the ceremonial in similar terms:

And when one wants to go from this second gate to where the pashas are, one has to pass from the middle of this court, and there again are *kapıcıs* who guard it, and it is their custom not to let anyone talk; otherwise they are hit with a stick. While one passes [through the court], at the right side are approximately ten or twelve thousand Janissaries, and they all stand, except for their Agha, who is seated with some other dignitaries under a gallery at the entrance to the second gate. At the left side, toward the stables, are the *sipahis*, *ulufecis*, *silahtars*, and all the other categories of salaried men whom we have previously mentioned. And all those who come for an audience with the pashas stand on the left beside the stables. And it is a beautiful thing to see such a handsome

42 Engraving of a banquet in honor of a European ambassador at the public Council Hall; the *tughras* of the ruling sultan flank the royal window. From Ohsson, *Tableau général de l'Empire othoman.*

assembly so well ordered, some clad in gold cloth, others in patterned velvet, with great pomp and grace.[20]

The fixed ordering of soldiers on the right and left sides of a public courtyard had Islamic precedents going back to Abbasid court ceremonial, where silence had been similarly emphasized. A tenth-century Buyid secretary reports in his *Rules and Regulations of the Abbasid Court* that it was "the rule for the people not to speak, and that neither sound nor clamor should be heard from them." To assure complete silence, the caliph's servants stood ready with bows in their hands to "shoot down any crow or bird lest they disturb the proceedings with their ominous crowing and noise."[21]

In general outline, the ceremonial order codified in Mehmed II's *kanunname* remained unchanged throughout the sixteenth century. After Süleyman remodeled the second court, its details were elaborated to an unprecedented degree and outdid every other court in splendor, winning the sultan his title of "Magnificent" in the West. The Venetian ambassador Pietro Bragadino, who came to the Topkapı in 1526 and had previously visited the Mamluk court in Cairo, found the Ottoman court much richer and more beautiful, with its horses in bejeweled caparisons and its courtiers dressed in gold cloth and precious silks.[22] In 1567 Marc'Antonio Pigafetta observed that the numerous courtiers standing in complete silence and obedience constituted the Ottoman court's unequaled grandeur and magnificence.[23] Another Venetian ambassador, Andrea Badoaro, compared the Topkapı in 1573 to the great palaces he had seen in Europe and concluded that no court in Christendom equaled its pomp and magnificence.[24]

Philippe du Fresne-Canaye, who visited the palace with a French embassy in 1573, provides a poetic description of the disciplined soldiers lined up around the court in an order that elaborated patterns already established in the fifteenth century:

At the right hand was seated the Agha of Janissaries, very near the gate, and next to him some of the highest grandees of the court. The Ambassador saluted them with his

head and they got up from their seats and bowed to him. And at a given moment all the Janissaries and other soldiers who had been standing upright and without weapons along the wall of that court did the same, in such a way that seeing so many turbans incline together was like observing a vast field of ripe corn moving gently under the light puff of Zephyr ... We looked with great pleasure and even greater admiration at this frightful number of Janissaries and other soldiers standing all along the walls of this court, with hands joined in front in the manner of monks, in such silence that it seemed we were not looking at men but statues. And they remained immobile in that way more than seven hours, without talking or moving. Certainly it is almost impossible to comprehend this discipline and this obedience when one

43 (opposite), 44 (above) A banquet in 1573 for the retinue of an Austrian embassy under the left portico of the second court and the parade of Austrian ambassadorial gifts in the second court, with the enthroned sultan seen behind the third gate. Album of Lambert Wyts, 1574, MS. Vienna, Österreichische Nationalbibliothek Cod. 3325*.

has not seen it ... After leaving this court we mounted our horses where we had dismounted upon arrival ... Standing near the wall beyond the path we saw pass all these thousands of Janissaries and other soldiers who in the court had resembled a palisade of statues, now transformed not into men but into famished wild beasts or unchained dogs.[25]

That the second court's ceremonies had the same impact on many European ambassadors is demonstrated by a description by Baron Wenceslas Wratislaw, who had seen the Topkapı in 1559: "Although there were some thousands of people there, nevertheless, there was no shouting, no conversation, no moving hither and thither, but all stood so quietly that we could not help wondering; nay, even the Janissaries, although furious and licentious people in war, here observed greater obedience towards their commander than boys towards their preceptor, standing as quiet as if they had been hewn out of marble."[26] This was no doubt precisely the kind of reaction the Ottomans were hoping to elicit at these Victory Councils, which could well convince embassies that the sultan was invincible.

Illustrations in the Lewenklau album of 1586, which record the reception ceremony of an Austrian embassy, capture the flavor of such Victory Councils in greater detail (Pls. 33j–o). They are accompanied by marginal notes that identify the courtiers, and in the process show how architecture acted as a stage for the theatrics enacted in it. Lackeys wearing plumed headgear, with rows of Janissaries behind them, are lined up along the right side of the court; their superiors sit under a portico in front of the Middle Gate, just as the texts describe. Under the porticoes to the left, a display of ambassadorial gifts appears as one lifts a paper flap of the album, on which wooden screens are drawn (Pls. 33j–l). According to Naili Abdullah Pasha's *Book of Ceremonies,* compiled in the eighteenth century from earlier texts, these gifts were brought to the palace the day before an official audience and arranged for exhibition behind protective wooden screens, on benches along the left portico, near the harem gate.[27] There the secretary of the Master of Ceremonies recorded them. That this practice had existed since the sixteenth century is proven by observers from that time, who relate that ambassadorial gifts were exhibited on carpet-covered stone benches under the left portico, where the ambassadorial retinues were also served their food (Pl. 33l).[28]

Illustrations in the Lewenklau album also show a ceremonial banquet offered to the retinues; in the foreground of one, veiled women and turbaned men seeking justice wait for their cases to be heard. Gatekeepers holding batons move about to ensure silence and order, striking those who do not behave properly,[29] as the ambassadors parade up the paved path toward the Council Hall (Pls. 33m,n). Under the marble colonnade that extended along the third gate, the leading eunuchs of the sultan's residence and officers of the palace's outer services are seated; a row of gatekeepers stands ready to carry the ambassadorial gifts to the sultan, who is seated inside the Chamber of Petitions in the third court.

Another group of Austrian drawings, from the Lambert Wyts album of 1574, depicts this ceremonial against the fantastic backdrop of a Europeanizing stage set (Fig. 44; see Fig. 43). The banquet is being served to the ambassador's retinue under the left portico, while Ottoman dignitaries in exotic costume exhibit in their hands the ambassadorial gifts, which include European clocks. They are about to bring them into the presence of the sultan, who is seated behind the third gate, here given a monumental Mannerist facade. These drawings wonderfully illustrate a European impulse to beautify and improve the second court's architectural framework, which they found rather unimpressive. The statement of an anonymous Venetian ambassador in 1579 that the Ottoman court was more impressive in its ceremonial pomp and its richly vested courtiers, which evoked incredulous amazement, than in its architecture reflects an opinion generally shared by Europeans.[30] The sixteenth-century visitors Ogier Ghiselin de Busbecq, Fresne-Canaye, and Michael Heberer von Bretten, all criticize the second court's lack of monumentality.[31] So does their contemporary, Salomon Schweigger, who complains of its haphazard layout, remarking that the small, low buildings look as if they had fallen out of a bag.[32]

When Europeans do praise the architecture of this court, they compare it to the cloisters of a monastery and refer to its precious marble revetments, its pavements inlaid with multicolored stones, its costly marble columns, and its gilt paintings on the portico ceilings.[33] The Habsburg ambassador Corneille Schepper, who saw the court in 1533, just after Süleyman's renovations, marveled at its "very beautiful colonnades, paved with an admirable artifice and elegance."[34] Caterino Zeno wrote in 1550 that the "pavements of all the colonnades were inlaid with multicolored stones," and that they had "beautiful columns and exquisite vaults."[35] In the last quarter of the sixteenth century, Reinhold Lubenau observes that the ceilings of colonnades and the vestibules of the main gates were painted with gold stars *(guldene Sternen)* on a blue background.[36]

In 1547 the Frenchman Jean Chesnau remarked that the architectural magnificence of the inaccessible inner palace was far greater than what ambassadors saw in the second court: "The said palace is marvelously beautiful for they have transported large multicolored marbles, porphyry, columns, and other unique materials not only from Constantinople, and Chalcedonia, but also from all over Greece and Asia to build it. One does not enter its chambers nor the rest of the building, except for a large court with some colonnades and low rooms, where they give audience four times a week. But from that place one can judge externally that this is a magnificent edifice."[37] Unlike the architecturally elaborate third court and the lavish garden pavilions, which were an extension of the sultan's private realm, the first two "exterior" *(birun)* courts were conceived as mere forecourts to the sultan's actual residence, the "interior" *(enderun)*, and as service areas for the extended royal household that regulated the sultan's relations with the outer world. For that reason, Ottoman descriptions of the second court, like foreign ones, concentrate on the ceremonies that took place in it, and make only tangential references to its architecture.[38]

Lokman's description of this court in the *Hünername* manuscript of 1584 analyzes its ceremonial in detail, and the accompanying miniature schematically depicts various administrative activities in the manner of the contemporary Lewenklau album illustrations (see Fig. 35). Although he praises the second court for its fountains, its large scale, and its tall columns, shining like mirrors, his description is otherwise nonarchitectural. Lokman sees the uniqueness of the Ottoman court in its ceremonial transactions between the interior and exterior zones of the palace, revolving around the theme of imperial justice. He praises the sober and strictly official nature of Ottoman court ceremonial, devoid of the "corruption of taverns and unorthodox entertainments," an indirect reference to court festivities at European and Islamic palaces characterized by royal banquets and drinking parties. Not only was there an absence of entertainment, but the ceremonies began with the recitation of the Sura of Victory (Koran, Sura 48).[39]

Lokman lists in detail the posts assigned to courtiers in the second court, and the fixed order in which members of the imperial council presented petitions to the sultan at the third court. This unchanging order came to be seen as a metaphor for the Ottoman state's traditional organization, based on dynastic principles, perpetuated by *kanun,* and codified by books of ceremonies. In 1588–91 Abu'l-Hasan al-Tamgruti, an ambassador from Morocco, expressed amazement at the rigidity of law and protocol: "All the affairs of the empire, interior or exterior, are regulated among the Turks by constitutions and written laws that have been codified. The grand vizier has to follow them to the letter and must never deviate from them. In doing so he does not need to consult at all with the sultan; he must only do so for important affairs." Noting the strict hierarchies and elaborate dress codes observed by Ottoman officials, al-Tamgruti continues, "Never should any one of them deal on an equal basis with his superior, be it in marching in the same row, in wearing a turban or clothes of the same quality, or in sitting on a similar seat. I have never seen men observe marks of precedence more scrupulously."[40]

Rigid rules of protocol, prescribing in minute detail the exact ordering of ceremonial functions and hierarchies of status, stressed the dynastic perpetuity of the empire and rendered it more majestic. Their message was directed to two audiences, insiders and outsiders. From an insider's point of view, they eliminated ambiguities within the sociopolitical order by giving visible structure and legitimacy to it. They confirmed the corporate unity of the ruling elite and its dependence on the sultan, while at the same time affirming distinctions of status within this privileged group. Not being hereditary nobles, the members of this artificially created elite derived their relative place in society from the office to which they were assigned by the sultan; they performed on the stage of the Topkapı Palace according to rules set by their master. The slave system that pervaded the military and palace services turned the dominant pattern of central government into a master-slave relationship. Ceremonial served to create a visual diagram of this hierarchically organized military state that was immediately graspable at a glance. This diagram accentuated the omnipotence of the sultan together with the transformation of the centralized state into a bureaucracy and a great army at the personal service of the sultan.

The perpetuation of ceremonial communicated a message of timeless order and stability, bestowing permanence and legitimacy on an arbitrary social construct. Its power lay in constant repetition, enacted in an eery silence, as if time had been temporarily suspended by an endless recurrence. It froze time into an eternal present and created the illusion of an order transcending mere human experience. The second court's ceremonial dramatized political concepts and a mentality of absolutism by making dignitaries act out their assigned roles within the ideal monarchical order. Dramatically portraying an ideological fiction about the nature of power, it mirrored a theory of absolute sovereignty in which the invisible, patrimonial monarch parceled out authority to his agents, the majority of whom were his household slaves. It was not a mere spectacle or game, but actively generated the empire's political reality. It also provided a potential stage for the rebellious exhibition of discontent when the social order was faced with crisis. The second court of the Topkapı Palace was, therefore, the arena in which relative rank and status were continually tested and challenged in a competitive fashion. Its ceremonial represented a male-dominated political order in which royal women, locked up in their harem, could participate only indirectly, through intermediaries.

For foreign audiences ceremonies provided a magnificent and intimidating backdrop to diplomatic negotiations. The bureaucrat and historian Feridun Ahmed Beg reports how "astonished, bewildered, stupefied, and completely enraptured" the Habsburg ambassador from Vienna was by the "order, decoration, and etiquette" he saw when he came to congratulate Selim II on his accession in 1566–67.[41] The same author records that Şahkulu, the Persian ambassador sent by the Safavid ruler Tahmasp that year, was also "lost in bewilderment," and became convinced of Ottoman superiority when he encountered the countless obedient courtiers all lined up in "order, majesty, magnificence, and greatness" around the broad court. He could not hide his astonishment at the silence of the massed Janissaries, which not even four or five Persians could sustain. The "order, ornament, luster, and magnificence" of the Council Hall was beyond description.[42]

Lokman describes another audience, given to the Safavid prince Haydar Mirza in 1591, in similar terms. When he entered the second court, the amazed prince looked down in embarrassment and knit his brows with shame when he beheld the thousands of orderly soldiers. After a sumptuous banquet in the Council Hall, where food was served on jewel-studded Chinese porcelain plates, with jeweled gold spoons, he emerged to join his attendants, who had been "exhausted" and "weakened" by the sight of the Janissaries and the display of imperial pomp; together they watched the Ottoman officials enter in their assigned order to present their petitions to the sultan.[43] An anonymous treatise, dated 1639–40, proposes some changes in the ceremonial to inspire even greater awe in the visitor. It suggests that the silverware stored in the Public Treasury be exhibited in front of it, that the

45 A parade of horses in the second court, with a band performing martial music before the sultan, enthroned under the third gate (Gate of Felicity) during a *bayram* ceremony. From Ohsson, *Tableau général de l'Empire othoman.*

gatekeepers should carry silver-coated batons, and that both the sultan's Chamber of Petitions and the vizier's Council Hall should be fitted out with silver-plated gates, wall panels, and window lattices. The reformer adds that staging a fencing tournament among four or five hundred Janissaries would also provide an effective spectacle.[44]

Such opulent displays for the benefit of foreigners also reinforced the imperial regime at home (Fig. 45). Their role in Ottoman court ceremonial was not so different from that outlined in the tenth-century *Book of Ceremonies,* compiled for the Byzantine emperor Constantine VII Porphyrogenitus: "As a result of this praiseworthy order the imperial power is revealed as more majestic and awe-inspiring and for that reason is honored by foreigners and by our own subjects." The imperial rituals, which were "like flowers picked in the fields to decorate the imperial splendor," had to be exercised with silence, rhythm, and order to reproduce the harmonious movement of the universe. The role of Abbasid palace ceremonial outlined by a tenth-century Buyid secretary was not that different either; the silent rhythm and perfect order of court rituals contributed to the dignity of the audience and made it "more awe-inspiring."[45]

Royal Kitchens

The boundaries of the second court's central ceremonial space were demarcated by two service courts lying behind its walls. The first of these comprised the palace kitchens, which extended along the right side of the second court and formed a subsidiary service court with living quarters for its staff (Pls. 5a,b, 9, 11 *[10]*, 12 *[5]*; Fig. 46). The kitchen court was separated from the second court by a wall containing several gates. Its layout was essentially established by Mehmed II, extended by Süleyman I, and extensively renovated by Sinan after the kitchens burned down in a fire in 1574. Their steep retaining walls and the first two domed units on the south end are the only fifteenth-century remains.[46]

According to Menavino, a page in the palace between 1505 and 1514, the original kitchens were divided into two sections, one private, for the sultan, the other public, for the household, staffed with about 160 servants.[47] This number increased considerably in the course of the sixteenth century, as the palace population grew, but even in Mehmed II's time the kitchens seem to have occupied the whole length of the second court, as is suggested by the continuity of their steep retaining wall with that of the third court. An elevation of a royal bath located along the right wing of the third court, drawn for a repair project after an earthquake in 1509, confirms that the kitchens extended up to the curtain wall separating the second court from the third (see Fig. 74).[48] An account book of 1474 listing expenses for Mehmed II's imperial kitchens (*maṭbāḫ-i ʿāmire*) provides information about the food cooked there, and a payroll of 1478–79 lists the officials employed, but neither document gives any hint of the architectural organization.[49]

Around 1550 Gyllius described the kitchens as having "eight arch'd Roofs, rising like a Cupola, in an hemispherical Manner; each of these Cupolas representing the figure of a little House, is nothing else but a chimney with Windows, light at Top, made in the Likeness of a Lantern."[50] We learn from Süleyman's account books that the extended imperial kitchens were divided into separate units catering to different groups of the palace hierarchy, as well as to those congregating within the second court during council meetings. They had a separate confectionary (*ḥelvaḫāne*) and an outer commissariat (*kilār-i bīrūnī* or *kilār-i ʿāmire*), each with its own staff and equipment.[51]

We learn how fire destroyed the kitchens in June 1574 through the account of the contemporary historian Selaniki:

46 Aerial view of the second court, with the stables, the Archaeological Museum, and the Tiled Kiosk in the foreground. Courtesy of Reha Günay.

> While kabob was being grilled at the imperial kitchen, by divine accident oil in the frying pan ignited, sending up flames of fire to the ceiling; which rendered extinguishing it impossible. The flame reaching the servants' rooms on the other side finally arrived at the commissary and the confectionary, creating a great fire that unexpectedly caused total confusion. And all the great viziers and the Agha of Janissaries arrived. Unable to find a remedy, they were helpful only insofar as they hindered its spreading to the inner imperial palace by immediately demolishing a wall.... In short, at the imperial commissariat and in the confectionary various agreeable rare objects and Chinese porcelain vessels, instruments, and other irreplaceable objects which had been inherited from previous sultans, were all wasted away.[52]

Although all contemporary sources say that the fire did not spread to the inner palace and affected only the general kitchen area,[53] architectural historians have continued to insist that it swept through the whole palace: Fanny Davis and Aptullah Kuran, for example, base their argument that Sinan built the Council Hall of the second court on the assumption that it was damaged in this fire; Barnette Miller claims that the conflagration swept away all but two or three of the palace's original structures; Godfrey Goodwin says the fire destroyed the harem.[54] But no such conclusions emerge from the documents themselves. A monthly account book lists, from July 1574 onward, the various expenses involved in replacing the imperial kitchen, confectionary, and imperial commissary, the rebuilding of which continued a few months into Murad III's reign, until March 1575.[55] Imperial decrees issued during the last year of Selim II's reign document in detail the supply of building materials and the number of construction workers employed. Firmans from August 1574, for example, concern the conscription of construction workers from Bilecik and the provision of marble and marcasite stone from Karamürsel.[56] Others from September order the transfer of half of the slaves working on the Selimiye Mosque in Edirne, ask for additional workers from Bilecik, and search for lead from Edirne, Thessaloniki, Sofia, and Plovdiv, for the kitchen roofs.[57]

Sa'i informs us that Sinan was charged with rebuilding the imperial commissariat, the kitchens, and their storage vaults after the fire.[58] Selaniki explains it this way:

> A few days later, the Admiral, the Agha of Janissaries, and the Agha of Istanbul came, and Mimar Sinan Agha made its plan and layout in accordance to its previous form [*ṭarz-i āḫir üzre resm ve ṭarḥ eyliyüb*]. Its site was cleared up and two and a half cubits of space were taken over along the length (*ṭulen*) of the court of the imperial council and added to the grounds of the imperial kitchens, which were thus enlarged.[59]

Sinan probably based his plan on the previous layout because the organization of the kitchens staff required it. Miller has argued that the 2.5 cubits he took from the second court meant that the wall separating the second from the third court must have been torn down,[60] but it is more likely that the extra space was made up by moving the right portico forward. The fire had spread so easily because the dormitories opposite were too close to the kitchens. By taking extra space, Sinan widened the path between them. That the marble colonnade in front of the kitchens was altered in this process is supported by the visible difference between its brick arcades and those around the rest of the court.

This portico is pierced by three double gates that correspond to the three main divisions of the kitchens; they are depicted in a *Hünername* miniature (see Fig. 35). Starting from the south they are the Gate of the Imperial Commissariat (*kilār-i ʿāmire ḳapusı*), the Gate of the Royal Kitchen (*ḫāṣṣ maṭbāḫ ḳapusı*), and the Gate of the Confectionary (*ḥelvaḫāne*) (Pls. 11 *[7–9]*, 12 *[2–4]*).[61] The portico served to screen the service area behind it. When its gates were locked at night the kitchen court became an independent area. It communicated through another door with the right wing of the first court, where related services such as the royal bakeries and water installations were housed.

Sinan's kitchens have been modified by frequent repairs, and most of the living quarters have been demolished. Their silhouette was altered in the 1940s, when the conical lead caps crowning the cylindrical chimneys were removed.[62] A seventeenth-century drawing by Scarella shows what they looked like from the outer garden, with multiple domes next to the sloping, pitched roof of the commissary at the south (Pl. 31b). Today the commissary is next to a masjid for cooks, identified with an inscription from 1626 as the "noble mosque of the royal kitchens at the lower end." Adjacent to it are ten domed halls, preceded by smaller vaulted furnaces in front. These end in a row of three small domed chambers at the north. Two of the latter are identified as the masjid for the confectioners in an inscription of 1613–14. The third, believed to be a soap manufactory, communicates with the ninth and tenth domed halls, which are separated from other kitchens by a wall. They are identified by various inscriptions as the confectionary kitchens, where sherbets, jams, and sweet pastes were prepared.[63] The remaining eight domes marked off eight individual kitchens that catered to different groups. Each produced food graded to match the status of its clientele: the southernmost unit was for the sultan's food, followed by those for the queen mother, the sultanas, the head gatekeeper, the imperial council, the royal pages, the lower-ranked male and female servants, and minor officers of the imperial council.[64] The facilities located across from these once included dormitories, baths, and masjids, but they have now been entirely replaced by modern buildings.

The kitchen complex also included a storage area for valuable tableware. Account books of 1527–29 mention the repair of the "ceramics room *(oda-i çīnī)* near the imperial kitchens."[65] Atâ attributes the establishment of these depots of rare vessels and Chinese ceramics across from the kitchens to Mehmed II, who entrusted them to the head commissar. This is supported by Angiolello's statement that during public banquets in the second court Mehmed II's food was carried from the kitchens on porcelain plates.[66] The İznik and Chinese ceramic tableware used at the circumcision ceremonies of princes at the Hippodrome in 1582 were loaned out from the same porcelain storeroom *(çīnī anbārı)*.[67] Since a document of 1581–82 refers to "the chamber of the ceramics official at the kitchen" *(oda-i çīnīci der maṭbāḫ)*, we know that the porcelain storeroom was rebuilt after the fire.[68] Large Chinese porcelain vessels were also used to store drinks and potions at the commissary, according to Domenico Hierosolimitano, who had to go there daily with other palace doctors to prepare drugs:

> The commissary is a very beautiful thing to see, being of great width and length. In it are thirty vases full of various kinds of liqueurs, syrups, electuaries, oils, ointments, and waters, and it is assisted by 300 youngsters, some of whom go each year to search for herbs, there being 18 masters and 4 leaders, called priors, who govern it.... At the right-hand side of the said commissariat are four large rooms full of diverse drugs, and at the left are two other rooms, where they are distilled.[69]

The porcelain wares in which ambassadors were served food during public banquets were also provided from the collection near the commissariat. In 1599 Baron Wenceslas Wratislaw described the ingenious way in which food was carried in porcelain dishes both to the sultan's private residence and to the Council Hall (see Figs. 34, 41–43):

> But, before they gave us anything to eat, we saw how the Turkish emperor is served. First came about 200 cup-bearers, or servers, dressed almost uniformly in red silk dresses, and with caps on their heads like those of the janissaries, except that about a span above the head they were embroidered with gold. These having placed themselves in a row from the kitchen to the Sultan's apartment, first did fitting reverence to all by an inclination of the head, and then stood close to each other, just as if they had been painted figures. When it was dinner time, the superintendent of the kitchen brought from the cook a porcelain dish, and another covered dish, handed it to the waiter nearest him, he to a third, and so on till it came to the one who stood nearest to the Emperor's apartment. There, again, stood other chamberlains, and one handed it to another, till the viands were carried very quickly, and without the slightest noise or clatter, to the Emperor's table. Several of them again placed themselves in a similar row to the place where the pashas and my lords the ambassadors were ready to eat, and handed the dishes from one to another till they placed them on the table.[70]

The monumental royal kitchens, whose ten pairs of cylindrical chimneys rising above the right colonnade dominated the second court, had more than just a practical significance.[71] Because eating food from the imperial kitchens played a central role in palace ceremonial, representing, as it had from the early days of the Ottoman dynasty, a commitment of allegiance to the sultan, the kitchens had considerable symbolic charge. They were a prominent element on the palace's skyline, and broadcasted the generosity of the sultan, who distributed food not only to his inner household and to the resident staff of his palace's public services, but to his slave soldiers and the imperial council officials who constituted his extended household, as well as to official guests visiting his palace.

Royal Stables

Angiolello describes the royal stables as long, vaulted structures covered with lead roofs and extending along the left behind the second court's walled enclosure (Pls. 5a,b, 9, 11 *[11]*, 12 *[6]*).[72] Another early source, Spandugino, says that they were reserved for the sultan's horses and located across from the kitchens. According to Menavino forty of the sultan's favorite horses were kept in them; others were stabled outside the palace.[73]

Unlike the kitchens, which are built on the same level as the second court, the stables are five to six meters below it (see Fig. 46). A chronogram cited by Karamani Mehmed Pasha and Kemalpaşazade indicates that they were appended to the second court in 1478–79.[74] They form a subsidiary service complex with living quarters, separated from the second courtyard by a wall pierced with a gate, called the Gate of the Imperial Stables (*ḫāṣṣ āḫūr ḳapusı*).[75] Two other gates along the curtain wall that separates the first court from the second communicate with the first court and with a maidan in front of the Tiled Kiosk (*Çinili Köşk*) (Pl. 11 *[12, 13]*).

The monumental masonry halls that make up these stables date from the time of Mehmed II, and frequent repairs over the centuries have not much changed their basic structure. Unlike the kitchens, with their domed, square modules, the long stable halls are covered by a continuous flat roof, accentuated with a single dome over a chamber that is thought to have been used as a treasury for precious trappings (Pls. 25d, 30a, 32a,b; see Fig. 46). The two longest halls stabled the horses; in the remaining, smaller chambers the stablehands lived.[76]

The stables were renovated with the rest of the second court during Süleyman's reign. An account book of 1527–28 mentions the repair of "the bath of the imperial stable" (*ḥammām-i isṭabl-i ḫāṣṣa*).[77] A small mosque is depicted in Dilich's 1606 bird's-eye view at the spot where the stables communicate with the first court (Pl. 26b). The eighteenth-century mosque that replaced it and the adjacent small bath were built by Mahmud I's chief black eunuch. An inscription on it records this sultan's extensive renovations at the royal stables.[78] A repair document from 1764 lists among its restored sections a treasury of horse trappings, to which new wooden galleries and shelves were added, a dormitory with individual chambers for officers of rank, several long rows of stalls for horses, stores for straw, a kitchen, bath, laundry, and a masjid.[79]

The most famous part of these royal stables was the domed hall used as a treasury for horse caparisons (*raḫt ḫazīnesi*), next to the stablemaster's chamber. Bon refers to the stables in 1608 as holding twenty-five to thirty horses for the sultan to use when he took exercise with his pages; at its upper end was a storage room for richly decorated "saddles, bridles, pectorals, and horsecloths inlaid with jewels of every kind, with so much grace, artifice, and in such great quantity that they astonish everyone who sees them because they exceed imagination."[80] The seventeenth-century historian Hezarfen describes this treasury in similar terms: "Near this royal stable are a number of rooms called the royal saddlery *[sarāchāne-i ḫāṣṣ]*, in which heavy gilded trappings, stirrups, jeweled bridles and jewels are beyond counting."[81]

These trappings were a source of great pride to the Ottomans and were sometimes exhibited on horses assembled in front of the left colonnade of the second court, near the Gate of Stables (see Fig. 39). During ceremonies or military parades the sultan and his pages rode on royal horses decorated with these jeweled furnishings. Sometimes ambassadors were given special permission to tour the stable treasury, and occasionally it was visited by the sultan himself.[82] On royal visits fur coats and robes of honor were bestowed on the officers in charge.[83] The historian Fındıklılı Silahdar Mehmed Agha recounts in 1685–86 that the French ambassador visited the treasury of the royal stables (*ḫāṣṣ āḫūr ḫazīnesi*) at the Edirne Palace, where he encountered a mountain of equipment, including a thousand pairs of stirrups, and trappings of gold and silver. When he marveled at it, he was told that this was nothing—the *real* treasury was in Istanbul.[84]

Dormitories of the Halberdiers with Tresses

Near the harem's Gate of Girls (*ḳızlar ḳapusı*), which communicates with the second court, are the quarters of the Corps of Halberdiers with Tresses. It was instituted sometime after the foundation of the palace (Pls. 9, 11 *[15]*, 12 *[7]*; see Fig. 46).[85] The functions of this corps were to carry wood into the male and female quarters of the third court, to clean the royal residence, and to serve the Council Hall. Like the sultan's male pages, the halberdiers wore long tresses to signify their privileged access to the third court. They were divided into two groups, one in the service of black eunuchs in the harem, the other in the service of the male quarters of the third court and of the Council Hall.[86] The dormitory where they lived was located between the three. Owing to lack of space it had to be built on an artificial terrace to the north of the royal stables. The door of this dormitory communicates with the left colonnade of the second court near the harem gate, as is clearly indicated in a *Hünername* miniature (Pl. 11 *[16]*; see Fig. 35). Its presence there confirms that it already existed by around 1584.

Although Hezarfen declares that the corps was founded toward the end of Murad III's reign, it is clear from account books that its quarters were built earlier, by Süleyman I, and coincided with the construction of the new Council Hall and with the enlargement of the harem to which they provided services. A document of 1527–28 mentions the repair of the "Chamber of Halberdiers and their bath," and cites the construction of a "kitchen, commissariat, beverage storeroom, the wall and courtyard of the platform near the Chamber of Halberdiers."[87] A document from the following year shows that the dormitory of halberdiers and its bath were still being repaired.[88]

Evliya Çelebi says that Süleyman built the Chamber of Halberdiers at the same time that he renovated the harem, the Chamber of the Black Eunuchs, the Council Hall, and the Tower of Justice.[89] It was expanded during Murad III's reign, through the efforts of leading harem officials. A series of sixteenth- and early-seventeenth-century inscriptions carved on stone slabs on the building help trace its history. It is the only extant example of the self-contained living quarters that once made up a large portion of the Topkapı Palace's structures, and which contributed to the *esprit de corps* permeating the lives of different groups of servants and pages attached to the inner and outer services of the palace.

One of these inscriptions above the main gate of the dormitory, which opens onto the second court, states that the Shadow of God, the Lord of the Happy Conjunction, the Polar Star of the Age, Sultan Murad III, the Conqueror of Tabriz, Shirvan, and Revan, who spread justice to his empire, ordered the expansion and rebuilding of the quarters, which the chief black eunuch Mehmed Agha had reported to be too small. Ibrahim Pasha, who was both vizier and admiral of the navy, provided galley slaves to construct it, and the chief matron *(kethüda kadın)* of the harem financed the building. The inscription ends with good wishes and prayers for the continuation of the sultan's justice and his conquests, and a chronogram, "Home of halberdiers," which yields the date 995 (1586–87).[90]

Another inscription over the inner gate of the dormitory, reached from the second court by descending a staircase, repeats the same information but adds some details. Here it is stated that the tight quarters that made the halberdiers suffer from overcrowding were ordered enlarged at the request of Mehmed Agha, the chief black eunuch. The building, financed by the chief matron, Canfeda Kadın, and the head treasurer, Mustafa Agha, was constructed by the chief royal architect, Davud Agha. Its chronogram is recorded as "Paradiselike [is] this peerless place," yielding the date 995 (1586–87).[91]

An inscription on a stone fountain tells us that Şehsuvar Agha, who entered the Corps of Halberdiers at the Edirne Palace, after participating in the campaign of Szigetvár in 1566, served there for eight years, until all of this corps was summoned from Edirne to the Topkapı Palace in 1574. After serving the council hall for nine years he was promoted to the post of head chamberlain *(odabaşı)*, which he occupied for two and one-half years, finally rising to the higher post of head of the corps *(bölükbaşı)*, which he occupied for three and one-half years, before his death in 1589. The inscription indicates that Şehsuvar Agha built this fountain, together with the marble floors in front of the dormitory, as a sign of corps solidarity when he was head chamberlain, and that he added ceramic revetments around the mihrab of the masjid when he was head of the corps. It ends with the chronogram

"May God bestow mercy on its builder," which contains the date 997 (1588–89). This inscription confirms the existence of a dormitory of halberdiers before 1574. Another inscription over the gate of the masjid, which carries the date 982 (1574–75), demonstrates that the architect Davud did not demolish all the former buildings when he expanded the dormitories in 1586–87.[92]

The dormitory complex, grouped around an open courtyard paved with stone, consists of a double-storied wooden masjid; ablution fountains; a triple-domed bath with a large furnace, adjacent to the masjid; latrines; a spacious recreation hall surrounded by wooden benches, with a brazier at the center for smoking pipes; an oven for roasting coffee; a small private chamber for the most important officers; and, finally, the large dormitory of the halberdiers, surrounded by wooden galleries resting on wood pillars painted red and green.[93] It seems that Davud expanded the southern dormitory toward the available space of the stables; the inner buildings at the north probably date from an earlier period.

The inscription on the northern masjid carries the date 982 (1574–75), when Sinan was chief architect. The triple-domed bath adjacent to it might well be the one mentioned in documents from Süleyman's reign, when the post of chief royal architect was occupied by Alaüddin. Detailed archaeological investigations are needed before this hypothesis can be confirmed, and to reach a better understanding of the building's chronology. The complex was apparently redecorated and repaired in the following centuries, without radical structural changes, according to the information provided in later inscriptions and waqf prescriptions preserved on its walls. The quarters of the Halberdiers with Tresses is now being restored. It is of particular value for the architectural historian as the only preserved residential complex from the sixteenth century in the Topkapı Palace. Built of ordinary materials, with wooden details colorfully painted red and green, its functional buildings were economically packed around a small, ill-lit courtyard and its rooms were dim. This was typical of the Topkapı Palace, where imperial architecture stood side by side with vernacular buildings. The dark, inward-looking halls of the complex of Halberdiers with Tresses contrast sharply with the outward-looking, light-filled buildings and belvedere pavilions of the royal residence, distinguished by their precious materials and marble columns. They also differ from neighboring administrative buildings in the ceremonial space of the second court, separated by walls from the service courts, which also boasted rich materials and lead-covered domes.

FOUR
The Second Court: Administrative Buildings

In the domed vestibule of the Middle Gate leading into the second court two army judges (*kazaskers*) held audiences after they had attended the vizier's council (Pl. 11 *[3]*). In 1433 Brocquière had observed in the palace at Edirne that the qadi heard cases of justice at the gate of the administrative courtyard in accordance with the ancient tradition that justice was dispensed at the monarch's gate,[1] and Spandugino tells us that in Istanbul the *kazaskers* did the same. After having presented petitions to the sultan in the third court, they went to the second gate to hear cases involving the military class.[2] This practice continued after Süleyman remodeled the Middle Gate,[3] and two raised platforms flanking the vestibule used for the purpose can still be seen there today.

It is tempting to identify the ten-columned portico at the gate's inner facade with the one described by Gritti's secretary in 1503, and by Spandugino about the same time, as the one under which the Agha of Janissaries sat with his lieutenants.[4] The two raised platforms under the portico on either side of the arched gateway are called by Atâ the "old council place" (*eski dīvān yeri*).[5] In the sixteenth century the leading officers of the Janissaries sat on a bench on the right platform, at the side of the kitchens; the aghas of the six cavalry corps sat on the left, toward the stables. An account book from 1618 refers to them jointly as "the council hall of the Aghas of the cavalry and the Agha of Janissaries at the Middle Gate,"[6] and another one of 1681–82, mentions "the seats of the Aghas of the cavalry, and the Agha of Janissaries at the imperial council of the Middle Gate."[7]

With its castlelike outer facade, its vestibule hung with shining weapons, its prison, and its various audience platforms for the administration of justice in the various branches of the military, the Middle Gate prepared the visitor for the themes of public justice and victory he would encounter in the ceremonial space of the second court. From there he had to proceed directly to the vizier's Council Hall.

Old Council Hall

In Mehmed II's time the Council Hall lay beyond the Tower of Justice (Pls. 11 *[25]*, 12 *[12]*), according to Angiolello, who refers to it as the "loggia and chancery" in which the grand vizier's council met four times a week to dispense justice in the sultan's name.[8] Any male or female subject of the sultan, Muslim or non-Muslim, could petition this high court of justice to have his case heard and decided. In 1503 Andrea Gritti's secretary places the same "loggia" and "chancery" at the far left corner of the second court. It was in this porticoed loggia that the grand vizier received Gritti; the Venetian secretaries accompanying him sat outside, under its portico. At the entrance ten officials seated on the ground weighed and counted the revenues brought to the sultan. The two *kazaskers* and the viziers sat on a carpet-covered bench that stretched along the wall opposite the entrance. The *nişancıbaşı*, who fixed the sultan's official monogram (*tuğra*) on imperial edicts, was seated on the left side; two *defterdars*, or finance ministers, sat across from them on the right.[9] This seating arrangement is also described in Mehmed II's *kanunname,* which refers to the building as the "imperial council" *(dīvān-i hümāyūn)* and to the long bench facing the entrance as the "lofty council's bench" *(ṣoffa-i dīvān-i ʿālī).*[10]

Behind the finance ministers, in a room at the right that communicated with the vizier's loggia through an iron-latticed window, sat fifty secretaries, taking notes. This is the chamber Gritti's secretary calls the chancery *(cancellaria);* in it imperial records and archives were stored inside a coffer sealed with the grand vizier's seal. Spandugino describes the same arrangement.[11] The chancery is also mentioned in Mehmed II's *kanunname,* in the passage: "And let my sacred seal be kept by the grand vizier. When it is required to seal and to open my treasury *(ḫazīnem)* and my chancery *(defterḫānem),* let them be opened and closed in the presence of my finance ministers." [12] At the end of each year the records that accumulated in the chancery were placed in leather sacks that were sealed by the *defterdar*s and taken to the treasury.[13] Also attached to the grand vizier's Council Hall was a small chamber where the council scribe *(divan yazıcısı)* recorded the sultan's decisions after the council members had left the Chamber of Petitions.[14]

In his seventeenth-century reform treatise, Koçi Beg says that the sultans continued occasionally to come to this building to hold extraordinary councils *(meşveret* or *ṭanışıḳ* or *danışıḳ)* until the reign of Süleyman, and to consult with grandees about important decisions.[15] These extraordinary meetings should not, however, be confused with the regular public appearances of sultans under a royal colonnade during communal banquets—a ceremony that Mehmed II abolished toward the end of his reign. After Süleyman's reign, even such extraordinary consultations started to take place inside the third court, as the principle of royal seclusion was interpreted ever more radically. Menavino provides the only known description of the vizier's Council Hall during such meetings:

> When the Grand Turk needs to hold a consultation about something, all his court is present ... Whenever he wants to hold council and to give audience the three viziers inform the courtiers, who immediately dismount, and the principle captains go to the large hall. There they sit according to rank, depending on their dignity, on the carpet-covered benches that have been prepared, and wait for the Grand Turk to arrive. First the two captains of the first gate, called *kapıcı başı,* enter the hall and with slow paces approach the Grand Turk's seat; after them comes the grand vizier, and then the Grand Turk, between the other two viziers, with the principle eunuchs of the palace following behind. And when the sultan arrives, everyone stands up without leaving his place, showing him great reverence. The two captains stand before the first step of the seat, each on one side. The carpet-covered seat, raised on many steps, is at the head of the hall, the wall tapestried with brocade. And to it mounts first the grand vizier, then the sultan with the two other viziers, who hold him under the arms, with three youngsters [pages] following behind, carrying his gold cushion on their shoulders. And at the right-hand side, two steps beneath the sultan's seat, sits the grand vizier with the *kazasker* of Greece, who maintains justice in the city. On the other side, the two viziers sit with the *kazasker* of Anatolia in an orderly fashion. The sultan begins to talk and everyone answers his questions according to his judgment and in this manner they reach decisions about matters of war and the maintenance of the state. And when the consultation is over, those who came with the sultan accompany him to his room.[16]

The grand vizier's Council Hall in the palace corresponded to a tent known as the "consultation tent" *(danışıḳ çadırı),* in which the imperial council congregated during campaigns.[17] The hall and its dependencies were, according to Spandugino, low and unassuming. In 1492 the Mantuan ambassador Alexis Becagut referred to the hall as a small loggia.[18] It was raised on a platform at the far left corner of the court that extended up to the point where the colonnade that extends from the third gate suddenly stops (Pls. 11 *[25],* 12 *[12],* 33o: Figs. 47, 48, see Figs. 33, 35, 40, 45). Its position is clearly indicated on eighteenth- and nineteenth-century Turkish plans, and on that of Gurlitt from 1910 (Pls. 15, 18, 19). Its foundation stones were discovered in 1943 between the second and third

47 Nineteenth-century watercolor illustration of the third gate and the Old Council Hall, Album, MS. Vienna, Österreichische Nationalbibliothek, Cod. 14.557*, fol. 17r.

windows of the eight-domed Public Treasury built by Süleyman.[19] Judging by them it must have been about ten meters wide. In the plans the steps leading up to its raised platform are not at the center of the building, but off to one side, adjacent to the treasury. This suggests that the platform originally extended all the way up to the corner of the second court. If it did, the steps would then have been exactly in the center. Süleyman I probably had part of Mehmed's Council Hall and its dependent chambers demolished. Its foundations continue under the wall of the eight-domed Public Treasury, suggesting that the latter building occupies part of the space originally taken up by the dependencies, but only further archaeological investigation can confirm this hypothesis.

48 Old aerial view of the third gate, with the Chamber of Petitions behind it; they are connected through the ceiling of the small forecourt extending in between. From Eldem and Akozan, *Topkapı*.

In 1706 Giuseppe Sorio wrote, "Between the upper corner of the [second] court and the [third] gate, the divan was once held. A section of the portico dedicated to that use still remains today, with its small window above the seat of the grand vizier for the appearance of the Grand Signor; it is called the old divan *[vecchio Divano]*." This implies that only a section of the original building was then preserved.[20] The iron-latticed window, which Solakzade calls the "cage" (*ḳafes*)[21] is still seen on a plan from 1748 (Pl. 19). It probably communicated with a royal chamber at the third court where the sultans must have sat to observe council meetings (Pl. 11 *[25, 31]*). It is tempting to identify this chamber with the "cell called the cage" (*ḳafes nām ḥücre*) through which, in the sixteenth century, the royal pages confined to the third court were occasionally permitted to speak with their relatives, who stood on the other side of the iron-barred window.[22]

After Süleyman I built his new Council Hall, that of Mehmed II came to be known as the "Old Council Hall" (*eski dīvānḫāne* or *dīvānḫāne-i ʿatīḳ*). Sixteenth-century miniatures show its remaining section as a small building with a red wooden portico and a pyramidal pitched roof (see Figs. 33, 35, 40, 45). Lokman identifies it as a "noble masjid" (*mescīd-i şerīf*) where the Sura of Victory (Koran, Sura 48), promising conquest to believers, was recited before public councils, and under whose portico grandees and ambassadors wishing to kiss the sultan's hand were made to wait.[23] A *Hünername* miniature depicts oil lamps hanging from the masjid's wooden porticoes (see Fig. 35). It was damaged in 1665 in a fire that started in the harem, and was repaired in a simpler form.[24] Later sources refer to it as "a low-quality" wooden masjid for the use of the Halberdiers with Tresses;[25] "the noble mosque called Old Council Hall";[26] or as "the noble mosque of the imperial council";[27] but in fact it also fulfilled a variety of other functions.

From the sixteenth century onward ambassadors frequently mention the Old Council Hall, adorned with carpets and tapestries, where they were made to wait after the vizier's audience. It was there that, with the Ottoman governors, they watched the Victory Divans before being received by the sultan in the third court,[28] and where the important members of their retinues were served food. Ambassadors were also vested there with robes of honor (*hilʿat*) brought out from the adjacent Public Treasury.[29] On religious holidays the *şeyhülislam* and the other leading ulama sat under the portico of the masjid.[30] Its various rooms served as offices of the palace steward and the head treasurer, who were the leading eunuchs of the third court.[31] There, according to an old custom, the head treasurer's secretary distributed wages to artisans attached to the royal workshops and his manager ordered the heads of these royal craft organizations to produce new objects for the palace, or to repair old ones.[32] The Old Council Hall, then, was a building that had entirely lost its original function after Süleyman's reign.

New Council Hall

The Venetian ambassador Marco Minio first saw the Topkapı Palace in 1521, on the occasion of Süleyman I's accession to the throne. When he returned six years later to congratulate the sultan on his victory in Hungary, he noticed that the palace was much more impressive than it had been before, and mentions in particular that Süleyman had demolished the Old Council Hall and Public Treasury in the second court in order to build a beautiful new structure.[33] Guillaume Postel credits the grand vizier İbrahim Pasha with overseeing the construction of the new Council Hall and with adding marble colonnades around the court (Pls. 11 *[20–24]*, 12 *[9–11]*).[34] Vigenère, writing during the last quarter of the sixteenth century, says that the hall was both constructed and paid for by İbrahim Pasha (probably from the Public Treasury under his control).[35]

The sixteenth-century historian Nişancı Mehmed Pasha writes, "The rebuilding and decoration of the Council Hall *[dīvānḫāne]* and imperial Treasury *[ḫizāne-i ʿāmire]* in Istanbul was ordered in the year 932"; that is, 1525–26.[36] Bostan Çelebi (Ferdi) confirms this, for he says that construction took place while the Hungarian campaign was going on in 1526:

> The Council Hall *[dīvānḫāne]* and Treasury *[dārü'l-ḫizāne]* within the grounds of the imperial palace at the capital, Istanbul, appeared deficient to the sovereign's glance. Immediately an imperial decree was issued for the mentioned Council Hall and Treasury to be rebuilt more monumentally, in masonry, and for the construction of some magnificent additions and majestic dependencies within the Courtyard of Justice. For the completion of this important task, different kinds of colored marbles, columns, lime, stone, and other building materials and building supplies were prepared. And after builders, carpenters, and stonecutters were gathered, its foundations were laid. By the time the banners of victory returned from the Holy War, its lofty roof and the high galleries of its porticoes, which reached the arch of Saturn and the dome of Heaven, were completed.[37]

Although the new Council Hall appears to have been built while the Hungarian campaign was going on, royal account books continue to list expenses for it after that time. Two from 1527–29 list expenses for final touches to the building, which is called the "outer council hall," as opposed to the inner, private one of the third court, known as the Chamber of Petitions. These items include iron lattices, a gilded globe to be hung from the dome, tables, benches, woodwork, and whitewashing (see Appendix A.2).[38] A gift of three thousand *akçes* and a robe of honor to the architect Alaüddin, presented between July and August 1528, shows that the building was officially finished by that time, as the account book notes: "Gift to the architect Alaüddin, the chief of architects, who completed the building of the imperial Council Hall *[dīvānḫāne-i ʿāmire]*."[39] The attribution of the new Council Hall and the colonnades around the second court to the architect Sinan by some scholars is problematic on both stylistic and chronological grounds.[40] Sinan became chief architect in 1538, long after the hall had been built. Its relatively squat proportions are not typical of his classical style. Since Alaüddin was

49 The public Council Hall and the Tower of Justice, with its neoclassical upper part.

50 (opposite) Drawings of a reconstruction of the triple-domed public Council Hall adjacent to the Tower of Justice, with the sultan's latticed window overlooking the first hall. From Eldem and Akozan *Topkapı*.

cated on the Nuremberg woodcut, which shows the tower with a conical cap (Pl. 24). The royal belvedere pavilion was, then, part of Mehmed II's original tower, but Süleyman I remodeled it extensively.

Although we do not know precisely when the building began to be known as the Tower of Justice, a poem by Cafer Çelebi that refers to the royal windows and towers of Mehmed II's New Palace suggests that from the very beginning this tower, like the window overlooking the Old Council Hall, might have been associated with the sultan's justice: "What is each window, but an eye opening to the whole world, to watch ceremonies and spectacles?/ What is each tower, but from head to foot a tongue to praise and eulogize the just shah?"[62] Like the tower pavilions of the Imperial Fortress surrounding the palace gardens, that of the second court signified the sultan's eternal vigilance against injustice. Rising high above the palace's skyline, it marked the corner of the second court where all the administrative buildings connected with the concept of justice were located.

When Süleyman built the eight-domed Public Treasury adjacent to his new Council Hall, the tower lost its original function as a treasury and was remodeled. Sixteenth-century sources refer to it as the "pavilion of justice" (*köşk-i ‹adl,*[63] *köşk-i ‹adālet,*[64] *köşk-i naṣfet,*[65] *ḳaṣr-i ‹adl,*[66] *ḳaṣr-i ‹adālet*[67]). The sultan's tent complex had a tall tent pavilion by the same name: "The royal tent complex resembles the imperial palace and the tent pavilion of justice (*‹adl köşki*) is a house of justice reserved for the person of the sultan and it corresponds to the sultan's latticed window at the imperial palace."[68] Account books recording Süleyman's repairs to the "kiosk of justice" between 1527 and 1529 include expenses for completing its ceiling, windows, lattices, doors, wooden porticoes (surrounding its upper belvedere), and painted decorations (see Appendix A.3). During this renovation Mehmed II's square tower of brick was heightened by the addition of an upper section of stone. It was also pierced with the latticed royal window that still overlooks the Council Hall. The original narrow stairs within the thick walls fell into disuse because their landings no longer corresponded to the new stories, adapted to the position of the window that looks into the Council Hall. A new set of wooden stairs replaced the old ones and connected the sultan's loggia above the grand vizier's seat to the belvedere pavilion upstairs.[69]

Several sixteenth-century illustrations depict the restored tower with its belvedere pavilion surrounded by porticoes with red-latticed wooden shutters and crowned by a conical lead cap (Pl. 33m; see Figs. 32, 35–40). From this tower pavilion, marked as "the kings' watchtower" on Melchior Lorichs's panorama of 1559, the sultan could observe ceremonies of the second court, political executions (for which he gave the signal by opening one of the latticed shutters), and the payment of his troops.[70] Donato notes that the royal belvedere commanding a view of the sea and of the whole city allowed the sultan to watch ceremonies in the second court unseen from behind its red shutters (Pls. 27–30, 32a,b).[71]

The royal window is mentioned for the first time by Celalzade, in a passage describing how Süleyman I watched the trial in 1527 of a Muslim who had publicly claimed that Christianity was superior to Islam:

> His Majesty, the prudent sovereign and asylum of justice, had built a high throne *[taḫt-i mu‹allā]* and a lofty loggia *[şāhnişīn-i bālā]* above the outer Council Hall *[ṭaşra dīvānḫāne]* where viziers sat, inventing a veiled window *[manẓara-i mestūre]* overlooking the Council Hall below. From this window, his Noble Excellency sometimes watched the events of the divan, checking the truth of affairs.[72]

In 1533 Schepper referred to the lookout as "a latticed window from which the grand Emperor had the habit of watching the banquet of ambassadors." According to Lokman the lattice was gilded.[73] Another early reference, that of Luigi Bassano, around 1537, describes the black-curtained window as accessible from a covered corridor in the harem.[74] This must be a reference to the Gold Path *(Altın Yol)*, a corridor built to connect the sultan's private apartments in the third court with the tower (Pls. 11 *[67]*, 12 *[38]*). Lubenau says that the sultans especially liked to sit at this latticed window on days when intelligence reports sent by Ottoman spies and agents from the courts of Christian monarchs were read aloud and translated.[75]

Koranic verses related to the theme of justice were once inscribed above the window, which was flanked by the ruling sultan's monogram *(tuğra)*. None of these original sixteenth-century inscriptions survive, but those of 1667–68, over the tower gate communicating with the harem and all around the harem vestibule, praise the justice of Mehmed IV, who repaired both the tower and the Council Hall after the harem fire.[76] Inscriptions about justice from Selim III's reign (1792–93) and that of Mahmud II (1819–20) flank the entrance gate of the Council Hall. Mahmud's compares the gold-latticed window from which the sultan inspected his ministers to the Sasanian king Anushirvan's legendary chain of justice, hung with bells, which those suffering from injustice had to pull to alert the sovereign (a device also used in Mughal palaces): "Its latticed window resembles the chain of justice / It shows the one who is right to the sovereign without having to be pulled."[77] The Tower of Justice thus continued to symbolize the unseen ruler's justice. Mahmud II, who adopted for himself the epithet "the Just," made the tower higher by adding a neoclassical pavilion crowned by a conical lead cap, which can still be seen there.

A gilded openwork globe, hung from the dome of the Council Hall, was yet another symbol of justice. Referred to in an account book of 1527–28 as a "gilded globe,"[78] according to Lokman it represented the earth, and the chain from which it hung was the "thread of reason." One end of this chain was placed into the hand of the grand vizier, the sultan's representative in the administration of justice. But if the vizier had wisdom on his side in dispensing justice, symbolized by his holding the globe in its proper place, the sultan had the ultimate executive power. The globe was hung in front of his royal window like a target, to indicate that the arrowlike imperial decrees shot from the bow of the prudent sovereign affected the whole world, passing from one side of the symbolic globe through to the other, to bring justice and order to every land. But the arrow did not cause any harm to the globe because it had been shot from the sultan's bow of prudence, which kept the grand vizier in check. According to Lokman this idea was exemplified when the Ottoman sultans came on council days to the "symbolic pavilion" *(ḳaṣr-i mermūze)* of justice with a bow in one hand. Afterward, they would rebuke unjust viziers during the presentation of petitions.[79] Several sixteenth-century miniatures depict this practice. Two from the *Hünername* show the sultan seated in front of the latticed window with a bow in his hand (see Figs. 34, 35). In a miniature in Lokman's *Shāhnāma* (book of kings) of Selim II, the sultan is accompanied by two royal pages carrying arrows and a sword as he watches a council meeting from the tower's latticed window, while holding a bow in his hand (see Fig. 51). The gilded openwork globe hanging from the dome is shown with an arrow passing through its interstices, without damaging it. Lokman's text explains that the miniature was painted to show both the sultan's talent in the royal sport of archery and his justice in the rule of empire.[80]

The window and globe embodied a central principle of Ottoman political theory, according to which the two types of justice (the secular, based on the dynastic law of *kanun,* and the religious, based on the Islamic law of Shari'a), both of which were dispensed in the Council Hall, had to be kept in balance and overseen by a strong authority in the person of the sultan, whose duty it was to protect both state and religion. The window overlooking the Council Hall and the belvedere pavilion atop the tower symbolized not only the presence of the omniscient, if invisible, sultan, but also his unseen omnipotence.

Public Treasury

The eight-domed Public Treasury of the second court, usually dated to Mehmed II's reign, was, as we have seen, in fact built by Süleyman along with his new Council Hall (Pls. 11 *[24]*, 12 *[11]*).[81] Minio tells us that the old treasury had already been torn down by the time he arrived in Istanbul around 1526–27.[82] Account books of 1527–28 list expenses for the finishing touches of this "outer treasury," which included seats, big cabinets, windowpanes, whitewashing, iron doors, and a raised platform (see Appendix A.4).[83] The last is probably a reference to the extant raised platform at its northwest corner. Under it a passage connects the third court to the building where the black eunuchs of the harem lived. The treasury also featured a small annex that was once partitioned into rooms. Either because of this inner annex or because of the building's inward position relative to the second court, some sources refer to it as the "inner treasury" *(iç ḫazīne),*[84] but since there was another inner treasury in the third court, it was more commonly called the "outer treasury" *(ḫazīne-i bīrūnī,*[85] *dış ḫazīne,*[86] *ṭaşra ḫazīne*[87]*),* to avoid confusion. The wooden galleries shown around the inner walls on Gurlitt's plan no longer exist, but holes mark where they were (Pl. 15 *[5]*).[88] The facade, with its high row of windows, once had wide projecting eaves supported by struts; they can be seen in later European engravings (see Fig. 45). Under these eaves several officials and guards of the treasury were stationed near the door (Pl. 33m; see Fig. 35).[89]

Inside the Public Treasury, the revenues transferred from the temporary treasury at the Imperial Gate were stored in subterranean vaults covered with stone slabs and chests marked with the names of the provinces where they had been collected. Old records were also kept there; current ones were stored in the archive of the Council Hall. A *kanunname* of 1676–77 required that this Treasury *(ḫazīne)* be locked with the grand vizier's seal after each council meeting, just like the neighboring archive of the finance department *(māliyye defterḫānesi)* and the chancery *(defterḫāne),* indicating that all of them were dependencies of the Council Hall entrusted to the grand vizier.[90] In wartime, when the court was away from the capital, the treasure was transported to the imperial fortress at Yedikule, whose fortifications made it more secure.[91]

In 1553 Navagero described the contents of this "extremely large building called *caznà*":

They place in it all the written documents of the Grand Signor's revenues, and put in many chests all the accounts that are sent from each of the provinces, and on the outside of every chest are attached labels indicating millesimals from year to year, and the accounts of various places, countries, and provinces. In this *caznà* they also keep ducats and money and everything that is brought during council days to the Porte. Moreover they place in the *caznà* robes sewn from wool cloth, silk, and gold brocades, furs of lynx and sable, and all the other sewn articles that have been either presented to the Grand Signor or bought for the needs of his court. This *caznà* is opened during the four council days ... otherwise it is locked with many keys and sealed with the seal of the Grand Signor.[92]

Navagero describes the ceremony the *çavuşbaşı* (chief herald) observed when he opened the Public Treasury, kissing the royal seal entrusted to the grand vizier. Andrea Badoaro, who saw it opened in 1573, writes, "from it they took out a large quantity of their coin in leather sacks to pay the Janissaries. In it is reportedly a large quantity of gold and silver coins, precious stones, jeweled objects of gold and silver such as swords, decorated knives, and other objects. But what is even worse, I have heard (even though it is a great secret) that there is a grand quantity of gold bars left from the past emperors."[93]

The *Hünername* miniature of the second court shows the sacks of money from which the salaried troops were paid their wages every three months on the ground in front of the Treasury (see Fig. 35). Before being paid out, coins given as tribute or from other revenues were tested for their metal content in a crucible in front of the new Council Hall's third domed chamber; then they were weighed inside the second chamber and placed in leather sacks. The Lewenklau album illustration of the second court shows both the furnace under the portico of the Council Hall and balances for weighing money in the second hall (Pl. 33n). The furnace for detecting counterfeit money, which is also depicted in a miniature from the *Süleymanname* (see Fig. 32), is described by Chesnau, writing in 1547:

Near the audience hall just mentioned there is another place where they authenticate the aspers that are brought to the said treasurers from duties, the sale tax, and other revenues of the emperor, which is a small coin of silver of the value of ten or eleven *deniers tournois*. There is a large crucible of iron filled with coal where they heat a stove

52 The third gate, known as the Gate of Felicity. Courtesy of Reha Günay.

until it turns red, on which they place the said aspers, and if they contain counterfeit ones up to a certain number, which is determined, those who have brought it pay it doubly.[94]

On those rare occasions when the sultan visited the Public Treasury, its floors were spread with carpets and its inner galleries hung with curtains; a royal throne was placed opposite the gate. Brocades were spread on the ground for the sultan to walk on from the place where he dismounted to his throne.[95] These royal visits were infrequent, however; except for the use of the imperial seal to close it, no ceremony was connected to the Public Treasury; as a consequence it was a functional building without much ornamentation. Its simple masonry walls and wooden struts contrasted with the marble revetments and colonnades of the adjacent new Council Hall.

Royal Colonnade and the Gate of Felicity

In Mehmed II's New Palace, the architectural equivalent of the umbrellalike open tent used in a military encampment for royal appearances was the royal colonnade extending along the second court's north wing in front of the third gate. This led to the private, residential court of the palace (Pls. 11 *[27]*, 12 *[13]*; see Figs. 48, 52).[96] The domed canopy in front of the double gate's domed vestibule reproduced the form of the royal umbrella tent, an obvious emblem of sovereignty (see Figs. 33–35, 38, 39, 45, 47, 48, 52). The monumental colonnade of alternating green and white marble columns is set off from other colonnades around the second court, which consist of shorter white columns added in Süleyman's time. Similar monumental arcades with alternating green and white marble columns are encountered in front of the main royal buildings constructed by Mehmed II in the third court.

A miniature from ca. 1560–70 depicts Ottoman dignitaries serving food to a ruler enthroned under a domed arcade, which resembles this colonnade (Fig. 53). The throne is shown between the first and second columns to the left of the gate, in front of

53 An enthroned ruler in front of the third gate. From Firdausi, *Tercüme-i Şehname,* ca. 1560–70, TSK, H 1522, fol. 494v.

54 Mehmed II enthroned in front of the third gate, with the Crimean scholar Mevlana Seyyid Ahmed seated on a lower seat, and the grand vizier Mahmud Pasha standing behind, TSK, R 406, fol. 12r.

which stands the sultan's swordbearer. On the two main religious holidays and for accession ceremonies a bejeweled gold imperial throne was brought out from the Inner Treasury in the third court and placed between these first two columns.[97] Sources give no explanation for this practice, but it can be traced to the sultan's early custom of making public appearances several times a week, which continued until the last years of Mehmed II's reign. Mehmed II appeared regularly during ceremonial banquets under an open colonnade in front of the third gate, which Promontorio referred to in 1475 as a "magnificent and excellent portico *[lobia]* roofed with lead." It ran in front of the door of Mehmed's private quarters, and under it the sultan sat on a "dazzling and high throne *[sedia]*."[98] Spandugino's description of the public appearances Bayezid II was compelled to make during Prince Cem's captivity indicates beyond doubt that they took place under the third gate's colonnade. He refers to it as "a monumental gallery which is at the far end of this court, made in marble, where, I remember, many years ago my lord Mannuel Palaeologos, who had been chased out of Greece, used to sit. There is no other lord in Turkey who is allowed to sit at this place, which has a door from which one enters the sultan's residence."[99]

A late-sixteenth-century miniature provides further confirmation that Mehmed II made his public appearances under this colonnade (Fig. 54). It shows the sultan seated cross-legged on a throne placed between the first two marble columns to the left of the third gate. This fits Angiolello's statement that the sultan sat there with his legs crossed "like a tailor" on a raised seat.[100] Sitting in front of him on a lower seat is a Crimean scholar; standing behind him is the grand vizier Mahmud Pasha (1455–67/1472–73), and the royal swordbearer stands in front of the gate.

That it was the site of the sultan's public appearances explains the special sanctity of this colonnade. This must be the *"loggia grande"* where, in 1492, the Mantuan ambassador Alexis Becagut sat with eight dignitaries on a bench to wait for the sultan's private audience in the third court, after the grand vizier's audience in a small loggia.[101] In 1503 Gritti noted that under the portico of the third gate the gatekeepers and other prestigious officers of the sultan were seated.[102] Important officials attached to the palace's inner and outer services continued to use the space in the sixteenth century (Pls. 33o–r; see Figs. 33–35). The leading eunuchs of the third court sat on a bench at the left side of the gate, followed by the chief officers of the palace's outer services, such as the head gatekeepers, stable masters, and the head butler. On the right were stationed the heads of the medical staff, joined on the two *bayram* festivals by royal tutors, imams, shaykhs, representatives of the sharifs of Mecca, and sons of the tributary khans of Crimea. The last two groups sat at the end of the row, next to a reservoir at the far right corner of the court which functioned as a guesthouse for distinguished visitors like them (Pls. 11 *[26]*, 15, 18, 19).[103] Dignitaries seated under the royal colonnade on ordinary council days represented the palace hierarchy. Together with a military contingent of foot soldiers, cavalry, and their chiefs stationed around the other colonnades, they embodied the state as an extension of the patrimonial sultan's household.

Miniatures capture the flavor of the ceremonies that took place around this royal colonnade, including *bayrams*, accessions, and public appearances during political crises (see Figs. 38–40). On these rare occasions rich hangings, carpets and curtains were brought out of storage to use as decorations (see Figs. 36, 39). Jewel-bedecked horses were lined up in front of the left colonnade, and a military band performed in front of the new Council Hall (see Fig. 39). The gold throne set with gems was brought out of the treasury in the third court, along with a celebrated imperial carpet which weighed more than 150 kilos.[104] The page who carried the heavy silk carpet won this honor in a contest held inside the third court, which is described by the seventeenth-century French ambassador Pierre Girardin on the basis of information derived from Bobovi:

> As the contestants carry the carpets, all their friends come out from their dormitories to look at them while the military band plays a concert of drums, fifes, and trumpets to encourage the carrier, and all the pages shout encouragement, *Allah, Allah kuvvet vire*—that is, "God give him strength." The one from whom I derived my memoirs told me that he saw among these brave carriers one who, finding the carpet's weight insufficient, made one of the palace dwarfs sit on top of it as well.[105]

Only on these rare festive occasions were the silence and the disciplined order of the second and third courts broken by cheering pages and by the sound of martial music. To pass the third gate's threshold on ordinary days was to enter a realm of such intense silence that it is said to have been like "the very silence of death itself." [106] One entered the third court through the third gate, variously called Sublime Porte *(bāb-i ʿālī)*,[107] Imperial Gate *(bāb-i hümāyūn)*,[108] Gate of Petitions *(ʿarż ḳapusı)*,[109] and Gate of Felicity *(bābü's-saʿāde)*[110] (Pls. 11 *[27]*, 12 *[13]*; see Figs. 47, 48, 52). The most common name was the last; it alluded to the inaccessible imperial residence located behind the gate, which was known as the Abode of Felicity *(dārü's-saʿāde)*. It signified that the sultan's residence was blessed with royal fortune, its heavenly mansions, gardens, ever-flowing fountains, pages, and concubines recalling those promised in paradise.[111]

The third gate is situated at the point where the key opposition between interior and exterior was most strongly articulated. A veil of secrecy surrounded everything that lay beyond this gate, which marked the dividing line between the inner palace *(enderun)* and the outer *(birun)*. Both interior and exterior had their own separate regulations, and their own hierarchies. The gate marked this important spatial and organizational boundary and controlled the access into the third court according to an order codified in Mehmed II's *kanunname*. With its domed vestibule behind a monumental marble colonnade, highlighted in the middle by a gilded, domed canopy, somewhat like a ciborium, it projected to the exterior the image of a *palatium* facade. Unlike the first two double gates, with their fortified appearance, this was the *porta regia* of a luxurious palace. Its vestibule, guarded by white eunuchs who were the sultan's trusted household servants, was not hung with military weapons but with carpets and brocade tapestries glittering with gold and precious stones.[112] It marked the place where the actual royal palace began (see Figs. 48, 52).

FIVE

The Third Court: Layout of the Sultan's Residence and the Chamber of Petitions

The third court was where the sultan lived with his family and his inner household (Pls. 4–9; Fig. 55a, b). The young male and female slaves selected to be educated in this court under the strict discipline of eunuchs and teachers learned to serve the sultan loyally before they were married off to one another and promoted to bureaucratic posts in the centralized administration of the empire. It was therefore both a royal household, with the sultan as its patriarchal head, and a palace school for the ruling elite. In this setting the sultan cultivated fatherly ties with the future administrators of his empire. The third court, roughly the same size as the second, is composed of three distinct parts: the first housed the male pages, entrusted to white eunuchs, the second housed the female population, guarded by black eunuchs, and the third is a walled hanging garden (known today as the fourth court), which communicates with the other two through gates (Pls. 11 *[B,C,D]*, 12 *[B,C,D]*).

Few fifteenth-century descriptions exist of the third court, where the most impressive royal buildings of the palace are concentrated. Its basic layout and most of its buildings had already been established by the end of Mehmed II's reign, as far as one can tell from Angiolello's description. He reveals that inside the court of pages, three royal structures—the Chamber of Petitions at the threshold of the third gate, the Treasury-Bath complex in the far right corner, and the Privy Chamber in the far left corner (with a view through its portico of the Golden Horn)—were arranged to form a triangle (Pl. 12 *[16, 21, 25]*). Since the Chamber of Petitions blocked the view of the court for someone entering through the third gate, the other two royal buildings were placed at the far corners in such a way that their colonnades could be seen obliquely from the sides of the small forecourt just beyond the gate's threshold. The outer portico of the Privy Chamber, where the sultan slept in the company of select male pages, opened onto a garden terrace featuring kiosks and a marble fishpond much like the one there today (Pls. 11 *[54, 55]*, 12 *[27, 28]*).[1] Kıvami, a contemporary of Angiolello, describes the third court as having "elevated domes, strange and wonderful marble columns, and gates at many places right and left." It was "a large private precinct with numerous beautiful windows, and a great pool flowing with the waters of life. Whoever stepped inside it would immediately think he entered paradise."[2]

Neither Angiolello nor Kıvami mention the inaccessible harem, which was at that time only a small appendage to the court of pages. Although some scholars doubt that Mehmed II's New Palace included any women's quarters, contemporary sources suggest the contrary. The notion that there was no harem hinges on the theory that the palace was a military stronghold, which we have already seen was not the case. It had both official and residential functions, including strictly separated zones for its male and female inhabitants.[3] When Kritovoulos saw the New Palace in 1465, it had "apartments for men and others for women, and bedrooms and lounging rooms and sleeping quarters, and very many other fine rooms."[4] At that

55*a* (above), *b* (opposite) Aerial views of the third court, with its hanging garden, and the harem. Courtesy of Reha Günay.

time women were assigned only a small court to the left of the court of pages, reached from the sultan's Privy Chamber through a secret passage. The off-center position of the harem contrasts with the centrality of the male court, which was placed on the main axis of the palace complex as defined by the processional sequence of the three main gates. This reflects the minor role women played in Mehmed II's overall scheme. Unlike the three main courts, arranged as ample and airy precincts, the women's quarters were constricting and sharply differentiated from the rest of the palace's ceremonial or domestic spaces.

Starting with the reign of Süleyman I the harem was enlarged, and it was completely transformed by successive sultans. Unlike Mehmed II, who resided in the Privy Chamber of the court of pages, sultans from the second half of the sixteenth century onward preferred to live in the harem's Privy Chamber, among women and black eunuchs. This new trend was to culminate in the so-called "Reign of Women" in the seventeenth century, when the harem became an important force in Ottoman politics. The sultan's residential quarters were transferred from the male section of the court into the female section at a time when the education of pages had begun to degenerate. Contemporaries complained that their number was drastically in-

creased and that they were no longer selected with care.[5] This important change coincided with the growing political influence of women and of the black eunuchs who served them over the white eunuchs who controlled the male quarters. These transformations were also part of the sultan's retreat into greater and greater seclusion within the palace's private quarters. As a result the male section of the third court lost its function as royal residence to the harem which had originally been conceived as a small dependency.

The third court of Mehmed II's New Palace differed in layout from the residential courts of the Edirne Palace and the Old Palace in Istanbul. In Edirne dormitories of pages surrounded several freestanding royal structures — a chamber of petitions, treasury, bath, and privy chamber (see Fig. 3 *[16–19]*). Mehmed II's privy chamber in the middle (known as Cihannüma Kasrı) dwarfed the other buildings.[6] The residential court of the Old Palace was similarly dominated by an imposing royal mansion, which can be seen on the Vavassore map and on a drawing by Dilich (see Figs. 4, 5). By contrast, the court of pages in the New Palace did not have a freestanding privy chamber soaring above every other building. It was, rather, surrounded by porticoed structures related to one another in scale. Its conception was closer to the modular planning of courts in contemporary Italian Renaissance palaces, despite its single-story elevation. Raised on high retaining walls and vaulted basements, these buildings have monumental outer facades with multilayered windows, balconies, and an impressive silhouette of lead domes, chimneys, and conical spires. Their single-storied inner facades, facing the porticoed court, however, create an intimate atmosphere, in stark contrast to the imposing monumentality projected to the outer world. The court of pages is about half the size of the second court and consists of a square garden surrounded by buildings of approximately the same height. Only a small mosque to the left, oriented diagonally to face Mecca, breaks the court's relatively regular layout (see Fig. 55).

Of all the courts in the New Palace, the third most clearly bears the imprint of Mehmed II's idiosyncratic taste. The striking variations in the design and materials of its individual buildings reveal how much unity was subordinated to variety. As Kritovoulos had observed in 1465, this section of the palace was designed "with a view to variety,"[7] an aesthetic preference that also characterizes the garden pavilions, to which we shall turn later. In the court of pages royal buildings featuring tall marble colonnades were built side by side with more modest structures with shorter or no colonnades that served as dormitories for the pages. Alternating green and white marble columns (like those of the third gate's outer colonnade) distinguished these royal structures from lesser buildings, which had lower arcades of white marble. The long, rectangular dormitories had flat roofs, while the royal buildings were punctuated with lead-covered domes and built of precious materials, to emphasize their importance. In contrast to the inward-looking dormitories, whose only windows faced the male court, Mehmed II's two main royal buildings—the Treasury-Bath complex and the Privy Chamber—were linked to the surrounding landscape and to the walled hanging garden in front by loggias, stately marble porticoes, and large windows (Pls. 4, 6–8). These spacious royal buildings and the pavilions of the hanging garden in front of them thus differed from the crowded, barracklike dormitories of the pages as spaces in which the sultan could enjoy some degree of privacy.

Unlike an inward-looking military stronghold, the third court of Mehmed's New Palace had an exteriorized orientation. It was designed to incorporate vistas of the surrounding landscape and sought an aesthetic relationship with nature through its belvederes and hanging garden. Contemporary Ottoman descriptions of Mehmed's New Palace are filled with descriptions of these belvederes and windows, which took full advantage of the spectacular views from the ancient acropolis. Bidlisi describes the sultan's residence as a collection of belvederes (*manāẓir* or *ghurfāt*) from which the sultan could watch each quarter of his flourishing capital and the sea, teeming with ships from all over the world. His contemporary, the poet Cafer Çelebi, likens the palace's windows to eyes surveying the whole world.[8] The third court of the New Palace was thus designed to provide the sultan—seeing all, but himself unseen—with multiple vistas of the two seas and the two continents over which his dominion extended. From the royal mansions of his private residence, the secluded ruler could survey his world empire; the vast kingdom he ruled fanned out from this nucleus of power, the Abode of Felicity.

The *Hünername* miniature (ca. 1584) of the third court and the surrounding outer gardens reflects the final form this section of the palace took after extensive renovations and enlargements during the second half of the sixteenth century (Fig. 56). Mehmed II's New Palace had not been designed for the leisurely life adopted by his successors; that required the expansion of the sultan's private domain as he ceased to venture forth into the world outside. The third court, hemmed in as it was by dormitories and the small harem, was too constricted for the sultan's pleasure. The *Hünername* miniature shows the compactly structured male section of the court as it had always been, unlike the harem area, which had burst its former boundaries. The miniatures of the first two courts in the same manuscript depict administrative and ceremonial activities (see Figs. 28, 35); that of the third court shows the sultan in his expanded private domain being entertained by a few male attendants in front of a shore pavilion (see Fig. 56). Lokman tells us that the sultan's "paradisical" residence remained hidden from the common eye. Since no words could describe its wonders, the text was accompanied by a beautiful painting executed in "hair-splitting de-

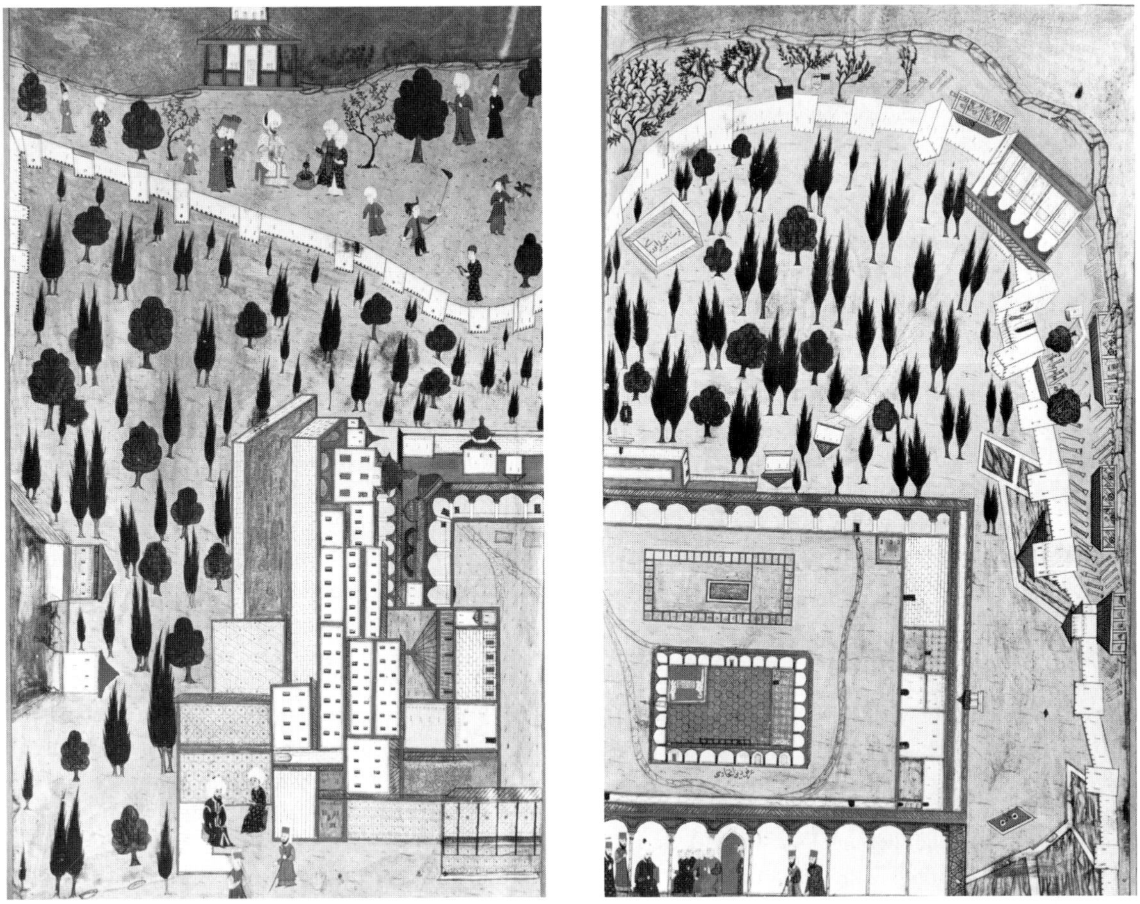

56 The third court and outer gardens, from Lokman, *Hünername,* ca. 1584–85, TSK, H 1523, fols. 231v, 232r.

tail," showing each building in both plan and elevation.[9] In the miniature of the third court not a figure is in sight, for none of the inhabitants were supposed to be seen. This requirement to observe the sultan's privacy at all times explains why Ottoman historical manuscripts almost never depict royal women or scenes in the harem. Their subject matter deals exclusively with public ceremonies or private activities of the sultan in the company of pages.

By the last quarter of the sixteenth century, the principle of royal seclusion had been carried to an extreme with the expansion of the harem quarters, into which the sultan voluntarily retreated. Contemporary accounts provide an intimate glimpse of the daily routine of Murad III, who rarely left the confines of his palace. The Venetian bailo Gianfrancesco Morosini wrote, in 1585:

> This sultan does not, in my opinion, live so desirable a life, for he stays almost continually enclosed in his seraglio in the company of eunuchs, boys, dwarfs, mutes, and slaves, which seems to me almost as bad as [the company of] women, without the conversation of any virtuous person with whom he can have a discussion....
>
> In the morning he arises quite late from bed, and as he comes out of the women's quarters, where he sleeps each

night without interruption, he dresses himself with other costumes, and as soon as he is dressed he eats. If it is a council day, he gives audience to the Agha of the Janissaries, to the army judges, and finally also to the viziers; and if anyone is newly made a provincial governor or something else, he goes to kiss his hand without uttering any word nor receiving any response. At that time the ambassadors and the other ministers of princes who go to that Porte also do the same....

When the viziers depart after a rather short time, most of the time he returns to the women, whose conversation delights him extremely, and when he remains outdoors, he retires to some part of his gardens to practice archery and to play with his mutes and buffoons. He frequently has noisy instruments played, and enjoys artificial fireworks very much.... He also frequently has comedies acted.... Then he always reenters the harem for dinner with the approach of night, both in the summer and winter.[10]

The court doctor Domenico Hierosolimitano describes Murad III's daily routine, punctuated by the five prayers, in similar terms. The sultan would arise at dawn for prayers, write for half an hour, have breakfast, then read for an hour. Four times a week he gave private audiences during the council meetings, after which he spent an hour in his gardens in the company of dwarfs and buffoons. Then he returned to his study until lunch. After the noon prayer, he usually spent time in the harem. Then he returned to the male quarters, either to read or to pass the time in the garden again, until evening prayers. These were followed by dinner and the last prayer, after which he returned to the harem for the night. Hierosolimitano tells us that the sultan rarely deviated from this routine.[11]

Besides the eunuchs, the sultan was the only person who could move freely and mediate between the strictly drawn gender boundaries of the third court, a rule that accentuated his role as master of the house. The spatial, architectural, and functional organization of the royal household was unified under one principle: the omnipotence of the sultan, whose relationship with the obedient boys, girls, and eunuchs of his household was that of a master to his slaves. The only inhabitants above slave status were the members of the royal family, including the princes, princesses, and the queen mother, who lived in dignified quarters in the harem.

Because the harem was strictly off limits to all outsiders—except for Jewish female intermediaries and female relatives of the royal family—Ottoman descriptions of the third court rarely refer either to women or to their quarters. They concentrate on the organization of the palace school for pages and on the sultan's reception ceremony in the Chamber of Petitions, where only the highest dignitaries and ambassadors were allowed. The placement of the chamber at the threshold of the third gate blocked the view of the residential court from the curious eyes of outsiders (Pls. 8, 9; see Figs. 48, 55a,b). Only the professors who taught the pages and the imams who led their prayers had permission to frequent the male section of the third court daily. Privileged Ottoman dignitaries were only occasionally invited into the court or to the kiosks of its hanging garden to participate in extraordinary consultations or ceremonies. These rare occasions provided a glimpse of the inaccessible inner palace to dignitaries, who often tried to imitate its architecture and decoration in their smaller palaces scattered through the capital and in the distant provinces. The sultan's legendary palace also served as a model for the grand mansions that former pages built after they had been promoted to the ranks of the ruling elite. No foreign ambassador, however, was allowed to go beyond the Chamber of Petitions, in which he finally encountered the secluded sultan after the public ceremonies of the first two courts.

Encountering the Sultan: The Chamber of Petitions and Its Ceremonial

Angiolello describes Mehmed II's Chamber of Petitions: "At the other end of [the second] court is another double portal, and as one enters it there is a loggia covered with lead, and here sits the Grand Turk when he gives audience; next comes the third court, which is as long and large as the other two."[12] This lost building is clearly the predecessor of the

tioned in the accounts of 1527 and 1528 may well be the ones later taken from an unspecified building and reused on the facade of the Circumcision Room (*Sünnet Odası*) near the Privy Chamber (see Figs. 111, 112). These include a group of hexagonal tiles, underglaze painted in blue, white, and turquoise, arranged with gold-stenciled ultramarine triangles to form stars. They would have perfectly matched the painted decorations of the Chamber of Petitions.[35] Contemporary illustrations of the interior of the sultan's audience chamber confirm the written descriptions, showing tile dadoes, the ornate fireplace, rich carpets and textiles, jeweled pendant globes with tassles, the ceremonial window opposite the sultan's seat featuring gilded iron lattices, the red iron lattices of other windows on the lower level, and stained-glass windows on the upper level.

The *cuerda seca* polychrome tile panels seen on the south facade of the building, which faces the visitor entering from the third gate today, are not mentioned in any contemporary descriptions; they were probably taken from another of Süleyman's buildings and fixed there at a later date (see Figs. 58, 59).[36] Their palette of manganese purple, dark blue, green, and yellow matches a group of tiles on the seventeenth-century kiosks of the walled hanging garden, which were removed from earlier structures built during Süleyman I's renovations in the late 1520s. The Lewenklau album drawing shows no tiles on the facade of the Chamber of Petitions; it was covered with marble revetments (Pl. 33o,p). All of the sixteenth-century observers agree that the outer walls of the building were faced with multicolored marble panels, and refer to it variously as a "beautiful marble palace," a "room covered with marble," and "a little house built of marble."[37] Its precious marble revetments probably matched the Mamluk-type Cairene marble paneling of Süleyman's new Council Hall in the second court, and were decorated with gold inscriptions.[38] Some of the remaining inscriptions record extensive repairs by Ahmed III in 1722, by Mustafa IV in 1807, and by Abdülmecid I in 1856, after a devastating fire. In 1740 Flachat provided a detailed description of the Chamber of Petitions and its small forecourt before its original decorations were completely destroyed by that fire:

> The walls are faced with porphyry panels and other exquisite marbles, where one sees a large number of Turkish inscriptions in gold letters. The pavement is unique. It is also of marble, with grooved joints so that horses do not slip when walking on it. The ambassadors go from there to the famous chamber where the *Grand Signore* gives them audience.
>
> It is in the form of a covered gallery, gilded, sculpted, well paneled. Columns of immense price are the most beautiful ornament of this isolated chamber. It is square in form, under a great dome that ends with a high, gilded pinnacle that bears a crescent.[39]

The Lewenklau album drawing shows the fountain on the facade facing the third gate, mentioned in Süleyman's account book (Pls. 33o,p). This exquisitely carved and painted marble fountain still exists today. Its inscription states in Persian that the "Solomon of the Age," who is the "fountainhead of generosity, justice and the sea of beneficence," ordered the installation of this fountain flowing with the "water of life" for the refreshment of the council members.[40] The same drawing shows a small forecourt with a checkered marble pavement stretching between the Chamber of Petitions and the vestibule of the third gate, lined with eunuchs. In 1606 the Habsburg ambassador Adam von Herberstein mentioned these pavements of black and white marble.[41]

Before they were escorted to the audience hall, the ambassadors were made to wait in the third gate's domed vestibule, where richly dressed eunuchs and pages stood. In 1591 Baron Wenceslas Wratislaw described this place as a "great saloon or hall, which was hung with valuable Persian tapestry and carpets interwoven with gold and silver."[42] After a short pause they were conducted to the colonnaded covered forecourt, where they had to wait again before being admitted into the sultan's presence. Under the colorfully painted ceiling of the forecourt silent courtiers were lined up on both sides; the singing of birds in the third court was the only sound.[43] In the mid sixteenth century Caterino

Zeno witnessed this part of the ceremonial, which he describes as follows:

> One goes to the place of the Grand Signor after leaving the Council Hall from a gate at the left. First the treasurers leave and ... go to the gate; after them enters the one who signs the commands, then [come] the army judges, and then, according to their rank and order, the viziers enter the gate, where they find a large chamber well adorned with stones, covered with a beautiful ceiling, in which stands a guard of eunuchs and some of [the sultan's] young slaves, all richly dressed; from that chamber one passes into a very beautiful loggia, the floor of which is of diverse fine stones of many colors, with a very fine vaulted ceiling of azure and ultramarine, full of stars of pure gold, in which is a very fine fountain resembling a holy-water basin; it has most beautiful windows with iron gratings and beautiful glass panes which overlook the gardens; from this very beautiful and pleasant place one enters the audience hall and the presence of that Grand Signor. At its door are two eunuchs of the highest rank, and two pages.[44]

In 1573 Fresne-Canaye described how the sultan's gifts were paraded in this marble-paved forecourt, before the ceremonial window that overlooked it:

> Then we entered a high gallery, under which, at the left side, were the aghas, or as we say, eunuchs, of the Grand Signor, about forty, ordered in such a fashion that they did not block one another from our view, and the youngest ones were behind all of the others. I do not know if they were dressed in gold, pearls, or rubies, for they appeared to me so brilliant, resplendent, and sparkling. Then we saw in a long and narrow court, all paved with very precious marbles of varied colors, a small gallery supported by very beautiful columns, and a very gentle fountain. As I waited at the door of the Grand Signor's chamber for the arrival of my turn to enter, I saw a *çavuş* who carried the gift of the king of France across this court; and after having passed twice in front of a small window from which it could be seen by the emperor, he went all around the seraglio to display this gift, so that the people, seeing that the foremost king of Christendom had sent those gifts to the Grand Signor, would recognize the power and incomparable grandeur of the sultan.[45]

The ceremonial window was named by later palace tradition "the window of displays" (*maʿrūżāt penceresi*).[46] In 1573 the Venetian ambassador Costantino Garzoni reported that not only ambassadorial gifts, but also war booty and the heads of enemies, were flourished before the sultan, seated on his throne. He added that the slave boys recruited from the Christian population to serve in the Ottoman army and administration also marched in procession in front of the same window, so that the sultan could choose the most handsome and noble-looking among them as pages for his palace.[47] An early-seventeenth-century treatise on the Ottoman state's administration confirms that the recruited youngsters were made to pass one by one in front of the sultan, who was seated inside the Chamber of Petitions, after which, upon the sultan's order, the head gatekeeper selected those of distinction to be royal pages. Âli explains that this process of selection on the basis of physical beauty — thought to be a sign of virtue — was supervised by an expert in the science of physiognomy.[48]

Inside the chamber, where the sparkle of gold and jewels was enhanced by a dim interior, the enthroned sultan sat like a divinity, immobile. The effect was striking, especially after Süleyman I's palace renovations, and the changes he made in the ceremony in order to aggrandize his imperial image and to emphasize the subordinate position of his visitors (see Fig. 61).[49] Süleyman no longer rose to honor ambassadors;[50] he did not allow them to sit in his presence, nor did he even address a single word to them.[51] He was the first sultan to sit majestically on a throne in the European manner, rather than cross-legged on a dais. In a letter dated 13 July, 1530, Pietro Zeno reports to the Venetian senate that Süleyman "sat in our manner on his throne ... resembling an idol displayed for adoration in that place."[52]

Marc'Antonio Pigafetta was received in a similar fashion by Selim II, who throughout the audience "remained immobile in a pose of extreme gravity and arrogance without looking at us at all" (Fig. 62). He notes that in the third court "one could hear no sound whatsoever," and likens this scene of "venerating silence" to a visit to the holiest sanctu-

62 Selim II receiving the Austrian ambassador in the Chamber of Petitions, furnished with jewel-embroidered carpets. From Feridun Ahmed Beg, *Nüzhet el-esrar der sefer-i Zigetvar,* 1568–69, TSK, H 1339, fol. 178r.

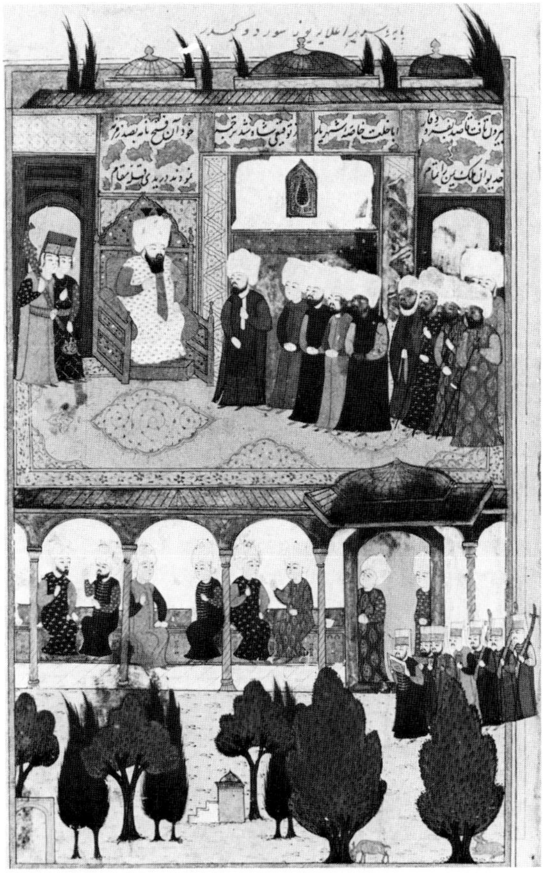

63 Murad III receiving the Morrocan ambassador, companion panel to Fig. 37. From Lokman, *Shahanshāhnāma,* 1592, TSK, B 200, fol. 143r.

ary in Jerusalem.[53] Describing Murad III's reception of an Austrian embassy in 1578, Schweigger complains of the "devilish arrogance and haughtiness" of the "barbaric" ceremony, so disrespectful to the representatives of the Holy Roman Emperor (Pls. 33o-q; Figs. 63, 64). He likens the sultan to a lifeless paper cutout sitting like an idol surrounded by viziers who stand like statues.[54] On one occasion the ceremony's austere proceedings were interrupted with laughter, when someone lost his shoe on the bejeweled carpet;[55] this gives the impression that the ambassador's retinue was hustled in and out with some haste. In 1621 Louis Deshayes de Courmenin complained of the discomforts of walking on carpets embroidered with jewels and having to stare at dazzling pendants hanging from the wooden throne's gilded canopy, supported on four jeweled pillars.[56]

By the late sixteenth century the ceremony in the Chamber of Petitions had been reduced to a momentary glimpse of the sultan in majesty, representing a symbolic act of tribute. "I cannot describe," wrote Wratislaw, "the apartment where the emperor sat, on a place about half an ell ele-

64 Murad III receiving Austrian ambassadors at the Chamber of Petitions. Album, MS. Vienna, Österreichische Nationalbibliothek, ca. 1590, Cod. 8626, fol. 122r.

65 Reception of the Austrian ambassador Hans Ludwig von Kuefstein at the Chamber of Petitions in 1628. From Teply, *Die kaiserliche Grossbotschaft an Sultan Murad IV*, pp. 122–23.

vated from the ground and covered with very beautiful gold brocade cushions, embroidered with precious stones and pearls, for it was impossible to notice it in a short time, and indeed, I looked more at the face of the emperor than at the beauty of the room; [I remember] only, [that] there were some balls hanging from the ceiling, which glittered very much, but I do not know whether they were made of looking-glass, or studded with precious stones."[57] Fresne-Canaye also lays his inability to describe the place to the abruptness of the ceremony.[58]

The throne where the sultan sat is still exhibited in the Chamber of Petitions, though by now it has lost most of its jewels (Fig. 65). Raised on a dais, it resembles the large canopied bed of state *(lit de justice)* of the French kings. The painting on its lacquered wooden dome represents a dragon and phoenix in combat, a Chinese-inspired theme with well-established auspicious royal associations that would have been transparent in the post-Mongol Islamic world. A Turkish poem inscribed around the dome says that the "just ruler" Sultan Mehmed III ordered this beautiful and artistic gilt throne, studded with jewels and set with gems, in order to dispense justice upon it. Its chronogram, "Throne of Felicity" *(serīr-i saʿādet)* dates its construction to 1005 (1597). A second poem inscribed on it praises the "new throne" *(serīr-i cedīd)*, completed upon the sultan's order in 1006 (1597–98), with jewels, paintings, and calligraphy. It ends with the wish that the enemies of state and religion arriving

from the seven climes should prostrate themselves in humility before the foot of this exalted throne, from which the sultan should rule forever in glory and honor.[59] A book of royal donations gives the precise date, 12 January 1598, for the completion of this new throne and notes that goldsmiths, tailors, and carpenters received payment for it.[60] It replaced a sofa with four cushions, which can be seen in some late-sixteenth-century illustrations and was probably modeled on Süleyman I's former jeweled gold throne, also surmounted by a domed canopy.

The throne was purposely placed at the corner of the Chamber of Petitions to heighten the drama of the reception ceremony. Its position across from the ceremonial window not only placed the sultan where he could watch the vestibule of the third gate, but also gave those waiting within the vestibule a "preview" of the sultan himself, sitting like an icon framed by the window (see Figs. 58, 59, 64). To the European viewer, used to axiality and symmetry, this oblique approach must have appeared strange. Two fantastic European prints, representing a sultan seated on a magnificent, centrally placed throne under a European-style baldachin, at the threshold of his palace, with impressive perspectival vistas on both sides, attempt to correct this discrepancy (Figs. 66a, b).

The throne was decorated with the jewel-studded gold insignia of sovereignty, consisting of a sword, bow, quiver with arrows, and a penbox, symbolizing the sultan's role as a "man of the pen" as well as a "man of the sword." Sketches of the Chamber of Petitions in later Ottoman Books of Ceremonies have written specifications concerning the correct position of royal insignia on the throne and the proper places for participants in the ceremony to stand. One of these plans, dating from the second half of the eighteenth century, indicates the location of doors, windows, and the fireplace, the sultan's position on the throne, the placement of the royal sword, and the inkpot next to which the ambassador's letter was put. The positions of the ambassador and other participants in the ceremony are also clearly marked, showing how carefully each reception was staged (Fig. 67). The large niches on the walls of the audience hall were used for exhibiting precious royal objects; the one adjacent to the throne contained the sultan's turbans with jeweled aigrettes.[61]

The viziers who accompanied the ambassadors into the Chamber of Petitions stood throughout the audience with the crossed hands that symbolized their subordinate status, and stayed on after the ambassadors had departed, to discuss affairs of state. They were allowed to sit across from the sultan's throne on a low, velvet-covered bench adjacent to the wall of the ceremonial window, which is clearly depicted in a *Hünername* miniature (see Fig. 60).[62] This practice was discontinued after the grand vizierate of Melek Ahmed Pasha (1650–51), because to show his respect this pasha had refused to sit in the sultan's presence — a precedent which was followed by later viziers.[63] To enter the

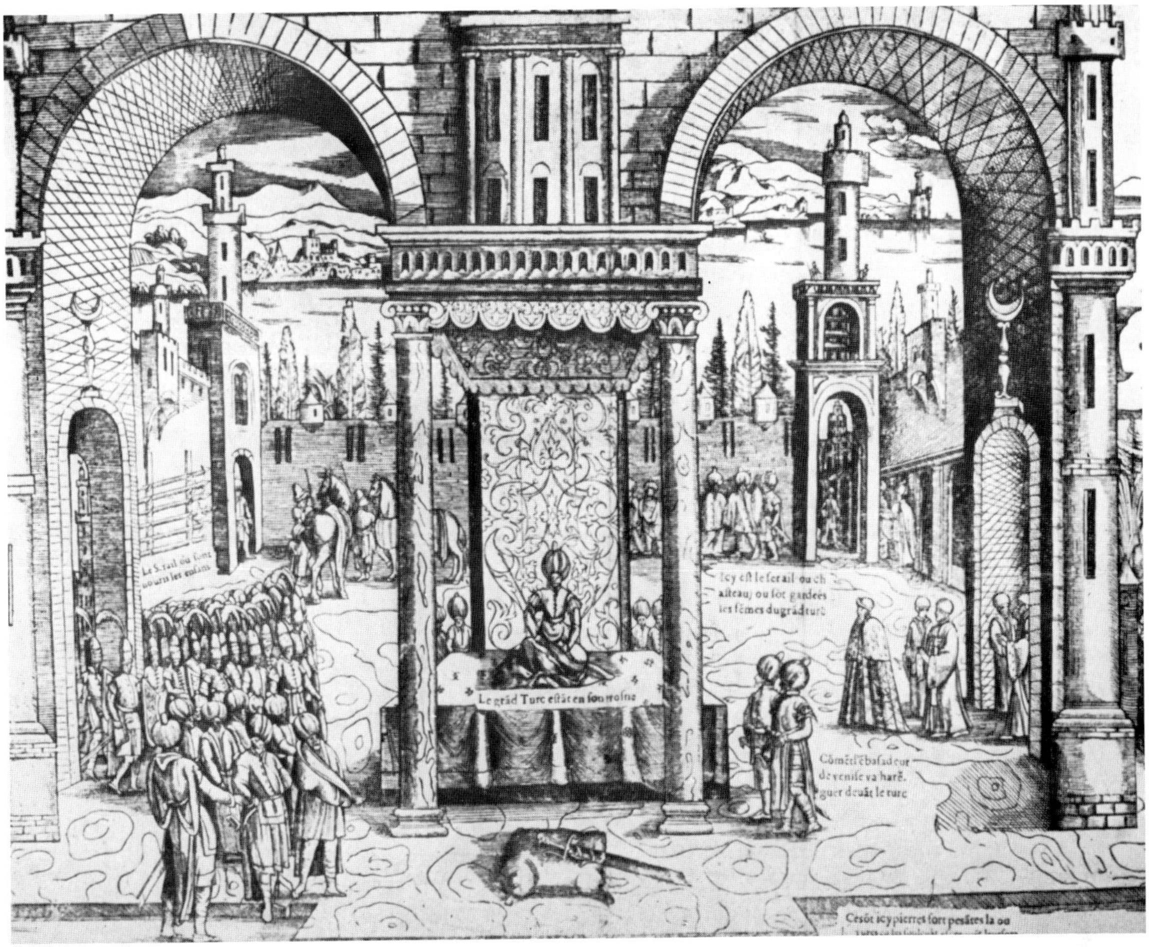

66*a* (opposite) An enthroned sultan, with the third court seen in the background. From Chalkokondylas, *L'histoire de la décadence de l'empire Grec.*
66*b* (above) Anonymous sixteenth- or seventeenth-century variant of the same print.

Chamber of Petitions could be a terrifying experience for the members of the imperial council, for the object of the sultan's inspection of council meetings from his "kiosk of justice" was to judge whether his officers conducted public justice according to the codified secular and religious laws. Occasionally they displeased him, which they learned only when they entered his presence, to discover that they were to be demoted, exiled, imprisoned, or (if the crime was serious) executed under the third gate's vestibule, a custom that preceded Süleyman's rebuilding of the Chamber of Petitions.[64] A sixteenth-century miniature depicts the execution of the sultan's grand vizier Kara Ahmed Pasha in 1555 in that very place (Fig. 68).

During the presentation of petitions in the chamber the head gatekeeper, the head treasurer, and several mutes stood by behind the gate, ready to execute the guilty dignitaries when the sultan stamped his feet on the ground as an indication of his displeasure.[65] These threatening executioners who lurked behind the walls are described by Fresne-Canaye: "All around this chamber were hidden I don't know how many mutes, who are the

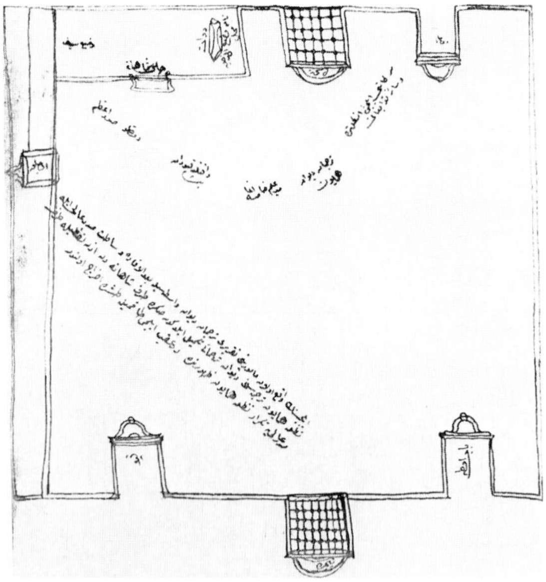

67 Eighteenth-century schematic plan of the Chamber of Petitions, with a description of its ceremonial for a particular reception, BA, KK Teşrifat 676M, fol. 146.

most loyal and the most experienced executioners of the atrocious commandments of this tyrant."[66] To a Western observer the sultan's executions appeared arbitrary and tyrannical, but from the Ottoman point of view they were performed within well-established norms of proper and improper conduct and represented the justice of their ruler. Those transgressors executed in the prison in the Middle Gate had been tried and found guilty in the Council Hall of the second court, which was a tribunal of public justice; those executed at the third gate were the judges themselves, who were sentenced by the sultan, as supreme judge of the empire. Therefore, to cross the threshold of the Gate of Felicity meant to suspend control over one's destiny, as one approached the omnipotent sultan. There was the danger of never coming out again, but also the enticement that one might emerge raised to the riches of still higher office, with accompanying robes of honor and other signs of status.

68 The grand vizier Ahmed Pasha executed in 1555, under the vestibule of the third gate, in front of the Chamber of Petitions. From Lokman, *Hünername,* ca. 1587–88, TSK, H 1524, fol. 177v.

The two small antechambers, connected to the audience hall by a single door, are indicated in the *Hünername* miniature, but not mentioned in the ambassadors' reports (see Fig. 60). Their function can be deduced from the layout of the Chamber of Petitions at the Edirne Palace, which was almost identical with the one in Istanbul, though smaller and built with wooden piers and less luxurious materials (see Fig. 3). Its two small antechambers are identified in repair documents as a latrine and an ablution chamber.[67] In a 1740 account, the Viennese lieutenant Schad describes the layout of the building in Edirne: "At the left is the audience chamber, smaller than the one in Istanbul, but otherwise it has the same chimney and the same gates; among them the one that is across from the throne never opens, except when a grand vizier is made *maʿzūl,* that is, deposed. Then he is pushed out through that frightful exit, which they open for that purpose, and which they shut again after him."[68] In his description of the Chamber of Petitions at the Topkapı, d'Ohsson says that when the sultan condemned a grand vizier to death, the disgraced dignitary was conducted through the inner door, called the Gate of Punishment *(mücāzāt ḳapusı),* to perform his last ablutions and prayers before his execution.[69]

Each of the building's four doors had its own specific ceremonial function. The one to the right of the south facade was the ordinary entrance; the one at the left of the ceremonial window on the same wall was used on rare occasions, when the sultan decided he wanted to keep in his Inner Treasury one or another of the gifts brought to him—ordinarily, they were sent to the outer Public Treasury of the second court to be redistributed. The door on the north, reached by a double staircase, was the sultan's royal gate. D'Ohsson describes the functions of these gates: "One is reserved for the sovereign, the second one serves as the ordinary entrance, the third is opened only for introducing the presents offered by foreign ambassadors in the name of their Courts, which during their audience remain exhibited in front of that gate; the fourth, across from the second, also remains closed; it is called the Gate of Punishment."[70]

As can be seen on the *Hünername* miniature, the staircase of the royal gate to the north was connected by a paved path to the Privy Chamber in the upper left corner of the third court (see Figs. 56, 57, 60). An account book for the year 1528–29 mentions "repairing the pavement of dressed stone from the vicinity of the chamber of His Majesty—may his reign last forever—to the inner audience hall."[71] The sultan was escorted down this path from his Privy Chamber to the Chamber of Petitions by the head gatekeeper and head treasurer.[72] It was the duty of the Halberdiers with Tresses to wash this white marble path with sponges soaked in a solution of rosewater, vinegar, and lemon juice, a custom called *pārs* (probably derived from the Persian *pārsā,* "pure").[73] The marble colonnades of buildings in the third court were also swabbed with lemon juice to make them shine. It was customary to chisel holes on the surface of royal paths so that they would not be slippery, an activity referred to in the sources as "pecking" *(ġaġalama).*[74] These holes can still be seen on the royal marble paths of the inner palace.

In addition to being a royal audience hall, the Chamber of Petitions functioned as a backdrop for the ceremonies enacted in its small, marble-paved forecourt. On the eve of the two major religious holidays the sultan sat on a special throne, called "throne of the eve" *(ʿarefe taḫtı),* placed under the marble colonnade at the spot still marked by a porphyry roundel. There he received greetings from the leading officials of the palace's inner and outer services. A wooden canopied throne, inlaid with ebony, ivory, and mother-of-pearl, was made for Ahmed I for this purpose in the 1610s.[75] During this ceremony, called the "eve celebration" *(ʿarefe muʿāyedesi),* he emerged through the common entrance of the Chamber of Petitions. Other important ceremonies also took place in front of the building. One was held at the departure of royal pages promoted to govern in the provinces. Once they stepped out of the Gate of Felicity, these new officers of the centralized state administration could no longer reenter their former residence in the inner palace, except during official visits.[76]

The ceremonies that took place around the Chamber of Petitions accentuated the strict boundary between the inner and outer zones of the palace. This building expressed the idea of imperial justice dispensed at the threshold of the royal residence, referred to in Ottoman imperial decrees as the "highest threshold" *(ʿatabe-i ʿulyā).* It was here that the world-conquering ruler received the emissaries who had come to his "court of world refuge" *(dergāh-i ‹ālempenāh)*. The administrative structures in the second court were an extension of this threshold, a spatial arrangement that signified the sultan's role as the omnipotent center of an empire governed by a bureaucracy mainly staffed by his household slaves.

Stripped of its original decorations and furnishings, the whitewashed Chamber of Petitions now gives a false impression of modesty; in its former, lavishly ornamented state it produced the opposite sensation.[77] Gone are the marble revetments, star-studded ceilings, elegant tiles, precious furnishings, rare fabrics, and gilded objects inlaid with jewels that made it legendary. One can no longer hear its playing fountains nor see the rich curtains and stained-glass windows that made it a dark, flickering, mysterious space, glittering with gold and gems. It was the culmination of every embassy's passage across the increasingly secluded thresholds and forecourts of the palace, the site of the final encounter with the sultan in majesty. The impact of its opulent interior, glistening, shining, and sparkling with ornaments, was dazzling. Despite its small scale, unusual in imperial architecture, this miniature building was not meant to express modesty but, on the contrary, unshakable confidence in the sultan's imperial grandeur.

SIX
The Third Court: The Palace School for Pages

The pages who lived in the dormitories grouped around the male section of the third court constituted an elite corps, educated and trained to be the future administrators of the empire. Their training took place in what amounted to a palace school, established in the New Palace from its very inception. According to Atâ it was Mehmed II who placed the inscription over the main gate of the third court that called it a "house of learning" *(dār al-ʿilm)*.[1] The origins of the palace school, which has been compared by scholars to that in Plato's *Republic*, are not clear.[2] The sixteenth-century historian Taşköprizade says that it was founded in the early fifteenth century by Mehmed I, who placed slave pages under the tutelage of eunuchs, a system perhaps inspired by the Mamluk model. The Byzantine historian Doukas tells us that both Bayezid I's palace in Bursa and Mehmed I's in Edirne kept young boys of great beauty, all of them Christian in origin, since Muslims could not be enslaved, according to Islamic law.[3]

This allowed part of the local Christian population (at that time constituting a majority in a frontier principality at the edge of the Islamic world) to be fully integrated into the ruling group as converts. The palace school, then, was based on an Ottoman institution that already existed, but that, under Mehmed II, came to be more fully organized. Its purpose was to consolidate the system of centralized government through a trained class of administrators that would hinder the development of a Muslim landowning aristocracy capable of challenging the sultan's absolute power. The palace school of the Topkapı complemented the madrasas of Mehmed II's mosque complex in Istanbul, which trained the highest-ranking ulama of the empire, and which replaced the Byzantine patriarchal university, built as a dependency of the Church of the Holy Apostles, that had occupied the same site. Given this striking parallel, it is tempting to propose that Mehmed II's palace school might have been partly inspired by the university in the Great Palace of the Byzantine emperors, which had also trained statesmen and administrators.

Kritovoulos writes that after conquering Constantinople in 1453, Mehmed II selected the noblest among the young boys in the conquered population, "according to their merits, to be his bodyguard and be constantly near him, and others to other service as his pages. He admired them for their prudence and other virtues and for their training. They were indeed of signal physical beauty and nobility and talent of soul, and in their manners and morals were outstanding, for they were of high and renowned ancestry and splendid physique, and well trained in the royal palace." Mehmed also selected young girls for his court with "the modesty, grace, and beauty of the virgins, and their superiority among their race in every sort of good trait."[4] According to Menavino, who was himself a page, the boys were placed under the strict discipline of eunuchs and instructed by tutors to become "the warrior statesman and loyal Muslim who at the same time should be a man of letters and polished speech, profound courtesy, and honest morals." The girls were entrusted to the strict supervision of matrons, who taught them the principles of Islam and trained them to be refined courtesans, skilled in sewing, embroidering, dancing, singing, playing musical instruments, storytelling, and reading. The organization and training for both sexes was essentially the same; the two institutions paralleled and complemented one another.[5]

Bobovi, a former page of Polish origin in the seventeenth century, says that the emphasis of the palace school was on religious indoctrination and instruction in court etiquette, the liberal arts, sports, and crafts, not on the training of distinguished scholars. Some of the pages studied more than others, each according to his own ability; but the sultan did not demand of them anything more than a great respect for books—especially the Koran, of which each of them owned a copy. The primary aim was to educate Christian-born slaves (now converted to Islam) destined for high office in a commonly shared Ottoman court culture and to instill complete obedience and loyalty to the sultan. The French translator of Bobovi's account compares the strict discipline of the palace school to "a Pythagorean school, where one learns silence; a Lacedaemonian school, where one learns austerity and wisdom, both in terms of good precepts and in the rigor of punishments; and a Spartan school, where one does not apply oneself to the sciences but rather to observing temperance and modesty and to rendering oneself capable of obeying and commanding."[6]

According to Deshayes de Courmenin, who wrote in 1621, the school and its pupils were completely isolated from the rest of society, like an independent republic with its own peculiar customs and way of life.[7] Throughout their education, the pages were never allowed to forget that they were slaves. The majority of them rarely had contact with the sultan. As a badge of their bondage they wore long tresses hanging from both sides of their caps, said to have been inspired by the long locks of hair Joseph wore during his years of slavery.[8] These tresses were seen as a symbol of rendering service to the person of the sultan. No page was permitted to grow a beard, because it was regarded as a mark of freedom.[9] According to Courmenin, even royal princes who governed provinces had to shave and send their beards to the sultan at frequent intervals to show that they were still under his custody, too young to govern by themselves.[10]

An initiation ceremony was held when a page first entered the inaccessible inner court and was sealed off from the outside world. Another ceremony marked his discharge back into the world, where he was finally allowed to grow his beard and take up the post for which he had been trained. The initiation ceremony, called *pārs* (probably also derived from *pārsā,* in the sense of a ritual of purification and abstinence), began when the novice entered the third gate where he stood all alone for three days in silence with nobody addressing him. At the end of his three days of solitude, the gate's leading eunuch announced that he had joined the ranks of the ruling elite and reminded him that he had entered the "gate of nobles" *(erkān ḳapusı).* Then he dressed the novice in the page's uniform.[11] Early sources fail to mention this initiation ceremony, but it may well have originated in the fifteenth century, when the palace school was founded.

While they lived in the sultan's palace, the pages' relations with the outer world were completely severed; they could not even leave the third court. Servants called "gate boys" *(kapı oğlanları)* were stationed at the third gate to run their outside errands. They relayed the wishes of the royal pages to novices *(acemi oğlanları)* in the first court—young slave boys attached to the outer palace's services—who then brought whatever was required from the city.[12] In the second half of the sixteenth century the ideal page system began to degenerate. The number of pages was increased drastically and they were no longer selected with care. Muslim-born pages whose relatives lived in the city began to infiltrate the system, which had originally been limited to Christian converts cut off from family ties to guarantee loyalty to the sultan. They began to find ways to communicate with the outside world through the latticed "cage" that the early sultans had once used to observe meetings in the Old Council Hall, or by pretending sickness, in order to visit the first court's hospital (Pl. 11 *[31]*).[13]

The page's daily schedule was strictly disciplined and regulated. Each one was assigned a small place on the platform in his dormitory, where he slept at night and studied during the day. Pages living in different dormitories came into contact with one another only in the communal mosque of the third court, where they prayed four times a day. In the interval between the fourth and fifth prayers, pages were allowed to talk quietly in their dormitories, where they also performed the last prayer. Before going to bed, roll was called, and then the chamber master struck the floor with his walking stick to signal the hour of repose. In all the dormitories, the pages slept in small beds in long rectangular halls that were illuminated the whole night with torches, so that the gate boys and eunuchs could monitor their behavior.[14]

Institutional Organization of Pages

The pages were organized into dormitories called chambers, or *oda*. The exact number of pages varied: in 1475 Promontorio mentions 400, his contemporary Angiolello counts 340, and Spandugino, also a contemporary, 300. In the mid sixteenth century their numbers had reached 500, and by the early seventeenth century, 700.[15] Wage registers of Mehmed II's court from 1478 to 1480 indicate that the royal pages (*ġilmān-i enderūnī*) were organized into five chambers: the Corps of the Chamber (*bölük-i oda*), the Corps of the Treasury (*bölük-i ḫazīne*), the Corps of the Commissary (*bölük-i kilār*), the Corps of Royal Falconers (*bölük-i şāhinciyān-i enderūn*), and the Corps of the Gatekeepers (*bölük-i rikābiyān* or *bölük-i rikābdārān*).[16] A similar classification appears in Promontorio's description, which mentions five leading eunuchs, the cupbearer (*şarābdār*), who was in charge of the Privy Chamber, the head treasurer (*ḫazīnedārbaşı*), the head of the commissary (*kilārcıbaşı*); the head falconer (*çakırcıbaşı*); and the head gatekeeper (*rikābdārbaşı*).[17]

The nomenclature varied over the years, but the organization remained almost unchanged from that established in Mehmed II's reign. By Âli's time the five chambers were called the Privy Chamber (*ḫāṣṣ oda*), the Treasury Chamber (*ḫazīne odası*), the Privy Commissary (*kilār-i ḫāṣṣa*), the Large Chamber (*büyük oda*), and the Small Chamber (*küçük oda*) (Pl. 11 *[30, 33, 46, 47, 53]*).[18] The Large and Small Chambers were the names given in the sixteenth century to two preparatory schools for the novice pages, housed in two dormitories that flanked the third gate. Together they comprised the Corps of the Gate (*bölük-i der*), placed under the head gatekeeper's control.[19] The head gatekeeper had a special room of his own, adjacent to the Small Chamber, to the left of the third gate's vestibule (Pl. 11 *[29]*).[20] His room, shown on Bobovi's plan, is mentioned earlier, in a repair document of ca. 1528–29, as "the room of the Agha of the Gate at the Small Chamber" (Pls. 16a,b *[3]*, 17 *[32]*).[21] As early as 1475 Promontorio observes that the head gatekeeper was the palace's highest-ranking eunuch, in whose chamber the largest group of novice pages was lodged.[22]

The Corps of Falconers had, by the sixteenth century, ceased to be one of the five chambers. A book of royal donations from the last quarter of the century indicates that its members were dispersed in different dormitories, including the Privy Chamber, the Treasury, and the Large Chamber. The seventeenth-century author Hezarfen mentions thirty falconers, three belonging to the Privy Chamber, seven to the Treasury, and twenty to the Large Chamber. Clearly the function still existed, but the falconers were among the pages known as "chamberless" (*odasız*).[23] Most of the chamberless pages were attached to the Large Chamber, and are mentioned in a treatise on the Ottoman court's organization from Mehmed III's reign.[24] One of these groups was called the "Expeditionary Pages of the Large Chamber" because its members followed the sultan to wars. There was also a group of chamberless falconers under the head falconer.[25] Still another group were the stokers, or *külḫāncıs*, whose duty it was to stoke the furnace for the sultan's bath.[26]

All these chamberless pages attached to the Large Chamber were eventually grouped together, and were given their own dormitory in 1606 by

Ahmed I (Pl. 11 *[38]*). It was known as the Chamber of the Expeditionary Force *(seferli odası),* and housed not only the expeditioners, but stokers, bath attendants, and some musicians. It was enlarged by Murad IV, and rebuilt in its present form by Ahmed III, in 1718–19.[27] The falconers were not included; instead, a new dormitory was built for them near the Privy Chamber in the mid seventeenth century.[28] It is shown as a freestanding structure on Bobovi's plan (Pls. 16a,b *[41]*, 17 *[16]*).

In their novice years the pages concentrated on studying, unlike the members of the three higher chambers, who were in active service to the sultan. When the youngsters reached puberty, they were assigned to the higher chambers, which were for the most part populated by pages in their mid to late teens. The details of the system of promotion from one chamber to the other are not known. The novices appear to have moved to the higher chambers according to merit; they could be both promoted and demoted, so the progression from the commissary to the Treasury and, finally, as the culmination of their training, to the sultan's Privy Chamber, was not routine for all. Untalented novices could be sent out of the palace to minor positions in the army, and not everyone who reached the upper chambers completed the full curriculum or was chosen in the end to serve in the prestigious Privy Chamber. Sometimes the less ambitious pages themselves requested to be assigned to lesser bureaucratic posts, not having the patience to endure the rigid lifestyle. Since promotion was not automatic, the pages had to attract the attention of the sultan or of their superiors with their talent, a system that turned the Ottoman political order into a meritocracy quite different from the aristocratic order in the West. The most talented slave pages eventually rose to the highest nonhereditary positions in the government and the military. Enjoying considerable freedom and opportunities denied to the general populace, they could get married and have offspring, but their legal status as slaves required that the lands they were given by the sultan and most of their accumulated property revert back to the state when they died or were demoted. Their freeborn Muslim children had no automatic rights to the high positions normally reserved for the household slaves.

Dormitories of Pages

The two preparatory schools for the novices were located on both sides of the third gate's vestibule, a position signifying the transitional status of the new arrivals who occupied them (Pls. 11 *[30, 33]*, 16a,b *[4,6]*, 17 *[21, 22]*).[29] The low rank of novices was expressed in the wages and robes they were issued by the sultan. Unlike the pages of the three upper chambers, who wore precious atlas, silk, or brocade caftans, and were called *kaftanlı* ("with caftans"), the novices, who wore simple wool robes, were called *dolamalı* ("with dolmans").[30] They were kept separate as a group from the pages promoted to the upper chambers and had little contact with them.

Promontorio explains that the novice was trained in religious doctrines, virtue, and—according to his talents—either singing, playing instruments, dancing, archery, or some other dignified activity.[31] His contemporary Angiolello says that the novice received his religious and cultural indoctrination while learning to read, write, and speak Turkish, after which he was placed in the sultan's service, depending on circumstances.[32] Menavino, a former page, writes that the novice had to learn to speak Turkish, to read the Koran and understand its prescriptions, and to read books in Arabic and Persian, for which purpose teachers were brought into the palace.[33]

Later, writing in the seventeenth century, the Polish page Bobovi provides a list of books included in the curriculum, starting with the Koran, and including books of Arabic grammar, Turkish books dealing with the Islamic faith and law, and Persian literary classics, including the works of Sa'di and Hafiz. He adds: "But they also read others in *mülemma* form. *Mülemma* is written in an ornate way and is the combination of Turkish, Arabic, and Persian words. It is used as much in prose as in verse, and is very elegant and filled with beautiful and rich thoughts." These *mülemma* works included such story collections as the *History of the*

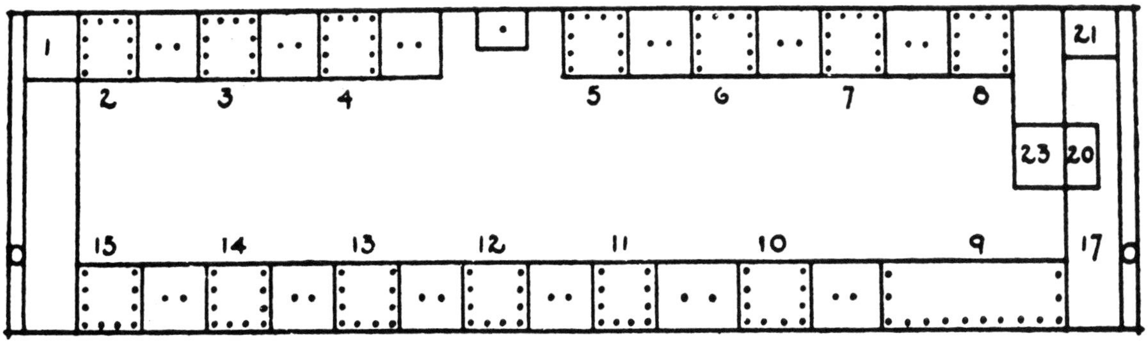

69 Schematic plan of the Large Chamber by Albert Bobovi. From Bobovi's German translation by Brenner, *Serai Enderum*. The explanations of functions listed below are summaries of Bobovi's much longer original text:
The places marked with ten dots denote the number of pages housed in each stall, while areas marked with two dots represent a *kerevet,* or raised platform, where two eunuchs are stationed to observe the behavior of pages. If they catch any irreverance they descend from the platform and bring the guilty page to the center of the hall, where they punish him.
KEY: *1.* Sand Door *(kum kapısı),* guarded by a leading eunuch; *2.* quarters of the newest recruits *(esfel mahallesi); 3.* formerly the quarters of Algerian slaves, presented to the sultan by corsairs, who no longer have separate housing, but are mixed with other pages *(Cezayir mahallesi); 4* and *5.* quarters near the Gate *(kapı mahallesi); 6.* the flea quarters *(bit mahallesi); 7.* the lice quarters *(pire mahallesi); 8.* station of the chamber master *(odabaşı mahallesi); 9.* stall of stokers who heat the furnace of the bath and the fireplace of the chamber *(17),* next to which is a furnace conducting heat to a small bath for ablutions *(gusulhane) (18); 10.* the learning quarter *(ilm mahallesi); 11.* the bed-lice quarter *(tahta biti mahallesi); 12.* two-story stall *(şirvan)* where formerly royal princes received their appointments to govern provinces, and where they were educated, together with royal pages. Since princes are no longer sent to provinces—having caused rebellions against their fathers—now those who fold the eunuchs' turbans *(sarıkçı)* and those who repair clocks *(saatçi)* are stationed there. Under the *şirvan,* which is a raised place, mutes and dwarfs are stationed; *13.* quarters of the Imam *(imam mahallesi); 14.* quarters of musicians *(sazende mahallesi); 15.* first quarter *(baş mahalle),* with the seat of the chief presiding officer *(baş kalfa);* each quarter has a supervising *kalfa* or presiding officer; *16.* (not on plan) Fountain Gate; *17.* furnace of the small bath for ablutions *(gusulhane); 18.* (not on plan) small bath for ablutions; *19.* (not on plan) latrines; *20.* fountains.

Forty Viziers (a compilation of Turkish folk tales), the *Hümayunname* (a book of Arabic fables), the *Thousand and One Nights,* and the epic tale of Seyyid Battal Gazi, an Arab hero who fought against paganism on behalf of Islam.[34] Their ornate literary language was invented in the Ottoman palace as a sign of distinction that would separate the ruling elite from the common people. *Mülemma* works, which were also read in the harem, formed the shared popular Islamic culture of a ruling elite chosen from disparate ethnic, linguistic, and religious backgrounds. Bobovi explains that some novices chose to study law, to become eligible for positions in local government or in the realm of justice; and those who had an inclination to learn Persian also tended to study calligraphy, eventually to become chancellors or secretaries.[35]

In the beginning the royal princes, along with a

chosen group of companions, were given their lessons with the novices. A wage register of Mehmed II's court from 1478 to 1480 lists under the "Corps of Gatekeepers" a subgroup called "Novices of Princes."[36] Bobovi's plan of the Large Chamber indicates a special two-storied stall with an upper gallery, where the princes once used to sit for instruction (Fig. 69 *[12]*). Bobovi says that this practice ended when the potentially rebellious princes were no longer sent to govern provinces. From the end of the sixteenth century onward, they were kept in the harem, under close supervision, and a separate school was built for them in the quarter of the black eunuchs.[37]

The next rank up from the novices was that of the commissary pages, under the custody of the head of the commissary. Mehmed II's *kanunname* states that their master was in charge of setting the royal table.[38] Their dormitory occupied the right half of the third court's north wing (Pls. 11 *[46]*, 17 *[14]*).[39] According to Promontorio its pages cared for the royal tableware of gold and silver studded with jewels and prepared delicacies served at the sultan's table.[40] We learn from Menavino that they were in charge of the nectars, juleps, confections, spices, and medicines stored in the commissary. They also continued their studies at a higher level, read books, and practiced archery.[41] Their dormitory is referred to in the sources as the inner commissary, or privy Commissary, to distinguish it from the other commissary, attached to the royal kitchens in the second court.[42] It had a separate storage area, used as a treasury for the objects needed for the royal table. Most of these were borrowed from the Inner Treasury, where unused objects were stored for safekeeping. Registers from 1546 to 1558, for example, list vessels loaned to the inner commissary by the head treasurer, and articles returned to the Inner Treasury from use in the inner commissary. They were gold or silverware, some of it jeweled, including trays, bowls, dishes, spoons, cups, colanders, frying pans, and grilling skewers.[43] Among the officers attached to the commissary's service were a napkin master, a master of candles, officers in charge of pickles, fruits, and tableware, and a guard for the storage area.[44] The gold, silver, and porcelain vessels, spices, syrups, and confections were entrusted to the head of the commissary, together with other edible items including drugs, aphrodisiacs, teriacs, and antidotes.[45] Atâ, who lived in this building as a page in the mid nineteenth century, says that gold, silver, and metalwares, celadons, and Chinese and European porcelain vessels were stored there.[46]

An account book of 1527–28 lists expenses for making large trunks *(anbār)*, cupboards *(dolāb)*, and chests *(ṣanādıḳ)* for storing objects in the Inner Commissary.[47] These objects were sometimes exhibited during festivities. After his accession ceremony in 1595, Mehmed III toured the Commissary, which had been decorated for the occasion, distributing largesse to its pages and officers. A later document, from 1791, reports that the sultan paid a visit to the ornamented commissary on the occasion of a royal birth.[48] Seventeenth-century sources describe the customs of the commissary corps pages, which probably originated earlier. One of these was to collect rain and rosewater during the month of April, which was offered in small bottles to the sultan in return for a reward.[49] Another ceremony involved carrying the sultan's drinking water from the inner commissary to the Privy Chamber door. When the sultan complained of thirst, his attendants signaled two commissary pages; one would run to the head of the commissary, shouting "water!" while the other rushed to the Privy Chamber door, where he was paid ten sequins. The water itself was brought by the head of the commissary, in a gold or porcelain bowl placed on a jeweled tray, as pages in his custody followed behind. Two of his retinue guided him by the arm, for etiquette dictated that he carry the water vessel above his head, and he could not see where he was going.[50] Âli says that, in addition to carrying water, confections, and food to the sultan, and setting the royal table, the duties of the head of the commissary included feeding the sultan his bone marrow —considered a delicacy worthy of the royal palate, but extremely difficult to serve.[51]

The Treasury Chamber was the third step up for

the page in training; its inhabitants were, according to Mehmed II's *kanunname,* under the command of the head treasurer. As the name implies, they were in charge of the sultan's Inner Treasury, as opposed to the outer one in the second court. The Inner Treasury itself was not attached to the pages' dormitory, which occupied the left half of the third court's north wing (Pls. 11 *[47]*, 17 *[13]*).[52] According to Angiolello, jewels, objects of gold and silver, textiles, robes of silk, precious artifacts, and the sultan's petty cash were entrusted to the head treasurer. Menavino confirms that the Treasury pages also continued their education while they maintained the royal vestments, jars of gold and silver, jewels, and money. They were required to carry to the sultan whatever he demanded from the Treasury.[53]

The Inner Treasury occupied the far right corner of the third court (Pls. 11 *[39–45]*, 12 *[21]*, 17 *[15]*). It was cleaned twice a year and the imperial clothes were laundered and left to dry in the sun.[54] Otherwise it was locked, and could be opened only by the head treasurer, in the company of pages, when an object was required by the sultan. Its leading officers included a bucket carrier, who was in charge of the imperial laundry, a superintendent of furs, scribes of registers and inventories, and a librarian in charge of royal books stored there.[55] The Treasury pages were also taught some art, depending on their talent or inclination. They were trained to be *valets de chambre,* and learned to wrap a turban, shave the sultan, cut the royal nails, wash and fold clothes neatly, and wait on the royal table. They were also taught how to train hunting dogs and falcons, and to be stable squires. By the time they were through, they were specialized in one of the services required for the sultan's Privy Chamber, to which they were then promoted.[56]

The Privy Chamber *(ḫāṣṣ oda)* was the fourth and most prestigious service (Pls. 11 *[48–53]*, 16a,b *[31]*, 17 *[12]*). Four of the most favored of its pages accompanied the sultan wherever he went, carrying his royal insignia. They also cleaned the royal bedchamber, lighted its fire, made the sultan's bed, and stayed inside the royal bedchamber at night, taking turns guarding the sleeping sultan in pairs.[57] Others slept in an antechamber containing the royal wardrobe, close to the royal bedchamber, from where they too guarded their master.[58] They took care of the royal vestments and carried the sultan's food to his table. Mehmed II's *kanunname* lists the titles of these four favored pages, the other pages of the chamber *(oda oğlanları)*, and the head of the chamber *(odabaşı)*.[59]

When those pages who had completed their training in the various chambers and proved their skill and loyalty in service to the sultan were finally ready to take up distinguished administrative posts in the outside world, a discharge ceremony marked this honored event. Menavino describes how the successful graduating pages submissively kissed the hand of the sultan, enthroned in front of his Privy Chamber. After a brief speech, in which they were exhorted to serve well in their new posts, the sultan gave each a vestment of honor, a horse, a turban, and some money, before they paraded out of the third court: "Approaching the grand gate [that is, the Gate of Felicity] to exit from it, dressed in brocade, each one of them carries a gold ornament on his forehead, studded with jewels worth three hundred scudi, and each holds a handkerchief in his hand, in which are about one thousand aspers, and at the gate they find horses on which they mount in great triumph, scattering the coins that they carry in the handkerchiefs as they ride ... carrying with them all the articles that they have acquired in the Seraglio."[60] By contrast, any disgraced page was unceremoniously chased away through another gate, communicating with the outer gardens.[61]

Bobovi describes the page's discharge ceremony as it was elaborated in the seventeenth century, using his floor plan as a reference (Pls. 16a, b *[42, 43]*):

And after he [the discharged page] obtains leave from His Majesty, it is the custom to have two large silver basins, filled with aspers and sequins, carried by the eunuchs, and to display them, one at the gallery of the audience chamber [the Chamber of Petitions, 42], at the spot marked *E*, and the other at the mark *F*, which is on the other side of the said chamber, and as soon as the martial musicians hit the drums and play the oboes and trumpets, the novices of the two chambers, the Large Chamber at the Section *F*, and the Small Chamber at the side *E*, come out, and the eunuchs throw down from the gallery the coins and the basins. It is then a marvelous pleasure to watch them scramble for the coins and fight with one another for the basin, which passes from hand to hand until one of them captures it and is able to throw it to the pages of the caftan *[kaftanlı]* who, having come out of their chambers, stand in front of the gate as spectators; they note the boy who throws it and safeguard it in order to return it to him after the fight.[62]

The graduating page was conducted to the Middle Gate with trumpets and drums as novices and his companions enviously watched him depart. This was one of the few festive occasions when the perfect silence in the third court could be broken. Ordinarily the pages not only had to remain silent, but at the sound of the whistle that announced the approach of the sultan or a high-ranking eunuch, they had to hide inside dormitories or behind columns until he passed by. This silence led to the invention of a sign language that was used in the palace after the middle of the sixteenth century.[63] Bobovi explains that during the religious holidays or celebrations of military victories the pages were permitted to play, chat, sing, freely visit all of the chambers, and amuse themselves with "all sorts of foolery which they can dream up." These games included boxing with handkerchiefs wrapped around the fists, dressing up in masks of fur and pretending to be some animal, and playing chess, backgammon, or other board games. Otherwise, Bobovi continues, "pages of one chamber do not dare to mix with pages of another chamber. Indeed, they can communicate with those of other chambers only by speaking with the sign language of mutes. Those in the Privy Chamber are always forced to communicate by signs and gestures, maintaining complete silence at all times in the sultan's presence."[64]

The dormitories, like all the buildings in the third court, were organized according to the increasing status of their occupants: the two preparatory schools flanked the third gate, followed, in a counter-clockwise direction, by the dormitories of the Commissary, Treasury, and Privy Chamber pages. The further along they were in their training, the closer was the building in which the pages lived to the Privy Chamber, with the four favorites lodged in the royal bedchamber itself. The degree of spatial proximity to the sovereign dictated not only a page's status, but the size of his salary and his type of dress.

Bobovi's plan of the Large Chamber shows clearly how these dormitories were laid out (see Fig. 69).[65] Two long, raised platforms placed across from one another along the length of the chamber, were partitioned off into fourteen stalls, each stall accommodating ten novices. These stalls were separated by twelve raised daises *(kerevet)*, upon each of which were two stations for surveillance, occupied by eunuchs. The pages were assigned stalls closer to or farther from the entrance gate according to seniority, so that the last stall (*no. 2* on Bobovi's plan) was occupied by the newest recruits. In addition to the entrance from the vestibule of the third gate, there was another gate in the center of the facade facing the third court. Across from it was the centrally placed double-storied stall *(no. 12)* with an upper gallery *(şirvan)* that had at one time been reserved for the royal princes, when they came for their lessons with the novices. The stall numbered *9* on the plan was occupied by the novices who stoked the furnace of the neighboring royal bath and tended the fire of the Large Chamber's fireplace. The spaces at the right *(nos. 17, 20, 21, 23)* were ablution fountains *(gusulhane)*, a furnace, and latrines.

Novices inhabiting the Large and Small chambers were more closely guarded, by white eunuchs called gate boys *(kapı oğlanı)*, than pages of the higher chambers. Âli confirms that they were subdivided into companies of ten, each watched over by a eunuch: "In the venerable palace are chambers, one of which is called the Small Chamber, and the other the Large Chamber, and each has daises, that is, flat estrades on which crowded flocks of novices are stationed. On each estrade sleeps a gate boy, in order to guard and watch over them, while oil lamps burn from night until morning to prevent and to hinder them from abominable temptations."[66] The vulgarity of the names by which several of the stalls were known "smacks of an army camp or barracks," just as the organization into groups of ten was reminiscent of the arrangement of the Janissaries.[67]

This system encouraged the development of an *esprit de corps* and comradeship, just as it reaffirmed status distinctions. Bobovi writes: "Most pages show great modesty and sweetness. When they chat together, they always show a great deal of affection. They usually call each other *kardeşim,* "my brother," or *canım,* "my soul," but they do not often have the chance to talk. They mostly remain seated in total silence with some book or writing in their hand and more often resemble statues rather than living figures."[68] This setting reinforced the ties among the pages, who were bound together as a group by their common relationship to the sultan, the symbolic father in whose name they would rule the empire. Their barracklike dormitories imposed behavioral routines and framed interpersonal relations. Architecture served as a circumscribed stage for fixed patterns of conduct, reflecting the concern to set rigid boundaries, to control, and to monitor actions.

Each rectangular dormitory was an autonomous, self-sufficient unit. A description by Abdullah bin Ibrahim Üsküdari, who was a page between 1651 and 1655, shows that, with the exception of the dormitories for the Falconers and the Expeditioners, which were not built until the seventeenth century, all the dormitories founded by Mehmed II were more or less alike. They were uniform in width (ten cubits *[ẕirāʿ]* or 7.58 meters), but varied in length. Each had two sofas running the length of the room and raised half a cubit above the ground. Each had windows facing the courtyard and blind walls toward the outside world, accentuating the isolation of the pages.[69]

The Large Chamber, to the right of the third gate, measured 65 by 10 cubits (49.27 by 7.58 meters) and featured twelve large windows, four facing the third court, the other eight overlooking the royal bath's furnace. The Small Chamber, to the left of the gate, measured 30 by 10 cubits (22.74 by 7.58 meters), about half as long as the Large Chamber. It had five large windows looking out onto the courtyard.[70] Its size was probably dictated by the placement of the royal loggia adjacent to the back wall of the Old Council Hall, from the iron-latticed window of which Mehmed II watched council meetings (Pl. 11 *[31]*). The Small Chamber may have gotten its name either from its small size, or because the youngest pages were lodged there. The latter possibility is suggested by Marc'Antonio Pigafetta's description in 1567: "It is called *küçükoda,* that is, small chamber, in which live fifty small youngsters.... These boys, being too young, never leave the palace, neither do they follow the person of the sultan in war, nor in other voyages of any sort, as do the others."[71]

The dormitory of Treasury Pages, adjacent to the Privy Chamber along the north wing of the court, measured 25 by 10 cubits, or 18.95 by 7.58 meters, and also featured large windows onto the court. The adjacent dormitory of commissary pages, near the Inner Treasury, was an exact replica of the former, except for a separate compartment to the east, where the sultan's valuable tableware was stored.[72] Tavernier, who obtained his information from two former treasurers, says that these two dormitories occupying the north wing each had an arcade of eight white marble columns, with checkered black-and-white marble pavements.[73] This arcade of sixteen columns, which still exists, is also described by Flachat in the mid eighteenth century: "The buildings that form the north facade are regular and uniform. This portion of architecture would be admired by all. A large number of isolated columns form a beautiful peristyle, which extends along all the apartments."[74] This continuous marble portico at the north wing is depicted in one of the *Hünername* miniatures. It accentuated the prestige of the higher-ranked dormitories, since the preparatory schools at the south wing were characterized by simple, uncolonnaded facades (see Fig. 56).

The original dormitories founded by Mehmed II were massively built structures, and survived to the middle of the nineteenth century, though with continual repairs and some minor changes. At that time they were replaced by the structures seen today, but the original basements still remain. Two nineteenth-century plans show these new structures (Pl. 18).[75] Tavernier describes the dormitory of Treasury pages before it was rebuilt as

> a long chamber, where one sees [running] from one side to the other a sort of estrade one and a half feet high, seven or eight feet wide. Each page has a place no more than four feet wide for the morning as well as the night.... Above the beds of pages one sees a gallery that extends around the chamber and is supported by wooden pillars, all painted with a red varnish, and this is where they keep their coffers.... At one end of the chamber there is a door that leads to the fountains where those attached to the treasury go to wash when they want to perform their prayers. There are seven yellow brass taps, and both the pavements and the walls of this place are of white marble. The places used as toilets follow at the right-hand side, divided into four small rooms, which are always clean and paved with white marble squares.[76]

Although Mehmed II's dormitories all had much the same layout—long daises, internal wooden galleries, a surveillance station with windows for privileged officers, latrines, and a paved court for ablution fountains, which was also used as a recreation space[77]—the higher the rank of its inhabitants, the more elaborately decorated its interiors were. Atâ, who lived in the first quarter of the nineteenth century in the Commissary dormitory, just before it was demolished and rebuilt, says that it had been built by Mehmed II in a solid manner and decorated with "very ornate gilt carvings." [78] After all, these spaces were frequently visited by the sultans, especially in the early years. Bayezid II, for example, took a great interest in his pages' education and sometimes visited them in their dormitories. Süleyman I also frequented the dormitories of pages while they were studying.[79] Before these announced visits, the pages would usually decorate their dormitories with precious textiles and carpets, and provide a royal throne. A book of royal donations from Murad III's reign records that the Small and Large chambers were decorated several times for that purpose. On these visits the leading eunuchs received gifts.[80]

The Mosque

Pages living in separate dormitories came into contact with one another on a regular basis only in the communal mosque of the third court, but even there, each group was allotted its own distinct space. The main mosque of the third court is a freestanding structure aligned toward Mecca (Pls. 11 *[36]*, 12 *[17]*, 15 *[11]*, 18). It has been extensively renovated, but the original building dates from Mehmed II's time. It is built of alternating courses of brick and stone, and consists of a large rectangular prayer hall with a central mihrab flanked by two windows. The prayer hall is still attached to two smaller ones at either end, to which it was once connected with windows and doors. Several restorations have transformed its upper structure. Its walls have been raised and its double-tiered windows enlarged. Nineteenth-century plans of the third court indicate that partition walls once subdivided the two smaller, annexed halls (Pl. 18).

The unusual, asymmetrical layout of this mosque has led some scholars to suggest that the annexed subsidiary chambers, which have a lower elevation than the raised central hall, must have been added later, but the archaeological evidence of the mosque's outer masonry shell does not support this. The *Hünername* miniature shows the central hall with a high, pyramidal, pitched roof—which probably had a wooden dome underneath—and clearly indicates the annexed halls as part of the original structure (see Fig. 56). The reconstruction suggested by some scholars, showing a domed, single-unit mosque, is therefore not supported by the evidence. One of the small, annexed halls, which has a mihrab of its own (today it is the reading room of the Topkapı Palace manuscript library), is not an

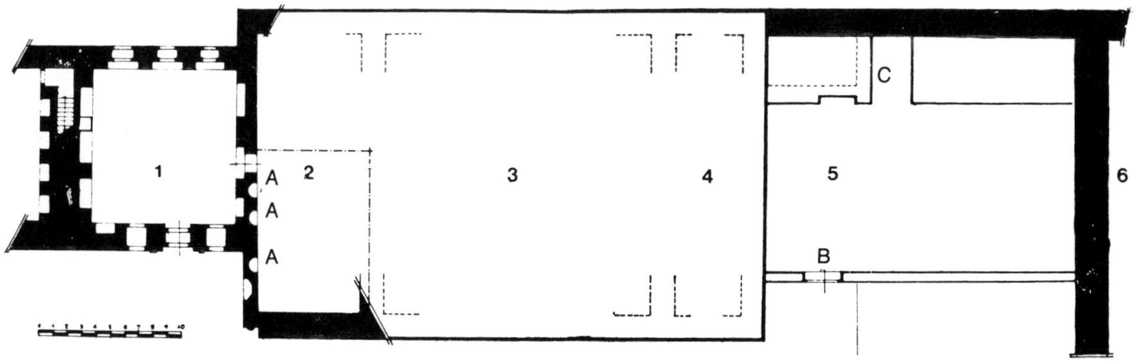

70 Hypothetical reconstruction of the Large Bath in the third court, by İlban Öz, based on a partial excavation. From Öz, "Topkapı Sarayının ilk Hünkâr Hamamı," p. 161.
KEY: *A.* excavated wall niches of the bath; *B.* wall separating furnace garden from the third court; *C.* wood storage; *1.* extant disrobing chamber adjacent to the Inner Treasury; *2.* excavated area; *3.* bath; *4.* furnace; *5.* the furnace garden; *6.* kitchens.

night, continually emitting smoke from its chimney, and was honored by the sultan whenever he felt like bathing. He would sit by the side of the pool, while the naked, well-proportioned bodies of the handsome bath attendants who served him made the "mouths of the fountains water," and the hot floors, burning with desire, kissed their bare feet.[14]

The royal bath was built as an annex to a suite of three rooms and a loggia that still occupies the far right corner of the third court. The domed fourth hall of the suite, which was once the disrobing chamber *(cāmekān),* is the only extant section of the bath, which was otherwise demolished to make room for the expansion of the Chamber of the Expeditionary Force in 1718–19 (Pls. 11 *[38, 45],* 12 *[20, 21]*); Figs. 70–72). A partial excavation in 1972 turned up the niched walls of the bath 1.85 meters below the foundations of the Chamber of the Expeditionary Force. The excavation was halted because it was endangering the foundations of the dormitory above the bath's remains (see Fig. 70).[15]

If we assume that the fifteenth-century bath was the same size as the dormitory that occupies the site today, there was an empty space between it and the facade of the Large Chamber. Today this is a small garden, separated by a partition wall with a gate from the third court. It was the site of Mehmed II's aviary and is clearly shown on the *Hünername* miniature (see Figs. 56, 70). Üsküdari calls it the area of the "furnace" *(külḫān),* onto which eight of the Large Chamber's twelve windows opened (Pls. 9, 11 *[34],* 12 *[19],* 15).[16] Bobovi's plan (Pls. 16a,b) identifies the space as a sand-covered open court where dishes were washed, and where the stokers of the bath's furnace (selected from among the strongest pages of the Large Chamber) practiced their military exercises *(15).* The plan also identifies the bath itself *(21),* the furnace, the room for its stokers *(19),* and neighboring buildings, including the mosque of the Large Chamber *(C),* a music chamber *(meşḫḫāne, 22),* a daytime retreat for mutes, where they were taught sign language *(D),* a recreation room for the chief eunuchs *(18),* and the Chamber of the Expeditionary Force, before it was enlarged *(20).*[17] Most of these buildings must have been added after the dormitory was built in 1606 and reorganized by Murad IV around 1636, but from the very beginning the site functioned as an extension of the Large Chamber, where the pages with duties in the bath furnace and aviary lived. The music chamber may also have existed from the beginning, since Promontorio mentions in 1475 that, among other skills, the novices were taught to sing,

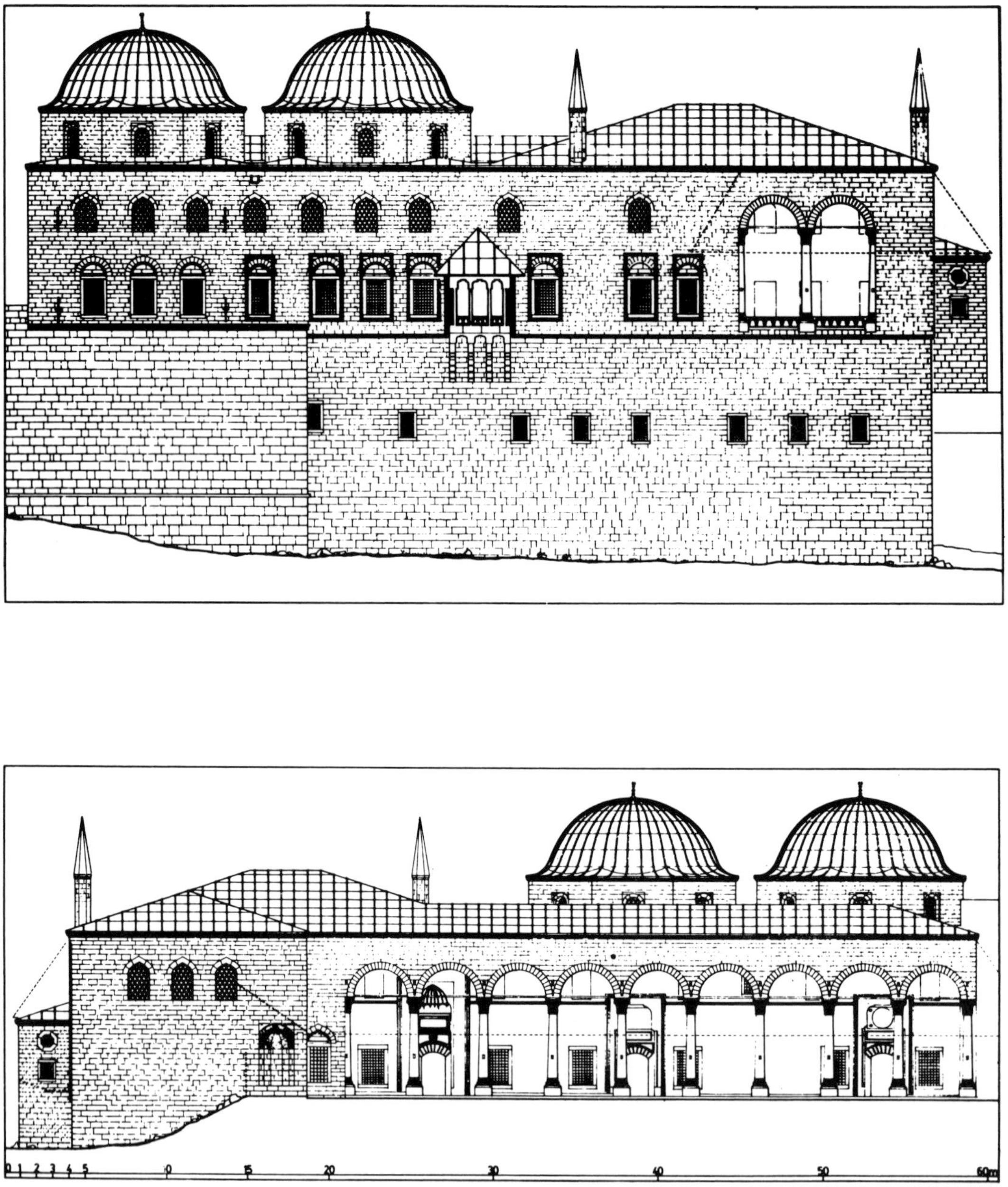

71 Elevations of the Treasury-Bath complex. From Eldem and Akozan, *Topkapı*.

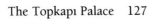

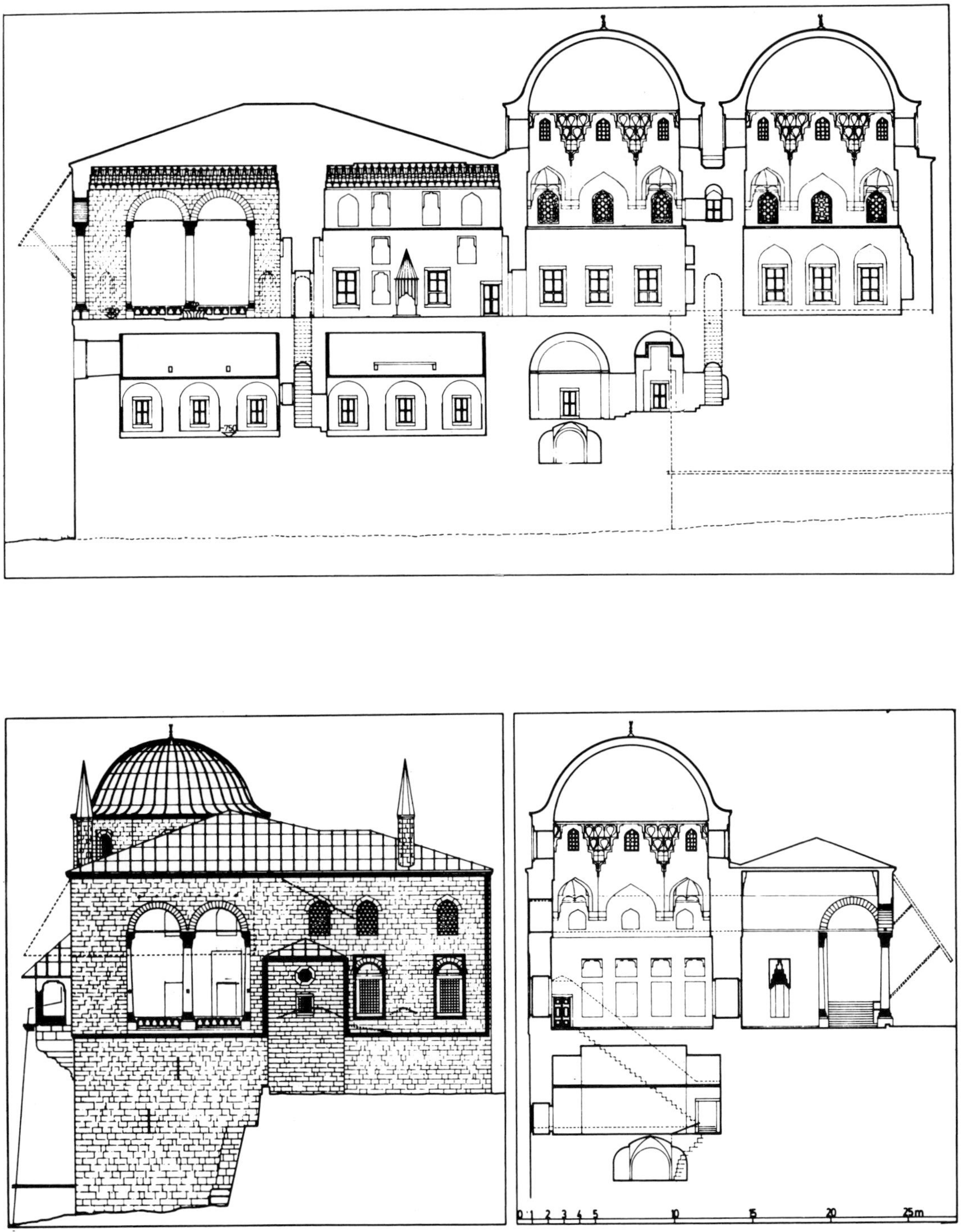

72 Elevations of the Treasury-Bath complex. From Eldem and Akozan, *Topkapı*.

73 An old photograph of the Topkapı Palace from the Sea of Marmara, showing the sea walls, the Treasury-Bath complex before its restoration, and the small mosque of gardeners, no longer extant, along the shore. From Eldem and Akozan, *Topkapı,* pl. 168.

dance, and play instruments. Bobovi tells us that it was an old custom of the musicians to perform each Tuesday, while the sultan was being shaved, which explains why the music chamber was an annex of the bath.[18]

Mehmed II's royal bath, built on top of a steep retaining wall, was seriously damaged in the 1509 earthquake, popularly called "The Little Doomsday." The contemporary historian Ruhi Edrenevi writes: "And there being no defect in the actual domed palace (*aṣl ḳubbe sarāy* [Privy Chamber]) of Sultan Bayezid, the sultan of Rum, Almighty God protected it, and it remained intact. But there was an inner bath *[içerü ḥammām]* on which some cracks appeared."[19] After the earthquake, monumental stone buttresses were added to the garden facade of the bath. In the spring of 1511, Bayezid II rewarded two men, named Solak Ali and Mehmed bin Kemal, after they had supervised the "construction of the buttress of the wall of the imperial palace." Before that, in the fall of 1510, a certain İbrahim had been rewarded for overseeing the "repairs of the imperial palace" necessitated by damage from the earthquake. The original buttresses can be seen on nineteenth-century photographs, but their upper section has since been demolished (Fig. 73).[20]

The buttressing is also shown on an elevation drawn on Italian paper that is datable to the early sixteenth century (Fig. 74). Its graphic information is imprecise, but its detailed annotations provide the basic dimensions and the name of Emin (overseer) Ali, who is probably the same Ali rewarded for his services in 1511. The three double-tiered windows of the domed chamber are identified as "the windows of the disrobing chamber of the bath" *(ḥammām cāmekānınuñ pencereleridür);* the upper section of the buttress to the left of the disrobing chamber is labeled "behind this wall is the bath" *(bu dīvāruñ ardı ḥammāmdur).* The buttress at the right blocks a pair of windows in the adjacent hall, identified here as the "windows of the imperial treasury" *(ḫizāne-i ʿāmire pencereleridür).* This drawing proves that the suite of chambers adjacent to the *cāmekān* of the bath comprised the Inner Treasury.[21]

Today the three double-tiered windows of the domed disrobing chamber differ in form from those

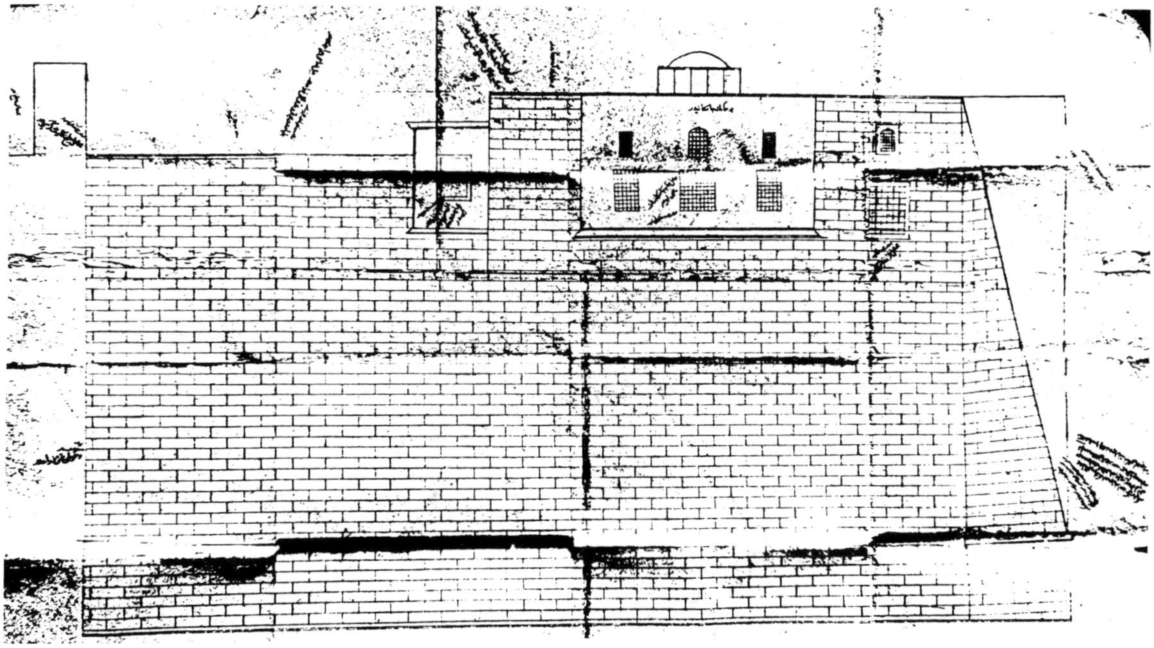

74 Early-sixteenth-century elevation drawing, recording the construction of buttresses in front of the garden facade of the Large Bath at the third court, after an earthquake in 1509, TSA, E 12307, no. 2.

seen on the facade of the Treasury, confirming that it was rebuilt (see Fig. 71). After 1509 the facade of the Treasury-Bath complex was no longer uniform. Süleyman also repaired the bath and increased its capacity. An account book of 1528–29 that refers to the building as the "Large Bath" (*ḥammām-i büzürg*) lists expenses for enlarging its reservoir, repairing its furnace and rooms, and cleaning its basins.[22] Another account book of 1527–28 mentions "Laying the dressed pavement of stone slabs from the room of His Majesty—may his reign last forever—up to the Large Bath of the New Palace," revealing that the sultan's Privy Chamber, occupying the third court's opposite corner, was connected to the royal bath across from it by a stone path.[23] The sultan would cross this path in the company of his favorite pages whenever he desired to bathe. A sixteenth-century miniature shows Süleyman undressing on a carpeted royal dais in the bath's domed disrobing hall, accompanied by his favorite pages, carrying the emblems of royalty, while other pages bathe in the attached secondary chambers, which are roofed with smaller domes, pierced with glass-fitted holes to provide light (Fig. 75).

Graffiti on the door of the adjacent Treasury record that the domes of the building were damaged in yet another major earthquake in 1556–57.[24] Selim II extensively remodeled the bath in 1574, as part of a project to rebuild the kitchens in the second court, which had burned down. His repairs that year are recorded by Âli as the "completion of the deficiencies of the buildings of the defective bath at the imperial palace."[25] Peçevi points out that "some domes of the royal bath, located inside the imperial palace, had recently been decorated, and others rebuilt," and remarks that, when drunk, Selim II slipped on its marble floors while carousing with his pages and died from the effects of the fall.[26] Thereafter, the building was known as the bath of Selim II (Pl. 17 *[19]*).[27] The two domes that crown the third and fourth halls of the

75 Süleyman I undressing in the disrobing chamber at the Large Bath of the third court, with his male pages and bath attendants, TSK, H 1524, fols. 147v, 148r.

Treasury-Bath complex, known today as the Conqueror's Kiosk *(Fatih Köşkü)*, probably date back to Selim II's renovation (they were rebuilt in concrete in the 1940s). The early-sixteenth-century elevation shows only one dome, raised on a blind drum over the disrobing chamber, suggesting that the adjacent Treasury was originally covered with a continuous pitched roof (see Fig. 74).

A royal account book of 1573 indicates that Selim's remodeling also involved adding "tiles and galleries to the interior and to the disrobing chamber of the royal bath, and balustrades and conduits to this bath's fountain, and some balustrades to the new royal kiosk [probably the kiosk-like projecting balcony of the adjacent Inner Treasury]."[28] Imperial decrees dated between July and September 1574 order the qadi of Karamürsel to quarry Marcasite stone and marble for the royal bath, and indicate that galley slaves were transferred from the construction site of the Selimiye Mosque in Edirne to work on the royal bath and other buildings at the palace.[29] Account books compiled in the fall and winter of 1574 mention carpets prepared for the "new royal chamber"

76 İznik tile panels of the Gold Path (*Altın Yol*).

(oda-i ḫāṣṣa-i cedīd), the "projecting balcony" *(ṣāhnişīn),* "daises" *(ṣoffayān),* and the "royal bath" itself *(ḥammām-i ḫāṣṣa).*[30]

Three spectacular İznik tile panels that create the illusion of gardens seen through arches (known as the *Altın Yol,* or Gold Path tiles, after a corridor in the harem to which they were later transferred) seem originally to have been made to decorate Selim II's renovated royal bath (Fig. 76). The date 982 (1574–75) appears in the Persian inscription on the first panel, which records the completion of the "projecting balcony of the lofty bath" *(shāhnishīn-i ḥammām-i ‹ālī).* The inscription on the second panel expresses the hope that the "building" *(binā')* and the sultan's reign will both last forever, and the third that the "high dais" *(ṣuffe-i ‹ālī)* will endure until Judgment Day.[31] An imperial decree addressed to the qadi of İznik on 16 September 1574 orders the completion in all haste of the tiles, which had been commissioned for the royal palace on the basis of a dispatched "model" *(numūne),* but it fails to specify what place in the palace they were intended for.[32] These were most likely the *Altın Yol* tiles. Some have argued that the panels were originally used in the royal bath of the harem, which communicates with a domed hall known today as the Imperial Hall *(Hünkâr Sofası),* but neither this bath nor the royal hall was built until the 1580s, as we shall see. It is therefore more likely that they were made for the royal bath in the male court than for the harem.[33]

A comparison of descriptions of this bath before and after Selim II's renovation confirms the impression that the sultan did no more than remodel and redecorate Mehmed II's bath. Evliya Çelebi, who saw it in the 1630s, when he was a page at Murad IV's court, describes it in terms similar to those used by Cafer Çelebi in his late-fifteenth-century poem:

> On its four sides are the bathing places of royal pages. The exemplary bath in the middle belongs to the emperor. At its corners are numerous pools, jets of water, and fountains. The water spouts and bowls of the fountains and basins are of gold and silver. Into some basins cold and hot water flow at the same time. Its pavements are all of pieces of valuable stone. Its walls are scented with musk and amber. The glimmer of the crystals and rock crystals in its domes floods the bath with light. On its walls not a drop of sweat forms. It does not make one feel too hot. In some of its private rooms there are bejeweled chairs of gold and silver. Its windows are on the east side. Most of them have a view of Üsküdar and Kadıköy [on the city's Asian shore]. To the right side of the door of the disrobing chamber is a room for musicians; the dome of the royal Treasury is to the left. To put it briefly, I have not seen such a bath on the face of this earth, except for the bath of Abdal Khan, the ruler of Bidlis [a lavishly decorated bath also adjoining a treasury].[34]

Another description by Üsküdari reveals that the centrally planned bath, with its private corner rooms, still had the same marble pools that were mentioned in earlier descriptions: "The large bath, which has five private chambers, two big pools, and walls decorated with tiles, has two windows overlooking the royal garden. It is a pleasant bath, with a fountain in the middle of its spacious disrobing chamber, and such a joy-increasing place that it would be fair to say that its like can not be encountered in the three towns [i.e., the Ottoman capitals, Istanbul, Edirne, and Bursa]."[35] Another page, Bobovi, describes the same bath as follows: "There is a hall capable of containing three hundred persons, covered with a very magnificent dome, worked in mosaic above, and paved with marble below. At the corners are an infinite number of small rooms, some filled with tepid water to the height of four or five feet, for bathing oneself, others serving as special pools for those who are the most honored: some function as retreats where one may go to be shaved, and others have waterspouts pouring hot and cold water into the basins, so that one can adjust the temperature ... "[36]

In 1675 Tavernier wrote that the domed disrobing chamber of this *grand bain* featured windows commanding a view and had a checkered marble pavement with a multitiered fountain of colored marble at the center. Its domed hall was surrounded by a gallery supported on iron brackets, protruding from the wall, where towels were left to dry. A door led from the disrobing chamber to the latrines and to the private bathing chambers, which were set around a central hall, also paved with multicolored, checkered marbles. This central hall had a raised royal dais and a white marble pool where three or four men could bathe together. It was filled from a double faucet that carried both hot and cold water. The small, variously decorated rooms surrounding this area included one for barbers. Some were paved with black and white marble squares, and had walls with tile revetments.[37]

The monumental building known as the Large Bath (*ḥammām-i büzürg* or *büyük ḥammām* or *ḥammām-i kebīr*)[38] was given over to the use of the pages after Murad III built a new royal bath in the women's quarters in the 1580s. Beauvau tells us in 1605 that Ahmed I no longer used the old one: "There are, in the inner seraglio, two baths, one for men and the other for women; the first serves the sultan's whole court, which goes there to shave. It is so beautiful and so magnificent, with so many diverse sorts of stones and extremely sumptuous decorations that I do not believe one can ever see anything like it in the world; its beautiful site renders it even more admirable. Nowadays the king does not use it any longer; instead, he uses the one for the women."[39] Writing in 1621, Deshayes de Courmenin confirms that the sultans preferred to use the harem's bath which was "even richer and more beautiful" than the old one.[40]

The male pages took turns using the Large Bath. The chief eunuchs had it on Friday, the Privy Chamber pages on Saturday, those of the Treasury on Sunday, the lesser eunuchs on Monday, the pages of the Expeditionary Force on Tuesday, and the commissary pages on Wednesday. On Thursday morning, the Large Chamber staff went there; on Thursday afternoon, that of the Small Chamber. The Falconers shared Wednesday with the Commissary, and Sunday with the Treasury pages. During the rest of the week, the pages used the small baths with ablution fountains attached to each dormitory.[41] The Large Bath was served by pages from the Large and Small Chambers and from the Expeditionary Force, supervised by three officials, the chief launderer (*çamaşırcıbaşı*), who directed the pages in charge of the royal laundry during campaigns; the bath master (*hamamcıbaşı*), who commanded the masseurs, barbers, and furnace stokers; and the music master (*sāzendebaşı*), who led the pages studying music, dance, and mime in the neighboring "exercise chamber" called the *meşkhane* (Pls. 16a,b *[22]*).[42]

Before the sultans moved to the harem and the bath lost its prestige, it was as much a center of royal entertainment as a bath, as Selim II's fall at a drinking party suggests.[43] In this respect, the third court's royal bath carries the distant memory of the Umayyad baths—based on Roman prototypes in the Mediterranean—which were also places for royal entertainment, musical performances, wine drinking, and the pleasurable relaxation associated with luxury and status. It is far more monumental and imposing than the modest mosque in the same court—another parallel to Umayyad palaces, where royal baths were architecturally more impressive than mosques.[44]

The Inner Treasury

The suite of three halls, its open loggia, and the attached domed disrobing chamber that constituted a fourth room were architecturally conceived, together with the royal bath (Pl. 12 *[21]*; see Figs. 70–72) as a unified whole (Pls. 11 *[39–45]*, 12 *[21]*). This monumental structure, occupying the far right corner of the third court, was originally covered with a pyramidal lead roof, which contrasted with the bath's domes. On Vavassore's map it dominates the terraced garden of Mehmed II's New Palace (Pl. 23). Its three square halls are provided with a protruding latrine, a magnificent loggia with a fountain, overlooking the outer garden, and a projecting balcony that have led some to postulate that it was originally built as Mehmed II's private quarters and only later converted into a treasury by Selim I, to house the enormous booty he brought back from the Safavid treasury in Tabriz and the Mamluk treasury in Cairo.[45] Contemporary sources yield no evidence to support that theory, however, and the pyramidal roof of the ashlar masonry building signals its secondary rank, relative to the multiple-domed Privy Chamber that occupies the opposite corner of the same court (Pls. 4–9). Nor do the sources mention that Selim I converted a building originally conceived as Mehmed II's privy chamber into a treasury. That Selim asked in his will that his successors continue to seal the Inner Treasury with his seal, so long as his record in accumulating treasures remained unbroken (a custom perpetuated until the end of the Ottoman dynasty),[46] does not necessarily mean he was its founder.

Promontorio, Angiolello, Menavino, and Spandugino all mention a private royal treasury in the third court, but fail to say where it was.[47] It is difficult to imagine a suitable site for the Inner Treasury other than the suite of halls with underground vaults adjacent to the Large Bath. According to Angiolello, jewels, gold and silver objects, precious textiles, silk robes, and other valuables were stored in several halls, under the care of a eunuch called the head treasurer.[48] These were apparently some distance from the Privy Chamber — Menavino says that the Treasury pages had to transport whatever it was the sultan required from his treasury to his private quarters.[49]

An early-sixteenth-century drawing of the buttressing added to the royal bath proves that the adjacent suite of halls (identified by an inscription as the imperial treasury *[ḫizāne-i ‹āmire]*) housed the royal treasury from at least 1509 onward, but probably from the beginning (see Fig. 74).[50] In his bath poem of 1493–94, Cafer Çelebi also alludes to the neighboring treasury, owing to which the bath's fountains flow not with water but silver — a subtle play on words, since *ḫazīne* can mean both reservoir and treasury.[51] Atâ says that it was Mehmed II who transformed the suite, originally designed as a *lieu de plaisance,* into his Inner Treasury. He cites a palace tradition that identified the building known as the *Fatih Köşkü,* or Conqueror's Pavilion, as the earliest royal mansion *(ḳaṣr),* built in the New Palace around 1462–63, and converted into a treasury after the completion of other structures.[52] It appears to have functioned as a temporary royal residence, until the actual Privy Chamber across from it was built, a few years later.

The three dim basements, reached by two narrow staircases from the second and third halls, appear to have been designed as a storage area and may even be the vaults mentioned in a 1476 inventory, which refers to a new treasury *(ḫizāne-i cedīde),* to which significant amounts of gold and silver had been transported from the fortress of Yedikule. The same document also refers to a "lower" and a "middle" treasury in which gold and silver coins and jewels were stored in jars, casks, and coffers.[53] Beginning in the sixteenth century, inventories refer to the basement as the Underground Treasury *(bodrum ḫazīnesi, bodrum-i ‹āmire ḫazīnesi,* or *bodrum-i ma‹mūre),* where gold and silver coins were stored in jars *(küp),* marble basins *(mermer muṣluḳ),* and iron coffers *(demür ṣanduḳ).*[54] The accounts for the gold and silver coins stored in this sealed section of the basement were kept separately from general inventories of the Inner Treasury. In 1675 Tavernier, who acquired his information from a former head treasurer, says that this sealed section could only be opened by the head treasurer in the presence of state dignitaries and the sultan.[55]

A general inventory of the imperial Inner Treasury *(ḫizāne-i ‹āmire-i enderūnī),* compiled for Bayezid II in 1496, lists various objects stored both upstairs and downstairs *(bālā-i ḫizāne-i ‹āmire* or *zīr-i ḫizāne-i ‹āmire).* It mentions, among objects stored in the basement, robes, caftans, swords, chessboards, incense burners, belts, sheets of paper, elephants' tusks, rhinoceros horns, sharks' teeth, arrows, Korans in kufic, attributed to the hand of 'Ali, pillows, floor spreads, prayer carpets, bed sheets, books, table spreads, shoes, and Menemen carpets. Objects stored upstairs included ceramic wares of İznik and China; Korans in kufic, kept in mother-of-pearl chests; objects of silver and gold; bed sheets; belts; cushions; books and illustrations *(taṣvīrāt)*; pitchers; metal cups; chandeliers; turbans; velvet, silk, brocade, and wool textiles; sheets of paper; archival documents and historic calendars; astrolabes and astronomical instruments, musical instruments; bows and arrows; chessboards; backgammon sets; incense; lapis lazuli; rosary beads; carpets; and chests full of miscellaneous objects.[56] An inventory made nine years later, in 1505, adds to these categories of objects chests full of manuscripts, maps, and architectural plans, and several sealed coffers containing the revenues from the imperial gardens, which were the sultan's personal spending money.[57]

The Inner Treasury was, then, not only a *Schatzkammer* for precious and exotic artifacts, but also a storage depot for archival documents, manuscripts, practical equipment, household furnishings, and clothing used in the palace. Its inventories suggest that little attempt was made to classify its contents systematically in distinct categories of natural and cultural curiosities, in the manner of the *Wunderkammer* or *studiolo* of Renaissance Europe. Objects loaned from it to various sections of the palace were recorded in registers. The head treasurer, who also oversaw the various court workshops attached to the palace, paid regular wages to the artisans (*ehl-i ḥiref*) whom he commissioned in the Old Council Hall of the second court to produce objects; this indicates that the arts and crafts were classified as part of the Inner Treasury's organization. Raw materials stored in that building, such as paper, gold leaf, lapis lazuli, multicolored marble, jewels, woods, and fabrics were given out to the craftsmen for such commissions. The royal craftsmen, centrally organized as an integral part of the palace administration, had diverse specialties, and included furriers, tailors, hatters, glovers, boot makers, jewelers, goldsmiths, damasceners, metalworkers, locksmiths, swordsmiths, armorers, arrow makers, bow makers, shield makers, carpet and textile weavers, embroiderers, intarsia workers, carpenters, glaziers, calligraphers, painters, and bookbinders.[58] Their products filled the Inner Treasury (which also included an international collection, accumulated as booty and gifts) and were widely used in the royal household. Among the leading officers of the Inner Treasury were a master of the wardrobe, charged with washing the imperial clothes, scribes of inventories, and a royal librarian. In the early nineteenth century d'Ohsson lists keepers of the keys, of jeweled turban ornaments, of ceremonial robes, of the imperial tableware and porcelains, and of weapons.[59]

The walls of the upper suite of halls are pierced up to the ceiling with large niches designed not only for storing, but also for displaying objects—the Ottoman counterpart of Timurid *chīnī-khānas* (Houses of China), which had walls completely covered with niche-shaped recesses to exhibit Chinese porcelains and other precious vessels (see Figs. 70–72).[60] That ceramics (mentioned in the earliest inventories of Bayezid II) were kept in this building is demonstrated by an account book of 1527–28, which refers to "large coffers and cupboards for storing royal porcelains in the chambers of the Inner Treasury."[61] The inbuilt niches suggest that Mehmed II must have conceived the building as an exhibition space when it was built. In function the Inner Treasury complemented both the Privy Chamber and the Large Bath, acting as a storehouse, a royal library, and a mansion for relaxation and intellectual contemplation, as well as a treasury. At least in its early years, before the Chamber of Petitions was built, it was probably also used as a hall where the ruler received important people. Before he enforced his own policy of princely seclusion, toward the end of his reign, Mehmed probably enjoyed showing his treasures to favorite courtiers and visitors. It was told of Kılıç Arslan, the last Anatolian Seljuk prince, who was captured by Mehmed II in 1471, that when he fled to Egypt he sent back to the grand vizier Gedik Ahmed Pasha a costly jewel that the sultan had given him on the occasion of a visit to the treasure house.[62]

The Inner Treasury's architectural prominence, approaching that of the Privy Chamber, reflects the prestige Mehmed II attached to collecting rare artifacts from all over the globe, to support his claim to universal monarchy—a theme reinforced by the spectacular views of two continents and two seas the building's belvederes commanded (Pl. 4). In this place Mehmed II could contemplate his rich collection of *objets d'art,* Byzantine regalia, manuscripts, incunabula, maps, albums, and paintings (which included works by such Italian artists as Gentile Bellini and Costanzo da Ferrara, whom he had invited to Istanbul, as well as works by Ottoman, Persian, and Chinese artists) that he had amassed. The remarkable and idiosyncratic collection included Christian relics. The armbone and skull of St. John the Baptist (the only remaining

77 The Treasury-Bath complex seen from the third court.

relics) are still on display today in one of the halls of the Inner Treasury. It was said that Mehmed II lit candles in front of them as a sign of veneration.[63]

The large collection of Christian relics is listed in an Italian inventory compiled in the time of Bayezid II, who offered them to the French king, and other European rulers, in exchange for holding his rival brother Prince Cem captive. The document specifies: "All of these relics are kept in Constantinople in the palace of the Grand Signor."[64] We know that they were kept in Mehmed II's library *(kitābḫāne),* for once, when the royal librarian, Molla Lutfi, stepped on a marble stone to reach a book on a high shelf, the sultan became greatly distressed; the stone, it turned out, was purported to be the cradle of Christ. It is mentioned in the relic inventory as "the stone on which our Lord Jesus Christ was born, for which the Venetians offered to the old Turk [i.e., Mehmed II] thirty thousand ducats to which the Grand Signor replied that he would not give it to them [even] for a hundred thousand." Mehmed was clearly deeply attached to his Christian relics.[65] He had collected them after the fall of Constantinople by issuing a public proclamation that ordered all the relics in churches to be brought to him intact, together with the Byzantine imperial regalia and vestments. The contemporary historian Guglielmo Caoursin confirms that the sultan firmly refused to sell any of the relics conserved in his royal treasury because he considered them "more precious than money," an attitude partly inspired by his Greek wife.[66]

The royal library in the Inner Treasury was also famous for its legendary manuscript collection, thought to include classical texts originating from the Byzantine imperial library. One of Bayezid II's treasury inventories refers to many "cultural and religious books" without specifying what they were, for they were recorded in separate registers by the head librarian. The colophons of many surviving manuscripts at the Topkapı Palace Library indicate that they once belonged to the Inner Treasury. An inventory from Selim I's reign lists historical manuscripts, 180 Korans, and 149 "non-Muslim books" *(kütüb-i gebrī),* which were probably the Greek and Latin manuscripts collected by Mehmed

78 Detail of the Ionic colonnade of the Treasury-Bath complex.

II.[67] Some of the latter were written between 1460 and 1480, for the sultan, who kept two readers, one for Greek and one for Latin. The few surviving examples of these, which are a mere fraction of the original classical collection (depleted by later sultans who did not share Mehmed's enthusiasm for classical antiquity and sent these volumes as gifts to European rulers) include texts of Hesiod, Homer, Ptolemy, Arrian, Diogenes Laertius, and Xenophon.[68] Selim I is said to have surveyed the "exquisite books at the imperial treasury" one by one.[69] An inventory from 1564 shows that the Turkish, Persian, and Arabic manuscripts were kept in separate cabinets in the second hall of the Inner Treasury, called the *dīvānḫāne* (Pl. 11 *[43]*).[70]

The *dīvānḫāne* is the main royal hall of the suite, and has an arched recess for the imperial throne that was carried to the Gate of Felicity for accession and *bayram* ceremonies (see Figs. 70–72). It opens onto both the projecting balcony and the loggia with a fountain, overlooking the outer garden. Its important function as the throne hall of the Treasury-Bath complex is heralded by its monumental marble portal crowned by a *muqarnas* (stalactite) hood, taller than the other three portals of the building that face the court, and by two green columns of its otherwise white marble Ionic colonnade (Figs. 77, 78). Tavernier describes this colonnade: "One walks in this gallery on large squares of marble and the ceiling is a remainder of antiquity and [has] excellent paintings in mosaic that represent diverse personages, and that are believed to have been made for the reception of some great prince in the time of the Greek Emperors." He adds that only the bodies of these personages remained; their faces had been effaced because of the Turk's disapproval of figural images.[71]

The architectural eclecticism of the Inner Treasury reflected the diverse stylistic trends favored by Mehmed II.[72] It had typically Ottoman Islamic elements, such as arches with pointed and Bursa-type profiles, *muqarnas* decorations, and woodwork inscribed with Persian poetry and Arabic phrases and intricately carved with geometric and vegetal arabesques, constituting an Ottoman variant of the international Timurid ornamental vocabulary.[73] These were juxtaposed to foreign motifs: a marble colonnade with Ionic volute capitals spanned by round arches and featuring unusual half-columns at both ends; a fountained loggia with matching columns, half-columns, and capitals; Italianate checkered marble floors, a Byzantine figural mosaic ceiling, and a Byzantine baptistery in the basement.[74] Later palace tradition attempted to account for these unorthodox features with the explanation that the building was originally a Byzantine structure, remodeled by Mehmed II.[75] It is tempting to propose that an Italian architect—possibly Filarete—contributed the unmistakably Italian flavor of the design and carved the composite Ionic capitals, which are not spolia, but were made for the building.[76]

The final product, however, was a hybrid creation of Mehmed II's eclectic imagination, expressing his claims to universal hegemony—a theme that also characterized the curious collection of objects housed in it. Architectural and decorative elements deriving from various sources were freely intermingled. The doors, windows, and niches were distributed on the walls asymmetrically, so that no two of the interior elevations or the four marble gates along the courtyard facade were alike. These architectural peculiarities bring to mind Kritovoulos's statement that all the royal apartments at the inner palace were built "with a view to variety."[77] This unconventional syncretism is also found in the portrait paintings produced under Mehmed II's patronage, which blend elements of European realism with the miniature format and the schematic treatment of the Persian painting tradition—again, a conscious effort to create an iconography that would reflect the universalism of Mehmed II's imperial idea.[78]

The Treasury-Bath complex, which carried the imprint of Mehmed's eclectic imperial taste, began to lose favor almost immediately. His son Bayezid II was a conservative, and his aversion to the figural arts is attested by Angiolello's report that he sold the painting collection of his father, whom he accused of not believing in the faith of Muhammad. The Italian merchant Tommaso di Tolfo's letter to Michelangelo in 1519 confirms Bayezid's hatred of figural images of any sort.[79] It was he who dispersed the Christian relics so valued by Mehmed, offering them to the rulers of Rhodes, France, and Italy in exchange for sequestering his brother Cem. Bayezid II must equally have disapproved of the figural ceiling mosaics, whose faces were probably effaced at that time, and any antipathy he might already have felt toward the building could only have been augmented by the damage caused in the 1509 earthquake. Crammed with objects accumulated over the years, the Inner Treasury gradually became a locked warehouse, visited by the sultans only on rare occasions.

That Mehmed II's successors no longer used the building as a *lieu de plaisance* is obvious from the sources. By 1584, the *Hünername* miniature (see Fig. 56) shows that the colonnade facing the courtyard had been walled up to provide extra storage space.[80] Scarella's 1686 panoramic view shows the loggia facing the gardens as also closed in by walls (Pl. 31b). By the nineteenth century photographs reveal that the belvederes and windows of Mehmed II's royal mansion were entirely walled in, to add extra space and security for the imperial treasures that had been gathered there over time (see Fig. 73).[81]

The Inner Treasury's collection was particularly augmented after Selim I's conquests of Tabriz and Cairo with new objects that added a strong Islamic flavor to it. These included relics presented to the sultan by the sharifs of Mecca and removed by him from the Mamluk treasury that had preserved the religious insignia of the Abbasid caliphs. The new conquests of Selim I and Süleyman I had transformed the character of the Ottoman lands from a frontier state into a vast Islamic empire, whose absolute ruler combined in his person the functions of sultan and caliph, a change reflected in the Inner

Treasury's contents. Süleyman's victorious campaigns brought new spoils both from the East and the West, including specimens from the great humanistic library of Matthias Corvinus, after the conquest of Hungary.

It is reported that Süleyman's grand vizier Rüstem Pasha (1544–53/1555–61) amassed such large sums of money that a new storage space had to be added to the Inner Treasury. In 1555 Ogier Busbecq reported that this special vault had an inscription on it, reading, "The moneys acquired by the care of Rüstem." Tavernier quotes the same words, inscribed over the gate of the fourth hall of the Inner Treasury, as a reminder to encourage zeal in collecting revenues.[82] During the reigns of Selim I and his son Süleyman I the inner and outer Public Treasuries became so full that the excess was sent to be stored at the Yedikule fortress, one of whose seven towers contained some of Selim's booty from Tabriz. Murad III had most of these treasures brought back to the palace, where he had built a new underground storage vault in the court of pages.[83] This transfer of treasures from Yedikule at a time of economic crisis, confirmed by several contemporary sources,[84] has led some to conclude that it was Murad III who first turned Mehmed's royal mansion into a treasury, but in fact he only added a new vault to the extant Inner Treasury to house the overflow funds that had accumulated in Yedikule.

From the early sixteenth century onward sources refer to the building as the Inner Treasury (*ḫazīne-i enderūnī, ḫizāne-i enderūnī, ḫizāne-i ʿāmire-i enderūnī,* or *iç ḫazīne*),[85] but it is not until 1564 that an inventory tells us how the objects were stored in its various halls. According to this source, the first hall, adjacent to the latrine, contained eight large storage coffers (*anbār*) filled with jars of (in order) electuaries; textiles; belts; objects and swords of silver (including the swords of the Prophet, Islamic heroes, and defeated kings); miscellaneous items, including bows, musical instruments, and turbans; tall caps, helmets, and belts; muslin pillowcases, underwear, napkins, sashes, and towels; and finally, in the eighth coffer, boots and shoes. The second hall, called the *dīvānḫāne,* contained two large coffers, one for royal furnishings, such as cushions, carpets, and sofa spreads; the other for the royal caftans, raincoats, and furs. The manuscripts were also kept there, in cabinets. The third hall, adjacent to the bath's disrobing room, had two large coffers. The first was filled with floor coverings—thick felt rugs, kilims, prayer carpets, Menemen carpets, and silk carpets. The second held royal insignia such as turban ornaments, bows, and arrows. One of the two large trunks in a fourth space, identified as a "bath furnace" (*külḫān*), contained miscellaneous objects, including tables, shields, water vessels, guns, plates, china (*fāġfūrī*), and musical instruments. The other held bedding and household furnishings. The inventory has a separate list of utensils, vessels, and weapons that were distributed among the various cabinets (*dolāb*).[86]

The seventeenth-century writers Tavernier and La Croix go into considerable detail about the Inner Treasury's contents in their time.[87] Tavernier notes that the arms and weapons on shelves or hung on the walls in the first hall were in a pitiful state and covered with dust. La Croix says the place was hung with tapestries, to which were attached the jeweled weapons of the sultans and the swords of the Prophet and the early caliphs. The second hall, considerably more orderly than the first, was a sort of museum, reserved for the robes and other personal belongings of previous Ottoman rulers and Islamic saints. Six huge coffers, each measuring twelve by six feet, were filled with imperial caftans, furs, magnificent turbans, and pearl-embroidered cushions. Some of the items were clothes of the Prophet and other saints, including Joseph's turban and Abraham's crown, which were considered precious relics. Six other coffers, measuring eight by four feet, contained precious textiles and embroidered sofa spreads; jeweled bridles and saddles were hung on brackets projecting from the walls.

The third hall contained mostly jewels. In it was a large coffer with three shelves, the bottom one reserved for the ceremonial furnishings of the Chamber of Petitions and throne covers, the middle one for jewel-embroidered saddle cloths, and the top one for jeweled horse trappings. Other coffers contained jewels, swords, sabers, ambergris, musk, lignum aloes, sandalwood, perfumes, drugs, bezoar stones, mastic, gold- and silverware, European clocks, inkstands, and a variety of objects decorated with precious stones. The walls were covered with scarlet cloth, and on them precious weapons were hung. The most valuable article in this hall was an iron coffer filled with rings, earrings, pendants, necklaces, and bracelets of inestimable value, and a casket of jeweled aigrettes for the sultan's turbans. At the center of this hall was a dais measuring nine by ten feet, covered with a European silk tapestry embroidered in gold thread. It depicted the emperor Charles V enthroned, with a globe in one hand and a sword in the other, with grandees paying homage to him. On this stand were dusty books in European languages, two globes, celestial and terrestrial, and maps drawn on vellum. The fourth hall was filled with coins collected by Rüstem Pasha, according to Tavernier, but La Croix maintains that it was a repository for weapons, an ambiguity caused by the fact that the numbers mentioned in the sources may not consistently have corresponded to the same halls.

All these objects were kept in coffers and cabinets or arranged inside wall niches reached by wooden galleries that ran around the walls.[88] The sultans are known to have visited the Inner Treasury on special occasions or sometimes simply to look at objects of particular interest. In 1580 a French ambassador was told that Murad III particularly enjoyed viewing gifts and letters sent by "his brothers and old friends" the French kings to his predecessors; they were kept in a gilt casket with an inscription identifying the contents.[89]

For special events the Treasury was elaborately decorated. Immediately after his accession ceremony, every new sultan went to pay homage to the Islamic relics and the personal belongings of his ancestors. Following his accession in 1595, on two consecutive days, Mehmed III visited the specially decorated Inner Treasury and distributed largesse to its pages, as custom dictated (*ḳānūn üzre*).[90] A late-sixteenth-century book of royal gifts records several visits by Murad III and Mehmed III when the yearly revenues from Cairo arrived. Descending to its basement, they distributed largesse to leading Privy Chamber pages, the head treasurer, and the Treasury pages, again an "old custom" (*ḳānūn-i ḳadīm*), before returning upstairs.[91]

When two hundred bags of gold had accumulated in the fourth hall, another ceremony took place. The sultan was conducted to it from his Privy Chamber by the head treasurer and swordbearer, between two rows of Treasury pages in dressed ranks, and down a staircase lit by torches. In the basement he watched the transfer of these bags to coffers. It was customary for the head treasurer to remind the sultan to distribute largesse to the Treasury pages before returning upstairs. In the meantime, the grand vizier and finance ministers, who were not allowed in the basement, admired the coffers filled with jewels on the upper floor.[92]

On the two religious holidays, Treasury pages laid sumptuous fabrics on the floors and decorated the walls of the Treasury with precious hangings, on which selected objects were hung, for the sultan's contemplation:

> The most tiring task of these pages is on the feast of the Bayram, when they take all the things that are most precious out of the coffers, to display them in four halls, ornamenting the walls and the ceilings with rich tapestries and gold- and silver-embroidered carpets strewn with gems. They append to these the swords that the Ottoman emperors have left in their treasury, and also arrange on them the gems, jewels, and all the rich harnesses, decorated with a large number of diamonds, rubies, emeralds, pearls, and turquoises, that are used in the Triumphs of the Grand Signors.
>
> His Highness, after the prayer, visits the first of these four halls, thanking God for making him the possessor of such riches.[93]

After the *bayram* ceremonies in 1613, Ahmed I went to admire the special decorations of the Inner Treasury.[94] In accordance with yet another "old custom," during Ramadan the Treasury pages worked for an entire month to adorn the building, pulling treasures acquired by gift and inheritance since the dynasty's founding out of coffers, chests, caskets, cupboards, and cellars. There were objects from Egypt, Damascus, Aleppo, India, Sind, Persia, Arabia, Samarkand, Bukhara, Khorasan, Russia, and Europe,—that is, all the "seven climes"; chief among these were the Prophet's sword, the swords of the four caliphs, and those of other holy men and noble kings. They were hung on colorful textiles suspended from the dome of the third hall.[95]

In a hall referred to as the "military campaign compartment" *(sefer ḫānesi),* every wall was decorated to the ceiling with gilded and jeweled horses' tack, armor, helmets, shields, and weapons. In the other halls jewels "that astonished the observer" were displayed so that each became a "sign of paradise." In one was a model of the Ka'ba, decorated with the *kiswa,* an old rainspout and keys that had once belonged to the actual Meccan shrine. On a dais decked with precious textiles were the alleged turbans of Joseph and Abu Hanifa—the founder of the Hanefi rite, to which the Ottomans belonged—the crown of Abraham, and the crowns or robes said to have belonged to other holy personages. When Ahmed I came to survey his riches, he was served halva and sherbets by the head treasurer. The treasurer and the Treasury pages who had spent the month mounting this exhibition then received gifts from the sultan for their efforts. Ahmed is reported to have visited the exhibit several times, deriving a lesson from each object on display. Contemplating the transitoriness of life, he thanked God for having given him all of these treasures.[96] In 1791 the Inner Treasury was decorated to celebrate the birth of a princess. It was visited by the sultan who sat on his imperial throne and the next day, after all the pages had been evacuated to the outer garden, by the harem ladies.[97]

Today the whitewashed Inner Treasury is stripped of its original decorations, but it still retains the air of a truly royal structure. It originally formed a unified, if severe, exterior facade with the Large Bath and the kitchens of the second court, the whole resting on a steep retaining wall. Seen from the sea by arriving ships, this vast expanse of masonry, crowned with chimneys, multiple domes, and a monumental pyramidal roof, must have been most impressive (Pls. 4, 23, 31b). The Inner Treasury projected to the outer world an image of imperial luxury, wealth, and power. It was a majestic structure, worthy of housing the enormous treasure gathered by the successive sultans. The carefully preserved personal belongings of each sultan, venerated by every subsequent ruler when he acceded to the throne, turned it into a sort of family museum celebrating Ottoman dynastic continuity. It enshrined the revered relics not only of royal forebears, but also of Christian saints and Islamic holy men, together with the captured regalia and precious possessions of defeated monarchs. Its contents, mementoes of the empire's past, embodied a historical consciousness that is also reflected in the Ottoman chronicles preserved in its royal library. Occasional thefts, the periodic discarding or sale of antiquated items, the melting down of precious metal objects for coins during economic crises, and the sultan's donations in the form of gifts or dowries in time would have reduced the immense holdings, had these losses not been counterbalanced by a constant influx of diplomatic gifts, confiscated properties, and booty.[98] One source compared the sultan's Inner Treasury to the Caspian Sea, continually fed by many rivers.[99]

Privy Chamber Complex

The Privy Chamber *(ḫāṣṣ oda)* mentioned in Mehmed II's *kanunname* was a domed building in the northwest corner of the third court, where the sultan lived.[100] Ruhi Edrenevi referred to it as Bayezid II's "domed palace" *(ḳubbe sarāy),* when he remarked that it had suffered no injury in the 1509 earthquake, thanks to its faultless construction, unlike the royal bath across the way.[101] Angiolello provides the earliest extant description of the building known today as the Pavilion of the Holy Mantle (Pls. 11 *[48–53],* 12 *[24, 25]*):

> On the left-hand side of the [third] court is the palace where the Grand Turk resides; most of that palace is vaulted in construction and has many chambers and summer and winter rooms. The part that looks toward Pera has a portico which is above the large garden, from which rise many cypresses that reach [the height of] the balconies of this portico, and that portico is built on two

79 The domes of the Privy Chamber complex, with added windows to bring in more light; the highest one, with a minaretlike fireplace chimney, crowns the throne room.

columns and is completely vaulted, and in the middle is a fountain that flows into a beautiful basin worked in marble with profiles and colonnettes of porphyry and serpentine, and in this basin are many sorts of fish, and the Grand Turk derives great pleasure from watching them.[102]

The Privy Chamber complex was differentiated from the pyramidally roofed Inner Treasury opposite by its many domes (Pls. 5–9). It commanded a view of the Bosphorus, the lively harbor of the Golden Horn, and Pera (Galata), in contrast to the Treasury-Bath complex, which overlooked the Sea of Marmara, into which the neighboring palace kitchens emptied their garbage, and was therefore less desirable as a residence. The latter had the further disadvantage of being too close to the chimneys of the bath furnace and the kitchens, which smoked night and day. The Privy Chamber has undergone many changes over the centuries, but the massive masonry core of today's Holy Mantle Pavilion belongs to Mehmed II's original building. It was once thought that Selim I had constructed it, but it is now generally accepted that he only remodeled an existing structure.[103] Certainly it seems unlikely that this important corner of the third court was left empty until the sixteenth century.

The quadripartite main core of the building is raised on a heavy, fortresslike basement of four square halls that reflect the layout above (Pl. 11 *[49–51]*; Fig. 79). The four domed square halls in the upper level occupy the court's northwest corner. Two lower rectangular wings, roofed with smaller domes, blend this blocklike core with the north and west wings of the courtyard (Pls. 8, 9, 11 *[48–53]*). A narrow staircase inside a thick wall connects the upper halls to the dark basement which communicates with the garden below. The building is constructed of alternating courses of stone and brick, unlike the Treasury-Bath complex, built of ashlar masonry (Fig. 80). Its inner facade, facing the third court, has a zigzag-shaped marble portico covered with small domes and spanned with pointed arches. This typically Ottoman portico of thirteen columns contrasts with the Italianate round-arched Ionic colonnade of the Inner Treasury across the way. The five columns at the two ends and at the points where the zigzagging portico changes direction are green; the others are

80 View of the Privy Chamber from the third court.

81 View of the Privy Chamber, the Circumcision Room *(Sünnet Odası)*, the marble terrace, and its pool, with the eaves of the Baghdad Kiosk in the foreground. Courtesy of Reha Günay.

white. The outer facade of the building, facing a hanging garden with a marble fishpond, is fronted by an L-shaped marble portico roofed with small domes, again of thirteen columns, resting on the projecting ceiling of the basement (Figs. 81, 82a,b). There is a second row of lower columns in front of these, creating a spacious portico—the "two columns" mentioned by Angiolello apparently refer to the double arcade of this stately portico overlooking Pera. The Privy Chamber, where the sultan slept, was the square hall at the northwest corner of the complex, accentuated with a dome higher than the others and sited to command the best view.

Except for a wooden door carved with the inscription *al-Sulṭān Meḥmed bin Murād Ḫān* ("the Sultan Mehmed, son of Murad Khan"),[104] none of the original decorations of the building remain, but a poem written by Cafer Çelebi in 1493–94, titled "Characteristics of the Imperial Palace," gives us some idea of what they looked like. The "dwelling of the world-commanding Shah," it says, had a gilded ceiling, multicolored marble pavements, and walls hung with precious fabrics. He compares the crenellated walls surrounding the hanging garden flanking it to a row of teeth (a play on the word *dendāne,* which can mean both "battlement" and "teeth") seen through the smiling "lips of the cheerful terrace *[ṣoffa]*" that beautifies the face of the royal mansion *(ḳaṣr)*. The mansion is then likened to a maiden combing her hair—the rows of battlements are the metaphoric comb. The poem also praises the high site of the paradisial royal residence and gardens overlooking the sea; its beautiful courtyard; its domes, resembling the heavenly spheres; its halls brightened by many windows and colorful paintings. The windows "opened their mouths [i.e., the shutters]" in astonishment, when they saw these paintings.[105]

Painted decorations are also mentioned by Bidlisi, who writes that the walls of the various royal structures at the inner palace were decorated with charming pictures *(tamāṣīl)* and extraordinary figures *(ṣuwar)*.[106] We know that the Inner Treasury did have figural mosaics, therefore, its interior walls and those of the Privy Chamber may well have featured figural frescoes. Some sources suggest that Gentile Bellini, who had been painting the murals of the Doge's Palace in Venice, was invited by Mehmed II in 1479–80 to paint some rooms in the New Palace.[107] But Bellini, who came to Istanbul with two assistants, stayed only a short time, not long enough to complete grand mural schemes. Besides, the sultan was already living in the Privy Chamber by 1479, and it is unlikely that he moved into the building with its walls still bare. Kritovoulos says that by 1465 the inner rooms of the palace were "shining and scintillating with an abundance of gold and silver, within and without and with precious stones and marble with various ornaments and colors, all applied with a brilliance and smoothness and lightness most attractive and worked out with the finest and most complete skill, most ambitiously. Both in sculpture and plastic work, as well as painting, they were the finest and

best of all.... And the whole was beautiful and adorned with myriads of other brilliant and graceful articles."[108] The "sculpture and plastic work" probably included carved stucco decorations in the international Timurid style that produced a rich textural and chromatic effect. These abstract ornaments may have been complemented with figural representations, but they were probably not painted by Bellini. If the Venetian artist did paint frescoes, he would most likely have been asked to decorate the pavilions in the outer garden or the belvederes of the Imperial Fortress, which had just been completed when he arrived.

The Privy Chamber was remodeled several times in the sixteenth century. Menavino says that Bayezid II built a two-story building to live in, descending to its basement on cold and hot days.[109] This was probably his father's Privy Chamber, which Bayezid must have remodeled according to his own taste, when the inner palace was repaired after the earthquake in 1509. Selim I also transformed and redecorated the building. He faced it with marble revetments taken from Cairene monuments when he conquered Egypt in 1517, and housed in it some of the Islamic relics removed from the Mamluk treasury (the rest were kept in the Inner Treasury). These changes explain why a nineteenth-century palace tradition attributes the building to him.[110]

Michael Meinecke dates the placement of the spoliated marble dadoes that still decorate the garden facade (believed to come from the *Diwan al-Kabir* in Cairo, where relics of the Prophet and his Companions were kept) to around 1518–20 (see Figs. 82a,b).[111] The blue-and-white tile borders around these marble panels, which appear to be

cording to a later source, Mahmud I visited this sealed treasury in 1735 to remove for repair some old harnesses, ornamental saddle covers, swords, and weapons, "which were souvenirs of Ottoman sultans' victories." Atâ says that in the nineteenth century the Swordbearer's Treasury still contained weapons and other souvenirs of military campaigns, valuable articles, coins, and holy relics.[160] Its contents were periodically checked by sultans, who ordered any surplus items transferred to the main Inner Treasury.

THE OUTER PORTICO, ITS MARBLE TERRACE AND POOL

The stately double-colonnaded portico attached to the outer facade of the Privy Chamber complex opened onto the hanging garden, with its fishpond and kiosks; it was also connected to the harem. This private royal garden, raised on a vaulted substructure, was planned as an extension of the Privy Chamber; its airy summer kiosks complemented the massive winter halls of the complex, and its vaulted portico functioned as an open hall for royal activities (Pls. 6, 8; see Figs. 81, 82a,b). On the outer walls of the Privy Chamber, faced with Cairene marbles and blue-white-turquoise underglazed tiles, hung bows, arrows, and other weapons, some of which were said to have been used by Selim I in the conquest of Egypt.[161] Others commemorated feats of strength by later rulers, who practiced archery and other royal sports there and in the walled garden below. They included a "ponderous round stone, which with one finger he [Murad IV] is said to have lifted by a ring fixt therein; likewise five thick and substantial shields, which being placed upon one another were pierced through by a cast of his *jirid* [javelin] still sticking in them; also several silver pellets thrown by him with that violence; as to stick in an iron door." [162] This iron door of the Privy Chamber, which opened to the outer portico, had a silver inscription commemorating Murad's having pierced it in three places in 1637–38.[163]

The garden portico of the Privy Chamber was also used as an entertainment hall. In 1599 the organ maker Thomas Dallam was asked to install there an organ sent by Queen Elizabeth to Mehmed III, although it was extremely rare for an outsider to be allowed to enter the sultan's private precinct. The Englishman who had this opportunity describes how the enthroned sultan listened to the automated organ, surrounded by pages:

> The Grand Signor, beinge seated in his Chaire of estate, commanded silence. All being quiett, and no noyes at all, the presente began to salute the Grand Signor; for when I left it I did allow a quarter of an houre for his cominge thether. Firste the clocke strouke 22; than the chime of 16 bells went of, and played a songe of 4 partes. That beinge done, ten personagis which stood upon the corners of the second storie, holdinge tow silver trumpetes in there handes, did lifte them to theire heades, and sounded a tantarra. Than the muzicke went of, and the orgon played a song of 5 partes twyse over. In the tope of the orgon, being 16 foute hie, did stande a holly bushe full of blacke birds and trushis, which at the end of the musick did singe and shake theire wynges. Divers other motions thare was which the Grand Signor wondered at.

After waiting in the basement, Dallam was summoned upstairs to play the organ for the sultan.[164] Later, the organ was moved to a garden pavilion called the Pearl Kiosk, probably because having automated figurines near the Privy Chamber where holy relics were stored was regarded as inappropriate. Mehmed III's son Ahmed I proved to be more scrupulous about the Islamic interdiction of images. He broke the organ in pieces on a visit to the garden pavilion.[165]

Dallam provides one of the earliest known descriptions of the Privy Chamber's groin-vaulted garden portico, where he had first installed the organ:

> Cominge into the house whear I was appoynted to sett up the presente or instramente, it seemed to be rether like a churche than a dwellinge house; to say the truthe, it was no dwellinge house, but a house of pleasur.... This great house it selfe hathe in it tow rankes of marble pillors; the pettestales of them ar made of brass, and double gilte. The wales on 3 sides of the house ar waled but halfe waye

to the eaves; the other halfe is open, but yf any storme or great wynde should hapen, they can sodonly let fale such hanginges made of cotten wolle for that purpose as will kepe out all kindes of wethere, and sudenly they can open them againe. The fourth side of the house, which is close and joynethe unto another house, the wale is made of purfeare [porphyry], or suche kinde of stone as when a man walketh by it he maye se him selfe tharin. Upon the grounde, not only in this house, but all other that I se in the Surralie, we treade upon ritch silke garpites, one of them as much as four or sixe men can carrie. Thare weare in this house nether stouls, tables, or formes, only one coutche of estate. Thare is one side of it a fishe ponde, that is full of fishe that be of diverse collores.[166]

The rolled-up curtains Dallam mentions are visible in later views and listed in repair documents, which also cite expenses for the straw mats that were placed under the carpets.[167] In the first decade of the seventeenth century Bon described the same portico as a *divano,* or hall of state. Near the window from which he peered into the royal bedchamber was a small fountain for washing hands and drinking, provided with a gold cup studded with turquoises and rubies. This must be the predecessor of the extant nineteenth-century wall fountain, which conducts water through a channel inlaid with multicolored marbles into the pool. Bon describes the pool as a delightful, small square lake surrounded by a path intricately paved with marbles, wide enough for two people to walk side by side. Thirty fountains were distributed along this paved border, spouting water with a "continuous and gentle murmur" into the pool, whose water was then drained out to the gardens. In the pool was a small boat that the sultan often rode in with his buffoons, making them row it and jump into the water to entertain him.[168] The extant pool, still surrounded with jets of water, was built on top of the one described by Bon during a mid-seventeenth-century remodeling of the marble terrace. The larger original pool was recently discovered under it.[169]

The Privy Chamber's wide portico, overlooking this pool, occasionally served as a council hall, which explains why Bon calls it *divano* and Lokman and Atâ refer to it as a *dīvānḫāne* (see Figs. 81, 82b).[170] Until Süleyman's time, extraordinary audiences *(meşveret)* were held in the Old Council Hall of the second court, but with the increasing emphasis on seclusion they began to take place under the outer portico of the Privy Chamber or in the kiosks of the hanging garden.[171] One miniature (Fig. 89) shows Osman II presiding over an extraordinary council meeting, seated on a large carpet in front of a building identifiable as the garden facade of the Privy Chamber. He is interviewing the dignitaries who had been invited in 1618 to advise him about an impending war.[172] A fountain directs water through a canal into a marble pool with steps on either side. Another extraordinary council, convened by Osman II in 1622 to subdue a rebellion, took place on this "large terrace" *(büyük ṣoffa),*

89 Osman II holding a war conference with grandees in 1618 on the pool terrace in front of the Privy Chamber, TSK, H 1124, fol. 49r.

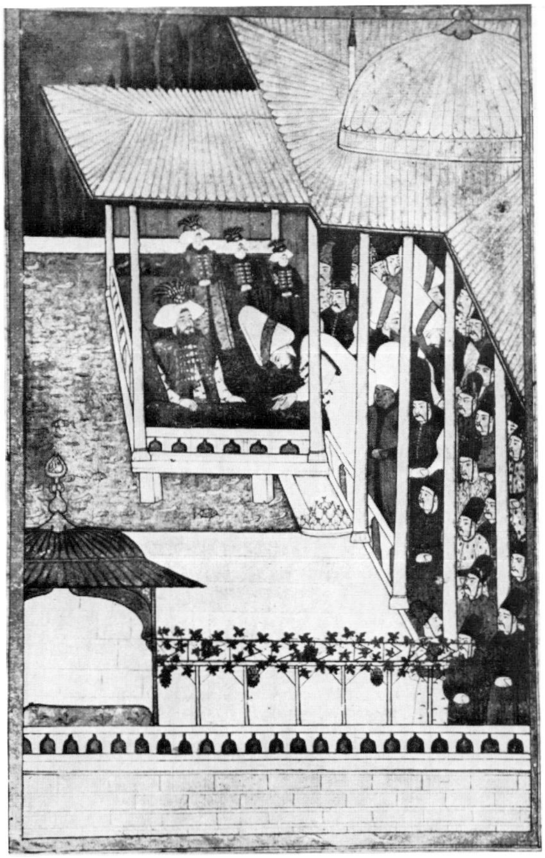

90 Levni, miniature painting, ca. 1720, showing Ahmed III seated on the marble throne overlooking the fish-filled pool of the marble terrace, in front of the Privy Chamber; princes waiting to be circumcised stand behind him, while pages and grandees are lined up under the portico to congratulate him. From Vehbi, *Surname,* 1720, TSK, A 3593, fol. 173v.

where the sultan was seated on a "chair inlaid with mother-of-pearl at the edge of the terrace." [173]

Earlier sources hardly mention the ceremonies that took place on this porticoed marble terrace, but by the beginning of the seventeenth century Safi writes that it was already an "old custom" for royal pages to congratulate the sultan there on religious holidays. For this ceremony a "noble throne was placed on the exhilarating terrace before the door of the Privy Chamber," and pages greeted him in hierarchical order.[174] The extant canopied stone throne attached to the Privy Chamber's portico and projecting over the marble pool was built in the mid seventeenth century to provide a permanent setting for these ceremonies. An eighteenth-century miniature by the Ottoman painter Levni depicts a circumcision of princes; in it, the sultan is seated on this throne overlooking a pool full of fish, as pages and grandees line up under the portico to kiss his hand (Fig. 90). Another double-page miniature by Levni shows the sultan scattering coins to his pages, while the circumcised princes rest in a pavilion (Fig. 91).

The terrace and its pool, where sultans were usually entertained by buffoons and male attendants, were occasionally reserved for the use of the harem women, for it is connected with the women's quarters through a passage and could be sealed off from the male court (Pls. 5–8). Ahmed I and his harem were entertained there with "comedies of voice and instruments." [175] According to Eremya, seated in a boat in the "sealike pool spacious enough for a boat ride," İbrahim I watched musicians, who performed around the edge of the water, and rewarded the girls of the harem for catching fish in their nets. Bobovi mentions musical and theatrical performances near this pool, where the sultan occasionally gave extraordinary audiences for the mufti and the grand vizier (Pls. 16a,b *[40]*).[176] Another seventeenth-century author, La Croix, writes:

> The emperor eats in the Privy Chamber ... and he then enjoys the pleasures of hunting, walking, exercising with the pages, wrestling, buffoons, mutes or dwarfs who jump one after the other into the basin of the fountain that is in the middle of the Privy Chamber to collect the coins that his Highness throws there; sometimes he gives audience in that place to the principal ministers of his empire.... The representations of comedies, marionettes, and other diversions occur in front of this basin, where his Highness also confers with the mufti, the grand vizier, and other ministers of his empire, about the most important affairs.[177]

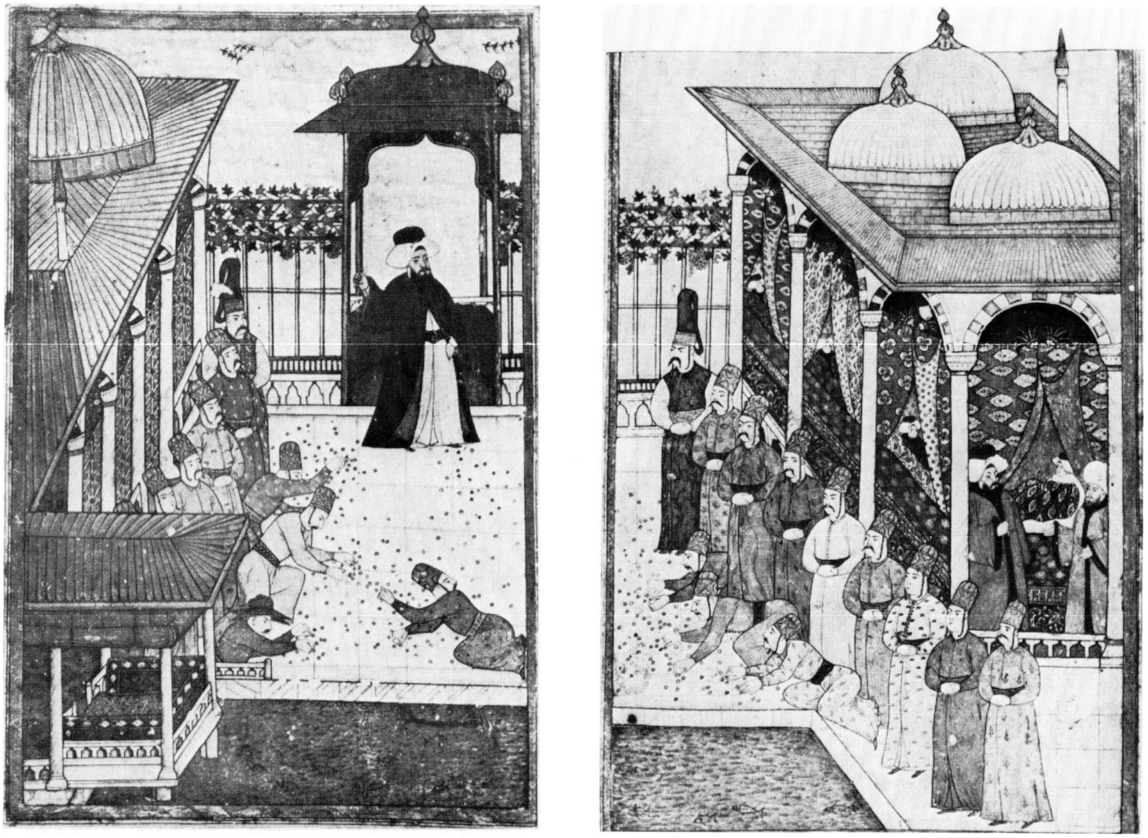

91 Levni, double-folio painting, ca. 1720, showing Ahmed III under the gilt-bronze canopy of the marble pool terrace, throwing coins to his pages; circumcised princes repose inside the Baghdad Kiosk. From Vehbi, *Surname,* 1720, TSK, A 3593, fols. 174r, 174v.

From the seventeenth century onward, sources frequently mention extraordinary audiences, investiture ceremonies for grand viziers and *şeyhülislams*, circumcisions of princes, reading sessions, and musical and theatrical performances taking place on the porticoed marble terrace or inside its kiosks, where the sultans also sometimes ate their meals.[178] The increasing frequency of ceremonies in this area reflected the growing reluctance of sultans, from the mid seventeenth century onward, to remain sequestered, a trend that provided dignitaries with an opportunity to see the magnificent royal quarters that they would otherwise never have been permitted to enter.

EIGHT
The Third Court: The Imperial Harem

The harem was an established institution throughout the Islamic world, associated with palace life. The term is derived from the Arabic word *ḥarīm,* meaning an inviolable area, and was used to refer both to the women of a household and to the secluded apartments in which they lived. The Ottoman harem differed from others in that it complemented the system of household slaves and paralleled that of pages. The harem of the Topkapı was always off limits to visitors and is consequently the section of the palace about which least is known. No ambassador, dignitary, or historian could enter it. Most of the information we have comes from fanciful accounts by curious Westerners, who had gathered their information from former palace inhabitants. Official Ottoman historians mostly avoided the subject of women, in keeping with their concepts of privacy and propriety; the central figure of their narrative was always the sultan. The miniatures that illustrated their texts also concentrated on the royal image of the sultan and his male court and, with very few exceptions, omitted women, who had no part to play in public court ceremonies (Figs. 92a,b).

Harem women figure in Ottoman histories only in the second half of the sixteenth century, and then as a negative force that disturbed the traditional order of society. Much to the resentment of those who wanted to preserve the old order, this was a period when royal women and black eunuchs joined forces and gained unprecedented power in politics, taking advantage of the increasing seclusion of the sultans, who had by then retired into the labyrinthine inner space of the harem. This abrupt emergence of women from obscurity to notoriety had its effects on the architecture of the harem in the Topkapı Palace, just as architectural transformations played a reciprocal role in bringing about such a change.

So rarely is the harem mentioned in the early sources that some scholars believe it did not even exist in Mehmed II's New Palace, an assumption based mainly on Evliya Çelebi's statement that "in this palace no harem had been established. Later, in the time of Süleyman Khan, a harem was built, together with a Chamber for Eunuchs, a Chamber for Halberdiers, a Kiosk of Justice, and a Council Hall." [1] This passage has convinced some that the harem remained in the Old Palace until it burned down in 1541 (and was rebuilt in reduced size, as the Süleymaniye Mosque took up much of its former site) or even until the reign of Murad III.[2] But such a theory cannot be correct, for archival documents show clearly that Süleyman I renovated a harem that already existed in the Topkapı Palace, around 1526–28, along with the other buildings rebuilt under Alaüddin's supervision.[3] Evliya's remarks must therefore refer to this sultan's extensive renovation of the harem and its services, including the quarters of the Halberdiers with Tresses and the black eunuchs, after which its prestige increased.

The scarcity of archival material from the fifteenth century does make it difficult to confirm the existence of a harem in Mehmed's palace, but a number of references in the early sources certainly suggest it. In 1465 Kritovoulos mentions women's apartments that complemented the quarters for men.[4] Promontorio says that in 1475, of the 400 women in the sultan's harem, only 150 lived with him in the New Palace; the remaining 250 stayed in the old one. Those selected for the sultan's palace were all slaves, the most splendidly fair and beautiful women to be found in the world, well dressed in silks and brocades of gold and silver, some adorned with pearls and jewels. They slept on individual beds in rooms they shared, three or four together. Each room was served by about twenty servants, and the harem itself was entrusted to twenty-five eunuchs, whose chief was an Agha. The harem of the Old Palace, which Promontorio refers to as the "second seraglio of damsels," was similarly run by eunuchs, but their chief ranked lower than the Agha in the New Palace.[5]

In 1499, Alvise Sagundino says, ten women lived in Bayezid II's palace, and eighty were housed outside of it, numbers that apparently refer to the royal consorts whose entourage of servants swelled the size of the harem. In 1507 Iacomo Contarini's report noted that women continued to live in the New Palace: "Inside his seraglio he [Bayezid II] continually keeps four aghas [chief white eunuchs] for the guarding of his person and of his household, who are three hundred persons; among whom there are eighty boys, and they say also some women." Contarini adds that Bayezid II occasionally visited the women who lived in the Old Palace.[6] When Menavino was a page in Bayezid's palace, the sultan used to stay there three or four days at a time before returning to his own apartments in the New Palace. Evliya writes that Mehmed II visited the Old Palace twice a week, and lived the rest of the time in the New Palace, a passage that has contributed to the notion that the latter was an administrative center, not a fully functioning residence.[7]

92*a* A prince offered wine by his consort, with attendant concubines and dancers in the imperial harem. From Baki, *Divan*, sixteenth century, MS. London, British Library, Op. 7084, fol. 101v.

There was a good deal of traffic between the crowded harem of the Old Palace and the smaller one in the New Palace. Mehmed II's grandsons were living in the Old Palace when their grandfather died in 1481. The sultan's body was carried in a procession that started at the New Palace, where his pages and soldiers had assembled, then passed the Old Palace, where the mourning wives and slaves of the deceased monarch watched from a gallery.[8] Angiolello and Menavino say that royal princes were brought up at the Old Palace by their mothers, before being sent off with them to govern the prov-

92*b* A late-sixteenth-century Austrian drawing of women in the harem, Album, MS. Vienna, Österreichische Nationalbibliothek, Cod. 8626, fol. 116r.

inces.[9] In the late fifteenth and early sixteenth centuries the Queen Mother was not yet living in the New Palace either; she wrote to her son, Bayezid II, complaining that she had not seen him for forty days and asking permission to visit.[10]

Taken together, these passages suggest that the Topkapı always had a harem, but that it was at first quite small, housing only slave concubines and not the royal family. Atâ, who attributes its foundation to Mehmed II, says that the white eunuchs in charge of the pages also ran the harem until the second half of the sixteenth century, when the two functions were separated. Until then, the head gatekeeper, who was the chief of the white eunuchs and resided at the Gate of Felicity, was the head of the entire inner palace household.[11] Bidlisi's description of that official as the gatekeeper of the "royal palace" *(devletḫāne-i ḫāṣṣ)* and of the "hidden palace of women" *(ḥarem-sarāy-i nihān)* supports this.[12] An important institutional change in the last quarter of the sixteenth century turned the chief black eunuch into the most important officer of the imperial household. Taking advantage of the increasing political influence of the harem in this period, the black eunuchs eventually usurped the power of the white ones.[13] A history of black eunuchs puts that turning point in 1574–75, the first year of Murad III's reign.[14]

Originally, Mehmed II had conceived the harem of his New Palace as a small appendage to the larger and more central court of pages, where he resided in the company of men. That the white eunuchs were responsible for both the male and female quarters of the inner palace shows that the two were considered part of the same household organization. Complementing the palace school for pages, the harem was a school for young slave girls who were recruited from all parts of the empire, carried off after conquests, or presented as gifts. These Christian slaves, selected for their physical beauty, were then converted to Islam and subjected to a rigid discipline, under which they were taught the principles of religion, etiquette, music, embroidery, sewing, dancing, singing, storytelling, reading, and writing as their talents and aptitudes led them. They were grouped in a hierarchy that paralleled the organization of pages, receiving wages and clothing from the sultan's treasury, according to rank.[15] Only a few of them became consorts of the sultan and bore him children; the rest were employed as servants or attendants. The early Ottoman sultans married princesses from the families of the Muslim principalities of Anatolia, the Christian despots of the Balkans, or the Byzantine imperial line. The establishment of a system of slave concubines paralleling that of pages, after the conquest of Constantinople, signaled the creation of a centralized empire that had swallowed up these neighboring small states; there were no princesses left in neighboring countries who could match the sultan in status. In other words, there were no rulers with whom the Ottoman family desired to be allied.[16] After the reign of Mehmed II, the dynastic lineage was perpetuated through the offspring of slave concubines brought up in the palace. Like the system of pages, this practice served to strengthen the autocratic power of the sultan, helping him curb the local autonomy of aristocratic families.

Like the pages, the female slaves of the sultan could hope to rise from anonymity to the highest position a woman could attain in a male-dominated sociopolitical order, by becoming mothers of princes and princesses. The woman whose son became sultan occupied the top of the hierarchy in the imperial harem, as Queen Mother.[17] The hope of achieving this status must have been entertained by every concubine taken into the harem; although the prospect was remote, it was not impossible. The slave concubines who loyally served the sultan or the royal family, but had no son, were given as wives to the highest dignitaries of the empire, most of whom had also been educated in the palace. The harem was, then, another institution established to generate a ruling elite, loyal to the sultan, and sharing a common upbringing, customs, and tastes. This elite constituted the patriarchal monarch's extended family of sons and daughters. The real daughters of the sultans were also married to the graduates of the palace school, in most cases to grand viziers who had reached the highest rank in the administrative hierarchy. This system created a multiethnic imperial elite with close marriage ties to the circle of the palace household.

With its living facilities for both male and female slaves, Mehmed II's New Palace was the nucleus of the system he established of absolutist rule through household slaves. As soon as a royal consort became pregnant, she was moved to the Old Palace, where the sultan's family, including his wives, children, and the Queen Mother, lived. If she had a son, the prince was brought up there, and she would then accompany him to the province he was assigned to govern as part of his education. Thus removed from the capital, her greatest hope was to return as Queen Mother, if her son succeeded in defeating his brothers and became the next sultan. There was no system of primogeniture in the Ottoman dynastic succession; therefore, princes born of different mothers had to fight among themselves to earn the throne, through merit and political acumen. The one who succeeded in winning the support of the military elite, and in taking possession of the Topkapı Palace with its treasury, was enthroned at the Gate of Felicity. He then had to kill all his brothers to ensure his absolute power, according to a clause legitimized in Mehmed's *kanunname*.[18] Exalted in her role as the sultan's mother, the queen could never marry again; she relinquished her sexuality to become a revered matriarch and the mistress of the Old Palace, where she lived.

This system continued well into the middle of Süleyman I's reign. As a young man, Süleyman, like his predecessors, frequented the Old Palace regularly.[19] At this time not only the Queen Mother, but also royal princes and princesses and their mothers were still living there. The Venetians referred to it as the "seraglio of the mother and wives of the sultan." Records indicate frequent visits between the sultan and its residents. Süleyman visited his mother and wives there before he left on a military campaign in 1532.[20] At the circumcision festival of 1530, the princes were conducted by a retinue from the Old Palace to the Hippodrome to kiss the sultan's hand.[21] In 1533 the oldest prince, Mustafa, was again accompanied by grandees from the Old Palace to the Topkapı to kiss his father's hand, before leaving with his mother to govern Manisa.[22] Süleyman's daughter Mihrimah was brought in a carriage with a red atlas curtain—the Ottoman royal color—with her retinue, from the Old Palace to the residence of her husband, Rüstem Pasha, in 1539.[23]

As the name implies, the "palace of girls [daughters]" (*sarāy-i duḫterān*) in the Topkapı that Süleyman maintained at the beginning of his reign must have been populated exclusively by young slave concubines, their servants, and black eunuchs, following the example of Mehmed II. Account books (see Appendix A.6) record its renovation between 1527 and 1529. They list expenses for a new room and a wooden penthouse near the chamber of girls, a bath for girls, a walled enclosure with an iron gate communicating with the imperial garden, a wooden house, a kiosk, a water channel, a fountain and pool, a stone staircase near the palace of girls on the side of the royal stables, and a new kitchen. The rooms for girls were provided with wooden floors, cupboards, seats, and large trunks. The use of the word "repair" and the reference to "pulling down the roof pavilion above the chamber of girls" demonstrate that this work involved the remodeling of a preexisting structure, not the construction of a new one.[24] The rebuilt harem can be seen on Melchior Lorichs's panorama of 1559 (Pls. 25c,d) as a long wing of buildings extending between the royal stables and the Privy Chamber, with a garden and trees contained in its walled enclosure.

Süleyman's favorite concubine, Hürrem, also known as Roxelana, gained undisputed control of the harem at the Topkapı after Prince Mustafa's mother went to Manisa with her son in 1533, and the Queen Mother died in 1534. Sources agree that she had convinced Süleyman actually to marry her, which went against the common practice of sultans;[25] when he did, she moved from the Old Palace to the new one with her children. Hürrem had several sons and a daughter, unlike previous royal consorts, who had to move with their only son to an assigned province. Daniello de' Ludovisi's report to the Venetian senate in 1534 shows that she was already living in the Topkapı; the passage remarks: "The Grand Signor has a son of about sixteen years, older than the other three, called Mustafa.... He holds the governorship of Manisa, near Chios, and with him is his mother, who is Albanian. The other sons are still in the seraglio, born of another mother, from Russia, who stays with the Grand Signor, who has married her as his wife."[26] The permanent move of Hürrem and her children to the harem of the Topkapı foreshadowed the complete abandonment of the Old Palace by the royal family in the post-Süleymanic era, when the sultans began to lead an increasingly secluded life in the familial atmosphere of the harem.

Around 1537 Luigi Bassano described Hürrem's impressive quarters at the harem in these terms:

> The Seraglio of the Sultana is in the same [complex] as the Grand Turk's, and one can go through secret rooms from one to the other. No one enters the palace of the Sultana except the Grand Turk, the eunuchs, and another person, highly trusted by the Grand Turk, called the procurator *[kethüda]* of the Sultana, who always comes and goes whenever he wishes, dressed extremely richly and accompanied by twenty slaves. The rooms of the Sultana are equally exquisite, with prayer halls, baths, gardens, and other comforts.[27]

Hürrem lived in the harem with one hundred ladies-in-waiting, he wrote; she never let herself be seen, and only went out at night, in a covered coach.[28] She was frequently visited by her daughter, Mihrimah, married to Rüstem Pasha, who twice occupied the post of grand vizier (1543–53 and 1555–61).[29] Bernardo Navagero's 1553 description confirms that her quarters could be reached from the hanging garden of the sultan's Privy Chamber, in the male section of the third court: "In the middle are the rooms of the Grand Signor and the Signora Sultana, whose room is separate; to go from one to the other one must pass through a small walled garden, belonging to the Grand Signor, and thence to another garden, belonging to the Sultana, which is also walled" (Pls. 6, 8, 11 *[66–70]*).[30]

Hürrem did not live to see the accession of her son Selim II to the imperial throne. Following Hürrem's example, the new sultan's legal Venetian wife, Nurbanu, continued to live with her husband after their oldest son, Murad, left for Manisa, while the princes under the age of ten (born of various concubines) were brought up in the Topkapı. Wage registers from Selim II's reign distinguish between concubines of the New Palace and the Old.[31] At that time, according to the Venetian ambassador Garzoni, about one hundred and fifty women lived in the Topkapı, guarded by eighteen black eunuchs (far fewer than the thirty-five white eunuchs who oversaw the male quarters). The Old Palace, in contrast, housed something like fifteen hundred women; this multitude was a kind of pool from which attractive women were recruited for the smaller, more select harem at the Topkapı. Selim, unlike his father, who continued to sleep in the male quarters of the palace, preferred to spend his nights in the harem. Garzoni writes that he used to enter "this seraglio of women each night for his pleasure, from a gate in his gardens."[32]

Selim II further enlarged the harem. Two imperial decrees of 27 January 1568 order the construction of "a room seven to eight cubits wide, featuring a staircase and an arch, behind the kitchen of the House of Felicity." Since they specify that the room "should not be very sumptuous," it was probably a utilitarian structure near the harem's kitchen.[33] Another decree, of 15 February 1568, addressed to the chief royal architect, Sinan, gives the sultan's approval for a drawing *(resm)* for this room and orders the architect to begin construction immediately.[34] Most of the account books record only minor repairs, such as adding a "cupboard for the mother of Prince Murad," in 1572–73, or repairing the commissary, kitchen, and the "palace of girls" *(sarāy-i duḫterān)*,[35] but one document in 1574 does list major expenses for building a "school for princes at the imperial House of Felicity," indicating that the princes no longer studied with the pages in the Large Chamber.[36]

When Murad III, under whom the architectural and institutional organization of the harem was to undergo drastic changes, arrived from Manisa to succeed his father in 1574, he sat on the throne of the Privy Chamber, where he received the congratulations of the grand vizier. Then he went into the harem to talk to his mother, Nurbanu, who had secretly kept her husband's corpse in an icebox until her son could arrive. That night he had his five younger brothers strangled, to eliminate them before his public accession ceremony the next day.[37]

The new sultan was dissatisfied with the harem. He set about rebuilding and enlarging it to provide new quarters for the Queen Mother, his numerous consorts, and the black eunuchs, whom he now granted more authority over the white ones. That Murad III's constructions in the harem included new quarters for his mother is shown in an account book of 1582–83, which refers to "building a new commissary for Her Majesty, the Queen Mother." The influential Nurbanu, whose correspondence with the Doge of Venice testifies to an affinity with her place of birth, remained the undisputed mistress of the harem between the accession of her husband, Selim II, to the throne in 1566 and her death in 1583, just before the harem's renovation under her son, Murad III, was finished.[38] Conscious of her power, through which she often influenced her son's political decisions (including his peace policy toward Venice), she exchanged letters with European monarchs and exploited patronage networks inside the Ottoman empire. To do this she used agents who acted as her intermediaries with the outer world, with which she had no direct contact.[39] Nurbanu thus became one of the first Queen Mothers to play a dominant role in politics, a trend that culminated in the seventeenth century with the "Reign of Women." She was the first officially to use the title "Queen Mother" *(valide sultan)*,[40] and her new quarters in the harem of the Topkapı Palace signaled her unprecedented authority.

The enlarged harem also included apartments for Murad III's many wives. Although the sultan was initially loyal to one woman, both his mother and sister (married to the grand vizier, Sokollu Mehmed Pasha) lured him into promiscuity by providing him with beautiful concubines, through whom they hoped to influence him.[41] The palace doctor Domenico Hierosolimitano reports that Murad had forty wives with separate quarters at the harem of the Topkapı Palace, a figure confirmed by Âli, who refers to these women as *hasekis*.[42] Before being promoted to the higher ranks, whose duties involved performing some specific service for the sultan or his family, young slave girls inhabited a large dormitory, where they were educated by old matrons, supervised by the head matron *(kahya kadın)*. Once a girl had slept with the sultan, she was given her own chamber, slave attendants, kitchen maids, a eunuch, and an increase in pay. Her income, servants, and rooms were increased again if she became pregnant. A *haseki* who bore the sultan's child received special privileges. She was crowned and moved to a larger private apartment with a more numerous retinue, instead of being transferred to the Old Palace, where royal women had brought up their children until the second half of the sixteenth century. The first woman to give birth to a son took precedence over the others.[43] If her son lived to become sultan, she would then be the Queen Mother, the absolute mistress of the harem.

Murad III's expanded harem, which now housed the sultan's family, provided a new, familial setting that differed significantly from the impersonal atmosphere of Mehmed II's original harem. The latter had been a training ground for slave concubines to complement that for slave pages, and excluded the sultan's wives, children, and mother, who lived in the Old Palace. The architectural and institutional changes Murad III brought about in the harem of the Topkapı (changes already foreshadowed in the reign of his father and grandfather) culminated with his construction of new apartments in the women's quarters that officially marked the abandonment of those in the court of pages. The new domesticity of the harem signaled the disintegration of the rigid *kul* system, which had replaced family ties and inherited power with a meritocracy. Now a completely sedentarized, unwarlike sultan retired into the seclusion of the inaccessible women's quarters, and the political vacuum he left was filled by strong women and the black eunuchs who acted as their intermediaries with the outer world.

Rebuilding the Harem in the Late Sixteenth Century: Royal Quarters

The several building campaigns involved in the harem's enlargement can be reconstructed from contemporary documents. Lokman's Persian *Shahanshāhnāma* (The King's *Book of Kings*), composed to eulogize Murad III's reign, has a chapter on "The Renovation *[tajdīd]* of the Imperial Palace." It recounts that the sultan was walking one day from his harem to the Council Hall and, as he looked at the walls and doors built over solid foundations by his forefathers, "in the old style" *(ṭarz-i qadīm)*, came to the conclusion that the harem was too small. Murad then ordered it enlarged and rebuilt in alternating courses of stone and brick. He moved into the Old Palace and sent for the grand vizier to explain the building project to the architect. The sultan's decorated furniture, goods, and household furnishings were all moved out, and the grand vizier summoned the architect to the public Council Hall and commissioned him to renovate the harem.[44] Dislodged from the Topkapı, Murad spent the year in the Old Palace; the summer palace of Üsküdar, built for Süleyman I in the early 1550s;[45] and the recently completed palace of his mother, built in a royal garden at Yenikapı.[46]

Lokman explains that the architect first gathered skilled craftsmen to prepare the stones and lime; when the necessary materials were ready, the construction was begun at an auspicious hour, and the old building was transformed "in an agreeable manner" from top to bottom. The role of the harem had changed so dramatically that it was enlarged to three times its original size. The construction began in Rebi' I 986 (May 1578) and reached completion in Receb 987 (September–October 1579). When two Georgian princes, newly converted to Islam arrived in Istanbul for their circumcision ceremony in 1579, their eyes were dazzled by the brilliance of the recently completed royal dome *(gunbād-i khāṣṣ-i shāh)*, which dominated the skyline of the harem from afar. The domed hall had a projecting balcony *(shāhnishīn)* and was decorated with gilt paintings rivaling the sun in brilliance, says Lokman; its alternating courses of brick and stone recalled "layers of gold and silver brick," and resembled the sun and moon (an allusion to the mansions of paradise described in *Hadith* literature as being constructed of gold and silver bricks), and it overlooked a marble pool whose continually flowing waters recalled the fountain of paradise. When the building that resembled the lofty heavenly palace *(qaṣr-i falak-i arjmand)* was finished, the sultan moved into his royal residence *(khāṣṣa manzil)*.[47]

Lokman's detailed description is accompanied by a miniature painting of ca. 1581–82 that depicts the rebuilt harem raised on vaulted substructures, in front of the Tower of Justice (Fig. 93a). The domed hall at the center of the miniature, with horizontal stripes denoting alternating courses of brick and stone, is known today as Murad III's bedroom pavilion; it also appears in a *Hünername* miniature painted ca. 1584 (Fig. 93b). It was added to the completely renovated and enlarged old core of the harem, represented in both miniatures as a large complex adjoining the right side of Murad III's bedroom pavilion (Pls. 11 *[69–71]*, 12 *[40, 41]*; Fig. 94 *[1, 2]*). Only the buildings adjacent to the Gold Path and stables seem to have been preserved from the earlier structures.[48] The pavilion of Murad III was built by the architect Sinan to overlook a large pool; on it are several foundation inscriptions with chronograms that yield the date 986 (1578–79).[49] Its construction is also recorded in several imperial decrees; in one of them, dated 24 January 1578, the

بهر جانبش باغ همچون بهشت
همه خاک او مشک عنبر سرشت
شده خاصه منزلگه پادشاه
برو مسند افکنده ظل اله

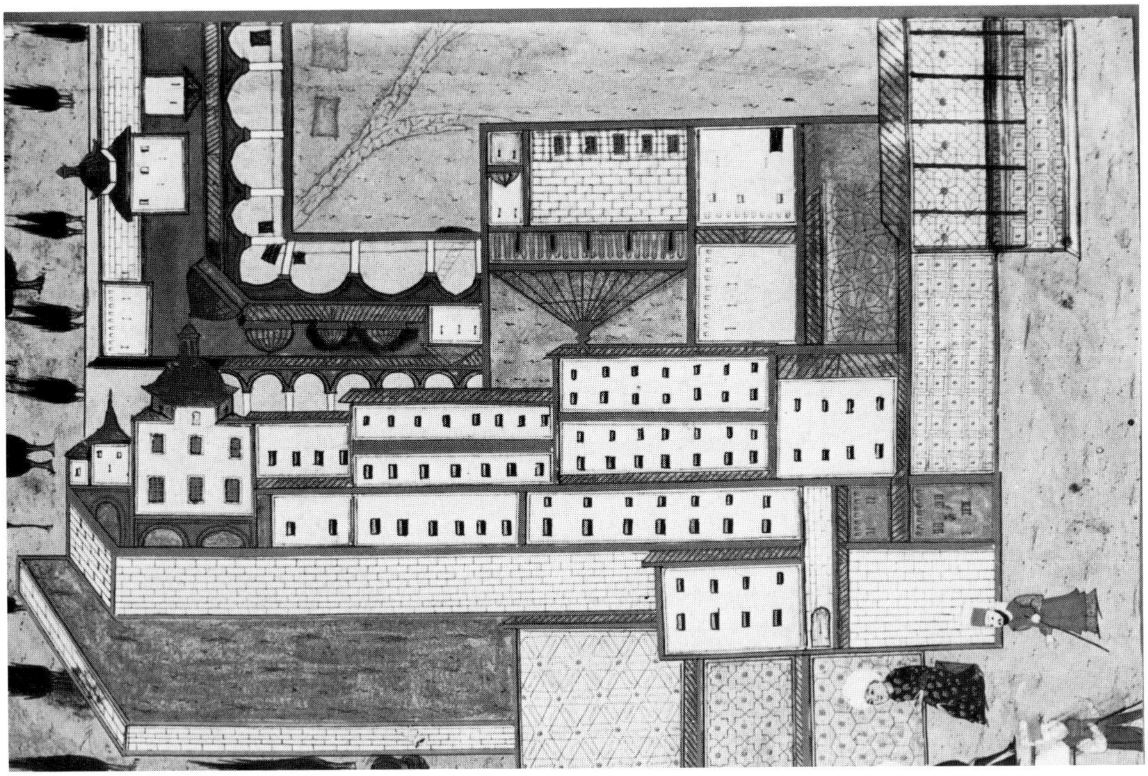

93*a* (opposite) Schematic representation of the harem facade, the hanging garden of the third court, and the outer garden with its pavilions. From Lokman, *Shahanshāhnāma,* 1581–82, İÜ, F 1404, fol. 118r.
93*b* (above) Schematic representation of the harem adjacent to the court of male pages and the hanging garden of the third court, detail of Fig. 56.

sultan orders the qadis of Gelibolu (Gallipoli) and İnoz to send "builders and carpenters required for the construction of a building at my private imperial domain."[50] Another, dated 25 June 1578, orders the qadi of Tire to return three marble cutters who, according to the chief royal architect, had abandoned their work at the imperial palace.[51]

The bailo Nicolò Barbarigo wrote, on 3 June 1578, to the Venetian senate that the admiral of the Ottoman navy, Kılıç Ali Pasha, was in charge of the building's construction, and was there all day long because the sultan wanted the work completed immediately. He must have been given that duty because the construction workers were mostly galley slaves from the arsenal under his jurisdiction. The bailo writes again, on 24 October 1578, that the admiral was still overseeing the construction, which was nearing completion.[52] Dispatches from Istanbul to the French court in 1578–79 repeat the same information.[53]

The inscription on the marble portal of the domed royal hall attributes the construction of this "noble pavilion" (*ḳaṣr-i şerīf*) to the "just" sultan Murad, likens its breezy site and flowing fountains beneath it to paradise, and provides the chronogram "Let this room always be auspicious to the Shah of the Age," which contains the date 986 (1578–79). Another inscription, over the gate of the antechamber in front of the main domed hall, says that Murad "ordered the construction in the

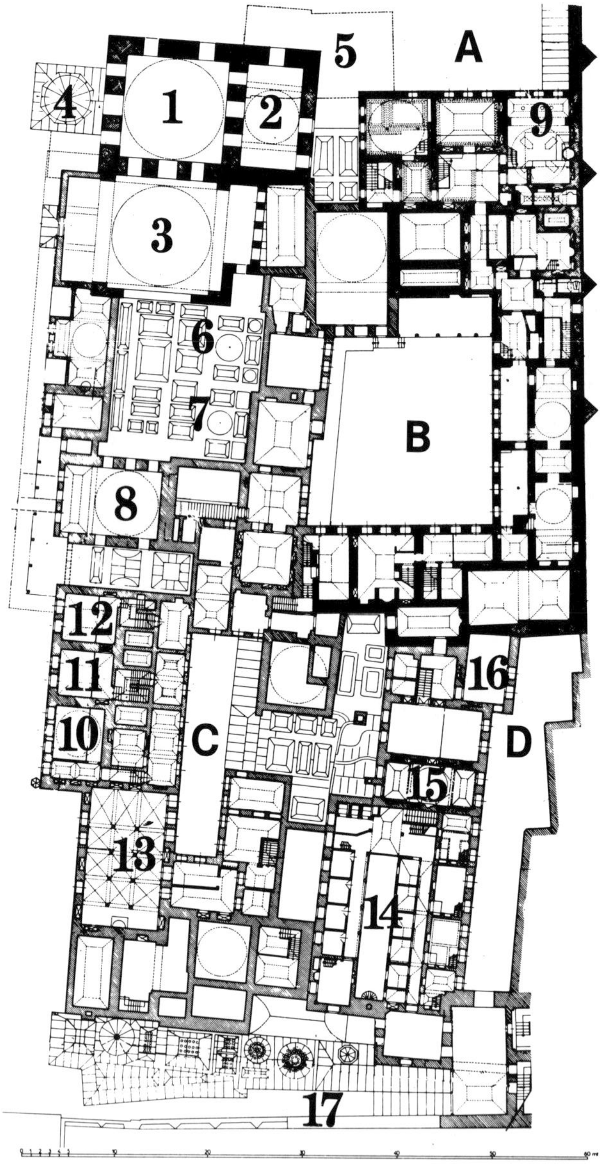

94 Hypothetical, reconstructed plan of the harem in the mid-seventeenth-century, showing the upper story, from Eldem and Akozan, *Topkapı*.

KEY: *A*. marble court overlooking a pool; *B*. court of the Queen Mother; *C*. court of concubines; *D*. court of the black eunuchs; *1*. Murad III's bedroom pavilion; 2. vestibule of Murad III's bedroom pavilion; 3. Imperial Hall *(Hünkâr Sofası); 4*. Ahmed I's pavilion; 5. twin pavilions; 6. sultan's bath; 7. Queen Mother's bath; *8*. Queen Mother's throne hall; *9*. quarters of the princes; *10*. quarters of the first *haseki; 11,12*. quarters of the second and third *haseki*s; *13*. dormitory of girls; *14*. dormitory of black eunuchs; *15*. school of princes; *16*. quarters of the chief black eunuch; *17*. ramp descending to the outer garden.

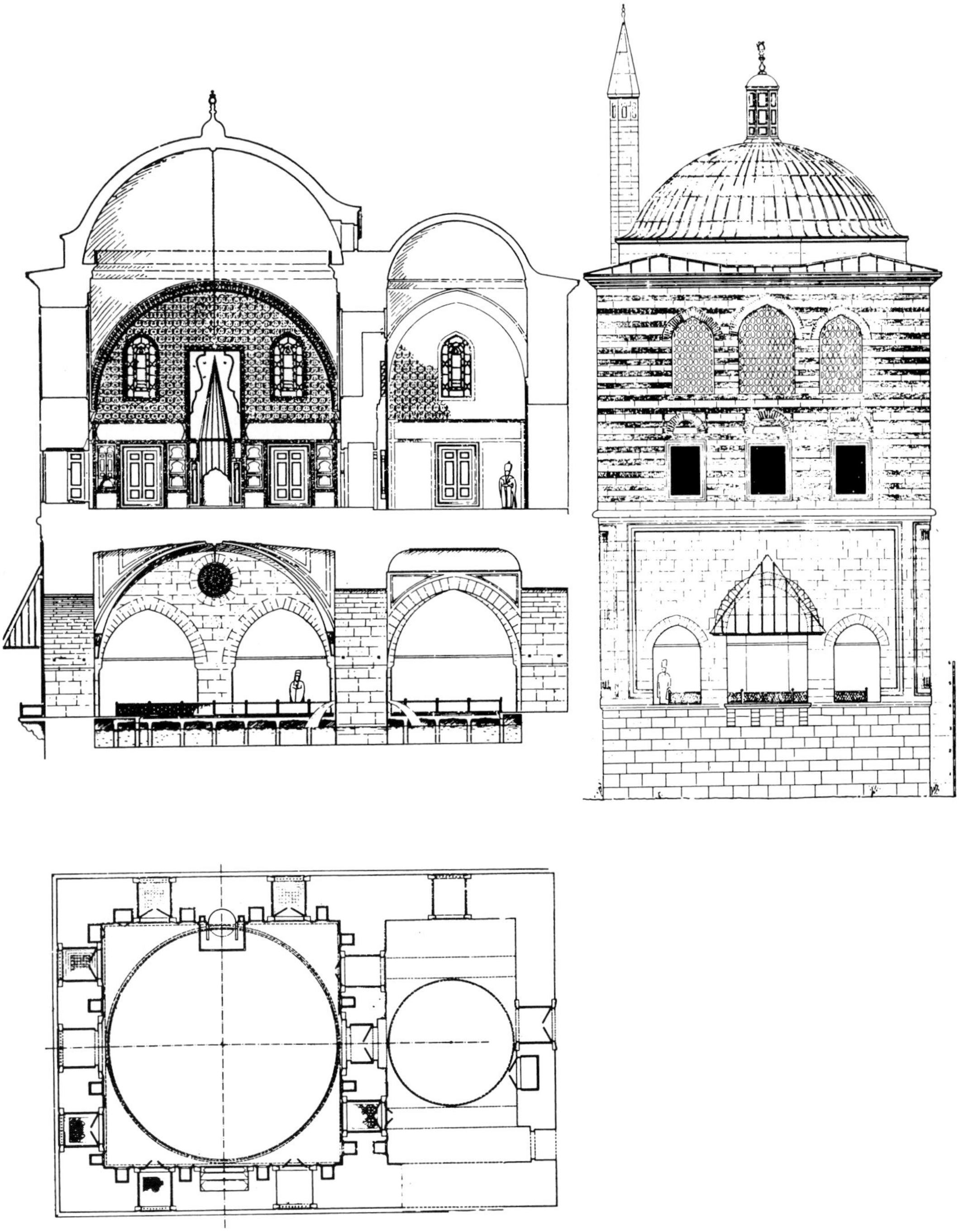

95 Plans and elevations of Murad III's pavilion in the harem. From Eldem and Akozan, *Topkapı*.

96a,b Interior views of Murad III's bedroom pavilion in the harem: *a.* the fireplace on the north wall; *b.* the fountain on the south wall. Courtesy of Reha Günay.

privy palace *[sarāy-i ẖaṣṣa]* of a beautiful, exhilarating, and unequaled pavilion *[ḳaṣr]*." Its chronogram reads "Thus, the pavilion of paradise became an excellent palace," which yields the same date. On a partition wall, added to the antechamber later, is an inscription on tile, referring to an unequaled building that is joy-increasing, pleasure-giving, and exhilarating. It asks the sultan to "make this mansion his felicitous dwelling place." [54]

Together with Lokman's description, these inscriptions show that the sultan had Sinan add a domed pavilion for his new bedchamber to the enlarged old core of the harem. Still known today as Murad III's bedroom pavilion, it is the only building in the harem from the sixteenth century that preserves some of its original interior decoration (Figs. 95, 96a,b). It has two stories and massive walls. Its vaulted basement features a pool and is surmounted by a square domed hall, preceded by a smaller antechamber, acting as a vestibule. According to Domenico Hierosolimitano, the antechamber of the sultan's bedroom, like the old one in the court of male pages, was lit by four large candles, one in each corner, but was now guarded at night by teams of three old women; the guard was changed every three hours.[55] The functions previously fulfilled by the pages of the old Privy Chamber in the men's court were now performed by female attendants.

Hierosolimitano also describes a ceremony that involved two lines of concubines, standing on both sides of a long corridor at the harem, most likely the Gold Path, which extends along the whole length of the harem (Pls. 11 *[67]*, 12 *[38]*). As the sultan passed between them they bowed in pairs. He would throw a handkerchief to the one who attracted his fancy, as a sign that she was destined to sleep with him that night. The chosen girl was then bathed, perfumed, and given instructions on how to behave by the head matron, before being conducted to the sultan's bedroom. A band of female musicians led her there and continued to perform outside the royal bedchamber.[56]

The main room where the sultan slept is decorated with İznik tiles up to the springing of the gilt dome (see Figs. 95, 96a,b). This dome originally had a lantern, like the dome of the throne room at the Privy Chamber in the men's quarters and those of the most prestigious royal kiosks. From its center hangs a gilt pendant globe with tassels, recalling those of the Council Hall, Privy Chamber, and the royal pavilions we will discuss later. A continuous band of tile inscriptions in *thuluth,* quoting the Koranic Throne Verse (2:255), surrounds this royal hall above the lower windows, each of which is flanked by marble niches. The verse reads, "Who is he that intercedeth with Him save by His leave?" referring to the absolute sovereignty of God in the heavens and earth, who provides legitimacy to rulers. At the center of the north wall is a gilt bronze fireplace framed by classical İznik tiles decorated with tiny plum blossoms, across from which is a three-tiered marble fountain, built into the wall. The window to the left of this fountain was replaced by a door when a domed throne hall was added next to Murad III's bedroom pavilion a few years later, blocking the latter's southern windows (Pls. 6–9; see Fig. 94 *[3]*). A small pavilion was later built for Ahmed I, in front of the west facade of the bedroom, whose vestibule was partly taken up by yet another structure, known as the Twin Pavilions (see Fig. 94 *[4, 5]*). Before these additions, Murad III's bedroom must have commanded a magnificent view and was no doubt much brighter. It is still an imposing specimen of palace architecture from the classical period, with its massive but elegant proportions, original İznik tiles, arched marble niches, and window shutters inlaid with mother-of-pearl and painted inside with naturalistic floral motifs and blossoming spring trees.

The pavilion's basement reflects the layout of the upper story and features a pool surrounded by a marble balustrade, into which water flows from fountains. It once functioned as a cool summer retreat, opening through arches onto the surrounding garden, which has another large pool nearby, with a pier for mooring the sultan's boat (Pls. 11 *[69]*, 12 *[40]*). Originally, a royal balcony, sheltered by a peaked eave, projected from the basement's west facade; Lokman calls it a *shāhnishīn.*[57] From this throne-shaped balcony, the sultan could see both the walled private garden of the harem and the pool below his bedroom, where he was often entertained in the company of women. Today, only corbels remain to testify to the existence of this projecting balcony (the top of whose eave is visible in a panoramic view of ca. 1590 [Pl. 27]), which established an intimate dialogue among architecture, garden, and water — a theme also found in the garden pavilions of the Topkapı. The royal throne was destroyed when Ahmed I added his kiosk in front of the pavilion and blocked its basement's view.

Murad III's bedroom pavilion communicated with the Privy Chamber in the male section of the third court through an L-shaped marble colonnade, which originally extended from a gate in the partition wall of the sultan's hanging garden to the main gate of the pavilion (Pl. 11 *[66, 67]*). In front of this colonnade (one arm of which belonged to the Gold Path) was built a marble-paved terrace, raised on vaulted substructures, which still overlooks the large pool and garden (known today as the Boxwood Garden, or *Çimşirlik*), below (Pls. 11 *[68, 69]*, 12 *[39, 40]*).[58] The remnants of İznik tiles that probably covered the facade of Murad III's pavilion (Fig. 97) are now found on the wall of the Twin Pavilions, which bisects its antechamber (see Fig. 94 *[5]*). These tile panels are decorated with blossoming spring trees seen through an illusionistic marble arcade. They pictorially echoed the actual L-shaped colonnade, which overlooked the gardens and provided access to the main gate of Murad III's pavilion. The ceramic inscriptions above these panels mention a beautiful gate resembling spring, apparently a reference to the gate of the pavilion flanked by tile panels. The royal colonnade also gave access to the harem's royal mosque, through a door located directly across from the gate of the pavilion. Behind this door the sultan and the royal women performed their prayers in a room whose latticed windows overlook the mosque of pages in the third court (Pl. 12 *[17]*).

Still another project at the harem — a new bath, built in 1580 — once again forced Murad III out of his palace temporarily. That year, the sultan occasionally came to the New Palace for special audiences, but the bailo Paolo Contarini complained in a dispatch dated 2 July 1580 that it was difficult to obtain an audience with him because "the seraglio was hindered by the building of a bath which His Majesty had ordered to be made, and which will be finished soon." [59] This time, the sultan stayed at his mother's palace while the work was being done.[60] Account books from the summer of 1580 list expenses for "covers for royal cushions for the new bath" made of Persian brocades.[61] Another source shows that by the end of that same summer two white eunuchs, the head treasurer and the palace steward, were rewarded with money and caftans "upon the completion of a bath and some buildings at the royal harem." [62]

Yet another large project in the harem, this time a new royal bath, for the sultan's own use, again moved Murad back to the Old Palace between 1583 and 1585 (see Fig. 94 *[6]*). After the completion of this bath the one in the male section of the third court was turned over to the use of pages. Materials were collected for this new building in 1582. In October of that year two royal decrees to the chief gardener ordered him to have a number of marble columns and marble panels removed from houses in the city, and to pay their owners for them. This marble was then to be supplemented by marble quarried in the Marmara Islands.[63] A decree addressed to the qadi of Midilli on 5 May 1583 ordered him to send six hundred masons and carpenters, whom the chief architect, Sinan, had requested; some of them would be employed in construction at the imperial palace.[64] Another decree, on 8 May 1585, ordered the qadi of Efsur to quarry "porphyry suited for making fountains" and to send to Istanbul the amount of marble specified in cubits by the chief royal architect.[65] On 1 September 1585 the qadi of Galata was ordered to send the various Greek masons and carpenters listed to work on the new bath under construction at the imperial palace, this time under the direction of the architect Davud, who was overseeing the construction.[66] Davud must have taken over management of the new constructions at the harem during Sinan's trip to Mecca in 1584.[67] A dispatch sent to the French court on 29 April 1585 reports that "the captain Kılıç Ali, immediately after his return from the Black Sea, was employed to supervise the construction of a bath at the grand seraglio." [68] This was the same admiral who had overseen the construction of Murad's bedroom pavilion in the harem in 1578–79.

Several royal decrees show that tiles were obtained for the new royal bath from İznik. Two dated 30 April 1585 order the qadis of İznik and Karamürsel to aid the chief officer of tiles, Silahdar Mehmed, who was sent from Istanbul to collect tiles required for the sultan's palace. If there were no available tiles, they were to be made quickly and sent to Istanbul by ship from the port of Karamürsel.[69] In a decree of July–August 1585 the sultan notifies the qadi of İznik that the previously ordered "tiles required for the new bath now under construction at my imperial palace" have not yet arrived. He commands him to have them made immediately, by forbidding ceramicists to fill orders for other customers until the sultan's requirements had been met.[70]

An account book of 1585 lists expenses for the carpeting of "the new bath of his Majesty, the world-protecting sultan" and "the dais of the new bath for his Majesty." It also mentions curtains for the sultan's "new room" and furnishings for his throne.[71] The latter must be the domed throne hall, known today as the *Hünkâr Sofası* (Imperial Hall), which adjoins the royal bath of the harem (Pl. 12 *[44, 45]*; see Fig. 94 *[3, 6]*). It was built next to Murad III's bedroom pavilion, which until then had remained open on three sides.

The *Shahanshāhnāma* miniature, which represents the harem around 1581–82 (see Figs. 93a,b), and the *Hünername* miniature, from around 1584 (see Fig. 56), do not yet show either the domed Imperial Hall or the bath. Both were completed in

97 Late-sixteenth-century İznik tile panels, representing an illusionistic marble arcade opening onto gardens with blossoming spring trees, in the vestibule of Murad III's bedroom pavilion.

September 1585, according to the contemporary historian Selaniki, who writes that Murad III "honored the completed royal hall, the comfort-giving bath, and pools built anew at the Imperial Palace."[72] They are clearly visible on a panoramic view of ca. 1590, which shows Murad III's harem extending from a stepped partition wall adjacent to the Privy Chamber to the royal stables (Pl. 27). The domed Imperial Hall is fronted by a portico with smaller domes. The multiple domes of the royal bath are visible behind the long, flat-roofed dormitory for women with a projecting balcony at the center of its facade—possibly that of the Queen Mother mentioned in a repair document of 1600–1601.[73]

The expansion of the harem during Murad III's reign was unprecedented. A Jewish doctor named Rabbi Salomone wrote that this sultan "did a great deal to the interior of the Palace, more than all the other kings preceding him had carried out. He adorned it with staterooms, baths, and fountains, porticos and loggias, and gardens, and decorated it with gilding and with royal magnificence."[74] In 1594 the Englishman John Sanderson made the same observation:

> Upon one of the corners of the citie (a poynt of the mouth of the streyght that divideth Europ and Asia) ... is the admirable habitation [Seraglio] of the Grand Signor ... built by great Mahumett the second, amplified and decked by all his successors. It is so replenished with faire pallaces, brave gardens, marble cesterns, fine fountayns, somptiouse banias [i.e., bagnos] that it weare an unwise part to describe them, espetially in regard that this present Soltan Moratt hath begonne so magnifically to replenish it; for he alone hath built therin more then all his predecessors together.[75]

Contemporary Ottoman sources agree. Âli writes that "at the time of previous sultans and glorious kings there was no lofty palace of this expanse, no Abode of Happiness of such pomp."[76]

Sinan's autobiographies mention the renovation of the harem as well: "At the New Palace: The private imperial domain was built anew," and "At the New Imperial Palace: The entire inner palace was built by Sultan Murad Khan; and its imperial commissary and kitchen were built after the fire."[77] The latter is the statement that has led some scholars to conclude that there was no harem before Murad III's reign, and others to link the renovation of the harem to the fire of 1574, which burned the kitchens of the second court.[78] The text makes no such connection, however; it merely lists Sinan's major constructions in the Topkapı Palace, one of which was expanding the harem between 1578 and 1585, and another rebuilding the burned-down kitchens in 1574.

An inscription over the gate of the harem that opens into the second court provides 996 (1587–88) as the termination date for Murad III's building activities (and not, as some have thought, the foundation date for the harem) (Pls. 11 *[18]*, 12 *[8]*). The inscription itself makes clear that the sultan had renovated a preexisting structure. After praising the "just" sultan's conquests, it points out that Murad III augmented the importance of this gate, which had previously lacked fame. Following the suggestion of the chief black eunuch, Mehmed Agha, he had built this "Audience Gate" *(bāb-i dīvān)* and provided it with the chronogram "Sultanic Gate at the high paradise of the harem" *(ḥarīm-i cennet-i ʿālīde bāb-i sulṭānī)*, with the date 996 (1587–88).[79] The neighboring door, leading to the dormitory of Halberdiers with Tresses, bears an inscription with the date 995 (1586–87), indicating that the dependencies of the harem, consisting of the quarters of the black eunuchs and halberdiers, were expanded at around the same time (Pl. 11 *[16]*).[80]

All this construction activity made manifest and at the same time augmented the new political power of the women and the black eunuchs whose quarters were located just behind the Audience Gate. In Murad III's reign, the chief black eunuch began holding weekly audiences at the gate on matters relating to royal waqfs, after Murad had transferred their administration from the white to the black eunuchs.[81] According to Âli, it was during this period that the grand viziers began to lose authority and independence as the eunuchs and royal women, thanks to their proximity to the secluded ruler, came to control appointments.[82]

Despite being hidden from the public eye, and so closely confined, the royal women could still wield power through black eunuchs and Jewish women. These were given the title of *Kira,* and lived outside the palace but had permission to enter the harem freely to teach embroidery or medicinal secrets to the royal women, sell them fashionable goods, and mediate their dealings with the outside world. Royal women advertised their power by commissioning monumental public buildings, supported with rich waqfs, and had almost as much access to political information as the secluded sultan did—an unforeseen consequence of the placement of the harem next to the public Council Hall. The hall could be reached from the Gold Path, originally built so that the sultan could go unobserved from his Privy Chamber in the court of pages either to his royal window overlooking the public Council Hall or into the room of a favorite. (Its name is thought to derive from a ceremony during which the sultan scattered gold coins to women lined up on both sides of the corridor, following his accession to the throne.)[83] This same corridor also enabled women and black eunuchs to watch political discussions in the Council Hall from a round hole above the sultan's royal window, probably made sometime in the late sixteenth century. It can still be seen there.

Another factor that allowed the harem to become a dominant political force in the seventeenth century was the change of policy in the education of princes after the end of the sixteenth century. They were no longer sent to govern provinces, but were instead confined as virtual prisoners to the women's quarters, within a group of halls called the Cage *(Kafes)*, a practice instituted to spare their lives. This not only made them more susceptible to the influence of women and eunuchs, in whose company they were raised, but also enabled the harem factions to enthrone and depose weak sultans who were either infants or mentally unfit to rule. While the sultans of the second half of the seventeenth century spent most of their time hunting in Edirne or in the pursuit of sensual pleasures (which gave rise to such popular verses as "His father is cunt-mad / His son is hunt-mad," written of İbrahim I and Mehmed IV), powerful women controlled politics.[84]

All this was foreshadowed by the changes Murad III had made in the structure of the harem. When he died in 1595, he left behind twenty sons, two daughters married to viziers, and twenty-seven unmarried daughters; many other of his children had died in infancy. The sultan's successor, Mehmed III, immediately had his nineteen brothers strangled, and banished the rest of the harem. The contemporary historian Selaniki vividly describes how these women, loudly lamenting their fate, were transported in carriages, together with their belongings, servants, and eunuchs, to the Old Palace.[85] Rabbi Salomone describes this pathetic scene:

> Directly after these poor princes, who people say possessed great beauty, had been buried, the populace waited at the gate to witness the departure from the Seraglio of their mothers and all the other wives of the king, with their children and their goods. All the carriages, coaches, mules and horses of the court were employed for this purpose. Besides the wives of the king and the 27 daughters, there were 200 others, consisting of nurses and slaves and they were taken to the Eschi Seraglio [i.e., Eski Saray, Old Palace], where the wives and daughters of the king reside, with their Aghas, that is eunuchs, who guard and serve them in royal fashion. There they can weep, as much as they like for their dead sons, a thing that was forbidden at the other Grand Seraglio, under penalty of capital punishment; and there by degrees they will marry according to the custom of the kingdom. Inside the Grand Seraglio there remained only the wives with child, and there they stay until their children are born.
>
> All the nurses and tutors of his dead brothers were also sent away together with a large number of eunuchs, and a great crowd of mutes and dwarfs who were there for the diversion of the Sultan's father.[86]

Not surprisingly, the Old Palace came to be known as the "Palace of Tears," a place of exile to which widows and disgraced women, fallen from the sultan's favor, were sent. Sometimes when a woman became too powerful she would also be sent there by a sultan, to keep her isolated from the center of government.[87] Moryson noted in 1597 that concubines and daughters of the deceased ruler Murad III lived in the Old Palace, together with the ruling sultan Mehmed III's less favored slave girls, "for the fairest and dearest to him are taken to live in his court."[88]

Mehmed III does not seem to have changed the harem's basic layout, which had reached its final form with his father's renovations. His only construction is recorded by Selaniki: "In the beginning of the month of Zilka'de 1003 [July 1595], the new bath at the inner House of Felicity cracked open and required renovation."[89] The sultan lived at the summer palace in Üsküdar while the repairs were made; from there, he occasionally crossed by boat to the Topkapı for audiences at the Chamber of Petitions. Toward the end of September he moved to the Old Palace; from there he continued to go to the Topkapı for audiences until "the bath and the privy chamber that were being renovated at the Imperial Palace reached completion."[90] The sultan and his harem returned to the Topkapı in November 1595, when "the ornamented and gilded tiled room and the charming bath ordered to be built anew at the Imperial Palace were finished."[91] These structures, renovated by the architect Davud, must have been the royal bath and the Imperial Hall *(Hünkâr Sofası)* adjacent to it, both of which had been completed in 1585 under his supervision, while Sinan was in Mecca.[92] Selaniki's statement that they "cracked open" suggests that the foundations of these structures, raised on vaulted substructures, had proven too weak.

Tile revetments for this renovation were again obtained from İznik. A firman dated 13 September 1595 orders the qadi of İznik once more to stop ceramicists from selling to merchants and from producing plates or cups so as not to slow down the production of the tiles immediately required by the chief royal architect, Davud, for the imperial palace and for Murad III's mausoleum behind Hagia Sophia.[93] Another firman, sent on the same date to the qadis of Sahib Karahisar and Lefke (who provided clay and other chemicals to the ceramic ateliers in İznik), orders them to stop merchants from hoarding these substances to make higher profits. The materials were to be sent to İznik without further delay.[94]

Some of these İznik tiles were used to decorate the Imperial Hall, usually referred to in late-sixteenth-century sources as the "privy chamber" *(oda-i ḫāṣṣa)* of the harem. The seventeenth-century page Bobovi and La Croix both call it the "ladies' privy chamber" (*khasodah des dames* or *l'as-oda des femmes*).[95] The hall and the adjacent bath were extensively repaired after a fire in 1665. Inside the Imperial Hall a fragment of a ceramic inscription band with the Throne Verse from the Koran (2:255) on it bears the date 1077 (1666–67). An account book for repairs in the harem after the same fire lists payments given in 1665–66 to workers who repaired "the domes of the baths and of the privy chamber at the inner imperial palace."[96]

Today the Imperial Hall has Europeanizing decorations and inscriptions dating from Osman III's renovations, done between 1754 and 1757, when a marble-paved hanging garden, resting on a vaulted substructure, was added in front of it (Pls. 11 *[72]*, 12 *[44]*; see Fig. 94 *[3]*). It is a spacious domed hall with a platform in front of its western windows, facing the garden terrace, over which a musicians' gallery is supported on thin columns. Next to this platform, furnished with cushions, is the sultan's canopied throne, placed in a corner, as it was in the Chamber of Petitions and the original Privy Chamber. The hall has three wall fountains and a door leading into the royal bath (see Fig. 94 *[6]*). The İznik tiles have by now disappeared from the bath; today it has white marble revetments and Baroque decorations. Other doors lead to the Queen Mother's quarters, Murad III's bedroom, and an antechamber with a fountain, which in turn leads to the central court of the harem, known

98 Court of the Queen Mother in the harem.

today as the Court of the Queen Mother *(Valide Sultan Taşlığı)* (Fig. 98, see Fig. 94 *[B]*). The recent discovery of four marble columns joined by three arches on the outer facade of the Imperial Hall, facing the Golden Horn, reveals that the domed space was originally fronted by a triple-domed open portico, with a balcony projecting from the central arch (Pls. 29, 30a, 32a,c).[97]

The Imperial Hall functioned as the formal assembly place of the harem, where official ceremonies and festivities took place in the enthroned sultan's presence. At *bayram,* after he had received the good wishes of pages in the old Privy Chamber, the sultan met with the women in this one. La Croix describes this ceremony, in which the sultan "sat on a small throne raised at the corner of the sofa of the women's privy chamber, where all those beautiful prisoners went to render homage to him in the retinue of the Queen Mother, who introduced them." [98] An earlier version of the same ceremony is described in more detail by Domenico Hierosolimitano:

> Then the Grand Signor gets up and goes to give holiday greetings to the female sultanas, who are all gathered in a large room waiting for him, and on his arrival they all stand up and make him a humble bow; saluting him with a cheerful expression, they wish him happy holidays, and he without answering them looks at them with a smile and turns to a eunuch, who carries as many jewels, all similarly made, as there are women, and equally to each of them he gives one with his own hands, together with a bag of gold coins, so that they have money to give to their slaves.[99]

The Imperial Hall was the harem's *Festhalle,* where the sultans listened to female musicians and were entertained by singers and comedians.[100] In 1608 Bon wrote that when a sultan wanted concubines to dance or play music for him, the harem's chief matron was sent for to provide them. Occasionally, pages were escorted blindfold to the harem by eunuchs, to perform when women were present.[101] The mid-eighteenth-century merchant Flachat, who saw this hall when the court was away, refers to it as the harem's "assembly hall, where all the women come to court His Highness and to try to please him with a thousand amusements, which succeed one after the other, and to which the inexhaustible fecundity of the genius of these women always gives an air of novelty." [102] Unfortunately, we know very little of how that genius manifested itself, for Ottoman codes of propriety did not allow any descriptions in literary or visual works of what must have been brilliantly inventive and amusing performances by women who remain anonymous to us. Several nineteenth-century accounts of such festivities say that the sultan sat on his throne with his favorites seated under the musicians' gallery, closer to or further from him, depending on their status, while lower-ranking members of the harem remained standing and motionless throughout the performance. According to a black eunuch's account, one of the popular dances consisted of girls leaping up to grab a pendant globe hanging from the dome in front of the sultan's throne. When they came down their skirts spread like parachutes.[103]

Courtyards of the Queen Mother, Concubines, and Black Eunuchs

After the sultan's quarters, those of the Queen Mother are the most imposing of the harem. Like her son, she lived in a suite consisting of a bedroom, throne room, and bath. Rooms for her retinue, a bakery, commissary, and kitchens are grouped around the largest court of the harem, the Court of the Queen Mother (see Fig. 94 *[B, 7, 8]*). Murad III built the Queen Mother's bath, which communicates with her domed throne room next to his own bath, adjoining his throne room, the Imperial Hall. Although seventeenth-century sources mention tile revetments in the "Queen Mother's bath," today its walls have no decoration.[104] A narrow corridor to the west of these two adjacent baths connects the Imperial Hall, and other royal chambers next to it, to the throne room of the Queen Mother, a domed hall featuring a fireplace, with a throne platform to the west, on its Golden Horn facade, which once had a projecting balcony like that of the sultan. Adjoining it is her small bedroom, faced with seventeenth-century tiles and her private masjid. All of these were remodeled after the 1665 fire, between 1666 and 1668, according to inscriptions, and redecorated in the eighteenth and nineteenth centuries in a Europeanizing style.[105]

The quarters for the princes, consisting of several domed halls with fireplaces and dependent rooms, some of them decorated with seventeenth-century tiles and marble niches, occupy the northeast corner of the Queen Mother's courtyard. Built above the colonnade that leads to Murad III's bedroom pavilion, they overlook the small Boxwood Garden (see Fig. 94 *[9]*).[106] These halls were connected by stairs both to the marble terrace overlooking the Boxwood Garden (a small court they shared with the sultan) and to the Gold Path, along which their school was located (see Fig. 94 *[15]*). No longer sent to provinces, seventeenth-century princes were allowed to maintain their own household of concubines and servants; they spent their years out of touch with the world in these halls with grilled windows, hoping that their turn to rule might come. This section of the harem, popularly known as the Cage *(Kafes)*, was appropriately situated at the edge of the women's residence; its windows faced a direction different from the Queen Mother's courtyard in order to preserve gender boundaries.

The first Queen Mother to live permanently in the expanded harem quarters of the Topkapı was Mehmed III's mother, the powerful Safiye. In her throne room she received gifts from the kings and queens of Europe, who hoped she would influence her son's decisions in their favor. Safiye probably also met in this hall with Esther Kira—one of the Jewish women allowed to enter the harem freely—who became her influential confidante, but could not escape being slaughtered by an angry mob for her role in the debasement of coinage that reduced the value of military pay.[107] In the mid seventeenth century La Croix reported that the sultan dutifully visited his mother there each morning to pay his respects and to report his daily schedule.[108] He usually chose his concubines from among the Queen Mother's slaves, "For it is only she who has the interest of the loves of her son at her heart. She always searches for beautiful girls to be presented to him. Also, she can more easily assure herself of their loyalty to both her and the sultan. Thus she appears to be the main superintendent of the pleasures of her son." [109]

After the sultan departed, the Queen Mother received the chief black eunuch, who was in charge of administering royal waqfs, and managed her business matters. Following lunch, attended by a large female retinue (including a treasurer, accountant, reader, pantry keeper, laundress, bather, stoker, taster, coffee maker, and water-ewer carrier), she was entertained by buffoons, dancers, and singers. Then a female reader read a chapter from the Koran or from a history book. On occasion, the sultan's wives also visited their mother-in-law in her reception hall.[110]

Second in rank to the Queen Mother was the sultan's first wife (*baş haseki* or *baş kadın*), who was also served by a large group of female attendants. Her quarters were in a separate courtyard, next to the Queen Mother's, known today as the Court of Concubines (*Cariyeler Taşlığı* or *Kadın Efendiler Taşlığı;* Fig. 99, see Fig. 94 *[C]*).[111] The lesser wives, ranked as second *haseki,* third *haseki,* and so on down the line, had progressively smaller entourages and more modest quarters.[112] The Court of Concubines, also restored extensively after the fire of 1665, is surrounded on three sides by arcades, living quarters for the *haseki*s and young slave girls, a laundry, kitchen, commissary, ablution fountains, a bath, and latrines. Three separate apartments that can be seen today in the Court of Concubines probably housed the sultan's favorite wives (see Fig. 94 *[10–12]*). Each has a large room with a fireplace overlooking the gardens and an antechamber entered from the court, with a small toilet on one side and a space for servants on the other, and stairs leading up to a gallery. The one at the center of the court's garden facade is the largest. It has more dependent rooms and is the only one, besides the Queen Mother's quarters, that has a domed hall. It probably housed the sultan's first wife (see Fig. 94 *[10]*).

99 Court of the concubines in the harem.

These three units are separated from the large, two-story dormitory for the young concubines by a steep staircase that descends to the garden (see Fig. 94 *[13]*). This may well be the stone staircase already mentioned in Süleyman's repair documents of 1528–29 at the "Girls' Palace," near the stables. The dormitory recalls those of the male pages; in it the girls slept on long sofas with an old woman posted between each group of ten, under lights kept burning all night to prevent Lesbian relations. In the daytime they were taught by elderly women to read and speak Turkish, to sew, and to play music, with some hours of recreation in between.[113] They wore robes resembling those of pages and were almost indistinguishable from boys, according to the Englishman Thomas Dallam, who secretly watched them playing ball in 1599, while he was installing Queen Elizabeth's organ in the palace:

Crossinge throughe a litle squar courte paved with marble, he [one of the pages] poynted me to goo to a graite in a wale, but made me a sine that he myghte not goo thether him selfe. When I came to the grait the wale was verrie thicke, and graited on bothe the sides with iron verrie strongly; but through that graite I did se thirtie of the Grand Sinyor's Concobines that weare playinge with a bale in another courte. At the firste sighte of them I thoughte they had bene yonge men, but when I saw the hare of their heades hange doone on their backes, platted together with a tasle of smale pearle hanginge in the lower end of it, and by other plaine tokens, I did know them to be women, and verrie prettie ones in deede.

Theie wore upon theire heades nothinge bute a litle capp of clothe of goulde, which did but cover the crowne of her heade; no bandes a boute their neckes, nor anythinge but faire cheans of pearle and a juell hanginge on their breste, and juels in their ears; their coats weare like a souldier's mandilyon, som of reed sattan and som of blew, and som of other collors, and grded like a lace of contraire collor; they wore britchis of scamatie, a fine clothe made of cotton woll, as whyte as snow and as fine as lane; for I could desarne the skin of their thies throughe it. These britchis cam doone to their mydlege; som of them did weare fine cordevan buskins, and som had their leges naked, with a goulde ringe on the smale of her legg; on her foute a velvett panttoble 4 or 5 inches hie. I stood so longe loukinge upon them that he which had showed me all this kindness began to be verrie angrie with me. He made a wrye mouthe, and stamped with his foute to make me give over looking; the which I was verrie lothe to dow, for the sighte did please me wondrous well.[114]

This is perhaps the only known description of concubines in the sixteenth-century harem. The androgynous costumes they wore would surely have disappointed those Orientalist painters who later imagined them sprawled naked on sofas and around pools. The scene described by Dallam shows that for the most part the harem resembled a monastery for young girls more than the bordello of European imagination. Just as in the court of male pages, silence was enforced. When the sultan walked down its silent halls, his shoes, studded with silver nails, clattered on the marble floor to alert the women to disappear from his path. Unintentionally to come face to face with him was an embarrassing incident, called "stumbling into the sultan" *(hünkara çatmak)* in the slang of harem inmates.[115]

Only a small number of the harem women were consorts of the sultan; the rest were girls in their teens who were educated full time, before being promoted to serve the sultan or his family. Dynastic continuity and procreation took precedence over sexuality in defining women's roles in the harem of the Topkapı Palace, which gradually evolved from a small residence for slave girls to one headed by the sultan's favorite wife, and finally to a spacious familial domain controlled by the Queen Mother, followed by the royal wives and the chief matron. The increasing size of the imperial harem was not necessarily a sign of promiscuity, as Westerners perceived it to be. In a polygamous society the sultans were expected to have many wives and concubines, but aside from Murad III most of them preferred to stay loyal to a few women — Islamic law allowed them four legal wives. Maintaining and supervising the collection of beautiful virgins from foreign countries required a carefully devised administrative structure that in itself was a visible sign of power, prestige, and wealth.

The quarters for the black eunuchs lie in a separate courtyard between the public Council Hall in the second court and the Court of Concubines (Fig. 100, see Fig. 94 *[D]*). They extend from a gate communicating with the second court at the south end of the harem, north to another gate, which opens into the chambers of the harem proper, grouped around the Court of the Queen Mother. They are entered from the second court through a gate that opens into a domed vestibule (Pl. 11 *[18]*). This room is lined with large cupboards, where the documents dealing with the royal waqfs administered by the chief black eunuch are thought to have been stored. A second vestibule behind the back wall of the Tower of Justice opens onto a narrow open court that leads to the Gold Path, extending all the way to the sultan's Privy Chamber in the court of pages. On the left side of this tiny court are a mosque, a long, three-story dormitory, much like that for the concubines, latrines, the chief black eunuch's apartment, which has its own latrine and bath, and the school for princes. The teachers of the princes were conducted each day by the black eunuchs to this school, so that they would not lay eyes on any of the women.[116] The domed schoolroom upstairs, now decorated with seventeenth-century tiles and gilded baroque wood paneling, was occasionally used for secret meetings. In 1600, for example, Mehmed III met there with the Şeyhülislam Sunullah Efendi to discuss the turmoil caused by a military revolt that had cost the Jewess Esther Kira her life, as the Queen Mother listened from behind a

100 Aerial view of the harem, separated by a wall from the court of male pages, with the Public Treasury at the lower right corner.

curtain.[117] Across from the school, on the right side of the narrow court, are small rooms thought to have been quarters for dwarfs. The bath for the eunuchs is located along a steep ramp that descends to the outer gardens. The function of a porticoed kiosk adjacent to it is unclear; the sultans may have visited it on their way to the outer garden. Most of these buildings are faced with seventeenth-century tiles and carry inscriptions from 1667–69, indicating that they too were rebuilt extensively after the fire.[118]

The Hierarchical Structure of the Harem's Layout

Today, although the four courts—the sultan's, the Queen Mother's, the concubines', and the black eunuchs'—can still be identified, it is no longer possible to determine the function of every room (see Figs. 94, 100). After the 1665 fire—an immense conflagration that spread all the way from the quarters of the black eunuchs and concubines to Murad III's bedroom—Mehmed IV hastily rebuilt the damaged harem according to its original layout, which was dictated by the hierarchical organization of its inhabitants. In this rebuilding, the wooden details were replaced with masonry, but a large part of the original walls was retained.[119] The quantities of stone, marble, columns, bricks, iron, and lead acquired for these extensive repairs are recorded in an account book of 1665–66, which also lists the wages for the construction workers.[120]

After these hasty repairs, most of the harem's walls were faced with inferior seventeenth-century tiles, except for Murad III's bedroom pavilion, which still retains most of its original decoration. The masonry fabric of the harem is completely covered with layers of paint and tile, hiding the clues necessary for solving its complex building history. The cramped, confined, and irregular layout the harem ended up with was as much a result of its additive development as it was of the limitations imposed by its sloping site. Since it had not been foreseen that the harem would expand so much, only a narrow plot was allotted to it in the beginning. It must originally have had a relatively regular layout, as the oldest buildings, adjacent to the Gold Path, suggest.[121]

The original garden wall of the harem probably formed a continuous line with the exterior facade of the stables, until it joined the crenellated wall of the sultan's hanging garden. By the sixteenth century, that section had long been filled up, and the limits of the ground suitable for building had been reached. As the harem expanded westward toward the outer garden, a new garden wall, protruding beyond the axis of the stables, was added in front of it. The new buildings had to be raised on high vaulted substructures to accommodate the steep slope, and each added building blocked the view of earlier ones (Pls. 5–9).

The harem was also continually remodeled according to changing fashions and requirements, and large halls were broken up into smaller rooms of irregular shape as the population increased. Unlike the other spaces of the palace, arranged around large ceremonial courts or open gardens, the harem consisted of a constellation of fragmented spaces enveloped by high walls and blocked from access with a large number of successive gates. No wonder it came to be associated in the West with a prisonlike, labyrinthine space designed for intrigue, where deprivation and sensual licentiousness lived side by side. The curiosity its enclosed spaces evoked in Europe is reflected in Orientalist paintings, plays, Mozart's opera *The Abduction from the Seraglio,* and in the widespread belief that the term *seraglio* (i.e., *sarāy*) derived etymologically from the Italian verb *serrare,* "to close, to lock."

Today the visitor must pass through dark vestibules and corridors before reaching the most prestigious royal halls with their magnificent views of the outer gardens, the Golden Horn, and the city (see Fig. 100). The contrast between the gloomy spaces, lit with a few skylights, and the sunlit royal halls overlooking gardens with pools, and opening onto porticoed courtyards, is a constant theme in this conglomeration of buildings constructed over the centuries. As if to compensate for the absence of a garden in the harem complex, the halls of the sultan were provided with multiple fountains and faced with İznik tile panels representing ever-blossoming gardens.

The harem, the "Abode of Felicity," was designed with a view to giving the utmost pleasure to only one person, the omnipotent sultan. Everyone else was deprived by degrees of the privileges and pleasures which he could enjoy. Only he and the eunuchs could mediate between the closely guarded and sharply delineated women's space and that of the men; everyone else was obliged to live a life of celibacy, except when the sultan desired a companion. The monastic spaces in the inner palace reflected an obsession with boundaries, the separation of opposite categories, and the rigid classification of ranks which only the sultan could transcend.

The sultan himself occupied the most spacious halls, whose lanterned domes highlighted the skyline of the harem (see Fig. 94 *[1–6]*). These were differentiated from the other halls by their richer building materials and more sumptuous decorations, furnishings, thrones, bronze fireplaces, and fountains; and by their site, which commanded the best view. The importance attached to large windows and projecting balconies with panoramic views, from which light poured into the royal interiors, is captured in the inscriptions in the pavilion Ahmed I built in 1608–9, to the west of Murad III's bedroom (see Fig. 94 *[4]*). Inscribed in gold between two of the many windows of this small, square, domed room is a couplet that praises the windows as manifestations of light and brightness. Other verses ask the sultan to enjoy eternal ecstasy and pleasure in his excellent pavilion (*ḳaṣr*).[122] This tile-decorated pleasure pavilion, open to the breezes and furnished with the "fountain of paradise," summarizes some of the main themes encountered in the royal spaces of the harem, which contrasted sharply with the dark, windowless, inward-turning, and undecorated nonroyal spaces, where eunuchs and female slaves were taught humility, obedience, and abstinence.

After the royal halls in importance came those of the widowed Queen Mother, exalted for her role of motherhood and hence her procreativity, which assured the propagation of the dynasty (see Fig. 94 *[7, 8]*). Her quarters, accentuated with a lower, unlanterned dome, were slightly smaller and less imposing, almost miniature versions of her son's apartments. The quarters of the princes, which did not have a separate court, but were inserted between those of the sultan and the Queen Mother, at the edge of the women's apartments, also had domes, though their siting reflected the subordinate role of their sequestered inhabitants (see Fig. 94 *[9]*). The mothers of princes, who came next in rank, lived in even smaller halls; only the quarters of the first wife boasted a dome, but smaller than that of the Queen Mother, and also without a lantern (see Fig. 94 *[10 – 12]*). Then followed the long, flat-roofed dormitory of the concubines at the southernmost edge of the harem, adjacent to the royal stables (see Fig. 94 *[13]*). The continuous outer facade of the harem architecturally expressed these status hierarchies, and could be read like a narrative from afar, just as the harem's ground plan encoded and reinforced a differential power structure (Pls. 29, 30a, 32a,b).

The imposing domed halls of the sultan at the northern edge of the complex formed a cluster of bubbles together with the domes of the men's Privy Chamber and the domed pavilions of its hanging garden (see Fig. 100). The Queen Mother's quarters occupied the middle portion of the facade, communicating her prestige through proximity to the apartments of the sultan. Like the royal apartments, hers too had a projecting balcony and arcades, regarded as signs of high status. The flat facades of the unbalconied quarters of royal wives, and the undistinguished mass of the dormitory of concubines came last. The quarters of the black eunuchs, who were officially the doorkeepers of the harem, had no outlook onto the gardens. No matter how influential the chief black eunuch was, his quarters had to be adjacent to the main gate of the harem, which provided access to the Court of the Queen Mother.

The constricted spaces of the prisonlike harem had several outlets to the outer gardens, which its inmates occasionally visited for recreation. During these outings, called *halvet* ("seclusion" or "retirement"), the pages and gardeners had to evacuate the gardens, so that no man remained in sight except for the sultan himself and the black eunuchs. One of these outlets is a steep staircase in the Court of Concubines, which leads to the private walled garden of the harem; several other staircases at different points descend to the vaulted substructures, which open onto this garden and its pools. There is also a ramp that connects the vestibule of the black eunuchs to the outer gardens; its door opens onto a terrace once studded with several pavilions, of which only the *Çinili Köşk* survives (Pl. 11 *[76, 77]*; see Fig. 94 *[17]*). Finally, a third passage, at the end of the Gold Path, links the harem to the sultan's hanging garden, fronting the Privy Chamber in the men's court (Pl. 11 *[66]*). This walled royal garden could be completely sealed off from the male section of the third court by closing several gates, so it was another garden setting that women could sometimes use. While the concubines played in the garden or swam in its pool, the sultan would retire with his favorite into one of the pavilions, hidden by shutters from the view of outsiders. On these outings the young girls would run about, playing and entertaining the sultan with amusing tricks, such as removing the eunuchs' turbans or pushing them into the water, or walking on their stomachs.[123] The gardens and their pavilions, then, offered an outlet for youthful spirits, a relative sense of freedom, and an escape from the constricting spaces of the harem and the stringent discipline it imposed on its inhabitants.

NINE
The Hanging Garden of the Third Court, Its Pavilions, and the Outer Garden

The three successive courts of the palace complex, proceeding from public to progressively more private zones, culminated in a small walled garden court with belvedere towers, pavilions, pools, fountains, terraces, and a breathtaking prospect of the Golden Horn, the Bosphorus, the Sea of Marmara, and the European and Asian shores of the capital (Pls. 4–9, 11 *[D]*, 12 *[D]*). This was the sultan's private hanging garden; it could be reached from the Privy Chamber in the court of pages and from the harem. It is known today as the "fourth court," but it was designed to be an integral part of the third, and is connected to the court of pages by two passages. The first of these passages is next to the Privy Chamber and leads into an upper garden that is raised on a vaulted substructure and was once surrounded by a crenellated wall, punctuated with tower pavilions (Pl. 11 *[56, 59]*). It contains yet another raised terrace, provided with a pool and paved with marble, that flanks the Privy Chamber and is connected to the garden below by two staircases (Pl. 11 *[54, 55]*). The second passage is a vaulted tunnel that runs between the Inner Treasury and the Commissary dormitory and leads to a lower garden platform (Pl. 11 *[57]*). This was once enclosed by a crenellated wall with a gate leading to the outer gardens (Pls. 11 *[62]*, 12 *[37]*, 27, 29, 30a, 32a,c; see Figs. 93a,b). Murad III's doctor, Domenico Hierosolimitano, describes it as a "narrow corridor" leading into a court with a flower garden.[1] Both passages seem to have existed from the beginning, and they are clearly shown on the *Hünername* miniature from 1584 (see Fig. 56).

In this court, garden and architecture subtly permeated one another, providing a zone of transition between the three aligned courts of the palace and the outer gardens beyond. From it, the sultan could survey the vast domains over which his rule extended. Passages in Ottoman sources describe in detail what Mehmed II could see from there, indicating the importance to the sultans and their architects of these panoramic vistas and of incorporating the outdoors into the design of the third court, with its hanging garden. Bidlisi, for example, writes that the sultan's residence overlooked the Bosphorus where the Black Sea met the Mediterranean, the Golden Horn, and all four sections of the capital: Istanbul, Eyüb, Galata, and Üsküdar.[2]

The terraced hanging garden, roughly the same size as the court of pages, was more elaborately designed than the gardens in the second and third courts. It was probably built with the rest of the inner palace in the 1460s, as a *giardino pensile*, reminiscent of those in such contemporary Italian palaces as Pius II's Palazzo Piccolomini in Pienza (1459–62) or Federico da Montefeltro's ducal palace in Urbino (ca. 1468). It exemplifies a renewed Renaissance interest in hanging gardens, whose history went back to the legendary gardens of Solomon's palace near the temple of Jerusalem and the

101 (opposite) Matrakçı Nasuh, ca. 1537, representation of the Topkapı Palace in a schematic map of Istanbul. From *Beyan-i Menazil-i Sefer-i Irakeyn*, İÜ, T 5964, fol. 8v.

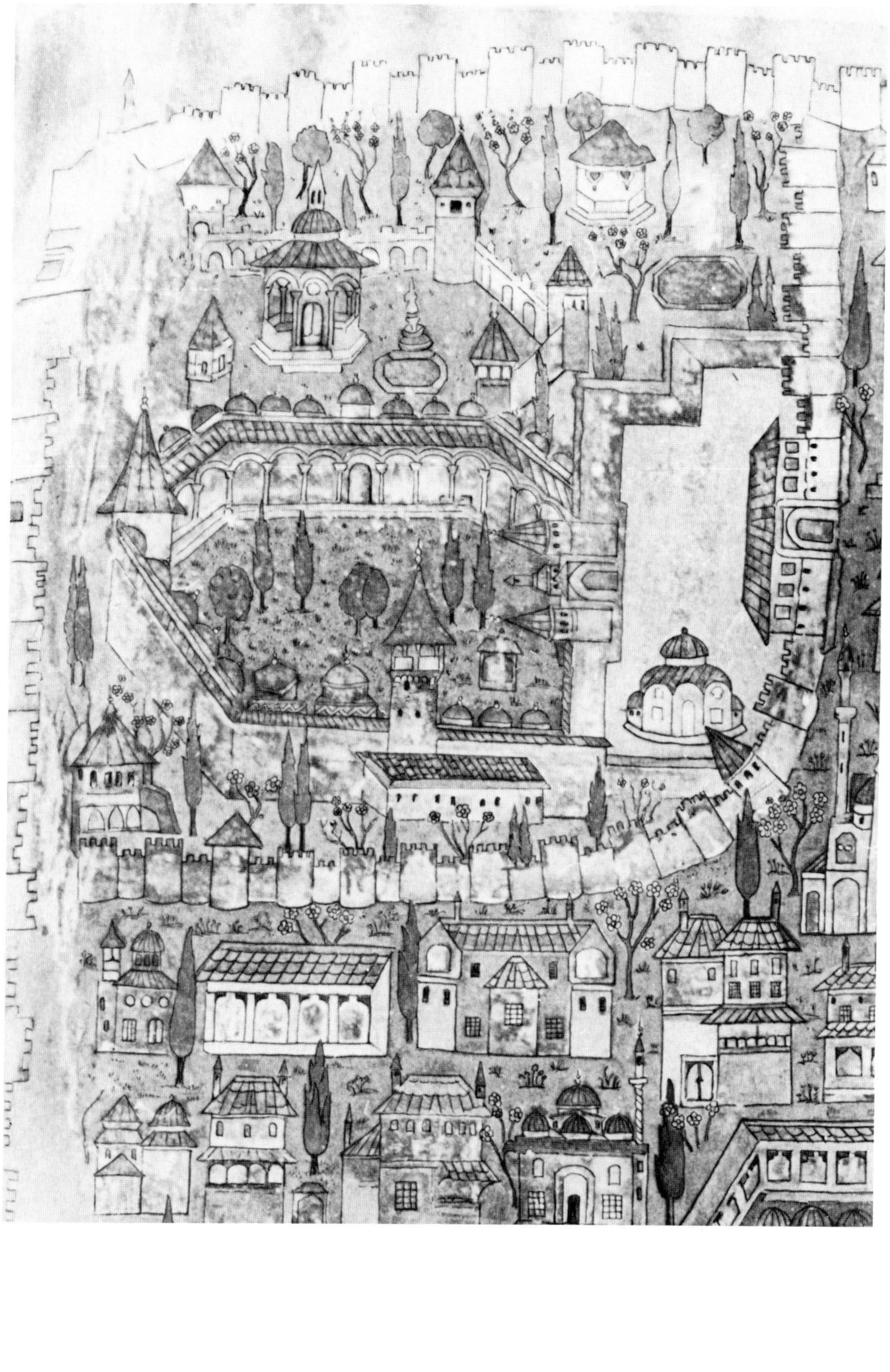

102 Jérôme Maurand, 1544, panoramic sketch of Istanbul. From Maurand, *Itinéraire d'Antibes à Constantinople.*

fabled Hanging Gardens of Babylon, which represented paradise on earth and were associated with royal power.

The design of Mehmed's walled hanging garden united a boundless view of nature with an enclosed space that had the quiet and meditative atmosphere of a "secret garden." In Ottoman court poetry the garden was commonly used as a metaphor for an inner, secure space where one was free to allow the private, emotional part of one's nature, suppressed in public, to emerge. In the *Asafname,* a treatise on statecraft composed by Lutfi Pasha, the deposed grand vizier of Süleyman I, who retired from political life to his estate in Dimetoka, wrote, "The kingdom of this mortal world is swift and passing and full of death. It is better to find wise but not heedless repose in the corner of leisure and the enjoyment of gardens and meadows."[3] Lutfi's praise of the contemplative life bore some resemblance to the ancient Roman distinction between the life of *otium* and that of *negotium.*

The setting for the leisurely life of pleasure and contemplation was the garden retreat idealized in Ottoman poetry as a sanctuary removed from worldly troubles.[4] Enclosed by secure walls, the Topkapı Palace's hanging garden was such a private royal space for repose, contemplation, and pleasure. The sultans spent the hours not taken up by ceremonial duties in its pavilions, with either male or female companions. They would often retreat into one of these pavilions with a favorite, eat meals there, read and write (part of the royal library was kept in the Revan Kiosk, built for Murad IV), compose poetry, listen to music, and watch sports activities in the gardens below (polo, archery, wrestling) from throne-shaped stone seats built into the colonnades. The garden pavilions, which were ideal settings for pleasurable relaxation, are often referred to in the sources as *teferrücgāh,* a place of recreation (*teferrüc,* or "recreation," was the source for the Italian word *tanfaruzzi*). The sultans themselves also played games in the hanging garden; an inscription on the lower platform of a stone throne praises Murad IV for having broken records in horseback archery and javelin throwing in 1636.[5]

Evidence adduced to argue that Mehmed II's New Palace was originally a fortress, with an inner citadel of seven towers, includes the remains of towers found in this garden court and images of towers in the miniature of Matrakçı Nasuh (Fig. 101), painted around 1537, and a sketchy drawing by Jérôme Maurand, dated 1544 (Fig. 102). The last two, however, can both be discounted. Maurand's drawing clearly depicts the seven-towered fortress of Yedikule, and not the Topkapı Palace at all. In it Thrace is represented by windmills near the towered fortress, Asia is in the upper right, across from the triangular cape of the palace, in front of Hagia Sophia. The legends *Trasia* and *Asia* on the drawing would have to be reversed for the seven-towered structure to be the Topkapı.[6]

This leaves Matrakçı's miniature of the Topkapı (see Fig. 101). There, the palatial complex is not shown as a complete ensemble seen from a single point of view, but as a series of selected units juxtaposed in unexpected ways. Matrakçı has omitted details and retains only the features readily recognizable to his contemporaries. He fragments space in an almost Cubist manner, to show different facets of each courtyard simultaneously; as a result the rectangular second court appears to be hexagonal. The first two courtyards are clearly identifiable, but the one with the problematic towers, which one would assume must be the third courtyard, shows none of the major buildings, and the crenellated walls between each tower are pierced

103 Remaining part of the walled enclosure around the hanging garden of the third court, with the Tower of the Head Physician (*hekimbaşı kulesi*). Courtesy of Reha Günay.

by arched windows with red iron lattices. The towers themselves have decorative brick patterns and are crowned by belvederes. Clearly this is not a defensive citadel, but a representation of the walled enclosure around the third court's hanging garden. A portion of this fifteenth-century garden wall pierced by arched windows with iron lattices still exists, and is far from being a fortified battlement. Its only remaining tower — known today as Başlala Kulesi (Head Tutor's Tower) or Hekimbaşı Kulesi (Head Physician's Tower) — was once crowned by a belvedere with a conical cap; it has thin walls and large, latticed windows designed to link the inner palace with the surrounding landscape (Pls. 11 *[59]*, 12 *[33]*; Figs. 103, 104).[7] Some late-fifteenth-century miniatures produced at the Ottoman court depict tower pavilions like this one, with arches opening onto panoramic vistas. These paintings show both towerlike kiosks and domed pavilions set in gardens enclosed by walls pierced with iron-latticed windows; they might well have been inspired by the Topkapı Palace itself (Figs. 105a,b, 106a,b).

104 Tower of the Head Physician, seen from the lower garden terrace.

It is curious that Matrakçı's miniature omits the residential zones of the third court and chooses instead to depict five decorative brick belvedere towers around its walled private garden. In the second court he shows the Tower of Justice and the two towers flanking the second gate, all of which add up to eight towers, and not seven.[8] These towers did not constitute a uniform inner fortress, but marked such highly charged areas of the palace complex as the hanging garden by the sultan's bedroom, the Council Hall of justice, and the ceremonial gate that provided access to the second court. That Matrakçı did not paint a fortress with seven

105*a* Bahram Gur with the princess of the white pavilion. From Amir Khusraw Dihlavi, *Khamsa,* 1498, TSK, H 799, fol. 196r.
105*b* Shirin sees Khusraw's portrait. From Hatifi, *Khusraw wa Shirin,* 1498–99, MS. New York, Metropolitan Museum of Art 69.27, fol. 22v.

towers is further corroborated by the total absence of references in the sources to an inner citadel. There are references only to paradise gardens with belvedere pavilions, from which the sultan could look over his capital and view the ships coming into the harbor from the four corners of the world.[9] In addition, had there been seven towers, one can be sure that that number would have been mentioned by poets; seven is a number pregnant with astrological significance.[10]

The upper parts of the garden towers were torn down in the sixteenth century and replaced with some of the palace's most lavish kiosks. Some scholars have argued that the towers were demolished after the women's quarters were built, to keep men from looking into the harem, but this assumes that no harem existed before the sixteenth century, and we know that there was one from the beginning. This transformation can better be attributed

106*a* Bahram Gur with the princess of the red pavilion. From Amir Khusraw Dihlavi, *Khamsa,* 1498, TSK, H 799, fol. 172.
106*b* Bahram Gur with the princess of the black pavilion. From Amir Khusraw Dihlavi, *Khamsa,* 1498, TKS, H 799, fol. 182.

to a change of fashion, from medieval tower pavilions to open domed kiosks surrounded by arcades (Pls. 25c, 27–32; see Figs. 56, 93a,b). Gradually the castellation of the hanging garden was replaced by the arcadian setting favored in the sixteenth century; it eventually lost whatever fortress appearance it may once have had.[11]

Pavilions of the Hanging Garden

The most impressive of these kiosks were those built on the raised marble terrace of the hanging garden in front of the Privy Chamber. Süleyman I remodeled the terrace and its fishpond, first mentioned by Angiolello.[12] His account books of 1527–29 (see Appendix A.7) list expenses for building a new marble-paved terrace, raised on vaults, with iron beams and subterranean water channels. A "new kiosk" and a "new room" adjacent to a small

107 The Revan Kiosk and the pool of the marble terrace, with its projecting canopy throne.

bath were built upon it, and the portico ceilings of the Privy Chamber were repaired and repainted.[13]

The *Hünername* miniature of 1584 shows three pavilions on the marble terrace by the Privy Chamber (see Figs. 56, 93b).[14] These must be the predecessors of the Circumcision Room *(Sünnet Odası)* and the Revan (Erevan) and Baghdad kiosks that stand there today (Pls. 11 *[63–65]*, 12 *[29–31]*; see Figs. 90, 91). All three of these still-extant pavilions were built after 1633, when a fire damaged their predecessors and led to the remodeling of the pooled terrace and its kiosks; an account book from that year cites expenses for "rebuilding the burnt pavilion."[15] The Baghdad and Revan kiosks were constructed between 1635 and 1638, while Murad IV was on a military campaign in the East: they commemorated the sultan's victories over the cities after which they were named (Figs. 107–9).[16] The neighboring gilt-bronze canopy, resting on four poles, over a marble throne was added by İbrahim I in 1640, according to its inscription, which identifies it as the *ḳaṣr-i ifṭāriyye,* or pavilion for breaking the fast during Ramadan (Pl. 8; see Figs. 90, 91).[17] The same sultan also transformed an earlier pavilion into the extant Circumcision Room, whose foundation inscription has a chronogram with the date 1051 (1641–42).[18] At the same time, the marble-paved terrace was again remodeled, and the new pool, still there today, was built on top of its larger predecessor.[19] In 1699, the English clergyman Reverend Edmund Chishull and a merchant companion were allowed to see this area, thanks to a Greek surgeon who attended the sultan's chief gardener. The reverend's description

108 The Baghdad Kiosk and the pool of the marble terrace.

shows that the marble terrace and its kiosks had already acquired their present form by the time of his visit:

Near a Corinthian pillar [i.e., the Goth's Column, in front of the gate of the hanging garden, which opens to the outer garden, see Pl. 10 *(24, 26)*] ... we were admitted through a gate, which opens into a green court, and that again into a garden kept in somewhat regular order. From hence we ascend by a few steps into an apartment of the *Grand Signior,* where are two rich *kiosks* [i.e., the Baghdad and Revan], a fish pond, a paved walk, and an open gallery.... The above mentioned gallery [i.e., of the Privy Chamber] is rich and splendid, adorned with various gilding of flower work, and supported with beautiful serpentine pillars. In the sides of one of the *kiosks* are three orbicular stones of fine porphyry, the middlemost of which is curiously polished, and thereby serves to reflect the prospect of the *seraglio* and adjoining city, in the nature of a looking glass.[20]

The seventeenth-century kiosks of the marble terrace provide us with an idea of what the earlier ones they replaced probably looked like. They all have a domed throne room with a bronze fireplace which usually opens onto smaller rooms containing a latrine and ablution fountain. Essentially, they were elegantly furnished, multiwindowed, free-standing royal rooms raised on foundations that lifted them so that they could command a better view. This is why these kiosks (*köşk*) are often referred to in the sources as "rooms" (*oda*). The most prestigious of them were surmounted with lanterned lead domes with pendant globes, also a distinguishing feature of the sultan's private chambers in both the male and female quarters of the third court.

These kiosks were showcases for the decorative arts of the time, with their rich textiles, carpets, tiles, objects on display in niches, bronze fireplaces, mother-of-pearl-inlaid wooden shutters, doors, and wooden ceilings with lavish gilt paintings. They had built-in alcoves, fitted with low sofas, from which a reclining person could comfortably enjoy the surrounding landscape, and were ringed with marble arcades equipped with stone thrones. Their outer walls were faced with marble dadoes, with elaborate tile revetments above. The interior walls were completely covered with tile panels, representing gardens seen through arches, alternating with large windows, a scheme that blurred the distinction between outside and inside, and between nature and art. Like the tiles and windows, fountains placed under the dome and inside the window recesses brought nature inside. Water played an important role in these luminous spaces, where interior and exterior met. Bobovi describes the general effect:

> I will tell you that these *köşks* are the most agreeable buildings that the Turks have. They are sometimes elevated on a number of columns; they have an octagonal or dodecagonal shape and are open on all sides. They are closed off with great canvases, which are lowered on pulleys on the side where the sun shines, so as to provide coolness in the summer. The floor is usually of marble, with fountains in the middle and in the corners, [with] water running from them and traversing the room in a series of small channels. There is an elevated platform running along the sides of the room, covered with rich rugs and large cushions made of the most beautiful materials from Persia and Venice, for comfortable seating.... It is always cool in these salons, which are ordinarily raised from the ground by five or six steps. All the rich families in the Empire have *köşks* in their gardens, where they sleep after dinner in the summer, or entertain their friends in their hours of leisure.[21]

One of the earliest structures to be built next to the Privy Chamber was a transparent crystal pavilion, first described by the Genoese page Menavino, who lived in the palace between 1504 and 1515:

> In this seraglio is a room entirely made of transparent glass squares joined and fastened together with tin rods, and it is in the guise of a round cupola, resembling a stretched tent when seen from a distance. In the past, water once ran over it with a marvelous artifice, flowing down from the cupola and descending to the garden. The king frequently used to go there in the summertime to sleep during the day, to the cool and sweet murmur of the resounding waters.[22]

The water conduits had already ceased to function by Bayezid II's reign, when Menavino saw it, so the crystal pavilion must have been built by Mehmed II.[23] Michael Heberer von Bretten, a galley slave who helped build another kiosk in the palace gardens in 1587, describes the same "transparent rotunda of crystal,"[24] and Domenico Hierosolimitano refers to it as a hexagonal pavilion with six large columns, surmounted by a lead dome with a lantern and covered inside with gilded silver plate. Its intercolumniations were spanned with plates of rock crystal, skillfully joined to appear as one piece; the lantern of its dome rested on crystal colonnettes and was made of joined pieces of coral that dazzled the eye in the sunshine.[25]

In 1621 Deshayes de Courmenin offered a somewhat different description, which firmly locates the pavilion near the marble pool of the Privy Chamber:

> One among the other [pavilions] is built on the edge of a small pool; the floor below it is all vaulted and enriched with marble incrustations of many colors. Above is a

109 Old photograph of the Baghdad Kiosk interior. From Eldem, *Köşkler,* 1:306.

room whose ceiling is supported on eight marble columns; the rest is completely open to daylight, for it is enclosed only by panes of very fine crystal. Around the room, there is a grand corridor, five feet wide and decorated with marble balustrades, from which thirty-two jets of clear water can be seen falling into the pool, making an agreeable murmur. The ceiling of this room is enriched with mother-of-pearl and with fine gems set in compartments [of wood]: the top is faced with plates of gilt silver and is so filled with turquoises, rubies, and other precious stones that never has anyone seen anything more dazzling.[26]

The pool, raised on a vaulted terrace and surrounded by jets of water, immediately recalls Bon's earlier description of the area fronting the Privy Chamber.[27] Because the sultan used the crystal pavilion for his afternoon siestas in the summer, it was built near the royal bedchamber, and is probably one of the domed summer rooms mentioned by Angiolello as being in the Privy Chamber complex.[28] It perhaps occupied the place where the Revan Kiosk stands today, at the edge of the pool (Pls. 11 *[64]*, 12 *[30]*). It must have been a wonderful curiosity in its time, for it was reproduced in the sixteen-century palace of the grand vizier Sokollu Mehmed Pasha at Üsküdar. Fresne-Canaye, writing in 1573, describes the grand vizier's pavilion as a small room beside a pool, made entirely of glass in the form of a lantern, so that his royal wife could look out onto the garden there without being seen.[29] Like its model, it blurred the boundary between interior and exterior space; the surrounding landscape was visible from within the glass rotunda, unobscured by walls.

An earlier pavilion also once occupied the site of the present Circumcision Room, one of the inscriptions of which reads, "He [İbrahim I] ordered a lofty and high pavilion to be made / In a new, joyful manner that should not be in the old style." Several panegyric poems commemorating the completion of this pavilion provide chronograms corresponding to the date 1051 (1641–42), and refer to it as a "renovated" *(tecdīd)* belvedere pavilion with numerous windows flanked by pairs of fountains, from which the sultan could watch javelin tournaments among the pages in the garden below (Pls. 6, 8, 11 *[63]*, 12 *[29]*).[30]

Eldem has confirmed that İbrahim did in fact renovate an existing building. An old photograph of the Circumcision Room shows that the masonry above its windows and on its garden facade is different from that on the rest of the building, proving that the original building was not entirely destroyed, but in part incorporated into İbrahim's new pavilion (Fig. 110). The original structure was rectangular; it featured two small rooms and a throne hall with a fireplace and a projecting bay window, supported from the garden side on two columns. İbrahim raised the height of the walls and demolished the bay window to extend the garden facade.[31] The renovated structure had essentially the same layout as its predecessor — a plan similar to that of Süleyman's Chamber of Petitions, built around 1526–28, which also has a throne room opening onto two smaller rooms, a latrine and a small bath for ablutions. The Circumcision Room's small bath across from the Privy Chamber was used by the sultans for ritual ablutions, shaving, and occasionally for royal circumcisions.[32]

Eldem thinks that the original pavilion was built for Selim I, when he renovated the neighboring Privy Chamber. He bases the argument on two interior *cuerda seca* tile lunettes over the north windows, which belong to the original structure and resemble those in Selim I's mosque in Istanbul.

110 An old photograph of the Circumcision Room, showing the different masonry of its original sixteenth-century core. From Eldem, *Köşkler*, 1:320.

However, contemporary sources state clearly that Selim I's mosque was built in his honor, but not by him; it was built by Süleyman I between 1521 and 1527 and dedicated to his father's memory.[33] Therefore, the color-glazed Persianate tile lunettes with a palette of blue, turquoise, green, and yellow should rather be dated to the early part of Süleyman's reign, when the entire palace was undergoing its major renovation under Alaüddin's supervision, between 1525 and 1529.

The predecessor of the Circumcision Room was probably the "new room *[oda-i cedīd]*, raised on a vaulted terrace, near the room of His Majesty [i.e., the Privy Chamber]" mentioned in Süleyman's account books of 1527–28. Its expenses included painted decorations, "a water channel" and a "small bath" whose conduit extended from the "new room up to the girls' garden" (i.e., the harem; see Appendix A.7). In Melchior Lorichs's panorama of 1559 the site of the Circumcision Room is occu-

111 Facade of the Circumcision Room with reassembled tiles.

pied by a conically capped, towerlike pavilion with a large window, adjacent to the left end of the Privy Chamber's portico, facing Galata (Pl. 25c). The same structure appears in the same place in a panoramic view from about 1590, with a tall chimney accentuating its conical roof and a bay window supported from the garden side by columns, which coincides exactly with Eldem's hypothetical reconstruction of the original pavilion (Pl. 27). It is possible that Süleyman's towerlike pavilion was built to replace one of Mehmed II's belvedere towers. Its solid masonry basement under the main hall might have been the base of a razed tower. The panoramic view from 1590 depicts a crenellated wall extending between it and another kiosk on the site of the present Baghdad Kiosk (Pl. 27). This wall must have been destroyed when the marble terrace was extended in the mid seventeenth century as far as the garden facade of the Circumcision Room. Another neighboring tower, adjacent to the gate connecting the Privy Chamber to the harem, was replaced by Abdülhamid I's Mabeyn Kiosk in the eighteenth century (Pl. 11 *[66]*).[34]

Dallam, who installed the clock organ in 1599, describes the predecessor of the Circumcision Room as a "little house" built next to the Privy Chamber's portico, "verrie curious bothe within and witheout; for carvinge, gildinge, good Collors

112 Detail of the Circumcision Room facade with its original door.

113 Detail of tiles on the Circumcision Room facade.

and vernishe, I have not sene the lyke. In this litle house, that emperor that rained when I was thare, had nyntene brotheres put to deathe in it, and it was bulte for no other use but for stranglinge of everie emperors bretherin" (see Figs. 81, 82a,b).[35] According to a contemporary report, Mehmed III had these nineteen young brothers brought out of the harem "and directly they had kissed his hand they were circumcised, then taken aside and dexterously strangled with handkerchiefs," an event which apparently took place in the building that once stood on the site of the Circumcision Room; but Dallam is certainly mistaken in his claim that that was the pavilion's sole function.[36]

The *cuerda seca* tile lunettes inside Süleyman's pavilion do not match the underglaze-painted blue, white, and turquoise tiles of its main facade facing the Privy Chamber (Figs. 111–13). Although various tiles were reassembled on this facade at a later date, the inset underglaze cartouches of the marble doorframe seem to be part of the original decorative scheme. This suggests that tiles of various techniques and color schemes were used in decorating Süleyman's kiosks. The facades of the structures grouped around the pool, however, appear to have been unified with a common decorative program consisting of blue, white, and turquoise underglaze-painted tiles and marble dadoes, matching the decoration of the Privy Chamber (see Fig. 82a,b).[37]

Account books of 1527–28 show that Süleyman also built a "new kiosk" *(köşk-i cedīd)* on the Privy Chamber's marble terrace. Expenses listed for it include a "subterranean water channel," passing underneath the vaulted basement of the kiosk, painted decorations, painted pendant globes, assorted tiles, a marble pavement in front of it, and glass for the lantern of its dome (see Appendix A.7). This may be the kiosk with a lanterned dome next to a pool depicted in Matrakçı Nasuh's miniature (see Fig. 101). The same kiosk appears in Lorichs's panoramic view of 1559 (Pl. 25c), on the *Hünername* miniature of 1584 (see Fig. 56), and on a panoramic view from 1590, where it occupies approximately the site of the Baghdad Kiosk, which later replaced it (Pls. 6–9, 27; see Fig. 108). It, too, was probably constructed on the base of one of Mehmed II's original belvedere towers; Eldem locates the remains of a tower base under the Baghdad Kiosk.[38]

Five tall tile panels, framed by arches and superbly painted in blue and turquoise over a white background, today decorate the facade of the Circumcision Room, but they were probably made for Süleyman's "new kiosk" (see Figs. 111–13). Four of them use two pounced designs for birds and *ch'ilins* (four-legged creatures deriving from Chinese mythology) among intertwined *saz* leaves, lotus palmettes, and rosettes; the fifth panel features *saz* foliage with birds springing from a vase. These tile panels were later copied, not very successfully, in the seventeenth-century tiles of the Baghdad Kiosk, which closely follows the layout and decorative program of Süleyman's domed kiosk, damaged in the fire of 1633. They are usually dated to the mid sixteenth century, but Banu Mahir has recently proposed a date for them of around 1530–40. She attributes their designs in the *saz* style, rooted in a Turcoman tradition developed in fifteenth-century Tabriz and Herat, to the Tabrizi artist Şahkulu, who is listed as Süleyman's highest-paid court painter in a wage register of 1526.[39] Even if this attribution cannot be documented, a close connection to the *saz* style as practiced by Şahkulu in black-line album painting is apparent in these tiles; they could not have been produced without the cooperation of tilemakers and court designers.

That this cooperation existed can be documented in Süleyman I's account books, which show that tiles were made in Istanbul for Süleyman's renovated palace in a "royal ceramics atelier" *(kāşīḫāne-i ḫāṣṣa)* in 1527–28, under the guidance of the chief ceramicist Usta Ali, assisted by court painters. This atelier was founded by a Tabrizi ceramicist named Habib, who was among the artisans brought to Istanbul after Selim I's conquest of Tabriz in 1514. Usta Ali, who was responsible for the tile revetments of Süleyman's palace, is listed as Habib's highest-paid assistant in a wage register of 1526.[40]

The five rectangular tile panels made for Süleyman's kiosk were the product of a collaboration between ceramicists and court painters trained in Tabriz, and represent a Timurid-flavored Persianate aesthetic different from the classical Ottoman style of tiles produced in İznik after the 1540s and 1550s. That these underglaze-painted blue, white, and turquoise tiles were used along with tiles based on a different color scheme is suggested by the niches of the Baghdad Kiosk, which are faced with old *cuerda seca* tiles, datable to the 1520s. Süleyman's new kiosk, built by Alaüddin (nicknamed Ali of Persia because Selim I had brought him to Istanbul from the conquered city of Tabriz), and decorated with tiles produced by ceramicists and painters steeped in Tabrizi traditions, represented the culmination of a Timurid-Turcoman taste patronized in the sultan's court during the 1520s and 1530s.[41] This Persianate aesthetic continued to flourish until the classical Ottoman style was formulated around the middle of the sixteenth century. Thereafter, the fashion for architectural tiles in a blue-white-turquoise color scheme was abandoned in Sinan's buildings in favor of a bold floral aesthetic, developed in İznik, that relied on more vivid, contrasting colors, adding red and green to the former limited palette influenced by prestigious Chinese blue-and-white ceramics.

114*a* (above) Michel-François Préaulx, Gardens of the seraglio with European visitors inspecting the Goth's Column, ca. 1800–20. From Briony Llewellyn, *The Orient Observed: Images of the Middle East from the Searight Collection*. London, Victoria and Albert Museum, 1989, p. 21.
114*b* (opposite) 1852 photograph, showing the Goth's Column and some structures, no longer extant, in the hanging garden of the third court, including its gatehouse, a classical column, and a cruciform pavilion; on the far left is the sultan's private stable. From Eldem and Akozan, *Topkapı*.

Pavilions were also built in the lower terraces of the hanging garden, but those from the fifteenth and sixteenth centuries no longer remain. A gate, once flanked by towers, connects the lowest terrace with the upper, walled section; today the gate is crowned by a wooden pavilion named after the seventeenth-century grand vizier Kara Mustafa Pasha. It is an eighteenth-century building with Rococo decorations whose walls are nearly transparent with tall windows overlooking both the upper and lower gardens; a repair inscription of 1704–5 refers to it as the Terrace Kiosk (*Ṣoffa Köşki*) (Pls. 11 *[58]*, 12 *[34]*).[42]

Along the eastern edge of the lower garden is the ground floor of a pavilion attributed to Mehmed II, a fifteenth-century structure built in alternating courses of brick and stone. Its upper floor was replaced in the nineteenth century by the neoclassical Mecidiye Kiosk (Pls. 11 *[60]*, 12 *[36]*). The extant basement of the original pavilion is buried under the garden terrace, making its walls blind on three sides. On the fourth side, facing the Sea of Marmara, it has a symmetrically composed facade with a large rectangular window topped by a round-arched lunette at the center, and two smaller windows of the same shape on each side, a scheme

recalling the facade of Mehmed's royal pavilion that once crowned the Imperial Gate (see Fig. 23). Inside is an oblong, barrel-vaulted hall with a fountain, behind a narrower hall with windows overlooking the garden and the sea beyond. A number of small rooms in the back, and the ruins of a staircase that once led to the upper story, complete the complex. The decorative pavement is composed of hexagonal bricks and triangular marbles, forming star patterns. The walls are said once to have been ornamented with rich stucco carvings in the fifteenth-century Bursa style, in keeping with the still-extant Bursa arched marble niches. Little is known about the upper story that once opened onto the lower garden terrace, but it probably repeated the plan of the ground floor.[43]

This building is the long pavilion occupying the eastern side of the garden court in Melchior Lorichs's panorama, where its facade is faintly shown with five rectangular windows topped by round arched lunettes (Pl. 25c). Its ground floor would have been used as a summer retreat; its upper story commanded an outstanding view. It is prominently situated and was probably built in the 1460s, along with the original core of the New Palace. It is located just in front of the open loggia of the Treasury-Bath complex and designed to exploit the view—demonstrating once again that Mehmed II's palace was far from being either inward-looking or a defensive fortress (Pl. 4). No attempt was made to match the facade of alternating stone and brick of the garden pavilion with the ashlar masonry facade of the neighboring Treasury-Bath complex. Its Byzantinizing exterior is combined with a typically Ottoman interior decoration, testifying once more to the eclectic architectural vocabulary of Mehmed II's palace.

Near the Mecidiye Kiosk is a small mosque, built in the nineteenth century; but we know from Flachat that there was also a mosque on that same site in 1740 (Pl. 12 *[35]*). Atâ calls it the "Terrace Mosque" (*ṣoffa Cāmiʿi*), and says that it and the neighboring dormitory (*ṣoffa ocāġı*) for gardeners in charge of the garden court were built by Süleyman.[44] We know from an account book dated 1564–65 that Süleyman's private hanging garden had an orange grove, jasmine planted in pots, and a field of carnations.[45] A later account book, from 1580, lists expenses for "renewing the jasmine pergolas near the terrace of the House of Felicity in the private garden."[46] Another one, from 1621–22, mentions "covering the orange and lemon trees in the private garden and in front of the Privy Chamber."[47] Documents also cite "vine pergolas";[48] in 1599, while Dallam was installing the organ under the portico of the Privy Chamber, he ate grapes that were grown there. No garden was "so well kepte in the worlde ...," he wrote. "Every ode [i.e., *oda,* chamber or kiosk] or corner hath som exelente frute tre or trees growing in them; allso thar is greate abundance of sweete grapes, and of diverse sortes; thar a man may gather grapes everie Daye in the yeare. In November, as I satt at diner, I se them gather grapes upon the vines, and theye broughte them to me to eate. For the space of a monthe I Dined everie day in the Surralia, and we had everie day grapes after our meate; but most sartain it is that grapes do grow thare contenually."[49]

In 1740 Flachat, who saw the planted parterres, wrote, "Water flows in abundance from the gardens above to the parterre of the orangery, into a large antique basin of marble decorated in a bas relief of admirable work";[50] this was one of the many antique sarcophagi Mehmed II had placed in the gardens to serve as basins for fountains. He had also preserved the antique Goth's Column in front of the gate that connected the private hanging garden to the more accessible outer garden (Pl. 10 *[26]*). The gardeners' dormitory was built on top of that gate, which marked the boundary between the two gardens (Pls. 10 *[24]*, 25c, 31a; Figs. 114a,b).[51]

Layout and Institutional Organization of the Outer Garden: Landscape as Microcosm

The outer garden extended along both shores of the triangular promontory on which the palace was built (Pls. 3, 10). It was connected by several gates to the first court, the walled hanging garden of the third court, and the private garden of the harem. Tavernier describes the triangular site of the palace: "This triangle is not equilateral, and it is divided into eight parts; the land side has three of them [i.e., the three main courts], and the five others are along the two seashores."[52] The nineteenth-century historian Şeref identifies the five "sections" of the outer garden that surround the main palace as the Shore Kiosk (*yālı köşki*), Seraglio Point (*sarāy burnı*), the Royal Garden (*ḫāṣṣ bāġçe*), the Rose Garden (*gülḫāne*), and the Arsenal (*cebeḫāne*), but their original names are unknown (Pl. 13).[53] The walls and screens that separated these gardens are visible in sixteenth-century miniatures and marked on nineteenth-century plans (Pls. 13, 14, 20a,b, 21a,b; see Fig. 56).

The old fortified Byzantine city walls along the shore separated the gardens from a narrow quay. Bayezid II had them repaired after the earthquake of 1509 and opened up several gates in them to provide access from the gardens to the shore. In front of the monumental double-towered Gate of St. Barbara, on the tip of the promontory called Seraglio Point, Mehmed II had mounted cannons for defense, giving this gate the new name of Cannon Gate (*ṭop kapu* or *ṭop kapusı*), which in the nineteenth century came to refer to a new shore palace that was built on that site, and finally to the whole palace (Pls. 10 *[48]*, 25–32).[54] Menavino describes this triumphal royal gate, as two towers "on the seaside ... well-furnished with large and small artillery and in the middle of these is the private gate of the king, and in front of the gate in a space five or six paces wide and thirty long are more than forty cannons which, when fired, rake the sea; when the Grand Turk wants to go to sea for pleasure, two brigantines come to that gate; the king boards one of them, and the other follows close by, in case of need."[55] By the sixteenth century, whatever defensive purposes they may originally have served, the cannons were used for announcing religious holidays, royal births, departures of the fleet, and the ceremonial boat processions of the sultans. Gradually, the towers of the Byzantine sea walls were replaced with belvedere pavilions, a trend already evident in the walled hanging garden of the third court.

Today the sea wall and the shore pavilions have for the most part disappeared; a railroad and highway now cut through the outer garden, which has largely been destroyed (Pl. 2). Originally, this garden was composed of a series of stepped terraces supported on vaulted substructures, some of which incorporated the ruins of the Byzantine acropolis. On the Vavassore map it looks like a multitiered mound, crowned by the palace (Pl. 23, see Fig. 6). Dilich's bird's-eye view shows these terraces cascading down to the shore, with some of the hanging parterre gardens planted in square beds in a grid pattern (Pl. 26b). The sultan's private hanging garden was a prelude to the several encountered beyond its walls.

Hanging gardens on terraces suggest the control of man over nature, a recurring theme in the design of the New Palace, where nature and architecture interpenetrated one another. The sultan's palace on the hilltop seemed to dominate the plant, animal, and mineral kingdoms represented in the outer garden by the flowers, fruits, vegetables, animals, and raw metals gathered, grown, or stored in it from all over the empire. These collected items were set in a position of subordination to the dominating residence of the sultan on the hilltop. Bidlisi wrote that the "three kingdoms of nature" *(mevālīd-i s̱elās̱e)* formed a castle around the sultan's palace.[56] The early-sixteenth-century poet Cafer Çelebi likened the orderly rows of cypresses and fruit trees in the outer gardens to obedient servants lined up around the sultan's palace to serve him; they reminded Bidlisi of troops on parade before the ruler.[57] The master-slave relationship of the sultan to his subjects, statesmen, and ambassadors, which was encoded in the architectonic structure and ceremonial of the palace's three main courts, was implied in the layout of the outer garden as well. The royal garden's symbolism of power and control, deeply rooted in ancient Near Eastern prototypes inherited by early Islamic culture, was enriched by its connotations as an earthy paradise containing the king's Abode of Felicity. The themes of paradise, pleasure, and power complemented one another in defining a garden setting that served as an appropriate backdrop to the palace of the universal monarch blessed with heavenly fortune.

These themes turn up in Ottoman descriptions of the New Palace's outer garden. Bidlisi praises the "paradiselike" terraced garden, studded with fountains, vineyards, and pavilions cascading down to the sea. When the sultan visited his heavenly garden with his handsome pages and beautiful concubines, recalling the ever-young *ghilman* and *khouris* of paradise, the replication of the Garden of Eden on earth was complete.[58] Tursun Beg compares the garden, filled with pavilions, fountains, and *kauthar*-like pools, and planted with roses, both cultivated and wild, tulips, narcissus, jasmine, and herbs to the "Garden of Eden, underneath which rivers flow" (Koran, Sura 20:76), and to the legendary garden of Iram.[59] Kemalpaşazade lauds its elaborate fountains and circular pools of marble, reminiscent of those in paradise. Cafer Çelebi describes roses, tulips, and herbs admiring their own reflections in these pools. Mehmed II's court poet Hamidi compares the garden's cypresses and pines to the mythical trees of paradise, which bore fruits of rubies and pearls and emerald leaves, and its patterned lawns to ornamental brocades.[60]

In 1465 Kritovoulos described the outer garden:

> Around the palace were constructed very large and lovely gardens, abounding in various sorts of plants and trees, producing beautiful fruit. And there were abundant supplies of water flowing everywhere, cold and clear and drinkable, and conspicuous and beautiful groves and

meadows. Besides that, there were flocks of birds, both domesticated fowls and song-birds, twittering and chattering all around, and many sorts of animals, tame and wild, feeding there. Also there were many other fine ornaments and embellishments of various sorts, such as he [Mehmed II] thought would bring beauty and pleasure and happiness and enjoyment.[61]

A decade later, Angiolello provided another detailed description of it as a sort of botanical and zoological garden:

And here in this garden there are many kinds of fruit trees planted in order, and similarly pergolas with grapevines of many kinds, roses, lilacs, saffron, flowers of every sort, and everywhere there is an abundance of most gentle waters, that is, fountains and pools. Also in this garden are some separate places in which are kept many kinds of animals, such as deer, does, roe deer, foxes, hares, sheep, goats, and Indian cows, which are much larger than ours, and many other sorts of animals. This garden is inhabited by many sorts of birds, and when it is spring it is a pleasure to listen to them sing, and likewise there is a marshy lake which is planted with reeds, where a large number of wild geese and ducks dwell, and in that place the Grand Turk derives pleasure in shooting with his gun.[62]

In 1499 Arnold von Harff again described the garden "in which grow many rare trees and fruits, and in which rare wild animals run loose."[63] Menavino says its gardeners, mentioned in Mehmed II's *kanunname,* numbered "two hundred boys 15 to 20 years old, called *bostancılar,* that is, gardeners, who are charged with pulling out weeds that grow in the garden, sweeping it, watering it, and all the other things needed for the cultivation and beauty of the plants and herbs." The gardeners were divided into nine groups, each differentiated by a belt of a particular color; each group had its own separate dormitory, bath, and kitchen distributed along the outer wall of the palace.[64]

Enormous quantities of flowers and trees were ordered for the royal gardens from all over the empire in the sixteenth century. An account book of Süleyman I, dating from 1527–28, cites among the expenses of the "imperial garden" *(bāġçe-i ʿāmire)* travel and sustenance for officials sent to "bring back flowers from Tripoli and elsewhere," and for transporting tulip bulbs from Caffa, in the Crimea. A document of 1528–29 also mentions travel expenses "for bringing tulips from Caffa and diverse flowers from various places."[65] Süleyman also imported pomegranate trees from Aleppo and Diyarbakır and had them planted along the seashore.[66] A decree of Murad III from 1577 orders the governor of Caffa to send three hundred thousand tulip bulbs.[67] Another decree, from 1576, orders the qadi and chief gardener of Edirne to send twenty loads of rose bushes, wrapped in felt;[68] in 1593 another four hundred *kantar*s (48,000 pounds) of red rose bushes and three hundred *kantar*s (36,000 pounds) of other colors were ordered.[69] In 1579 five hundred thousand hyacinth bulbs were supplied by the governor of Uzeyr, who was paid by the treasurer of Aleppo;[70] finally, in 1593 the governor of Maraş had to send fifty thousand white and fifty thousand blue hyacinth bulbs.[71]

Flowers, usually planted in square beds, were found mainly around the kiosks; their grid pattern is shown on Dilich's bird's-eye view (Pl. 26b). The mid-seventeenth-century author La Croix calls them "quelques carrez de fleurs." They were surrounded by red wooden railings, and often featured wooden pergolas.[72] In 1573 Fresne-Canaye described the mixed grouping of flowers in these beds, which must have inspired the distinctive floral aesthetic that appeared in the decorative arts of the Ottoman court around the middle of the sixteenth century:

One can scarcely believe how much the Turks love flowers, how they always have them in their hands and turbans, and value them like a sacred thing. And if the Grand Signor has any tree that pleases him more than the others, he plants under its shadow many flowers of all types and scents. And in all his gardens there is such a quantity of all kinds of them that merely by extending one's hand one plucks a mixed and varied bouquet of all the colors that one can imagine. The alleys are lined with cypresses so high that their sight excites admiration; but they are narrow, for the Grand Seigneur always walks alone.[73]

About twenty years later Baron Wenceslas Wratislaw wrote of the outer garden of the Topkapı:

Here we saw most delightful spots, many kinds of flowers, most pleasant parterres and lawns, delightful vales, flowing streams, and an abundance of groves, not so much artificially constructed by men, as growing spontaneously by nature. Here goddesses formerly dwelt; here the muses had their seats; here learned men selected spots for meditation in private. Thus, after gazing on everything thoroughly, and gathering nosegays of sweet-scented flowers, we sincerely lamented that this most beautiful spot, and the whole of this delightful region, should remain in the power of the Turks.[74]

In 1610 the English traveler George Sandys observed that this garden contained "goodly Groves of Cypresses intermixed with Plaines, delicate gardens, artificiall Fountaines, all varietie of fruit-trees, and what not rare? Luxurie being the Steward, and the Treasure unexhaustible."[75]

Some European writers disapproved of the cultivation of vegetables, cucumbers, fruits, and melons in the palace gardens, but they were in fact an important source of revenue and represented a productive agricultural landscape.[76] According to an ancient custom of the Ottoman dynasty, the money made from selling the produce grown in the royal gardens (including those along the Bosphorus and Golden Horn) had to meet the expenses of the sultan's table. Menavino says that it was sold by the head gardener in the public square in front of the Imperial Gate: "When it is the season for fruits, he [the head gardener] has them gathered and sold in the piazza outside the seraglio, and he gives all the collected monies to the Grand Turk, who spends them for the expenses of his own mouth, for he says that these are well-acquired monies and not [coming] from the sweat of poor men." A 1505 inventory of the Inner Treasury lists one coffer of 150,000 *akçes* and another of 100,000 *akçes* as representing the proceeds of the royal garden.[77]

Besides the fields, vineyards, pastures, woods, and flower beds, the outer garden contained several pens and game preserves, filled with a variety of wild and domestic animals.[78] The sultan's private menagerie (complementing the one in the Hippodrome) was kept in a walled enclosure near the Rose Garden, by the Sea of Marmara (Pl. 10 *[36]*). It is mentioned in an account book of 1564–65 as the

115 Bayezid II watching an animal fight from a kiosk at the Topkapı Palace. From Lokman, *Hünername,* ca. 1584–85, TSK, H 1523, fol. 189r.

"animal keep" *(ṭoḳat ḥavlısı),*[79] and was probably installed in Mehmed II's time. He had similar ones at the Old Palace and in the Tokat Garden on the Bosphorus, where he and his successors went hunting.[80] A small wooden kiosk with wide eaves and wooden piers, called the Tokat Kiosk *(köşk-i ṭoḳat, ṭoḳat ḳaṣrı)*[81] in the seventeenth-century sources may be the one in which Bayezid II is shown in a miniature watching a fight between a lion, sent by the ruler of Tunisia, and a buffalo. The accompanying text says that he sat on a "gilded seat" at the "place of recreation *[teferrücgāh]* reserved for such events in his imperial palace" (Fig. 115).[82]

Both animal fights and hunts continued to be held in the outer garden of the Topkapı and the Old Palace throughout the sixteenth century (Fig. 116). Referring to Murad III, Lorenzo Bernardo writes, "He holds hunts in his garden, having first stocked it not only with deer and goats but also wild boar, bears, and lions, and standing at a window he watches his novices *[acemi oğlanı]* hunt. He also has birds of every kind brought there, and riding a horse in his garden he watches them fly; and in short, all the pleasures of the hunt that the other princes have in the countryside, he has within his seraglio and enjoys them at his convenience."[83]

In 1621 Deshayes de Courmenin described these hunts, which had distinct political overtones:

> He [the sultan] sometimes holds small hunts in his palace that are quite pleasant. He has many live wild boars caught, which they bring there into a place that is enclosed by canvas screens. When he wants to give them the pleasure, he has the Sultanas, eunuchs, and others whom he likes the most come there. He gives to each wild boar the name of one of his enemies, such as the King of Spain, whom he calls the Signor of Spain, the Duke of Florence, the Grand Master of [the Knights of] Malta, and others in this manner.[84]

According to Şeref's map, the area was still a menagerie *(arslanḫāne)* in the nineteenth century (Pl. 13). Nearby was stationed a group of gardeners called the "Corps of Sacrificial Sheep," who tended the sheep destined for sacrifice at each *bayram*.[85] A stone's throw away, on the Marmara shore, at the point where the sea and land walls meet, was the royal aviary (Pl. 10 *[37]*).[86] Atâ says that the feathers for the royal arrows were supplied by the swans, who were fed by gardeners attached to the Corps of the Aviary *(ḳuşḫāne ocāġı)*, adjacent to the Gate of Stables (Pl. 10 *[3, 37]*).[87] A woodcut from the *Nuremberg Chronicle* shows that around 1490 this site was occupied by a domed Byzantine chapel marked "S. Grovus" (Pl. 24). The same building also appears on later views of the palace (Pls. 22b, 31b), but its identity is unclear. Many monastic foundations were once located there, and Saint Grovus may have been a saint buried on this site.

Just as Mehmed II had converted other churches near the Hippodrome into a lion house and an elephant house, according to Angiolello,[88] he seems to have transformed this chapel into an aviary. The mid-seventeenth-century Armenian author Eremya Çelebi locates it between the Gate of Stables on the land wall and the Gate of the Fishing Station on the sea wall of Marmara: "Let us pass beyond the Gate of Stables, toward the south, you can observe a magnificent Greek church near the sea walls. This was once the Church of St. John, but now it is converted to an aviary *[kuşhane]*, and here various types of birds are fed ... a little further ahead along the seashore is the Fishing Station *[balıkhane]*." Eremya goes on to say that three saints were buried in the church, and he identifies one as "Saint Menas."[89] The names of the other two are mentioned in an eighteenth-century description by İnciciyan of the same aviary: "This building in which the birds of the palace are given shelter, was once an old church named after St. John the Baptist, being at the same time the burial place of the saints Menas, Ermoukine, and Karpos."[90] Hagia Karpos may well be the "S. Grovus" of the Nuremberg woodcut.

In 1699 the English clergyman Edmund Chishull saw "at the further end of the garden of the Seraglio ... the intire walls of an antient Christian church, and near to that the aviary of the Grand Signior, where I observed the hens of Grand Cairo, having blue gills and feathers curiously colored with grey circles, and in the center of each a spot of black."[91] Account books mention a number of pools near the aviary, one of them perhaps the reed-lined lake populated by wild geese and ducks, where Angiolello says Mehmed II practiced his shooting.[92] Both Matrakçı's miniature and Şeref's map show a large pool there (Pl. 13; see Fig. 101).

In one of the towers of the Byzantine sea wall facing Marmara, past the aviary, was stationed the Corps of Fishermen, in charge of the fish in the ponds and in the surrounding sea. They tended a fishgarth that was set up in a small bay, protected

116 Süleyman I hunting in the game preserve of the Old Palace. From Lokman, *Hünername,* ca. 1587–88, TSK, H 1524, fols. 88r, 88v.

from strong currents (Pls. 10 *[38],* 13. 14). In the 1550s Gyllius writes, "There is a fifth Port or Gate, where is built a Room, though it is only rafter'd, whence you may have the *Diversion* of seeing the Fish catch'd; as it is also a kind of Repository, where the *Grand Seignor's* Fishermen lay up their Tackle."[93] An account book of 1580 mentions "repairing the fishery of the royal fishgarth [and] rebuilding the stairs of its tower, and the sultan's dock."[94] A new wooden kiosk was built above this tower in 1610.[95]

In a 1686 illustration Scarella depicts the wooden fishing station, raised on piers in the middle of the sea, a dock, and some functional buildings along the shore, in front of two towers with conical caps (Pl. 31b). Eremya describes it at around the same time: "Further along the shore, inside the sea is the kiosk of the chief fisherman *[balıkçıbaşı köşkü].* In front of stretched fishing nets watchmen sit at the fishgarth. Here delicious fish are caught for the sultan."[96] The tall tower with a bay window seen on Scarella's drawing was probably the small royal kiosk known as the Fishery Pavilion (*ḳaṣr-i balıḳḫāne* or *balıḳḫāne ḳaṣrı*). Sometimes the sultans came to the kiosk to watch the fishermen cast their nets.[97] Deposed grandees were brought there to await the ship that would carry them off to exile.[98] A nineteenth-century inventory of its furnishings mentions a "royal seat on a raised platform," an "ablution chamber," a "small balcony attached to the kiosk," and "the room of the pashas," namely the waiting room where the disgraced dignitaries stayed until the boat arrived.[99] It was the task of the Corps of Fishermen to guard this kiosk and its temporary prisoners, as well as to catch fish for the royal table.[100]

The outer garden was used for other royal sports besides hunting. It had two large arenas, one below the kitchens on the side overlooking the Sea of Marmara, the other in front of the stables, facing the Golden Horn. The *Hünername* miniature shows the former with a pumpkin-shaped target attached to a pole in it, used by the sultan and his court to practice horseback archery (Pl. 10 *[32]*; see Fig. 56). It was known as the Maidan of the Gourd (*meydān-i ḳabaḳ* or *ḳabaḳ meydānı*) in the sixteenth century.[101] A stone marker with an inscription dated 909 (1503–4) praises Prince Ahmed's talent in mace throwing.[102] The seventeenth-century sources refer to it as the Maidan of the Cavalry (*meydān-i cündiyān*)[103] or the Javelin Maidan (*meydān-i cirīd* or *cirīd meydānı*).[104] Tavernier says it was used for the horseback javelin tournaments of grandees after Friday prayers.[105] The gardeners stationed near the maidan guarded its kiosks and cultivated the small gardens attached to them.[106]

In front of the Tiled Kiosk (Çinili Köşk), in the second large maidan, built over immense vaults, wrestlers and lion tamers performed on religious holidays before the sultan (Pl. 10 *[41]*).[107] Since the royal stables were connected to this maidan by a gate, it is likely that the sultan also inspected his horses there (see Fig. 46). Eighteenth-century sources mention polo among the various games played, which also included snowball fights between pages and lion watching.[108] This sand-covered playing field was known as the Sand Maidan (*ḳum meydānı*).[109]

The most important of the royal pavilions and the most elaborate formal gardens overlooked the Golden Horn. Sixteenth-century miniatures show that only this part of the outer garden was planted with rows of cypresses, unlike the side facing Marmara, directly below the kitchens and covered with meadows, vineyards, and vegetable gardens (Pls. 20b, 21b; see Fig. 56). The gardeners stationed near the meadow (*çayır*) on the Marmara side included the Corps of Vine Grafters, the Corps of the Haystore, near the Gate of Stables, and the Corps of Okra and Cabbage (two rival groups, thought to have been modeled on the Blue and Green factions of Byzantium who, when not tending their crops, practiced horsemanship in the Maidan of the Gourd). This area also housed the various corps of gardeners who tended the animal keeps, the aviary, and the fishing station that supplied the royal kitchens.[110] In it were a number of Byzantine cisterns and some cellars Sinan had built to store ice, tin for retinning cooking utensils, and copper, used for casting cannons and minting coins.[111] The Corps of Garbage Collectors was also housed there, in one of the Byzantine sea-wall towers, between the fishing station and the Cannon Gate on Seraglio Point. Eremya Çelebi writes, "Under this fortified wall, dirty waters flow into the sea. Nearby, from a hole in the wall the garbage from the kitchens and other departments of the palace is thrown out, scavengers *[arayıcılar]* who wander there poke through the rubbish in hope of finding some things.... Here, it is possible to turn up pieces of gold and silver, earrings, rings and precious stones carried by waters from the bath [i.e., the Large Bath]. Three times a year, these scavengers dive into the sea hoping for good luck and sift the sands with a sieve."[112] Evliya Çelebi calls these treasure hunters the "guild of scavengers" (*arayıcıyān eṣnāfı*), and Flachat claims that some of them made fortunes from the refuse of the palace.[113]

Nearby, along the Marmara shore close to the Cannon Gate, lived the Corps of the Windmill. Their dormitory, a windmill for grinding flour, storehouses for flour and wheat, a bakery, a rosewater distillery, an infirmary for gardeners, and a small mosque known as the Masjid of the Hospital, or of the Gardeners' Hospital (*Tabhane*, or *Bostancılar Tabhanesi Mescidi*; Pl. 10 *[29, 30]*) can be seen in a triangular enclosure outside the sea wall in Scarella's 1686 panoramic view (Plate 31b). The same triangular wall surrounding these utilitarian structures and a mosque with a single minaret and pitched roof appear in nineteenth-century photographs and plans (Pls. 13, 14; see Fig. 73), and the pyramidal roof of the mosque and its minaret can be seen in Matrakçı's miniature in the same place near the Cannon Gate (see Fig. 101).[114] According to Hafız Hüseyin Ayvansarayi, this small mosque, built by Süleyman I, was a communal prayer hall for all the gardeners who served the gardens on the Marmara side.[115]

A second mosque, on the Golden Horn, served the gardeners who tended the other half. It is known as the Green-Tiled Masjid (*yeşil kiremidli mescid*) and is near the dormitory of royal gardeners. Ayvansarayi attributes its construction to Süleyman I. Its name derived from a green-glazed tile (*çīnī kiremīd*) roof, which no longer exists; today, the mosque, rebuilt in the second half of the eighteenth century, has a lead-covered dome.[116] The neighboring dormitory housed the Corps of Royal Gardeners, who tended the flower gardens attached to the royal kiosks. The *Hünername* miniature identifies it as the Chamber of Gardeners (*bostāncılar odası*) and shows it as a cloisterlike building with an internal courtyard (Pl. 10 *[47]*; see Fig. 56). The same building is seen on several other late-sixteenth-century miniatures (Pls. 20b, 21b; see Fig. 93a).

This walled enclosure with towers is also seen on Melchior Lorichs's 1559 panorama (Pl. 25d) and on a 1590 Austrian panoramic view (Pl. 27). Both panoramas show a tall tower pavilion, attached to a walled enclosure, that may have been the chief gardener's residence. The chief gardener also had police functions; a prison for convicts brought to labor on construction projects around the palace was located near his quarters. The dormitory complex included a kitchen, bakery, and bath, as well as the Green-Tiled Masjid.[117] The complex dated from the time of Mehmed II and endured until the nineteenth century, when it was replaced by a medical school. The ruins of the bath and the rebuilt mosque still stand nearby (Pl. 13).[118]

Giovanni Battista Donato, after he saw the gardeners' dormitory in 1681, wrote, "There one can also see a nearly ruined church, in the vaults of which one can still see mosaics, and it now serves as the habitation for the above-mentioned gardeners."[119] In 1740 Flachat included the chief gardener's residence and a colonnaded "old palace," decorated with Byzantine mosaics, among the various buildings that could be reached from the harem gate, which opened onto the maidan by the Tiled Kiosk: "From there, one goes through different paths to the apartment of the Bostancı Başı [chief gardener] ... to the old palace, which is decorated with a beautiful colonnade and with mosaics. Some claim that this was the palace of Constantine; others assert with some likelihood that it was a famous college which the Byzantine emperors honored with a special protection."[120] Taken together, these descriptions make it clear that the dormitory complex of gardeners was some kind of converted Byzantine structure, possibly the church and monastery of St. Demetrius, near Seraglio Point, once elaborately decorated by the Palaeologi.

The Corps of Oarsmen, who rowed the sultan's ceremonial boat, had the greatest prestige of the outer-garden servants. They are mentioned in Mehmed II's *kanunname*.[121] The boathouse in front of the Green-Tiled Masjid, which they served, is called the *ḳāyıḳḫāne* or *ḳāyıḳḫāne-i ḫāṣṣa* in Süleyman's account books; in it the red-painted royal galleys were built and kept.[122] Lorichs's panorama shows it in 1559 as a long wooden building on the seashore, identified as "the house of the king's galleys, in which he takes rides" (Pl. 25d). The oarsmen's dormitory, bath, and kitchen were located near the boathouse (Pls. 10 *[46]*, 27–30a, 31a, 32a,c).[123] Şeref's map shows a number of workshops and warehouses in that area as well (Pl. 13).[124] An account book of 1527–28 mentions a "warehouse on the shore" (*anbār-i yālı*), and Sinan later built another "imperial warehouse" (*anbār-i ʿāmire*) there.[125] They appear to have been used for storing the boatbuilding equipment and other building materials. An account book of 1681–82 mentions "workshops for the sawmill, restorers, painters, and boatmakers near the boathouses along the New Imperial Palace's seashore." Ayvansarayi says that whitewashers, sawyers, and the makers of bows and arrows worked there as well.[126] Eremya Çelebi writes:

Further ahead [along the seashore] are the chief gardener's boathouse and the rooms where the chief restorer *[meremmetçibaşı]* and his men sit. All kinds of supplies required for repairing the palace are kept there. [The boathouse's] skilled workers are always ready to be called upon for any sort of repair in the palace. Further ahead are the residence of the palace's chief limeburner *[kireççibaşı]* and the rooms of the fettered convicts employed as construction workers. Adjacent to this is a prison where the convicts are heavily guarded. The chief gardener punishes those who disobey orders by having them beaten there.[127]

All these warehouses and construction-related workshops supplemented the ones attached to the imperial warehouse on the west side of the first court, and occupied with them a continuous zone extending along the land wall from the hilltop to the shore.[128]

At Seraglio Point, beyond the boathouse, was stationed the group of gardeners known as the Corps of the Cannon Gate (Pl. 10 *[48]*). Their dormitory was inside the double-towered gatehouse itself. In addition to guarding the cannons mounted in front of the gate, they acted as a kind of coast guard. One of their tasks was to throw stones to chase off boats that sailed too close to the royal shore pavilions. In 1573 Fresne-Canaye sailed along the shore near the palace and saw Selim II riding in the outer garden in the company of two or three pages, some mutes, and two dwarfs. After the sultan dismounted from his horse, he sat on a carpet-covered platform near Seraglio Point and the chief gardener handed him a bouquet of flowers. The Frenchman then saw no more because he had come too near, and the gardeners had begun to stone his boat (see Fig. 128).[129] The Cannon Corps also used boathooks to rescue the occasional unwary seafarer who fell out of his boat into the swift current of Seraglio Point, and freed ships from the strong current, using ropes and windlasses.[130]

The *Hünername* miniature shows the cannons under wooden sheds in front of the Cannon Gate. On the gate hangs what appears to be the skeleton of a tall man, a large fish spine, and the head of a beast (see Figs. 56, 126). Eremya Çelebi identifies these objects as a "large tortoise shell and a spine which is as long as two people, hanging horizontally."[131] Similar objects—said to be the leg bones of a stone-throwing giant and a large stone ball—hung at another gate on the Byzantine sea wall below Hagia Sophia.[132] Perhaps both were talismans protecting the gates from intruders.

The vast garden surrounding the palace had, then, a complex and populous organization complementing the outer services provided by the first and second courts. The palace on the hilltop dominated this microcosmic garden in which flowers, agricultural products, livestock, metals, and construction materials were gathered from various provinces categorically ordered, stored, and used. The plants and animals, though serving the monarch's pleasure, were essentially there to provide food for the royal table. The functional contents of the garden were at the same time a manifestation of the powerful sultan's control over nature and the resources of the lands under his rule. The raw materials deposited in the warehouses and cisterns were used up in the royal workshops that represented the various crafts; thus, in the garden work and royal pleasure were allotted their respective places. The outer garden fused idyll with economic activity in the manner of the Roman tradition exemplified by Hadrian's villa in Tivoli.

Antiquities were displayed in the outer garden as yet other signs of power and victory (the mosaic-decorated churches, converted to new functions, were viewed in the same way). Among these were sarcophagi, most of which appear to have been spoils from the Church of the Holy Apostles, where the Byzantine emperors had been buried (demolished to make way for Mehmed II's mosque complex), and the Goth's Column, which still stands in front of the third court's hanging garden (Pl. 10 *[26]*; see Fig. 114a,b). The latter, originally surmounted by a statue of Byzas, the founder of ancient Byzantium, commemorated the victory over the Goths with an inscription that reads: FORTUNAE / REDUCI OB / DEVICTOS GOTHOS / IC XC NIKA. It was preserved as a trophy of victory, reminding the viewer that the site of Mehmed's palace had once been the walled acropolis of Byzantium.[133] One of the many Byzantine sarcophagi used as basins for fountains could still be seen in the middle of the seventeenth century, near the Goth's Column; it had a low-relief carving of two angels holding a roundel of laurels.[134] Others are still *in situ,* but most of them have been taken to the Archaeological Museum, a modern building in the outer garden of the palace, across from the Tiled Kiosk. These cultural artifacts complemented the garden's natural collection in communicating a consistent message of power, as did the pavilions that Mehmed II had constructed in the outer garden.

TEN
The Pavilions of the Outer Garden

Fifteenth-Century Garden Pavilions: Metaphors of Universal Empire

When the main buildings of the New Palace were finished, Mehmed II ordered three pavilions to be built in the outer garden in differing architectural modes, representing the kingdoms incorporated into his world empire — a theme picked up again by Murad IV in the 1630s, when he built the Baghdad and Revan kiosks to commemorate his conquest of those two cities. Mehmed's three pavilions are shown on the Vavassore map (Pl. 23; see Fig. 6) and described by Angiolello in these terms:

> Around the palace is a garden that embraces all the three courts mentioned above.... In this garden are some small, vaulted churches, and the Grand Turk has had one of them, which is decorated in mosaic, repaired. And in this garden there are three pavilions about a stone's throw distant from one another, and they are built in various modes. One is built in the Persian mode *[alla Persiana]*, decorated in the mode of the country of Karaman, and is covered with wattle and daub; the second is built in the Turkish mode *[alla Turchesca]*; the third in the Greek mode *[alla Greca]*, covered with lead.[1]

In his description of the outer garden, Tursun Beg also identifies two neighboring pavilions built for Mehmed II in different styles. One was a "tile palace" (*ṣırça sarāy*), constructed in the mode of the Persian kings (*ṭavr-i ekāsire*); the other, across from it (*muḳābilinde*), was a pavilion (*ḳaṣr*) constructed in the Ottoman mode (*ṭavr-i ʿos̱mānī*). This last was a "wonder of the age," embodying the science of geometry.[2]

Mehmed's three pavilions may be regarded as the architectural counterparts to his medals and painted portraits with Latin inscriptions celebrating his victories over the kingdoms of Greece (Constantinople), Trebizond, and Asia (Iconium, or Karaman), in which the conquered kingdoms are represented by three emblematic crowns.[3] The sultan's invitations, in the winter of 1480, to a Venetian master builder and Florentine interior decorators for inlaid woodwork *(maestri d'intaglio e di legname, e di tarsie)* may have been related to a projected Italianate *alla Franca* pavilion in the palace, which would have been "both technically and decoratively European."[4] The presence at the sultan's court that year of Gentile Bellini, who is reported to have been involved in painting some rooms in the palace, makes this likely. Mehmed's hypothetical Italianate pavilion may well have been conceived to celebrate the conquest of Otranto in the summer of the same year (August 1480).[5] It was the sultan's grand plan to seize the rest of the Italian peninsula and to unite East and West by conquering Rome, but he died in 1481, too soon to achieve it.

Of Mehmed's three pavilions only the Persian one, known today as the *Çinili Köşk* (Tiled Kiosk), remains (Pl. 10 *[41]*; see Fig 6).[6] It overlooks the Golden Horn from the edge of a hanging garden supported by high vaults, under which an artificial lake — seen in the *Hünername* miniature (see Fig. 56) — once mirrored its west facade. The maidan in front of the Tiled Kiosk's east facade, around which Mehmed II's three pavilions were apparently grouped, could be reached from the first court, the royal stables of the second court, and the Gold Path of the harem. It forms a lower platform parallel to the west side of the first court, to which it is con-

117 Aerial view of the royal stables of the second court and the Tiled Kiosk in the outer garden.

nected by a path and gate, once guarded by a special group of gardeners (see Figs. 46, 117). Mehmed favored this part of the garden both because of its view and because it was well away from the kitchens, whose garbage was emptied into the Sea of Marmara. The raised terrace of the Tiled Kiosk enjoyed about the same view as the walled hanging garden in front of Mehmed II's Privy Chamber, which also had a collection of pavilions reflected in a large pool.

It is tempting to identify one of the two kiosks overlooking the large pool in a *Hünername* miniature (see Fig. 53) as the Ottoman pavilion, which Tursun Beg locates in the outer garden, "across from" the Tiled Kiosk. These two neighboring kiosks, resting on a high retaining wall, can be seen in several sixteenth-century miniatures (Pls. 20b, 21b; see Figs. 93a,b), as well as in European panoramic views (Pls. 25d,e, 26–28, 30a). On Melchior Lorichs's 1559 panorama, the Tiled Kiosk can be identified by its apselike projection. The building with a pyramidal pitched roof, to its right, below the Church of St. Irene, may be the Ottoman pavilion (Pl. 25d,e). A similar pavilion with a pitched roof is depicted on the same spot south of the Tiled Kiosk on the Vavassore map (Pl. 23; see Fig. 6), perhaps the site now occupied by the modern Museum of Ancient Near Eastern Archaeology, which replaced an older structure (Pl. 10 *[39]*). An unidentified building occupies this site on the southwest corner of the maidan, to the south of the Tiled Kiosk, in Dilich's bird's-eye view (Pl. 26b) and in an anonymous nineteenth-century painting (Fig. 118).

Dilich's print and the anonymous painting also

118 Anonymous painting of the Tiled Kiosk, showing structures, since destroyed, around its maidan. From T. Öz, *Guide to the Museum*.

depict a third pavilion, perhaps the Greek one, across from the Tiled Kiosk, on the present site of the Museum of Classical Archaeology (Pl. 10 *[40]*). The pavilion shown in this area on Vavassore's map has domes and towerlike elements, suggesting that it was constructed in the Byzantine manner, not in the post-and-lintel system of classical Greek monuments that Mehmed is said to have admired on the Acropolis of Athens.[7] Unfortunately, neither textual nor archaeological evidence allows us to determine what the Greek pavilion was like. It is unclear whether it was adapted from an older Byzantine structure, or newly built for the sultan. Menavino does mention an ancient cloister near the Cape of St. Demetrius (i.e., Seraglio Point) that had once belonged to the priests of Hagia Sophia, and that Mehmed II had converted into his summer residence. It had "an antique colonnade with more than two hundred chambers," but this was more likely the mosaic-decorated complex identified by later observers as the dormitory of gardeners, discussed in the last chapter. Angiolello clearly distinguishes Mehmed's three pavilions *(Palazzi)* from the Byzantine churches *(Chiesiole)* he restored in the outer garden.[8] This suggests that the Greek pavilion was in all likelihood a new building commissioned by Mehmed II in the architectural mode of a defeated empire. Placed around a maidan with other pavilions, built in the Ottoman and Persian styles, it could be read as a statement of victory, reflecting the international character of Mehmed's universal empire.

TILED KIOSK

The Tiled Kiosk is the Persian pavilion, which Angiolello says was decorated in the mode of the Karaman region (Pl. 10 *[41]*; Figs. 119–21). Tursun Beg provides its original name, the "tile palace" (*ṣırça sarāy*); Menavino comes close by referring to it as "*Sercessarai*."[9] The same name appears on a late-sixteenth-century fountain inscription inside the

ish poems composed in its praise, which show that the heavenly associations of the Tiled Kiosk, built as a variant of the Hasht Behisht pavilion type, were recognized by contemporary observers. Typical of them is Veliyüddin Ahmed Pasha's long poem, which says that the lofty pavilion reproduced the structure of the heavens on earth with its arches and multiple domes. Its gilt tiles resembled the sun and the moon, the cypresses painted on its walls were like the Tuba tree in paradise, and the projecting alcove (*ṣāhnişīn*) where the sultan sat on his throne, provided a vision of the gardens of paradise, which had a pool (*ḥavż*) and a waterwheel (*dolāb*).[25] A poem by Cafer Çelebi also refers to this "magnificent throne at the head" of the pavilion, cited in a seventeenth-century repair document as "the noble throne of the tile pavilion."[26]

Cafer says that the arches of the pavilion bent so as to observe more closely the walls, full of charming paintings.[27] Except for some elaborately carved plaster in a dome on the lower story, the painted decorations of the Tiled Kiosk have completely disappeared. We know, however, that in general Timurid pavilions featured narrative murals with subjects ranging from reception ceremonies, hunting scenes, and military campaigns to erotic themes. The figural wall paintings of Timur's palaces in Samarkand are mentioned in texts. Uzun Hasan's Hasht Behisht palace in Tabriz was decorated with gilded ultramarine tiles and narrative scenes— battles, hunting expeditions, and Ottoman embassies—identified with Persian inscriptions. At Isfahan the palace of Uğurlu Mehmed Mirza, who joined the Ottoman court in 1474, also featured murals with historical scenes, including the beheading of a grandee.[28] It is likely that the walls of the Tiled Kiosk were also decorated with narrative scenes, but the poems mention only flowers and cypresses that supported its paradisal associations.

As the poems suggest, the Tiled Kiosk was mainly used as a royal pleasure pavilion, located as it was beyond the ceremonial boundaries of the palace, though it may occasionally have been used for royal receptions—at least before the *kanunname* was codified in the last years of Mehmed II's reign. The poets mention nocturnal entertainments (*bazm*) where musicians played, and the sultan drank wine under the starry night sky with his royal pages. He also sought recreation (*tafarruj*) in it with the "virgins of paradise."[29]

İSHAKİYE KIOSK

Although Mehmed built most of the important outer garden pavilions to overlook the Golden Horn, at least one of them faced the Sea of Marmara. It is shown on Şeref's plan near the sports maidan and is identified as *Isḥāḳiye köşki*, the Kiosk of İshak Pasha, but it is often referred to in the sources as the Kiosk of Sultan Mehmed the Conqueror (Pl. 10 *[28]*, 13). After his first grand vizierate in the 1450s, İshak Pasha served as Mehmed II's grand vizier for a second time between 1470 and 1472; it is thus probable that the kiosk was built around the same time as the Tiled Kiosk. No trace of it remains, but inscriptions on eighteenth- and nineteenth-century stone archery targets near the Maidan of the Gourd tell us that the sultans used to practice shooting from the *ḳaṣr-i Isḥāḳiye*.[30]

Matrakçı's miniature (see Fig. 101) shows a small colonnaded structure crowned by a conical lead roof in the outer garden facing Marmara which may be the kiosk. The archives provide some data as well: a document of 1682 locates the "pavilion of the Father of Conquest, His Majesty Mehmed Khan" near the Meadow Pavilion (i.e., the Pearl Kiosk, built along the Marmara shore later, for Murad III; Pl. 10 *[31]*),[31] and mentions repairing its wooden roof (probably provided with an internal dome) and lead-covered eaves, polishing its marble columns and capitals, its red-and-green wooden throne, and its fountain with a marble basin. It was built of rubble masonry (*kārgīr dolma dīvār*), and featured many wooden details painted red and green. A nineteenth-century document mentions replacing the eleven green canvas curtains with red linings that protected its porticoes, suggesting that it may have had twelve columns.[32] An eighteenth-century repair document mentions its repainted eaves, lead sheets replaced on its roof, and tiles (*kāşīler*) refixed.[33] That it was rather small can be deduced from the minimal furnishings listed in 1710 as being in the "Kiosk of the Father of Conquest Sultan Mehmed": a royal seat *(taḫt-i hümāyūn)* with a long mattress and four small cushions in the back, and an old Uşak carpet.[34] According to Atâ a group of gardeners called the Corps of İshakiye guarded the kiosk, which was demolished together with its neighbors in the second half of the nineteenth century.[35]

Sixteenth-Century Shore Pavilions: The End of Universalism

In the sixteenth century four new pavilions were added along the seashore, outside or on top of the fortified walls" (Pl. 10 *[31, 44, 45, 49]*). The first was built for Selim I early in the sixteenth century, the remaining three by the grand vizier Sinan Pasha for Murad III, in the last quarter of the same century. Sinan Pasha, the conqueror of Yemen, had accumulated immense treasures in various military campaigns before he was appointed to the post of grand vizier; through the pavilions he paid for, he must have hoped to win the sultan's favor at a time when financial troubles led to the frequent downfall of grand viziers. Sinan himself was deposed and reinstated five times. These shore pavilions demonstrate that the secure empire no longer needed the symbolic protection of the fifteenth-century castellated walls that gave the palace a medieval aspect. In this period—which roughly coincides with the development of the High Renaissance villas in Europe—the secluded sultan's private domain on the hilltop was extended to the seashore. Stretching outward from the medieval Byzantine sea wall these new pavilions commanded a majestic view. Domenico Hierosolimitano writes of them:

> There are around the wall which extends along the sea four rooms *[stanze]* which are inhabited by servants and are called in the Turkish language kiosks *[chiostri]*, that means coops *[gabbie]*, to which the Grand Signor often goes to watch the sea, and in the time of Sultan Murad [III], Sinan Pasha built one of them (besides many others which are of great value) for one hundred fifty thousand sequins.[36]

The sultans usually frequented these pavilions in the company either of a few pages or of female attendants, sometimes inviting a dignitary or scholar to discuss politics, philosophy, or religion. A miniature depicts Süleyman seated on a carpet with a sheikh in a domed pavilion in front of the harem with his favorite pages, dwarfs, and gardeners, wearing conical hats nearby (Fig. 122). Another miniature (Fig. 123) shows the same sultan praying in the outer garden near a pavilion along the seashore, in the company of his pages, a religious scholar, and one of his sons. The tall building in the background shows a striking similarity to the Inner Treasury of the third court, with its projecting balcony and double-arched loggia (see Fig. 72).

Sixteenth-century miniatures also represent enthroned sultans being entertained in pavilions in the company of pages, buffoons, and dwarfs (see Fig. 56), and sometimes depict extraordinary audiences, similar to receptions at the Chamber of Petitions, given to some privileged guest (Figs. 124a,b). When the sultan announced his intention to visit a pavilion, the cypress-lined royal alley leading to it was cleaned and its fountains put in operation.[37] When these outings involved women, they were called *ḥalvet,* or seclusion, and all the gardeners evacuated the garden, which was kept under the strict surveillance of black eunuchs using spyglasses. On these occasions the gardeners had to wait along the quay outside the sea walls.[38] Even the muezzins of the neighboring mosques were not allowed to mount their minarets. When women were to travel by boat to other royal gardens, a temporary passageway was made out of canvas walls held on both sides by gardeners, leading from the harem down to the shore.[39]

Like the garden pavilions built for Mehmed II, Selim I's Marble Kiosk on Seraglio Point incorporated into its design elements from the styles of newly defeated kingdoms and exemplified the universalism of a rapidly expanding empire. The shore pavilions built for Murad III by the architect Davud, however, no longer quoted the styles of conquered kingdoms; instead, they signaled the establishment of a classical Ottoman pavilion type, decorated with İznik tiles. The formative period of the empire

122 Süleyman I conversing with a sheikh, in a domed pavilion in front of the harem. From Lokman, *Hünername,* ca. 1587–88, TSK, H 1524, fol. 232v.

123 Süleyman praying in the outer garden, in front of a shore pavilion, with the Treasury-Bath complex of the third court seen in the background. From Lokman, *Hünername,* ca. 1587–88, TSK, H 1524, fol. 212r.

had come to an end and imperial expansion had ceased. The Ottoman empire now became a territorially defined entity that had to express its identity through its own distinctive architectural style.

Unlike the monumental, multichambered garden pavilions of Mehmed II, which Angiolello called *palazzi,* palaces, those built in the classical Ottoman style were small domed structures that Domenico Hierosolimitano appropriately called *stanze,* the equivalent of the Ottoman *oda,* or room, often used interchangeably with *köşk,* kiosk. The shore pavilions built by Davud, like Süleyman I's pavilions in the hanging garden of the third court, were essentially domed halls with windowed projections, incorporating the natural surroundings as much as possible. Increasing royal seclusion made monumental pavilions like the Tiled Kiosk—suited to the public nature of Timurid ceremonial and its Safavid or Mughal offshoots—impractical. The sultan could not use his garden pavilions for lavish

124*a* Murad III interrogating his vizier Osman Pasha at the Shore Kiosk. From Lokman, *Shahanshāhnāma,* 1592, TSK, B 200, fol. 156v.
124*b* Murad III in the Shore Kiosk, rewarding the vizier Osman Pasha with a robe of honor for his report about the defeat of the rebellious Crimean Khan. From Lokman, *Shahanshāhnāma,* 1592, TSK, B 200, fol. 149r.

banquets and festivities because he no longer appeared in public. What he needed were buildings for his own contemplation and pleasure in the company of a few slave pages or concubines. Even his rare consultations with guests in them were entirely private occasions. The peculiar character of Ottoman ceremonial dictated a preference for smaller pavilions, with a main domed throne hall and a few tiny dependent chambers, reminiscent of the layout of the Chamber of Petitions.

MARBLE KIOSK

"With marble columns and colored marbles sent from Egypt, [Selim I] caused to be built an unequaled kiosk *[köşk]* close to the garden, by the seashore, in front of the Cannon Gate of the imperial palace's garden," wrote Lokman, adding that this shore pavilion was commissioned together with the redecoration of the Privy Chamber with Cairene marble revetments (Pl. 10 *[49];* Figs. 125, 126).[41] Both projects used the spoils of the Egyptian campaign, which had vanquished the last of the Mamluk sultans in 1517 (see Figs. 82a,b).

According to the late-sixteenth-century historian Hoca Sadeddin, whose father was one of Selim I's favorite pages, a plague in Edirne in 1518 forced the sultan to return to Istanbul, where his treasurer, Defterdar Abdüsselam—an Egyptian Jew whom the sultan had brought to the capital as his commis-

125 Marble Kiosk in front of the Cannon Gate, detail from Pl. 31b.

126 Marble Kiosk in front of the Cannon Gate, detail from Fig. 56.

sioner of royal expenditures — had been overseeing the kiosk's construction. When the sultan complained about its high cost, Abdüsselam told him that he had paid for it himself. The pleased sultan bestowed three robes of honor and some land near İzmit (Nicomedia) on him for this service.[42] We learn from another sixteenth-century historian, Lutfi Pasha, that this structure was known as the Marble Kiosk *(mermer köşk),* and that Selim I died on the road back to Edirne in 1520, before it was completed.[43]

Lutfi's remark suggests that the kiosk may have been completed at the beginning of Süleyman I's reign, and some eighteenth-century European sources do attribute its construction to him.[44] However, Lokman says that the kiosk was finished in 1519.[45] Sixteenth- and seventeenth-century Ottoman sources consistently refer to it as the "Kiosk of Sultan Selim Khan" or the "Kiosk of Sultan Selim near the Cannon Gate."[46]

The Marble Kiosk appears in a number of sixteenth-century illustrations, which show a single-storied pavilion with a pyramidal lead roof, built adjacent to the sea wall by the Cannon Gate, and surrounded on three sides by a colonnade of twelve marble columns (Pls. 25a, 27, 31b, 32a; see Figs. 125, 126). European travelers praised these precious marble columns, which were reused in a two-story kiosk that replaced the Marble Kiosk in the eighteenth century. According to the nineteenth-century traveler Edward Daniel Clarke, these twelve green columns were "of that beautiful and rare breccia, the *viride Lacedoemonium* of Pliny, called by Italians *il verde antico.* These columns are of the finest quality ever seen; and each of them consists of one entire stone. The two interior pillars are of Green Egyptian breccia, more beautiful than any specimen of the kind existing."[47]

Scarella's panoramic view shows that in Selim I's kiosk six of these columns were used on the main facade; the narrower lateral facades had three each (see Fig. 125). The kiosk probably had a main royal hall with an internal wooden dome and smaller dependent rooms, including a latrine, at the back.[48] Miniatures from the *Hünername* suggest that the arcades had cushion voussoirs typical of Cairene architecture (Figs. 127a,b). In addition to the columns from Egypt the portico dadoes were faced

127*a* The coffin of the grand vizier İbrahim Pasha (d. 1536) being carried out of the Cannon Gate by the Marble Kiosk. From Lokman, *Hünername,* ca. 1587–88, TSK, H 1524, fol. 165v.
127*b* Selim I practicing archery at the Marble Kiosk. From Lokman, *Hünername,* ca. 1584–85, TSK, H 1523, fol. 217r.

with thin strips of marble paneling in the Mamluk mode, resembling those visible today in the Privy Chamber (and the lost marble revetments of Süleyman's Chamber of Petitions and public Council Hall; see Figs. 82a,b, 126). They are mentioned in a document of 1681 as the "marble revetments of porphyry on the walls of the kiosk." The document also mentions "changing the lead sheets on the roof," "renewing the marble balustrades between the columns," and "repairing the arm of His Majesty's seat."[49] Other seventeenth-century account books mention the same royal seat inside the kiosk.[50] In one of the *Hünername* miniatures wooden lattices painted red surround the garden of the kiosk to protect its privacy (see Fig. 126), as they do in several European images (see Figs. 125, 128). Account books refer to them as the "lattices *[ḳafes]* near the Cannon Gate," and periodically mention renewing their red-ocher paint.[51]

The Venetian secretary Francesco della Valle, who arrived at Istanbul in 1531, praises the magnificence of this prestigious kiosk: "Above that point [Seraglio Point] there is the seraglio of Süleyman, with a perfectly superb loggia raised on columns that shine with marvelous artifice, to which he oftentimes comes for diversion, and this loggia is of a grandeur and pomp equal to his state."[52] Today it

128 The shore of the Topkapı Palace, facing the Golden Horn, with *(top)* gardeners throwing stones at boats coming too near in front of the Marble Kiosk, and *(bottom)* the Shore Kiosk. Lewenklau Album, MS. Vienna, ca. 1586, Österreichische Nationalbibliothek, Cod. 8615, fols. 122v, 123r.

may seem strange that a tiny pavilion could be seen as representing the magnificence of Süleyman's world empire, but clearly that judgment took into consideration the symbolic significance of its site on Seraglio Point, where two seas and two continents meet, its lavishly gilded decorations, and its precious marbles, the spoils of conquest. An anonymous Venetian *Relazione* of 1579 is, however, considerably less enthusiastic about the kiosk: "By the harbor of the Seraglio there is a loggia, about which they say great things: yet it has no more than some columns."[53] The French antiquarian Petrus Gyllius wrote:

'Tis very large, has a Porch with an arch'd Roof before it, is gilded, and adorn'd in a surprizing manner with Persian Paintings, supported with Pillars of *Ophitick* Marble, and looks into the *Bosporus*.... If he [Süleyman I] has an Inclination to take a View of his *Seraglio,* from that Point of Land which projects so far into the Sea [Seraglio Point], and which, as I observ'd, divided the *Bosporus;* here he beholds it in all its Glory, strengthen'd with large Pillars of Marble, and fann'd with gentle refreshing Breezes, where he often sits with small Osier Lattices before him; so that, like another *Gyges* [the fabled king of ancient Lydia, whose ring gave him the power of invisibility], he discerns all that sails near him, though he himself is visible to no one.[54]

This description demonstrates that the symbolic significance of the marble pavilion's siting was transparent even to foreigners. In 1607, Thomas Gainsford described the kiosk *(Caska)* as a "delicate banquetting-house" with "a roome of great riches, yet small capacity, set all over with inlayed worke of mother of pearle, rubies, opals, emeralds, and had the metall beaten into thin plates layd counter-company, which with the borders answered one another in graceful proportion."[55] It was apparently decorated with thin plates of gilt inlaid with jewels, as were the Privy Chamber and the Chamber of Petitions in the third court, all of them works of the Persian architect Alaüddin, whose bejeweled aesthetic was characteristic of the 1520s and the 1530s.[56]

The "Persian Paintings" mentioned by Gyllius

are also noted by later travelers,[57] and by Hoca Sadeddin, who, in his history of Sultan Selim I, says this about them:

> One day, as he [Selim I] was having the kiosk along the seashore, which is known as Sultan Selim's Kiosk *[Sulṭān Selīm köşki]*, built, he descended to the garden and came to look at this pavilion *[ḳaṣr]*. Painters were occupied with painting it. A portrait painter *[muṣavvir]* had depicted the well-proportioned figure of the late Sultan Mehmed [II].... When the mute showed that picture *[taṣvīr]*, the sovereign said: "In fact, he must have wanted to portray the late Sultan Mehmed, but has not been able to capture his likeness. The deceased used to make us sit on his blessed lap in our childhood; his noble countenance is still in our memory: he was falcon-nosed. This painter has not captured his likeness at all.[58]

The passage suggests that the walls of the kiosk were painted with historical scenes. This is not unlikely, for a letter written from Edirne by Tommaso di Tolfo to Michelangelo on 1 April 1519, urges the latter to come to the Ottoman court because Selim I, unlike his father, Bayezid II, is not opposed to the figural arts.[59] Selim I's appreciation of figural painting is also apparent in several other royal kiosks built for him along the Bosphorus, whose historical paintings are described by foreign observers. Busbecq writes, "Well, we had a delightful voyage [along the Bosphorus], and I was allowed to enter some of the royal kiosks. On the folding doors of one of these palaces, I saw a picture of the famous battle between Selim and Ismael, King of the Persians [the Çaldıran war of 1514, when the Safavids were defeated], executed in masterly style, in tesselated work." In 1587, Lubenau saw a kiosk with an artistic painting *(kunstliche Tafel)* that depicted the same victory.[60] This was probably the one built for Selim I in the Karabali Garden near Beşiktaş, a typical Persian quadripartite garden *(chahār-bāgh)*, divided into quarters by two intersecting main paths lined with trees, each quarter further subdivided into smaller square flower beds (Fig. 129).[61]

The Marble Kiosk, too, appears to have been painted with historical murals in the manner of Persian pavilions, which Selim I certainly saw when he conquered Tabriz in 1514. The sultan greatly admired the mural paintings of Uzun Hasan's Hasht Behisht palace there, and brought Persian painters, tile makers, and builders (including the architect Alaüddin) with him from the conquered city.[62] It was probably they who executed the murals of the Marble Kiosk. Its Persian paintings and Egyptian marbles filled the kiosk with reminders of Selim I's victories over the Safavids in 1514 and the Mamluks in 1517.

The Marble Kiosk, built on a platform on the very spot where the two seas merged, functioned as a belvedere, as the identical legends of Melchior Lorichs's and Dilich's panoramas show:

> By the [Cannon] gate Sultan Selim had had a beautiful building of marble built, so that he could occasionally enjoy himself and observe the ships arriving from all places. On the right he had the White Sea or Propontis, now generally called the Sea of Marmara, from which arrive Christians from Spain, Venice, Genoa, Italy, Nicomedia [İzmit], Arabia, Egypt, and Syria and also from other places which lie beyond that sea; at the left, the Black Sea or the Euxine ... from which many kinds of heathen people of Asia as well as Europe arrive down the Danube and other rivers.[63]

Lokman remarks that Selim I frequently sat there on a chair to listen to reports from the various parts of his empire. It was there that he rewarded the messengers of Şehsuvaroğlu Ali Beg, who brought him the head of a heretical rebel named Kızılbaş Celal. The sultan questioned one of the rebel's followers to find out why he had joined up with this heretic, who had claimed to be the Mahdi. The man answered that Celal's skill in archery had convinced him of his superhuman powers. A miniature depicting this event shows Selim, seated in his shore pavilion, shooting arrows at a target to demonstrate that he is as skilled with the bow as the heretic was, while still remaining a faithful servant of God (see Fig. 127b). After watching the sultan's feats, the rebel's follower admitted his error, and the sultan decided to punish him with imprisonment rather than death.[64] Lokman narrates this ep-

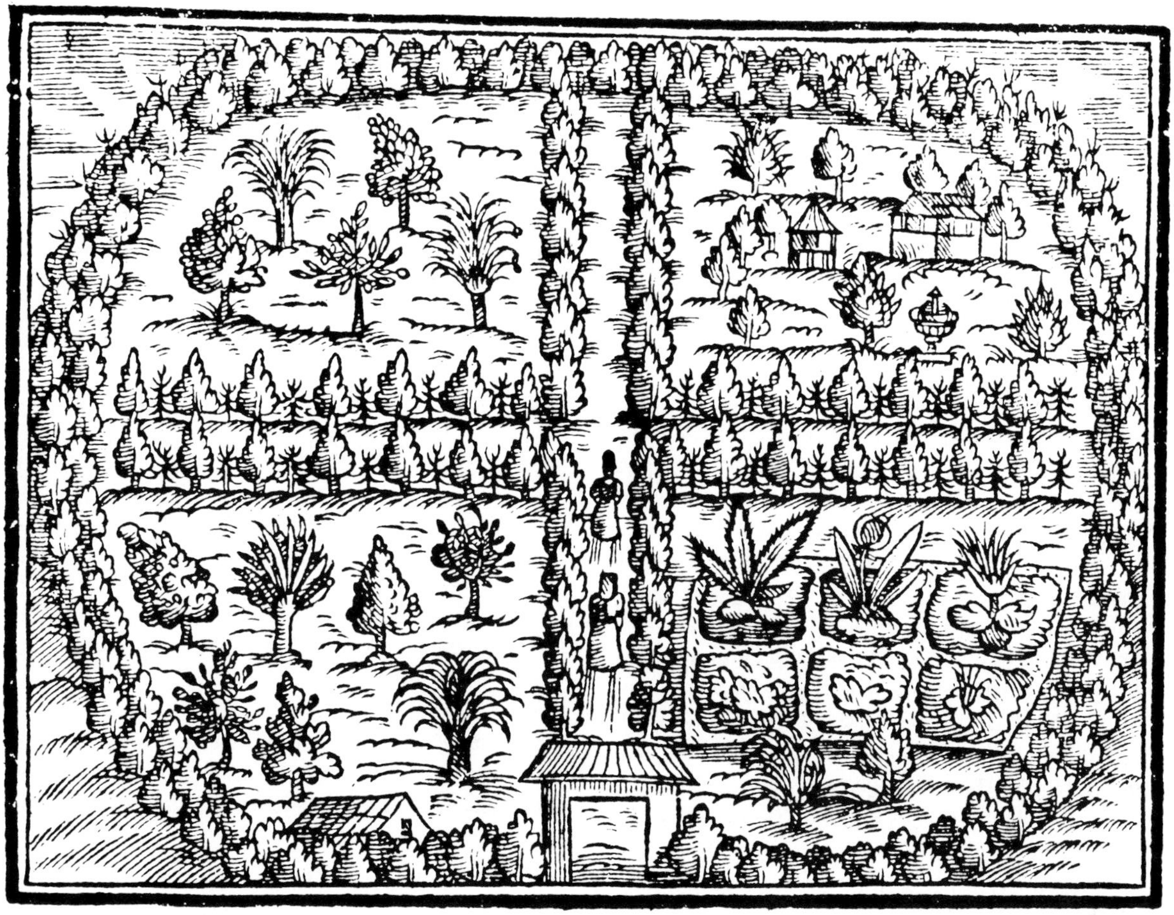

129 Schematic drawing of the Karabali Garden on the Bosphorus. From Schweigger, *Ein newe Reyssbeschreibung auss Teutschland nach Constantinopel und Jerusalem,* p. 127.

isode as an example of the sultan's justice, so at least on this occasion the Marble Kiosk was used as a court of law. It brought the otherwise secluded ruler into contact with the outside world, since it was built beyond the palace walls. A 1638 document ordering some repairs even refers to it as "the kiosk of justice at the Cannon Gate."[65]

Seventeenth-century rulers continued to frequent the Marble Kiosk with their wives, concubines, and musicians. On those visits the black eunuchs waved handkerchiefs as a warning that the sultan was there and threw large stones at boats passing too close, supplementing the efforts of the gardeners at the Cannon Gate.[66] The French Orientalist Antoine Galland describes one of these occasions, when the Queen Mother arrived to watch a French ship come into the harbor, while the gardeners threw stones at the overly curious, who offended her privacy.[67] Until Murad III had his more monumental pavilions constructed along the shore, Selim I's Marble Kiosk remained a favorite spot for royal outings. It was eventually replaced by the monumental summer palace called the Cannon Gate, or *Topkapı,* built in the eighteenth and nineteenth centuries and destroyed by a fire in 1862–63.[68]

PEARL KIOSK

The Pearl Kiosk was built by the grand vizier Sinan Pasha for Murad III between 1588–89 and 1591. It stood atop the Byzantine sea wall facing Marmara, between the windmill and the fishing station (Pls. 10 *[31]*, 13, 14). It was known as the Pearl Kiosk (*incüli köşk*[69] or *incüli ḳaṣr*[70]), after exquisite pendant globes with clusters of pearl-strung tassels that hung from its dome. There was a great fashion for pearls in Murad III's reign, and several royal decrees demanding large pearls from the governors of Baghdad, Basra, and Bahrain were issued.[71] Sometimes the Pearl Kiosk was called the Kiosk of Sinan Pasha (*Sinān Pāşā köşki*[72] or *Sinān Pāşā ḳaṣrı*[73]) after its builder, or the Meadow Kiosk (*çayır ḳaṣrı, ḳaṣr-i çayır,* or *çayır köşki*), after its location.[74] There are no known sixteenth-century illustrations of it, but it can be seen on drawings from the seventeenth century onward (Pl. 31b; Figs. 130, 131). It was demolished in 1871 to make way for a railroad which the government deliberately laid out to pass along the outer garden of the abandoned palace, as a symbol of Westernization.

Today, only its vaulted basement, with a fountain built into it, remains. The fountain's carved-stone Turkish verse inscription states that Sinan Pasha "built this unequaled pavilion *[ḳaṣr]* high" on the sultan's order, and that the architect Davud exercised his talents to make it artistic. It asks those drinking water from it to pray for the sultan, and provides the chronogram "life-bestowing water," to yield the date 997 (1588–89).[75] The date, however, refers solely to the fountain, which must have been built along with the basement, and not the entire kiosk, which took another two years to complete. In a royal decree issued between April and May 1590, the sultan orders the qadi of İznik to oversee the production of tiles "needed for a newly built kiosk in my imperial palace." A royal gardener was sent there with fifteen thousand *akçes* and a model *(numūne)*, on the basis of which the ceramicists were ordered to produce the tiles.[76] Another decree, from September 1590, orders the qadi of Karahisar to send raw materials to İznik for the tiles that were being prepared for the imperial palace.[77]

130 Detail from Pl. 31b, showing the Pearl Kiosk.

Lokman writes that the kiosk Sinan Pasha built for the sultan with his own money was completed in 1591. It stood solidly on top of a tower of the sea wall and resembled the mansion of paradise with its pleasant waters, breeze, and windows overlooking the garden on one side, and the sea on the other. With its high lead dome reaching to the skies and its gilt decorations, the kiosk resembled the Khawarnaq, an ancient Near Eastern palace built by the Lakhmid ruler Nu'man (d. ca. 418) for his Sasanian suzerain, and famed for its domed construction echoing the structure of the heavens.[78] Another contemporary historian, Selaniki, describes the "lofty pavilion" *(ḳaṣr-i muʿallā)*:

131 Watercolor illustration of the Pearl Kiosk with the kitchens and Treasury-Bath complex in the background. From J.N. Huyot, *Croquis de voyages,* 1817–20, MS. Paris, Bibliothèque National, Fr. Nouv. Acq. 5080, pl. 7.

His Majesty the world-protecting Sovereign had desired the construction of a pavilion with no peer, near the wharf of the Gate of Stables in the imperial palace, on top of the city walls of Istanbul, along the seashore, so that it would overlook both the horsemen's Maidan of the Gourd, inside the imperial palace, and the sea. For that purpose, the grand vizier Sinan Pasha summoned the chief of the world's architects, Davud Agha. To obtain the materials required for the construction of this pavilion through royal decrees, he provided a substantial amount of gold from his own funds. Working many days with great effort, he caused to be built a lofty pavilion, unequaled [in splendor], which became an exemplar to the world. In the month of Şa'ban in 999 [May, June 1591], artisans completed the above-mentioned pavilion, notable for its elegance and beauty. The gilt finials *[ʿalemler]* of its exterior were fixed, and its glitter dazzled the glances of the literati and common folk alike. It was so delightful that words fall short of its description. Its interior was decorated with tilework *[kāşī-kār],* gilt *muqarnas [mukarnes-i ḥal-kārī],* and gilded paintings *[zer-endūd nuḳūş].* It was furnished with silk carpets, embroidered spreads, gold-embroidered cushions, and jeweled pendant globes of mirror *[mücevher ṭob avīzeler ve āyineler]* encrusted with jewels and pearls.[79]

According to the seventeenth-century historian Hasanbeyzade, the "lofty pavilion" *[ḳaṣr-i bülend]* had a dome *[ḳubbe]* studded with infinite stars *[encüm-i bī-pāyān]* and ornamented with colorful paintings and shining jewels: "From this dome representing the revolving vault of the heavens hung bejeweled and gilded pendant globes with pearl-strung tassels that resembled the celestial spheres." The windows were inscribed with beautiful poems *(tevārīḫ-i zībā)* and *qasidas,* praising the kiosk *(ḳaṣā'īd-i ḳaṣriyye).* The monumental arched portals and window frames were all silver gilt. The balustrades of the veranda in front of the kiosk were of white marble. Sinan Pasha had furnished it with floor spreads and cushions of gold cloth, gold-embroidered brocade, atlas, velvet, and silk, and Persian silk carpets. The week-long festivities organized by the grand vizier for the kiosk's inauguration included concerts, sports activities, boat races, and fireworks.[80]

Selaniki says that the sultan rode to the kiosk with pages walking on either side of his mount and the grand vizier in front, holding a scepter. The sultan so admired Sinan Pasha's gift that he regretted it was not "inside the imperial palace." He then bestowed three robes of honor on the grand vizier. The admiral who had supervised the construction received two; the chief architect, secretary, city commissioner, officers of the grand vizier and admiral, and chief overseer of the galley slaves were given one each. Coins were scattered from gold and silver trays; then came a banquet accompanied by music. Inside the kiosk, the sultan, served by royal pages, ate alone off gold plates; the guests ate in the garden, seated on precious rugs spread on the ground, or in tents. The next day, the sultan watched a race between the boats of some grandees from the new kiosk. The grand vizier's boat won the first prize. On the third day, horsemen displayed their prowess on the Maidan of the Gourd, and there was another boat race. On the fourth day, the garden was curtained off and the harem women were given a banquet and a tour of the kiosk.[81]

Seventeenth-century drawings show the kiosk with a pyramidal roof (Pls. 22b, 31b; see Fig. 130), but this was later replaced with a domical vault whose curved surfaces tapered to a pointed finial (see Fig. 131). The mid-seventeenth-century page Üsküdari says the kiosk was "covered with a pyramidal cap of lead,"[82] and a document recording repairs between March and April 1681 mentions the same cap, surrounded by wide eaves, but says it was demolished by royal decree and "replaced with a new domical vault."[83] The dome mentioned in the sixteenth-century sources must have been a wooden dome beneath the original pyramidal cover, which gave the kiosk the appearance of a tower on top of the castellated sea wall. In 1599

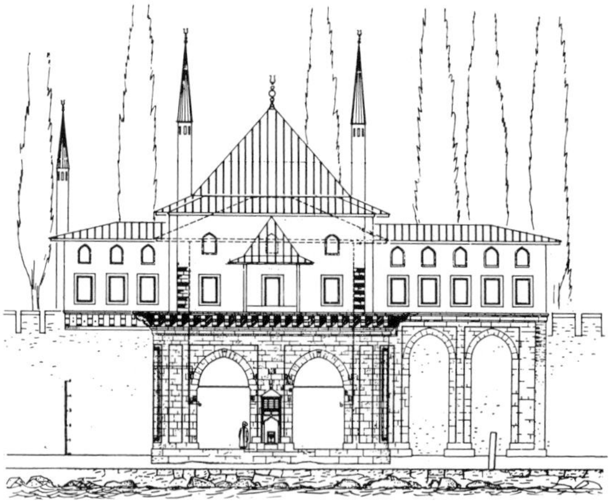

132 Hypothetical reconstruction of the Pearl Kiosk. From Eldem and Akozan, *Topkapı*.

Dallam, who installed Queen Elizabeth's clock organ in the Pearl Kiosk, provides a detailed description of the building:

The waye was verrie pleasante throughte the garthens, whear did grow store of siprus trees and many other good frute trees in verrie comly and desent order. Beinge paste the gardens, we entered upon a faire grene, wheare we founde som galland Turks ridinge horses on the easte sid of that grene or plain upon the wale of the surralia. Close to the sea sid Dothe stande a prittie fine litle buldinge which theye cale a Cuske [kiosk], made for a bancketinge house; but espetially, as I persaved, it is a place wheare the Grand Signor dothe use to meet his Congquebines twyse in the weeke. It is finely covered with Leade, and bulded squear on the topp; in the midle a litle square tour like a peramadease [pyramid] on a greate heighte, and on the top of that a litle turrett well gildede, and on the side nexte to the sea a faire large gallarie wheare men may stande and se bothe up and doune the rever of Hellisponte, and lik wyse over it into Asia.

On the other 3 sids towards the grene ar verrie larg pentazis [penthouses], supported with fine marble pillers, the flore spred with fair carpites, the roufe under the pentas verrie Curiously wroughte withe gould and collors; but cominge into it it is a little wonder, I cannot duly discrib it, but the roufe is a round hollo.[84]

Unfortunately, the next page in Dallam's diary, containing a description of the kiosk's interior, has been lost.

R. Demangel and E. Mamboury's excavations after the First World War, which explored the Byzantine remains of the Mangana quarter near the kiosk, yielded a large number of İznik tiles. Eldem's partial excavation in 1964, combined with the visual and written sources, makes a hypothetical reconstruction of the rest of the kiosk possible (Fig. 132)[85] It was built on a monumental arched basement; its central domed hall (approximately eleven meters wide), crowned by the pyramidal cap, was flanked by side wings. In the mid seventeenth century Joseph Pitton de Tournefort wrote, "It is built on arches that support three halls covered with gilded domes."[86] Three minaretlike chimneys, visible in nineteenth-century drawings, show that each hall, crowned with an internal wooden dome, had a fireplace. Hasanbeyzade mentions a seaside terrace with a marble balustrade, which can be seen in several drawings. Eldem discovered remnants of this terrace or veranda, supported by a row of large stone brackets; it extended along the entire facade and was paved with large slabs of stone.[87] The small bay window in the center of the sea facade on Scarella's drawing was later replaced by the larger projecting alcove seen in nineteenth-century drawings (see Figs. 130, 131). The vaulted basement with a fountain is the only part of the pavilion that remains today.

Eldem's excavations yielded little information about what the garden facade may have looked like. The architect A. I. Melling's cruciform plan of the kiosk, drawn in the early nineteenth century (Pl. 14), shows the central domed hall with four projections. The eighteenth-century Armenian author İnciciyan describes the kiosk as having five domes, suggesting that the projecting alcoves facing the garden and the sea were also covered with internal domes that gave the kiosk a cruciform plan.[88] The centralized, cross-shaped pavilion, raised on a high battlement that was incorporated into a vaulted basement, ideally served the function of a belvedere from which one could survey all directions. To the south, next to the sea wall, was a simple, low building with a tiled roof; this was the dormitory for the gardeners attached to the kiosk's service. The Pearl Kiosk's carefully proportioned architecture owed a great deal to Davud's earlier experience during the 1580s in renovating the harem, where the Imperial Hall and the royal bath next to it are also set on a high, vaulted basement and fronted by a veranda (with projecting balconies) that rests on a row of brackets under a wide eave (Pls. 30a, 32a,c).

In addition to the central throne room, the Pearl Kiosk had rooms in the side wings for the favorites, black and white eunuchs, and the harem matrons, a prayer room, a kitchen, a small bath, and latrines. Inside the throne room there were low sofas on both sides of the seaside alcove, which also had its own cushioned sofa, mentioned in an eighteenth-century inventory of the Pearl Kiosk's furnishings as "the imperial seat facing the sea."[89] On the garden side, sofas flanked the main gate facing the meadow. Outside the gate an open, domed baldachin projected from the center of a raised terrace (probably featuring a columned portico), supported from the garden on marble pillars; it was also furnished with cushions. Inventories refer to it as "the legged royal seat overlooking the meadow."[90] In 1763 this was described in a royal journal as an "external silver royal seat facing the maidan"; it had replaced an older one in 1747.[91]

In the eighteenth century the central domed space of the throne room was furnished with cushioned sofas, large Uşak and Persian carpets, and a royal throne with a domed canopy, from which hung four silver globes *(sīm ṭob-i taḫt)*. Wall niches held silver and Chinese porcelain objects; there was also a fountain with four large and two small silver bowls and copper balls playing on top of its water jets. It was probably in the center of the hall, below the dome, with its nine pendant globes strung with pearls *(incü püskülli āvīze ṭob)*.[92] The exact numerical correspondence of these pendants to the nine celestial spheres demonstrates that the contemporary descriptions of the dome as a replica of the dome of heaven cannot be dismissed as mere hyperbole. Descriptions in *Hadith* literature of bejeweled waterfront pavilions in paradise, with bulbous domes of pearl, must also have reinforced the

Pearl Kiosk's heavenly allusions, which its poetic inscriptions no doubt stressed.

A separate prayer space with a mihrab had another "pendant globe with pearl tassels" hanging from its dome. Its floors were spread with small Uşak prayer carpets *(seccāde-i Uşaḳ)*.[93] The presence of this prayer hall in the kiosk was what prompted Ahmed I to have Dallam's organ, with its automated figurines, destroyed. Mustafa Safi, the sultan's imam, wrote that its strange figures and queer representations, suited to heathens' temples, could "not be tolerated in a place of prayer and mansion of the caliphate."[94]

In 1593–94 the British ambassador Edward Barton recounted that Murad III used to visit the kiosk several times a week to perform his prayers and to watch ships:

Hear the agent appointed the master of the *Ascension* to stay with the shippe untill a fitte winde and opportunity served to bring her about the Seraglio to salute the Grand Signor in his moskyta or church: for you shall understand that he hath built one neere the wall of his Seraglio or pallace adjoyning to the Sea side; where unto twice or thrice a weeke hee resorteth to perform such religious rites as their law requireth: where hee being within few days after, our shippe set out in their best manner with flagges, streamers and pendants of divers coloured silke, with all the mariners, together with most of the Ambassadours men, having the wind faire, and came within two cables length of this moskita, where (hee to his great content beholding the shippe in such bravery) they discharged first two volies of small shot and then all the great ordinance twise over, there beinge seven and twentie or eight and twentie pieces in the ship.[95]

A similar display took place in 1599, when another English ambassador, named Thomas Glover, arrived at the port of Istanbul in a ship called the *Hector*. Dallam describes how Mehmed III watched the ship's arrival from the Pearl Kiosk:

Heckter, our ship, made hire salutation to the Great Turke, thare called Grande Sinyor, on the northe side of the Surralya, the Grande Sinyor beinge in his Cuske [kiosk], upon the wale which is close to the sea.

This salutation was verrie strange and wonderfull in the sighte of the Great Turke and all other Turkes ... our gonores [gunners] gave fiere, and discharged eighte score great shotte, and betwyxte everie greate shott a vallie of smale shott; it was done with verrie good decorume and true time....

The seconde day, the Grand Sinyor desieringe to take a better vewe of our shipp, he came in his goulden kieke [caique] upon the watter, and wente round a boute the shipp; but he came so sodonly that his beinge there was not knowne till 2 or 3 houres after.

One houre after him came the Sultana his mother, in the lyke manner....[96]

Dallam says that Murad III used to come to the Pearl Kiosk twice a week with his harem and describes how one day the sultan paid an unexpected visit to it, while he was installing the organ:

By chance I caled to my drugaman [translator] and asked him the cause of theire runinge awaye; than he said the Gran Sinyor and his Conquebines weare coming, we muste be gone in paine of deathe; but they run all away and lefte me behinde, and before I gott oute of the house they weare run over the grene quit out at the gate, and I runn as faste as my leggs would carrie me aftere, and 4 neageres or blackamoors cam runinge towardes me with their semetaires drawne; yf they could have catchte me theye would have hewed me all in peecis with there semeteris.... Now, as I was runinge for my life, I did se a litle of a brave show, which was the Grand Sinyor him selfe on horsbacke, many of his conquebines, som ridinge and som on foute, and brave fellowes in their kinde, that weare gelded men, and keepers of the conquebines; neagers that weare as black as geate [jet], but verrie brave; by their sides great semeteris; the scabertes seemed to be all goulde.[97]

In the eighteenth century the sultan often visited the kiosk with women or pages, to watch javelin contests on the maidan, to pray in the little mosque, or simply to enjoy the view and watch the ships embark and make port. Sitting on one of the thrones, he would sip coffee while listening to music.[98] After distributing gold coins among his attendants and drinking coffee, he performed his afternoon prayers, and went off to visit yet another kiosk.[99]

Another spectacle the sultans enjoyed was watching Christian pilgrims visit a nearby miraculous fountain *(ayazma)*, believed to have curative powers, on the Feast of the Transfiguration (6 August). Its source was a well in the palace garden near the ruined Church of the Savior, still visible today on the sea wall. In the middle of the seventeenth century the Chevalier Laurent d'Arvieux wrote:

> This place was formerly occupied by a church, a wall of which is preserved where the remnants of some crosses can still be seen. Very nearby is a fountain where the Greeks go on the day of the Transfiguration; this is one of their devotions which so resembles a carnival that it entertains the Grand Seigneur and some of his court. The Greeks hold the water of this fountain to be miraculous; they make their sick drink from it, and after having dug deep pits in the sand, they bury them there up to the neck, and it is said that many regain their health there.[100]

Eremya Çelebi describes how the afflicted would bury themselves in the sandy quay *(kumluca)* in front of the Pearl Kiosk, and Greeks and Armenians would play drums and horns. While they amused themselves eating, drinking, and swimming, Sultan Murad IV—in a gesture of generosity and tolerance toward his non-Muslim subjects—would scatter coins from behind the window shutters, without showing himself to them.[101]

The Pearl Kiosk remained mainly a private retreat, although from the seventeenth-century onward rulers occasionally met state dignitaries there.[102] One day in 1595, Murad III went there and ordered his musicians to perform a song; its lyrics said, "I am sick, come, destiny, take my life tonight," and as they sang, some ships from Alexandria fired their guns to salute the sultan as custom required. The explosion was too powerful: the windows of the kiosk were shattered and the whole building shook. The sultan, himself ill, took this as an omen, and he died that very night.[103]

SHORE KIOSK

Murad III so admired the Pearl Kiosk that he asked his grand vizier, Sinan Pasha, to rebuild another shore kiosk, originally built for Bayezid II across from Galata, in the same style (Pl. 10 *[44]*). It had already been renovated by the admiral Kılıç Ali Pasha, but the sultan found the results unimpressive.[104] Again Davud was appointed architect, and work began in June 1591. The historian Selaniki writes:

> The kiosk of the late Sultan Bayezid—may God bless him—which is comparable to this beautiful pavilion [Pearl Kiosk] had been restored from its foundations up by the late admiral Kılıç Ali Pasha. It was demolished, and the construction of a lofty kiosk superior to it was ordered in its place. A noble decree was issued to the greatest engineer of the age, the chief architect Davud Agha. He was ordered and reminded that, given its location on the seashore, he should devote extreme care to make it firm to the utmost degree, with strong foundations. It was begun at the end of Şa'ban in the year 999 [13–22 June 1591]; its provisions and expenses were likewise to be covered at the grand vizier's expense.[105]

The kiosk that Bayezid II had originally built is mentioned in sixteenth-century sources as the Kiosk of Sultan Bayezid.[106] Several drawings show that it was raised on a platform jutting into the sea (Pl. 25c; see Figs. 101, 128). It had a pyramidal lead roof (probably surmounting an inner wooden dome), surrounded by wide overhanging eaves and supported on wooden struts. Lorichs's panorama identifies it as "the king's small pleasure house."[107] A repair document of 1572–73 cites the expenses for renovating the piers of its foundations, pavement, and balustrades, and for whitewashing its walls and ceilings.[108] It was a relatively simple building with many wooden details, and must have appeared too modest for Murad III, who ordered Kılıç Ali Pasha to rebuild it in 1583. The reconstruction was extensive: historians refer to it as a "rebuilding from the foundations up."[109] The result can be seen in the *Hünername* miniature executed around 1584 and on a panoramic view of around 1590 (Pl. 27; see Fig. 56). The rebuilt kiosk was surrounded by a wooden portico with wide eaves and surmounted by a lanterned pyramidal roof (probably featuring an inner wooden dome underneath), decorated with a gilded finial. Like several kiosks in the summer palace of Üsküdar, visible on two seventeenth-century maps, it had a pagodalike appearance (Pls. 22b, 30b). It was so completely overshadowed by the splendid Pearl Kiosk, then just recently completed, that it was demolished once again and rebuilt in 1591.

This next replacement is the wide-eaved kiosk with a lanterned dome depicted for the first time in a panoramic view published by George Sandys in 1610 (Pl. 28). It is also shown in later seventeenth-century views and numerous panoramic views from the following centuries (Pls. 10 *[44]*, 22b, 29, 30a, 31a, 32a,c). Unlike its two predecessors, which had jutted into the sea, this one had a wharf in front of it, artificially constructed on wooden piers and columns.[110]

Selaniki writes that the "lofty pavilion" (*ḳaṣr-i ʿālī*) ordered rebuilt on the site of the Kiosk of Sultan Bayezid was completed on 4 Şevval 1001 (4 July 1593). He adds that the chief architect, Davud, started its construction during the grand vizierate of Sinan Pasha (23 June 1591–2 August 1591). After his deposition, the grand viziers Ferhad Pasha (3 August 1591–5 April 1592) and Siyavuş Pasha (6 April 1592–29 January 1593), who replaced him, also devoted a great deal of money and effort to the building. It was finally finished after Sinan Pasha was reinstated (1 February 1593). The pavilion, commonly known as the Shore Kiosk (*yalı köşki* or *yalı ḳaṣrı*), was also called the Kiosk of Sinan Pasha or the Kiosk of Sultan Bayezid. The ulama and other pious men (probably prominent sufis) were invited to its inauguration banquet. When the sultan arrived, animals were sacrificed and alms were distributed to the poor.[111] Grand Vizier Sinan Pasha himself, the chief architect Davud, and various other officers were given their rewards on July 17, 1593.[112]

Most of the history of this kiosk's construction can be traced from an account book that records its daily costs in materials and wages. Extracts from it have been published, but all of its more than two hundred pages deserve attention. It covers expenses incurred between 1 Ramadan 999 (23 June 1591) and 25 Cumada II 1000 (8 April 1592) by Sinan Pasha and Ferhad Pasha. It was compiled by Siyavuş Pasha's manager, Kethüda Mustafa Beg, to keep track of previous expenses, and does not include construction that went on during Siyavuş Pasha's tenure and Sinan Pasha's second term in office.[113] The account book actually records expenses for two pavilions (it uses the Arabic dual form of *ḳaṣr, ḳaṣreyn*)[114] built at the same time. The other was a tower pavilion that once occupied the site of the present Basketmakers' Kiosk, just behind the shore pavilion. The latter is referred to as the "lofty pavilion," the "new pavilion at the Shore Gate," or the "imperial pavilion at the Shore Gate" (Pl. 10 *[45]*).[115]

As always, many of the building materials had to be brought from afar. Iron beams and nails came from Samakov; white and red marbles from the Marmara Islands, Darıca, and Rodoscuk (Tekirdağ); tiles from İznik, and lead from Thessalonika. The lead of the demolished "old pavilion *[ḳaṣr-i ʿatīḳ]* of the late Sultan Bayezid Khan" was also reused.[116] A royal decree of 23 June 1591 commands the qadis of Thessalonika and Sidrekapsa to send three thousand *kantar*s of lead by ship;[117] a firman of 6 January 1592 orders the qadi of İznik to warn Osman, the chief of ceramicists, to stop the production of tiles for merchants, because the chief architect, Davud, was complaining that it delayed the delivery of the imperial tiles.[118] In another firman of the same date the sultan orders the qadi of Gelibolu (Gallipoli) to send thirteen experienced non-Muslim carpenters—whose names are specified by Davud—"to work on my imperial pavilion under construction."[119] A similar decree, issued on 14 February 1592, orders the qadi of Istanbul and the chief architect to recruit the carpenters and masons required for "the imperial pavilion ordered

133 (opposite) Hypothetical plan and elevations of the Shore Kiosk, from Eldem and Akozan, *Topkapı*.

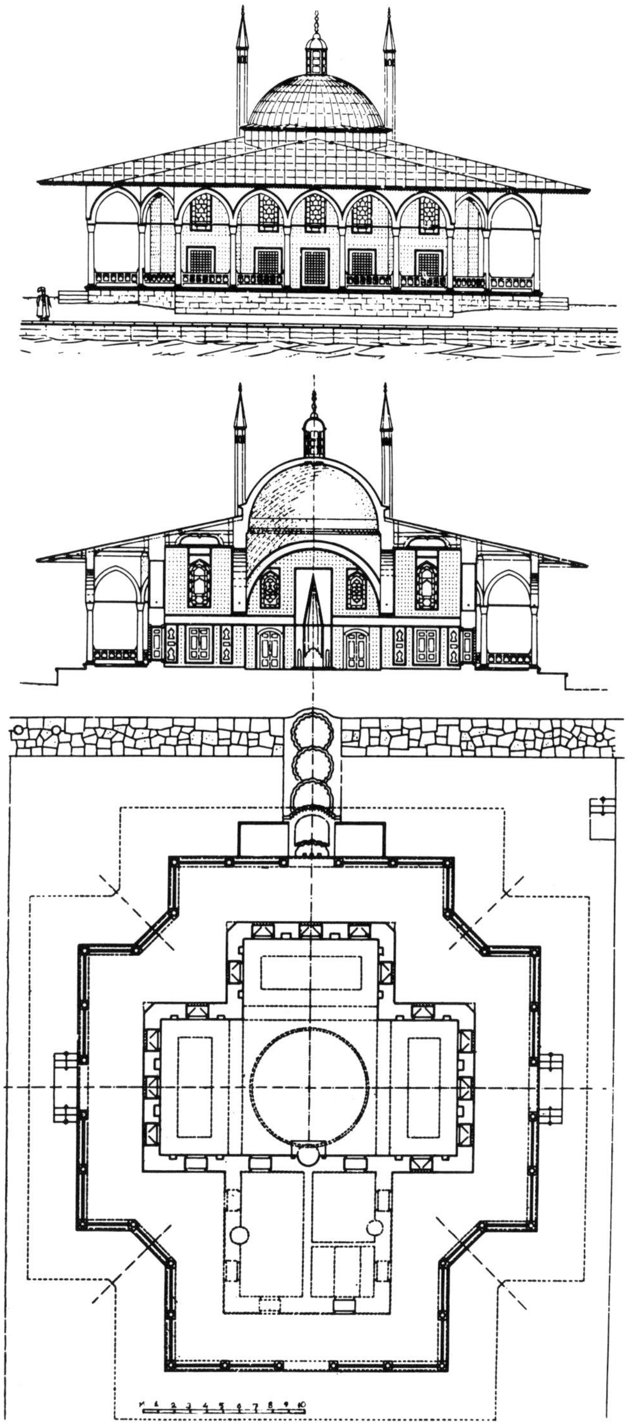

to be built anew on the shore." They are asked to inquire through the imams of each district in Istanbul about construction projects going on in various neighborhoods, and to take carpenters and masons employed on them away to work on the imperial pavilion.[120]

Most of the masonry core of the kiosk had been finished by the point where the incomplete account book ends; the latest date recorded is 25 Cumada II 1000 (8 April 1592). A second unpublished account book from the personal archives of Sinan Pasha, compiled by the kiosk's financial supervisor *(emīn-i binā')* Yusuf Agha, covers its final expenses between 15 Cumada I 1001 (17 February 1593) and 7 Receb 1001 (7 July 1593). It confirms that the kiosk was completed in Şevval 1001 (July 1593) by Sinan Pasha, who had commenced its construction.[121] Taken together, the two account books allow us to reconstruct the entire building. Using only information from the first book, Eldem has shown that the domed kiosk had a cruciform plan and was surrounded by a portico *(dihlīz)* with thirty-four white marble columns (Fig. 133).

This arcade had voussoirs *(ḳālıb-i kemerhā)* of alternating red and white marble, thirty simple white marble capitals *(ser-sütun-i sāde)*, and four more expensive *muqarnas* capitals *(ser-sütun-i muḳarnes)*.[122] The throne room *(oda-i ḫāṣṣ)* consisted of a central domed hall *(ṣoffa-i kebīr)* with three windowed projecting alcoves *(şāhnişīn)* facing the sea, forming a T-shape.[123] In a fourth alcove at the back were a prayer chamber *(ḫāne-i ʿibādetḫāne)*, a small room *(ḫāne-i küçük* or *oda-i sağīr)*, and other dependencies, including a latrine.[124] The T-shaped main hall was surrounded by eleven windows whose recesses were flanked by pairs of *muqarnas*-decorated white marble fountains. It had a large white marble cupboard on its east wall. On the lateral sides were two large white marble doors opening onto the portico; the pavilion, raised on a high platform, was reached by marble stairs that led to these two doors. The first account book also lists plain marble windows without built-in fountains, doors, and cupboards in the small dependent rooms.[125] It gives a detailed inventory of 5,887 assorted tiles, featuring *ḫitāyī* (chinoiserie) and *rūmī* (arabesque) motifs, and seminaturalistic grapevine, tulip, and marbled designs. All were produced in İznik between 10 November 1591, and 14 February 1592, and brought to Istanbul by the gardener Hasan Çavuş.[126] There are no references in this first account book to the fireplaces or to the lanterned dome surrounded by wide eaves, from which it may be inferred that the kiosk was incomplete.

The second account book covers expenses for decoration, including the gilding on the fireplaces, seven brass chains to be hung from the large dome, thirty-six brass chains for the small domes, woodwork for the ceilings and the furniture, and marble for doorframes, windows, cupboards, and balustrades.[127] This document also mentions a fountain in the central domed hall, a smaller fountain in the head gatekeeper's room, an ablution room, a large gilded pendant globe for the central dome, and a small globe for the other room.[128] A kitchen of rubble masonry, probably a separate dependency for the special group of gardeners, known as the Corps of the Shore Kiosk *(yalı köşki ocāğı)*, was attached to the kiosk's service.[129] Expenses are listed for materials used by unspecified court painters for decorating the kiosk, including sponges, white lead, red lead, various kinds of containers, sheets of Istanbul paper, cobalt blue, vermilion, turpentine, scissors, lining, verdigris, gum, isinglass, and lavish amounts of gold leaf.[130]

The largest portion of this second account book is taken up with the expenses for İznik tiles manufactured between February and June 1593, using designs sent from the capital. The royal gardener Hasan Çavuş brought them to Istanbul in several shipments. The chief of ceramicists, Osman, was paid for the "tiles of the imperial pavilion" between 23 February and 4 March 1593. At the same time, a non-Muslim silk textile designer named Bali *(Bālī ẕimmī eş-şehīr be-kemḫācı)* received payment for the designs he had made for tiles *(resm-i kāşī)*. A month later, the painter Mehmed Çelebi *(Meḥmed Çelebi ressām)* was paid for forty-nine drawings *(rusūm)* for the tile designs *(resm-i ḫuṭūṭ-i kāşī)*.[131] In other words, the revetments for this kiosk followed a unified program, and were not mass-pro-

134 Adalbert de Beaumont, mid-nineteenth-century engraving of the marble-columned portico surrounding the Shore Kiosk. From Eldem, *Köşkler,* 1:181.

duced, as were some of the ceramic revetments hastily purchased for the renovated harem, but made to fit specific dimensions. That a textile artist contributed to their design helps to explain the close parallels between classical İznik tiles and Ottoman textiles.

The tiles themselves are listed in various categories: inscription tiles, border tiles, grapevine tiles, tulip tiles, *rūmī* tiles, marble-patterned tiles, *muqarnas* tiles, cornice tiles, skirting tiles, cresting tiles, beveled border tiles, double-beveled corner tiles, small or large tile roundels, and curved lunette tiles. Tile revetments were also made for particular places in the kiosk, such as a fountain, a small door, the fireplace in the head gatekeeper's room, and the fireplace in the main domed hall.[132] The kiosk's tiles must have resembled those of the Takkeci İbrahim Çavuş Mosque in Istanbul (built ca. 1592), celebrated for their high-quality arched panels alternating with windows, and for their unusual grapevine motifs. A nineteenth-century print by Adalbert de Beaumont shows that they were also used in the outer dadoes of the kiosk (Fig. 134), which are mentioned in a repair document of 1813 as "exterior tiles."[133]

In 1672–73 the French Orientalist Antoine Galland described the Shore Kiosk in some detail:

This is a building which on the exterior is square, with a small dome in the middle of its lead roof. Inside, before entering the apartment, one encounters a gallery that extends around the interior apartment; it is open and supported by marble pillars, and is about ten feet wide. From there one enters a large room which on the sea side

135 Engraving of the Shore Kiosk. From Choiseul-Gouffier, *Voyage pittoresque.*

has a *sofa* [projecting alcove] accompanied by two others on the sides, and across from it a fireplace with a hood covered from top to bottom with bronze plaques. The *sofas* were not furnished with their cushions and mattresses; all of them were stacked one on top of the other in a corner. The ceiling of each *sofa* consisted of a small dome painted with arabesques in gold and colors, and these three *[sofas]* accompanied a much larger one, which was raised in the middle of the kiosk, ornamented and enriched with the same paintings. The rest of what one saw on the walls was white marble or tiles painted with branches and arabesque inscriptions, which took the place of the tapestries we use. There were also jets of water in three or four places, with a sort of small cascade, which they operated when His Excellency was there.... The Ambassador was then allowed to go through a door near the fireplace into a closet where there were three large chairs of gilt wood, made for the Grand Seigneur to sit on.... From there one went to the private area across from the door, in front of which was a cupboard filled with a variety of furniture.[134]

Another contemporary French visitor, Guillaume Grelot, wrote: "There is nothing in the world more fitting: the marble, the columns, the artificial jets of water, the precious carpets, the galleries that extend all around, the charming view that one has from all sides outside, and the richly gilded and carved woodwork inside make this kiosk a place of enchantment."[135]

When its portico curtains were pulled down to protect its decorations, the pavilion resembled a

lead-covered pyramidal roof and probably had a single room; only a new staircase in its interior is mentioned in the accounts.[159] It was painted with murals by a distinguished group of court painters, under the supervision of the chief court painter, Lutfi Agha. Fourteen painters worked for a total of 1,042 workdays "painting the new pavilion above the tower of the castle." They were each paid six *akçes* a day; their chief *(ser-naḳḳāşīn)*, Lutfi Agha, his leading assistant *(ḫalīfe-i naḳḳāşīn)*, Ali Çelebi, and the painters Osman, Ali Beg, İbrahim, and Ayas worked 86 days each. The rest of the group, Sefer, Hamdi, Ümmi, Mehmed, Frenk, Acem Yusuf, Tiflisi, and Divane Ahmed worked between 55 and 70 days each, for the same pay. The materials used included red lead, vermilion, glue, sandarac resin, cobalt blue, yellow, brushes, gum arabic, lining, verdigris, size, turpentine, soot, ocher, and indigo.[160] Unlike the Shore Kiosk, in which a lavish amount of gold leaf was used to complement a rich tile program, the tower pavilion was simply painted with primary colors, an indication of its lesser status.

Although the functions of the original tower pavilion are not known for certain, it does not appear to have had any ceremonial purpose. Perhaps it was used by the harem women for watching the departure and arrival of the fleet; this would explain why it was built close to the Shore Kiosk, from which the sultans watched the same ceremonies. Certainly the second Basketmakers' Kiosk—with its cruciform, domed throne hall, resembling those of the Pearl Kiosk and the Shore Kiosk—was used for that purpose, besides functioning as a royal belvedere from which the sultans watched passing ships.[161]

Together with the three sixteenth-century shore pavilions built earlier, the new Basketmakers' Kiosk exemplified an original Ottoman pavilion type, specifically designed for the ceremonial code of the Ottoman court and the topography of Istanbul.[162] The seascape of the promontory on which the palace stood thus became decked with shore pavilions, no longer protected from the outer world within walled gardens, but standing beyond and atop the palace walls. The shore pavilions of the sixteenth century provided an ideal private space for the secluded sultan, who could watch both the gardens and the sea from behind latticed windows, without being seen. Unlike the multichambered, monumental brick pavilions of Iran and Turan, built to house elaborate public court festivities, these stone shore pavilions were essentially intimate, domed throne halls, often provided with projecting alcoves and marble colonnades, lavishly decorated with İznik tiles, marble panels, mother-of-pearl-inlaid wood shutters, gilt wooden ceilings, rich furnishings, and playful fountains as private spaces for the sultan.

ELEVEN
Conclusion: The Topkapı and Other Palatine Traditions

Mehmed II built the New Palace as both a royal residence and the official seat of government for the Ottoman empire, combining in its structure areas for *otium* and *negotium,* zones of ceremonial ostentation and zones of retreat for pleasurable relaxation. Its construction, between 1459 and 1478, coincided with a period of territorial expansion, empire building, and centralization of power during which the Ottoman imperial image was redefined. It was meant to outshine all previous Ottoman palaces in both plan and conception, and its design was essentially conceived by its founder. The palace was not only an architectural manifestation of Ottoman absolutism; its architecture in turn actively informed the discourse and conceptualization of empire for generations to come.

Standing isolated from the rest of the metropolis on top of a pyramidal, tiered hill that seemed formed by nature to act as the pedestal of a great monarchy, the main core of the palace was majestically raised over the Byzantine acropolis, the new order superimposed upon the old. The relationship of one building to another was based on the traditional order of the Ottoman royal encampment, in which tents fulfilling specific functions were lined up according to a predetermined scheme, an organization paralleled in the layout of the palace. The similarities could hardly have been a coincidence; the sultan's military camp and his palace were both recognized as symbols of imperial power in the Ottoman world. "The sultan's imperial tent *[otāḳ-i pādişāhī]* is the counterpart of the imperial palace *[sarāy-i ‹āmire],*" wrote an Ottoman writer.[1] The buildings of the palace did not necessarily copy tent forms, but they were akin to them in scale, single-story elevation, and in their use of minimal furniture, with temporary furnishings such as awnings and tent curtains attached to the porticoes and doors. They also comprised a vast conglomeration of large or small, detached or adjoining, rectilinear modular units arranged around courts and ranging from freestanding pavilions to suites of rooms, representing a lively juxtaposition of royal and vernacular architecture. The palace complex was a paratactical system of separate buildings dedicated to specific functions, not so far removed from the tents of a royal encampment, which defied integration into a single monumental edifice. The interpretation of the Topkapı Palace by Orientalist travelers as a collection of tents lacking grandeur, but reflecting a love of nature, an instinct for beauty of site, and the memory of an ancestral past is therefore not far from the mark.

The main facades of the three courts on the spine of the hill were turned outward. These immense facades, with their multistoried windows, projecting balconies and arcades, crowned by lead domes with gilded finials and accentuated by chimneys and turrets, displayed to the outside world a monumentality that the interior of the palace lacked. The blocklike mass of the Topkapı, so effective from a distance, and its magical panoramic impact, were lost once the visitor had entered its courts. Unlike contemporary multistoried European palace forts, the courts of Mehmed II's New Palace were surrounded by single-storied structures. The irregular topography of the triangular promontory made it necessary for most of the trapezoidal complex to be constructed on top of artificial terraces and vaulted substructures, which contributed to its deceptively monumental external appearance. The internal spaces, experienced sequentially through a processional ceremonial, were surrounded by low structures, unlike the compact external blocks, which presented a unified monumental appearance. In the eighteenth century an English traveler named John Richards wrote that from afar the Topkapı afforded "a most pleasant prospect," but its interior was disappointing to visitors: "One would scarcely believe it to be the same place they saw at a Distance." Two mid-seventeenth-century travelers, Sir George Wheeler and Dr. Jacob Spon, were similarly disappointed once inside the palace, which had wonderfully raised their expectations at a distance.[2]

From the outside the palace appeared to extend over a vast area, but a large proportion of that space was made up of open courts and gardens. Buildings took up only a small part of the great space enclosed by the castellated Imperial Fortress. Modular square or rectangular halls, accentuated with domes or towers and grouped according to their functions around different courts, were usually preceded by porticoes, but no attempt was made to create a unified arcade around each court. The architecture of the palace was characterized by the repetitive use of elementary forms acting as surfaces for decoration applied with varying degrees of elaboration. The brilliant royal aspect with which the Topkapı announced itself to the outer world—especially to those arriving from the sea or approaching from the opposite shores of the city—could only be sustained at a distance, where the complex could be contemplated as an aesthetic object. To be viewed as an object in the urban fabric and, in turn, to provide a spectacular view of the surrounding landscape were two central themes characterizing its design.

The contrast between the exterior and interior of the Topkapı made the visitor, who could never hope to penetrate beyond the threshold of the third gate, aware of the secret that the inner palace possessed, and this inner mystery rarely failed to intrigue. The nineteenth-century traveler Edward Clarke wrote, "In vain does the eye, roaming from the towers of Galata, Pera and Constantinople, attempt to penetrate the thick gloom of cypresses and domes, which distinguishes the most beautiful part of Constantinople. Imagination magnifies things unknown: and when, in addition to the curiosity always excited by mystery, the reflection is suggested, that ancient Byzantium occupied the site of the Sultan's palace, a thirst of inquiry is proportionably augmented."[3] Unlike most palaces, which display their royal apartments to visitors with the objective of overwhelming them through riches, splendor, artifice, and illusion, the magnificence of the invisible royal space at the Topkapı was whatever the visitor's own imagination could create.

The palace was skillfully adapted to the uneven topography of its site, and not subjected to the rational, geometric planning principles that governed the design of Mehmed II's royal mosque complex, built around the same time (see Figs. 9, 10). Symmetry and axiality were not at the time seen as components necessary to achieve grandeur in palace architecture. In the Ottoman world palatial monumentality was expressed, not by dominating verticality (more appropriate for the royal mosques, which sought to emulate Hagia Sophia), but through sprawling horizontal spaces that had to be crossed at great length by the official visitor before he could approach the secluded monarch. The spaces experienced in a processional sequence had a cumulative effect; their seemingly incoherent architectural units became integrated through a fixed ceremonial, which underlined the narrative experience of architecture. Gates carrying the distant memory of Roman triumphal portals were the most monumental elements of each court. They focused attention, marked and bridged boundaries, and funneled the ceremonial procession through three trapezoidal courts of diminishing size, toward the ruler, where all movement converged.

The vast area and numerous buildings the palace complex encompassed reflected the complexity of its institutional organization and the variety of functions it housed. This had distant Roman roots;

imperial villas such as that in Piazza Armerina, Nero's Domus Aurea, and Hadrian's villa in Tivoli were all elaborately landscaped agglomerations of buildings and pavilions informally arranged around courts, gardens, and pools. The Roman imperial tradition had been inherited in early Islamic times and synthesized with comparable ancient Near Eastern concepts. The Topkapı is therefore typologically linked both to earlier Islamic prototypes and to the Romano-Byzantine heritage preserved in the Great Palace of Constantinople (see Fig. 2). The latter was a city within a city, impressive for the huge area it covered; a law of the year 490 had proclaimed that only imperial authority had a right to claim such vast spaces and to keep them inaccessible to the public.[4] The horizontal emphasis of the Great Palace, which contrasted sharply with the mountainlike vertical mass of the neighboring Hagia Sophia, formed a striking analogue to the layout of the Topkapı.

The deliberate asymmetry of compositional schemes and the nonaxial organization of buildings in the Topkapı Palace exemplify a kind of "picturesque" planning that is neither informal nor formal, but a sensitive interpenetration of architecture with nature. Gates, porticoes, loggias, and pavilions—never large enough to dominate the open spaces—were conceived in relation to gardens, water, light, and the expansive view. Rigid axiality was softened by subtle tensions between nature and structure. A monument or pavilion was never the centerpiece of a composition. Instead of dramatic axial vistas, one encountered indirect diagonal movement and a symbiotic relationship between natural and constructed forms.

This intimate merging of architecture with nature and the emphasis on commanding vistas were not just aesthetic preferences, but important components of the iconography of power. Behind the Imperial Fortress, which gave the palace its symbolic castellated appearance, and beyond the first two walled, relatively austere public courts, lay a fanciful private palace that opened out onto a hanging inner garden and surrounding outer gardens through belvedere towers, airy loggias, arcades, large windows, and pavilions. The sultan's private residence, whose royal halls were distinguished from others by their higher lanterned domes, featuring pendant globes, combined prisonlike confinement with the decorum and gay abandon of the countryside. It took full advantage of its imperial site, ideal for symbolizing the authority of a "Ruler of the Two Seas and the Two Continents," whence the invisible but omnivoyant sultan could command his world empire and extend his gaze, literally and metaphorically, over his vast dominions. The royal pavilions, raised on view-commanding platforms in the gardens or along the seashore; the belvederes crowning the towers and gates of the Imperial Fortress, of the hanging garden of the third court, and of the second court's Tower of Justice, all signified the omniscient presence of the sultan, hidden behind latticed windows that stressed his power to see without being seen. The iconic sultan's mastering gaze, architecturally framed by ceremonial windows of appearance, implied a form of domination and control that accentuated the spatial and sociopolitical distance between subject and object, ruler and ruled. The absent ruler could not be perceived directly, but his invisible potency became known indirectly, through its effects. The power of the privileged gaze was so fully embodied in the architectural discourse of the palace that to catch a glimpse of the hidden monarch became the propelling force of the ceremonial narrative.

The palace was originally made up of a collection of stylistically diverse units that reflected the universalism of Mehmed II's imperial idea. Its ingeniously heterodox building program deliberately subordinated unity to variety. This eclectic vocabulary, a veritable catalogue of the architectural and decorative styles available in the empire, should not be interpreted as a failure to develop a coherent aesthetic program. Variety was not the accidental result of unplanned organic development, but a major theme in the original building program. Like the variegated structures of the third court, Mehmed's garden pavilions were built in the architectural modes of conquered kingdoms and juxtaposed to a pavilion in the Ottoman style, in order to represent the pluralistic outlook of a sultan who ruled over a rapidly expanding, international empire. Their symbolism would have been obvious to contemporaries, who regarded them as comparable to royal tents. The captured tents of defeated monarchs were traditionally recognized as symbols of power and victory. A visible demonstration of this concept was a ceremony in which the tent of a disgraced official or defeated ruler was publicly dismantled by the cutting of its ropes to signify loss of power. This ancient practice had its roots in the Turco-Mongol heritage, which regarded the collapse or capture of a ruler's tent, seen as a symbol of ṣovereignty, as a bad omen. At the marriage feast of İbrahim Pasha in 1524, and at the circumcision ceremonies of Süleyman I's sons in 1530, the captured domed tents of defeated monarchs such as the Akkoyunlu ruler Uzun Hasan, the Safavid ruler Shah Ismail, and the last Mamluk sultan, Qansu Gauri, were proudly displayed as trophies of victory at the Hippodrome, alongside Süleyman I's own imperial tent in the Ottoman style.[5]

Mehmed II's garden pavilions no doubt carried the same message. Placed in the terraced outer garden of the palace, in which a collection of Byzantine antiquities was displayed amidst plants, wild and domestic animals, and warehouses filled with raw materials gathered from different realms, these pavilions proclaimed Mehmed's microcosmic vision of empire. The imperial symbolism embodied in the outer garden of the Topkapı can also be seen as a descendant of the Roman palatine tradition. Its striking parallel to the gardens of Nero's Domus Aurea, described in a famous passage by Suetonius, may not have been accidental: "There was a pond, too, like a sea, surrounded with buildings to represent cities, besides tracts of country, varied by tilled fields, vineyards, pastures and woods, with great numbers of wild and domestic animals." Mehmed II's three pavilions representing the Greek, Persian, and Ottoman kingdoms unified under his empire, like Nero's pavilions representing various cities, were grouped near a large pool and were surrounded by both formal and functional gardens and flocks of animals. This fusion of idyllic pleasure with the functional needs of the royal table and economic profit had its origin in a Roman tradition described by Pliny. However, Mehmed's palace, unlike that of Nero, did not boast illusionistic mechanical devices such as rotating domes of heaven, nor were there the mercury-filled pools that could be stirred to create dramatic effects, roaring lions, or golden trees with artificial singing birds that overwhelmed the visitors of Byzantine, Abbasid, and other early Islamic palaces. Still, the domed pavilions of the Topkapı continued to carry heavenly associations expressive of the cosmic nature of royalty, a concept that went back to classical Mediterranean and ancient Near Eastern palatine traditions. These traditions of cosmic rulership had been synthesized in the formative period of Islamic architecture, in such centers as Baghdad, Cordova, and Cairo, and finally culminated in the fourteenth century with the Alhambra Palace in Granada. The Fatimid palace in Cairo, for example, had twelve square garden pavilions, according to the eleventh-century traveler Naser-i Khosraw, a design with obvious heavenly and zodiacal allusions. A similar scheme characterized the early-fourteenth-century palace of the Ilkhanid ruler Oljeytu in Sultaniya, where twelve pavilions surrounded a larger, free-standing residential royal pavilion in the center of a marble-paved court.[6]

The Topkapı Palace's formal gardens, with their pools, flowing fountains, and pavilions were constantly compared by fifteenth- and sixteenth-century Ottoman historians, poets, and inscriptions to the gardens of paradise and its heavenly mansions. These analogies, so common in Islamic architecture, could not have been mere clichés; the architectural and decorative forms of the domed pavilions and royal halls were pervaded with paradisal and heavenly allusions transparent to contemporaries. Their brocade furnishings, their gilded walls and domes, studded with stars, jewels, and pearls, or hung with globe-shaped pendants (compared in the sources to the heavenly spheres), were reminiscent of the luxurious, bejeweled pavilions of gold and silver promised to believers in paradise. Their siting along the seashore, around or in the midst of pools with jets of water; their gushing internal fountains; and their sixteenth-century İznik tile panels, schematically representing eternally blossoming gardens seen through arches, were all evocative features that did not fail to move contemporary observers. These pavilions, with their comfortable cushioned sofas to recline upon, their multiple windows, projecting throne-shaped balconies, and colonnades opening onto actual gardens, seemed to be a preview of the heavenly mansions, populated by unaging *ghilmans* and *khouris*, whom the sultan's young male and female companions impersonated.

The cosmic analogy was also repeatedly emphasized by such court poets as Hamidi, who likened Mehmed II's New Palace to the Haft Paykar, the "Seven Portraits," a legendary palace built in the image of the heavens for the Sasanian ruler Bahram Gur (see Figs. 105a, 106a,b). As described by the Persian poet Nizami and other poets, including Amir Khusraw Dihlavi, Jami, and Navai, this palace had seven domed pavilions, each painted a different color, corresponding to the seven days of the week and the seven planets, and inhabited by the beautiful daughters of the seven kings ruling the seven climes of the world. Bahram Gur used to visit one of these heavenly pleasure pavilions each day of the week, wearing a costume that matched its color. The themes of universal rule (signified by control over the seven climes), heavenly symbolism, and royal pleasure made the Haft Paykar analogy particularly appropriate for Mehmed's New Palace—the Abode of Felicity, where the protection of the heavens was coupled with the heavenly bliss and sensual pleasures associated with kingship and the charisma of royal fortune. In conceptualizing the architectural program of his palace, the sultan may have drawn some of his inspiration from such mythical palaces. If he did, he was not the only Muslim ruler to do so. The Mughal emperor Humayun (r. 1530–40/1555–56) followed the Haft Paykar model much more literally when he built a seven-domed palace in Dinpanah, near Delhi. Like Bahram Gur, he used to give audiences in a different room each day of the week, varying the color of his robe to match the decor of that day's room.[7]

Mehmed II's lost domed crystal pavilion near the Privy Chamber's marble pool may also have been inspired by legendary palaces, possibly those described in the *Shāhnāma,* such as the pleasure house of crystal with a cupola of onyx that Kai Kaus built on Mount Albruz, or another crystal palace, with a fountain in its center, that Alexander the Great encountered on his travels. It may also have been a direct descendant of now-lost Islamic pavilions, such as the domed crystal pavilion standing at the center of a pool in the palace of the Ta'ifa king of Toledo, Yahya al-Ma'mun (r. 1043–75), which presented a dynamic spectacle of light and sound when bright rays were refracted through the water cascading over its dome, under which murmured a gushing fountain; a similar domed crystal pavilion stood in the middle of a pool in Granada. Another prototype for Mehmed's pavilion may have been the crystal pavilion of Solomon.[8]

The legendary palace of Solomon is an image one frequently encounters in descriptions of the New Palace. Bidlisi, for example, refers to the palace of Solomon—known for his justice and his subjugation of the animal kingdom—when he mentions the wild animals on view in the second court of the Topkapı, where imperial justice was administered.[9] Tursun Beg, on the other hand, compares the gleaming floors of the Tiled Kiosk *(sırça sarāy)* to the glass floors of the crystal pavilion built by Solomon for the Queen of Sheba, so like water that she lifted her skirts before crossing them. Moreover, the site of Mehmed's Palace, believed to have once housed a pavilion built by Solomon, was endowed with yet another mythical Solomonic reference.[10]

Concrete historical inspirations are difficult to trace because unfortunately few of the palaces Mehmed II saw or could have known about through descriptions have survived. Little is known about the contemporary Timurid palaces in Herat and Samarkand, the Hasht Behisht ("eight paradises") in Tabriz, built by the sultan's rival Uzun Hasan, the palace of the Mamluk sultans in the Citadel of Cairo, or the palaces of the defeated Anatolian Seljuk and Karamanian dynasties in Konya. The Alhambra in Granada is the only major late-medieval Islamic palace that remains; it is built, like the Topkapı, on a dominating hilltop and surrounded by extensive gardens, contained in a castellated enclosure punctuated with belvedere towers. Its origins have been traced to the Mediterranean tradition of the fortified Roman villa, which was also the source of the early Islamic chateaux of Syria and Palestine and the medieval palaces of Baghdad, Samarra, Cairo, and Cordova—all of them exemplifying an Islamic synthesis of classical Mediterranean and ancient Near Eastern palatine traditions.[11]

The Alhambra is typologically related to the Topkapı Palace, with its courts arranged informally in a natural environment and its progression from public to private zones, defined by an increasing luxury of interior spaces. These, like the Topkapı's, include baths, fountains, pools, garden pavilions, and belvedere towers, constituting a lavish setting for royal pleasure, permeated with heavenly and cosmic themes. The Alhambra's raised belvederes, or *miradors,* providing vistas into the gardens and overlooking the city below, similarly represented the monarch's dominating gaze, an important element in the architectural iconography of rulership also encountered at the roughly contemporary Mamluk palace in the Citadel of Cairo, preserved in a fragmentary state. The now-lost structures of the Cairo Citadel were also elevated loggias and belvederes, with grilled ceremonial windows displaying on all sides a panoramic view of the city, contributing to the Mamluk sultan's sense of power and control over his subjects. This feature can be traced back to earlier Islamic models, such as the eighth-century domed belvederes of al-Mansur's round city of Baghdad, from which he could survey the four directions of his empire, and the ninth-century palaces of Samarra, whose elevated royal belvederes, oriented along the Tigris, provided panoramic vistas of the river and the countryside. The taste for such belvederes, embodying the symbolic gaze of the vigilant ruler over his domains, had spread from the central Abbasid domains to such distant palaces as the Lashkari Bazar in Afghanistan, the Qal'a of the Bani Hammad in North Africa, and the Madinat al-Zahra near Cordova. This last foreshadowed the Alhambra, with its position on a terraced hillside, the uppermost level of which was reserved for the view-commanding royal belvedere pavilions.

While there are genetic links between the Alhambra and the Topkapı, the two palaces embody diametrically opposed aesthetic experiences. With its complex grouping of continuous halls and antehalls around symmetrically planned intimate courts, the Alhambra is more closely related to early-medieval Islamic palaces than the Topkapı, whose simple, disjointed modular units are asymmetrically organized around vast irregular courts. The Alhambra's overwhelming splendor represents a different taste, one that treats architecture as an almost magical, precious object with illusionistic qualities. Built by the shrinking Nasrid dynasty, cut off in distant Spain from new aesthetic developments in the rest of the Islamic world, it was both a nostalgic revival and a culmination of the early-medieval Islamic palace tradition. As Grabar has pointed out, its contrast with the fourteenth-century architecture of Anatolia, Iran, and, to a slightly lesser degree, Egypt and Syria illustrates that "the Alhambra stands at the end of a historical development and is, despite all its perfection, a formal dead end."[12]

The Topkapı Palace, built for the expanding Ottoman empire, is more closely related to a new Turco-Mongol palace tradition, introduced into the Islamic world with the fall of the Abbasid Caliphate in the middle of the thirteenth century. The Ilkhanid palaces in Tabriz and other Iranian cities, with their origins in the nomadic encampment and their connections to the Mongol palaces of China, have not survived. German excavations at Takht-i Sulayman, the site of a palace complex built by the Ilkhanid ruler Abaqa in the 1270s, have uncovered a vast square central courtyard with a lake surrounded by rectangular halls, cross-shaped pavilions, iwans, and kiosks in a loose arrangement. A royal garden built for Ghazan Khan in Ujan near Tabriz in 1302 is described by his vizier, Rashid al-Din, as a square formal garden *(bāgh)* with flowing waters and pools enclosed by a wall, in the middle of which were built "pavilions and towers and a bath and a high building in such a way that they might pitch the golden tent in the middle of that *bāgh,* with the audience hall *[bārgāh]* and parasols that are appropriate to it." The centerpiece of this summer palace-cum-encampment was a golden tent with a golden throne, where the ruler gave audiences. The Ilkhanid use of impermanent structures in a garden setting was directly related to the Chinese-flavored Mongol imperial palaces. For example, the one built for Khubilai (Kublai) Khan (1215–94) in Shangdu (known in the west as Xanadu) was a roughly square walled enclosure, created under the supervision of Chinese craftsmen and painters; it included a game reserve, a number of separate halls, and impermanent mobile structures that could easily be dismantled. Marco Polo writes, "In the middle place of that park thus surrounded with a wall, there is a most beautiful grove, the great Kaan has made for his dwelling a great palace or loggia which is all of canes, upon beautiful pillars gilded and varnished, and on top of each pillar is a great dragon all gilded.... The roof of this palace is also of canes gilded and varnished. ... Moreover the great Kaan had made it so arranged that he might have it easily taken away and easily set up,... for when it is raised and put together more than two hundred ropes of silk held it up in the manner of tents all round about."[13]

Dadu, another imperial palace built in 1267 for Khubilai Khan, was also a square enclosure with axially aligned monumental gates, audience halls, residential quarters, and an artificial mound, described between 1325 and 1328 by the Franciscan friar Odoric of Pordenone:

> And within the enclosure of the great palace there hath been a hill thrown up on which another palace was built, the most beautiful in the world. And this whole hill is planted over with trees, wherefrom it hath the name of the *Green Mount.* And at the side of this hill hath been formed a lake [more than a mile round], and a most beautiful bridge built across it. And on this lake there be such multitudes of wild geese and ducks and swans, that it is something to wonder at.

The royal mound, surmounted by palatial structures, and the lake with its flocks of geese not only recall features of the Topkapı but also those of a garden palace Timur had built in Samarkand. The Spanish ambassador Ruy Gonzalez de Clavijo described it in 1404 as a walled enclosure, featuring palaces on top of an artificial hill, planted with fruit trees and watered by canals issuing from six great tanks:

> In the exact center there is a hill, built up artificially of clay brought hither by hand: it is very high and its summit is a small level space that is enclosed by a palisade of wooden stakes. Within this enclosure are built several very beautiful palaces, each with its complement of chambers magnificently ornamented in gold and blue, the walls being panelled with tiles of these and other colors. This mound on which the palaces have been built is encircled below by deep ditches that are filled with water.... To pass up unto this hillock to the level of the palaces they have made two bridges.... There are to be seen many deer which Timur has caused to be brought hither, and there are pheasants here in abundance.

The Timurid palaces in Iran and Turan, which elaborated upon and further Islamicized the Mongol tradition, have largely disappeared, but descriptions and miniatures show that they too consisted of a series of tiled domed pavilions set in extensive walled garden estates, entered through monumental gates, but conceived on a gigantic scale that would dwarf the structures of the Topkapı. They must have recalled royal tent enclosures, for the seminomadic Timurid rulers continued to live in tents during most of the spring and summer; receptions and festivals were often held in meadows enclosed by walls of cloth, in which colorful domed tents were pitched.[14]

The layout of the Topkapı Palace, reflecting the organization of the Ottoman imperial encampment, partly grew out of this nomadic Turco-Mongol palace tradition, synthesized with earlier Islamic precedents encountered in Anatolia, and Romano-Byzantine elements inherited from Constantinople. By merging Turkic, Islamic, and Roman imperial traditions, the palace complex signaled that the Ottoman state was no longer a nomadic tribal confederation in the Mongol or Timurid manner, but a sedentary empire that had replaced tribal ties with a centralized bureaucracy of slave servants, stationed in a fixed capital. In this respect it bore an affinity to the Mamluk sultanate, firmly established in its capital, Cairo, as the last bulwark of the slave system, harking back to the Abbasid caliphate. Unlike Timur's peripatetic court and harem, which continually moved about with him and rarely stayed in the capital, Samarkand, the Ottoman court established Istanbul as a permanent base, where the sultan left his harem when he was briefly away on seasonal military campaigns.

Mehmed II may well have borrowed ideas from the Byzantine palaces he came across on his conquests, not only in Constantinople, but in such centers as Trebizond and Mistra as well. Like the Topkapı, the Byzantine palaces were composed of a series of loosely organized courts, monumental gates, porticoes, pavilions, and chapels in various styles, lacking strict axiality. Cardinal Bessarion describes the palace in Trebizond that Mehmed II conquered, also built on top of an acropolis, as a collection of massively constructed vestibules and halls with balconies facing in all directions, notable for their "variety, size, and beauty"—phrases reminiscent of the general spirit of the Topkapı Palace, described by Kritovoulos as built "with a view to variety, size, and magnificence."[15]

There are also striking parallels between Mehmed's palace and the Great Palace built by Constantine next to the Hippodrome and continually remodeled by his successors (see Fig. 2). While the sultan's New Palace was being constructed near the Hippodrome and Hagia Sophia, his mosque and tomb complex replaced the Church of the Holy Apostles, where Constantine and subsequent Byzantine emperors had been buried (see Figs. 9, 10). These two grand building projects were undertaken simultaneously, perhaps to show that the founder of the Christian city had been superseded by the founder of the Islamic city. The sultan no doubt meant to announce that, following in Constantine's footsteps, he was the legitimate heir of the Roman emperors. Among the titles he assumed was that of "Roman Caesar" (*ḳayser-i rūm*), a title that reflected his ambition to conquer Rome and to revive the Roman empire by reuniting East and West. Mehmed did not take as his model the weakened late-Byzantine empire which he had defeated, but the Eastern Empire in the golden age of Constantine and Justinian, whose imperial monuments he either appropriated or rebuilt. The lives of Alexander, Hannibal, and Caesar, daily read to him by a Greek and Latin reader, inspired a dream of *renovatio imperii* that would bring the whole Mediterranean basin under a single monarch and a single religion.

Part of this grand vision involved restoring the dilapidated city, which was not renamed but continued to be called *Kostantiniyya* in imperial documents and coins, to its old splendor. Kritovoulos wrote that Mehmed "was constructing great edifices which were to be worth seeing and should in every respect vie with the greatest and best of the past."[16] Referring to the New Palace, he wrote, "Both as to view and as to enjoyment as well as in its construction and its charm, it was in no respect lacking as compared with the famous and magnificent old buildings and sights."[17] The ruins of the Byzantine Great Palace, next to which the New Palace was meaningfully juxtaposed, could not have been ignored by the sultan, whose buildings were meant to compete with those of the past.

The Great Palace, which remained the Byzantine imperial residence until the fortified Blachernai Palace took its place in the eleventh century, is thought to have had some features in common with Diocletian's palace at Split, but its exact form is unknown (see Fig. 2). Its main courts progressed from public to private areas, and around them were grouped halls, pavilions, and chapels, connected by galleries and separated by gardens. Its outlying terraced gardens, cascading toward the Sea of Marmara, had pavilions and shore palaces just as the Topkapı did.[18] They too were built in various styles, reflecting the universalism of the Byzantine empire. One of them, the Moukhroutas, is identified in the sources as being Persian (Anatolian Seljuk) in design. Thought to have been erected in the twelfth century, it was a centrally planned pavilion with a conically shaped *muqarnas* dome (*makhrūṭ*), from which its name derived, gilded and painted with figures of Persians. It must have resembled the *muqarnas* vault of the Capella Palatina in Palermo, built by the twelfth-century Norman ruler Roger II, a royal chapel that unconventionally juxtaposed Islamic and Byzantine elements in its decorative program. Roger's eclectic blend of different artistic traditions paralleled Mehmed's search for an imperial iconography expressive of his universal empire.[19] Like the Norman kings before him, the sultan set out to fuse and reconcile the various cultures and imperial traditions he was heir to, a synthesis that would formally express the diversity of an empire that had neither ethnic, cultural, religious, nor linguistic homogeneity.

In the Istanbul that Mehmed created, as in the rapidly expanding Ottoman empire, largely populated by Christian subjects, Muslims were still a minority. The sultan had turned his capital into a microcosm of his cosmopolitan empire by transplanting inhabitants of every conquered city to it and assigning to each a separate quarter named after their original city. This policy of forced resettlement, going back to Mongol precedents, had also been used by Timur to develop Samarkand as an imperial capital, with its suburbs named after the great cities of Islam, Damascus, Baghdad, Sultaniya, Shiraz, and Cairo. Foreshadowing Mehmed II's collection of artists and architects from different regions, Timur had gathered—like the Mongols before him—artisans from Azerbaijan, Iran, Iraq, Egypt, Syria, and India in Samarkand. His palaces in that city exhibited an eclectic mix, like the Topkapı; one of them was built by Egyptian and Syrian stonemasons who were assisted by tile makers from Fars and Persian Iraq. This conscious eclecticism also had its roots in the Mongol heritage, as exemplified in the palaces that Mengü (Möngke) Khan (r. 1251–58) ordered to be built in Karakorum by a mixed group of Chinese (Cathayan) and Muslim builders, who constructed and decorated separate buildings in their own respective traditions. Once again, the juxtaposition of differing architectural styles was meant to connote the universalism of an empire.[20]

Kritovoulos describes how Mehmed had gathered in his capital people "from all parts of Asia and Europe" and "people of all nations." Angiolello says that each quarter that carried the name of a conquered city used its native language, retained its own customs, and had its own baths, mosques, and marketplaces, built in the style of each region; the Greek, Armenian, European, and Jewish communities had their own churches and synagogues.[21] The cosmopolitan capital Mehmed created became the stage on which new monuments and ceremonies shaping the Ottoman state's imperial image developed. The New Palace was a microcosm within the microcosmic city that articulated Mehmed's vision of a world empire. The palace complex was built by artisans from both the East and the West, captured from conquered lands or enticed to the Ottoman court by generous fees and invitations. A number of satirical poems express resentment at the sultan's preference for foreign talent and complain that one had to be either a Persian, a Jew, or a "Frank" (i.e., European) to find employment at his court.[22]

Mehmed's attempt to import foreign styles by employing artisans of international origin was, however, bound to remain an eclectic experiment with little impact on the future developments of Ottoman architecture. His stylistically diversified New Palace was suited to the cosmopolitan character of his empire, which emerged from the ruins of the Byzantine empire as a syncretic cultural and political entity (see Map I). Together with its new ceremonial code, so different from the customs of the old Ottoman frontier principality, the palace marked the inauguration of a new imperial era. Mehmed's creation served as the foundation of the Ottoman dynasty for generations to come. The new imperial image he defined set the sultans well apart from other men. The New Palace was built as an architectural frame for that image, codified in Mehmed's *kanunname*.

Designed as a theatrical stage for the representation of imperial authority, the plan of the palace read like a diagram of absolutist rule, with the sultan occupying the focal point from which all power radiated, and to which it converged. This was a coercive space, the space of power. Both architecture and ceremonial mutually translated into visual form a hegemonic imperial ideology. Dignitaries regularly acted out their place in the ideal monarchical order as portrayed in the ceremonial, which amplified absolute royal authority by organizing people and space into relationships of service and overlordship. The political order was constructed around the symbolic center occupied by the sultan at the innermost, private core of his palace; the higher one moved in the ruling hierarchy, the closer one came to that locus of power, which was the source of status. Rank was thus conceptualized and defined in spatial terms; the royal women (relegated to the private space of the harem) were excluded from the central ceremonial space, designed for the dominant male order.

Palace ceremonial reflected the master-slave relationship that pervaded the structure of the central government. As Marshall Hodgson has noted: "Ottoman absolutism built upon the tradition of looking upon the central power, including all its administrative branches, as one great army; and of regarding this army as at the personal service of the monarch.... With a well-supported dynasty solidly established in Istanbul, then, something of the Byzantine political idea reasserted itself: the same strategic opportunities and problems were reproduced. But the political idea had been reasserted in a thoroughly Islamicate form."[23]

The court ceremonial codified in Mehmed's *kanunname* must have been inspired to a certain degree by the model of the Byzantine absolute monarchy, as recorded in its Books of Ceremonies —a model that was synthesized with the Turco-Mongol and classical Islamic heritage. Perhaps the most prestigious Islamic precedent was Abbasid court ceremonial, some of whose elements the Ottomans indirectly inherited from the Anatolian Seljuks and the neighboring Mamluk sultanate, but which they also knew intimately from historical texts. The serried ranks of perfectly still Abbasid slave soldiers lined up on both sides of the public court in Baghdad known as al-Salām, where only the caliph could ride; the custom of watching the vizier's council of justice from behind a curtain; the emphasis on silence guaranteed by officials armed with bows, "to prevent and shoot down any crow that flew or croaked"—all found their counterparts in Ottoman ceremonial. The seclusion of the Abbasid caliphs, which was particularly elaborated in the tenth century, found close parallels in the Fatimid as well as Byzantine courts, signaling the existence of a shared language of imperial ceremonial in the post-Roman Mediterranean world, regardless of religious identities. Mehmed II, who dreamed of reviving the Roman empire by uniting his capital, Constantinople, with Rome, inherited this tradition, which was redefined according to existing Ottoman dynastic practices. In 1573 Fresne-Canaye perceptively observed that "those who imagine the Ottoman Porte as a copy of the court of Byzantine emperors are clearly mistaken." True, the Byzantine Books of Ceremonies had promoted imperial aggrandizement through the studied use of hieratic calm, solemnity, secrecy, and silence, but the self-image Mehmed defined was more secular than that of the basileus, who came near, at times, to playing the role of Christ. Byzantine rituals emphasized the link between the emperor and Christ. Royal ceremonies involved frequent visits to chapels within the palace grounds or processions to churches in the city, and had undeniably religious overtones. They were completely intertwined with the Christian liturgical calendar, involving constant movement between sacred and profane contexts.[24]

Although Mehmed's *kanunname* respected the two Muslim holidays, when he presented himself in the public court of the palace, and the requirement of Friday prayers, when he paraded from his palace to the imperial mosques, the rest of the court ceremonial was almost entirely nonreligious in tone. There were no public ceremonies in the palace grounds involving the extensive use of mosques; the sultan's mosque in the third court was a modest structure for private prayer, completely overshadowed by other royal structures. The Ottoman sultan was the protector of Islam at the frontiers of the Christian world, and by the sixteenth century he could claim the ambitious title of caliph, but his imperial image was relatively worldly. He was the victorious and just ruler in the service of Islam, the "Servant of the Two Sacred Sanctuaries" (i.e., Mecca and Medina), who like a servant washed the Prophet's mantle, which the Abbasid caliphs had proudly worn in state ceremonies. The tenth-century Buyid secretary Hilal al-Sabi' describes the Abbasid caliph in his *Rules and Regulations of the Abbasid Court:* "The Caliph, may the mercy of Allah be upon him, had the Qur'ān in front of him [ʿUthmān's copy]. On his shoulder he had the Garment [of the Prophet]; and in his hand, the Stick [of the Prophet]. He was girded with the sword of the Apostle of Allah, may God bless him."[25] Unlike the Abbasid caliph, who almost impersonated the Prophet by carrying his insignia, in a ritual that paralleled the implied Byzantine equation of the emperor with Christ, the Ottoman sultan did not regularly display signs of religious sanctity in his ceremonial. And unlike the Abbasid caliphs, who boasted ties of lineage to the Prophet's family, the Ottoman sultan could claim to be a staunch defender of Sunni Islam only by means of military might and administrative justice. To stress the legitimizing role of the sultan in protecting Islam, the Prophet's holy mantle and his other relics were preciously guarded in the Topkapı, where Ottoman grandees were allowed to visit them once a year.

Mehmed's *kanunname* defined an original concept of early modern absolute monarchy that prefigured the rise of sixteenth-century absolute monarchies in the West. About a century after its composition, in 1547, the sultan was presented as an ideal ruler in Ivan Peresvetov's "Biography of Sultan Mehmed," thought to have been written for the young czar Ivan the Terrible. The text urges Ivan to curb the power of the landowning boyars by replacing them with a paid central army like that of the Ottomans, and to create a meritocracy that would replace the corrupt aristocracy. The downfall of the last Byzantine ruler, Constantine, is blamed on the degenerate aristocracy and its injustice. By contrast, Mehmed—a philosopher-king who owed his wisdom to the Greek classics—is praised for his impeccable justice and his promulgation of systematic law codes. The author urges Ivan to imitate the sultan's empire and to improve upon it with the Christian religion. The Ottoman system was thus presented to the heir of the Byzantine imperial tradition, who was to turn Moscow into the "Third Rome," as a model to emulate. The palace fort of the Kremlin, built roughly around the same time as the Topkapı, also with the help of architects imported from Italy, was to become the center of another absolute monarchy with strong roots in the Byzantine past. Its constellation of domes, protruding from behind a castellated outer wall punctuated by belvedere towers, and its rigid ceremonial code that elaborated Byzantine precedents make the Kremlin comparable to the Topkapı. However, its architecture, dominated by multiple domed churches, provided a framework for predominantly religious rituals, closer in spirit to those of the Byzantine emperors than to the official state ceremonies enacted under the domes of the Ottoman palace. Another contemporary palace complex in the Soviet Union, the Bahçe Saray (Garden Palace), built for the Crimean Khans after they had become tributaries of the Ottoman sultan, provides a more direct comparison with the Topkapı, since it was inspired both architecturally and ceremonially by the latter.[26]

The Ottoman empire was one of the first major absolute monarchies to establish itself, not only in Europe but also in the Islamic world, after the break-up of the Timurid empire in the late fifteenth century. Other contemporary Islamic dynasties held relatively small territories, fitting a general pattern outlined by Fernand Braudel for a fifteenth-century Mediterranean world dominated by city-states. By the late fifteenth and early sixteenth centuries, these city-states were losing ground: Constantinople fell in 1453, Barcelona in 1472, Granada in 1492, and Cairo in 1517. Mehmed's centralized empire (see Map I) exemplified an emerging pattern that culminated in the sixteenth century with the growth of vast territorial empires in both the Christian West and the Islamic East, when the Safavids in Iran and the Mughals in India established their domains.[27] The Ottoman empire, too, continued in the sixteenth century to extend its dominions in eastern Europe, western Iran, Azerbaijan, Mesopotamia, Arabia, Egypt, and North Africa, becoming one of the leading world powers in the Mediterranean basin (see Map II). Its territories came to approximate those of the late Roman empire, with the exception of Italy and Spain. The possession of the holy cities of Mecca, Medina, and Jerusalem turned the sultans into the protectors of the holiest sanctuaries of Islam. This new context, in which the Ottomans were no longer a Muslim minority in predominantly Christian lands, required the reinforcement of the Islamic imperial tradition. By the middle of the sixteenth century, the eastern and western boundaries of the empire were by and large set, and the hope of creating a world empire that included Rome receded. The Ottomans abandoned the active pursuit of universalist claims and focused their energies on consolidating their territorially defined state.

Mehmed II's palace was adapted to this new context by sultans who saw themselves as successors to the caliphate. Its quotations from foreign architectural traditions, inherited from Byzantium or imported from Renaissance Italy and the Timurid world, became exotic curiosities as the Ottoman character of the palace took over. Despite his receptiveness to Byzantine, Italian, and Persian culture, the imperial message of Mehmed II's palace was nonetheless deeply rooted in Ottoman Islamic traditions. Had it not been, it would not have remained relevant to his successors who, though they adapted it to changing conditions and fashions, retained its essence, just as they perpetuated the basic outline of its ceremonial. By doing so they consolidated the imperial tradition invented by Mehmed II, which came to represent and legitimize their dynastic continuity.

Unlike the fifteenth-century buildings, so diverse in character, those added to the Topkapı in the sixteenth century by the architects Alaüddin, Sinan, and Davud eventually came to bear the unifying stamp of the classical Ottoman imperial style, replacing, in many cases, structures with colorful wooden details that seemed to lack monumentality. The Persian architect Alaüddin's buildings, whose decorations were deeply embedded in a Timurid-Turcoman aesthetic, and continued to incorporate foreign elements imported from the Mamluk and Safavid lands conquered by Selim I, represented a transitional phase. Their painted plaster or wood ceilings (often decorated with gold stars and thin gold plates studded with jewels) were unified by a limited palette of blues, white, and gold, a color scheme that harmoniously pervaded the whole palace of Süleyman in the 1520s and 1530s, from the portico ceilings of the second court to the royal structures beyond.

Inspired by the strong element of chinoiserie in the international Timurid style, these decorations recalled eastern prototypes, such as the fifteenth-century Zarnigar Khaneh (gilded room) in the shrine of Gazurgah in Herat, decorated with paintings on plaster in light blue, dark blue, and gold. Such paintings (also preserved in the late-fifteenth-century 'Ishrat Khaneh and Aq Saray mausoleums at Samarkand), were no doubt widespread in the now-lost Timurid palaces. The figural narratives of Uzun Hasan's Hasht Behisht Palace in Tabriz, for example, were accompanied by painted decorations and tiles dominated by blues and gold, just like those in the Chini Khaneh, an early-fifteenth-century garden pavilion Ulugh Beg had erected in Samarkand. The latter's walls were completely covered with hexagonal porcelain tiles painted in cobalt blue on a white ground (thought to be imported from Ming China); its walls must have been provided with multiple niches to display the ruler's prestigious Chinese porcelain collection, like those of many later pavilions of the Chini Khaneh type built in Timurid Herat, and in the Safavid and Mughal capitals.

The royal structures Alaüddin added to the Topkapı Palace between 1525 and 1529 also featured Persianate *cuerda seca* tiles (based on a dark blue, turquoise, green, and yellow scheme), used together with blue-white-turquoise underglaze, and gilded dark blue tiles cut in various shapes, a Timurid-flavored mixture. The architectural decorations of Alaüddin's buildings, created by the court workshops (painters, ceramicists, and goldsmiths) of Istanbul, mostly headed at that time by the artists Selim I had imported from Tabriz, were also faced with Cairene marble panels in the Mamluk mode. Unlike the direct quotations of foreign elements in Mehmed II's eclectic architecture, however, Alaüddin's buildings successfully synthesized these decorative details with stonemasonry buildings in the Ottoman style to reflect the aesthetic pluralism of a rapidly expanding empire that still continued to incorporate new kingdoms into its territories.

Buildings constructed at the palace in the second half of the sixteenth century by Sinan and his student Davud signaled the formation of a classical Ottoman synthesis no longer receptive to foreign models, a synthesis that reflected the separate identity of a self-confident world empire. They were conceived on a more monumental scale, but still did not equal the imposing dimensions and vertical emphasis of the multistoried palaces with stately staircases built in sixteenth-century Europe. Featuring marble revetments, precious columns, classical İznik tiles in a novel color scheme and design vocabulary, and building materials imported from various parts of the empire, they were the products of a mature centralized construction industry.

The loose organization of the architectural profession in the late fifteenth and early sixteenth centuries had accommodated foreign architects and decorators. By the second half of the sixteenth century, the organization of royal architects trained in the palace had grown rigidly centralized; its products bore the unmistakable stamp of an imperial architectural style perpetuated by the school of Sinan. In most cases their construction was overseen, and even paid for, by the grand viziers, under whose jurisdiction fell the court architects, now part of the palace's outer service organization. Other high officials, such as the admiral (who commanded the galley slaves used in construction), or eunuchs of the inner palace (the head treasurer and palace steward, who commanded the centralized institution of court artisans, or *ehl-i hiref*), also supervised the construction and decoration of palace buildings, since the aloof sixteenth-century sultans, unlike Mehmed II, had little direct contact with architects and artisans.

Paralleling the formation of a classical Ottoman synthesis in architecture in the 1540s and 1550s was the notable development of the decorative arts that furnished the palace, an important source of patronage for artists working in any medium. The Topkapı was not only the nucleus of patronage for Ottoman art, but also a vast showroom for the best of the luxury items produced in the palace workshops. These *objets de luxe* cannot be understood independently of the palace and the court ceremonial that constituted the context for which they were produced. By the second half of the sixteenth century, in the court workshops a distinctive Ottoman decorative style, dominated by boldly magnified, seminaturalistic floral motifs, was formulated. The minutely rendered, intricate abstract arabesques and chinoiserie motifs of the international Timurid aesthetic were thus relegated to a subordinate role.

This new Ottoman decorative language flourished in almost all media, particularly in royal textiles and İznik tiles (based on a polychromatic scheme of two blues, turquoise, green, and red over a white background, with large, clearly legible patterns outlined in a black contour) that were widely used in palatial settings. Vibrantly contrasting colors, dominated by red, thus replaced the earlier, restrained blue-and-white schemes. This distinctive Ottoman taste was the creation of centralized court workshops, no longer dominated by Persian artisans, but by recruited *(devşirme)* slaves *(kul)*, trained at the capital as full-time, salaried employees of the palace. It represented a unified visual language that the sultan's administrators then dispersed to the four corners of the empire. The Topkapı Palace itself provided a model for the smaller residences of statesmen in the capital and of governors in the provinces and set the taste for the Ottoman ruling elite. Fashions created in it were disseminated from the center to the periphery of the Ottoman world.

The Topkapı Palace and its ceremonial set the Ottoman dynasty apart not only from fifteenth-century Islamic dynasties, but also from later post-Timurid empires such as those of the Safavids and Mughals. By the end of the sixteenth century, the principle of royal seclusion had been carried to its ultimate conclusion, with the sultan transformed into a mute and immobile idol, almost too sacred to be seen. The depersonalized monarch became an invisible signifier of pure potency at the symbolic navel of his empire, the Abode of Felicity in the innermost core of his palace. The late-sixteenth-century historian Âli likened the secluded sultan, sealed up in his private residence, to a pearl hidden in an oyster shell, observing that the Islamic rulers of Persia, Central Asia, and India set no stock in such aloofness and haughtiness, which were attributes better suited to God.[28]

The Venetian ambassador Giacomo Soranzo wrote around the same time that the Ottoman sultan's seclusion contrasted sharply with the practice of the Safavid rulers of Persia. The Turkish sultan "did not speak to anyone and was visible rarely," whereas the Persian king "constantly stayed in public," and held public audiences three times a week.[29] So foreign was the Ottoman royal etiquette of silence that when Süleyman I's son Prince Bayezid sought refuge in the court of the Safavid ruler Shah Tahmasp his behavior was interpreted as

139 Seventeenth-century mural painting from the Chehel Sutun Palace in Isfahan, depicting a Safavid reception ceremony.

haughtiness. The Persian historian Iskandar Munshi writes:

Bayezid, however, was an arrogant, reticent, and cold natured man. It has reached me from a variety of sources that at the official receptions of Tabriz and Qazvin, despite all the performances put on by skilled craftsmen, despite the festival crowd and the lavish hospitality, he looked neither to right nor to left as he rode, but gazed straight ahead between his horse's ears.... When he reached the place of audience, he dismounted and Shah Tahmasp advanced a few paces and shook hands with him, greeted him with warmth and affection and displayed the utmost friendliness. But Bayezid maintained his haughty and arrogant demeanor. He spoke not a word, and did not join in that cultured dialogue which every occasion of this sort demands.[30]

In contrast to the Ottoman sultans, who remained nearly invisible, Safavid and Mughal rulers appeared regularly in public audiences and at festivities, surrounded by their noble courtiers. Seventeenth-century murals at the Chehel Sutun Palace in Isfahan depict some of these courtly banquet scenes, in which Safavid rulers, seated with ambassadors and other dignitaries, are shown holding wine cups and being entertained by dancers in the foreground (Fig. 139). The Mughal rulers held similar banquets, as well as public audiences or *darbars* (Fig. 140) and other regular public appearances, in which they stood at ceremonial windows called *jharoka,* with dignitaries, common people, and elephants gathered below (Fig. 141). The ceremonies of the Safavid and Mughal courts had a common root in Timurid *majlises,* famed for their lavish banquets, wine drinking, musical performances, dancing, and poetry recitations, ultimately going back to the definition of royalty in the *Shāhnāma*. No such lighthearted public ceremony could be found in the Ottoman court.

The unique ceremonial of the Topkapı stressed the difference of the Ottoman imperial system from the Timurid and post-Timurid empires with which it shared a common Turco-Mongol nomadic heritage. The centralized Ottoman system envisioned by Mehmed II was no longer dependent on the loyalty of nomadic tribes and landowning local chieftains. By replacing the latter with an elite of household slaves and turning the ulama into salaried employees of the centralized state, the sultan brought about a radical change in the power base of his empire, as Machiavelli noted when he defined the Ottoman state as an absolute monarchy based on slavery, unlike the aristocratic French system. "The whole monarchy of the Turk is governed by one master; the rest are his servants," he wrote. "But the King of France finds himself in the midst of a great number of established lords, acknowledged and beloved of their subjects." The sultan's relation to his dignitaries was that of a master to his slaves, in contrast to the other rulers of the post-Timurid era, whose power depended on the fickle allegiance of landowning nobles, local chiefs, ulama, and Sufi sheikhs, who had to be entertained at court. The Ottoman sultan had no equal within his realm to invite to a banquet or even to converse with; he was beyond any relations of reciprocity. Ceremonies at the Ottoman court stressed the unbridgeable gap between master and slave; they were not for hereditary nobles but for household slaves and dependent ulama appointed to fixed offices by the sultan. In the last quarter of the sixteenth century, Giacomo Soranzo informed the Venetian senate about this crucial difference between the government of the Safavid shah, whose counselors, called *sultans*, were influential landowners, and the slave-based Ottoman system.[31]

This explains why neither the Safavid nor the Mughal empire ever attained anything like the Ottoman state's degree of centralization. Safavid and Mughal palaces, which elaborated Timurid models, resemble the Topkapı, with their public and private

140 The Mughal emperor Jahangir in a *darbar* scene at the public audience hall. From the *Tuzuk-i Jahangiri,* ca. 1620, Boston, Museum of Fine Arts, Francis Bartlett Donation of 1912 and Picture Fund, 14.654. Reproduced from S. C. Welch, *India, Art and Culture 1300–1900,* New York, 1985, p. 184, fig. 115.

audience halls, their successive courtyards and monumental gates, arranged in progression from public to semipublic to private areas, culminating in formal gardens with pavilions, surrounded by high walls. But unlike the Topkapı, where the most architecturally elaborate area was primarily accessible to the secluded sultan, his family, his silent eunuchs, and obedient slaves, the Safavid and

141 The Mughal emperor Jahangir appearing at the *jharoka* window, with dignitaries gathered below. From the *Tuzuk-i Jahangiri,* ca. 1620, Collection of Prince Sadruddin Aga Khan, Geneva. Reproduced from Welch, *India,* p. 186, fig. 116.

Mughal palaces, like those of the West, had more accessible private zones, where the ruler constantly entertained guests. The dignitaries and ambassadors waited on the ruler in his magnificent private domain, in contrast to the courtiers of the Ottoman sultan, whose ceremonial allowed only a brief and usually silent official encounter. When a privileged dignitary informally entered the private quarters of the Topkapı it could be regarded as a serious breach of etiquette. The permission Süleyman granted to his favorite grand vizier, Ibrahim Pasha, to frequent the third court and to sleep there generated resentment as a violation of the accepted rules. In 1553 the grand vizier Rüstem Pasha, the sultan's son-in-law, was prohibited from entering the third court, except during official audiences. When Süleyman's wife Hürrem and his daughter Mihrimah tried to intervene, he rejected their request, declaring that one mistake of that kind was enough.[32]

The ceremonial practice of the Topkapı also differed from that of European courts. Like several other Europeans who detected an ancient Near Eastern flavor in the Ottoman court's foreign practices, Gyllius compared the secluded sultan to Gyges, the legendary Lydian king whose ring gave him the power of invisibility. Flachat contrasted the invisibility of Ottoman sultans, adopted to inspire fear in their subjects, with the exhibitionism of the French kings, who wanted to be liked by them; one entered Versailles with a "tender respect," but would not even dare to approach the seraglio except with "the chill that a master who is feared produces in all hearts."[33] Ottoman subjects, however, did not entirely feel that chill; their awe was combined with a warm and affectionate respect for their emperor. Writing around the same time as Flachat, the official historian Naima therefore still advised the sultans to remain aloof and hidden behind the "curtain of reverence and sanctity," because too much contact with people would lessen their majesty and dignity.[34]

The architectural, institutional, and ceremonial organization of the Topkapı Palace perfectly reflected the system of Ottoman absolute monarchy and helped to perpetuate it. Its layout, obsessed with clearly delineated boundaries and codified functions, was designed to classify, to assign roles, and to impose rigid behavioral patterns that influenced the perception of government as it was inherited from one generation to another. Created at the height of centralized imperial power in the fifteenth and sixteenth centuries, it did not change much until the second half of the seventeenth century, after which the sultans began to spend most of their time in Edirne. By the reign of Mehmed IV (r. 1648–87), nicknamed Hunter ("Avcı"), who moved his court to Edirne to enjoy its good hunting, the system of slave pages had begun to degenerate, the power of the grand vizier, who had once occupied the apex of the hierarchy of household slaves, was challenged by the harem factions, and the sultan no longer followed the rule of seclusion as rigidly as before. These changes signaled the new decentralizing tendencies that had begun to threaten the old order.

When the court was forced to move back from Edirne to Istanbul by a rebellious populace in the early eighteenth century, the Topkapı was extensively remodeled and its buildings received a new decorative skin. With a few exceptions, however, these were mostly cosmetic and not important structural changes.[35] The eighteenth century also marked an increased relaxation of the ceremonial code, as the sultans deviated more and more from the principle of seclusion, a trend that culminated in the construction of waterfront palaces along the Golden Horn and the Bosphorus. Impatient with the formality of the Topkapı, whose ceremonial had become a straightjacket, the sultans emerged from seclusion and began to spend most of their time in these relatively informal seaside residences, visiting the Topkapı only for state ceremonies. In a letter to his grand vizier, Ahmed III (r. 1703–30) complained about the rigid rules with which he was hampered while living in the Topkapı: "[If] I go up to one of the chambers, forty Privy Chamber pages are lined up; if I have to put on my trousers, I do not feel the least comfort, [so] the swordbearer has to dismiss them, keeping only three or four men so that I may be at ease in the small chamber."[36]

As the nature of absolute power that had crystallized in the architecture and ceremonial of the Topkapı Palace gradually changed, it left behind the residues of an anachronistic ritual. The eighteenth-century seasonal waterfront palaces of Istanbul were a prelude to the final abandonment of the Topkapı, along with the system of government and lifestyle it had come to represent, for the neoclassical shore palace of Dolmabahçe in 1853. This happened in the wake of the momentous Westernizing reform effort ushered in by the declaration of the imperial edict known as Tanzimat in 1839. Nineteenth-century reformist sultans, in the midst of their frantic attempts to cure the Ottoman state, the "sick man of Europe," of its ills, needed palaces built in a different image. It is reported that when the court architect of Mahmud II (1808–38) tried to assure him that no palace in Europe could hope to rival the Topkapı in splendor, the sultan pointed at the plans of European palaces before him and vehemently declared, "None save a rogue or fool could class that palace ... hidden beneath high walls, and amid dark trees, as though it would not brave the light of day, with these light, laughing palaces, open to the free air, and pure sunshine of heaven. Such would I have my own, and such shall it be."[37] This criticism of the Topkapı echoed the views of Europeans, who by the seventeenth century had come to see the palace as a symbol of oriental despotism; for example, Tavernier had compared it to a prison, lacking the cheerful atmosphere of French or Italian palaces, and Benvenga had interpreted its shadows that shunned the sun's truth as a sign of the sultan's tyranny.[38]

The new rulers, who were increasingly prepared to depart boldly from their heritage in favor of Westernization, were quick to be influenced by such views and to realize that the Topkapı had exhausted its role within the new order. Ironically, they chose grandiose schemes modeled on monumental European palaces just at the moment when the empire was on the verge of collapse. The abandoned Topkapı Palace was, however, preserved as a monument to the glory of the Ottoman dynasty. It continued to exercise a legitimizing role in royal affairs—accession ceremonies, *bayram* celebrations, and religious rituals centering on the Prophet's mantle were held there until the final collapse of the empire.

Today the inner core of the palace complex, a sad shadow of its former self, is a museum that houses the accumulated treasures of the Ottomans. Its buildings, stripped of most of their original decorations and used as exhibition spaces, give little idea of the functional and ceremonial uses they once served. Yet the legacy of the palace is not altogether violated by its present function. After all, the original building complex, with its treasuries, libraries, archives, and samples of architecture in different styles from different periods, was also in its own way a museum, a *lieu de mémoire* in which the collective memory of the Ottoman dynasty was enshrined.

Appendices

Appendix A: Excerpts from two account books in the Başbakanlık Arşivi, MM 17884, dated 934–35 (1527–29), and KK 7097, dated 935 (1528–29), recording renovations and rebuilding by Süleyman I of some of the major structures in the Topkapı Palace.

1 The Middle Gate

MM 17884, fols. 54, 69:

"For the completion of repainting the ceiling porticoes of the Middle Gate in the imperial palace, including the construction of its ceiling, its borders, and its scaffolding to place the porticoes *[Tetimme-i naḳş-kerden-i pīşḫūnhā-i tavan-i bāb-i miyāne der sarāy-i ‹āmire ki sāḫten-i tavan ve ḥāşiyehā ve sāḫten-i iskele-i nihāden-i pīşḫūnhā]*."

"For repairing the room of gatekeepers at the Middle Gate *[Becihet-i meremmet-i oda-i bevvābān-i bāb-i miyāne]*."

KK 7097, fols. 23, 33, 99:

"For building a scaffolding to place the porticoes of the Middle Gate's ceiling, and some repairs of its painting *[Becihet-i sāḫten-i iskele berā-yi nihāden-i pīşḫūnhā-i tavan-i bāb-i miyāne ve ba‹ẓı meremmet-i naḳş-i o]*."

"For expenses of the royal workshop of painter-designers for painting the porticoes of the Middle Gate *[Becihet-i ḫarc-i naḳḳāşḫāne-i ḫāṣṣa berāy-i nuḳūş-i pīşḫūn-i bāb-i miyāne]*."

"For repairing the wall of the imperial garden near the Middle Gate of the imperial palace *[Becihet-i meremmet-i dīvār-i bāġçe-i ‹āmire der nezd-i bāb-i miyāne der sarāy-i ‹āmire]*."

"For repairing the rooms and latrines of gatekeepers at the imperial palace's Middle Gate *[Becihet-i meremmet-i odahā ve ḥelāhā-i bevvābān-i bāb-i miyāne der sarāy-i ‹āmire]*."

2 The New Council Hall

MM 17884, fol. 52:

"For making iron lattices for the outer Council Hall *[Becihet-i sāḫten-i ḳafeshā-i āhen berā-yi dīvānḫāne-i bīrūnī]*."

"For making a gilded globe to be hung from the dome of the outer Council Hall at the mentioned palace *[Becihet-i sāḫten-i ṭob-i müẕehheb berā-yi āvīḫten-i ḳubbe-i dīvānḫāne-i bīrūnī der sarāyi'l-mezbūr]*."

"For making a table and seat for placing the food of the exalted viziers of the imperial council *[Becihet-i sāḫten-i pīştaḫta ve iskemle berā-yi nihāden-i ṭa‹ām-i ḥażrāt-i paşayān-i ‹iẓām der dīvān-i hümāyūn]*."

KK 7097, fols. 23–24:

"For making the carpentry of the outer Council Hall *[Becihet-i sāḫten-i necrān berā-yi dīvānḫāne-i bīrūnī]*."

"For repairing the outer Council Hall and whitewashing it *[Becihet-i meremmet-i dīvānḫāne-i bīrūnī ve baṭana-kerden-i o]*."

3 The Tower of Justice

MM 17884, fol. 69:

"For constructing the ceiling and window frames and western doors and lattices and painting the kiosk of justice *[Becihet-i sāḫten-i tavan ve zār ve bābhā-i ġarbī ve ḳafeshā ve naḳş-kerden-i köşk-i ʿadl]*."

KK 7097, fol. 99:

"For repairing the kiosk of justice and constructing a scaffolding to place its porticoes and for painting *[Becihet-i meremmet-i köşk-i ʿadl ve sāḫten-i iskele berā-yi nihāden-i pīşḫūnhā-i o ve naḳş-kerden]*."

4 The Public Treasury

MM 17884, fols. 51, 69:

"For making seats and big cupboards and glass panes and the plastering of the outer treasury and the western door for safekeeping the seal and repairing the iron gate at the above mentioned palace *[Becihet-i sāḫten-i iskemlehā ve dolābhā-i büzürg ve cāmhā ve ṣıva der ḫazīne-i bīrūnī ve bāb-i ġarbī berā-yi ḥıfẓ-kerden-i mühr ve meremmet-i bāb-i āhen der sarāyi'l-mezbūr]*."

"For preparing materials to build a concave raised platform in the outer treasury *[Becihet-i müheyyā-kerden-i esbāb berā-yi sāḫten-i ṣoffa-i mücevvef der ḫazīne-i bīrūnī]*."

5 The Chamber of Petitions

MM 17884, fols. 53, 69:

"For preparing various types of materials for the exalted council hall of the interior *[Becihet-i iḥżār-kerden-i esbābhā-i mütenevviʿa berā-yi dīvānḫāne-i ʿālī der enderūn]* (366,920 *[akçe]*)."

"For making the iron tie beams required for the inner council hall *[Becihet-i sāḫten-i kirişhā-i āhen berā-yi mühimmāt-i dīvānḫāne-i enderūn]* (23,747 *[akçe]*)."

"For casting a hood for the fireplace of the inner council hall *[Becihet-i rīḫten-i yaşmaḳ-i āteşdān berā-yi dīvānḫāne-i enderūn]* (27,239 *[akçe]*)."

"For constructing a ceiling between the Gate of Felicity and the inner council hall *[Becihet-i sāḫten-i tavan-i mābeyn-i bābü's-saʿādet ve dīvānḫāne-i enderūnī]* (8,060*[akçe]*)."

KK 7097, fol. 58:

"For expenses of repairing the inner council hall of the imperial palace, together with the expense of gilding the metal rings of the marble column capitals *[Becihet-i ḫarc-i taʿmīr-kerden-i dīvānḫāne-i enderūnī der sarāy-i ʿāmire maʿa ḫarc-i ṭilā-kerden-i perāzvānehā-i ser-i sütūn-i mermer]* (435,894 *[akçe]*)."

"For making the silver hood of the fireplace and its latticework and its outline and gilding and enameling and the drawing of its design and the molding of its cornice and the table and else for the inner council hall of the imperial palace *[Becihet-i sāḫten-i yaşmaḳ-i āteşdān-i sīm ve müşebbeḳ-kerden ve guzār ve ṭilā ve mīnā ve resm-i naḳş ve ḳālıb-i gilvi ve pīştaḫta ve ġayri berā-yi dīvānḫāne-i enderūn der sarāy-i ʿāmire]* (129,246 *[akçe]*)."

"For expenses of painting the ceiling and [wall] borders and window frames and [window] lattices and the surrounding eaves and the burnished gilding of the iron window lattice, and coloring the iron tie beams of the inner council hall of the imperial palace *[Becihet-i naḳş-kerden-i tavan ve ḥāşiyehā ve zārhā ve ḳafeshā ve ṭurre-i eṭrāf ve zer mühre-i āhen-i pencere ve renk-kerden-i kirişhā-i āhen berā-yi dīvānḫāne-i enderūnī der sarāy-i ʿāmire]* (330,778 *[akçe]*)."

"For expenses of making assorted ceramic tiles for the inner council hall of the imperial palace *[Becihet-i ḫarc-i sāḫten-i kāşīhā-i mütenevviʿa berā-yi dīvānḫane-i enderūnī der sarāy-i ʿāmire]* (63,363 *[akçe]*)."

"For constructing the water channel of the fountain of the inner council hall of the imperial palace *[Becihet-i sāḫten-i rāh-i āb-i çeşme-i dīvānḫāne-i enderūnī der sarāy-i ‹āmire]* (3,178 *[akçe]*)."

"For quarrying marble from Istanbul for the inner council hall of the imperial palace *[Becihet-i iḫrāc-kerden-i mermer der Istanbul berā-yi dīvānḫāne-i enderūnī der sarāy-i ‹āmire]* (3,856 *[akçe]*)."

Total expenses of the inner council hall *[Yekūn-i dīvānḫāne-i enderūnī]* (966,314 *[akçe]*)."

6 The Harem

MM 17884, fols. 53–54, 69, 71:

"For repairing the new room near the chamber of girls *[Becihet-i meremmet-i oda-i cedīd der nezd-i oda-i duḫterān]*."

"For repairing the bath of girls at the imperial palace *[Becihet-i meremmet-i ḥammām-i duḫterān der sarāy-i ‹āmire]*."

"For building a walled enclosure, and constructing a wooden house, and kiosk, and fountain, and a water channel for the fountain of the water tank near the girls' palace at the side of the imperial garden *[Becihet-i sāḫten-i dīvār-i ḥavlı ve sāḫten-i ḫāne-i çatma ve köşk ve şādırvān ve rāh-i āb-i şādırvān-i ābḫāne der nezd-i sarāy-i duḫterān ‹an ṭaraf-i bāğçe-i ‹āmire]*."

"For making the iron gate of the enclosure wall near the girls' palace at the side of the imperial garden *[Becihet-i sāḫten-i bāb-i āhen berā-yi dīvār-i ḥavli der nezd-i sarāy-i duḫterān be-ṭaraf-i bāğçe-i ‹āmire]*."

"For repairing the rooms of girls and laying wooden floors and making cupboards, seats, large trunks, and fireplace wood, and frames, and carpentry, and pulling down the roof pavilion above the chamber of girls at the imperial palace *[Becihet-i ta‹mīr-kerden-i odahā-i duḫterān ve döşeme-i taḫta-i pāzu ve sāḫten-i dolāb ve iskemlehā ve anbār ve taḫta-i āteşdān ve çerçeve ve necrān ve ḳal‹-kerden-i çārdāḳ der fevḳ-i oda-i duḫterān der sarāy-i ‹āmire]*."

KK 7097, fols. 22, 24, 58:

"For building a stone staircase near the girls' palace at the side of the royal stables *[Becihet-i sāḫten-i nerdübān-i seng der nezd-i sarāy-i duḫterān der ṭaraf-i āḫūr-i ḫāṣṣa]*."

"For building a walled enclosure around the pool and its water channel near the girls' palace at the side of the imperial garden *[Becihet-i sāḫten-i dīvār-i ḥavlı der eṭrāf-i ḥavż ve rāh-i āb-i o der nezd-i sarāy-i duḫterān der ṭaraf-i bāğçe-i ‹āmire]*."

"For repairing the rooms of the girls' palace and its bath and making a penthouse together with the roof of the penthouse *[Becihet-i meremmet-i odahā-i sarāy-i duḫterān ve ḥammām-i o ve sāḫten-i ṣundurma ma‹a tavān-i ṣundurma]*."

"For repairing the new room near the palace of girls *[Becihet-i meremmet-i oda-i cedīd der nezd-i sarāy-i duḫterān]*."

"For expenses of building a new kitchen, and doors of the masonry wall, and its water tank, and a walled enclosure and a stone staircase at the palace of girls *[Becihet-i ḫarc-i sāḫten-i maṭbaḫ-i cedīd ve bābhā-i dīvār-i kārgīr ve ābḫāne-i o ve dīvār-i ḥavli ve nerdübān-i seng der sarāy-i duḫterān]*."

"For repairing the terrace of the privy garden near the girls' palace *[Becihet-i meremmet-i sedd der bāğçe-i ḫāṣṣ der nezd-i sarāy-i duḫterān]*."

7 The Hanging Garden of the Third Court

MM 17884, fols. 52–53:

"For making a new water channel and a small bath from the vicinity of the new room up to the girls' garden in the above mentioned palace *[Becihet-i sāḫten-i rāh-i āb-i cedīd ve ḥammām-i kuçek der nezd-i oda-i cedīd ilā bāğçe-i duḫterān der sarāyi'l-mezbūr]*."

"For repairing the marble pavement in front of the

new kiosk, together with painting it and glass panes for the top [i.e., lantern] of the kiosk's dome *[Becihet-i meremmet-i döşeme-i ferş-i mermer der pīş-i köşk-i cedīd maʿa naḳş-i o ve cāmhā-i ser-i ḳubbe-i köşk]*."

"For making the terrace of the above mentioned garden *[Becihet-i sāẖten-i ṣoffa der bāġçeyi'l-mezbūr]*."

KK 7097, fols. 58, 99:

"For expenses of building the new kiosk and the marble terrace and the subterranean water channel of the vault underneath the above mentioned kiosk and the new room in the vicinity of the room of His Majesty [i.e., Privy Chamber]—may his reign be everlasting—at the privy garden *[Becihet-i ẖarc-i sāẖten-i köşk-i cedīd ve ṣoffa-i mermer ve kārīz-i toloz der taẖt-i köşki'l-mezbūr ve oda-i cedīd der nezd-i oda-i ḥażret-i hüdāvendigār ẖullide mülkuhu der bāġçe-i ẖāṣṣa]*."

"For expenses of making iron beams for the marble terrace of the privy garden *[Becihet-i ẖarc-i sāẖten-i kirişhā-i āhen berā-yi ṣoffa-i mermer der bāġçe-i ẖāṣṣ]*."

"For casting the glass panes of the new kiosk in front of the room of His Majesty [i.e., Privy Chamber]—may his reign be everlasting *[Becihet-i rīẖten-i cāmhā-i köşk-i cedīd der pīş-i oda-i ḥażret-i ẖullide mülkuhu]*."

"For expenses of painting the [portico] ceilings of the marble terrace and the kiosk and the new room at the privy garden *[Becihet-i ẖarc-i naḳş-kerden-i tavan-i ṣoffa-i mermer ve köşk ve oda-i cedīd der bāġçe-i ẖāṣṣ]*."

"For making assorted ceramic tiles for the privy garden's new kiosk near the marble terrace *[Becihet-i sāẖten-i kāşīhā-i mütenevviʿa berā-yi köşk-i cedīd der bāġçe-i ẖāṣṣa der nezd-i ṣoffa-i mermer]*."

"For making a water channel required for the new room at the imperial garden *[Becihet-i sāẖten-i rāh-i āb berā-yi mühimmāt-i oda-i cedīd der bāġçe-i ʿāmire]*."

"For expenses of painted globes to be hung at the new kiosk at the imperial garden *[Becihet-i ẖarc-i ṭobhā-i münaḳḳāş kim āvīẖten-i ḳaṣr-i cedīd der bāġçe-i ʿāmire]*."

Appendix B: Chronological Table of the Reigns of the Ottoman Sultans (1281–1924)

Osman I (1281–1324)
Orhan (1324–60)
Murad I (1360–89)
Bayezid I (1389–1401)
Interregnum (1402–13)
Mehmed I (1413–21)
Murad II (1421–44/1446–51)
Mehmed II (1444–46/1451–81)
Bayezid II (1481–1512)
Selim I (1512–20)
Süleyman I (1520–66)
Selim II (1566–74)
Murad III (1574–95)
Mehmed III (1595–1603)
Ahmed I (1603–17)
Mustafa I (1617–18/1622–23)
Osman II (1618–22)
Murad IV (1623–40)
İbrahim (1640–48)
Mehmed IV (1648–87)
Süleyman II (1687–91)
Ahmed II (1691–95)
Mustafa II (1695–1703)
Ahmed III (1703–30)
Mahmud I (1730–54)
Osman III (1754–57)
Mustafa III (1757–74)
Abdülhamid I (1774–89)
Selim III (1789–1807)
Mustafa IV (1807–8)
Mahmud II (1808–39)
Abdülmecid I (1839–61)
Abdülaziz (1861–76)
Murad V (1876)
Abdülhamid II (1876–1909)
Mehmed V (1909–18)
Mehmed VI (1918–22)
Abdülmecid II (Caliph, 1922–24)

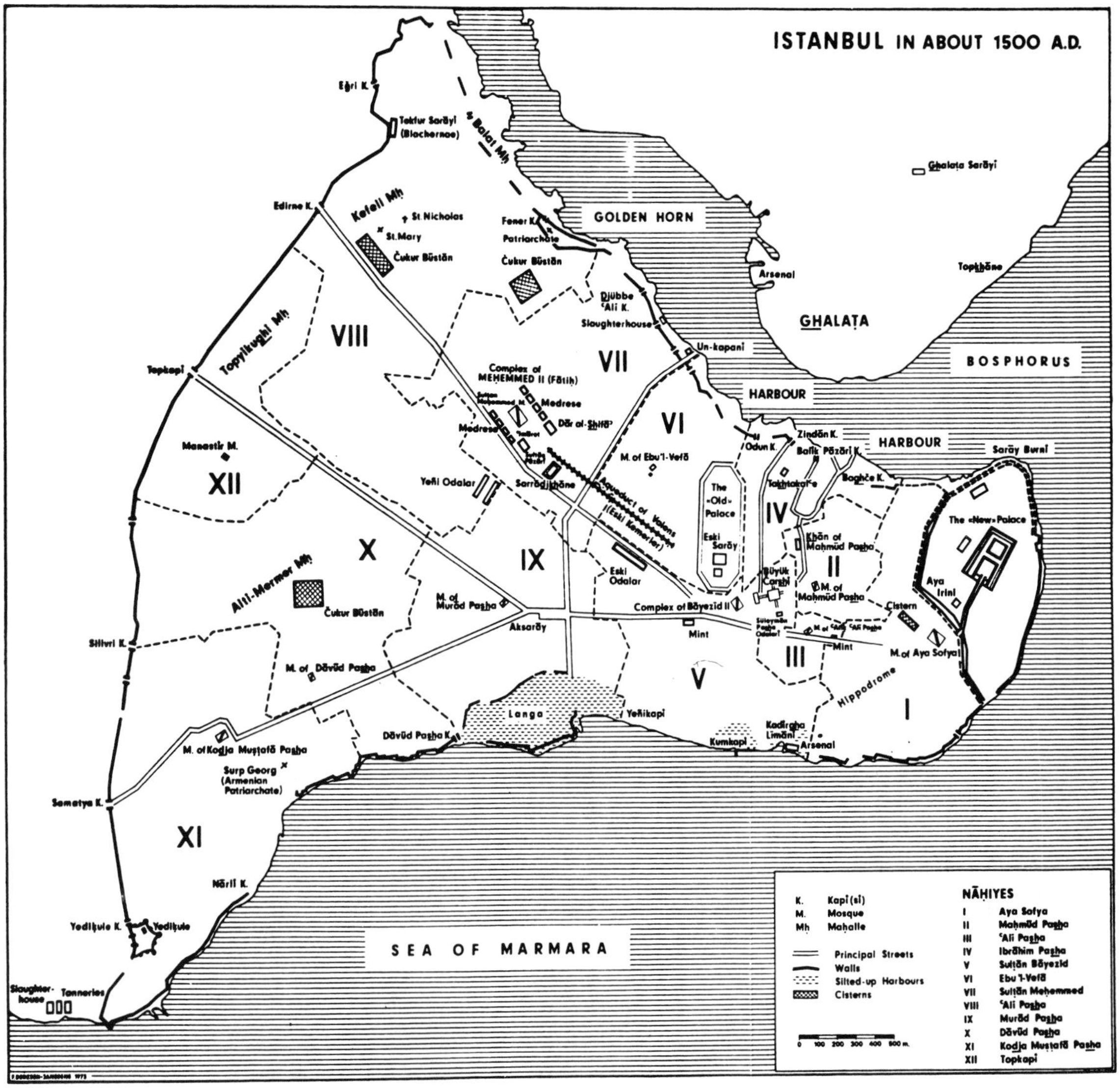

PLATE 1 Map of Istanbul, ca. 1500, from İnalcık, "İstanbul," *EI 2*, vol. 4, opp. p. 232.

PLATE 2*a,b* Aerial views of the Topkapı Palace, Hagia Sophia, and the Hippodrome.

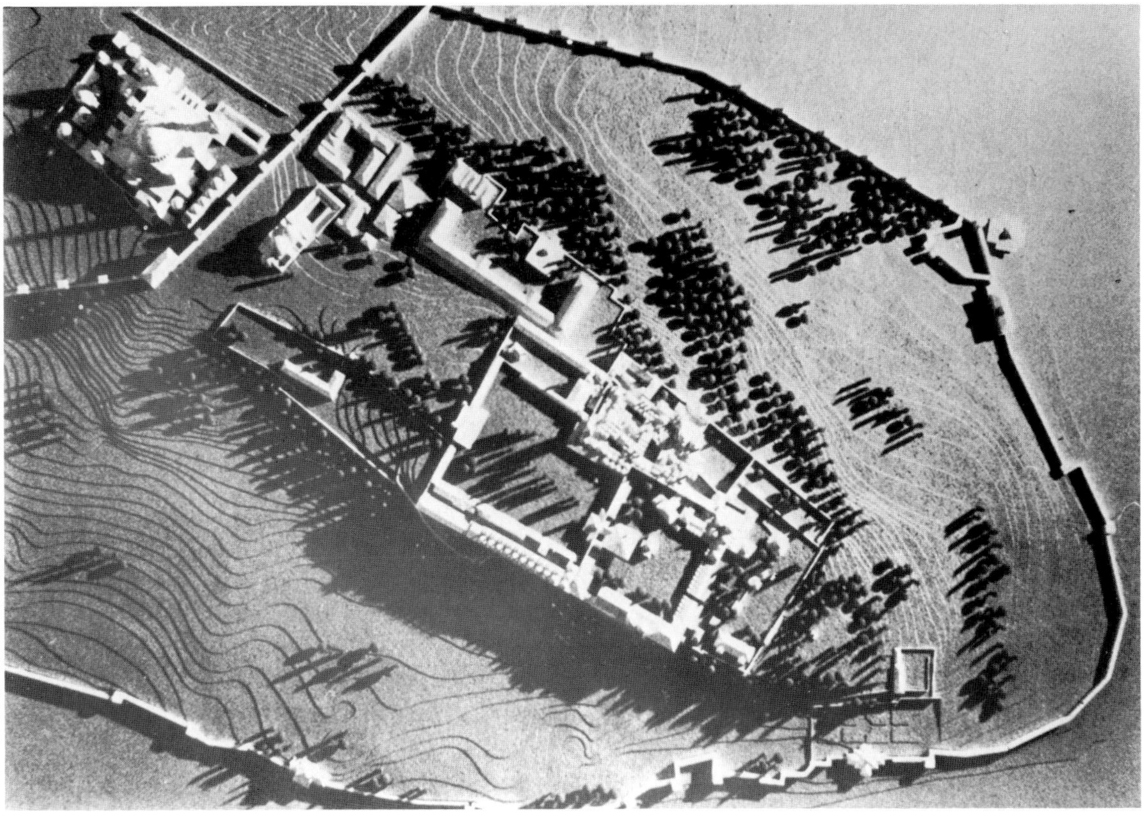

PLATE 3 Model of the Topkapı Palace in relation to Hagia Sophia. From the exhibition catalogue *Türkische Kunst und Kultur aus osmanischer Zeit,* Museum für Kunsthandwerk, Frankfurt, 1985.

PLATE 4 Bird's-eye view of the Topkapı Palace with Hagia Sophia in the background. Courtesy of Reha Günay.

PLATE 5*a*,*b* Bird's-eye views of the main core of the Topkapı Palace: the second and third courts and the walled hanging garden. Courtesy of Reha Günay.

PLATE 6 Bird's-eye view of the third court in the Topkapı Palace, showing the Golden Horn facade of the harem. Courtesy of Reha Günay.

PLATE 7 General view of the Topkapı Palace from the Golden Horn.

PLATE 8 (above) Bird's-eye view of the third court in the Topkapı Palace, showing the court for male pages, the harem, and the hanging garden with royal pavilions. Courtesy of Reha Günay.

PLATE 9 (opposite) Bird's-eye view of the main core of the Topkapı Palace. From Eldem and Akozan, *Topkapı*.

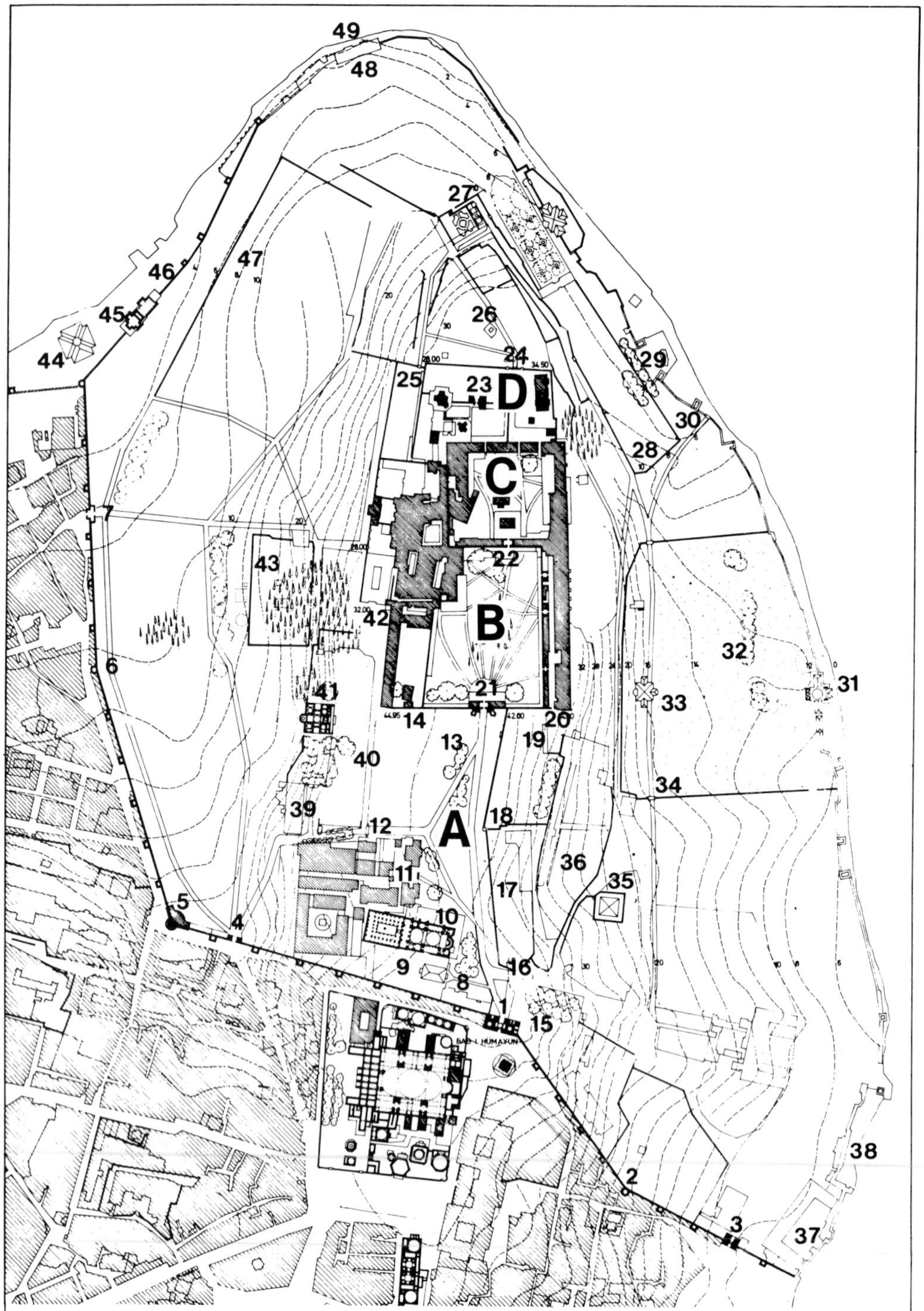

A
B
C
D
BAB-I HUMAYUN
1
2
3
4
5
6
7
8
9
10
11
12
13
14
15
16
17
18
19
20
21
22
23
24
25
26
27
28
29
30
31
32
33
34
35
36
37
38
39
40
41
42
43
44
45
46
47
48
49
0 50 100 150 200 250 300 400 500 600 700 800 mt

PLATE 10 Hypothetical reconstruction of the palace grounds in the nineteenth century. Drawing from Eldem and Akozan, *Topkapı*.

KEY: *A*. first court; *B*. second court; *C*. third court; *D*. the terraced hanging garden; *1*. first gate, or Imperial Gate; *2*. octagonal tower; *3*. Gate of the Stables, or Haystore Gate; *4*. Gate of the Cool Fountain, opening to a path that leads to the first court; *5*. dodecagonal tower, crowned by the Kiosk of Processions; *6*. octagonal tower of the Royal Band; *7*. Iron Gate; *8*. site of the dormitory of novices; *9*. site of the wood storehouse and workshop of mat makers; *10*. St. Irene, or royal armory; *11*. site of the imperial warehouse, the royal mint, and workshops of artisans, extending to the Gate of the Cool Fountain; *12*. gate connecting the first court to the outer gardens and to the maidan of the Tiled Kiosk (Çinili Köşk); *13*. site of the tower of the paper commissioner; *14*. gates of the stables; *15*. site of the hospital for pages and the launderers, with various functional workshops extending along the land wall up to the Gate of the Stables (Haystore Gate); *16*. gate connecting the first court to the outer garden; *17*. site of the royal bakery; *18*. water tower; *19*. site of the palace waterworks and related workshops; *20*. gate connecting the first court and the kitchens; *21*. second gate, or Middle Gate; *22*. third gate, or Gate of Felicity; *23*. gate from the sultan's private garden to the lower garden terrace; *24*. gate connecting the hanging garden of the third court with the outer garden; *25*. gate to the outer garden; *26*. the Goth's Column; *27*. site of an eighteenth- and nineteenth-century summer palace, with formal gardens; *28*. site of the İshak Pasha Pavilion, associated with sultan Mehmed II; *29*. site of the Corps of the Windmill, bakery, hospital for gardeners, and the gardener's mosque; *30*. Gate of the Windmill; *31*. Pearl Kiosk and the holy spring, called the *Ayazma Christos Sotiros; 32*. site of the sports maidan; *33*. Gülhane Kiosk; *34*. Gülhane Gate; *35*. antique cistern used as an arsenal; *36*. menagerie; *37*. site of the Byzantine chapel converted into a royal aviary; *38*. fishing station; *39*. present location of the Ancient Near East Museum *(Şark Eserleri Müzesi); 40*. present location of the Classical Archeology Museum *(Arkeoloji Müzesi); 41*. Tiled Kiosk *(Çinili Köşk); 42*. harem gate communicating with the maidan of the Tiled Kiosk; *43*. hanging garden *(çemen soffa); 44*. Shore Kiosk; *45*. Basketmakers' Kiosk; *46*. site of the Corps of Oarsmen, the boathouses, construction-related warehouses, and workshops; *47*. site of the dormitory of gardeners (replaced by a medical school) and the Green Tiled Mosque; *48*. site of the Cannon Gate; *49*. site of the Marble Kiosk.

PLATE 11 Hypothetical reconstruction of the main core of the Topkapı Palace in the early eighteenth century. Drawing from Eldem and Akozan, *Topkapı*.

KEY: *A.* second court; *B.* third court (court of male pages); *C.* harem; *D.* terraced hanging garden of the third court; *1.* second gate, or Middle Gate; *2.* dormitories of gatekeepers; *3.* domed vestibule; *4.* prison of executioners; *5.* execution fountain; *6.* gate connecting the kitchens with the first court; *7.* Gate of the Imperial Commissary; *8.* Gate of the Royal Kitchens; *9.* Gate of the Confectionary; *10.* court of the kitchens; *11.* court of the stables; *12.* gate connecting the stables to the first court; *13.* gate connecting the stables to the maidan of the Tiled Kiosk *(Çinili Köşk); 14.* mosque and bath of the stables; *15.* quarters of the Halberdiers with Tresses; *16.* gate connecting the quarters of Halberdiers to the second court; *17.* Gate of Stables; *18.* gate connecting the harem to the second court; *19.* three salutation stones on the path connecting the Middle Gate to the public Council Hall; *20.* Council Hall of the grand vizier, with the sultan's latticed window; *21.* chancery; *22.* archives; *23.* Tower of Justice; *24.* Public Treasury; *25.* Old Council Hall; *26.* water distribution reservoir with a guesthouse; *27.* third gate, or Gate of Felicity, with the royal portico; *28.* domed vestibule of the third gate; *29.* chamber of the Head Gatekeeper; *30.* Small Chamber; *31.* hypothetical position of the royal loge, with a latticed window overlooking the Old Council Hall; *32.* gate connecting the harem with the third court; *33.* Large Chamber; *34.* small court of the Large Bath's furnace, hypothetical site of the fifteenth-century aviary; *35.* Chamber of Petitions; *36.* mosque; *37.* early-eighteenth-century library, built for Ahmed III on the approximate site of the Pool Pavilion; *38.* site of the Large Bath, later occupied by the Chamber of the Expeditionary Force; *39.* Ionic colonnade of the Treasury-Bath complex; *40.* first hall of the Inner Treasury; *41.* projecting latrine; *42.* open loggia with fountain; *43.* second hall of the Inner Treasury (throne room, containing the royal library); *44.* third hall of the Inner Treasury; *45.* fourth hall of the Inner Treasury, originally the disrobing hall of the Large Bath; *46.* Chamber of Commissary Pages; *47.* Chamber of Treasury Pages; *48.* Treasury of the Swordbearer and small room with a spiral staircase, once leading to a roof pavilion; *49.* petition hall; *50.* Privy Chamber, or throne hall; *51.* fountained hall; *52.* domed space continuous with fountained hall; *53.* Chamber of Privy Chamber Pages; *54.* marble pool; *55.* marble terrace; *56.* privy garden; *57.* lower garden platform; *58.* gate connecting the privy garden with the lower garden platform; *59.* Head Physician's Tower, with the remaining walls of the sultan's privy garden; *60.* site of a fifteenth-century pavilion replaced by the Mecidiye Kiosk; *61.* site of cruciform pavilion; *62.* gate connecting the hanging garden of the third court with the outer garden, originally surmounted by the dormitory of privy gardeners; *63.* Circumcision Room; *64.* Revan Kiosk; *65.* Baghdad Kiosk; *66.* site of a former tower with a gate, connecting the Privy Chamber to the harem; *67.* Golden Path *(Altın Yol); 68.* marble terrace; *69.* large pool overlooking the Boxwood Garden; *70.* harem garden; *71.* Murad III's bedroom pavilion; *72.* Imperial Hall; *73.* court of the Queen Mother; *74.* court of concubines; *75.* quarters of black eunuchs; *76.* ramp descending to the outer gardens; *77.* harem gate communicating with the maidan of the Tiled Kiosk; *78.* garden gate; *79.* garden gate.

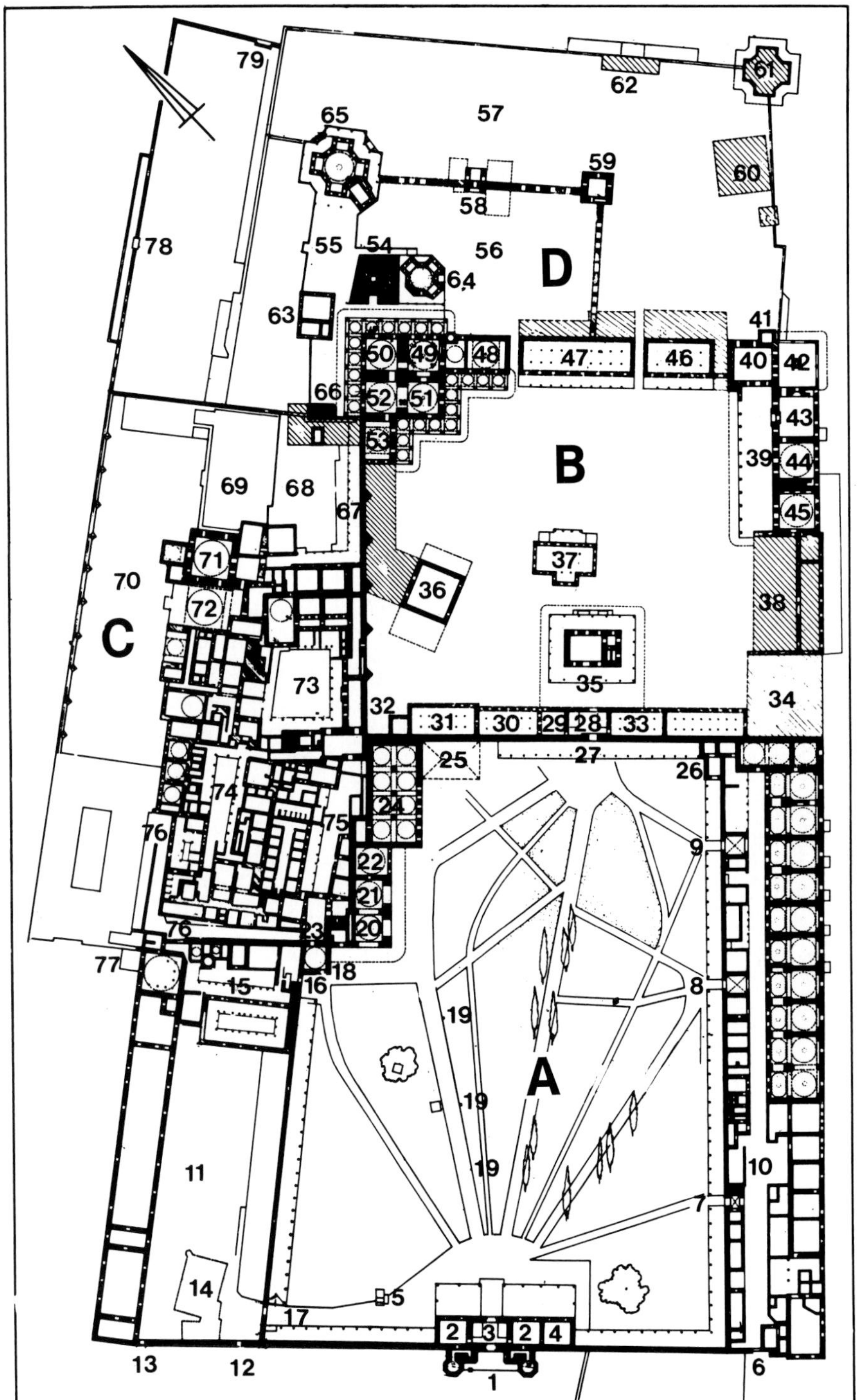
A
B
C
D
1
2
3
4
5
6
7
8
9
10
11
12
13
14
15
16
17
18
19
20
21
22
23
24
25
26
27
28
29
30
31
32
33
34
35
36
37
38
39
40
41
42
43
44
45
46
47
48
49
50
51
52
53
54
55
56
57
58
59
60
61
62
63
64
65
66
67
68
69
70
71
72
73
74
75
76
77
78
79

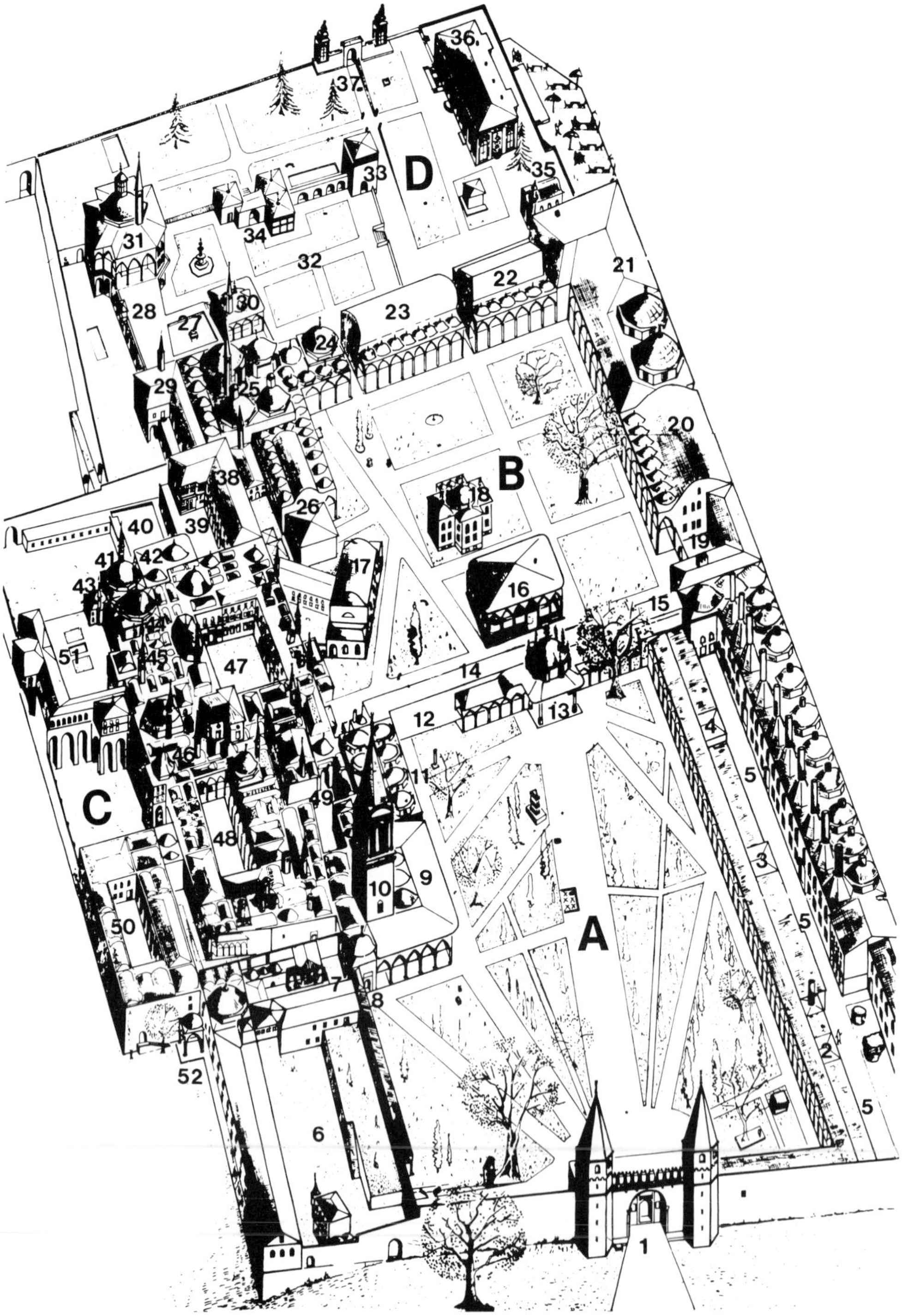
A
B
C
D
1
2
3
4
5
6
7
8
9
10
11
12
13
14
15
16
17
18
19
20
21
22
23
24
25
26
27
28
29
30
31
32
33
34
35
36
37
38
39
40
41
42
43
44
45
46
47
48
49
50
51
52

PLATE 12 Isometric drawing of the main core of the Topkapı Palace as it stands today, drawn by İlban Öz.
KEY: *A.* second court; *B.* third court (court of male pages); *C.* harem; *D.* hanging terraced garden of the third court; *1.* second gate, or Middle Gate; *2.* Gate of the Imperial Commissary; *3.* Gate of the Royal Kitchens; *4.* Gate of the Confectionary; *5.* court of the kitchens; *6.* court of the stables; *7.* quarters of the Halberdiers with Tresses; *8.* gates connecting the quarters of Halberdiers and the harem to the second court; *9.* public Council Hall; *10.* Tower of Justice; *11.* Public Treasury; *12.* site of the Old Council Hall; *13.* third gate, or Gate of Felicity, with the royal colonnade; *14.* formerly the Small Chamber; *15.* formerly the Large Chamber *16.* Chamber of Petitions; *17.* mosque; *18.* library of Ahmed III; *19.* small court of the Large Bath's furnace; *20.* Chamber of the Expeditionary Force; *21.* Treasury-Bath complex; *22.* formerly the Chamber of Commissary Pages; *23.* formerly the Chamber of Treasury Pages; *24.* Treasury of the Swordbearer; *25.* main core of the Privy Chamber complex; *26.* mid-nineteenth-century dormitory of Privy Chamber Pages; *27.* marble pool; *28.* marble terrace; *29.* Circumcision Room; *30.* Revan Kiosk; *31.* Baghdad Kiosk; *32.* privy garden; *33.* Head Physician's Tower and remains of the garden wall, pierced by round-arched, latticed windows; *34.* gate pavilion, leading to the lower garden platform; *35.* mosque of the garden terrace; *36.* Mecidiye Kiosk; *37.* gate leading to the outer garden; *38.* Golden Path *(Altın Yol); 39.* marble terrace raised on vaults; *40.* marble pool; *41.* Murad III's bedroom pavilion; *42.* twin pavilions; *43.* Ahmed I's pavilion; *44.* Imperial Hall *(Hünkâr Sofası); 45.* double bath of the sultan and the Queen Mother; *46.* Queen Mother's quarters; *47.* court of the Queen Mother; *48.* court of concubines; *49.* quarters of black eunuchs; *50.* hospital; *51.* marble terrace added in the eighteenth century; *52.* harem gate, communicating with the terrace of the Tiled Kiosk.

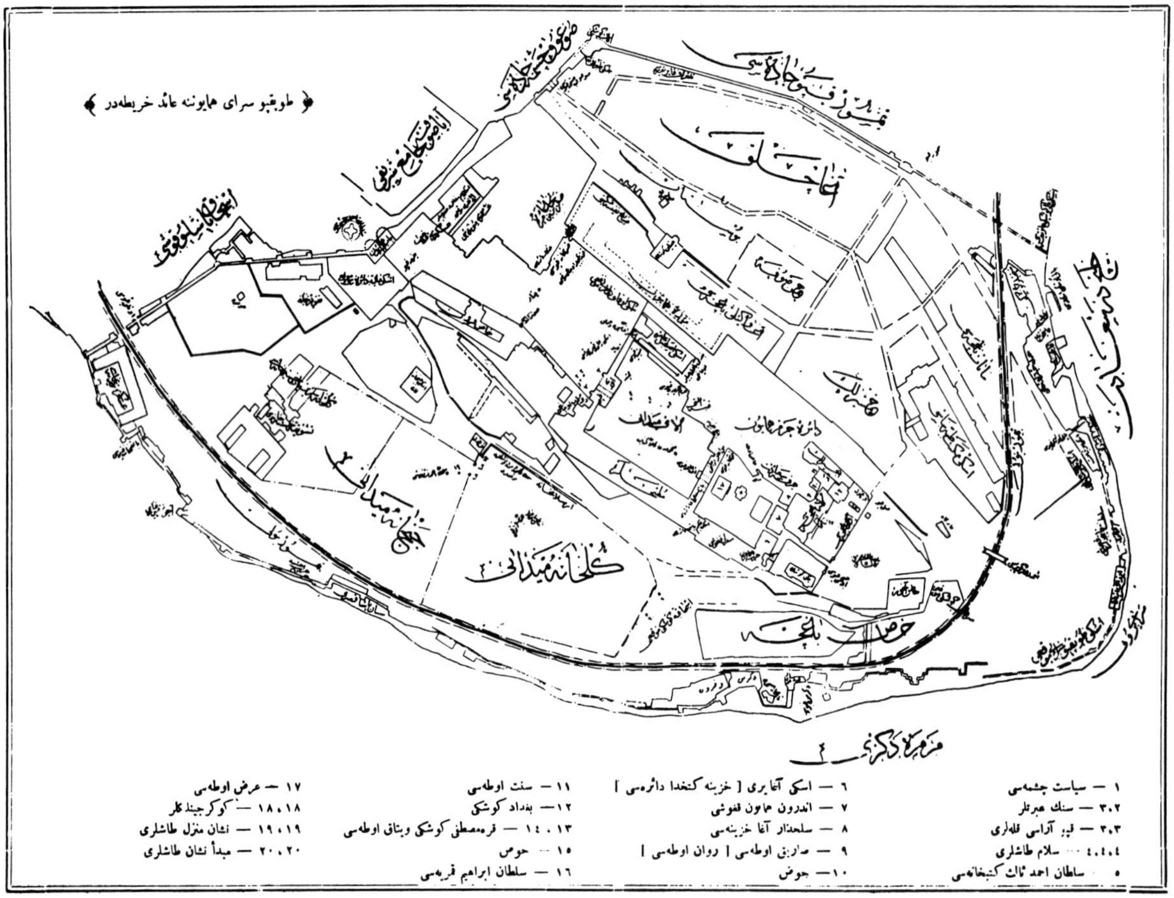

PLATE 13 Schematic plan of the palace grounds around 1910. From Şeref, *Topkapu*.

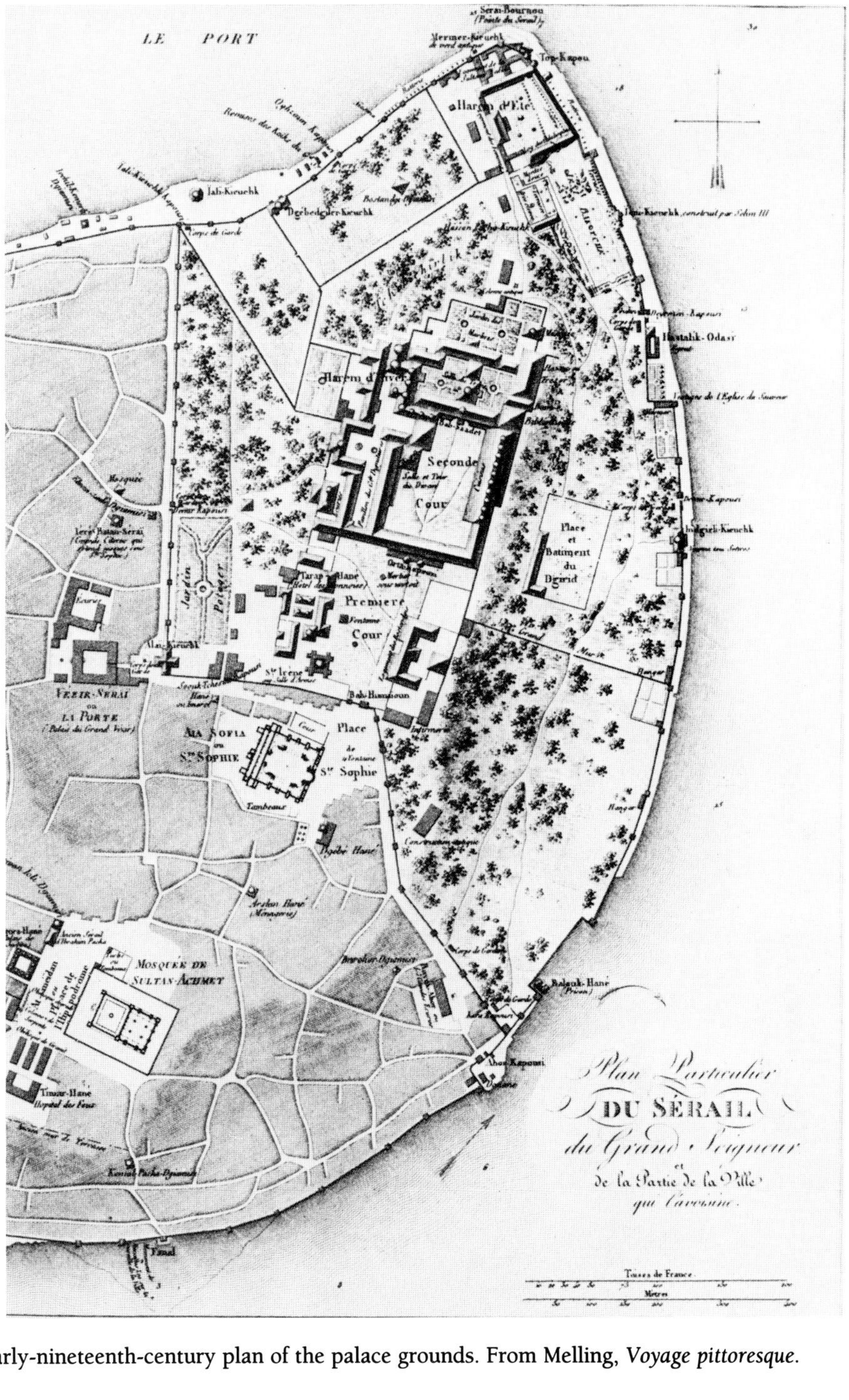

PLATE 14 Early-nineteenth-century plan of the palace grounds. From Melling, *Voyage pittoresque*.

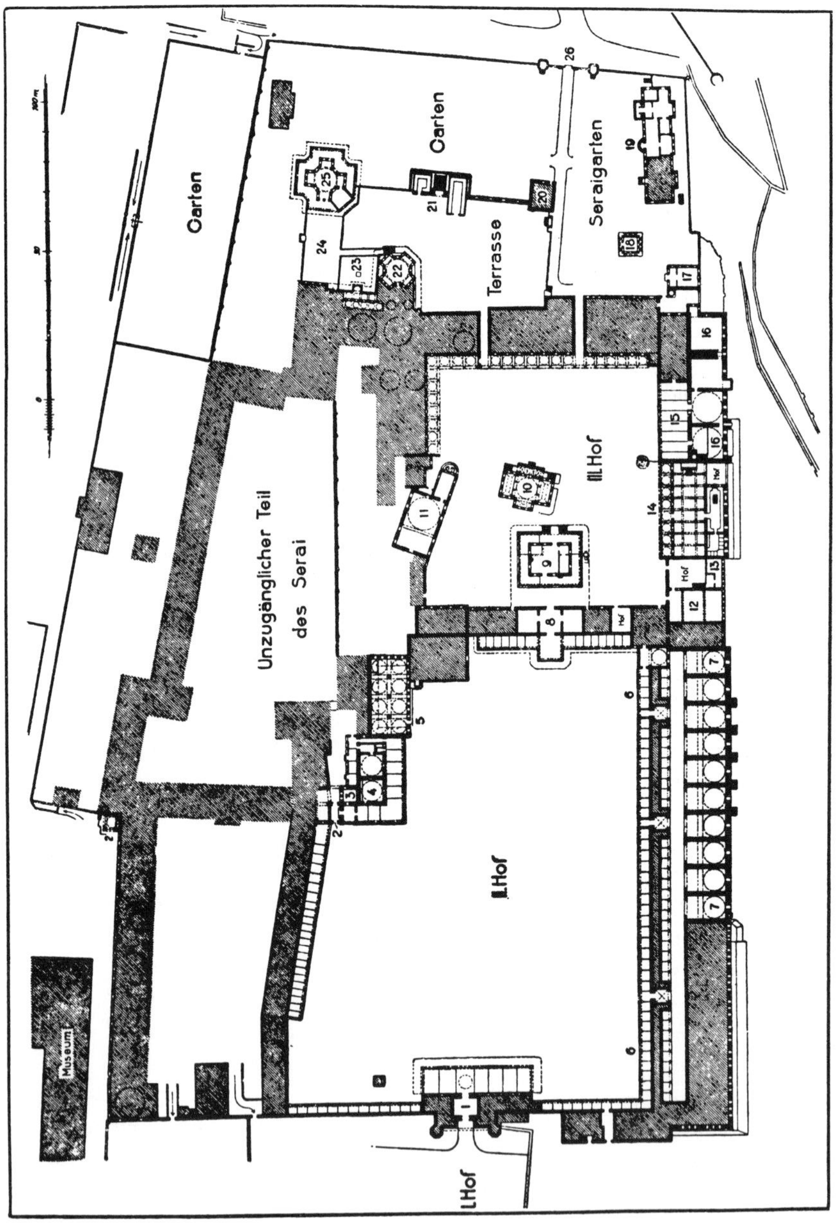

PLATE 15 Plan of the main core of the Topkapı Palace in 1910. From Gurlitt, *Baukunst.*
KEY: *1.* second gate; *2.* Harem Gate; *3.* tower; *4.* divan; *5.* old library; *6.* Janissary dormitories; *7.* kitchens; *8.* third gate; *9.* throne room; *10.* new library; *11.* mosque; *12.* dormitory for eunuchs; *13.* pharmacy; *14.* dormitory for eunuchs; *15.* Treasury vestibule; *16.* Treasury; *17.* mosque; *18.* pavilion; *19.* Mecidiye Kiosk; *20.* summerhouse; *21.* pavilions; *22.* Pavilion of the Holy Mantle; *23.* pool in front of the sultan's apartment; *24.* terrace; *25.* Baghdad Kiosk; *26.* garden gate; *27.* Goth's Column.

PLATE 16 (overleaf) *a*. Schematic plan of the main core of the Topkapı Palace by Albert Bobovi, from *Mémoires sur les Turcs,* 1666, MS. Harvard University, Houghton Library, French 103.

b. Schematic plan of the main core of the Topkapı Palace by Albert Bobovi, from *Description du Serail du Grand Seigneur,* 1666, MS. Paris, Bibliothèque Nationale, Fr. Nouv. Acq. 4997.

KEY: for Bobovi's plan (summarized from Bobovi's longer text):

A. The letter *A* represents the second court (the first court and outer gardens have been omitted, to concentrate on the organization of the inner palace); *B*. court of the harem, where women hang their laundry; *C*. small oratory, or masjid, of pages of the Large Chamber, where they pray four times a day; *D*. daytime retreat of mutes, where they study sign language; *E,F*. third court; *G*. latticed window from which the sultan watches private councils; *H*. small daytime chamber of the head falconer; *1*. Imperial Gate; *2*. gate of the chief black eunuch; *3*. chamber of the head gatekeeper, where he sleeps, eats, and guards the gate; *4*. dormitory of pages of the Large Chamber; *5*. back door of the Large Chamber, called the "Sand Gate," opened only at night, and guarded by two pages of that chamber; *6*. the Small Chamber, whose pages pray in the sultan's mosque, unlike pages of the Large Chamber; *7*. back door of the Small Chamber, like the Sand Gate used only at night; *8*. gate of the Large Chamber at the harem, opening into court *B; 9*. chamber of the chief black eunuch, where he sleeps and eats; *10*. bath where pages and eunuchs perform their ablutions; *11*. gate of the Small Chamber, communicating with the third court, marked *E,* which is kept open in the daytime and closed at night; *12*. inner door of the Imperial Gate; *13*. gate of the Large Chamber, communicating with the third court, marked *F,* which is kept open in the daytime and closed at night; *14*. chamber of the palace steward, where all pages and eunuchs receive their salaries every three months; *15*. open court for washing dishes and for military exercises of the bath stokers; *16*. No explanation provided in Bobovi's text; *17*. No explanation provided in Bobovi's text; *18*. recreation room of eunuchs and of the nine masters of petitions (allowed to give written petitions to the sultan); *19*. furnace of the bath and chamber of bath stokers; *20*. Chamber of the Expeditionary Force, whose pages are charged with washing the sultan's laundry during campaigns, and his turban every Tuesday; *21*. bath reserved for the use of pages of a different chamber each day of the week; *22*. music chamber; *23*. portico in front of the Inner Treasury, where they measure gold and silver; *24*. Inner Treasury; *25*. Chamber of Treasury Pages [*sic:* Chamber of Commissary Pages]; *26*. daytime office of the head treasurer's lieutenant, where artisans come to find him when they are summoned to melt gold and silver objects into coins; *27*. Chamber of Commissary Pages [*sic:* Chamber of Treasury Pages]; *28*. daytime office of the head of commissary's lieutenant, where he receives goods brought to the commissary; *29*. storeroom of the commissary, where sweets, perfumes, candles, and drugs are stored; *30*. a kiosk guarded by a corps of gardeners, from which one descends to the garden, called the Guard's Kiosk *(Kioschk Bektschysy); 31*. hall where pages of the Privy Chamber are lodged; *32*. portico in front of the Privy Chamber; *33*. Imperial Hall *(Khunkiar Odahsy),* consisting of richly decorated rooms where the sultan sleeps, located between the men's Privy Chamber *(Khasodah des Pages)* and the women's Privy Chamber *(Khasodah des Dames); 34*. Long Chamber *(Ouzounodah),* inhabited by royal favorites called *haseki; 35*. daytime cabinet of the swordbearer, where he receives visitors; *36*. royal mosque, where the sultan, his mother, women, and black eunuchs pray with the whole court; *37*. daytime cabinet of the master of the wardrobe; *38*. aviary, where small birds are nourished, with a gate connecting the court of male pages to the harem; *39*. inner gate of the harem; *40*. large pool at the Privy Chamber, where music and plays are performed to entertain the sultan, who sometimes gives audiences there to the mufti and grand vizier *(g); 41*. Chamber of Falconers *(h); 42*. chamber where the sultan receives ambassadors; *43*. portico in front of the aforementioned chamber; *44*. Chamber of the Halberdiers with Tresses; *45*. public Council Hall; *46*. portico of the public Council Hall, for lesser officers and plaintiffs; *47*. confectionary kitchens; *48*. kitchens; *49*. section of the royal garden; *50*. infirmary of pages; *51*. chamber of the chief eunuch in charge of the infirmary; *52*. chambers of old slave laundresses, called "mothers" *(analar),* attached to the infirmary, who wash the laundry of pages; *53*. infirmary of Privy Chamber pages and the masters of petitions; *54*. infirmary of Treasury and commissary pages; *55*. infirmary of Large Chamber pages; *56*. infirmary of pages of the Expeditionary Force; *57*. infirmary of Small Chamber pages; *58*. bath of invalids; *59*. infirmary of eunuchs; *60*. gate of the infirmary; *61*. infirmary formerly serving as the chamber of cavaliers; *62*. chamber of novices; *63*. first gate of the palace.

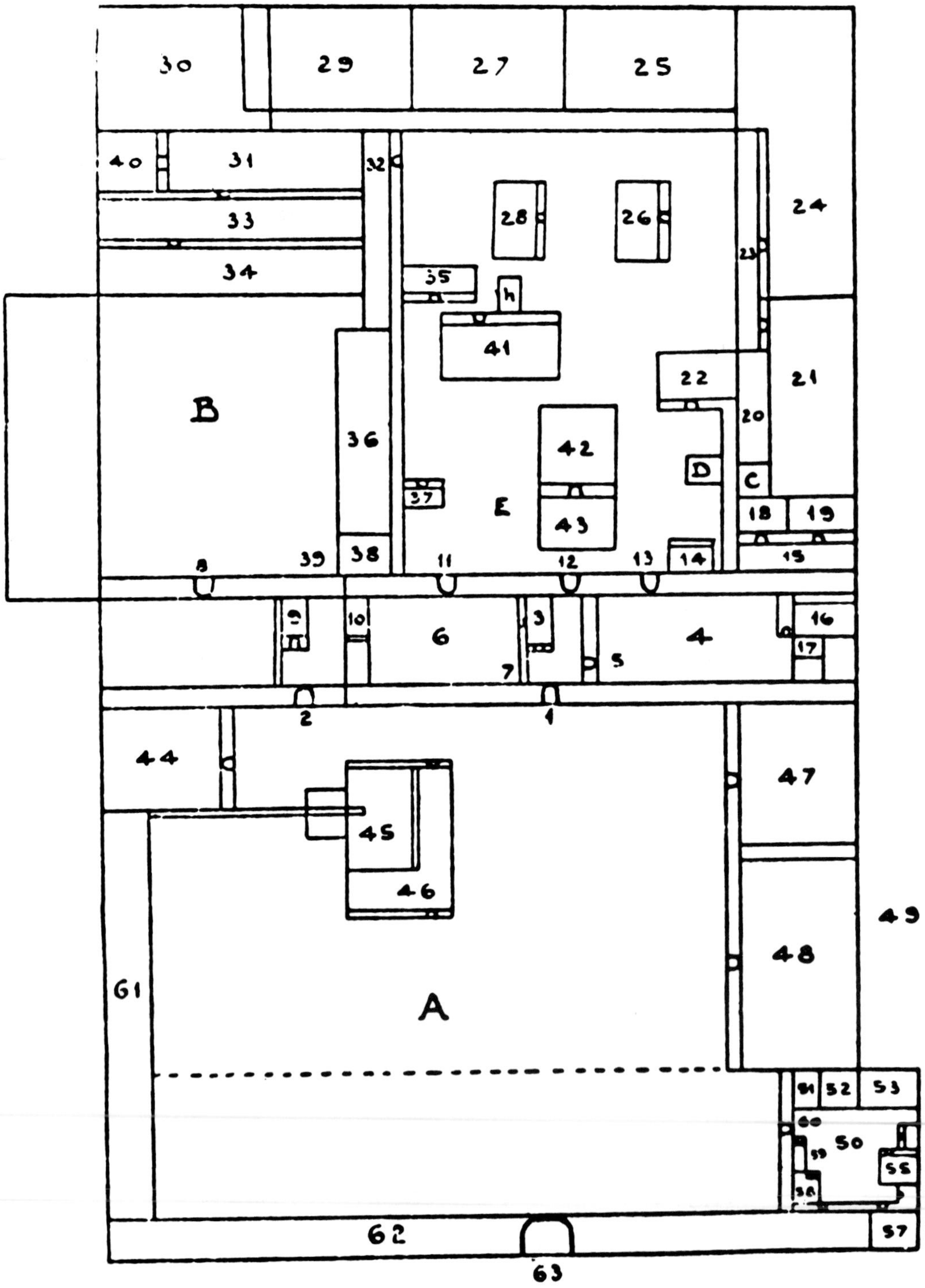
30
29
27
25
40
31
32
33
34
28
26
24
23
35
h
41
22
21
20
B
36
42
D
C
37
E
43
18
19
8
39
38
11
12
13
14
15
9
10
6
3
4
16
17
7
5
2
1
44
47
45
46
49
48
61
A
51
52
53
60
50
54
59
55
58
56
57
62
63

Plan du serail neuf.

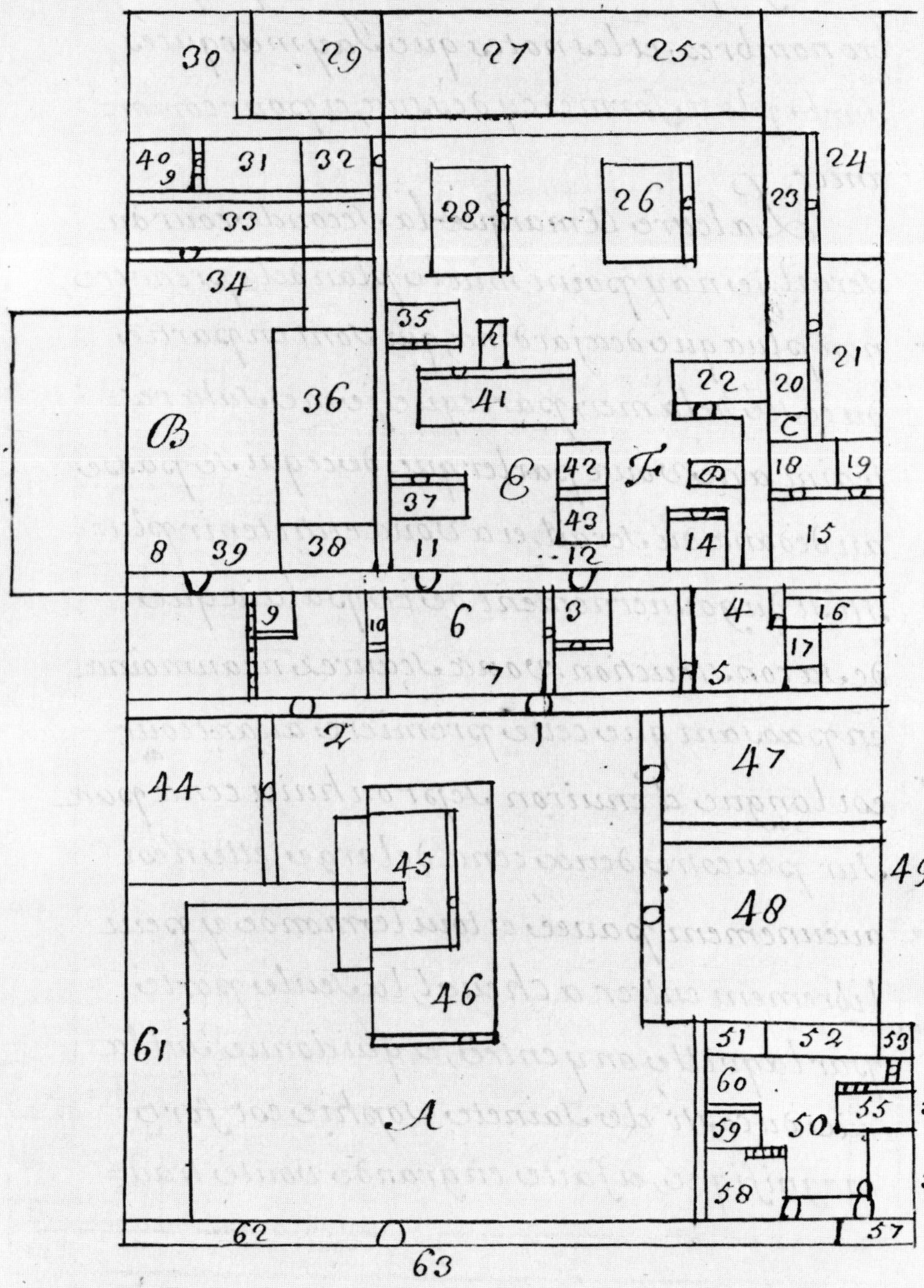

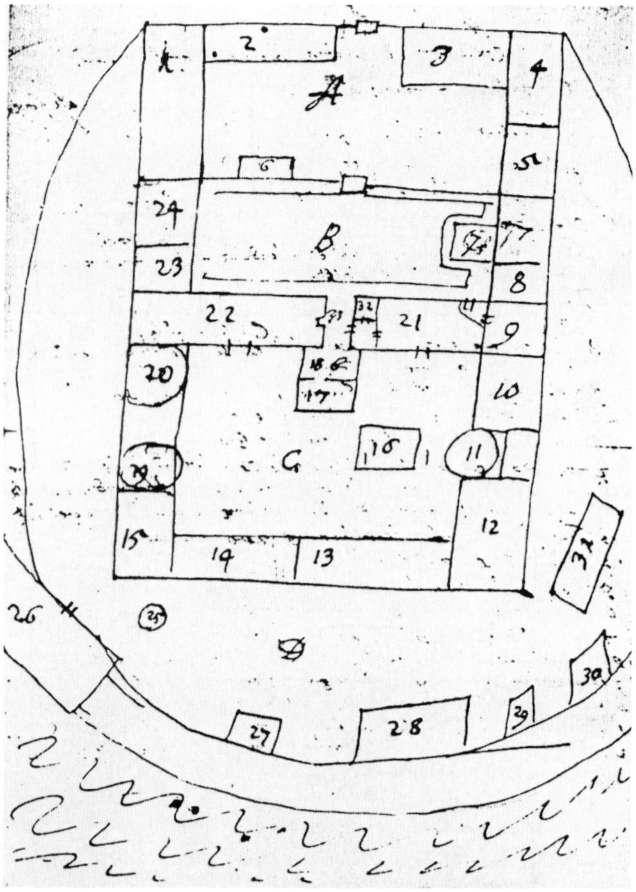

PLATE 17 A variant of Bobovi's plan, from Claes Ralamb, *Diarium ... 1657–58.*

KEY: *A.* first court; *B.* middle court; *C.* inner third court; *D.* garden; *1.* hospital; *2.* wood storehouse; *3.* arsenal; *4.* dormitory; *5.* mill and bakery; *6.* place for dismounting horses; *7.* Council Hall and chancery; *8.* Halberdiers; *9.* black eunuchs and their chief; *10.* harem; *11.* sultan's mosque; *12.* sultan's Privy Chamber; *13.* head treasurer; *14.* dormitory of the commissary; *15.* sultan's treasure chamber; *16.* falcons; *17.* divan for audiences; *18.* little forecourt with fountain; *19.* bath of Selim II; *20.* mosque of pages; *21.* Small Chamber of pages; *22.* Large Chamber of pages; *23.* confectionary bakery; *24.* kitchen; *25.* Sinan Pasha's mosque (destroyed); *26.* larger stable; *27.* Erivan (i.e., Revan) Kiosk; *28.* house of the chief gardener; *29,30.* kiosks for private audiences: Sinan Pasha Kiosk and Kara Mustafa Pasha Kiosk; *31.* smaller stable; *32.* head gatekeeper and white eunuchs; *33.* passage to the audience chamber, the Gate of Felicity; *34.* animal keep (next to *B*).

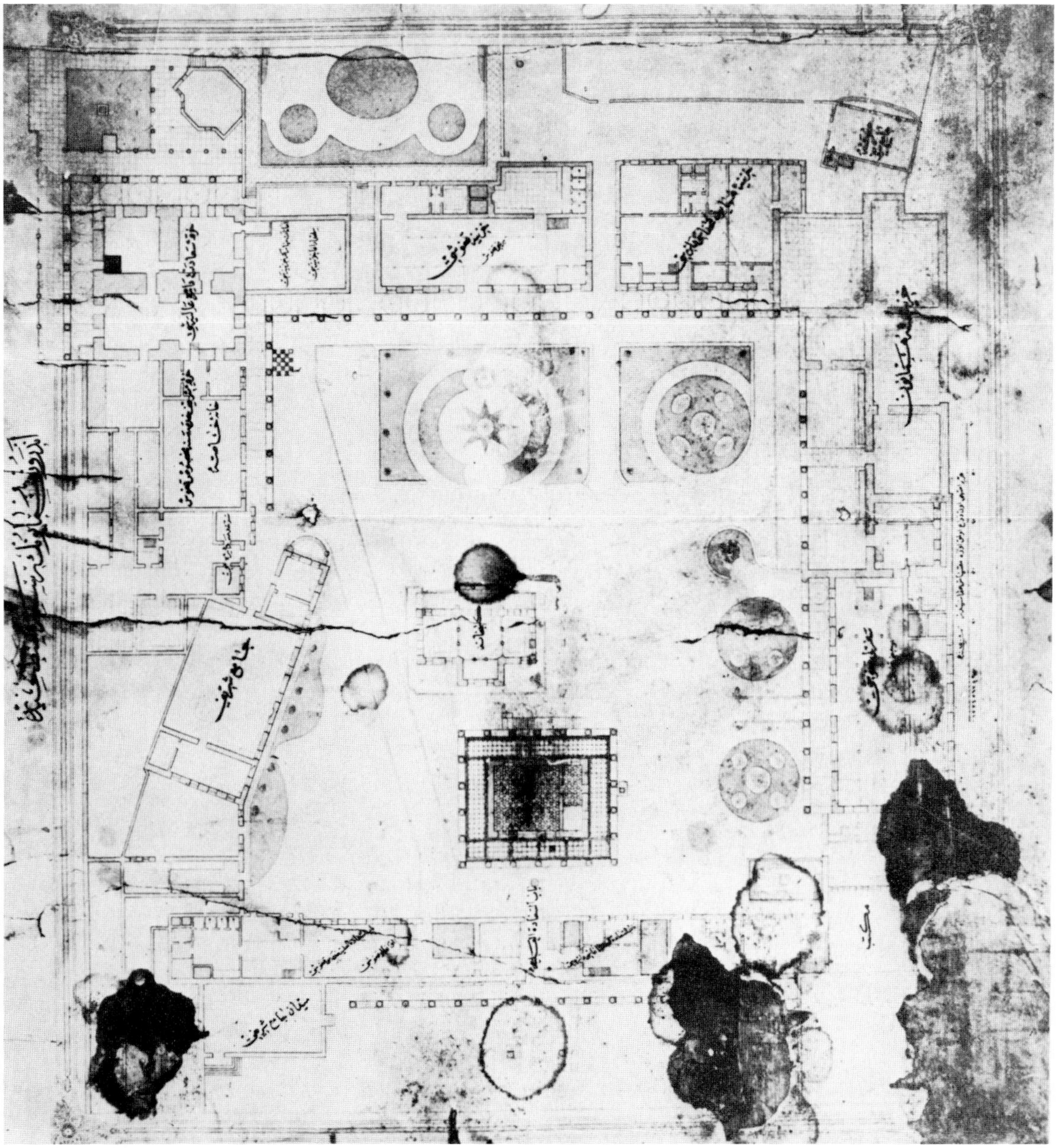

PLATE 18 (above and overleaf) Two mid-nineteenth-century plans from the Topkapı Palace Archives of the third court, recording a major remodeling project. From Eldem and Akozan, *Topkapı*.

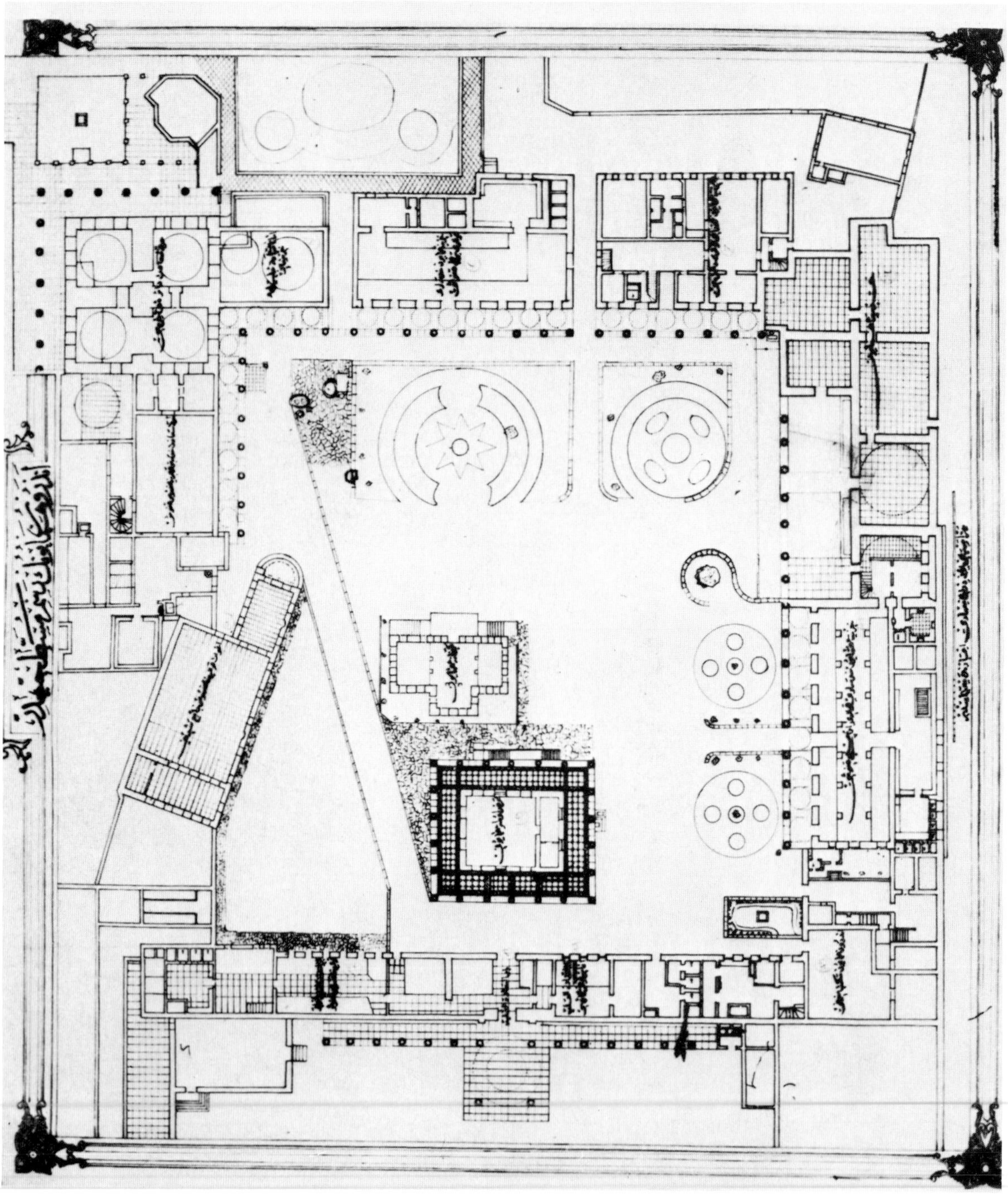

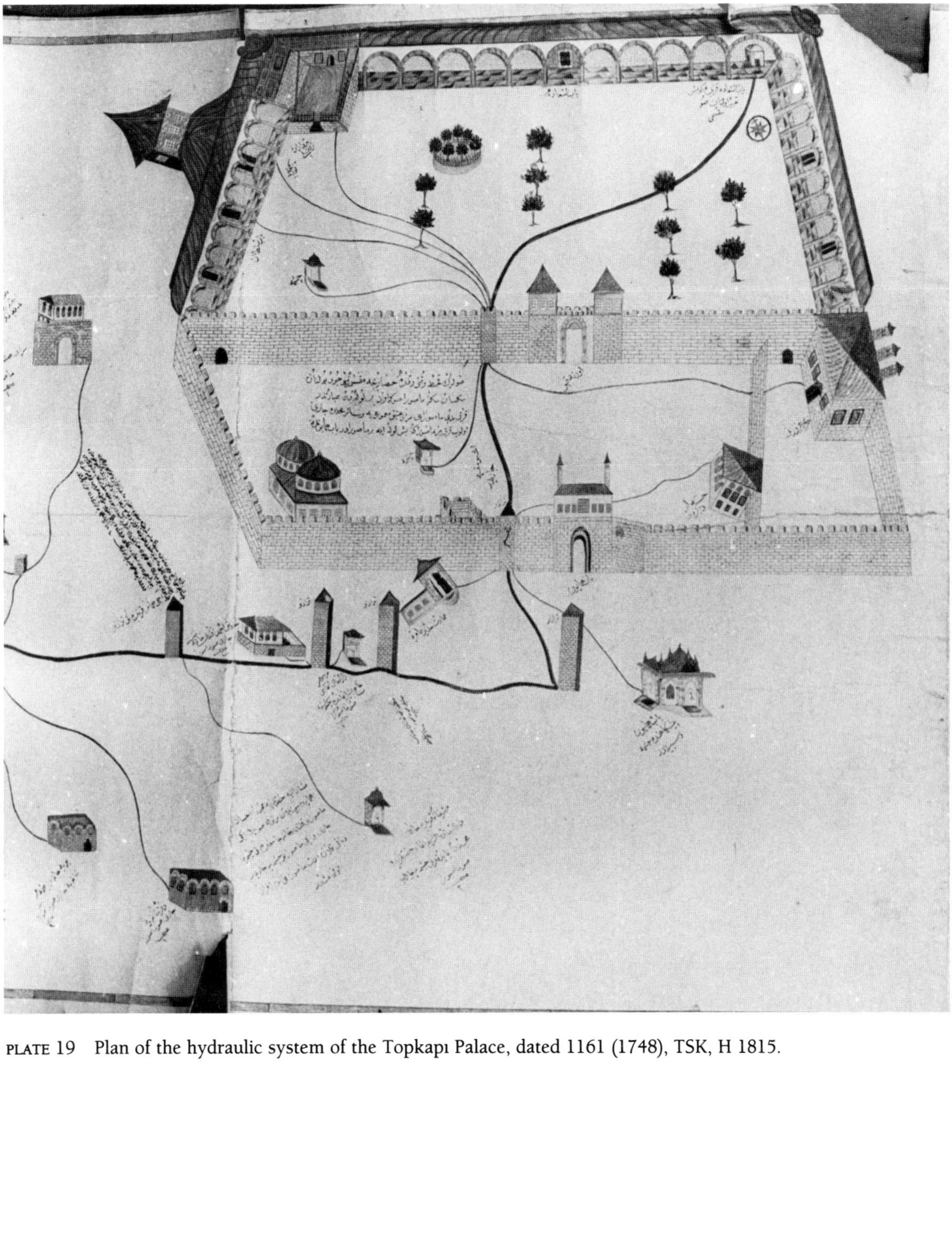

PLATE 19 Plan of the hydraulic system of the Topkapı Palace, dated 1161 (1748), TSK, H 1815.

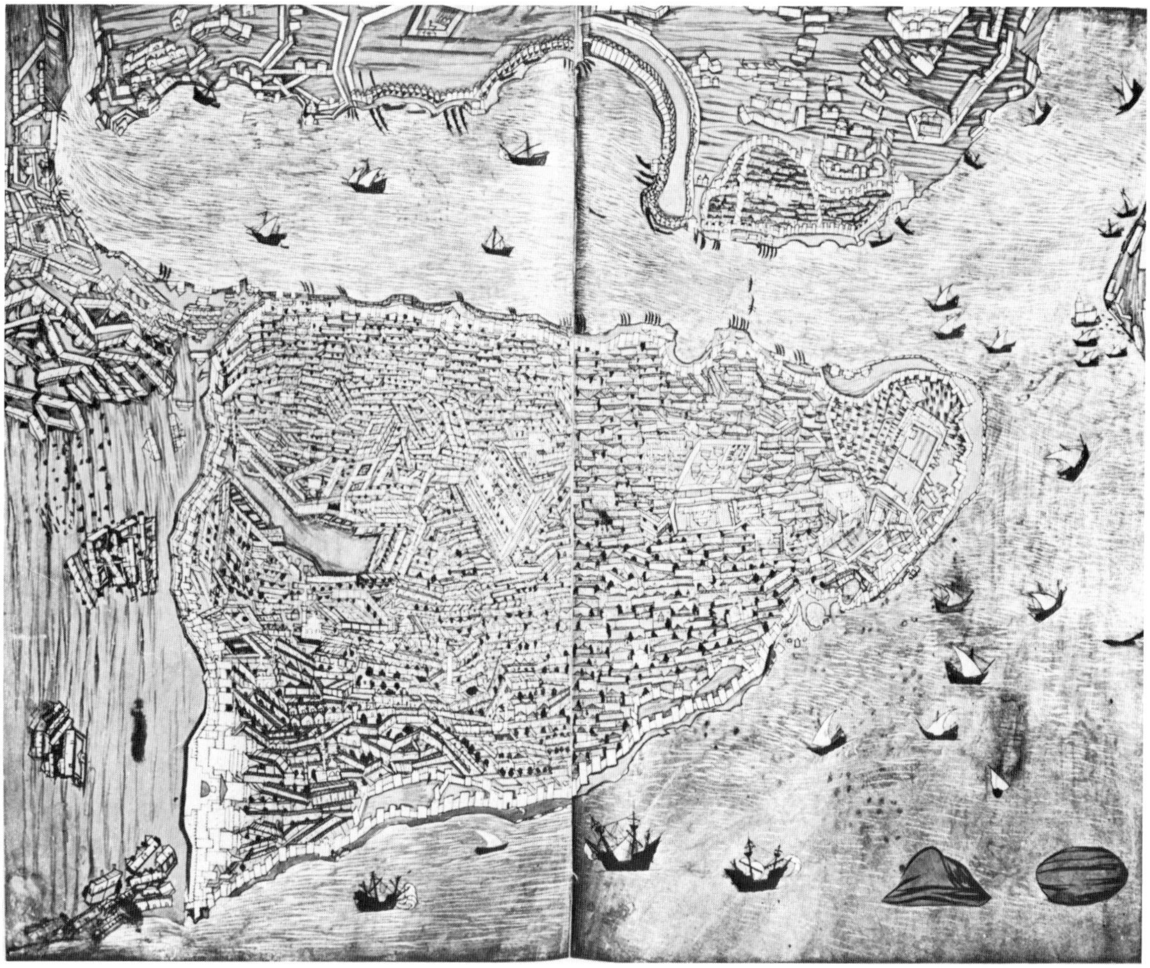

PLATE 20*a* Map of Istanbul ca. 1584–85. From Lokman, *Hünername,* TSK, H 1523, fols. 158v, 159r.

PLATE 20*b* Detail of *a*, showing Seraglio Point (*Saray Burnu*).

PLATE 21*a* Map of Istanbul in 1581–82. From Lokman, *Shahanshāhnāma,* İÜ, F 1404, fol. 58r.

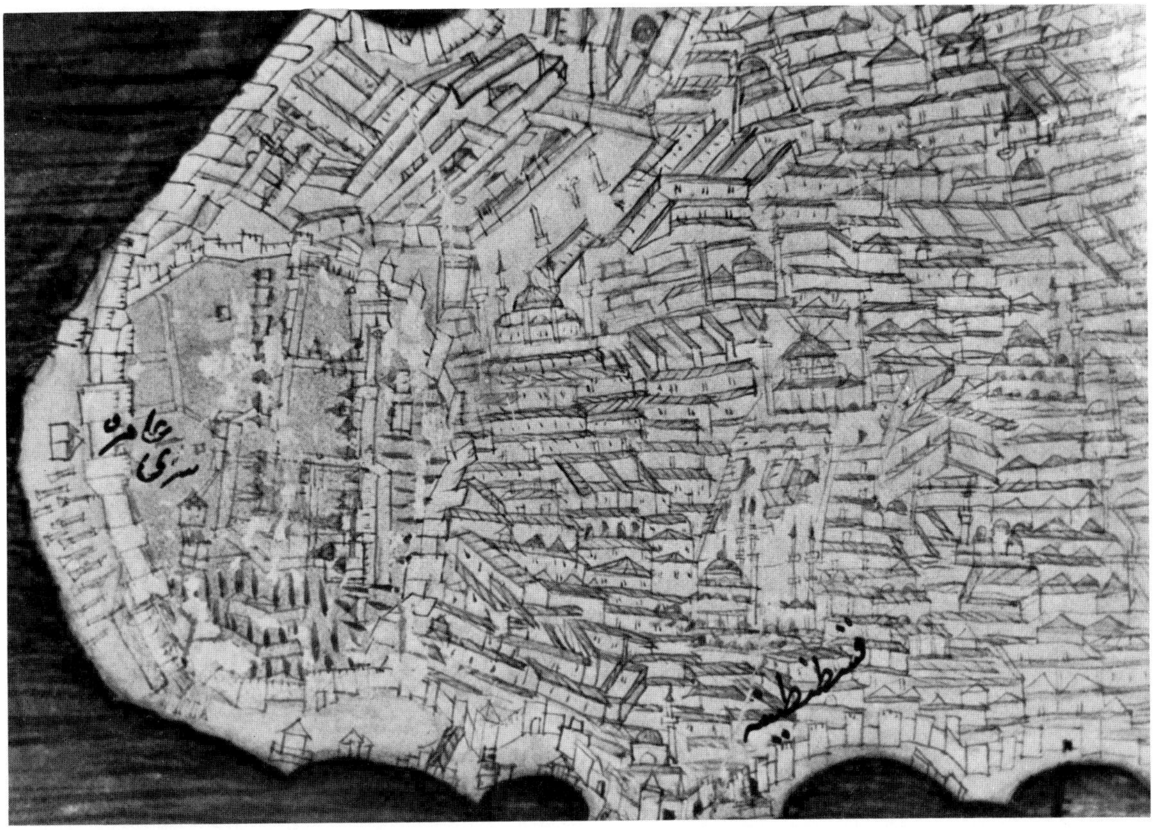

PLATE 21*b* Detail of *a*, showing Seraglio Point.

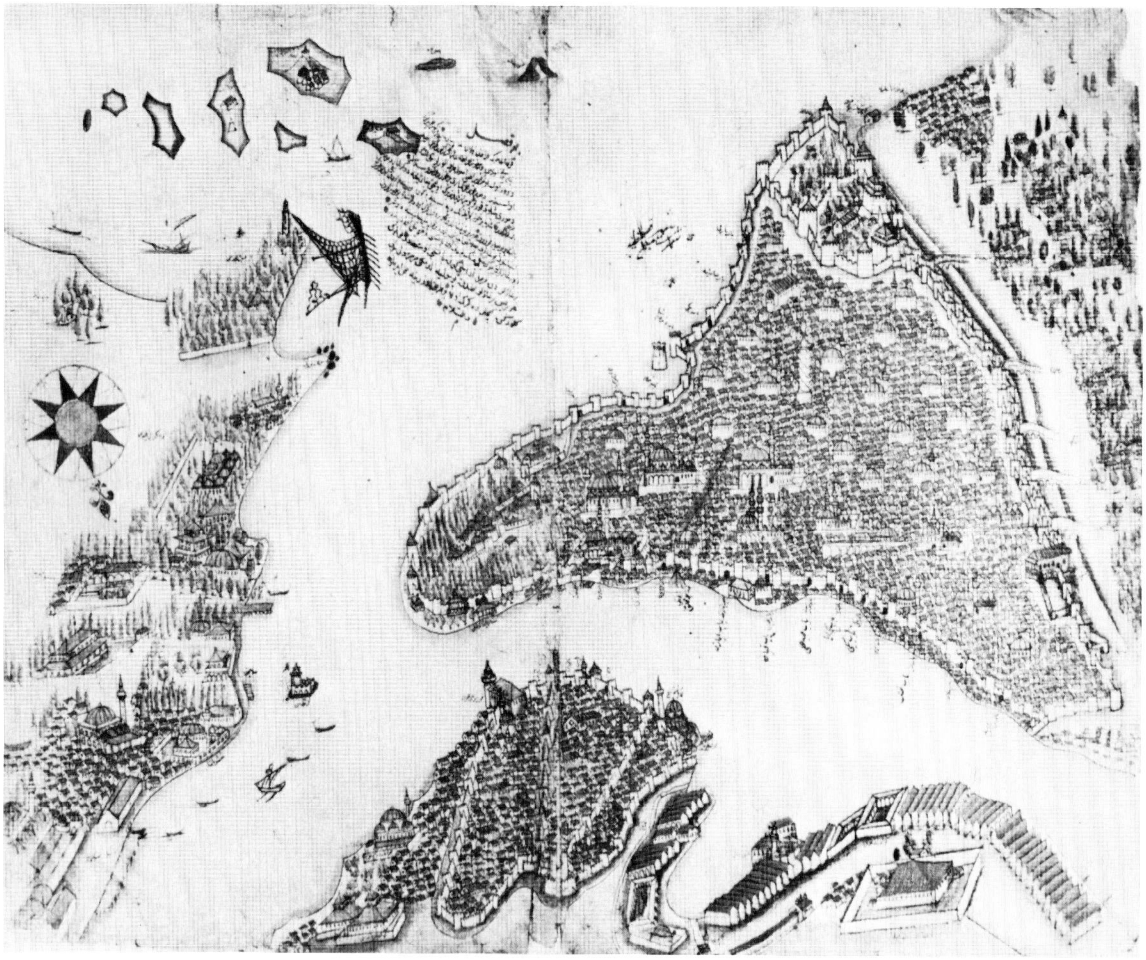

PLATE 22*a* Seventeenth-century map of Istanbul. From Piri Reis, *Kitab-i Bahriye,* MS. Berlin, Königliche Bibliothek.

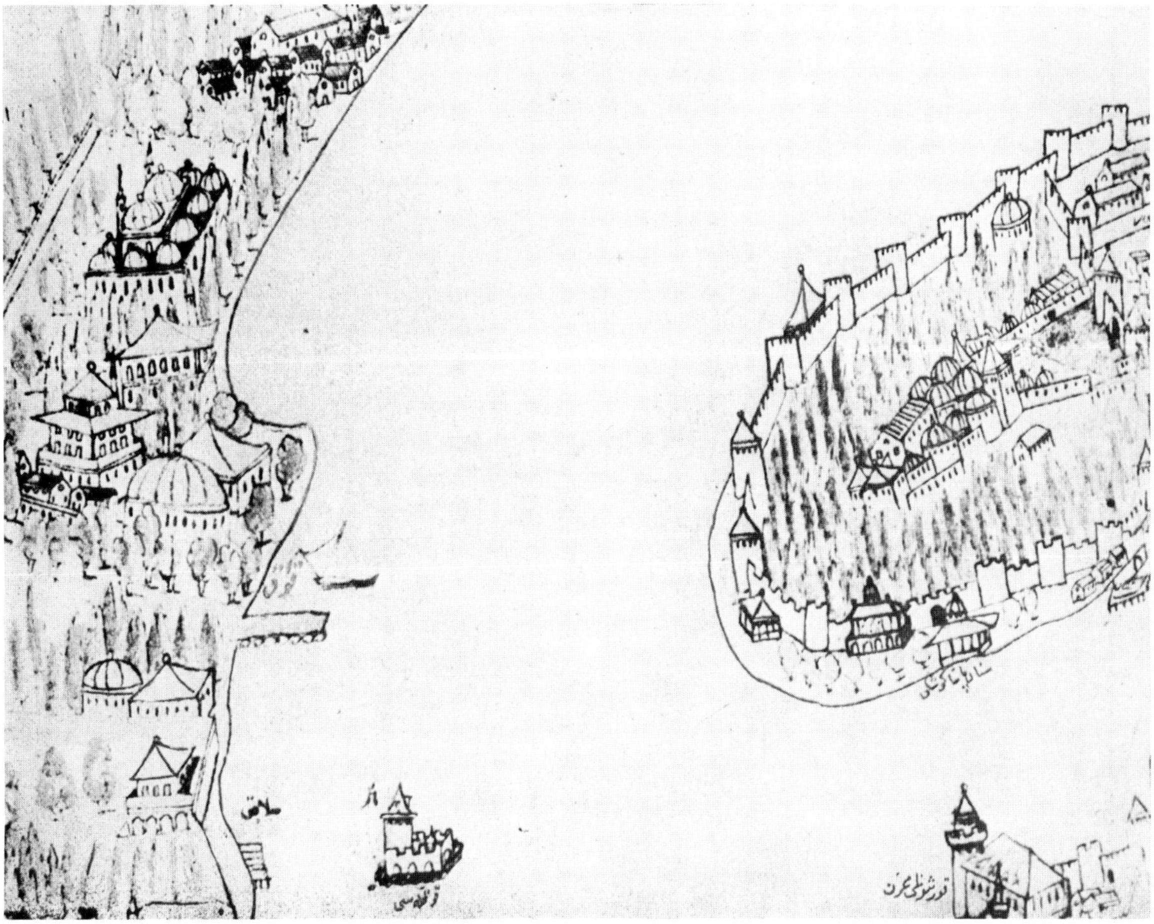

PLATE 22*b* Detail of *a,* showing Seraglio Point and the summer palace of Üsküdar across from it.

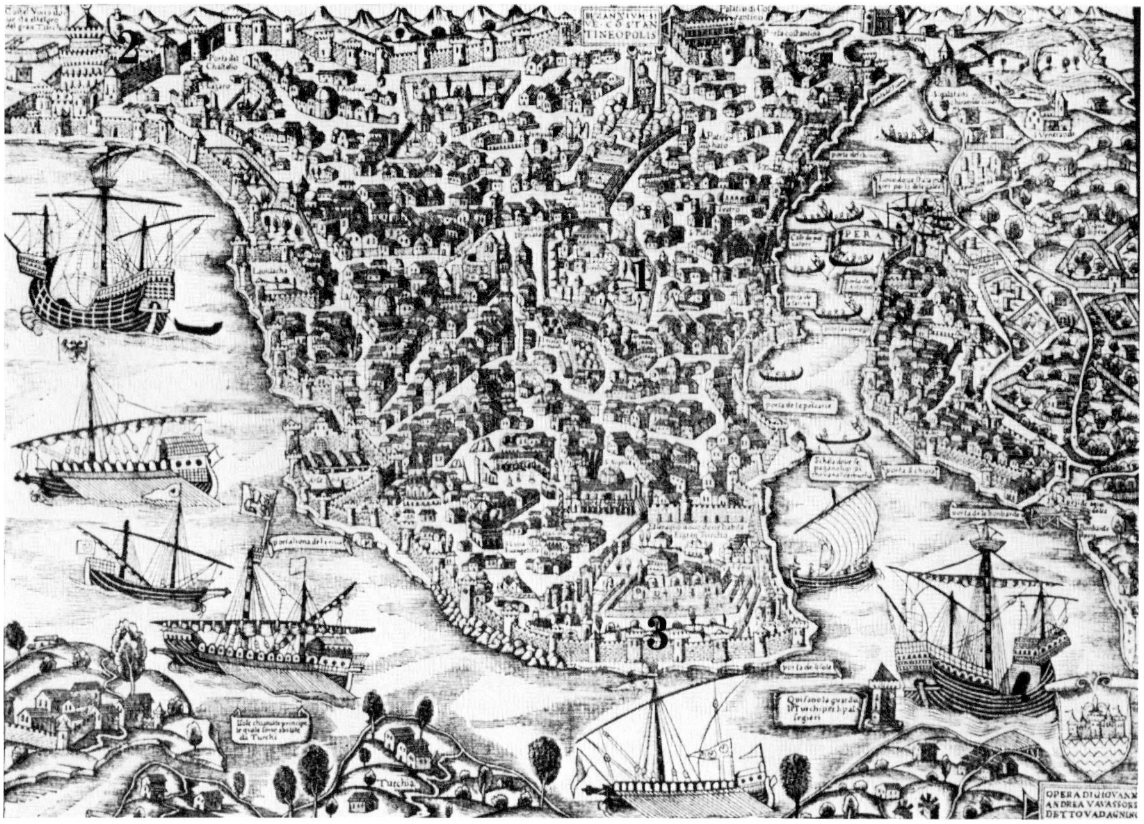

PLATE 23 Map of Istanbul published in 1520 by Giovanni Andrea Vavassore on the basis of a lost drawing of ca. 1479. 1. *Seraglio Vecchio* (Old Palace); 2. *Castel novo dove sta el tesoro del Gran Turcho* (Yedikule Fortress); 3. *Seraglio novo dove habita El Gran Turcho* (New Palace).

PLATE 24 Woodcut from Hartmann Schedel's *Nuremberg Chronicle,* published in 1493, depicting the destruction by lightning of Güngörmez Kilisesi in 1489–90, with a partial view of the Topkapı Palace next to the Hippodrome and Hagia Sophia.

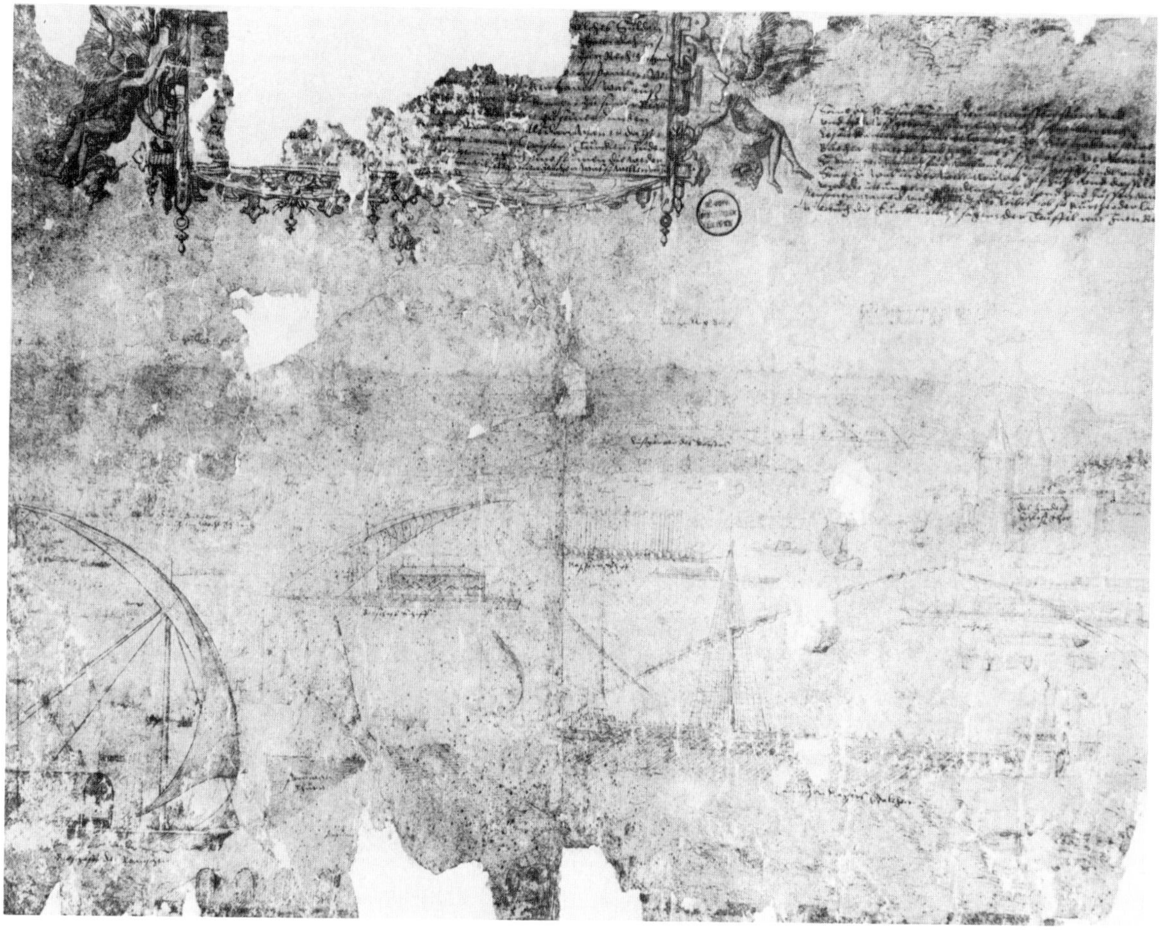

PLATE 25*a*–*f* The Topkapı Palace in Melchior Lorichs's panoramic view of Istanbul from the Golden Horn, 1559, Leiden University Library Cod. 1758, reproduced from Oberhummer, *Konstantinopel*.

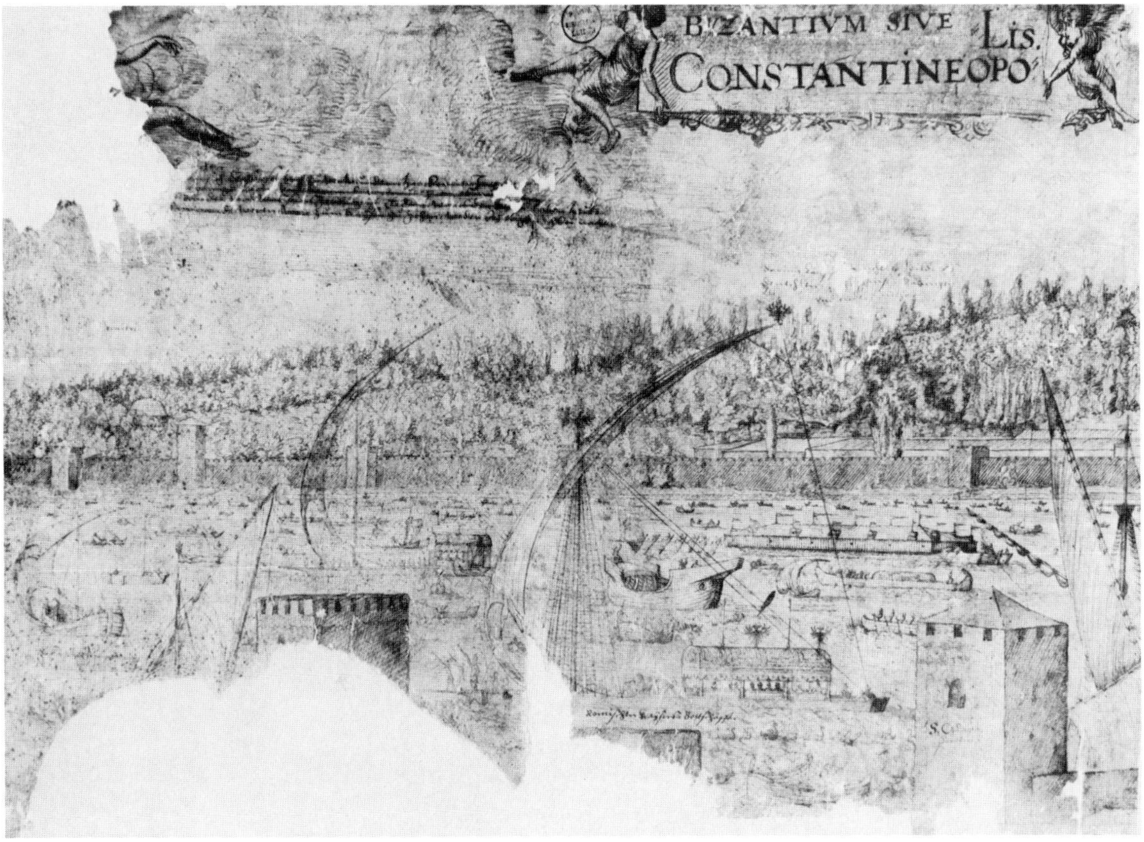
B ZANTIVM SIVE
LIS.
CONSTANTINEOPO

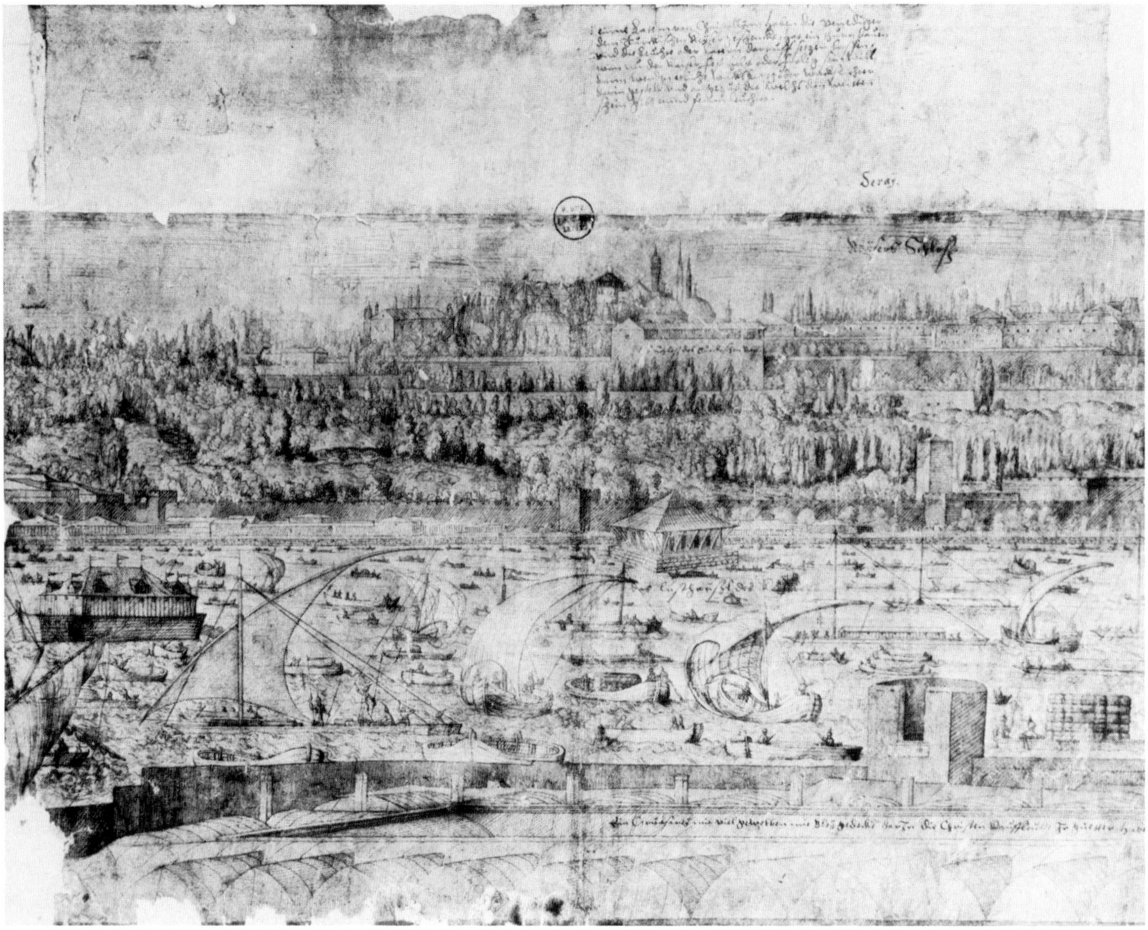
Seray.

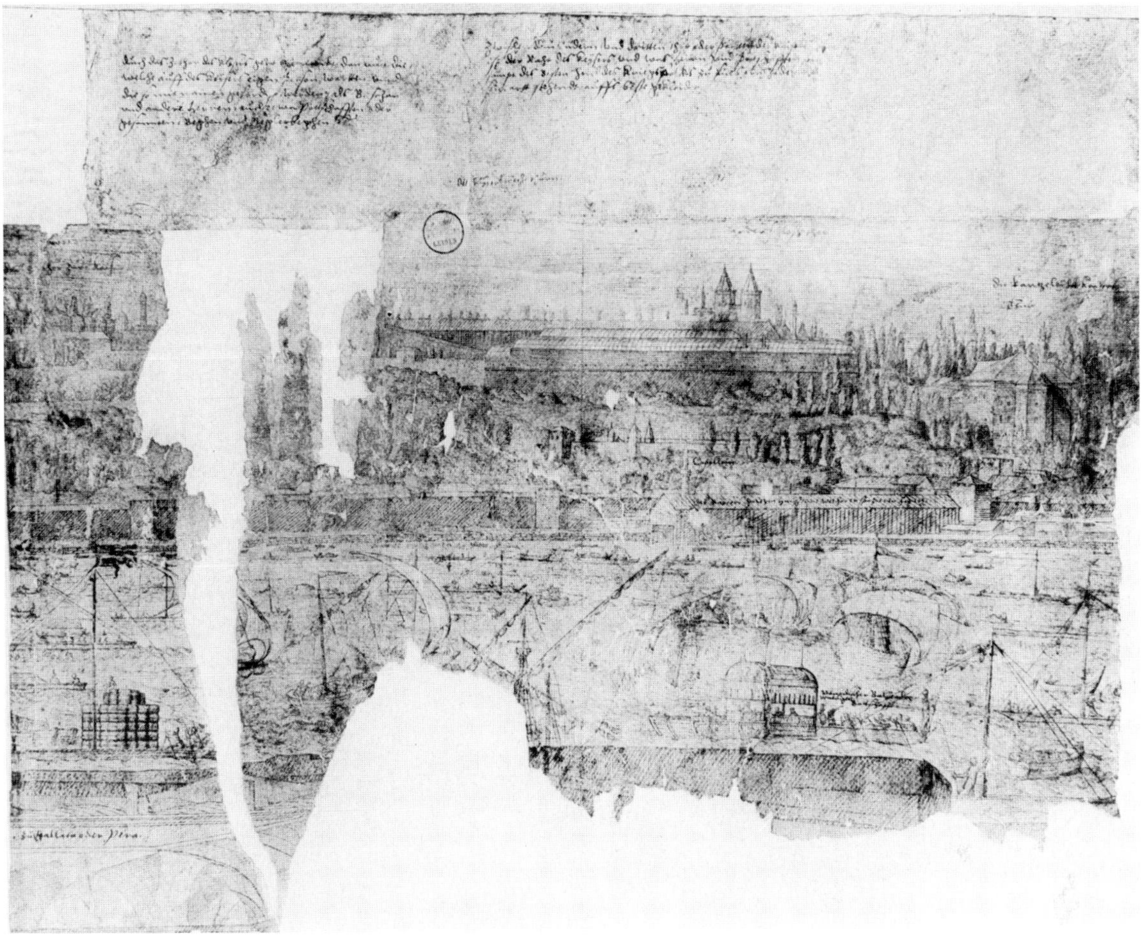

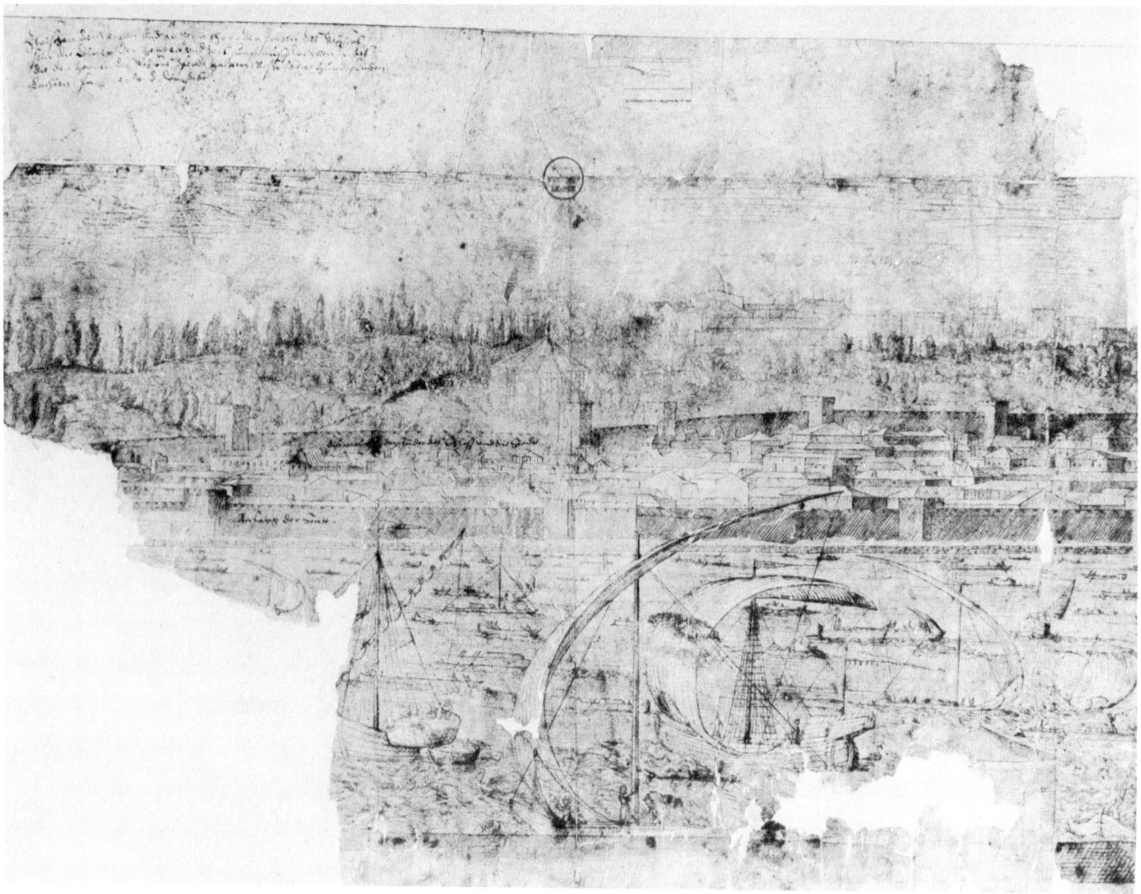

S. Sophia
S. Sophia

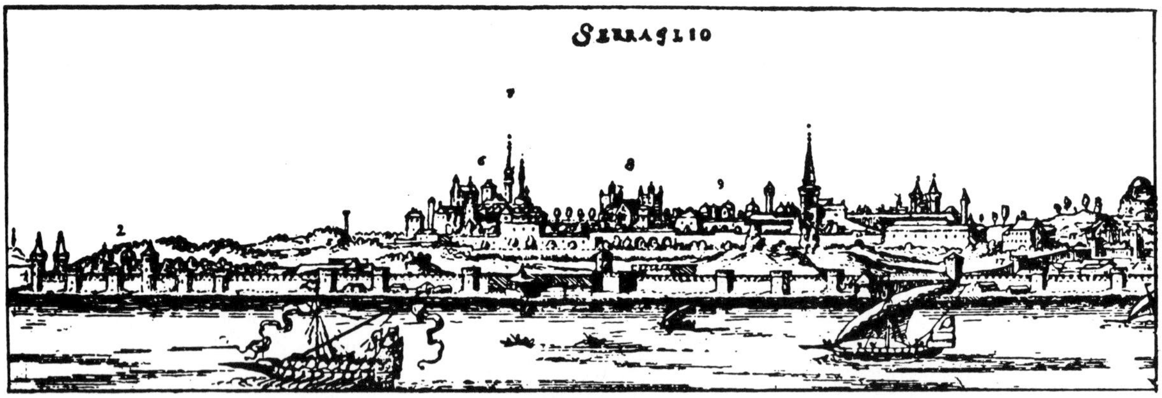

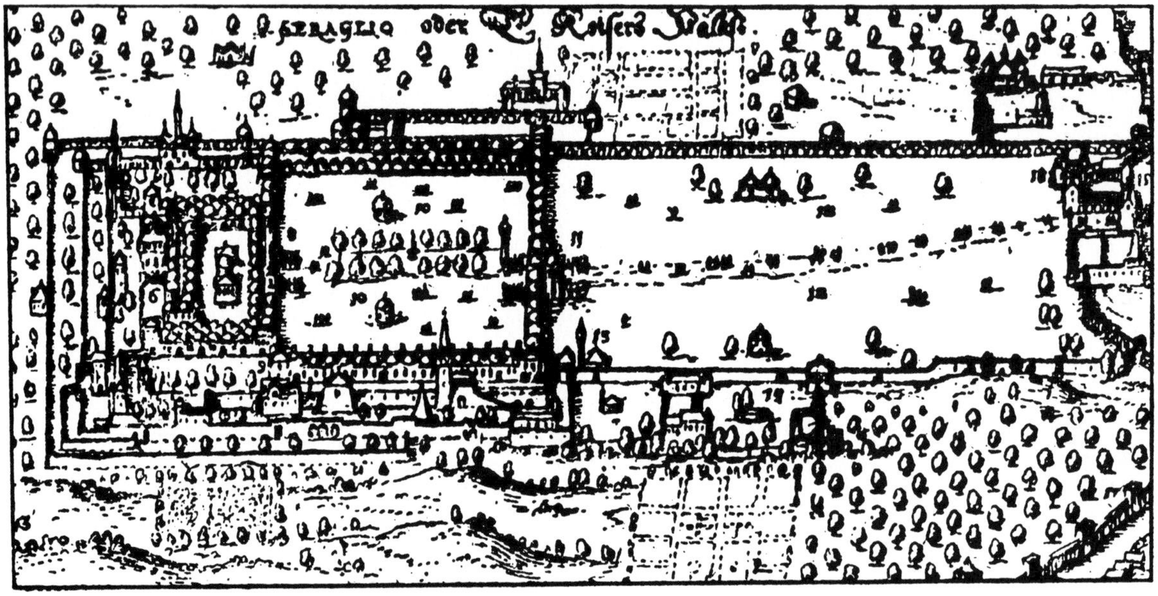

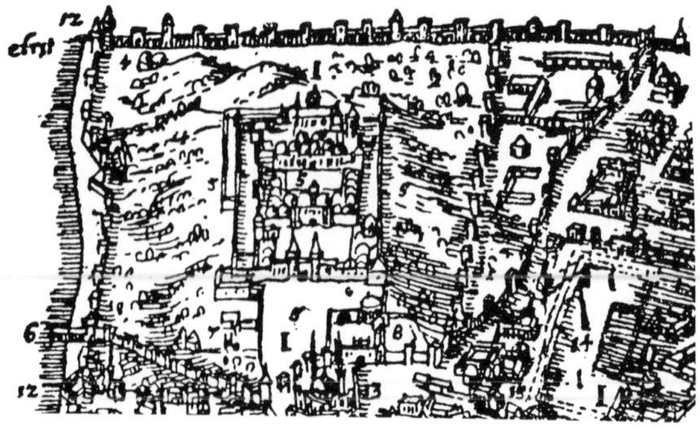

PLATE 26*a*–*c* Views of the Topkapı Palace published in 1606 by Wilhelm Dilich. From *Eigentliche kurtze beschreibung*. The legends of the panoramic view repeat verbatim those of Melchior Lorichs from 1559, suggesting that Dilich, who never visited Istanbul, used drawings by Lorichs, now lost, for his other prints as well.

PLATE 27 Panoramic view of the Topkapı Palace from the Golden Horn, ca. 1590. Detail from a view of Istanbul in MS. Vienna, Nationalbibliothek, Cod. 8626*, fols. 159v, 160r.

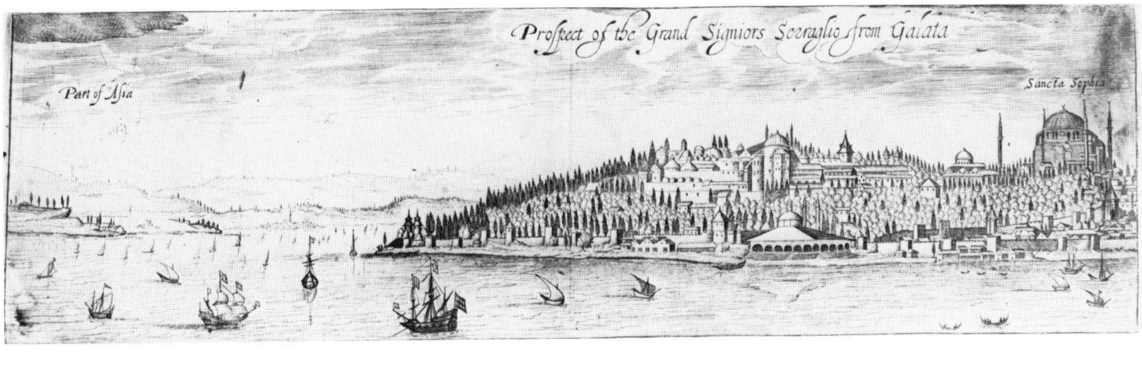

PLATE 28 Panoramic view of the Topkapı Palace from the Golden Horn. From George Sandys, *A Relation of a Journey begun An Dom ... 1610*. London, 1615, p. 33.

PLATE 29 Willem Van de Velde, ca. 1665–70, panoramic view of the Topkapı Palace from the Golden Horn. Private Collection, reproduced from Eldem and Akozan, *Topkapı*.

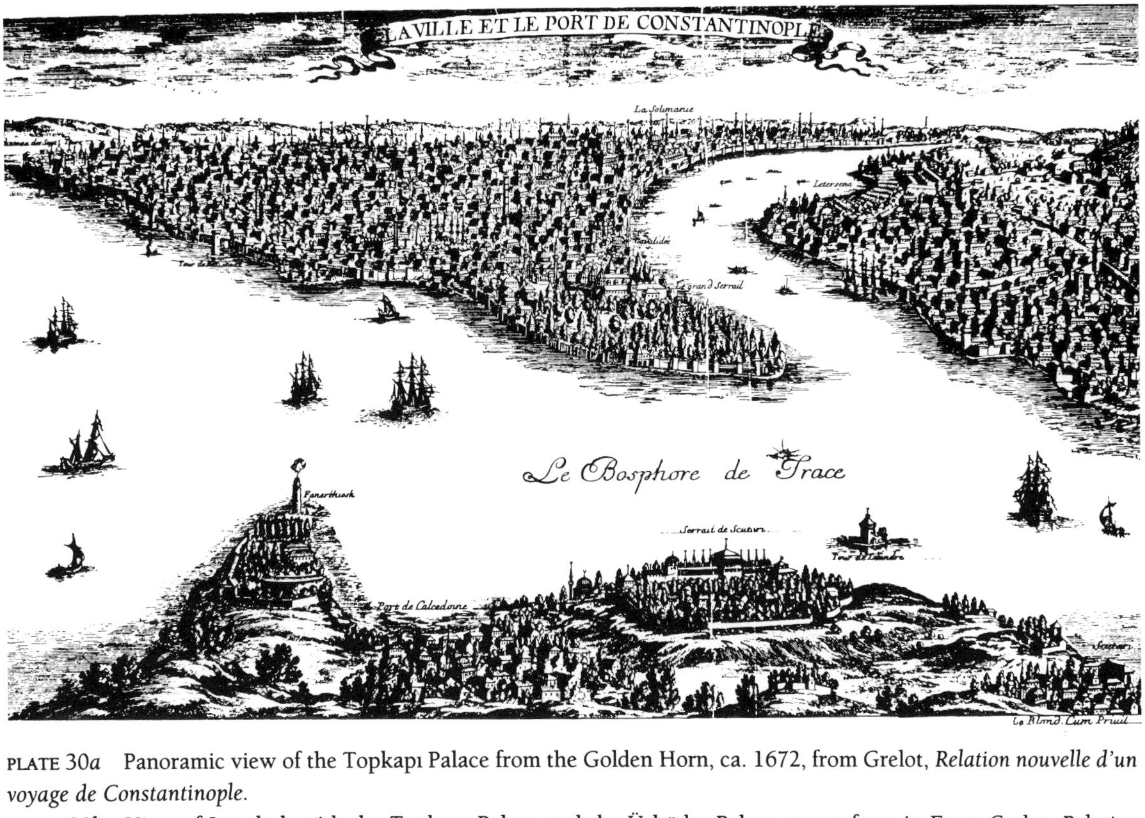

PLATE 30*a* Panoramic view of the Topkapı Palace from the Golden Horn, ca. 1672, from Grelot, *Relation nouvelle d'un voyage de Constantinople.*

PLATE 30*b* View of Istanbul, with the Topkapı Palace and the Üsküdar Palace across from it. From Grelot, *Relation nouvelle.*

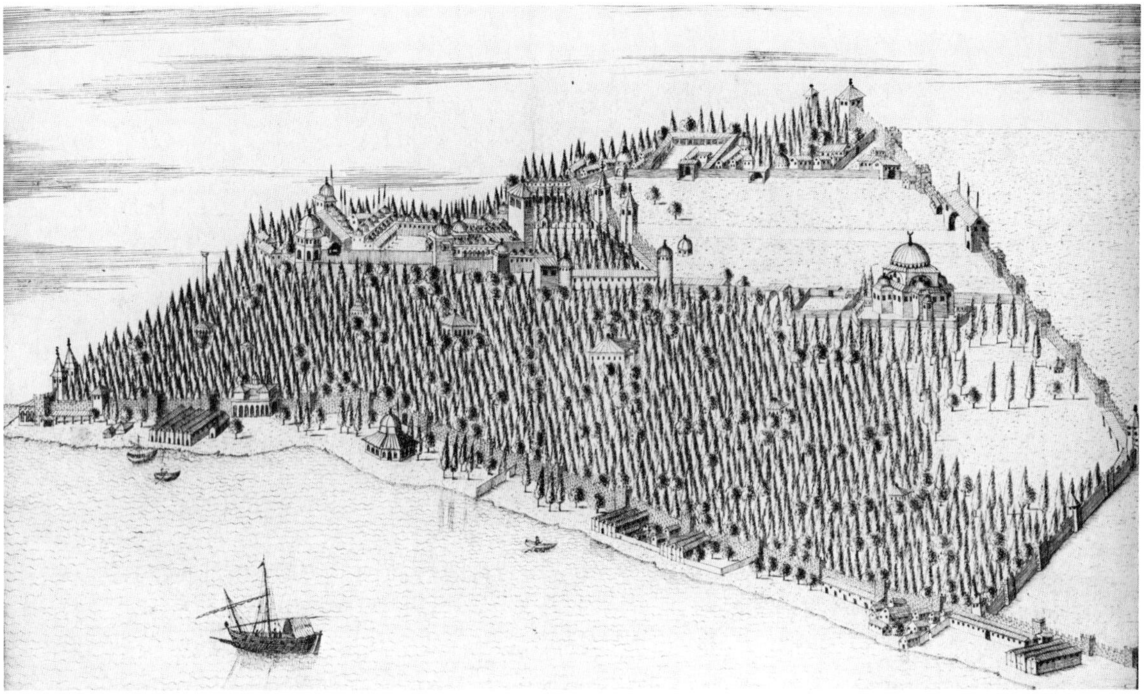

PLATE 31*a* Francesco Scarella, drawing of the Topkapı Palace from the Golden Horn, 1686. From Album, MS. Vienna, Österreichische Nationalbibliothek, Cod. 8627, fol. 3.

PLATE 31*b* Francesco Scarella, drawing of the Topkapı Palace from the Sea of Marmara, 1686. From Album, MS. Vienna, Österreichische Nationalbibliothek, Cod. 8627, fol. 4.

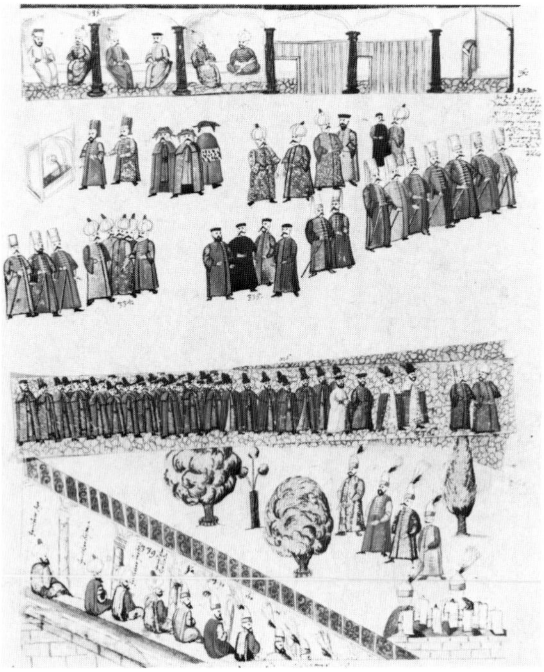

Notes

Abbreviations

Encyclopedias, archival documents, and manuscripts cited in the notes, bibliography, and captions in abbreviated form, are listed here:

ASV
Archivio di Stato di Venezia

BA, Ali Emiri
Başbakanlık Arşivi, Ali Emiri (Classification in the Prime Ministry Archives)

BA, BNE
Başbakanlık Arşivi, Bab-i Defteri, Başmuhasebe Kalemi, Bina Emini (Classification)

BA, Cevdet
Başbakanlık Arşivi, Cevdet, Saray (Classification)

BA, KK
Başbakanlık Arşivi, Kamil Kepeci (Classification)

BA, MD
Başbakanlık Arşivi, Mühimme Defterleri (Classification)

BA, MM
Başbakanlık Arşivi, Maliyeden Müdevver (Classification)

EI1
Encyclopedia of Islam, 1st ed., Leiden, 1913–42

EI2
Encyclopedia of Islam, 2nd. ed., Leiden, 1956

İÜ, F
İstanbul Üniversitesi Kütüphanesi, Farsça Yazmalar (Persian Manuscripts Collection in the Istanbul University Library)

İÜ, T
İstanbul Üniversitesi Kütüphanesi, Türkçe Yazmalar (Turkish Manuscripts Collection)

TSA, D
Topkapı Sarayı Arşivi, Defter (Registers in the Topkapı Palace Museum Archives)

TSA, E
Topkapı Sarayı Arşivi, Evrak (Single Documents)

TSA, SP
Topkapı Sarayı Arşivi, Sinan Paşa Arşivi (Documents from the Personal Archive of Sinan Pasha)

TSK, A
Topkapı Sarayı Kütüphanesi, Ahmed III (Collection in the Topkapı Palace Museum Library)

TSK, B
Topkapı Sarayı Kütüphanesi, Bağdad (Collection)

TSK, EH
Topkapı Sarayı Kütüphanesi, Emanet Hazinesi (Collection)

TSK, H
Topkapı Sarayı Kütüphanesi, Hazine (Collection)

TSK, R
Topkapı Sarayı Kütüphanesi, Revan (Collection)

TSK, YY
Topkapı Sarayı Kütüphanesi, Yeni Yazmalar (Collection)

Introduction

1 Âli, *Mevaid,* pp. 211–13.
2 Âli, *Counsel,* 1:59–61. Besides the main palace of Topkapı, Âli points out that there were several other, secondary palaces in Istanbul which the sultan occasionally visited, such as the Old Palace, once occupying the site of today's Istanbul University, the İbrahim Pasha Palace at the Hippo-

drome, the Palace of the Queen Mother at Yenibahçe, the Galata Palace, and the Üsküdar Palace. He proposed to reduce their unnecessarily large staffs, since the sultan rarely visited them. Writing in the early eighteenth century the historian Mustafa Naima also recognized the necessity of exhibiting royal magnificence and pomp through palaces and luxury objects, Naima, 1:54–57.

3 Tavernier, p. 56.

4 For a partial translation of the French text into English, see Fisher, pp. 5–81.

5 La Croix, *Serrail,* pp. 2–10.

6 For an analysis of Western texts that interpret the palace as the heart of despotic rule, see Grosrichard.

7 Miller, *Beyond the Sublime Porte,* p. xv.

Chapter 1

1 According to the contemporary historian Tursun Beg, Mehmed II quoted this famous Persian distich during his visit to Hagia Sophia, but the seventeenth-century author Hezarfen says that the sultan cited it during his tour of the ruins of the Great Palace, Tursun, text fol. 51a; Hezarfen, *Tenkih,* fol. 118v; cited in Miller, *Beyond the Sublime Porte,* p. 24; and Babinger, *Mehmed,* p. 96. It seems that the distich was quoted with reference to both buildings, which were in the same area.

2 For Mehmed II's New Palace in Edirne on the Tunca River (completed in 1452–53), where his father, Murad II, had previously constructed several pavilions, see Doukas, p. 189; Kritovoulos, p. 22; Neşri, II:841; Oruç, *Frühosmanischer Jahrbücher,* p. 64; Beşir Çelebi, pp. 2–9. The most detailed information about the Edirne Palace is in Osman. He saw the palace before it was destroyed and had access to a now-lost treatise written by Aşık Ali Ağa in 1085 (1674) that recorded repairs made to the palace during the reign of Mehmed IV. For a general review of sources and two descriptions of the Edirne Palace, see Kreiser, *Zwei unbekannte Beschreibungen,* pp. 119–42; Babinger, *Mehmed,* pp. 61, 74; Eldem, *Köşkler,* 1:21–57. The Old Palace of Edirne was replaced by the Selimiye Mosque (1569–75).

3 For information on the monastery, which caused the death of several Janissaries as it was being demolished, see Anonymous Chronicles (Giese, ed.), 1:104, 2:139; Evliya, 1:117–18; Atâ, 1:511. This may be the Franciscan monastery where the sultan stayed immediately after the conquest of Constantinople, since he did not want to reside in the Byzantine Blachernai Palace, Spandugino, "De la Origine," p. 154.

4 Doukas, pp. 243–44.

5 Kritovoulos, pp. 83, 93–95, 104.

6 Evliya, 1:117–18. Other Ottoman sources only give the date 858 (1454): Âli, *Künh,* fol. 84v; Hezarfen, *Telhis,* fol. 9r; Mehmed Aşık fol. 354r.

7 Tursun, text fols. 52b–53a.

8 Angiolello, *Inedito manoscritto,* p. 25.

9 Menavino, p. 134. For the Old Palace see also Harff, *Pilgerfahrt,* p. 207; Harff, *Pilgrimage,* p. 242.

10 The palace came to be called Topkapı after a popular shore palace, built in the eighteenth and nineteenth centuries near the seaside gate of the complex, known by that name. That palace was destroyed by fire in 1862–63; Şeref, p. 266.

11 Âli, *Künh,* fol. 84v; Bidlisi, *Tercüme-i Heşt Bihişt,* fol. 52v.

12 Bidlisi, *Hasht Behisht,* fols. 71v–72v; Bidlisi, *Tercüme-i Heşt Bihişt,* fols. 52r–53v.

13 For the foundation of the outer wall in 881–82 (1477–78), see Anonymous Chronicles (Giese, ed.) 1:115, 2:153; Kemalpaşazade, 1:474, 2:430; Hamidi, p. 213; Ahmed Pasha, p. 369, nos. 6–8. Several chronograms of the court poet Halimi that yield the same date are cited in Ünver, *Istanbul,* pp. 27, 29, 30. The completion date 883 (1478–79) is provided in Karamani, p. 324; Ahmed Pasha, p. 370, no. 13; Kemalpaşazade, 1:474, 2:430; and Sadeddin, 1:448.

14 For the inscription on the Imperial Gate, see Şeref, p. 274; Ayverdi, *Fatih Devri Mimarisi,* pp. 310, 315; Miller, *Beyond the Sublime Porte,* p. 42; and Carbognano, pp. 20–21. A longer version of this Arabic inscription is recorded in TSA, E 12019. This document is cited in T. Öz, "Topkapı Sarayı," p. 56; Atasoy, "Matrakçı's Representation," p. 95; it is published with a German translation in Kreiser, "Archivalisch uberlieferte Inschriften," pp. 260–66.

15 Promontorio calls the public administrative court the "primo serraglio," or first seraglio, and the residential one "l'altro serraglio, dove sta lo Signore," the other seraglio, where the [Grand] Signor dwells, Promontorio, pp. 34, 37–39.

16 Kritovoulos, p. 140.

17 Evliya, 1:115. The nineteenth-century historian Atâ cites the source *Es̱mārü't-tevārīḫ* as providing roughly the same foundation date of 862 (1457–58) Atâ, 1:59.

18 Kritovoulos, p. 140.

19 Ibid., pp. 147, 149.

20 For the mosque's inscription, see Ayverdi, *Osmanlı Mimarisinde Fatih Devri,* 3:386.

21 Nişancı (p. 169) and Mehmed Aşık (fol. 354r) both cite 867 (1462–63); Âli, *Künh* (fol. 84v) has 866–74 (1462–70). For a general discussion of historical sources that refer to the foundation date of the palace, see Şeref, pp. 268–74; Ayverdi, *Osmanlı Mimarisinde Fatih Devri,* pp. 682–87; and Raby, "El Gran Turco," pp. 291–92.

22 Kritovoulos, pp. 207–8; Karamani, p. 362; Evliya, 1:115; Gurlitt, *Baukunst,* 1:44. Enveri, who dedicated his history to the grand vizier Mahmud Pasha in 1464–65, mentions two palaces *(ḳaṣr)* built for Mehmed II in Istanbul, probably the Old Palace and the recently completed new one, Enveri, p. 102. Two seventeenth-century sources cite the completion date of 872 (1467–68): Hezarfen, *Telhis,* fol. 14v; and Katib Çelebi, fol. 258r. On the basis of an un-

known Greek source, Atâ writes that Mehmed II moved to the New Palace in 872 (1467–68), Atâ, 1:51.

23 The inscription on the Çinili Köşk is published in Ayverdi, *Fatih Devri Mimarisi,* pp. 358–68; see also Ayverdi, *Osmanlı Mimarisinde Fatih Devri,* p. 686. For the kiosk of İshak Pasha, see Eldem, *Köşkler,* 2:226. Atâ writes that it was built during İshak Pasha's second grand vizierate, in Bayezid II's reign, but this second vizierate, 875–77 (1470–72), falls into Mehmed II's reign. İshak served as grand vizier for a third time under Bayezid II, Atâ, 1:303.

24 For the lost inscription, see Gurlitt, *Baukunst,* 2:44. The building chronology of the palace is controversial. Ayverdi's hypothesis that the garden pavilions were the earliest buildings of the palace, the main courts of which were added as an afterthought between 1472 and 1478, is not tenable, see Ayverdi, *Fatih Devri Mimarisi,* p. 294; Ayverdi, *Osmanlı Mimarisinde Fatih Devri,* p. 686. Others have also taken the date of the Tiled Kiosk as the foundation date of the whole palace and have placed all building activities between 1472 and 1478, Anhegger-Eyüboğlu, "Fatih Devrinde," p. 26; Sertoğlu, p. 3; Tansuğ, p. 147. Şeref and Babinger date the palace complex to the years 1465–79. For the statement that the main palace buildings were constructed between 1465 and 1470, and that the outer wall was added in 1478–79, see Müller-Wiener, pp. 495–96. The main buildings were finished by 1472, according to Goodwin, pp. 107–8.

25 For this argument see Ayverdi, *Fatih Devri Mimarisi,* p. 289; Miller, *Beyond the Sublime Porte,* p. 27; and Raby, "El Gran Turco," p. 291.

26 Lokman, *Hünername,* 1: fols. 173r–v. The early-sixteenth-century historian Ruhi states that Bayezid II laid the foundations of his mosque "inside his own palace known as the Old Palace" in 907 (1501–2), Ruhi, *Tarih,* fol. 180v, Ruhi, "Edirne," p. 331. According to Lokman it was a religious dream that inspired Bayezid II to build his mosque on the grounds of the Old Palace, Lokman, *Hünername,* 2: fols. 193v–96r. The French antiquarian Pierre Gilles, who saw the Old Palace when he twice visited Istanbul, in 1544–49 and 1550–51, says that it extended more than two miles before Süleyman I decided to build his mosque complex there, Gyllius, p. 201.

27 For this hypothesis, see Örs, "History of the Topkapı Palace," pp. 6–8; and Çığ, "Fatih Topkapı," pp. 22–24. In the taped recording of a symposium held at the Topkapı Palace Museum in 1982 (kept at the palace library), Şehabettin Tekindağ similarly argued that the palace was built as a fortified castle against a Venetian sea attack. Fanny Davis writes that the site of the palace was chosen in order to build a fortress that "could guard the entire city," Davis, pp. 4, 6.

28 For the treaty, see Babinger, *Mehmed,* pp. 369–88.

29 Angiolello, *Inedito manoscritto,* pp. 28–29.

30 For contemporary descriptions of the Yedikule fortress, see Angiolello, *Inedito manoscritto,* p. 16; Menavino, p. 90. For the Italian influence on the plans of Mehmed's fortresses, see Restle, p. 361; Raby, "Sultan of Paradox," p. 7. Mehmed's fortress of Rumeli Hisar, built along the Bosphorus prior to the conquest of Constantinople, also had royal quarters. Wenceslas Wratislaw writes that Mehmed II "caused apartments, handsomely floored with marble, to be constructed in that tower, and dwelt there till he took Constantinople," Wratislaw, p. 83.

31 Âli, *Künh,* fol. 84v.

32 İnalcık, "Rise of the Ottoman Empire," pp. 40–45; Shaw, 1:55–70; Werner, pp. 5–8.

33 Commynes, 2:431, cited in Babinger, *Mehmed,* p. 377.

34 Aşıkpaşazade, pp. 9–10.

35 Mihailović, pp. 145–47.

36 Teply, "Kızıl Elma," pp. 78–108; Teply, *Türkische Sagen,* pp. 34–73. Teply argues that the sources of the Ottoman golden-apple tradition can be traced back to both classical antiquity and the Turco-Mongol Central Asian heritage.

37 Using Giacomo Languschi as his source, Zorzi Dolfin writes that the sultan had histories of antique heroes read to him daily, see Languschi, pp. 172–73. Other contemporary sources record that Mehmed had histories of Alexander and Julius Caesar read to him, Anonymous (Kreutel, ed.); p. 164; Anonymous (Baştav, ed.), p. 173. For the sultan's emulation of Alexander, see the contemporary reports compiled in Pertusi, *Caduta di Costantinopoli,* and Pertusi, *Testi inediti.*

38 Babinger, *Mehmed,* p. 500; Raby, "Mehmed the Conqueror," pp. 18–19.

39 Pertusi, *Testi inediti,* p. 81.

40 Languschi, pp. 172–74. Raby argues that an Italian friend of Cyriacus of Ancona was Mehmed's Greek reader and that the Jewish physician Jacopo da Gaeta was his Latin reader; Raby, "Mehmed the Conqueror," p. 25. Sagundino says that the sultan had three readers, a philosopher for Arabic texts, and two Jewish and Greek doctors for antique histories in Greek and Latin, see Pertusi, *Testi inediti,* pp. 131–32. Angiolello does not identify these readers, to whom he refers as "persons who used to read to him" (persone che gli legeva), Angiolello, *Historia Turchesca,* p. 119.

41 For George of Trebizond's writings addressing Mehmed II and promising him world dominion through conversion to Christianity, see Pertusi, *Caduta di Costantinopoli,* 2:75–79; George of Trebizond, pp. 491–569, 757. For Pius II's letter, which apparently was never sent to the sultan, but was published in several editions during his lifetime, after the first edition of Cologne (1469), see Babinger, *Mehmed,* pp. 198–201, 417, and Piccolomini.

42 Pertusi, *Caduta di Costantinopoli,* 2:73.

43 Kritovoulos, p. 3. According to Raby, Arrian's life of Alexander, found among Mehmed's books, was written by the same scribe as Kritovoulos's unicum manuscript (presumed to be the author's autograph and dedication copy). He argues that the text of Arrian was a pendant volume

to Kritovoulos's history of Mehmed, intended to enable the sultan to appreciate the validity of his neo-Alexander image; Raby, "Mehmed the Conqueror," p. 18.

44 Cited in İnalcık, "Policy of Mehmet," p. 233.

45 The text is incorporated into Anonymous (Giese, ed.), 1:fol. 74, 2:99–100. For its Turkish and Persian versions, see Tauer, "Notice," pp. 487–94; Tauer, "Les Versions persannes," pp. 1–20; Wittek, pp. 266–70. For Mehmed's copy of the *Diegesis* written by Michael Aichmatoles in 1474, see Raby, "Mehmed the Conqueror," p. 19. One of the Turkish versions dating from 1491 is translated into French, and is discussed in terms of its relation to the other known texts in Yerasimos.

46 Bidlisi, *Tercüme-i Heşt Bihişt,* fols. 52r–v.

47 Neşri, 2:711; Anonymous, *Fatih Mehmed* II *Vakfiyeleri,* pp. 33 (fol. 40), 201; Bidlisi *Tercüme-i Heşt Bihişt,* fol. 52v; Âli, *Künh,* fol. 84v; Kemalpaşazade, 1:102, 2:103; Sadeddin, 1:448.

48 Şemseddin, fols. 3–4.

49 Kritovoulos, p. 140. Around 1550 Gilles also identified the site as that of ancient Byzantium and described at length its view-commanding position, Gyllius, pp. 40–41.

50 Kritovoulos, pp. 136–37. The same information is given in Chalkokondylas, p. 632.

51 Tursun, text fol. 58a; Bidlisi, *Tercüme-i Heşt Bihişt,* fol. 52v.

52 Garzoni, p. 393. In 1675 the French traveler Tavernier wrote that from his palace the sultan could simultaneously view both Europe and Asia, over which his dominion extended, Tavernier, p. 61. The text of İlyas Efendi is cited in Yerasimos, pp. 225–26.

53 For contemporary Italian rulers who actively participated in the design process, see Hollingsworth, pp. 398–406; Heydenreich, pp. 1–6.

54 Tursun, text fol. 58a.

55 Kemalpaşazade, 1:102, 2:103.

56 Kritovoulos, pp. 19–20; cited in Gabriel, p. 63.

57 Kritovoulos, p. 149.

58 Âli, *Künh,* fol. 84v. According to Âli, the sultan, like a real overseer, personally inspected the construction of his palace where slaves of viziers and other dignitaries were employed.

59 The sultan's patronage of manuscripts fell in the same two periods, see Raby, "Mehmed the Conqueror," p. 28.

60 Kritovoulos, p. 149; Kıvami, p. 70; Kemalpaşazade, 1:102, 473, 2:103, 429.

61 Tursun, text fol. 58b; Kemalpaşazade, 1:475, 2:430.

62 Cited in Mango, *Byzantine Architecture,* p. 190; and Raby, "Sultan of Paradox," p. 7.

63 For Mehmed's invitation to Florentine interior decorators specializing in inlaid woodwork "maestri d'intaglio, e di legname, e di tarsie," see Dei, p. 176, cited in Babinger, *Mehmed,* p. 386, and Raby, "Sultan of Paradox," p. 5. About the master builder invited from Venice, see Babinger, *Mehmed,* p. 378; Raby, "Sultan of Paradox," p. 4.

64 In the sixteenth century Francesco Negro wrote that Gentile Bellini was sent to decorate the sultan's palace, and Francesco Sansovino reported that he was invited to paint some rooms for the sultan "per dipingere alqune sue sale," cited in Raby, "El Gran Turco," p. 51. For the Venetian artist's activities in Istanbul, see Meyer zur Capellen, pp. 9–39, 87–103.

65 For Corvinus's palace, see Moos, pp. 126–27; Białostocki, pp. 7, 13–14.

66 Cited in Babinger, *Mehmed,* pp. 246, 465; Restle, pp. 361–67.

67 Restle, pp. 361–67.

68 Anonymous (Giese, ed.), 1:fols. 100–101, 2:133–34; Ruhi, *Tarih,* fol. 149v.

69 Ruhi, *Tarih,* fol. 120r; Ruhi, "Edirne," pp. 329–30. An anonymous source confirms that the paralyzed architect of the Üç Şerefeli Mosque had also built a palace for Mehmed II on the Tunca River in Edirne, see Beşir Çelebi, p. 7.

70 Ruhi, *Tarih,* fols. 149v, 152v, 177v; Ruhi, "Edirne," pp. 330–31. The waqfs of Mimar Murad and Mimar Sinan bin Abdullah are recorded in the Hagia Sophia endowment register of 1519, *Ayasofya Tahrir Defteri,* Istanbul, Belediye Library, MS. Muallim Cevdet 0.64, fol. 270. Mimar Hayreddin bin Mimar Murad, who repaired the walls of Galata after an earthquake in 1509, appears to have been the same architect's son; Ruhi, *Tarih,* fols. 193v–94r. About Mimar Hayreddin, see also Meriç, pp. 27–28.

71 Kemalpaşazade, 1:477, 2:432.

72 Bidlisi, *Tercüme-i Heşt Bihişt,* fols. 52r–v. For this episode see also Âli, *Künh,* fol. 84v.

73 Bidlisi, *Tercüme-i Heşt Bihişt,* fols. 51v–52r.

74 Only two sixteenth-century copies of Mehmed II's *kanunname,* composed by Nişancı Leysizade Mehmed Efendi during the grand vizierate of Karamani Mehmed Pasha, are known. The Vienna manuscript was published by Mehmed Arif in 1912, and the Leningrad manuscript by A.S. Tveritinova in 1961. Abdülkadir Özcan's critical edition of these two texts, published in 1982, is cited throughout this book as Leysizade.

75 Aşıkpaşazade, p. 38; cited in Dilger, pp. 42–43; Uzunçarşılı, *Merkez ve Bahriye Teşkilatı,* p. 1.

76 Taşköprizade, 1:24–25.

77 Cited in Uzunçarşılı, *Merkez ve Bahriye Teşkilatı,* p. 1; Dilger, p. 43; Mumcu, p. 23.

78 Taşköprizade, 1:34; cited in Uzunçarşılı, *Merkez ve Bahriye Teşkilatı,* p. 2; Dilger, 1:43.

79 Aşıkpaşazade, pp. 84–85; Doukas, pp. 127–30; Neşri, 2:552–54.

80 Brocquière, pp. 187–89.

81 Ibid., pp. 190–93.

82 Ibid., pp. 193–94.

83 Ibid., pp. 195–96.

84 Cited in Babinger, *Mehmed,* pp. 29–30.

85 Cited in Babinger, *Mehmed,* pp. 44–45; Dilger, p. 43.

86 Mihailović, p. 195. For Mehmed's public reception of Dra-

cula's brother in 1462, see ibid., pp. 129–31.

87 Ibid., p. 157; see also pp. 25–27 for a description of the grand vizier Mahmud Pasha presiding over a public council where food was served.

88 Promontorio, pp. 37–38; cited in Dilger, p. 44.

89 Promontorio, pp. 38–39. For Mehmed II's appearances before his courtiers during a public banquet, on days when the imperial council met, see also Angiolello, *Inedito manoscritto,* pp. 37–38: "Et quando il Gran Turco vol mangiar il giorno di udienza, lui senta solo sopra una sedia un puoco alta da terra, et sta al modo che stano li sarti a cusire, et poi li predetti vinti Scuderi li portano la vivande inanti ... et fino che il Gran Turco mangia, li quattro Vixir, lo Cadilescher, et li due Testerdari con assai altri Baroni stano là in piedi dinansi esso Gran Turco, et le squadro da Cavalo et da piedi stano ali suoi luoghi deputati attorno la corte, li quali sono circa persone due milia ... et come il Gran Turco comincia a mangiar, tutti questi vintimilia mangia anco loro, et dapoi levati li piati, et che il Gran Turco ha finito di mangiare si leva in piedi, et con il capo chino fa riverenza a tutti, et poi entra nella sua camara, et partito il Gran Turco li Vixir, lo Cadilescher et li altri, li quali sono stati in piedi et hano mangiato, vano poi a'suoi luoghi deputati ... et dopo che questi maggiori hano mangiato, mangiano li Secretari et Cancelleri et li altri, et fino che la brigata mangia, siascuno va a far quello che è deputato: nei quattro giorni della settimana si tien quest'ordine, cioè il Sabato, la Dominica, il Luni et il Marti."

90 Aşıkpaşazade, p. 14; Mihailović, p. 29.

91 Aşıkpaşazade, pp. 13–14; Neşri, 1:106–9; Lokman, *Tomar,* fols. 33r–v.

92 Âli's passage is cited in Uzunçarşılı, *Merkez ve Bahriye Teşkilatı,* p. 274. See also Neşri, 1:106–7; Lokman, *Tomar,* fol. 33v; Atâ, 1:6.

93 Leysizade, pp. 44–45.

94 Ibid., pp. 33–34, 42.

95 Solakzade, pp. 268–69.

96 Lokman, *Hünername,* 1:fols. 14r–15r; Taşköprizade, 1:45. Uzunçarşılı traces the origin of Mehmed II's curtained window to the Abbasid caliphs, who observed councils of public justice from behind a curtain made from the Ka'ba's *kiswa,* Uzunçarşlı, *Osmanlı Devleti Teşkilatına Medhal,* p. 5; for this late-Abbasid practice, see Sourdel "Questions de cérémonial," p. 132. According to Köprülü this practice was inherited by the Ottomans from the Khwārazmshāhs, see Köprülü, pp. 185–86.

97 Leysizade, p. 42.

98 Ibid., p. 10. A later *kanunname,* compiled in 1676, describes the rules of ceremonies at the Chamber of Petitions (*ḳānūn-i ‹arż*) with more detail. It shows that the Agha of Janissaries had begun to present petitions to the sultan, a change from fifteenth-century practice, Tevki'i, pp. 511–12.

99 Dilger, pp. 14–36, 47–49, 88–92, 113–16.

100 On the methodological problems posed by Dilger's conclusion, see Fleischer, pp. 197–200. Özcan convincingly argues that one cannot ignore the *kanunname*'s consistent attribution to Mehmed II by sixteenth-century historians such as Bidlisi, Mustafa Âli, and Taşköprizade; he also demonstrates that some of the elements listed by Dilger as anachronisms are in fact authentic, Leysizade, pp. 7–28. İnalcık dates the *kanunname* to Mehmed II's reign, despite his awareness of minor anachronisms in it, and he perceptively notes the connection between the *kanunname* and Mehmed's new policy of centralizing the state government through a system of household slaves, İnalcık, "Osmanlı Hukukuna Giriş," pp. 112–16; İnalcık, "Ḳānūnnāme," pp. 562–66; İnalcık, "Ḳānūn," ibid., pp. 558–62; İnalcık, "Rise of the Ottoman Empire," pp. 45–48. Repp also accepts that the main body of legislation in the *kanunname* must have been promulgated by Mehmed II, despite the presence of some sixteenth-century details, Repp, pp. 41–42. Beldiceanu argues that Mehmed II's *kanunname* concerning the ceremonial functions of the palace was composed as part of a vast movement of codification, simultaneously with another law code, covering penal and fiscal issues, Beldiceanu, p. 18. The evidence for Mehmed II's construction of a window overlooking the public Council Hall and the Chamber of Petitions is discussed in chapter 4 (Old Council Hall), and chapter 5 (Chamber of Petitions).

101 Kemalpaşazade, 2:531; Leysizade, pp. 8–9; Beldiceanu, p. 18.

102 Philippe de Commynes reported that a strange abscess had formed on the sultan's leg which kept him in his palace, whence he appeared in public as little as possible, cited in Babinger, *Mehmed,* pp. 377, 424.

103 Aşıkpaşazade, p. 182.

104 For a description of the sultan's modest procession and prayer in a mosque in the early part of his reign, see Georgius de Hungaria, pp. 27–28. The royal tribune in Mehmed II's mosque is mentioned in a poem by Cafer Çelebi, p. 81.

105 İnalcık, "Rise of the Ottoman Empire," pp. 47–48. In Bayezid II's reactionary reign many centralizing policies initiated by his father, such as the confiscation of properties and waqfs, were reversed, İnalcık, "Policy of Mehmet," pp. 244–46, 273–87.

106 Spandugino, *Petit Traicté,* pp. 137–39; Spandugino, "De la Origine," p. 224. Some sultans were forced to appear in public during political crises, when they sat on a throne under the portico of the third gate. For such a "divan on foot" (*ayaḳ dīvānı*) in 1011 (1602–3), see Naima, 1:307; another one, during Mehmed III's reign, is recorded in Taşköprizade, 1:87. Also see Ohsson, 7:232.

107 Bidlisi, *Tercüme-i Heşt Bihişt,* fol. 53v.

108 Ruhi, *Tarih,* fols. 190r–91r.

109 Uğur, p. 38.

110 For Bayezid II's pavilions, see Necipoğlu-Kafadar,

"Account Book," pp. 31–45. For his shore pavilion facing Galata at the New Palace, see Eldem, *Köşkler,* 1:173–207, and chapter 10 (The Shore Kiosk).

111 See chapter 7 (The Privy Chamber Complex) and chapter 10 (The Marble Kiosk).

112 Helaki, chronogram no. 13, p. 11. For Süleyman I's extensive constructions in the palace, see chapters 2–9, and Appendix A.

113 See chapter 3 (The Royal Kitchens), chapter 7 (The Treasury-Bath Complex), and chapter 8.

114 See chapter 8.

115 See chapter 10 (The Pearl Kiosk, the Shore Kiosk, the Basketmakers' Kiosk).

116 Bassano, fol. 16v; Sanderson, p. 72.

117 Leysizade, p. 29.

118 Ibid., p. 41.

119 Minio, "Copia di una lettera," p. 291.

120 T. Contarini, p. 380.

121 Minio, "Relazione [1521]," p. 22; Minio, "Relazione [1527]," p. 176. For the observation that the custom of silence was not practiced before Süleyman, see P. Zeno, "Itinerario," pp. 114, 117; Ramberti, pp. 306–7.

122 For a detailed discussion of these ceremonial changes, see Dilger, especially pp. 55–59, 70–74, 75–77, 81–84, 96–104.

123 Moro, p. 330. The sultan's increasing arrogance is also noted in Fresne-Canaye, pp. 69–71, Schweigger, p. 55.

124 Fresne-Canaye, p. 129.

125 Bernardo, pp. 373–75. For the isolation of Selim II, also see Barbaro, pp. 321–22: "Tanto usano quelli imperatori Ottomani star ritirati dalle pratiche degli uomini, non conversando con altri che con eunuchi, paggi, e donne, le quali persone sono tutte affatto prive d'intelligenza delle cose del mondo, essendo allevate ristrette in quei serragli, dove non hanno mai commercio o pratica alcuna con altre persone di fuori, perchè mai è permesso, nè anco al primo visir, sopra il quale stà appoggiato tutto il governo di quell'impero, di poter entrar nel serraglio del Gran-Signore."

126 Vigenère, pp. 43–44.

127 Âli, *Counsel,* 1:38.

128 About sign language Moro (p. 330) writes: "... secondo l'uso degl'imperatori ottomani, di farsi servire piu con cenni che con parole, essendo tre soli, fra tutti quelli che servono, che abbiano libertà di parlargli, che viene usata anche da essi rare volte, per riverenza."

129 La Croix, *Serrail,* fols. 168ff.

130 For Melchior Lorichs's panorama, see Oberhummer, pl. 1; Beauvau, p. 68; Bon, pp. 86–87. For the practice of sign language, also see Bernardo, p. 352; Dallam, p. 70, and Bobovi, *Mémoires,* fols. 296–97.

131 Baudier, p. 19: "Sultan Mustapha oncle d'Osman, qui regnoit ces mois passez, tenant sur la fin de l'année mil six cens dix-sept, le Sceptre de l'Empire Turc, pour ne se pouvoir accoustumer à cette gravité muette, donna suiet aux Turcs du Conseil d'Estat de se plaindre de luy, & de dire que parler librement aux siens, comme faisoit Mustapha, estoit plus propre d'un Ianissaire, ou d'un Marchand Turc, que de leur Empereur: ils le mépriserent, & iugerent sa franchise & familiarité indigne de l'Empire. Pour bien faire le Sultan, il ne faut point parler, mais par une extraordinaire gravité faire trembler les hommes d'un clin d'oeil: car la sourcilleuse arrogance des Princes Turcs est montée à telle insolence, que de vivre parmy les siens comme quelque grande Divinité, adorée par les muettes admirations de ces esclaves."

132 Ramberti, p. 308. The depersonalization of administration under Süleyman is analyzed in a forthcoming book by Cornell Fleischer, who kindly shared his ideas with me.

133 For the description of a hunting parade staged by Murad III to impress a Persian ambassador, see Schweigger, pp. 77–79.

134 Fresne-Canaye, p. 126.

Chapter 2

1 Tursun, text fols. 40a, 64b.

2 Promontorio, pp. 45–48. For the parallel between the sultan's palace and his tent encampment, also see Lutfi, *Asafname,* pp. 26, 31.

3 For the name Imperial Fortress *(qalʿat al-sulṭāniyya),* see TSA, E 12019. Ruhi calls it "the Fortress named Sultaniya" *(sulṭāniyye nām ḥiṣār);* Ruhi, *Tarih,* fol. 149v; Ruhi, "Edirne," p. 330. For a general description of the castellated wall and its gates, see Eldem and Akozan, pp. 68–69; Şeref, pp. 267–68; Atâ, 1:310; Eremya, pp. 5–13; İnciciyan, pp. 27–29; Evliya, 1:59–60; Gyllius, pp. 39–40; Menavino, pp. 91–92; Angiolello, *Inedito manoscritto,* pp. 22–23. Around 1550 Gilles counts twelve iron gates (seven on the land wall, five on the sea wall) that were kept locked and used only by privileged dignitaries.

4 Angiolello, *Historia Turchesca,* pp. 134–35.

5 Harff, *Pilgerfahrt,* p. 205; Harff, *Pilgrimage,* p. 240.

6 Tursun, text fol. 58b; Kemalpaşazade, 1:473–74, 2:429–30. Kemalpaşazade says that skilled architects, engineers, carpenters, stonemasons, painters, blacksmiths, and lime burners were gathered from neighboring countries for the construction of the Imperial Fortess; the painters must have been employed in decorating the belvedere pavilions that crowned some of the towers and gates.

7 Hamidi, pp. 212–13; Karamani, p. 361. Three chronograms composed for the completion of the castle surrounding the New Palace refer to it as a symbol of the sultan's glory, Ahmed Pasha, p. 369. For other poems about the Imperial Fortress, see Ünver, *İstanbul,* pp. 27–30; Cafer Çelebi, p. 76.

8 Evliya, 1:621; Uzunçarşılı, *Osmanlı Devletinin Saray Teşkilatı,* pp. 449–52. Archival documents refer to it as

"tower of the military band near the iron gate," *(kulle-i nevbethāne der kurb-i bāb-i āhen)* or, "outer military band at the Iron Gate," *(demür kapuda taşra nevbethāne)*, BA, MM 1250, fol. 24; MM 424, fols. 43–44. This might be the tower of royal musicians mentioned in Menavino, p. 120.

9 The tower pavilion is referred to as the "tower of processions" *(kulle-i alāy),*" in a document from 1634, BA, MM 403, fols. 14, 16. For the custom of listening to the complaints of rebels, see La Croix, *Serrail,* fols. 22–23, Tavernier, p. 58; Thévenot, pp. 214–16.

10 For the inscription, see Şeref, p. 283.

11 For the tower in Bursa, see Taşköprizade, 1:34; and Uzunçarşılı, *Merkez ve Bahriye Teşkilatı,* p. 2. The tower pavilion in Konya is described in Sarre, *Kiosk von Konia.*

12 Şeref, p. 283.

13 Before the campaign of Erlau in 1596 Mehmed III watched the parade of his army from there, see Topçular Katibi, fols. 15v–16r, 37v.

14 For the inscription, see Şeref, 274; Ayverdi, *Fatih Devri Mimarisi,* pp. 310, 315; Miller, *Beyond the Sublime Porte,* p. 42. The gate is described as "ung grand portail de marbre bien ouvré de menuyseie avec lectres moresques qu'il faict moult beau veoir," in Spandugino, *Petit Traicté,* p. 133. Its ornaments are described as "di sotto, & di sopra lavorato di colori variati con lettere d'oro, & con foliaggi alla Damaschina," in Menavino, p. 91.

15 Şeref, 274.

16 For these weapons, see Bassano, fol. 16v; Lubenau, 1:161; Gyllius, p. 38. For the notion that they symbolized the peace that reigned in the palace, see Borderie, fol. 34v, and Bobovi, *Mémoires* fol. 29.

17 Angiolello, *Inedito manoscritto,* p. 23.

18 In this "latticed window over the gate" *(das vergitterte Fenster oberhalb des Tores)* Bayezid II once appeared holding a bow and arrow, the insignia of sovereignty, to appease the rebellious Janissaries, Oruç, *Sultan Bayezid;* see also Sanuto 6:374, 8:12. A seventeenth-century document refers to the repair of two "rooms" *(oda),* a "formal hall" *(dīvānhāne),* and a "large portico" *(dihlīz-i kebīr)* upstairs, BA, MM 1947, fol. 17. An eighteenth-century repair document lists above the Imperial Gate's vestibule a "treasury" *(hazīne),* "rooms" *(otalar),* a "formal hall" *(dīvānhāne),* a "portico" *(soffa)* whose "intercolumniations were spanned with iron lattices and glass panes" *(direk araları kafesleri, direk aralarınuñ camları),* and a painted wooden "eave on the inner facade" *(derūnī tarafında saçak),* BA, Cevdet 1853; Cevdet 2370. For a hypothetical reconstruction of the gate pavilion without its inner portico, see Eldem and Akozan, pp. 68–69, pls. 31–33.

19 Hezarfen, *Telhis,* fol. 15r. This information is repeated in Atâ, 1:60.

20 "Le Cabinet que fait construire Mehemet 2e est au dessus de cette porte soustenu par une espece de voute dorée, il estoit ouvert de tous costés, mais son successeur le fit fermer, y laissant seulement deux fenestres pour éclairer ce lieu destiné a déposer les biens de ceux qui mouroient sans heritiers l'on les y conservoit sept ans apres les queles s'il ne parois soit point d'heritiers, ils estoient acquis au Sultan qui en disposoit," La Croix, *Serrail,* fols. 24–25; La Croix, *Mémoires,* p. 134.

21 BA, Cevdet 1853; Cevdet 2370, see note 18

22 Lutfi, *Asafname,* pp. 12–13.

23 Peçevi, 1:6.

24 Ayvansarayi, 1:105–6.

25 It is mentioned as the "treasury of the vestibule" *(kapu arası hazīnesi)* in Atâ, 1:60. BA, KK 7097, fol. 23; MM 17884, fol. 61. For finance officers collecting revenues near the vestibule, see also İnciciyan, p. 29; Carbognano, p. 22.

26 Lokman, *Hünername,* 1:fol. 15r; Donato, 2:83–84. Donato describes the gate as follows: "Tiene due gran Nicchi, senza ornamento di statue ad ambi li fianchi, e sopra essa è alzata una Torre di mezzana grandezza, con gran finestroni per ogni solaro, che servono ad illuminare le Camere, che sono in essa, nelle quali si conservono i Libri, e le Scritture delle rendite, che dalle contributioni de'Regni, e Provincie soggette a quell'Impero si ricavano. S'ascende sopra questa Torre per piccola scala de pietra, e sotto di essa nel piano, che serve come campo di Guardia, commorano alcuni Capigì," Donato, 2:84.

27 When Süleyman I left his capital during military campaigns, council meetings were held twice a week at this gate, which then served as a court of justice, Trevisano, p. 120. The gate pavilion was also used as a council hall in 1595–96, during the campaign of Erlau, Topçular Katibi, fol. 14r.

28 Salahi, fols. 72v, 81r, 161v; Tavernier, pp. 232–33.

29 Spandugino, *Petit Traicté,* p. 133.

30 Anonymous, "Testament," pp. 15–17.

31 In 1433 a large crowd of attendants and horses waited outside the first gate of Murad II's palace in Edirne, since no forecourt existed there, Brocquière, p. 187.

32 Gritti, "Relazione fatta in Pregadi," p. 456.

33 "Et a man destra di questo cortivo vi è un mureto con lastre di sopra, che tiene quanto la lungheza del cortivo, et da quella parte si sentano gli Schiavi, et famigli, li quali si congregano il giorno di corte, et sopra le dette lastre vi sono alcuni muraletti di legno larghi per modo che si puol vedere il gran Giardino da quella parte," Angiolello, *Inedito manoscritto,* p. 23.

34 Menavino, p. 91; Spandugino, *Petit Traicté,* p. 133.

35 "*Sāha-i ‹ālīyye-i bāb-i hümāyūn-i sa‹ādet meşhūn,*" Lokman, *Hünername,* 1:fol. 15r. For the panorama of Lorichs, see Oberhummer, pl. 5.

36 The reception ceremony shown in the Lewenklau album, compiled in 1586, is thought to be based on drawings brought to Vienna by the Austrian Habsburg ambassador David Ungnad, who was in Istanbul between 1573 and 1578. Two of the decapitated heads on spears are identified in the legends as those of Herbart von Auesperg and Friedrich von Weixelburg, who died near Bosnia in 1575.

The same reception ceremony is depicted in a scroll executed by Zacharias Wehme in 1582, which copies in edited form the original drawings in Vienna. For this copy, preserved in the Sächsische Landesbibliothek in Dresden (12a), see Bernus-Taylor, p. 302.

37 Lokman, *Hünername,* 1:fols. 15r–v; 2:fol. 25r.

38 Hoberdanacz, p. 3; Jurischitsch and Lamberg, p. 39; Curipeschitz, *Yolculuk Günlüğü,* pp. 45, 47.

39 In 1544 the French visitor Jérôme Maurand described the horses lined up on both sides of the court: "De côté e d'autre, pendant que mon très illustre seigneur passait pour aller à la seconde porte du Palais, se tenaient les chevaux des spahis, dont une partie étaient montés et très richement vêtus. Nous ne vîmes aucun de ces chevaux (qui étaient au nombre d'environ deux cents) qui n'eût des rênes d'or ou d'argent, ainsi que les étriers; la plupart avaient sur le front une lame d'or ou d'argent, en forme de rose, dans laquelle était enchâssé un rubis, une hyacinthe ou une turquoise; et ils avaient les brides faites à la turque, brodées d'or et de soie cramoisie, enrichis de turquoises. Chacun de ces chevaux avait le sous-barbe faite en forme de chaîne d'or ou d'argent, estimée d'une valeur de 500 ducats ... Ils avaient de petites selles à la turque, toutes dorées; sur la croupe, trois palmes de brocart d'or ou de velours brodé d'or avec des rangs de boutons pendants de chaque côté et faits de fil d'or et de soie cramoisie. Les chevaux étaient de très beaux turcs et barbes, de robe noire ou more, baie, grise, pommelée ou blanche, et dont le prix était au moins de 200 ducats," Maurand, p. 211.

40 Lubenau, 1:161; Heberer, p. 378; Schweigger, p. 62. The court is described by Baron Wenceslas Wratislaw, attached to an embassy sent by Rudolf II to Murad III in 1591, "Having been admitted into the first square, we saw handsome buildings everywhere at the sides, in which the court artisans have all kinds of shops and workshops, just as in front of the palace at Prague," Wratislaw, p. 58.

41 Maurand, p. 211.

42 Flachat, pp. 168–69: "L'architecture en est simple & uniforme. J'en excepterai un grand kiosque de figure octogone; il mérite un peu plus d'attention. Il est bâti en pierre de taille sur une vaste plate-forme; on peut en faire le tour. On croit qui'il étoit destiné pour aller à la priere dans le temps que les troupes s'assemblent dans cette vaste cour, où l'on pourroit aisément faire faire l'exercice à quarante mille hommes."

43 For its function, see Anonymous, "Administrative treatise," fol. 20r; Anonymous, *Kitâb-u Mesâlih,* 1:134–381, 2:38–39; Hezarfen, *Telhis,* fol. 15v.

44 Lokman, *Hünername,* 1:fol. 15r.

45 Beauvau, pp. 31–32.

46 Flachat says that prayers were once performed in this kiosk with up to forty thousand soldiers gathered at the first court, Flachat, pp. 168–69.

47 Moryson, 2:93. Some late sources refer to this structure as the "kiosk of plaintiffs" *(deāvī ḳaṣrı)* where viziers once took turns to collect the petitions of citizens seeking justice, see Atâ, 1:60–61; Şeref, p. 281.

48 They are described as "lunghe fabriche, dove sono Stanze senza finestre, che rispondono sopra esso, ma solo di quando in quando alcuni portoni, che introducono in quelle," in Donato, 2:84–85.

49 Moryson, 2:93.

50 For the corps of gardeners stationed at these two gates, see Atâ, 1:165, 304.

51 Pigafetta, p. 138; C. Zeno, p. 24.

52 Bon, p. 61, describes it as "un solo porticale a mano sinistra fatto per starvi li cavalli e servitori al coperto in tempo di pioggia."

53 Angiolello, *Inedito manoscritto,* p. 22.

54 Angiolello, *Inedito manoscritto,* pp. 21, 23. For the popular belief that St. John Chrysostom was buried in the Church of St. Irene, see the report of an anonymous pilgrim, of 1424–53, in Majeska, p. 227; İnciciyan, p. 57. For the church, see Müller-Wiener, pp. 112–17.

55 Sandys, p. 113; Courmenin, p. 130; İnciciyan, pp. 57–58. Flachat writes, "Je n'y ai point vu le bras de S. Jean-Baptiste, dans le grand nombre de pieces curieuses & d'effets rares qu'on a enlevés aux successeurs de Constantin, quoique les Grecs m'aient affirmé plusieurs fois qu'on l'y conserve dans une cassette d'or," Flachat, p. 165.

56 Clarke, p. 5.

57 Anonymous, "Administrative treatise," fol. 20r.

58 Barkan, *Süleymaniye,* 2:24, no. 46. For eighteenth-century repair inscriptions at St. Irene, see Şeref, pp. 276–77.

59 Lokman, *Hünername,* fol. 15r; BA, MM 148, fol. 96r; MM 17884, fol. 61; KK 7097, fol. 99.

60 Tavernier, p. 68. See also Evliya, 1:563; Hezarfen, *Telhis,* fol. 21r; Wheeler, p. 180.

61 BA, MM 17884, fol. 61; Barkan, "İstanbul saraylarına," p. 48.

62 Anonymous, "Administrative treatise," fol. 20r.

63 Bobovi, *Mémoires,* fol. 281; Wheeler, p. 180; Atâ, 1:301; Ralamb, pp. 703–4; Bon, p. 61; Eremya, p. 13.

64 Atâ, 1:94, 299; Şeref, p. 278; Ralamb, pp. 703–4; Hezarfen, *Telhis,* fol. 15v; Evliya, 1:116. About the transport of rushes from Manyas Lake for straw mats, see BA, Cevdet 325, 353, 8097.

65 BA, MM 17884, fol. 61; KK 7098, fol. 37r.

66 "Becihet-i nev-sāḫten-i kārḫāne-i ḥaṣīrcıyān der nezd-i gāvān-i hīmekeşān," BA, MM 487, fol. 63. In a firman of 3 Şa'ban 984 (27 October 1576), addressed to the city commissioner, the sultan orders that the "dormitory of novices in the service of oxen" *(öküzler ḫidmetinde olan ‹acemī oğlanlar odası)* be given to the "mat makers" *(ḥaṣīrcılar),* since "my imperial palace's mat workshop is not large enough" *(sarāy-i ‹āmirem ḥaṣīrḫānesi vasī‹ olmamağın),* and that "a new dormitory" *(yeñiden bir oda)* be built for the novices, MM 7534, fol. 1218.

67 BA, MM 699, fol. 24; TSA, D 10384, fols. 1r–2v; D 10587, fol. 3r.

68 The "imperial warehouse" *(anbār-i ‹āmire, anbār-i ḫāṣṣa)*

is mentioned in an early document of 893 (1488), TSA, D 10587, fol. 3r. See also BA, MM, 17884, fols. 2, 61; Barkan, "İstanbul saraylarına" p. 48.

69 It is mentioned as "the imperial warehouse vault near the armory" *(cebeḫāne ḳurbinde anbār-i ‹āmire maḫzeni),* in Sa'i, *Mimar Sinan,* pp. 47, 123.

70 Barkan, "İstanbul saraylarına," pp. 56–59, 83; BA, KK 7097, fol. 125; MM 422, fol. 176; MM 5530, fol. 84; MM 855, fol. 6. A document of 1555–56 refers to the repair of the "atelier of carpenters" *(kārḫāne-i neccārān)* near the warehouse, BA, KK 7098, fol. 37r.

71 "Becihet-i meremmet-i kārḫāne-i naḳḳāşān ma‹a kemer der fevḳ-i arslānḫāne der ḳurb-i meydān-i esb," BA, MM 17884, fol. 61. For the menagerie, see Mango, *Brazen House,* pp. 154–69, Müller-Wiener, p. 81.

72 These artists are referred to as "painters and their assistants at the imperial warehouse," or "painters belonging to the imperial warehouse," *(naḳḳāşān ve şāgirdān-i īşān-i anbār-i ‹āmire, naḳḳāşān ... tābī‹-i anbār-i ‹āmire,"* BA, MM 5530, fol. 84; MM 855, fol. 6; KK 7097, fol. 125; MM 422, fol. 176.

73 Evliya, 1:569; Şeref, p. 280. The warehouse, also known as "şehremin," was used for storing "all the construction supplies of the palace," Eremya, p. 13. It is referred to as the "city commissioner's warehouse" *(şehr emīni anbārı)* in Hezarfen, *Telhis,* fol. 15v; as the "warehouse for palace repairs" *(sarāyıñ tā‹mīrāt anbārı)* in Atâ, 1:60; and as "le magasin des provisions," in La Croix, *Serrail,* fol. 26; 295–96.

74 The warehouse had "appartements, magasins & atteliers" and artisans "les charpentiers & menusiers qui travaillent sans cesse à réparer ou à embellir le serrail," Flachat, pp. 165–67.

75 Ibid., pp. 165–67.

76 Lokman, *Hünername,* 1:fol. 15r.

77 Anonymous, "Administrative treatise," fol. 20r. See also İnciciyan, p. 29; Carbognano, p. 22; Flachat, p. 167.

78 Lokman, *Hünername,* 1:fol. 16r.

79 Cafer Efendi, p. 34.

80 "Bāġçe-i ‹āmire kārḫānesinde," TSA, E 9704.

81 For the "workshop of goldsmiths and gold-thread embroiderers at the imperial palace," or the "workshop of engravers at the imperial garden," *(kārḫāne-i zergerān der sarāy-i ‹āmire, zerdūzān der sarāy-i ‹āmire,* or *kārḫāne-i ḥakkākān der bāġçe-i ‹āmire),* see BA, KK 7097, fols. 23–24, 100; Şeref, p. 280.

82 BA, KK 1772, fols. 29r, 40v; BA, MM 5633, fols. 65, 82, 83.

83 It is referred to as "inner mint near the Tiled Kiosk" *(żarbḫāne-i enderūn der ḳurb-i sarāy-i sırça),* in BA, MM 5633, fol. 82; and as the "mint at [or inside] the Tiled Kiosk" *(sırça sarāy içindeki żarbḫāne, sırça sarāyda żarbḫāne)* in Selaniki (İpşirli, ed.) pp. 137, 157–58.

84 "Çeşme ḳurbinde dīvānḫāne-i defterdārān ve āna maḳrūn anbār-i mühimmāt ve kārḫāne-i üstādān," Lokman, *Hünername,* 1:fol. 15r. A contemporary document of 1581–82 cites an "archive" *(defterḫāne)* near the "imperial warehouse" *(anbār-i ‹āmire);* BA, MM 422, fol. 176. The royal mint and warehouse near a fountain are also mentioned in Flachat, p. 167.

85 Eremya, p. 13; Hezarfen, *Telhis,* fol. 15v; Donato, 2:85. The abandoned mint is referred to as "le lieu où l'on battoit anciennement la monnoye," in La Croix, *Serrail,* fol. 26.

86 For the eighteenth-century mint, see Küçükçelebizade, p. 443.

87 Şeref, pp. 278–80.

88 Lokman, *Hünername,* 1:fol. 15r; Menavino, p. 103.

89 Atâ, 1:60; Âli, Mevaid, pp. 26–27. Âli refers to the hospital as the "chamber of invalids" *(ḫastalar sarayı, ḫastalar odası).* A repair document of 1582–83 mentions it as "house of invalids" *(sarāy-i bīmārān),* BA, MM 148, fol. 96r.

90 "Oda-i marīż der nezd-i bāb-i hümāyūn," BA, KK 7097, fol. 99; "room of sick pages and [its] bath near the Imperial Gate" *(oda-i ġılmān-i marīż ve ḥammām der nezd-i bāb-i hümāyūn),* MM 17884, fol. 54; see also, KK 7098, fol. 37r.

91 Bobovi, *Mémoires,* fols. 278–80. Bobovi's plan shows that the infirmary had individual rooms for each group of pages, for eunuchs, and for the chief eunuch of the infirmary, a bath, and rooms for launderers, where old female slaves washed the laundry of the pages. A workshop for launderers is mentioned earlier by Menavino, who does not specify its location, Menavino, p. 101. A repair document of 1581–82 mentions the "workshop of launderers" as *(cāmeşūyān),* BA, MM 422, fol. 176. For a detailed study of Bobovi's description of the hospital, see Terzioğlu, "Alberto Bobovio," and *Hofspitäler.*

92 Üsküdari, 2:fols. 315v–16r. See also Anonymous, "Administrative treatise," fol. 20r.

93 Bobovi, *Mémoires,* fols. 278–79; Üsküdari, 2:fols. 316r–18v.

94 Âli, *Mevaid,* pp. 26–27; Tournefort, 2:212; Tavernier, pp. 63–65.

95 For the inscription, see Şeref, p. 275. For this bakery, see Tavernier, p. 69; La Croix, *Serrail,* fol. 26; Eremya, p. 14; Carbognano, p. 22; Atâ, 1:60, 297; Ralamb, p. 704; İnciciyan, p. 29.

96 The document also mentions the installation of new water pipes, and the construction of other dependent buildings, BA, MM 653, fols. 1, 4. Another source, from 1617, cites the repair of "walls of the royal and common bakeries" *(dīvārhā-i furun-i ḫaṣṣa ve ḫarcī),* MM 858, fol. 67.

97 Miller, *Beyond the Sublime Porte,* p. 164. Without specifying its location, Menavino describes the bakery as "quattro forni insieme in una casa, dove si fa il pane per la bocca del Signore, & di tutta la famiglia," Menavino, p. 99.

98 Âli, *Künh,* fol. 84v. Mehmed II had also chosen the site of the Old Palace after testing its source of water, which was found to be the best in the city, Evliya, 1:117–19. The

sultan had similarly decided to build his palace on the Tunca River in Edirne when a fountain was discovered there, Beşir Çelebi.

99 For the water supplies of the palace, see Bilge, pp. 216–18; Nirven, pp. 45–53; Ayverdi, *Osmanlı Mimarisinde Fatih Devri,* 616–17.

100 There are two plans of the Topkapı Palace water installations, TSK, H 1816, H 1815. They are discussed in Bilge and Çeçen.

101 Tavernier, pp. 81–82.

102 Sa'i, *Tezkiretü'l-bünyan,* pp. 65–68.

103 Çeçen, pp. 108, 112. For the Kırkçeşme Channel, see Nirven, pp. 76, 103; Bilge, p. 101; Ayverdi, *Osmanlı Mimarisinde Fatih Devri,* 613–15.

104 This gate is mentioned in Hezarfen, *Telhis,* fol. 15v.

105 For these lost buildings, see BA, Cevdet 355; Cevdet 7063; Cevdet 355. Some documents mention a "royal pavilion at the Corps of the Water Wheel" *(dolāb ocāğında vāḳīʿ ḳaṣr-i hümāyūn, ḳaṣr-i hümāyūn der dolāb ocāğı),* BA, Cevdet 6182. According to Atâ, this was the "pavilion of the head gatekeeper" *(ḳapu ağası ḳaṣrı),* where he held audiences concerning the imperial waqfs under his control; Atâ, 1:301.

106 Spandugino, *Petit Traicté,* pp. 133–34. Spandugino observes that viziers suffering from gout were allowed to enter on horseback. The Akkoyunlu prince Uğurlu Mehmed was also given permission to enter the gate on a horse, Angiolello, *Historia Turchesca,* p. 167.

107 Menavino, p. 91.

108 For the inscription, see Şeref, p. 331; Ayverdi, *Fatih Devri Mimarisi,* p. 315. It was misread as "ʿamel-i ġaybın Meḥmed," in Miller, *Beyond the Sublime Porte,* p. 170; for the correct reading, see Davis, p. 40; Akdağ, p. 73. For the assertion that the towers were added in the sixteenth century, see Ayverdi, *Fatih Devri Mimarisi,* p. 315; Ayverdi, *Osmanlı Mimarisinde Fatih Devri,* pp. 683, 701; Koçu, p. 31; Akdağ, 73.

109 Kemalpaşazade, 1:475, 2:430. For the argument that the towers were added to the original core of the gate between 1482 and 1500, see Eldem and Akozan, pp. 69–70, pls. 36, 37.

110 For the ceremonial functions of the gate of St. Barbara and the Golden Gate, see Millingen, pp 178–93, 248–67; Demangel and Mamboury, p. 7; Müller-Wiener, pp. 297–300. For Chalke, see Müller-Wiener, pp. 81, 229–37, 269; Mango, *Brazen House,* and Smith, *Architectural Symbolism,* pp. 134–41.

111 Postel, pt. 3, p. 50.

112 The list of materials used by the workshop of "royal painter-designers" *(naḳḳāşḫāne-i ḫāṣṣa),* headed by Nakkaş Hasan, for painting the Middle Gate included, sandaracha *(sandalus),* paper *(kāğıd),* cobalt blue *(lāciverd),* pots *(tās),* knives *(kārd),* vermilion *(zencefre),* brushes *(furça),* straw *(ḥasīr),* wire *(ḥām tīl)* and silver leaf *(varaḳ-i nuḳra),* BA, KK 7097, fol. 33. A later document, of 1603–4, mentions "repairing the paintings of the Middle Gate and the Imperial Gate" *(meremmāt-kerden-i naḳş-kerden-i bāb-i miyāne ve bāb-i hümāyūn),* MM 6019, fol. 78. Repairs in 1172 (1759) of the Middle Gate's painted ceiling are recorded in an inscription cited in Şeref, pp. 331–32.

113 Gyllius, p. 39; Vigenère, p. 17; Breuning, p. 50.

114 BA, KK 7097, fols. 23, 33, 43, 99; MM 17884, fols. 54, 69; MM 422, fol. 176; MM 148, fol. 96r; MM 1946, fol. 14; MM 6019, fol. 78; Eremya, p. 14; Hezarfen, *Telhis,* fols. 15r–v.

115 Lokman, *Hünername,* 1:fols. 15r, 16r; Âli, *Künh,* fol. 91r.

116 İnciciyan, p. 30. For the inscription, see Şeref, p. 331.

117 For the al-Salām court in Baghdad, see Hilāl al-Sābi', pp. 63–64. For the inscription on the Middle Gate, see Şeref, p. 332.

118 For the assumed defensive function of the gate, see Örs, *History of the Topkapı Palace,* p. 8; Miller, *Beyond the Sublime Porte,* p. 171. For the argument against a defensive function, see Davis, p. 39; Raby, "El Gran Turco," p. 301; Tansuğ, pp. 152–56.

119 Gyllius, p. 38. See also Fresne-Canaye, p. 62; Schweigger, pp. 64, 153; Bon, p. 62.

120 BA, Cevdet 8627.

121 He refers to "a masjid for gatekeepers above the Gate of Felicity and below it two facing stations for gatekeepers," *(fevḳānī-yi bābü's-saʿādet-meāb mescīd-i bevvābān ve taḥtānīsinde ḳarşulı menāzīl-i ḳapucıyān),* Lokman, *Hünername,* 1:fol. 16r. A document of 1527–28 cites the repair of the "gatekeepers' rooms at the Middle Gate," *(oda-i bevvābān-i bāb-i miyāne),* BA, MM 17884, fol. 54. Another one, from 1528–29, mentions the "rooms and latrines of gatekeepers at the Middle Gate" *(odahā ve ḥelāhā-i bevvābān-i bāb-i miyāne),* BA, KK 7097, fols. 43, 49.

122 A document of 1528–29 mentions the "prisoners inside the Middle Gate" *(maḥbūsān der enderūn-i bāb-i miyāne),* BA, KK 7097, fols. 43, 99. For the prison and the dormitories of gatekeepers, see Eremya, p. 14; La Croix, *Serrail,* p. 27; Hezarfen, *Telhis,* fol. 15v; İnciciyan, p. 30; Carbognano, p. 23; Şeref, p. 330. For prisons attached to Chalke, see Mango, *Brazen House,* p. 31.

Chapter 3

1 For the animals, see Lokman, *Hünername,* 1:fol. 16r; Fauvel, p. 63; Maurand, pp. 213, 215; Bon, p. 62; Lubenau, 1:162, 2:10; Courmenin, p. 130; Donato, 2:86–87. The railings are mentioned in Bon, p. 62; Tavernier, p. 73; Hezarfen, *Telhis,* fols. 16r, 29r; BA, MM 3780, fol. 140; MM 443, fol. 45; Cevdet 8026. Ottaviano Bon describes the second court as "un altro cortile poco minore del primo ma molto più bello per diverse nobilissime fontane, per esservi strade compartite da altissimi cipressi e per ritrovarsi alcuni quadri di prato, dove nascendo l'erba

pascolano diverse gazelle, che fruttano, e sono tenute per delizia ... Dall'una e l'altra parte di esso, vi sono porticali sostentati da nobilissime colonne," Bon, p. 62. Fauvel (p. 63) writes, "Les chemins y sont pavez, le reste est en preau avec des barrieres à costé, où reposent plusieurs oiseaux d'Inde, Cerfs, Biches, Gazelles, & autres animaux." For the red ocher paint *(āşı)* of wooden "railings" *(dizmehā-i parmaḳ, dizme parmaḳlıḳlar, parmaḳlıḳlar)*, see BA, MM 3780, fol. 140; MM 443, fol. 45; Cevdet 8026.

2 Maurand, p. 223.

3 Kritovoulos, pp. 207–8.

4 Angiolello, *Inedito manoscritto,* p. 23.

5 Spandugino, *Petit Traicté,* pp. 156–57. For the identical layouts of the sultan's palace and his camp, where the public council tent was pitched next to the public treasury tent, see Lutfi, *Asafname,* pp. 26, 31.

6 Mihailović, p. 157.

7 In 1537 Baron de Saint-Blancard wrote, "Tant vault dire Porte comme lieu où se tient conseil, audience et faict justice," Saint-Blancard, p. 347. In 1621 Deshayes de Courmenin wrote, "La Cour du *Grand Seigneur* est appelée *Porte,* parce qu'au lieu qu'en Chrestienté chacun entre dans la cour des Palais des Princes, il faut que tout le monde demeure à la porte de ses *Serrails,* où personne n'entre que huict ou dix de ses principaux ministres, & les Ambassadeurs en arrivant, & en s'en retournant," Courmenin, p. 235.

8 Bidlisi, *Hasht Behisht,* fol. 72r.

9 Bostan, fol. 99v; Lokman, *Hünername,* 1:fol. 16r.

10 For Âli's statement on justice and Ottoman legitimacy, see Fleischer, pp. 290–92.

11 Gyllius, p. 38.

12 Selaniki (İpşirli, ed.), pp. 357, 368–69, 385–86. For the Executioner's Fountain, see Thévenot, p. 66; La Croix, *Serrail,* fol. 28; Beauvau, p. 32; Arvieux, p. 477.

13 Gritti, "Relazione fatta in Pregadi," p. 457.

14 Selaniki, *Tarih,* pp. 142, 182, 195, 227; Ohsson, 7:222–25; Atâ, 1:269–73; Hezarfen, *Telhis,* fol. 30r; Naili, fols. 99v–103v. Bon calls this ceremony "divano grande," Bon, p. 68.

15 Bon, 69; Naili, fol. 99v, 110v. Naili writes that the Council Hall was not decorated for the inferior ambassadors of Wallachia and Dubrovnik.

16 Naili, fol. 99v; Hezarfen, *Telhis,* fol. 16r; Anonymous, "Administrative treatise," fol. 19v; Wratislaw, p. 58.

17 Lamberg and Jurischisch, p. 40; Curispeschitz, *Yolculuk Günlüğü,* p. 46.

18 For the salutation stones and the ceremonial procession through the second court, see Hezarfen, *Telhis,* fol. 28r; Naili, fols. 43r–49r; Esad, pp. 68–69, 80–81; Atâ, 1:269ff. These stones are described as "trois petites colonnes de marbre" in Ohsson, 7:215–16.

19 Gritti, "Relazione fatta in Pregadi," pp. 456–57. Angiolello observes that the courtiers had fixed positions: "Le squadre da Cavalo et da piedi stano ali suoi luoghi deputati attorno la corte," Angiolello, *Inedito manoscritto,* pp. 37–38.

20 Gritti, "Relazione [1503]" in Albèri, p. 27; Spandugino, *Petit Traicté,* p. 135.

21 For the ceremonial in the al-Salām courtyard in Baghdad, see Hilāl al-Sābi', pp. 64–66, 73–74.

22 Bragadino, "Sommario" in Albèri, p. 106.

23 Pigafetta, p. 138.

24 Badoaro, pp. 355–56.

25 Fresne-Canaye, pp. 62–64, 71–72. The silence of the second court is also noted in Lubenau, 1:161, 2:12; Borderie, fol. 35r.

26 Wratislaw, pp. 59–60.

27 Naili, fol. 99v.

28 Naili, fol. 101v; Lokman, *Hünername,* 1:fol. 16v; Palerne, p. 447; Lubenau, 2:10. For the serving of food under the same portico, see Saint-Blancard, pp. 377–78; Fresne-Canaye, p. 63.

29 Those who made noise were bastinadoed: "Chi fa rumore nell'udienza publica, è bastonato acerbissimamente," Bassano, fol. 28r.

30 Anonymous, "Relazione anonima," p. 467.

31 Busbecq, pp. 124–25; Heberer, p. 252; Fresne-Canaye, p. 55.

32 "... Ist sehr unordentlich und ungeschickt gebaut die Gebau stehn überzwerch krumm und schreg durcheinender als wie sie einem aus eim Sack ungefehr gefallen weren sie seyn auch nicht so hoch gros weit und so ansehlich gebaut," Schweigger, p. 62.

33 For the monastery comparison, see Maurand, p. 213; Bassano, p. 16v; Sandys, p. 113; Thévenot, p. 66; Donato, 2:87. For the marble revetments and painted portico ceilings, see Saint-Blancard, p. 376, who describes the second court as "une grande basse-court toute pavée de marbres, excepté les belles grandes allées; a bien de loing mil cinq cens pas ou plus, large troys cens, a tout autour une allée en forme de gallerie couverte, toute paincte le ciel et entredoré; soubz ladicte gallerie, et plus oultre du costé est la porte faicte de voulte, de grandz coulonnes et marbres, riche et superbe, où l'on tient l'audience et faict l'on les expédicions de justice: tel lieu où se faict justice appelle l'on la Porte."

34 Schepper, p. 168.

35 C. Zeno, p. 25.

36 Lubenau 2:10. For the blue-and-gold scheme, see also Saint-Blancard (n. 33) and Breuning, p. 50.

37 Chesneau, p. 26. A similar passage is found in Deffens, fol. 9v.

38 Lokman, *Hünername,* 1:fols. 16r–18r; Anonymous, "Administrative treatise," fols. 18v–20r; Hezarfen, *Telhis,* fols. 15r–16r; 28v–29v.

39 Lokman, *Hünername,* 1:fols. 16r–18r.

40 Tamgruti, pp. 61–63.

41 Feridun, fols. 175v–76r.

42 Ibid., fols. 249r–v.

43 Lokman, *Şehname,* fols. 138v–47v.

44 Anonymous, *Kitâb-u Mesâlih,* 1:99–101; 2:132–34.

45 The ceremonial prescribed in the Byzantine *Book of Ceremonies* is cited in Cameron, p. 118; for the Abbasid cere-

monial, see Hilāl al-Sābi', p. 64.

46 For a general discussion of the kitchens, see Ayverdi, *Fatih Devri Mimarisi,* pp. 296, 298; Ayverdi, *Osmanlı Mimarisinde Fatih Devri,* pp. 686, 705–13; Eldem and Akozan, pp. 71–73; T. Öz, "Topkapı Sarayı Müzesi Onarımları," p. 34; Davis, 46–49, 59–60; Miller, *Beyond the Sublime Porte,* pp. 185–203; Goodwin, p. 135.

47 Menavino, pp. 99–100.

48 For this elevation drawing, dated to the early sixteenth century through its watermark, see Necipoğlu-Kafadar, "Plans and Models," pp. 234–36.

49 A section of the payroll is published in Refik, "Fatih Devrine Aid Vesikalar," pp. 24–58. For fifteenth-century account books of the kitchens, see Barkan, "İstanbul saraylarına." For descriptions of the kitchen personnel, see Angiolello, *Inedito manoscritto,* pp. 31–32, 37; Angiolello, *Historia Turchesca,* pp. 126–27, 136; Spandugino, *Petit Traicté,* pp. 73–76, 129; Promontorio, pp. 34–35; Menavino, pp. 99–100, 131–33.

50 Gyllius, p. 38.

51 BA, KK 7097, fols. 22, 99.

52 Selaniki, *Tarih,* pp. 114–15.

53 Lokman, *Tomar,* fol. 145r; Âli, *Künh,* fol. 460v.

54 Davis, pp. 59, 69; Kuran, "Palace of the Sultans," p. 111; Miller, *Beyond the Sublime Porte,* pp. 33, 39, 105–6, 176; Goodwin, pp. 321–22. Miller (p. 106) and others repeat Atâ's erroneous statement that the fire occurred in Murad III's reign, Atâ, 1:71.

55 BA, KK 1770, fols. 30v, 31r, 32r, 34r, 35v, 36r, 42v, 47v, 50r, 52r, 69v, 71v, 76r, 79r, 82v.

56 BA, MD 26, nos. 353, 362.

57 Ibid., MD 26, nos. 449, 454, 565, 571, 590, 596, 606, 607, 736, 737, 746.

58 Sa'i, *Mimar Sinan,* pp. 40, 48, 123.

59 Selaniki, *Tarih,* pp. 114–15.

60 Miller, *Beyond the Sublime Porte,* p. 107.

61 For the gate names, see Hezarfen, *Telhis,* fol. 15v.

62 For these repairs, see T. Öz, "Topkapı Sarayı Müzesi Onarımları," pp. 33–41, 49–50; Akdağ, p. 85.

63 For the inscriptions, see Şeref, pp. 335–38.

64 Hierosolimitano, *Vera relatione,* pp. 40–41; Bon, p. 62; Courmenin, p. 131; Tavernier, pp. 73–75.

65 "Repairing the room for ceramics near the imperial kitchen" *(meremmet-i oda-i çīnī der nezd-i maṭbāḫ-i ʿāmire)* BA, MM 17884, fol. 54. See also BA, KK 7097, fol. 99; MM 17884, fol. 54. Selaniki writes that the ceramic wares kept in the commissary and confectionary were destroyed in the fire of 1574, Selaniki, *Tarih,* pp. 114–15.

66 Atâ, 1:62; Angiolello, *Inedito manoscritto,* p. 37.

67 TSA, D 9715; see also Raby and Yücel, pp. 41–42.

68 BA, MM 422, fol. 176; Uzunçarşılı, *Osmanlı Devletinin Saray Teşkilatı,* p. 381.

69 Hierosolimitano, *Vera relatione,* pp. 37–39, 66.

70 Wratislaw, pp. 62–63. For the ceremonial banquet, see also Maurand, pp. 222–23.

71 The monumentality of the kitchens was admired by foreigners. "The Kitchens seem too stately for the Turkish Cookery," commented Wheeler, p. 181. Flachat (p. 173) wrote, "Elles sont sous des dômes couverts de plomb. Leur distribution est admirable. On y reconnoît l'intelligence des anciens, & l'art qu'ils avoient à associer l'agréable à l'utile."

72 Angiolello, *Inedito manoscritto,* p. 23.

73 Spandugino, *Petit Traicté,* pp. 124–25; 134–35; Menavino, pp. 112–13. For the stables, see also Angiolello, *Historia Turchesca,* pp. 142–43; Angiolello, *Inedito manoscritto,* p. 42; Promontorio, pp. 32–33. Another royal stable was located outside the Gate of Stables, one of the three main gates of the Imperial Fortress, Menavino, pp. 112–113. It is identified as *stabula* on the Nuremberg Chronicle woodcut (see Pl. 24).

74 Karamani, p. 362; Kemalpaşazade, 1:476–77, 2:431–32; cited in Şeref, p. 273; Ayverdi, *Osmanlı Mimarisinde Fatih Devri,* pp. 685, 708.

75 Lokman, *Hünername,* 1:fol. 16v; Anonymous, "Administrative treatise," fol. 19v; Hezarfen, *Telhis,* fol. 16r.

76 For the seventeenth-century function of the stables as a hospital, see Miller, *Beyond the Sublime Porte,* p. 202; Şeref, p. 340; Tezcan, "Sur-u Sultanî," p. 387.

77 BA, MM 17884, fol. 71; see also KK 7097, fol. 99.

78 For repair inscriptions, see Şeref, pp. 339–42.

79 BA, Cevdet 7709. For restorations in the 1940s, see T. Öz, "Topkapı Sarayı Müzesi Onarımları," pp. 8, 13, 19–29.

80 Bon, p. 62; see also T. Öz, *Guide to the Museum,* p. 86.

81 Hezarfen, *Telhis,* fol. 16r. See also Tavernier, p. 82; Fauvel, p. 64.

82 Sandys, p. 114; Bon, p. 62.

83 TSA, D 34, fol. 186v; E 12359, no. 1, fol. 5r.

84 Silahdar, 2:232–33.

85 Hezarfen, *Telhis,* fol. 20r.

86 Âli, *Künh,* fol. 94r; Bobovi, *Mémoires,* fol. 274; Beauvau, pp. 65–66; Üsküdari, 1:fols. 257r–v; Atâ, 1:265, 297, 305.

87 "Meremmet-i oda-i teberdārān ve ḥammām," "sāḫten-i maṭbāḫ ve kilār ve şerbetḫāne ve dīvār-i sedd ve ḥavlı-yi sedd der pīş-i oda-i teberdārān," BA, MM 17884, fols. 54, 69.

88 It mentions the "repair of the chambers of halberdiers and its bath," *(meremmet-i odahā-i teberdārān ve ḥammām-i o),* BA, KK 7097, fol. 24.

89 Evliya, 1:116.

90 Cited in Şeref, p. 343; Atasoy, "Topkapı Sarayı Zülüflü," p. 629.

91 Cited in Şeref, p. 344; Atasoy, "Topkapı Sarayı Zülüflü," p. 631.

92 Cited in Şeref, pp. 344–45; Atasoy, "Topkapı Sarayı Zülüflü," pp. 629, 632.

93 For a description of these buildings, see Atasoy, "Topkapı Sarayı Zülüflü," pp. 627–32; Eldem and Akozan, p. 72, pls. 57–60.

Chapter 4

1 "Le grant cadi, et les autres qui sont commis avec luy, tenoit la raison pour faire justice à ung chascun, à l'entrée de la porte de ladite court," Brocquière, p. 196.

2 "Les Cadilesquier partent les premiers, car quant ilz se partent du Seigneur, ilz s'en vont ung petit seoir avec les Bassa et apres ilz vont donner audience dessus la seconde porte, laquelle est faicte en sorte que chascun a son siege pour juger la banque de sa province," Spandugino, *Petit Traicté,* pp. 96, 140.

3 Lokman, *Hünername,* 1:fol. 18r; Âli, *Künh,* fol. 91r; Navagero, pp. 96–97.

4 Gritti, "Relazione fatta in Pregadi," p. 456; Spandugino, *Petit Traicté,* p. 135.

5 Atâ, 1:61. Also mentioned in Şeref, p. 333.

6 "Dīvānḫāne-i aġa-yi ebnā-i sipāhiyān maʿa aġa-yi yeñiçeriyān der bāb-i miyāne," BA, MM 861, fol. 115. See also Lokman, *Hünernāme,* 1:fol. 16r; Hezarfen, *Telhis,* fol. 15r; Anonymous, "Administrative treatise," fol. 19v; Şeref, p. 333.

7 "Oturaḳ-i aġa-yi sipāhiyān ve aġa-yi yeñiçeriyān der dīvān-i hümāyūn-i bāb-i orta," BA, MM 1947, fols. 14, 15.

8 Angiolello, *Inedito manoscritto,* p. 23.

9 Gritti, "Relazione fatta in Pregadi," p. 457. For this seating order, see also Spandugino, *Petit Traicté,* p. 100.

10 Leysizade, p. 33.

11 "Da l'altro ladi [i.e., the right side] sentano i duo defterdari, *scilicet* thesorieri, apresso un balcon *cum* ferri de una camera dove stanno da circa 50 scrivani che scriveno; et lì hano le scripture pertinente al stato, poste quelle de importantia in una cassa ligata et sigilata *cum* l'anello del primo bassà—el qual loco se pò reputar et è la sua cancellaria, benché, *etiam* lì se tegnino: libri de le intrade et uscide del Signor," Gritti, "Relazione fatta in Pregadi," p. 457. Spandugino refers to the vizier's council hall as "une petite chambre où lesdictz Bassa tiennent leur audience," and to the chancery as "ung petit cabinet qui respond à ladicte chambre," Spandugino, *Petit Traicté,* pp. 100, 136–37.

12 Leysizade, p. 46.

13 Angiolello, *Inedito manoscritto,* p. 35; Angiolello, *Historia Turchesca,* p. 132.

14 This place is referred to as "une petite chambre separée des autres escripvains," Spandugino, *Petit Traicté,* p. 140.

15 Koçi Beg, p. 24. For a council meeting Selim I held in the second court, see Uğur, pp. 230–33. Ohsson writes, "Ces conseils se tenaient autrefois au sérail, présidés par le Sultan autour duquel les membres de l'assemblée formaient un demi-cercle, assis sur des petits tapis," Ohsson, 7:228–32. Taşköprizade states that it was Murad I (1360–89) who initiated such consultations; Taşköprizade, 1:24–25. Ruhi Edrenevi refers to a "consultation" *(ṭanışıḳ)* of Murad II in 1442–43, when the ruler explained the need for a campaign to gathered soldiers, Ruhi, *Tarih,* fol. 122r.

16 Menavino, pp. 92, 127–28.

17 "And also the imperial council does not deliberate in the presence of the emperor, but far from the emperor ... and in a different room. If outside, however, a special tent is pitched called *danissik czaderi* [i.e., danışık çadırı], which would mean in our language 'council tent,'" Mihailović, pp. 145–47, 157.

18 "Les petites chambres des Bassa sont toutes par bas," Spandugino, *Petit Traicté,* p. 137. The vizier's Council Hall is referred to as "una logietta dove sedono gli Signori Bassa," in Becagut, fol. 16v.

19 Ayverdi, *Fatih Devri Mimarisi,* p. 317; Ayverdi, *Osmanlı Mimarisinde Fatih Devri,* p. 714; Eldem and Akozan, p. 70; T. Öz, *Guide to the Museum,* p. 34; Akdağ, p. 99. For the location of the Old Council Hall between the Public Treasury and the third gate, see Hezarfen, *Telhis,* fol. 15v; TSA, E 12359, no. 1, fol. 5v; D 4462, fol. 2r.

20 "Tra l'angolo e la porta una volta si faceva il Divano, è resta ancora una parte del portico compartito a quest'uso colla piccola fenestra sopra la sede del Gran Vizir per affaciarvisi il Gran Signore, il che si chiama ancora il vecchio Divano," Sorio, p. 35.

21 Solakzade, pp. 268–69.

22 Âli, *Mevaid,* pp. 25–26.

23 Lokman, *Hünername,* 1:fol. 17r. For these functions, see also Hezarfen, *Telhis,* fol. 28v; Naili, fol. 43v; Esad, pp. 43, 70.

24 Atâ, 1:61; Şeref, p. 355.

25 Şeref, p. 355. This "oratoire des Baltagis" is described thus: "C'est une grande salle dont le plafond est soustenu par des colonnes de bois peintes en rouge. Il ressemble assez à des halles. Il tient à la façade du septentrion de la troisieme porte du serrail," Flachat, p. 174. The mosque was demolished in 1917, T. Öz, *Guide to the Museum,* p. 34. Repair documents cite the red and green paint of its wood, BA, MM 1947, fol. 17; TSA, D 4462, fol. 2r.

26 "ʿAtīḳ dīvānḫāne tāʿbīr olınan cāmiʿ-i şerīf," BA, KK 7140, fol. 3v.

27 "Dīvān-i hümāyūn cāmiʿ-i şerīfi," TSA, D 9916, no. 1, fol. 2r.

28 In 1573 the Venetian ambassadors waited in a hall "dove anticamente solevano dare audientia, non molto discosto della porta del serraglio del Signore che era preparato con Tapeti," Barbaro and Tiepolo, fol. 34. In 1567 it was described by Pigafetta as "uno appartamento adorno di tapeti, sotto ad una di quelle loggie," p. 138. See also Fresne-Canaye, pp. 66–67; Garzoni, p. 377; Bon, p. 69; Courmenin, p. 138. In 1596 the Venetian ambassador complained of having to wait under its portico *(loggia aperta)* in the blazing sun for an hour, Donà, p. 272. Tavernier writes, "Un peu plus haut que le Sale du Divan en voit une autre élevée comme une maniere de Belveder, où les Ambassadeurs se rendent quand ils assistent au Divan, & ils y assistent de trois en trois mois, & les jours qu'on paye les Janissaires. On les avertit de s'y trouver pour une vaine ostentation, & pour leur faire voir la quantité d'argent qui sort du tresor," Tavernier, pp. 99–100.

29 For the food and robes of honor, see Naili, fols. 101v, 103r, 105r–6v, 108r, 110v; Esad, p. 74; Atâ, 1:273.

30 Hezarfen, *Telhis*, fol. 30v; Safi, 1: fol. 136r; Lokman, *Hünername*, 1:fol. 17r; Naili, fols. 166r–v; Esad, pp. 43–44.

31 Hezarfen, *Telhis*, fol. 15v.

32 Üsküdari writes, "In the place called Old Council Hall *[eski dīvānḫāne]* the head treasurer and head of the commissary have rooms of their own adjacent to one another *[birbirine muttaṣıl maḫṣūṣ hücreleri]*, where the wages of the royal artisans *[ehl-i ḥiref]* are distributed inside the Old Council Hall in the head treasurer's presence, according to an ancient custom whereby their wages have come to be distributed by the secretary who keeps the accounts of the above mentioned agha [i.e., head treasurer]," Üsküdari, 2:fols. 133v–34r. For the payment of court artisans, also see Lokman, *Hünername*, 1:fol. 17r; Âli, *Künh*, fol. 93r.

33 "Trovai la Porta benissimo ad ordene, altramente di quello trovai l'altra volta veni de qui ambasiator ... È grande differentia da questa a l'altra volta," Minio, "Copia di una lettera," p. 291. "Disse come il Signor havia fatto ruinar nel Serraio ... che è gran cosa, dove li bassà dava audientia, per far una bella fabrica, et ruino il casnà," Minio, "Relazione [1527]," pp. 116–17; cited in Dilger, p. 51.

34 Referring to İbrahim Pasha, he writes, "Et hors guerre faisoit les plus braves entreprises du monde, comme il fist faire le portail doré du Serrail du Seigneur. Les allées avec colonnes de marbre. Le Divan ou auditoire dudit lieu ... " Postel, pt. 3, p. 50.

35 Vigenère, pp. 17–18.

36 Nişancı, p. 249. Dilger makes the hasty assertion that no reference is to be found in contemporary Ottoman sources from Süleyman's reign to the construction of this Council Hall, Dilger, p. 50. Without specifying his source, Öz writes that the divan was built in 933 (1525), T. Öz, *Guide to the Museum*, p. 34.

37 Bostan, fol. 99v. Evliya writes that the Council Hall *(dīvānḫāne)* and the Tower of Justice, adjacent to it, were built by Süleyman, Evliya, 1:116. See also Ohsson, who states that the "new Council Hall," the public "outer treasury," and "archives" were built by Süleyman, Ohsson, 7:211–12.

38 BA, MM 17884, fols. 52–54, 69, 71; BA, KK 7097, fols. 22–24, 99.

39 The entry from Zilka'de 934 reads: "İnʿām be-miʿmār ʿAlā'ü'd-dīn ser-mīʿmārān ki tamām-kerden-i binā'-i dīvānḫāne-i ʿāmire," BA, KK 1764, fol. 22.

40 This attribution is based on the faulty assumption that Süleyman's Council Hall was built to replace that of Mehmed II, destroyed in the fire of 1574, see Miller, *Beyond the Sublime Porte*, p. 175; Davis, p. 69; Kuran, "Palace of the Sultans," p. 111.

41 A wage list from 932 (1525–26) shows that the "chief architect Alaüddin" *(miʿmārbaşı ʿAlā'üd-dīn)* received forty-five *akçes* a day, and gives the names and daily wages of other members of the corps of royal architects: ʿAlī neccār, twenty-three; Maḥmūd miʿmār, twenty-two; Bālī miʿmār, twenty-one; Ḫüdāverdi miʿmār, eighteen; Süleymān miʿmār, thirteen; Şeyḫī miʿmār, thirteen; Dervīş ʿAlī miʿmār, eleven; Yūsuf miʿmār, nine; ʿAlī Eflāḳ, nine; ʿAlī bin Süleymān, eight; İsḥāḳ kiremīdī, eight; İbrāhīm ġulām-i Murād ḫalīfe, eight; ʿAlī Küçük, eight; Ḫıżır miʿmār, seven; Seydī miʿmār, seven; Muṣṭafā bin Şücāʿ, seven; ʿAlā'üd-dīn miʿmār, twelve, TSA, D 9706/2, fols. 2v, 10r. The same list appears in D 10141, fol. 5v. Alaüddin's wage as chief architect was later raised to fifty-five *akçes*, see TSA, D 7843, fol. 2v. A document of 942–43 (1536), just before Sinan became chief architect, refers to "ʿAlā'üd-dīn ser-i miʿmārān," BA, MM 559, fol. 3.

42 He refers to them as "le Camere dell'Archivio, e della Tresoreria, che si congiungono con quelle della Segretaria, ò Cancellaria, le quali finalmente s'uniscono alla stanza del Divano," Donato, 2:88.

43 For these repairs, see T. Öz, "Topkapı Sarayı Müzesi Onarımları," pp. 27–33; Akdağ, p. 102. For the fire, see Silahdar, 1:384; Rycaut, p. 185. For repair inscriptions, see Şeref, pp. 352–54, 461. A repair document from 1208 (1794) refers to "Europeanizing paintings imitating marble," *(efrenckārī ṣomāḳī taḳlīdi)*, which still exist, BA, KK 7140.

44 For example, Eldem and Akozan, pp. 70–71, pls. 42, 43.

45 Saint-Blancard, pp. 376–77; "Questa stanza, lavorata di bellissimi marmi, et bellissime colonne, ha al di fuori banchi da sedere," Navagero, p. 94; Bassano, fol. 24r; "Una bellissima loggia, con un portico davanti, ne piu ne meno come un gran Capitolo de Frati, davanti al quale vi è poi il suo chiostro." The colonnade is described as "una gran loggia in colonne larga et alta più di le altre, la qual è davanti il divan," C. Zeno, p. 25.

46 Teply, *Kaiserliche Großbotschaft*, pp. 120–21.

47 Gudenus, p. 118, illustration p. 171; Tevki'i, p. 513.

48 For the Holy Mantle Pavilion (Privy Chamber Complex), see chapter 7. C. Zeno, p. 25, describes the hall as "una stanza ben salligiata di pietra di diversi colori, et li muri bianchi in volto"; see also Navagero, p. 94, n. 45.

49 "Diese Hauptwand ist bis zum Gewölbe hinauf mit Marmormosaik verkleidet, die Nebenwande vergoldet und in türkischem Stil rot, blau und weiss bemahlt, ebenso die Kuppel aber auf weissem Grund," Gudenus, pp. 117–18.

50 For the Marble Kiosk, see chapter 10; for the palace of Mustafa Pasha, see Pietro Zeno's letter in Sanuto 50:472, 51:622–23: "Questo bassa ha uno belissimo palazo, fato per lui in Constantinopoli, adornato di pietre portate del Cayro, che è cosa bellissima et in bel sito."

51 BA, KK 7097, fol. 100 *(mermerhā ki ʿan Mıṣır amede, ḫazīne-i mermer der bağçe-i ʿāmire)*; MM 17884, fol. 55, "carrying royal marbles coming from Cairo from the boat gate to the mentioned garden" *(keşīden-i mermerhā-i ḫāṣṣa ki ʿan Mıṣır amede ʿan bāb-i ḳayıḳ ʿilā bāġçe-yi'l-mezbūr)*. For the marbles Selim I brought to Istanbul from Cairo, see Ibn Iyas, 2:156, 173–76; Meinecke, "Mamlu-

kische Marmordekorationen," pp. 207–20. Various letters of 1517–18 refer to these spoliated marbles; see Sanuto, 24:600; 25:68; 25:123; 26:146.

52 Hezarfen, *Telhis,* fol. 28v; Donato, 2:88; Anonymous, "Administrative treatise," fol. 18v, 19r. The "archive" *(defterḫāne)* is also mentioned in Lutfi, *Asafname,* p. 41; Âli, *Künh,* fol. 90r.

53 For the benches, and the officers sitting on them, see Hezarfen, *Telhis,* fol. 28v; Anonymous, "Administrative treatise," fols. 18v–19r; Navagero, p. 94. For the red ocher paint, see BA, MM 1947; TSA, D 4462, fol. 2r.

54 "Elle est ouverte dans toute sa façade ... l'on y entre de plein pied pour montrer que l'entrée est libre à tout le monde, la face qui est ouverte, se ferme avec des toiles, et il paroit en fin que ce lieu retient quelques choses de la guerre où il a pris son origine," La Croix, *Serrail,* fol. 322. Atâ says that the hall was deliberately left open on its three sides, Atâ, 1:60.

55 Saint-Blancard, p. 347.

56 See "Account of building expenses for the new council hall in the well-protected city of Edirne," *(Muḥāsebe-i icārāt-i binā'-i cedīd-i dīvānḫāne der mahrūsa-i Edirne),* BA, Ali Emiri 308. Another document of 935–36 (1527–29) mentions "building the royal council hall at the Edirne Palace," *(sāḫten-i dīvānḫāne-i ḫāṣṣa der sarāy-i Edirne),* BA, KK 7097, fol. 98. For the old audience hall in Edirne, see Osman, pp. 64–65.

57 Angiolello, *Inedito manoscritto,* p. 23. For the remaining parts of Mehmed II's tower, see T. Öz, "Topkapı Sarayı Müzesi Onarımları," p. 33; Ayverdi, *Fatih Devri Mimarisi,* p. 298; Goodwin, p. 135.

58 Gritti, "Relazione fatta in Pregadi," p. 463; Spandugino, *Petit Traicté,* pp. 65, 119–20.

59 TSA, D 9176.

60 For the treasures stored in each tower of Yedikule, see Hierosolimitano, *Vera relatione,* pp. 2–5.

61 For the tower treasury of the Belvedere Pavilion in Edirne, see Osman, p. 73; Eldem, Köşkler, 1:26, 34–35, 42.

62 Cafer Çelebi, pp. 72–73.

63 BA, MM 17884, fol. 69; KK 7097, fol. 99; Lokman, *Hünername,* 1:fol. 16v, 2:fol. 235v.

64 Lokman, *Hünername,* 1:fol. 14v; Hezarfen, *Telhis,* fol. 15v.

65 Lokman, *Hünername,* 2:fol. 7v.

66 BA, MM 1947, fols. 17, 26; MM 443, fol. 37.

67 BA, MM 443, fol. 37.

68 "Otāḳ-i pādişāhī sarāy-i ʿāmireye naẓīrdür ve ʿadl köşki vücūd-i pādişāhīye maḫṣūṣ dārü'l-ʿadl menzīlesidür ki sarāy-i ʿāmirede ḳafes-i hümāyūna naẓīrdür," Anonymous, *Risale,* fol. 39v.

69 BA, MM 17884, fol. 69; KK 7097, fol. 99.

70 For Melchior Lorichs panorama legends, see Oberhummer, tafel 4; for the signal, Selaniki (İpşirli, ed.), pp. 357, 368–69, 385–86.

71 Donato, 2:137. The "royal belvedere pavilion" is referred to as "cihānnümā-yi hümāyūn" in Ömer Efendi, fols. 2r, 7r, 17r, 18r.

72 Celalzade, *Tabakat,* fol. 173v. Dilger is wrong when he asserts that Süleyman I was the first sultan to institute the practice of listening to divan meetings from behind a window, Dilger, pp. 14–36, 48–49, 113–16. In 1556 the Venetian bailo Domenico Trevisano wrote that Süleyman's predecessors had used the window more often, "Solevano li passati imperatori, e questo ancora era solito, andare nelli giorni del divano ad una finestra [i.e., at the Old Council Hall], dalla quale udite e vedute tutte le cose che si facevano e dicevano nelli predetti divani, provvedevano poi sopra di quella al meglio che loro pareva. Ma questo Gran Signore, sono già alcuni anni, non volendo aver pensiero a simili affari, lasciando il carico del tutto al signor Rustan [i.e., Rüstem Pasha] suo genero e primo pascià, ha rimesso d'andarvi, e si riduce nelli prefati giorni in una camera nel suo serraglio [i.e., the Chamber of Petitions], aspettando che da esso pascià gli sia riferito il tutto, ovvero a bocca, ovvero in scrittura, il che loro chiamano in lingua turco fare *arz,*" Trevisano, p. 119.

73 Schepper, p. 169. Lokman refers to it as "gilded lattice" *(müşebbek-i zerrīn, müşebbek ḳafes),* Lokman, *Hünername,* 1:fol. 16v; Lokman, *Shāhnāma* (TSK, R 1537), fol. 10r; see also Hezarfen, *Telhis,* fol. 29r.

74 "Il gran Turcho mai non interviene à questa publica udienza: ma egli ha una finestra quadra coperta d'Ormisi nero, laquale risponde sopra il luogo dove sedono i Bassà dove puo senza esser da persona veduto andar per un certo corridoio coperto," Bassano, fol. 24v. See also Postel, pt. 1, p. 123, "Souvent le Prince est a escouter a une fenestre qui respond l'auditoire." For the black curtain, see Vigenère, p. 20; Courmenin, p. 136; Thévenot, p. 182.

75 Lubenau, 1:162.

76 The Koranic inscriptions above the window are described by Ohsson: "Elle est couronnée de versets du Cour'ann, en gros caractères qui recommandent les vertus nécessaires pour bien administrer; aux deux côtés est placé le chiffre en or du Sultan," Ohsson, 7:214. For the window, also see Donato, 1:13; Gudenus, p. 118.

77 For these inscriptions, see Şeref, pp. 352–54, 461–62.

78 BA, MM 17884, fol. 52, and see Appendix A.2.

79 Lokman, *Hünername,* 1:fols. 14v–15r.

80 Lokman, *Shāhnāma,* TSK, R 1537, fols. 10r–v. A repair document from 1682 shows that the gilded globe was attached on its exterior to a smaller ball, and also contained a small ball within. The document mentions "the renewed solid-gold plating of the large stone globe hanging from the dome's center" *(ḳubbe ortasında aṣılan kebīr seng ṭob cedīd ṣom altun işi),* "the vermilion paint of the small globe contained within it" *(mezbūruñ içinde olan ṣaġīr ṭobuñ zencefre boyası),* and "the gold plating of another small globe attached under the mentioned globe" *(mezbūruñ ṭobuñ altında ṣaġīr ṭobuñ ṣom altun işi),* BA, MM 1947, fol. 26. Apparently the gilded globe was carved in filigree openwork, in order to make visible the smaller,

red-colored ball contained within it, and to allow arrows to pass through it.

81 Nişancı, p. 249; Bostan, fol. 99v; Ohsson, 7:211–12.

82 "Ruino il casnà, ... fu visto portar fuora un gran numero di dinari," Minio, "Relazione [1527]," pp. 116–17.

83 BA, MM 17884, fols. 51, 69.

84 TSA, D 9823; Şeref, p. 355; T. Öz, *Guide to the Museum,* p. 86.

85 BA, MM 17884, fols. 51, 69; Âli, *Künh,* fols. 216v, 241r, 504v.

86 Hezarfen, *Telhis,* fol. 15v; Naili, fol. 50v.

87 Naili, fols. 62v, 50v; Orhonlu, p. 109, Hezarfen, *Telhis,* fol. 28r.

88 T. Öz, "Topkapı Sarayı Müzesi Onarımları," pp. 40–41.

89 Lokman, *Hünername,* 1:fol. 17r; Anonymous, "Administrative treatise," fol. 19r.

90 Tevki'i, pp. 499, 509–10.

91 Trevisano, pp. 120–21.

92 Navagero, pp. 94–95.

93 Badoaro, p. 357. See also Lubenau, 1:162; Hierosolimitano, *Vera relatione,* p. 31; Courmenin, p. 132; Garzoni, pp. 427–28; Thévenot, p. 182; Lokman, *Hünername,* 1:fol. 16v; Hezarfen, *Telhis,* fol. 29v; Naili, fol. 43v.

94 Chesneau, p. 42.

95 Naili, fol. 62v; Akif, fols. 43v–44v; TSA, E 12359, fol. 5v.

96 Mihailović, p. 157, calls this tent "segiwan" (i.e., *sayeban,* or *sayevan,* "awning").

97 Hezarfen, *Telhis,* fol. 30r–v; Safi, 1:fol. 136v; Üsküdari, 1:fol. 255v. For the extant sixteenth-century throne, see Atıl, *Age of Sultan Süleyman,* pp. 115–16.

98 Promontorio, pp. 37–39.

99 Spandugino, *Petit Traicté,* pp. 137–38.

100 Angiolello, *Inedito manoscritto,* p. 37.

101 Becagut, fol. 16v.

102 Gritti, "Relazione fatta in Pregadi," p. 457.

103 Lokman, *Hünername,* 1:fol. 17v; Anonymous, "Administrative treatise," fol. 19r–v; Donato, 2:87. For the guesthouse *(chambre d'hoste),* see La Croix, *Memoires,* pp. 135–36; and Hezarfen, *Telhis,* fol. 15v, where it is mentioned as *misāfirḫāne.*

104 Hezarfen, *Telhis,* fols. 30r–v; Safi, 1:fols. 135v–36r; Üsküdari, 1:fols. 255v–56r.

105 Bobovi, *Mémoires,* fols. 125–27; 370–80.

106 Cited in Miller, *Beyond the Sublime Porte,* p. 158.

107 Lokman, *Hünername,* 1:fols. 16r–18r, 230r.

108 Üsküdari, 1:fols. 251r, 253v–54r, 258v.

109 Hezarfen, *Telhis,* fol. 15r.

110 Hezarfen, *Telhis,* fol. 15r; Üsküdari, 2:fol. 316v; Âli, *Künh,* fol. 91r; Selaniki, *Tarih,* p. 136; Anonymous, "Administrative treatise," fol. 19r; Evliya, 1:116; BA, MM 17884, fol. 53.

111 For the broad implications of the concept of felicity *(saʿāde),* which also entailed the notion of the heavenly charisma of royal fortune, see Bombaci, "Qutlug Bolzun! Pt. One," pp. 284–91; Bombaci, "Qutlug Bolzun! Pt. Two," pp. 13–43.

112 The precious carpets and textile hangings of the vestibule are described in Wratislaw, p. 61; Herberstein, p. 126. According to Flachat, the royal colonnade had a gilded dome with floral paintings and its walls were pierced with windows through which the white eunuchs could watch the second court from their two dormitories flanking the gate's vestibule, Flachat, 174–75.

Chapter 5

1 Angiolello, *Inedito manoscritto,* pp. 23–24.

2 Kıvami, pp. 70–71.

3 For the theory that no harem existed in Mehmed II's New Palace, since it was built as an administrative center, see Atasoy, "Matrakçı's Representation," pp. 93–101; Miller, *Beyond the Sublime Porte,* p. 25; Goodwin, p. 132; Akdağ, p. 23; Davis, p. 7; Anhegger-Eyüboğlu, "Fatih Devrinde," pp. 26–27; Tansuğ, p. 149; Durukan, p. 7. Some have argued that Mehmed II built the New Palace as a summer residence, leaving most of his court at the Old Palace: Evliya, 1:116; Atâ, 1:56–57; Ohsson, 7:3; Baykal, p. 45; Babinger, *Mehmed,* p. 245. Some architectural historians, however, attribute the construction of the harem to Mehmed II: Ayverdi, *Osmanlı Mimarisinde Fatih Devri,* p. 683; Eldem and Akozan, pp. 81–82.

4 Kritovoulos, pp. 207–8.

5 For the degeneration of pages, see Âli, *Mevaid,* pp. 25–26.

6 For the Edirne Palace, see Osman; Eldem, *Köşkler,* 1:21–57; Kreiser, *Zwei unbekannte Beschreibungen,* pp. 119–42.

7 Kritovoulos, p. 207.

8 Bidlisi, *Tercüme-i Heşt Bihişt,* fol. 53r; Cafer Çelebi, p. 72.

9 Lokman, *Hünername,* 1:231r.

10 Morosini, pp. 281–82.

11 Hierosolimitano, *Vera relatione,* pp. 55–59.

12 "Dall'altra parte di questo secondo cortivo si trova un'altra porta doppia, et entrati entro di quella vi è una Loggia coperta di piombo, et qui senta il Gran Turco quando il dà udienza; poi si trova il terzo Cortivo, il quale è lungo et largo, come li altri doi," Angiolello, *Inedito manoscritto,* p. 23.

13 "Entrai per uno andito, dove a mezo a man dextra era una camarella in volta tutta bianca, et senza ornamento alcuno, salvo che gli era uno quadro, dove sedeva la Mta del Gran Sr. molto ben apparato de tapeti, et brocati a la loro guisa," Becagut, fol. 17r. For Becagut's several missions at the Ottoman court, see Kissling, pp. 8–36.

14 "Li doni che sono fatti alla Mta del Gran Sr sono portati per alcuni deputati alla Porta per uno certo Andito di fore de la Camera dove la Mta del Gran Sr sede, quando da audientia, et sua Mta gli vede per una fenestra passar per il detto Andito," Becagut, fol. 16v.

15 "Messo l'hordine per el Signor si aviono li bassa verso dove era il Signor, qual visto venir esso orator per il bal-

con si levo in piedi e intrando dentro, l'orator li tocho la man," Zancani, pp. 599–600.

16 "Taking off their caftans, two executioners and some gatekeepers came inside. As the seated sultan was watching from the iron-latticed window of the small chamber of petitions *[maḥall-i ʿarż olan hücrenüñ demür ḳafesine ḳarşu ki hüdāvendigār oturduġı yirden temāşā idermiş]* they first executed İskender Pasha, then Tacizade Cafer Çelebi, the Kazasker of Anatolia, and Balyemez Sekbanbaşı," Haydar Çelebi, fol. 124r. Mehmed Refik had noted this incident in his article on the Chamber of Petitions but, Dilger, unable to find its source, dismisses it as a fable and argues that the Chamber of Petitions was not built until the time of Süleyman I; see M. Refik, "Enderun," pp. 115–16; Dilger, p. 89. Dilger (pp. 88–89) interprets a letter of March 1525 that refers to "una bellissima caza" prepared by Süleyman I as evidence for the construction of the Chamber of Petitions, but clearly *caza* here refers to a hunting party (i.e., *caccia*) and not to a *casa*. For another hunting party *(caza bellissima)*, which Selim I organized in Edirne in 1519, see Sanuto, 28:106.

17 Gritti, "Relazione fatta in Pregadi," p. 458: "Sopra un mastabe coperto de veludo negro, *cum* oro, *cum* algune pelle de liompardo integre nel mezo et altri lavori de cuorame, sentava el prefato excellentissimo signor a la *turchesca*, chavendo driedo le spale due cussini d'oro soprarizo."

18 An eighteenth-century inventory of the furnishings of the Chamber of Petitions lists "two leopard-skin spreads" *(ḳaplan postlu iki maḳʿad)*, TSA, D 7851. For the audience hall at the Byzantine palace, see Clavijo, p. 61; and Tafur, p. 117.

19 BA, MM 17884, fols. 69, 53; KK 7097, fol. 58; MM 422, fol. 176; MM 7668, fols. 21, 23, 24; MM 5530, fol. 82; MM 1947, fol. 15; TKS, D 7851 nos. 1, 2, D 4462, fol. 1v; Leysizade, p. 42; Selaniki, *Tarih*, p. 134; Anonymous, *Müstetab*, p. 6, fol. 11; Üsküdari, 1:fol. 254r; Evliya, 1:116; Atâ, 1:312.

20 The three entries read: "Casting the windows [i.e., lattices] of the private royal portico" *(rīḫten-i pencerehā-yi eyvān kim hümāyūn-i ḫaṣṣa)*; "curtains of the council hall at the private imperial palace" *(perdehā-yi dīvānḫāne-i sarāy-i ʿamire-i ḫaṣṣa)*; "metal rings for the exalted council hall at the imperial palace" *(perāzvānehā-yi dīvān-i ʿālī der sarāy-i ʿāmire, 44 ḳıṭʿa)*, BA, MM 7668, fols. 4, 21.

21 BA, MM 17884, fols. 53, 69.

22 BA, KK 7097, fol. 58.

23 Evliya, 1:116.

24 Ayverdi, *Fatih Devri Mimarisi*, pp. 298; Ayverdi, *Osmanlı Mimarisinde Fatih Devri*, p. 715; Eldem, *Köşkler*, 1:81–86. For other attributions of the Chamber of Petitions to Mehmed II, see Miller, *Beyond the Sublime Porte*, pp. 210–11; M. Refik, "Enderun," pp. 115–16; İnalcık, "Rise of the Ottoman Empire," p. 46; Uzunçarşılı, *Merkez ve Bahriye Teşkilatı*, p. 30.

25 Schepper, pp. 172–73. A small fountain still exists inside the hall, on the north wall, next to the throne; it is referred to as "la fontaine de cristal" in Fresne-Canaye, p. 69.

26 Saint-Blancard, pp. 378–79. See also Bassano, fol. 17r: "Vi sono piu sale, & tra l'altre una molto bella, con lavori d'oro, e musaichi ricchissimi, con una sedia regale dove il gran turcho siede nel dare udienza àgli Oratori della Città, o Provincie."

27 Giovio, p. 345. The 1538 version of Spandugino's text similarly reads, "Lo imperatore Suleiman ha fatto una camera precioso soffitata d'oro et pietra pretiose," Spandugino, "De la Origine," p. 223.

28 Gyllius, p. 39.

29 Badoaro, p. 358: "Un focone alla nostra usanza, tutto tirato d'oro massiccio a similitudine di mosaico, con bellissimi lavori d'intaglio, e con preziose gioje di rubini, diamanti, smeraldi, e perle, che in verità per comune opinione ascende alla valuta di un milione d'oro"; Fresne-Canaye, p. 69: "La cheminée est en argent doré"; Bon, p. 60: "Una caminiera apparente tutta coperta di lastre di argento perfilate d'oro." It is referred to as an "enameled and latticed silver fireplace" *(mīnā-kārī müşebbek gümiş ocāḳ)* in an eighteenth-century inventory, which lists its removable furnishing as "One fireplace curtain *[ocāḳ yaşmaġı]* of pearled gold brocade embroidered at one place with five big and three medium, and at another place with 106 small gold plates *[altun pafta]* inset with 1,107 emeralds and 1,108 rubies," TSA, D 7851, pts. 1, 2.

30 For the eighteenth-century furnishings, see TSA, D 7851, pts. 1, 2. Tavernier writes that eight different throne covers were kept at the Inner Treasury. The richest was of black velvet embroidered with pearls, the second was of white velvet embroidered with rubies and emeralds, and the third of violet velvet adorned with turquoises and pearls, while the other three were of different colored velvets with embroideries of gold thread, the last two being of gold brocade, Tavernier, pp. 108–10.

31 Saint-Blancard, pp. 349.

32 For these tent audiences and the Venetian helmet, see Necipoğlu-Kafadar, "Süleyman the Magnificent," pp. 401–27.

33 The wooden dome of the hall is described as "il cielo in volto d'azzuro oltra marino finissimo con le stelle d'oro, cosi come qui le se fanno di legno"; the ceiling of the marble-paved small forecourt between the Gate of Felicity and the Chamber of Petitions is referred to as "soffitada in volto d'azzuro oltra marino, pieno di stelette d'oro schieto," C. Zeno, p. 26. For the ceilings of the second court, which were painted with "guldene Sternen," see Lubenau, 2:10. For the blue-and-gold color scheme at the Chamber of Petitions, see Schepper, p. 172; Saint-Blancard, pp. 378–79; Omichius, p. 19r. The gilt decorations are likened to the manner of Perugino in a *relazione* of 1573: "Il detto luoco è tutto lavorato d'oro alla Perugino, et nelli muri adornato di Maiolichi bellissimi alla loro usanza," Barbaro and Tiepolo, fol. 34. Referring to the gilt ceiling, Courmenin writes (p. 139), "le plancher en est

tellement doré, que l'on croit qu'il soit d'or massif."

34 Matteo Venier wrote, in 1582, "Il muro intorno era di quelle maioliche loro dorate," Venier, Sala Monico Cod. 34, fol. 52v; and "Le mura della camera, incrostate di quelle loro Maioliche indorate," Venier, Marciana Cod. 8505, fol. 42v. Schepper refers to the blue-gold tiles as "d'ouvraiges mosaicques semés d'azur et d'or," Schepper, p. 172. Pietro della Valle writes (1:112), "Les ornemens des murs tout autour sont diverses pièces de fayance fine, ou de porcelaine, qui sont fortement enchassées dedans avec des Arabesques d'or & de très-belles couleurs, le tout d'un ouvrage exquis." The white-ground tiles are described as "pietre bianchi cotte con colori diversi a fogliami, e molto ben composte insieme, delle quali essendo tutta incrostata la muraglia, si fa bellissima vista," by Bon, p. 60. In 1572 Omichius referred to the walls as "die Wandt mit Lazur und Golde köstlich gezieret," fol. 19r. Süleyman's account books of 1527–28 show that the tiles were made by an "atelier of royal ceramicists" *(kāşīḫāne-i ḫāṣṣa)* in Istanbul under the direction of Usta Ali. The list of materials they used included "gold leaf" *(varaḳ-i zer)*, "white lead" *(isfidāc)*, and cobalt blue *(lāciverd)*, suggesting that the assorted tiles made for the palace included underglaze-painted blue-white-turquoise ones, BA, KK 7097, fols. 22, 33; MM 17884, fol. 50. For the tiles produced in this atelier before İznik became the preferred center for tile production, see Necipoğlu-Kafadar, "From International Timurid to Ottoman."

35 For these tiles, see Lane, pp. 265–66; Denny, "Ceramics of the Mosque of Rüstem Pasha," pp. 112–23; Erdmann, pp. 144–53. For the hypothesis that some of the underglaze-painted blue-white-turquoise tiles on the Sünnet Odası may originally have come from the Chamber of Petitions, see Necipoğlu-Kafadar, "From International Timurid to Ottoman," and chapter 9.

36 For these *cuerda seca* tiles, see Necipoğlu-Kafadar, ibid.

37 Gerlach, p. 129, "ein schöner Palast von Marmelstein"; Omichius, p. 19r "einen mit Marmorstein gepflasterten Sahl"; Barton, p. 13.

38 An account book from 1601–2 mentions "repairing the marble wall of the Chamber of Petitions," *(meremmet-kerden-i dīvār-i ruḫām-i oda-i ʿarż)*, BA, MM 5530, fol. 82. For the marbles with gilt inscriptions, see P. della Valle, 1:112. For inscriptions that record later repairs, see Şeref, pp. 396–98.

39 Flachat, p. 175.

40 For the inscription, see Şeref, p. 398; M. Refik, "Enderun," p. 113; Eldem, *Köşkler*, 1:81–82.

41 Herberstein, p. 127.

42 Wratislaw, p. 61. Precious carpets and textile hangings are also mentioned in Herberstein, p. 126.

43 Pigafetta, pp. 139–40.

44 C. Zeno, p. 26.

45 Fresne-Canaye, pp. 67–68.

46 Osman, p. 68.

47 Garzoni, pp. 379, 396. For the window also see Badoaro, pp. 357–58; Omichius, p. 19r; Barbaro and Tiepolo, fol. 34.

48 Anonymous, *Müstetab*, p. 6, fol. 11; Âli, *Mevaid*, pp. 25–26. Âli complains that in his time the boys are no longer selected with care.

49 For transformations in ceremonial that were already foreshadowed at the end of Selim I's reign, see Dilger, pp. 55–59, 70–74, 75–77, 81–84, 96–104.

50 Minio, "Relazione [1521]," p. 22.

51 P. Zeno, "Itinerario," pp. 114, 117; Ramberti, pp. 306–7; Minio, "Relazione [1527]," p. 176; "Et hanno posto questo ordine, che niun orator parli, ne il Signor li rispondi, ma *solum* li basi la man."

52 In 1523 the sultan was still sitting on a cushioned sofa in the manner of his ancestors, P. Zeno, "Itinerario," pp. 114, 117; in 1530 he was sitting on a throne, see Pietro Zeno's letter of 1530 in Sanuto 53:445; Minio, "Relazione [1527]," p. 176.

53 "Quivi tratanto non si sentiva suono di cosa veruna, ma d'ogn'intorno vi si scorgeva una veneranda taciturnità, come è più, se qualche luogo santissimo di Gierusalem si fosse andato a visitare ... A questa modo dunque più a simiglianza d'esser condotti da i birri in prigione, che alla presenza di un tanto signore ad uno ad uno fummo appresentati dinanzi a quello ... stando lui nel resto immobile et con gravità et superbia grandissima senza punto guardarci," Pigafetta, pp. 140–41. In 1567 Marino Cavalli said that Selim II's grandeur consisted in not talking and in staying motionless with an extremely affected gravity, Cavalli, pp. 8–9.

54 Schweigger, pp. 55, 57.

55 Lubenau 2:11–12.

56 Courmenin, p. 139.

57 Wratislaw, pp. 61–62.

58 Fresne-Canaye, pp. 69–70.

59 For the inscriptions, see M. Refik, "Enderun," pp. 111–12; Akdağ, p. 181. For the dragon combatting a phoenix, see Çığ, "Decoration on the Ceiling," pp. 57–60.

60 TSA, D 34, fol. 232v.

61 Ohsson, 7:221.

62 For the vizier's bench, see Schepper, p. 176: "Et apres les salutations faictes au grand Empereur et aux Bassas, lesquels icy avoient tousiours estez debout, mais à nostre départ commençoyent de s'asseoir sur ung banc à l'opposite d'icelluy Empereur, nous nous sommes retirez." Moro writes (pp. 330–31), "Vicino a detta finestra v'è una banchetta posata al muro, sopra la quale siedono poi li bassà quando vanno a lui per rendergli conto delli negozi pubblici." For the fixed order in which dignitaries presented petitions to the sultan, see Leysizade, pp. 33–34, 42; Lokman, *Hünername*, 1:fol. 17v; Tevki'i, pp. 510–17.

63 The velvet-covered bench is referred to as "the bench covered with a velvet cushion opposite the sultan," *(müvācehe-i pādişāhīde vāḳīʿ ḳadīfe maḳʿadla puşīde ṣoffa)*,

Abdi Pasha, fol. 68r; Silahdar, 1:257; Uzunçarşılı, *Merkez ve Bahriye Teşkilatı*, p. 35.

64 For executions in the sixteenth century in front of the Chamber of Petitions, see Lokman, *Hünername*, 2:fol. 177r; Peçevi, 1:334; Hasanbeyzade, p. 256; Uzunçarşılı, *Merkez ve Bahriye Teşkilatı*, p. 35.

65 Courmenin, pp. 139–40.

66 Fresne-Canaye, p. 70. See also Ralamb, p. 684.

67 Cited in Osman, pp. 67–68, 147. For the layout of the Chamber of Petitions in Edirne, see Eldem, *Köşkler*, 1:1–19.

68 Kreiser, *Zwei unbekannte Beschreibungen*, p. 138.

69 Ohsson states that behind the gate was an ablution fountain and oratory, Ohsson, 7:221; cited in Uzunçarşılı, *Merkez ve Bahriye Teşkilatı*, p. 30.

70 Ohsson, 7:221. For the gates, see also Uzunçarşılı, *Merkez ve Bahriye Teşkilatı*, p. 30.

71 "Meremmet-i döşeme-i yonma ‹an pīş-i oda-i ḥażret-i ḫullide mülkuhu ilā dīvānḫāne-i enderūnī," BA, KK 7097, fol. 24.

72 Beauvau, pp. 33–34; Courmenin, pp. 139–40.

73 Beauvau, p. 66: "C'est encor leur charge de laver avec des esponges d'eau rose, de vinaigre, & du jus de lymon, un chemin pavé de marbre blanc qui va depuis la chambre Favorite iusques au Tribunal où il donne audience aux Visiers." The marble path is mentioned as "the marbles paving the path of His Majesty from the Privy Chamber to the Chamber of Petitions," (*ḫāṣṣ odadan ‹arż odasına gelince rāh-i ‹ālempenāhda mefrūş olan mermerler*), and the term *pars* is provided in Üsküdari, 1:fol. 257v.

74 For the custom of cleaning columns with lemon juice, see Bobovi, *Mémoires*, fol. 275. For "pecking," see TSA, D 9916, no. 11, fol. 2v; D 9916, no. 58, fol. 6r.

75 For this ceremony, see Atâ, 1:221–22; TSA, E 12358, fol. 5v; D 10749, fol. 5v. For the throne, see Atıl, *Age of Sultan Süleyman*, p. 116.

76 For the departure ceremony of promoted pages, see Bobovi, *Mémoires*, fols. 233–35; Hezarfen, *Telhis*, fol. 18r; La Croix, *Serrail*, fol. 161.

77 Inscriptions record repairs by Ahmed III (1722) and Mustafa IV (1807), and the *tuğras* of Abdülmecid commemorate repairs after a fire in 1856 that seriously damaged the building, see Şeref, pp. 396–98; Gurlitt, *Baukunst*, 1:46; Akdağ, pp. 178, 183.

Chapter 6

1 Atâ, 1:67.

2 Lybyer, 1913, p. 71; Miller, *Beyond the Sublime Porte*, pp. 65–66.

3 Taşköprizade, 1:35–36; Doukas, pp. 87, 146.

4 Kritovoulos, pp. 85–86.

5 For the quote from Menavino and the educational system of the palace, see İnalcık, *Ottoman Empire*, pp. 79–80, 85–87.

6 Bobovi, *Mémoires*, fols. 283–92, 301–2.

7 Courmenin, p. 155.

8 For the symbolism of tresses, see Bobovi, *Mémoires*, fols. 34–35; La Croix, *Serrail*, fols. 87–88.

9 Bon, p. 83.

10 Courmenin, p. 176.

11 Üsküdari, 1:fols. 257v–58r.

12 Angiolello, *Inedito manoscritto*, p. 30; Angiolello, *Historia Turchesca*, p. 125; Menavino, p. 104; Âli, *Künh*, fol. 94r; Beauvau, p. 56.

13 Âli, *Mevaid*, pp. 25–26.

14 Promontorio, p. 41; La Croix, *Serrail*, fols. 89–94; Courmenin, p. 148.

15 Promontorio, p. 39; Angiolello, *Historia Turchesca*, p. 125; Angiolello, *Inedito manoscritto*, p. 31; Spandugino, *Petit Traicté*, p. 59. Geuffroy (1540s) and Ramberti (ca. 1534) mention about 500 pages, Geuffroy, p. 230; Ramberti, p. 266. Ayn-i Ali Efendi's *Ḳavānīn* of 1609 cites about 700, see Ayn-i, p. 97.

16 BA, KK 7154. A section of this document has been published in Refik, "Fatih Devrine Aid Vesikalar," pp. 5–6.

17 Promontorio, pp. 41–43.

18 Âli, *Künh*, fols. 93r–94r. In his 1553 *relazione* Navagero mentions the Privy Chamber *(cassodà)*, the Treasury Chamber *(caznà)*, the commissary *(chiler)*, the Large Chamber *(casa grande)*, and the Small Chamber *(casa piccola)*, Navagero, p. 44. Sixteenth-century sources identify the palace's chief eunuchs as: the palace steward *(ağa-yi sarāy* or *sarāy ağası)*, who was in charge of the Small and Large chambers, and the maintenance and repairs of the palace; the head of the commissary *(ser kilārī* or *kilārcı başı)*, who was the master of the inner commissary, charged with setting the sultan's table and preparing delicacies; the head treasurer *(ser ḫāzin* or *ḫazīnedār başı)*, who was the master of the Inner Treasury, charged with commissioning court artisans to produce objects for use in the palace; the head gatekeeper *(ağa-yi der* or *ḳapu ağası)*, who was the master of the palace school, charged with guarding the third gate and the whole inner palace; BA, MM 903, fol. 5; Âli, *Künh*, fol. 93r; Navagero, p. 44; Ramberti, pp. 265–66.

19 BA, KK 1863, fols. 14, 23; KK 1765, fols. 2v; AE 250, fol. 3v.

20 Âli, *Künh*, fol. 93r.

21 *(Oda-i ağa-yi der der oda-i küçük)*, BA, KK 7097, fol. 58. See also Hezarfen, *Telhis*, fol. 20r; Tavernier, p. 107.

22 Promontorio, p. 41.

23 TSA, D 34 fol. 56r; Hezarfen, *Telhis*, fol. 18v. The chamberless pages are mentioned in La Croix, *Serrail*, fols. 85–86.

24 Anonymous, "Administrative treatise," fols. 20r–21v.

25 Beauvau, p. 57.

26 Ibid., pp. 64–65, 71.

27 For Ahmed I's foundation of this dormitory, see Baykal, p. 26; Atâ, 1:153; Miller, *Beyond the Sublime Porte*, p. 56; T. Öz, *Guide to the Museum*, p. 68. Murad IV's restoration

is mentioned in Hezarfen, *Telhis,* fol. 19v, La Croix, *Serrail,* fols. 85–86; La Croix, *Mémoires,* p. 142. Expenses of Ahmed III's new dormitory are recorded in an account book, TKS, D 2001.

28 Üsküdari, 1:fols. 254r, 258r; Tavernier, pp. 197–201; Evliya, 1:116.

29 For their location, see Bobovi, *Mémoires,* fols. 34–37; Üsküdari, 1:fols. 254r, 258v; Evliya, 1:116; Hezarfen, *Telhis,* fol. 20r. The dormitory of newly recruited pages is referred to as the *saraglio da piccioli* in Angiolello, *Inedito manoscritto,* p. 31; Angiolello, *Historia Turchesca,* p. 126. It is called the school *(schola)* known as *Lengioda* (i.e., *yenioda,* or novice's chamber) in Menavino, pp. 96–97.

30 The two preparatory schools were called *dolama altı* because their pages wore simple wool *(çuḳa)* clothing. Pages of the higher chambers, called *ḳaftan altı,* wore clothes of atlas *(aṭlās)* and silk *(sereng).* Pages of the Privy Chamber were distinguished by more valuable caftans of atlas, brocade *(dībā),* and gold brocade *(serāser),* Üsküdari, 1:fols. 253r–v; 256v–57r. Bobovi states that pages were divided into two classes on the basis of clothing; that is, novices in wool cloth *(tschoukahlu),* and pages of higher chambers, in silk or brocade caftans *(kaftanlu,* or *kaftan altında),* Bobovi, *Mémoires,* fols. 21–23.

31 Promontorio, p. 43.

32 Angiolello, *Inedito manoscritto,* p. 31; Angiolello, *Historia Turchesca,* p. 126.

33 Menavino, pp. 96–97.

34 See Fisher, pp. 77–79, for the English translation.

35 Ibid., p. 79.

36 Bölük-i ġılmān-i çelebiyān, ġılmān-i şehzādegān, şehzāde oğlanları, BA, KK 7154, fols. 2, 18, 38, 54, 70.

37 "Schirvan: Est un lieu élevé, où on avoit anciennement coustume de placer les enfans des grands seigneurs dans le temps qu'ils estoient admis dans les gouvernemens, et qu'on leur donnoit des apanages et des principautez. On les mettoit là, pour les instruire et les faire passer par les mesmes degrez que tous les autres qui sont elevez dans le Serail: mais quelques uns de ces princes aiyans causé plusieurs fois du trouble dans l'Empére, et excité des revoltes contre leurs peres ou parens qui regnoient, on jugea à propos, et on decerna mesme un decret pour les éloigner de toutes les charges, et les exclure de l'administration de l'Estat," Bobovi, *Mémoires,* fol. 104.

38 Leysizade, pp. 34, 43.

39 For the location of this dormitory, see Üsküdari, 1:fols. 254r, 258r; Evliya, 1:116; Tavernier, pp. 186–96. Bobovi's plan shows the commissary and Treasury dormitories in reversed order, but another version of it, published by Ralamb, indicates the correct order, figs. 8A, B, nos. 25, 27, 29; fig. 9, nos. 13, 14.

40 "Lo terzo monocho si chiama chilerihibasi, id est dispensiero. Tiene tutta la necessaria argenteria del Signore, cioè lo predicto bacile d'oro, con altri infiniti bacili d'oro et argento, coppe d'oro cum balasci dentro per bevere, barchette d'oro cum balasci di gran valuta etiam per bevere, taze d'oro et argento infinite, stagnare grandissime mediocre et parve d'oro et d'ariento con altre cope, saline et candelabri d'oro et d'ariento sine fine, et così diverse pretiose cose, simile munitione di cose comestive confectione etc.; infine ha cura d'ogni cosa pertinente a la mensa et credenza del Signore," Promontorio, p. 42.

41 Menavino, p. 95.

42 *Iç kilār, kilār-i ḫāṣṣa-i enderūn, kilār-i enderūnī, kilār-i ḫāṣṣa,* TSA, D 1085; Anonymous, "Administrative treatise," fol. 20r; Evliya, 1:116; Hezarfen, *Telhis,* fol. 19v; BA, KK 7097, fol. 24; MM 17884, fols. 51, 53.

43 TSA, D 1085.

44 For these officers, see Atâ, 1:166–67, 174–75, 193–94; Üsküdari, 1:fol. 253r; Hezarfen, *Telhis,* fol. 19v; Bobovi, *Mémoires,* fols. 215–16; Uzunçarşılı, *Osmanlı Devletinin Saray Teşkilatı,* pp. 313–15.

45 Badoaro, p. 360.

46 Atâ, 1:174.

47 BA, MM 17884, fol. 51.

48 TSA, D 34, fol. 186r; D 10749, fol. 17r.

49 Bobovi, *Mémoires,* fol. 237; Flachat, pp. 188–89; Atâ, 1:183; Uzuncarşılı, *Osmanlı Devletinin Saray Teşkilatı,* p. 315.

50 Tavernier, pp. 186–88.

51 Âli, *Künh,* fol. 93r.

52 Leysizade, pp. 34, 43. For the location of this dormitory, see note 39.

53 Angiolello, *Inedito manoscritto,* p. 30; Angiolello, *Historia Turchesca,* p. 124; Menavino, pp. 94–95.

54 Bobovi, *Mémoires,* fols. 201–14; La Croix, *Serrail,* fol. 126.

55 For these officers, see Atâ, 1:165–67; Uzunçarşılı, *Osmanlı Devletinin Saray Teşkilatı,* pp. 315–22; Tavernier, pp. 138–39; Üsküdari, 1:fol. 253r.

56 Bon, p. 82.

57 Menavino, pp. 93–94. For the four favorite pages, see Menavino, pp. 92–93; Spandugino, *Petit Traicté,* pp. 60–62. Mehmed II's *kanunname* identifies them as: the swordbearer *(silahdar),* who carried the sultan's sword; the stirrup holder *(rikabdar),* who held the royal stirrup while the sultan was mounting for outings; the coat carrier *(çuhadar),* who carried the sultan's raincoat; and the page of the turban *(dülbend oğlanı),* in charge of carrying the sultan's turban, Leysizade, pp. 42–43. Also see Âli, *Künh,* fol. 93v.

58 Promontorio, pp. 40–41.

59 Leysizade, pp. 42–43. According to Âli, the head of the chamber *(odabaşı),* charged with dressing the sultan, was sometimes chosen from among the eunuchs, but more often from among the pages, Âli, *Künh,* fol. 93v.

60 Menavino, pp. 104–5. Before departing, the pages had to kiss the hand of the sultan, who was enthroned majestically "inanzi la porta della sua stanza, sopra una piazzetta ov'è un grandissimo e richissimo tappetto di seta e d'oro, posto a sedere sopra un seggio alla turchesca, con gran

maestà," Navagero, pp. 46–47. By the end of the sixteenth century the sultans no longer personally delivered the parting speech, which was read out from a decree at each dormitory. A decree in the sultan's handwriting of 1009 (1600–1601) advises the pages to remain obedient in their new posts, warning them otherwise to beware damnation in the other world, Orhonlu, pp. 9–10.

61 Bobovi, *Mémoires,* fols. 233–35; Hezarfen, *Telhis,* fol. 18r; La Croix, *Serrail,* fol. 161.

62 Bobovi, *Mémoires,* fols. 233–35.

63 Atâ, 1:288. For the sign language, see chapter 1.

64 Translation from Fisher, pp. 79–80.

65 This plan is published in Brenner's German translation of Bobovi's text (p. 42); it is missing from the incomplete Italian and French manuscripts. It is reproduced in Eldem and Akozan, pl. 64; and Miller, *Palace School,* p. 56. The higher dormitories were not as closely guarded by eunuchs, but their architectural layout approximated that of the Large Chamber, Bobovi, *Mémoires,* fol. 107.

66 Âli, *Künh,* fols. 93r–v. For the division of novices into companies of ten, see Junis, p. 263; Ramberti, p. 266; Geuffroy, pp. 229–30.

67 Miller, *Beyond the Sublime Porte,* p. 55. Angiolello describes the Janissaries in Istanbul as: "... dieci milia persone, le quali stantiano in questo cortivo, cioè undeci per casa, un caporale et dieci compagni," Angiolello, *Inedito manoscritto,* p. 27.

68 Translation from Fisher, pp. 80–81.

69 Üsküdari, 1:fols. 258r–v.

70 Ibid., fols. 258r–68v.

71 Pigafetta, p. 177.

72 Üsküdari, 1:fol. 258r.

73 It is described thus: "Devant l'appartement du *Kilar* on voit une galerie carrelée de marbre blanc & noir, & soustenue de huit belles colonnes de marbre blanc, & elle vient aboutir à un petit cartier qui est la demeure du grand Echanson ... Le *Kilargibachi* a en garde toute la vaissele d'or & d'argent, les bassins, les aiguieres, les coupes, les soûcoupes & les chandeliers, la plus grande partie de cette vaiselle est garnie de diamans, de rubis & d'emeraudes, & d'autres pierres de prix," Tavernier, pp. 187–92.

74 Flachat, pp. 186–92. Eldem claims that these dormitories had wooden pillars prior to the eighteenth century, Eldem and Akozan, pp. 66, 74.

75 For a large-scale repair of the third court in 1712, see TSA, D 4462. For the mid-nineteenth-century demolition of most of the dormitories by Dayezade Mehmed, see Atâ, 1:313; Şeref, p. 403. The new dormitories, carrying inscriptions of Abdülmecid, were built after a fire in 1856–57, and subsequently remodeled by the museum.

76 Tavernier, pp. 191–94. Another seventeenth-century author describes the higher-ranking dormitories as follows: "Chaque ordre des Itch-oglans [i.e., *içoğlan,* boys of the interior] a son appartement separé, composé de plusieurs chambres, longues et larges qui aboutissent en croisée, et forment au milieu, une espece de salle quarrée, où est l'estrade du Gouverneur et d'où il peut decouvrir ce qui se passe par tout. Il y a deux Gardiens à chaque extremité, il regne autour de ces chambres a chaque estrade, sofa elevée de terre d'un pied, fermée d'une balustrade et ornée du tapis de pied, les Itch-oglans y habitent jour et nuit, et n'occupent pas plus de place qu'il en faut pour un petit lit et deux cassettes; leurs lits sont composés de deux grosses couvertures et d'un coussin, l'une sert dessous en guise de matelas, et l'autre desus pour couvrir; ils couchent deux à deux et se tournent le dos, ne leur estant pas permis de se retourner. Ils ont chacun leurs cassettes au prés d'eux pour serrer leurs livres, leurs ecritoires et d'autres bagatelles; leurs grosses hardes et leurs petits Tresors sont dans d'autres coffres marqués de leurs noms, posés sur des galleries qui regnent en haut come en bas; l'on allume dans chaque chambre de gros flambeaux de cire qui brulent toute la nuit, les Eunuques de garde veillent tour à tour." The same author adds that at the end of each dormitory were marble ablution fountains: "des fontaines qui sont à l'éxtremité des chambres avec plusieurs robinets et des bassins de marbre," La Croix, *Serrail,* fols. 89–90.

77 The estrades are referred to as *sedir* or *kerevet,* the wooden galleries as *şirvan,* the windowed surveying station as *cāmekān,* and the fountained court as *çeşme ḥavlısı* in Atâ, 1:140, 145–47, 158–59, 166. The upper galleries for storing chests were occupied by deaf and dumb pages, according to Üsküdari, 2:fol. 316v. During the nineteenth century these galleries were reserved for privileged pages, Atâ, 1:147, 158–59. Ohsson mentions in each dormitory a windowed compartment for leading personages; "une pièce vitrée au fond de chaque salle sert de logement à l'un des premiers officiers ..." Ohsson, 7:49.

78 "Yaldızlı oymalı ġāyet müzeyyen," Atâ, 1:313.

79 Ohsson, (7:49) says that the dormitories were beautifully decorated, since the sultans visited them occasionally. For Bayezid II's visits, see İnalcık, *Ottoman Empire,* p. 79; for those of Süleyman I, see Postel, pt. 3, pp. 10–11.

80 These occasions are mentioned as "being ornamented" *(donanma)* or "to beautify" *(şenlik),* TSA, D 34, fols. 60r, 111r, 114r, 186r.

81 For this small mosque, known today as Ağalar Camisi, see Kuran, *Mosque in Early Ottoman Architecture,* pp. 185–88; Ayverdi, *Osmanlı Mimarisinde Fatih Devri,* p. 106; T. Öz, *İstanbul Camileri,* 1:19. For the annexed rooms, which existed at least as early as the seventeenth century, see Üsküdari, 1:fol. 254v; Tavernier, pp. 207–9. Although Kuran has argued, on the basis of a late inscription, that the annex functioning today as a reading room was added in the eighteenth century, it must have belonged to the original building, as Ayverdi has pointed out.

82 Menavino, pp. 106–7. The same information is provided in Schweigger, p. 154; Courmenin, p. 154.

83 Spandugino, *Petit Traicté,* p. 72. The imam of Ahmed I refers to this mosque as the "noble masjid of the vast

inner court," *(mescīd-i şerīf-i ḥarem-i vasīʿ),* Safi, fols. 15v–16r, 21r. In 1581 the Small Chamber pages, who were attached to the service of the mosque, were rewarded by the sultan for decorating it with roses, TSA, D 34, fol. 186r.

84 Bobovi, *Mémoires,* fols. 36–37, 273; also see Üsküdari, 1:fol. 254v. Tavernier also mentions the little room in the back, where the sultan and his ladies prayed behind latticed windows, and the palace steward's room, adjacent to the main prayer hall, Tavernier, pp. 207–9.

85 Bobovi, *Mémoires,* fols. 36–37, 43. This mosque is referred to as "noble masjid of the Large Chamber pages," *(mescīd-i şerīf-i ġılmān-i enderūnī der oda-i kebīr),* in BA, MM 1690, fol. 56. It is called "masjid of the Large Chamber," *(büyük oda mescidi),* in Üsküdari, 1:fol. 254v.

Chapter 7

1 "A man destra vi è una bella Colombara, nella quale vi sono colombi assai, et di più sorte, con picagli di perle alli piedi, et questi colombi sono ammaistrati, che con sifoli si levano tutti in aria, et secondo che vi si sifola fanno alcune tombole in aria voltandosi sotto sopra, et poi li fanno poner tutti a baso, cioè in terra, et questo glielo può far fare a sua requisitione, et vi sono alcuni di questi colombi, che nella prima pena fano il scapocio, come quello delli frati," Angiolello, *Inedito manoscritto,* pp. 23–24.

2 For Ahmed I's building, see Baykal, p. 26; Atâ, 1:153; Miller, *Beyond the Sublime Porte,* p. 56; T. Öz, *Guide to the Museum,* p. 68.

3 Üsküdari, 1:fols. 254r, 258r. For the royal falconers who paraded with jewel-decorated birds, see Tavernier, p. 200: "Ils marchent tous en bel ordre l'oyseau sur le poing, & chaque oyseau porte au col ou un diamant ou une autre pierre de prix avec le chaperon tout brodé de perles; ce qui ne peut estre qu'un tres-beau spectacle." From the seventeenth century onward, sources also mention an "aviary" *(kuşhane)* at the southwest corner of the third court; it was attached to a kitchen in the harem where fowl, and the favorite royal dish of doves, were prepared (see Pl. 16a,b [38]).

4 Eldem, *Köşkler,* 1:99–107. For this kiosk, see also T. Öz, *Guide to the Museum,* p. 68.

5 "Kitābḫāne-i hümāyūn maḥallinde muḳaddemā olan ḳaṣrdan iḫrāc olınub teslīm olınan ʿatīḳ ḳurşun," TSA, D 2002, fol. 30r.

6 Küçükçelebizade, pp. 128–29, 176–77.

7 "ʿArż odası ardında ikinci Selīm inşāsı ḥavż bāġçesi denen ṣaġīr bāġçe içinde ṣāfī mermerden ḥavż ve üsti tekne ḳubbe ve oniki ʿadet kebīr ṣomaḳī direkli ol köşk," cited in Eldem, *Köşkler,* 1:99; Akdağ, p. 187. For the eighteenth-century renovation of the Chamber of the Expeditionary Force by Ahmed III, see TSA, D 2001, nos. 1–13.

8 See note 7.

9 "Ḥavż köşkiñ eṭrāfında olan parmaḳlıḳ meremmatı aşı boyalı," BA, MM 424, fol. 42.

10 Tavernier, pp. 197–98, 201.

11 "Et poi alla detta parte del cortivo, un puoco più avanti, vi è una statua fatta in volto coperta di piombo, et dentro selesata di marmo con fontane fredde et calde con suoi lavelli, et in questo luogo si lava il gran Turco, et poi li suoi cortigiani ogni Venere," Angiolello, *Inedito manoscritto,* p. 24.

12 Kritovoulos, p. 207; Barkan, "İstanbul saraylarına," p. 210.

13 Menavino, pp. 102–3.

14 Cafer Çelebi, pp. 73–75.

15 For the excavation, see İ. Öz, pp. 157–65. For the disrobing hall of the royal bath, see Ayverdi, *Fatih Devri Mimarisi,* p. 326; Goodwin, p. 134; Davis, p. 124; Eldem and Akozan, pp. 75–77, pl. 72.

16 Üsküdari, 1:fol. 258v.

17 Bobovi, *Mémoires,* fols. 108–201. Also see Evliya, 1:116; Tavernier, pp. 117–20.

18 Promontorio, p. 43. Bobovi, *Mémoires,* fols. 77–80, 137–39, 161–92.

19 Ruhi, *Tarih,* fol. 119r.

20 "Binā'-i ṭayama-i dīvār-i sarāy-i ʿāmire," "meremmet-i sarāy-i ʿāmire," Meriç, pp. 34–36, 70, nos. 162, 176, 177. For the damages of the bath, see Akdağ, p. 134; Ayverdi, *Fatih Devri Mimarisi,* p. 326. Kemalpaşazade mentions damages inside the third residential court, without specifying the buildings involved, Uğur, p. 38. See another photograph published in Eldem and Akozan, pl. 168.

21 For the plan (TSA, E 12307, no. 2) see Necipoğlu-Kafadar, "Plans and Models," pp. 234–35.

22 "Ḫarc-i vasīʿ-kerden-i ḫazīne-i āb-i ser ve ḥammām-i büzürg ve meremmet-i külḫān ve ḥammām ... ve oda-i pīş-i külḫān ve ḫarc-i pāk-kerden-i ḳurna," "meremmet-i ḥammām-i büzürg ve külḫān," ("expenses for enlarging the main water reservoir, and the large bath, and repairing the furnace, and bath ... and the room in front of the furnace, and cleaning the basin," "repairing the large bath and furnace," BA, KK 7097, fol. 58.

23 "Sāḫten-i döşeme-i ḳaldırım-i yonma ʿan seng-i ḳapaḳ ʿan oda-i ḥażret-i ḫullide mülkuhu ilā ḥammām-i büzürg der sarāy-i cedīd," BA, MM 17884, fols. 53, 69.

24 For these faintly visible graffiti, see Akdağ, p. 138; T. Öz, "Topkapı Sarayı Müzesi Onarımları," p. 53. The earthquake is mentioned in Busbecq, 1:200; İnciciyan, p. 89.

25 "Sarāy-i ʿāmiredeki ḳuṣūr ḥammām binā'larınuñ ḳuṣūrı tamām oldı," Âli, *Künh,* fol. 460v.

26 "Sarāy-i ʿāmirede vāḳiʿ ḥammām-i ḫāṣṣanuñ baʿżi ḳubābı tezyīn ve baʿżıları daḫı tecdīd olunmış idi," Peçevi, 1:503.

27 The bath was identified by palace tradition as that of Selim II, see Atā, 1:198, 312; Şeref, p. 402.

28 "Becihet-i sāḫten-i kāşīhā ve pervāzhā-i enderūn ve cāmekān-i ḥammām-i ḫāṣṣa ve tırābzonhā ve oluḳhā-i şādırvān-i ḥammām-i mezbūre ve baʿżi tırābzonhā-i köşk-i cedīd-i ḫāṣṣa," BA, KK 7100, fol. 10r.

29 BA, MD 26, nos. 280, 362, 565. A large number of decrees

from Cumada I to Cumada II 982 (1574) command the dispatch of lead for the superstructure of the bath, ibid., nos. 590, 591, 596, 606, 607, 736, 737, 746.

30 BA, KK 1769, fol. 83r; KK 1770, fol. 52v. Sixteenth-century bath plans show that daises were called *ṣoffa*, see Necipoğlu-Kafadar, "Plans and Models," pp. 225–26.

31 For bibliography on these tiles and for their inscriptions, see Çağman, "Osmanlı Sanatı," p. 201.

32 BA, MD 26, no. 592; published in R. Anhegger, no. 4; A. Refik, "İznik Çinileri," p. 36, no. 1.

33 For the argument that these tiles came from a bath in the harem, see T. Öz, *Guide to the Museum*, pp. 161–62. They are correctly associated with Selim II's bath at the third court in Goodwin, p. 134. The "high dais" was probably the one in the domed disrobing hall, where the sultan sat.

34 Evliya, 1:245, 333.

35 Üsküdari, 1:fol. 254r.

36 Bobovi, *Mémoires*, fols. 166–67.

37 Tavernier, pp. 120–26.

38 BA, MM 17884, fols. 69, 53; MM 148, fol. 69r; MM 403, fol. 113; TSA, D 4462; Atâ, 1:198, 312; Üsküdari, 1:fol. 254r.

39 Beauvau, pp. 70–71.

40 Courmenin, p. 154.

41 Bobovi, *Mémoires*, fols. 165–66.

42 Ibid., fols. 77–80, 137–39, 161–92.

43 For this incident, see Âli, *Künh*, fol. 460v; Peçevi, 1:503.

44 For Ummayad baths and palaces, see Ettinghausen and Grabar, *Art and Architecture of Islam*, pp. 45–71.

45 Ayverdi, *Fatih Devri Mimarisi*, pp. 324–26; Miller, *Beyond the Sublime Porte*, p. 37; Davis, p. 124; Eldem and Akozan, p. 76; Goodwin, p. 135; Koçu, p. 75; Akdağ, pp. 134, 157.

46 For Selim I's seal, see Atâ, 1:98, 198, 255; Şeref, p. 401; Ohsson, 7:39–43.

47 Promontorio, p. 42; Angiolello, *Inedito manoscritto*, p. 30; Angiolello, *Historia Turchesca*, p. 124; Menavino, p. 94; Spandugino, *Petit Traicté*, pp. 65, 119–20.

48 "Da poi ve è un altro Eunuco chiamato Haxenadarbassi, et questo ha in governo le camere et altri luoghi dove sta le Zoglie et lavori d'oro et d'argento, drapi et veste d'ogni sorte di seta, et assai altre cose appressiate," Angiolello, *Inedito manoscritto*, p. 30.

49 "Il loro ufficio è haver buona cura alla camera del thesoro; percioche in quella sono veste di broccato in varie guise, & vasi di piu sorti d'oro, & d'argento; & gioie, & danari, & per questo sono messi à quel servigio: & deono stare preparati per portare queste cose sempre, che'l Gran Turco le domandasse," Menavino, p. 94.

50 For this plan, see Necipoğlu-Kafadar, "Plans and Models," pp. 234–35.

51 Cafer Çelebi, p. 73.

52 Atâ, 1:59–60, 92. Öz agrees that the treasury was founded by Mehmed II, rather than by Selim I, T. Öz, *Guide to the Museum*, pp. 87–88.

53 TSA, D 9813, published in Sahillioğlu, pp. 29–31.

54 TSA, E 12009; D 1085; D 34, fols. 52v, 55v, 47v, 187r. Also see T. Öz, *Guide to the Museum*, pp. 86–87.

55 Tavernier, pp. 130, 148–53. The head treasurer, who had the keys of the treasury, could open it only in the presence of the *defterdar* and *nişancı*, who sealed its gate and coffers, Menavino, p. 95. The head treasurer was entrusted with the "key of the imperial vaults," (*kilid-i maḫāzen-i sulṭānī*) Bidlisi, *Tercüme-i Heşt Bihişt*, fol. 29v.

56 TSA, D 4.

57 For the treasury inventory of 910 (1505), see T. Öz, *Topkapı Sarayı Müzesi Arşivi Kılavuzu*, facsimile no. 21.

58 For the *ehl-i hiref*, see Uzunçarşılı, *Osmanlı Devletinin Saray Teşkilatı*, p. 316.

59 For these officers, see Atâ, 1:165–67, 172, 199; Ohsson, 7:39–43; Bobovi, *Mémoires*, fols. 201–14; La Croix, *Serrail*, fol. 126; Uzunçarşılı, *Osmanlı Devletinin Saray Teşkilatı*, pp. 315–22; Tavernier, pp. 138–40; Üsküdari, 1:fol. 253r.

60 For the one built by Ulugh Beg in Samarkand in the 1430s, see Babur, 1:49. Other examples are those in the Safavid shrine at Ardebil, in the palace of Isfahan, and in Mughal palaces.

61 "Anbār ve dolāb berā-yi nihāden-i çīnīhā-i ḫāṣṣa der oda-i ḫazīne-i enderūnī," BA, KK 7097, fol. 23. See also MM 17884, fols. 51, 52.

62 Cited in Babinger, *Mehmed*, p. 300.

63 On the basis of a report by Gentile Bellini, some sources record that the sultan venerated the relics and lit candles in front of a Madonna painting, Suriano, pp. 94–95; Spandugino, "De la Origine," p. 169. For the same report, see Friar Bartholomew of Foligno's *Sermonale* of 1482, in Mgr. Faloci, *Miscellanea Francescana*, 3:65–69.

64 For the published inventory, see Babinger, "Sultanischer Reliquiensacher," pp. 110–13. Based on Cuspinianus's (1523) report, Babinger states that the imperial regalia found in the Byzantine palace and in the cloister of St. John the Baptist entered the sultan's collection, ibid., pp. 97–98.

65 Sehi, pp. 149–51. The story is cited in Raby, "Sultan of Paradox," pp. 5–6. Raby convincingly argues against Babinger's statement that Mehmed had accumulated the relics merely to bargain with Christian princes, Raby, "Mehmed the Conqueror," p. 23.

66 Caoursin, pp. 114–17.

67 TSA, D 3, no. 2, fol. 12r.

68 For these Greek and Latin manuscripts, see Raby, "Mehmed the Conqueror," and Jacobs.

69 Sadeddin, 2:398.

70 TSA, D 4855.

71 "On marche dans cette galerie sur de grands carreaux de marbre, & le plat-fond est un reste d'antiquité, & d'excellentes peintures à la Mosaique qui representent divers personages, & que l'on croit avoir esté faites pour la reception de quelque grand Prince du temps des Empereurs Grecs," Tavernier, pp. 129–30.

72 Ayverdi, *Fatih Devri Mimarisi*, p. 339; Eldem and Akozan, pp. 76–77, pl. 75.

73 Similar patterns appear on late-fifteenth-century blue-and-white İznik tiles and in an album dating from Mehmed II's reign, in the Istanbul University Library, F 1423; see Ünver, *Fatih Devri Saray,* pp. 33–53.

74 For the baptistery, see Tezcan, "Sur-u Sultanî," pp. 79–80.

75 Atâ, 1:55; Şeref, p. 401.

76 For the hypothesis that Filarete contributed to the design of Mehmed II's mosque complex, see Restle, pp. 361–67, and chapter 1.

77 Kritovoulos, p. 207.

78 For Mehmed's painted portraits and medals, see Atıl, "Ottoman Miniature Painting," pp. 103–20; Andaloro, pp. 185–212; Thuasne, pp. 46–59; Karabacek, pp. 1–64; Raby, "Sultan of Paradox," pp. 4–5, and Raby, "Pride and Prejudice," 171–94.

79 Angiolello, *Historia turchesca,* p. 121; Sarre, "Michelangelo," pp. 61–66.

80 For the unconvincing argument that the colonnade was a Europeanizing eighteenth-century addition, see Gurlitt, *Baukunst,* 1:95; Davis, p. 110. There could have been no incentive to add an impressive colonnade at a time when the Inner Treasury was rarely visited by the sultans. It belonged to Mehmed II's original building, according to Ayverdi, *Fatih Devri Mimarisi,* pp. 336–39; Ayverdi, *Osmanlı Mimarisinde Fatih Devri,* p. 716; Eldem and Akozan, pp. 75–77.

81 For the photographs, see Eldem and Akozan, pl. 168, top, 172, bottom.

82 Busbecq, 1:114; Tavernier, p. 143. Also see Lubenau, 1:162, "In diesem Gewelbe leidt der grose Schatz, der von Rustano mitt seiner Vorsichtikeit dem Sultan oder Keiser gesamlet." Rüstem's accumulation of treasures is also mentioned in Navagero, p. 89.

83 For the abundance of treasures prior to Murad III's reign, see Âli, *Künh,* fols. 216v, 241r; Taşköprizade, pp. 68–69. For the transfer of treasures from Yedikule, see Hierosolimitano, *Vera relatione,* pp. 2–4, 34–35.

84 P. Contarini, p. 226; Donà, pp. 310–12; Âli, *Künh,* fol. 460v; Bernardo, p. 348.

85 BA, KK 7097, fol. 23; MM 17884, fols. 51, 54; Üsküdari, 1:fol. 254r; TSA, D 3, no. 1, fol. 1v; D 3, no. 2, fol. 1r; D 4, fol. 1r; D 5, fol. 1v; D 34, fols. 52v, 55v, 186r; Naima, 2:107; Orhonlu, p. 82; Anonymous, "Administrative treatise," fol. 20r; Âli, *Künh,* fol. 460v; Evliya, 1:116.

86 TSA, D 4855, fols. 1v–4v.

87 La Croix, *Mémoires,* pp. 140–42; Tavernier, pp. 129–53.

88 "Les apartements du Casné sont immenses. Il y a beaucoup de chambres souterrains, qui ne sont éclairées que par des fenêtres que l'on ouvre du côté de la mer. On y enferme tout ce qui ne craint point l'humidité. Dans les chambres qui vont de plain-pied à la cour du serrail, on étale sur des planches à plusieurs étages, ou dans des armoires, des étoffes de toutes les especes, des harnois d'un prix infini, des pierreries de choix brutes ou mises en oeuvre, en un mot tout ce que les Sultans ont de précieux. Le détail seroit immense, & paroîtroit incroyable," Flachat, p. 181. For the destroyed wooden galleries, see Ayverdi, *Osmanlı Mimarisinde Fatih Devri,* p. 721; Eldem and Akozan, p. 76. Tavernier mentions "des bras qui sortent de la muraille," p. 132.

89 Charrière, 3:896.

90 TSA, D 34, fol. 186r. See also Atâ, 1:255–56.

91 TSA, D 34, fols 55v, 187r.

92 Tavernier, pp. 152–53.

93 La Croix, *Serrail,* fols. 127–28; La Croix, *Mémoires,* pp. 141–42.

94 Naima, 2:107: "The decorations of the imperial treasury were observed" ("Ḫazīne-i ʿāmire zīneti seyr ve temāşā olundı").

95 Safi, fols. 138v–39v. This information is repeated in Hezarfen, *Telhis,* fols. 18v–19v. Cited in Uzunçarşılı, *Osmanlı Devletinin Saray Teşkilatı,* p. 320. Donato similarly writes: "... i muri, quali hanno tele diverse, con quantità di gioie attaccate dall'alto al baso," Donato, 2:91.

96 Safi, fols. 138v–39v.

97 TSA, D 10749, fol. 17r.

98 For the occasional sale of objects from the Inner Treasury in front of the Imperial Gate, see La Croix, *Serrail,* fol. 127; Atâ, 1:173–74. For thefts, see Tavernier, pp. 140–42; Ohsson, 7:40; Uzunçarşılı, *Osmanlı Devletinin Saray Teşkilatı,* pp. 318–19.

99 "C'est une mer que je puis comparer à la mer Caspienne, où il entre plusieurs rivieres que l'on n'en void point sortir," Tavernier, p. 130.

100 Leysizade, p. 42. Later sources refer to it as "ḫāṣṣ oda," "oda-i ḫāṣṣa," "ḫāne-i ḫāṣṣa," Anonymous, "Administrative treatise," fols. 13r, 20r; Anonymous, *Müstetab,* p. 6, fol. 13; Evliya, 1:116; Âli, *Künh,* fol. 94r; Üsküdari, 1:fol. 252r, 254r; Hezarfen, *Telhis,* fol. 18r; Safi, fol. 127v; TSA, D 34, fols. 24r, 32v, 187r, 227v.

101 Ruhi, *Tarih,* fol. 119r.

102 "A man sinistra del cortivo vi è il Palazo, dove stanzia il Gran Turco, il qual Palazo la maggior parte è lavorato in volto, et ha molte camare, et stanze da estate, et da inverno. Dalla parte che guarda verso Pera, vi è un portico, il quale è sopra il gran giardino, et da quello ascendono molti ancipressi, i quali vengono a referire alli balconi del detto portico, et questo portico è edificato sopra due colone, et è fatto tutto in volto, et in mezzo vi è una fonte, la quale spande in un bel lavello lavorato di marmo con profili et colonele di porfido, et serpentina, et in questo lavello vi sono più sorte pessi, et il Gran Turco se ne piglia gran piacere a vederli," Angiolello, *Inedito manoscritto,* p. 24.

103 Ayverdi, who was among the first to date the basement to Mehmed II's reign, argues that it is capable of supporting a tower eight to nine stories high, similar to the one in the Edirne Palace, Ayverdi, *Fatih Devri Mimarisi,* p. 300, Ayverdi, *Osmanlı Mimarisinde Fatih Devri,* p. 729. Others have supported this early date of foundation:

Akdağ, p. 148; Goodwin, p. 183; Davis, p. 97; T. Öz, *Hırka-i Saadet,* p. 5; Eldem and Akozan, pp. 74–75, 77. The thesis that the Privy Chamber was built by Selim I originates from Atâ, 1:30, 92–93.

104 For this door, see T. Öz, *Hırka-i Saadet,* p. 5; Davis, p. 148; Akdağ, p. 148; Ünver, "Süsleme Sanatı Bakımından," pp. 112–13.

105 Cafer Çelebi, pp. 71–73.

106 Bidlisi, *Hasht Behisht,* fol. 5.

107 Cited in Babinger, *Mehmed,* p. 379; Raby, "El Gran Turco," p. 51; see also chapter 1.

108 Kritovoulos, p. 207.

109 "Fece Sulthan Paiaxit una bella habitatione per la sua persona; dove continuamente dimorava: nel tempo della invernata viene nelle stanze piu basse, & questa fa per fuggire il vento, procedente dal mar Maggiore: & anchora perche sono luoghi assai piu caldi," Menavino, p. 91. For the sultan's sleeping habits, see also Spandugino, *Petit Traicté,* p. 60.

110 Atâ, 1:30, 92–93, 255.

111 Meinecke, "Mamlukische Marmordekorationen," pp. 208–12.

112 For the assertion that the marbles were mounted by Süleyman I around 1524, see Goodwin, pp. 182, 325; Davis, p. 148; Denny, *Ceramics of the Mosque of Rüstem Pasha,* p. 123.

113 Aslanapa, *Osmanlı Devri Mimarisi,* pp. 155–57.

114 Lokman, *Hünername,* 1:fol. 219r.

115 Atâ, 1:313; Bon, pp. 63–64: "Il divano, cioè la sala aperta dalla parte di levante, posto sopra colonne bellissime che guardava sopra un laghetto."

116 One account book cites "large trunks and cupboards" *(anbār-i büzürg ve dolāb),* "goldsmith's chests with mother-of-pearl" *(ṣanādıḳ-i zergerān maʿa ṣedef),* "a tongue-and-groove-construction wooden door" *(bāb-i muḳaṭṭaʿ-i çatma),* "a casket of sandalwood and ebony for storing jewels" *(ṣanduḳçe-i ḫurde ʿan ṣandal ve abanos berā-yi nihāden-i cevāhīr),* "an inlay-work cupboard" *(dolāb-i fisoskārī),* "a seat, sofa, and throne" *(iskemle ve kerevet maʿa taḫt),*" "a table" *(pīştaḫta),* and "a table and chest for placing books" *(pīştaḫta maʿa ṣanduḳ berā-yi nihāden-i kitābhā).* The same document cites "repairing the room of His Majesty—may his reign last forever—and repairing its paintings and making window frames and wooden floors" *(meremmet-i oda-i ḥażret-i ḫullide mülkuhu maʿa meremmet-i naḳş ve sāḫten-i çerçevehā-i revzen ve döşeme ʿan taḫta-i bāzū),* "repairing the basement under the room of His Majesty—may his reign last forever" *(meremmet-i bodrum der zīr-i oda-i ḥażret-i ḫullide mülkuhu),* and laying a marble path between the Privy Chamber and the Large Bath of the third court, BA, MM 17884, fols. 51–54, 69. Another account book, of 935 (1528–29), lists "a painted marble cupboard" *(mermer dolāb-i münaḳḳāş);* "cupboards of jeweled inlay-work" *(dolāb-i fisos-kārī ve cevherī);* "a table inlaid with gold" *(pīştaḫta-i zernişān);* "a walnut cupboard" *(dolāb-i taḫta-i ceviz);* "royal chests" *(ṣanduḳhā-i ḫāṣṣa);* "repairing the painting, together with hanging and making a finial above the throne, and a walnut sofa" *(meremmet-i naḳş be avīḫten ve sāḫten-i ʿalem-i fevḳ-i taḫt ve kerevet ʿan taḫta-i ceviz);* "making a bronze fireplace hood" *(sāḫten-i yaşmaḳ-i āteşdān ʿan nüḥās);* and laying a path between the Privy Chamber and the Chamber of Petitions, BA KK 7097, fols. 22–24, 58.

117 Kürkçüoğlu (ed.), *Süleymaniye Vakfiyesi,* p. 22, transliteration, pp. 37–38.

118 Bragadino "Sommario" in Albèri 3, p. 106; Bassano, fol. 17r.

119 For Melchior Lorichs, see Oberhummer, pl. 3. For this roof pavilion, no longer extant, where the sultan ate and enjoyed the view in summer, see Bassano, fol. 17r.

120 TSA, D 34, fol. 75v. The palace steward was in charge of repairs and constructions at the sultan's palace.

121 For the attribution of these tiles to Murad III, see Davis, p. 148; Goodwin, p. 325. "Nev-sāḫten-i kāşīleme-i oda-i ḫāṣṣa-i ḥażret-i hüdāvendigār," BA, MM 4435, fols. 50, 57.

122 "Ḫāne-i ḫāṣṣada ḳış odası kāşī olduḳda," TSA, D 34, fol. 227v.

123 Tavernier, p. 210.

124 Bon, p. 64.

125 Üsküdari, 1:fols. 252r–v.

126 "Les murs incrustés de Porcelaine que l'on couvre l'hyver de Tapis de velours brodés d'or qui s'ostent l'été. Les planchers sont carelés de marbre, l'hyver l'on y étand de riches Tapis semblables à ceux dont on orne les murailles," La Croix, *Serrail,* fol. 247. For the rich furnishings, see also Bassano, fol. 17r. The checkered marble pavements are also mentioned in Tavernier, pp. 209–10.

127 "Suo lecto che è picolo da due persone, alto da terra due spanne, formato di lagioni di porceletta, tutti deaurati con tapeti sopra tapeti di seta di Persia dignissimi deaurati et rachamati a leopardi con straponta di bombice, batuto, alto due spanne di camocato cremisi lis [cremisino] de Bursia, qual straponta rimova di 3 in 3 giorni," Promontorio, pp. 39–40.

128 Menavino, pp. 93–94; the baldachin is described thus: "& sopra tirano con cordoni di seta, fatti à posta, un baldachino d'oro, il quale copre il letto."

129 Ramberti, p. 265; Navagero, p. 45; Junis, p. 262; Geuffroy, pp. 227–29.

130 Selaniki, *Tarih,* p. 126; see also Peçevi, 1:27.

131 Naima, 3:452.

132 Safi, fols. 127r–29v.

133 Atâ states that the relics were divided between the Privy Chamber and Inner Treasury by Selim I, Atâ, 1:255–56.

134 Lokman, *Tomar,* fols. 163r–64v.

135 For the holy standard, see Uzunçarşılı, *Osmanlı Devletinin Saray Teşkilatı,* pp. 248–60; Miller, *Beyond the Sublime Porte,* p. 73; Safi, 1:fols. 128v–29r; Silahdar, 2:14–15.

136 The relics were embellished in the late sixteenth and early

seventeenth centuries, T. Öz, *Hırka-i Saadet,* pp. 40–45.

137 Atâ, 1:207–8, 215, 288; T. Öz, *Hırka-i Saadet,* p. 9; Salahi, fol. 44v.

138 Tavernier, pp. 211–13.

139 Safi, fol. 128v. Also see Hezarfen, *Telhis,* fol. 17r; Tavernier, pp. 213–15; Bobovi, *Mémoires,* fol. 237; La Croix, *Mémoires,* p. 139; Donato, 2:89; Atâ, 1:219.

140 Naili, fols. 2r–3r; Esad, pp. 14–18.

141 TSA, D 34, fol. 32r.

142 Çağman, "Serzergerân Mehmed Usta ve Eserleri" pp. 58–61, 75–77.

143 Safi mentions a gilt casket on a high shelf *(raff-i mükellef)* near the throne, where the mantle was kept; the Prophet's standard, sword, and bow and relics of the early caliphs were hung on the "walls of the throne of the caliphate" *(taḫt-i ḫilāfet raḫt dīvārları),* Safi, fol. 129r. They were "kept or hung on the shelves and walls of the throne room" *(taḫt oṭasında rufūf ve cidārda ta‹biye ve ḥıfẓ olunmışdur),* according to Naima, 2:106. For the relics, see also T. Öz, *Hırka-i Saadet;* Üsküdari, 1:fol. 252v; Hezarfen, *Telhis,* fol. 18r; Donato, 2:90–91; Tavernier, pp. 211–16; Atâ, 1:255–56; Bobovi, *Mémoires,* fols. 236–37.

144 Tavernier, pp. 210–11.

145 Evliya, 1:571; Cevri, pp. 289.

146 Bon, p. 64.

147 For this hall, see Atâ, 1:201; TSA, D 448; Bostanzade, fol. 26r; TSA, E 12359, no. 1, fol. 1v; D 2233, fol. 3v; D 9917, no. 10, fol. 10r; D 10749, fol. 2r; Salahi, fol. 111r, 162r; Esad, pp. 112ff.

148 Bostanzade, fol. 23r. For a description of the three-tiered fountain, see Tavernier, pp. 209–10.

149 Hierosolimitano, *Vera relatione,* pp. 36–37, 39. For the library, see also Jacobs, pp. 62–74.

150 "Fıskiyehā-i ejder ağzı ve lālehā-yi eğri ve lālehā-i ṭoğrı," BA, KK 7104, fol. 10v. For the metal spout, see Binney, p. 227, no. 2.

151 For Mehmed II's readers, see Pertusi, *Caduta di Costantinopoli,* 2:131–32; Raby, "Mehmed the Conqueror," p. 25. For readers to later sultans, see Bassano, fols. 20v–21r; Courmenin, p. 173; Ramberti, p. 299; Abdi Pasha, fols. 101r, 106v. For the custom of eating in the Privy Chamber, see Safi, fol. 138r; La Croix, *Mémoires,* pp. 376, 383–88; Beauvau, pp. 33, 62–63; Bon, pp. 63, 67, 93–94.

152 He calls it a *guardarobba,* Menavino, pp. 93–94. For the Privy Chamber's *guardarobba,* where the sultan was dressed every morning, see also Geuffroy, p. 228; Junis, pp. 262–63; Ramberti, p. 265; Morosini, pp. 281–82.

153 Atâ, 1:92–93, 312–13. For chronograms commemorating Murad IV's repairs of the Privy Chamber, see Cevri, pp. 286, 290, 302.

154 For these inscriptions, see Şeref, pp. 406–10. Tavernier states that there were many inscriptions at the dormitory of Privy Chamber pages, Tavernier, pp. 204–6.

155 Flachat, pp. 185–86. In front of the original dormitory a larger masonry building, serving as a new dormitory, was built in the middle of the nineteenth century, see Atâ, 1:312–13, 30, 92–93.

156 Promontorio, p. 40.

157 "Mevcūdāt-i ḫizāne-i ‹āmire-i enderūnī der enderūn-i anbārhā-i şimşīr der nezd-i oda-i ḫāṣṣa," TSA, D 3, no. 2, fols. 14v–15v.

158 "Oda-i ḫāṣṣada olan iç ḫazīne," "ḫāne-i ḫāṣṣada olan ḫazīne," "ḫāne-i ḫāṣṣa ḫazīnesi," "oda ḫazīnesi," "odada olan ḫazīne-i ḫāṣṣa," TSA, D 34, fols. 24r; 29v; 55v, 187r.

159 Ibid., fols. 55v, 72r, 187r.

160 Salahi, fol. 5r; Atâ, 1:313, 209–10. For the contents of this treasury, see also Şeref, p. 405; T. Öz, *Guide to the Museum,* p. 86; Silahdar, 2:15.

161 T. Öz, *Hırka-i Saadet,* p. 9. Atâ writes that a special group of pages was charged with periodically cleaning these weapons, Atâ, 1:195–96.

162 Chishull, p. 46.

163 Atâ, 1:311.

164 Dallam, pp. 71–72, 76–80.

165 Safi, fols. 39r–v.

166 Dallam, pp. 62–63.

167 For straw mats, carpets, and curtains on the marble terrace, see BA, MM 511, fols. 6, 23, 48; MM 861, fols. 106–7; MM 403, fols. 10, 130; MM 1756, fol. 66; MM 858, fols. 70–71.

168 Bon, pp. 63–64: "Un laghetto di forma quadra fatto artificiosamente da alcune fontane in no. di 30, tirate e compartito sopra un corridore di pietre di marmo finissime, che circondava detto lago, sì che le fontane gettavano l'acqua da quel corridore nel lago, e l'acqua di esso si scolava poi con serioli in alcuni giardini, che rendevano il luoco deliziosissimo: per il corridore potevano camminare due uomini pari, e girandolo godere di quelle fontane, che facevano un continuo e soave mormorio, e nel lago vi era un brigantino assai piccolo nel quale mi fu detto, che entrava spesso la Maestà Sua con buffoni, per farli volgare a ricreazione, e per far loro qualche burla di sbalzarli nell'acqua, come spessissimo camminando con loro nel corridore gli faceva far tombole per trabalzarli nel lago."

169 For the original pool, see Eldem and Akozan, pls. 77, 85.

170 Bon, pp. 63–64; Lokman, *Hünername,* 1:fol. 219r; Atâ, 1:313.

171 Koçi Beg writes that Süleyman stopped holding consultations at the Old Council Hall, Koçi Beg, p. 24.

172 Nadiri, fols. 47v–48r.

173 "Kenār-i ṣoffada bir kürsi-yi sedefkārī," Bostanzade, fol. 22r.

174 "Ḫāṣṣ oda ḳapusı öniñde vāḳı‹ ṣoffa-i pür safā üzre taḫt-i şerīf ḳonub," Safi, 1:fol. 138r. See also Üsküdari, 1:fol. 256r; Hezarfen, *Telhis,* fol. 32r; Atâ, 1:313; Salahi, fol. 63v; TSA, E 12359, no. 1, fol. 1r; E 12358, fol. 3r, 6r.

175 Cited in Miller, *Beyond the Sublime Porte,* p. 224.

176 Eremya, p. 11; Bobovi, *Mémoires,* fols. 239, 263. See also Tavernier, pp. 218–21.

177 La Croix, *Mémoires,* pp. 376, 384–88; see also La Croix, *Serrail,* fols. 122–23.

178 For these activities, see Evliya, 1:245–48; Bobovi, *Mémoires,* fol. 192; Dallam, pp. 61–63, 67–73. For an eighteenth-century concert in the Privy Chamber, see TSA, E 12358, fol. 1v.

Chapter 8

1 Evliya 1:116. For the hypothesis that Mehmed II's New Palace was merely an administrative center, built to separate official and residential functions, see Miller, *Beyond the Sublime Porte,* p. 25; Goodwin, p. 132; Akdağ, p. 23; Davis, p. 7; Anhegger-Eyüboğlu, "Fatih Devrinde," pp. 26–27; Tansuğ, p. 149; Durukan, p. 7; Kuran, "Palace of the Sultans," p. 115. Some have argued that Mehmed II built the New Palace as a summer residence and that he left most of his court at the Old Palace; Atâ, 1:56–57; Ohsson, 7:3; Baykal, p. 45; Babinger, *Mehmed,* p. 245.

2 For the argument that Süleyman I transferred the harem to the Topkapı Palace, see Evliya, 1:116; Ohsson, 7:3; Atâ, 1:56–57; Miller, *Beyond the Sublime Porte,* pp. 86–90; Penzer, p. 134; Alpay and Schneider, p. 44; Durukan, pp. 7–8; Koçu, p. 236. Others propose a later date of transfer during Murad III's reign, Örs, "History of the Topkapı Palace," p. 9; Davis, p. 207; Anhegger-Eyüboglu, "Fatih Devrinde," pp. 23–27; Atasoy, "Matrakçı's Representation," p. 96; Tansuğ, p. 149; Erkins, *Topkapı Sarayı Müzesi,* p. 43; Çığ, "Fatih Topkapı," pp. 26–27.

3 BA, MM 17884, fols. 53–54, 69, 71; KK 7097, fols. 22, 24, 58; see Appendix A.6.

4 Kritovoulos, p. 207; cited by Ayverdi, who believes that a harem existed during Mehmed II's reign, Ayverdi, *Osmanlı Mimarisinde Fatih Devri,* p. 683. Tursun writes that after the completion of the New Palace the old one, which had become "antiquated," was abandoned for the use of women, Tursun, text fol. 59b. Âli says that Mehmed II abandoned the Old Palace to invalids, women, servants, and retired personnel, Âli, *Künh,* fol. 84v.

5 He refers to the harem in the New Palace as "Serraglio di damiselle del Signore, tutte schiave propinquo a dicto serraglio del Signore"; and to the one in the Old Palace as "Secondo Serraglio di Damiselle," Promontorio, pp. 44–45.

6 Sagundino, p. 600; I. Contarini, pp. 7–8.

7 Menavino, pp. 135–36; Evliya, 1:118. See also Atâ, 1:72–73, 137. Ohsson writes that Mehmed II lived only with a select number of male attendants at the New Palace, leaving his harem and the rest of his courtiers at the Old Palace, Ohsson, 7:3.

8 For Mehmed II's grandsons who lived in the Old Palace, see Sehi, p. 107; for the procession, see Anonymous, "Testament," p. 17.

9 Angiolello, *Inedito manoscritto,* p. 33; Angiolello, *Historia Turchesca,* p. 128; Menavino, pp. 134–35.

10 For the queen's letters, see Uluçay, *Haremden Mektuplar,* pp. 18–20.

11 Atâ, 1:62, 159–60; Şeref, pp. 394–95.

12 Bidlisi, *Tercüme-i Heşt Bihişt,* fols. 261r, 262r.

13 İnalcık, *Ottoman Empire,* p. 86.

14 Ahmed bin İbrahim, fol. 3v.

15 Promontorio, pp. 44–45. For the women, see Angiolello, *Inedito manoscritto,* p. 33; Angiolello, *Historia Turchesca,* p. 128; Menavino, pp. 134–35.

16 Uzunçarşılı, *Osmanlı Devletinin Saray Teşkilatı,* pp. 146–47.

17 İnalcık, *Ottoman Empire,* p. 86.

18 Leysizade, p. 46.

19 "Lui va spesse fiate al seraglio delle donne," Minio, "Relazione [1521]," p. 22; Minio, "Relazione [1522]," p. 78; Postel, pp. 31–32.

20 "Seraio di la madre del Signor," "Seraio da la madre et moier del Signor," Sanuto, 41:526, 473; 56:883; Anonymous, *Coppia di una lettera,* p. 2r.

21 Sanuto, 53:446; Celalzade, *Tabakat,* fol. 199v; Âli, *Künh,* fol. 314r.

22 Sanuto, 57:632.

23 Selaniki, *Tarih,* pp. 205–9; Donini, p. 184.

24 BA, MM 17884, fols. 53–54, 69, 71; KK 7097, fols. 22, 24, 58. The term "palace of girls" also appears in the account books of Mehmed II's kitchens at the New Palace. These kitchens supplied food to the harem population *(cemaʿāt-i dārü's-saʿāde)* only during the two religious holidays, when certain goods and vessels were carried "from the commissary up to the Palace of Girls" *(ez kilār ilā sarāy-i duḫterān),* suggesting that the harem had its own kitchen; Barkan, "İstanbul saraylarına," pp. 99, 194, 196, 226, 229.

25 For the marriage, see Ludovisi, p. 29; Navagero, pp. 74–75; Bassano, fols. 18r–v; Dernschwamm, pp. 136–37.

26 Ludovisi, pp. 28–29. For the princes living at the Topkapı, see Bassano, fol. 18v; Trevisano, p. 117; Navagero, p. 75. For the Ottoman politics of reproduction, see the unpublished Ph.D. thesis of Leslie Peirce, Princeton University, 1988.

27 Bassano, fol. 17v.

28 Ibid., fol. 17v.

29 Navagero, p. 90.

30 Ibid., pp. 52–53. Other sources confirm that Hürrem lived in the Topkapı, see Chesneau, p. 40; C. Zeno, p. 28; Nicolay, p. 67. At the time of her death in 1558, however, she was staying in the Old Palace, Dernshwamm, pp. 36, 136–38; Kamil, pp. 72, 78. Hürrem probably moved to the Old Palace because there was no women's hospital at the Topkapı at that time. The Old Palace had become the residence of widow princesses, the sultan's unmarried relatives, children of nobles, and slave girls, see Ludovisi, p. 13; Bassano, fol. 18r; C. Zeno, p. 28; Nicolay, p. 67; Âli, *Künh,* fol. 84v.

31 These concubines are mentioned, in 1569–70, as "cevārī-yi sarāy-i cedīd," "cevārī-yi sarāy-i ʿatīḳ," BA, KK 1767, fol. 72r. Another wage register, of 1572–73, lists two dis-

tinct groups of women, "cemāʿat-i dārü's-saʿāde-i ʿatīḳ," "cemāʿat-i dārü's-saʿāde-i cedīd," BA, KK 7100, fol. 4v.

32 Garzoni, pp. 403, 395. See also Badoaro, pp. 359–62.

33 "Dārü's-saʿādede maṭbaḫ ardında kademe ile ve kemer ile yidi sekiz zirāʿ bir oda yapılmaḳ lāzım olub ... ġāyet mükellef olmaya," BA, MD 7, nos. 758, 759.

34 Ibid., no. 878; published in A. Refik, *On Altıncı Asırda*, p. 3, no. 6.

35 BA, KK 7100, fol. 10r.

36 "Muʿallimḫāne-i ḥażret-i şehzādegān der dārü's-saʿāde-i ʿāmire," BA, KK 1769, fol. 83r.

37 Peçevi, 1:27; Selaniki, *Tarih*, p. 124, 126; Hezarfen, *Tenkih*, fol. 134v.

38 "Nev-sāḫten-i kilār-i cedīd berā-yi ḥażret-i vālide sulṭān," BA, MM 148. For the Queen Mother's monthly trips to the Topkapı from her own palace in a gilt carriage, before the rebuilding of the harem was completed, see Heberer, p. 287; Hierosolimitano, *Vera relatione*, p. 63.

39 For Nurbanu's letters to Venice, see Skilliter, pp. 515–36.

40 Uzunçarşılı, *Osmanlı Devletinin Saray Teşkilatı*, p. 154.

41 Âli, *Künh*, fols. 497v–498r; Morosini, pp. 283–84; Moro, p. 328; Peçevi, 2:4–5; Salomone, p. 20, 27–28; Bernardo, p. 352.

42 Hierosolimitano, *Relatione*, fols. 111v–12r; Âli, *Künh*, fol. 460r.

43 Hierosolimitano, *Vera relatione*, pp. 33–34.

44 Lokman, *Shahanshāhnāma*, 1:fol. 66v–67r.

45 Lokman, *Tomar*, fols. 179v–81v; Lokman, *Silsilename*, fols. 105r–6v; Breuning, pp. 56–57; Charrière, 3:809–11; TSA, D 34, fols. 39r–40v.

46 The garden at Yenikapı was located between the Topkapı and Edirnekapı gates of the city wall; Lokman, *Silsilename*, fols. 105r–7r, 111r–12v; Lokman, *Tomar*, fols. 180r, 189v, 208r, 212r.

47 Lokman, *Shahanshāhnāma*, 1:fols. 67v, 117v–18r. For the arrival of the Georgian princes in 1579, see also Schweigger, p. 82; Lokman, *Tomar*, fols. 185v–86r.

48 For the domed building, see Eldem, *Köşkler*, 1:124–42.

49 For the inscriptions, see Şeref, pp. 651–52.

50 "Sarāy-i ʿāmirem içinde ḫāṣṣa-i hümāyūnım içün binā' olınacaḳ binā' mühimmātıyçün bennā' ve neccār lāzım olmaġın," BA, MD 33, no. 655.

51 BA, MD 35, no. 145.

52 ASV, Dispaccio al Senato, Secreta, Costantinopoli, Filza 12, fols. 108v, 289r. Barbarigo refers to the building as "una fabrica che fu nel seraglio," and writes, "Il Capitano del Mare ... per lo piu sia nel serraglio del Signore soprastante à quella fabrica, la qual però per quanto si dice presto sarà finita."

53 A dispatch of 3 June 1578 reads, "Aussy qu'il se faict une nouvelle fabrique au Grand Sarrail, de laquelle ledit cappitaine est surintendant et n'en bouge ordinairement depuys le matin jusques au soir, faisant faire une merveilleuse diligence à ceux qui y travaillent, de sorte qu'on a dit au seigneur que s'il manquoit de là elle ne s'achèveroit de cest esté, comme il désire qu'elle fasse, s'estant cependant retiré avec toutes ses femmes à Scutary, où il ne veult demeurer l'hyver," Charrière, 3:743–44. Another dispatch, of 18 August 1579, reads, "Le G.S. est toujours au sarrail de sa mère, où il se trouve si bien (pource qu'il est en bel ayr et commode pour monter à cheval et aller chasser ou se promener hors la ville, comme il faict quasi tous les jours sans estre veu, d'aultant qu'il est près l'une des portes de la ville), qu'on dit qu'il ne passera à Scutary comme il pensoit faire, ainsi achèvera là cest esté, et puys se retirer à son grand sarrail et logis ordinaire où se tient le divan, estant presque achevés quelques nouveaulx édifices qu'il y a faictz fair pour la comodité de ses femmes," ibid., 3:810.

54 For these inscriptions, see Şeref, pp. 651–52.

55 Hierosolimitano, *Vera relatione*, p. 59. Contemporary accounts confirm that Murad III always slept in the harem, Morosini, p. 282. Seventeenth-century sources show that the sultan's bedroom was located between the Privy Chamber of the male quarters and the Privy Chamber of the female quarters, Bobovi, *Mémoires*, fols. 240–42; La Croix, *Mémoires*, p. 376.

56 Hierosolimitano, *Vera relatione*, pp. 56–58. For the handkerchief ceremony, also see Menavino, p. 135; Bobovi, *Mémoires*, fols. 243–45; La Croix, *Mémoires*, pp. 391–92.

57 Lokman, *Shahanshāhnāma*, 1:fol. 117v.

58 For a hypothetical reconstruction of the L-shaped colonnade, see Eldem and Akozan, pl. 109.

59 "Il seraglio era impedito per certa fabrica d'un bagno che faceva far sua Mᵗᵃ, la qual saria finita presto," ASV, Dispacci al Senato, Secreta, Costantinopoli, Filza 14, fol. 155r. Süleyman I had commissioned the architect Sinan to build only three baths in the palace, Sa'i, *Mimar Sinan*, pp. 45, 124; Sa'i, *Tezkiretü'l-bünyan*, pp. 43–44.

60 A dispatch of June 1580 reads, "Il loge à présent avec la royne sa mere hors son serrail ordinaire, où il fait bastir, près la porte d'Adrinople," Charrière, 3:915, see also 922.

61 "Puşīş-i minder-i ḫāṣṣa ki ḥammām-i cedīd," BA, KK 682, fol. 63.

62 Receb 988 (August–September 1580): "Ḥarem-i ḫāṣṣada bir ḥammām ve baʿżi yapular binā' olundıḳda," TSA, D 34, fol. 52r.

63 BA, MD 48, nos. 318, 371. For the sultan's abandonment of the bath in the court of male pages, see Beauvau, p. 70; Courmenin, p. 154.

64 Published in A. Refik, *On Altıncı Asırda*, p. 29, no. 28.

65 BA, MD 58, no. 172.

66 "To serve at the bath being built anew at my Imperial Palace," *(sarāy-i cedīd-i ʿāmiremde müceddeden binā' olınan ḥammāma ḫidmet içün)*, ibid., no. 633.

67 A decree from 16 Safer 992 (24 February 1584) shows that the chief architect Sinan was setting out to Mecca, BA, MD 52, no. 714.

68 "Le cappitaine Oluchaly, sitost après son retour de la mer Noyre, a esté employé à l'intendance de la fabrique d'un baing au grand serrail de ce seigneur," Charrière, 4:381.

69 Without specifying a building, these firmans refer to "tiles being required for my private imperial domain," (*Ḥāṣṣa-i hümāyūnım mühimmi içün ḳāşī lāzım olmaġın),* BA, MD 58, nos. 117, 119. Published in A. Refik, "İznik Çinileri," p. 39, nos. 5, 7; translated in R. Anhegger, nos. 8, 9.

70 "Ḥāliyā sarāy-i ‹āmiremde binā' olınan ḥammām-i cedīde lāzım ḳāşī," BA, MD 58, no. 393. Published in A. Refik, "İznik Çinileri," pp. 39–40, no. 8; translated in R. Anhegger, no. 10.

71 "Niḥālī-yi ḥammām-i cedīd-i ḥażret-i pādişāh-i ‹ālempenāh" ("carpets of the new bath of his Majesty, the world-protecting sultan"); "niḥālī-yi ṣoffa-i ḥammām-i cedīd berā-yi ḥażret-i pādişāh" ("carpets of the dais of the new bath for his Majesty, the sultan"); "perde-i oda-i cedīd der sarāy-i cedīd saḫte," ("curtains of the new room made in the new palace"); "perde-i pencere-i oda-i cedīd-i ḥażret-i pādişāh-i ‹ālempenāh" ("curtains of the windows of the new room of his Majesty, the world-protecting sultan"); "niḥālī-yi taḫt-i ḥażret-i pādişāh-i ‹ālempenāh" ("carpets of the throne of his Majesty, the world-protecting sultan"), BA, KK 2284, fols. 42v, 43v, 49v.

72 "Sarāy-i ‹āmirede müceddeden yapılan oda-i ḫāṣṣ ve ḥammām-i rāḥat-baḫşā ve ḥavzlar temām olmaġın teşrīf buyurdılar," Selaniki, *Tarih,* p. 193.

73 "The projecting balcony of her Majesty the Queen Mother" (*Şehnişīn-i ḥażret-i vālide sulṭān),* BA, MM 5633, fol. 65.

74 Salomone, p. 4 (Italian facsimile), p. 22 (English translation).

75 Sanderson, p. 72.

76 Âli, *Counsel,* 1:59.

77 "Sarāy-i cedīd, hümāyūn-i ḫāṣṣa tecdīden binā' olundı," "Sarāy-i cedīd-i ḫāḳānī, iç sarāyı cümle sulṭān Murād ḫān binā' itmişdür ve kilār-i ‹āmire ve maṭbaḫı hod ba‹de'l ihrāḳ binā' olunmışdur," Sa'i, *Mimar Sinan,* pp. 40, 117.

78 Davis, pp. 59–60; Örs, "Haremin Muamması," pp. 2–12; Anhegger-Eyüboğlu, "Fatih Devrinde," pp. 23–36.

79 This Carriage Gate (*‹Araba Ḳapusı)* is also known as the Gate of Girls (*Ḳızlar Ḳapusı),* or Harem Gate (*Ḥarem Ḳapusı* or *Ḥarem-i Hümāyūn Ḳapusı),* Atâ, 1:311; Esad, pp. 66–67, 115, 121; Naili, fols. 99v, 101v; Hezarfen, *Telhis,* fol. 16r. For the inscription, see Şeref, p. 458. A variant of this inscription of 996 (1587–88) is cited in Atâ, 4:136–37.

80 For the inscription on the gate of the dormitory of Halberdiers with Tresses, see chapter 3.

81 Ahmed bin İbrahim, fols. 3v–4r.

82 Âli, *Künh,* fol. 501v. For the transferral of the administration of waqfs from white to black eunuchs at the end of the sixteenth century, see Selaniki, *Tarih.* MS. Gökbilgin, fol. 114v; Şeref, pp. 342–43.

83 For the scattering of gold, see Durukan, p. 92; Hierosolimitano, *Vera relatione,* p. 61. Hierosolimitano (pp. 32–33) notes that the sultan could visit the separate quarters of his wives from the secret corridor without being seen, and describes the corridor as follows: "Da una parte di detto Giardino vi sono le stanze del Gran Signore quando stà con le donne, dove si và per corridori alti, con chiave alle porte, che solo egli tiene, ò il capo di Eunuchi, che assiste alla custodia della porta di esse donne." For the name "Gold Path" (*altun yol* or *altun sokak),* see TSA, D 474, fol. 2v; D 2233, fols. 2v, 9v; D 9916 (no. 56), fol. 5v; D 9916 (no. 1), fol. 2r, D 9916 (no. 19), fol. 3v. It is called the "Long Path" (*rāh-i dırāz, rāh-i tavīl,* or *uzun yol)* or "Sultan's Path" (*rāh-i pādişāhī* or *ṣoḳāḳ-i ḥażret-i pādişāh)* in BA, MM 403, fols. 51, 96, 100, 103, 130; KK 7104, fols. 20v, 22v; MM 861, fol. 89, 107; MM 1947, fol. 15; MM 2126, fol. 118; MM 1501, fol. 21; TSA, D 4467, fol. 3r.

84 "Babası am delisi, oğlu av delisi," Bobovi, *Mémoires,* fol. 120.

85 Selaniki, *Tarih.* MS. Gökbilgin, fol. 53r. See also Âli, *Künh,* fol. 497v.

86 Salomone, pp. 28–29.

87 Bon, pp. 101–2; Sandys, p. 74; P. della Valle, p. 37; Hierosolimitano, *Vera relatione,* p. 28; Courmenin, pp. 114–15. For the banishment of women, see La Croix, *Serrail,* fol. 187; Bon, p. 102; Uluçay, *Padişahların Kadınları,* pp. 43–44, 48–49.

88 Moryson, p. 99.

89 "İçerü dār'üs-sa‹ādede vāḳī‹ olan yeñi ḥammām binā'sına ḫalel geldi tecdīde muḥtāc oldı," Selaniki, *Tarih.* MS. Gökbilgin, fol. 74v.

90 For the sultan's stay in Üsküdar, see ibid., fols. 77v–79v. For his stay in the Old Palace, see ibid., fols. 88r, 90r. "Sarāy-i ‹āmirede müceddeden ābād olınacaḳ ḥammām ve oṭa-i ḫāṣṣa itmām bulınca," ibid., fols. 93r–v.

91 "Sarāy-i ‹āmirede müceddeden binā'sı fermān olınan mükellef ve müẕehheb ḳāşī oṭa ve ḥammām-i laṭīf kemāl-i leṭāfetde yapılub itmām buldı," ibid., fol. 74v.

92 For the faulty attribution of this building of the architect Davud to Sinan, see Akdağ, p. 164; Köseoğlu, p. 13; Erkins, *Topkapı Sarayı Müzesi,* p. 58; T. Öz, *Guide to the Museum,* p. 162. Kuran attributes it to Süleyman I, and the adjacent royal bath to Selim II; Kuran, "Palace of the Sultans," p. 115.

93 BA, MD 73, no. 118.

94 BA, MD 73, no. 117.

95 Selaniki, *Tarih.* MS. Gökbilgin, fol. 88r; Selaniki, *Tarih,* p. 193; Bobovi, *Mémoires,* fol. 240; La Croix, *Serrail,* fol. 316.

96 For the repair inscriptions, see Şeref, pp. 585–86. "Ḳubbe-i ḥammāmān ve oda-i ḫāṣṣ-i enderūn-i sarāy-i ‹āmire," BA, MM 908, fol. 45.

97 Eldem and Akozan, pp. 67–68, pls. 107, 127–30.

98 La Croix, *Serrail,* fol. 316.

99 Hierosolimitano, *Vera relatione,* p. 76. For this ceremony, see also Üsküdari, 1:fol. 256r; TKS, E 12358, fol. 3r.

100 Âli, *Künh,* fol. 497v; Peçevi, 2:22–25.

101 Bon, p. 71. For the blindfolded pages, see Bobovi, *Mémoires,* fol. 192.

102 Flachat, pp. 199–200.

103 For descriptions of games popular in the harem, see Uluçay, *Harem II,* pp. 154–57; Şeref, p. 585; Durukan, pp. 58–60.

104 BA, MM 1947, fol. 23; MM 7370, fols. 9, 14.

105 For the inscriptions, see Şeref, p. 723.

106 The princes lived with their mothers until the age of six; then they were placed in separate quarters and assigned teachers: "Attacato all'appartamento delle donne vi sono le stanze, dove si allevano li figliuoli del Gran Signore cioè li maschi, perche le femine stanno con le madri, & li maschi, quando sono in età di sei anni, si levano da le madri, & si mettono all'altre stanze loro deputate, co'loro maestri, che li insegnano," Hierosolimitano, *Vera relatione,* pp. 33–34. Bon says that the princes lived with their mothers till the age of five or six and were then assigned a teacher, who was conducted every day by a black eunuch to a schoolroom in the harem, Bon, p. 92.

107 For Jewish women associated with the palace, see Bon, p. 76; La Croix, *Mémoires,* pp. 358–59.

108 La Croix, *Mémoires,* pp. 356–57, 360–62.

109 Quote from Bobovi translated in Fisher, p. 73.

110 La Croix, *Mémoires,* pp. 356–57, 360–62.

111 For this court, see Eldem and Akozan, pls. 145–46.

112 For the quarters of the *haseki,* see Hierosolimitano, *Vera relatione,* pp. 59–60; La Croix, *Serrail,* fols. 180, 193; Bobovi, *Mémoires,* fols. 245, 263, 37.

113 "Hanno li suoi refettorj e dormitorj lunghissimi, che capirebbono fino al numero di cento di esse; dormono sopra li sofà posti al lunga della stanza dall'una e l'altra parte, si che resta in essa una capacissima strada nel mezzo da poter camminare; li loro letti sono di schiavine e filzade, e per ogni dieci di giovani, dorme una vecchia; nella stanza vi stanno la notte diversi fanali accesi, pendenti dal cielo di essa, e così compartiti, che dappertutto si può comodamente vedere, e ciò per divertire il male, e per il bisogno che potesse occorrere; appresso detti dormitorj vi sono li bagni, le cucine, l'uso per la necessità, con abbondanza di fontane per il bisogno delle acque, e diverse stanze sopra essi dormitorj, dove si riducono a cucire e ove tengono li forzieri per custodire li loro vestimenti. Mangiano poi a camerata nelli refettorj sopra il piano delli sofà, e sopra corami di bulgaro, che servono per mantili, e vengono servite da altre donne secondo il loro bisogno, sì che non restano in mancamento di cosa alcuna; hanno il loro luochi da ridursi alle scuole per imparare a leggere ed a parlare turco, ed a cucire, a sonare, e con le loro maestre che sono donne di età vivono e stanno tutte il giorno con qualche ora di ricreazione, perchè non mancano giardini e piaceri quanti ne vogliono fra di esse," Bon, p. 71. For harem dormitories, see also La Croix, *Serrail,* fols. 180–84; La Croix, *Mémoires,* pp. 354–55; Tavernier, p. 253; Bobovi, *Mémoires,* fol. 264ff.

114 Dallam, pp. 74–75.

115 Uzunçarşılı, *Osmanlı Devletinin Saray Teşkilatı,* p. 149.

116 Bon, p. 92.

117 It is mentioned as the "school of princes" *(şehzādeler muʿallimḫānesi),* located near the "harem gate" *(dārü's-saʿāde ḳapusı)* in Selaniki (İpşirli, ed.), p. 410.

118 For the inscriptions, see Şeref, pp. 461–63, 465–78, 481. For these buildings, see Eldem and Akozan, p. 83, pls. 100–104, 149–55.

119 For repair inscriptions in the harem after the fire, see Şeref, pp. 461–65, 478, 481, 523, 593, 723. For the fire and the rebuilding of wooden structures in masonry, see Silahdar, 1:384, 390; Hezarfen, *Telhis,* fols. 14v–15r; La Croix, *Serrail,* fol. 17.

120 BA, MM 908.

121 These are generally accepted to be the oldest structures in the harem; Ayverdi, *Fatih Devri Mimarisi,* p. 301; Goodwin, p. 135; Eldem and Akozan, pp. 81–82, pls. 19–21; Anhegger-Eyüboğlu, "Fatih Devrinde," pp. 26–27.

122 For inscriptions stressing the view-commanding nature of royal chambers in the harem, see Şeref, pp. 592–93, 655–56. The inscriptions of Ahmed I's pavilion are cited in Rogers, *Topkapı Saray Museum,* pp. 33–34.

123 La Croix, *Serrail,* fols. 184–87.

Chapter 9

1 Hierosolimitano, *Vera relatione,* p. 32.

2 Bidlisi, *Tercüme-i Heşt Bihişt,* fol. 52b.

3 Cited in Andrews, pp. 150–58.

4 For an interpretation of the garden in Ottoman poetry, see ibid.

5 Sultan Süleyman used to watch the exercises of pages in the garden from a gallery "par quelques galleries les peut voir sans etre veu," Postel, pt. 3, pp. 10–11. For later sultans watching sports activities on the lower garden platform from the raised pavilions, see Courmenin, p. 172; Cevri, pp. 290–91. For the inscription on the stone throne, see Şeref, p. 420. A repair document from 1089 (1678–79) refers to "the wrestling field facing the Baghdad Kiosk" *(Bāġdād ḳaṣrı muḳābelesinde güreş meydānı),* BA, fol. 39.

6 For the hypothetical seven-towered inner fortress, see Atasoy, "Matrakçı's Representation," pp. 93–101; Örs, "History of the Topkapı Palace," pp. 6–18; Davis, p. 4; Anhegger-Eyüboğlu, "Fatih Devrinde," pp. 27–28; Tansuğ, pp. 135–69; Raby, "El Gran Turco," pp. 300–301; Çığ, "Fatih Topkapı," pp. 17–27. Confusing the Topkapı Palace with the fortress of Yedikule, Kemal Çığ refers to a passage from Tursun Beg's history that mentions a "citadel" *(aḥmedek)* built by Mehmed II with fortified towers. This citadel is not even mentioned in the chapter describing the New Palace; it could only have been Yedikule, which the historian Kemalpaşazade does identify as an *aḥmedek* (Çığ, "Fatih Topkapı," p. 24; Tursun, text fol. 60b; Kemalpaşazade, 1:99, 2:101).

7 For a hypothetical reconstruction of this towered enclosure, see Ayverdi, *Fatih Devri Mimarisi,* pp. 296, 300; Eldem and Akozan, pp. 78–79, pl. 92. Although Ayverdi argued in 1953 that the crenellated wall turned south at the Hekimbaşı Tower, his hypothetical reconstruction

plan from 1974 shows this wall extending beyond the tower, up to the Mecidiye Kiosk, where it turns south to meet the Inner Treasury, Ayverdi, *Osmanlı Mimarisinde Fatih Devri,* p. 727. For the only remaining tower, which functioned later as a royal pharmacy, inhabited by the head physician, if the sultan was ill, see Atâ, 1:174ff, 193–94; T. Öz, *Guide to the Museum,* p. 124; Davis, p. 174.

8 Atasoy has counted seven towers on Matrakçı's miniature, Atasoy, *Matrakçı's Representation,* pp. 93–101. When her list of possible locations in which these towers formerly stood is plotted on a plan, they fail to show a rational relationship to one another. Moreover, not all of them could have been remains of towers. The hypothesis that the fountained loggia of the Inner Treasury was formerly the base of a tower is based on the assumption that such an open balcony would necessarily contradict the military spirit of Mehmed II's defensive castle. The "defensive loopholes" of the basement of this loggia are in fact the narrow slits commonly used in minarets for admitting light.

9 Bidlisi, *Hasht Behisht,* fol. 5.

10 Poems cited as evidence for the existence of an inner citadel can be dismissed because they all refer to the outer fortified enclosure known as the Imperial Fortress, which was completed in 1478. (The poem of Hamidi that describes a fortress resembling the "heavenly castle of the seven heavens" ["ḥiṣn-i sipihr-i haft paykar"], Hamidi, pp. 212–13, 336, is cited in Atâ, 5:190–94; Atasoy, *Matrakçı's Representation,* pp. 94–95; Çığ, "Fatih Topkapı," pp. 22, 24.) The inner core of the palace was completed by around 1465, when Kritovoulos described its towers as follows: "In it he had towers built of unusual height and beauty and grandeur, and apartments for men and others for women, and bedrooms and lounging rooms and sleeping quarters, and very many other fine rooms. There were also various out-buildings and vestibules and halls and porticoes and gateways and porches, and bakeshops and baths of noble design," Kritovoulos, p. 207.

11 The crenellated wall of the hanging garden is seen on several drawings (Pls. 25c, 27, 29, 32c). The nineteenth-century traveler Edward Clarke (p. 9) mentions the "walls with turrets." For Abdülhamid II's destruction of this crenellated wall, see Şeref, p. 420; Ayverdi, *Fatih Devri Mimarisi,* p. 300. Cannons placed in the outer garden in front of this wall were fired to announce religious holidays and births of princes and princesses, Esad, p. 112.

12 Angiolello, *Inedito manoscritto,* p. 24.

13 BA, KK 7097, fols. 58, 99; MM 17884, fols. 52–53.

14 The terrace is mentioned in the sources as the "marble terrace" *(ṣoffa-i mermer),* "imperial terrace" *(ṣoffa-i ḫāṣṣa, ṣoffa-i hümāyūn),* "terrace of the Privy Chamber" *(ṣoffa-i oda-i ḫāṣṣa),* or the "large terrace" *(büyük ṣoffa, kebīr ṣoffa);* see BA, MM 511, fols. 3–6, 23, 26, 39, 44, 48; MM 403, fol. 9; KK 7097, fols. 58, 99; MM 17884, fol. 53; MM 858, fols. 69–71; MM 672, fol. 73; MM 648, fol. 77; MM 847, fol. 41; TSA, D 10749, fol. 16r; D 12360, no. 4, fol. 1r; D 12360, no. 6, fol. 1r; D 2157, fol. 4r; E 12359, no. 4, fol. 40v; Atâ, 1:313; Bostanzade, fols. 22r–23v.

15 "Nev-sāḫten-i ḳaṣr-i muḫteriḳ," see BA, MM 2097, fols. 9–13.

16 For a detailed description of these seventeenth-century kiosks, see Eldem, 1:287–318. Their date of construction is recorded in Cevri, p. 287; Topçular Katibi, fols. 229v–303r; Karaçelebizade, p. 605; Naima, 3:398, 447–48. For their inscriptions, see Şeref, pp. 410–14.

17 The inscription is published in Şeref, p. 414. For a description of this canopy, see Eldem, *Köşkler,* 1:329–34. An account book of 1050 (1640) refers to the construction of the "gilded dome of the noble throne for breaking the fast, near the Privy Chamber" *(Becihet-i nev-sāḫten-i ḳubbe-i taḫt-i şerīf-i ifṭāriyye-i muṭallā der nezd-i oda-i ḫāṣṣ)* and lists expenses of new curtains for the "ḳaṣr-i ifṭāriyye," BA, MM 373, fols. 63, 42. It is mentioned as "ḳaṣr-i ifṭār" in Üsküdari, 1:fols. 252v–53r.

18 The chronogram is published in Şeref, pp. 415–16.

19 For the discovered remains of the earlier pool, which was larger than the present one, see Eldem and Akozan, pls. 77, 85. The pool is referred to as the "large pool" *(ḥavż-i büzürg, büyük ḥavż, ḥavż-i kebīr, kebīr ḥavż)* in the sources, BA, MM 511, fols. 4, 5, 39, 51; MM 861, fols. 106–7; MM 858, fol. 69; Atâ, 1:313; Naima, 3:398.

20 Chishull, p. 46; cited in Miller, *Beyond the Sublime Porte,* p. 223. For another description of the same area, see Tavernier, pp. 218–23.

21 Translation from Fisher, pp. 60–61.

22 "Similmente in questo Serraglio é una stanza fatta tutta quanta di vetri bianchi quadrati, con verghe di stagno commesse, & legate insieme, & é in guisa di cupola ritonda, che vedendola di lontano rende sembianza d'un padiglione disteso; sopra la quale gia anticamente passava una acqua con mirabile artificio, che giu spargendosi per la cupola, discendeva nel giardino, dove andava à starsi sovente il Re ne i tempi della State per dormirsi il giorno al fresco, al dolce mormorio delle risonanti acque; ma al presente, percio che sono rotti quei condotti; l'acqua altrove s'è rivolta." Menavino, p. 91. Later travelers plagiarize this passage; see Nicolay, p. 66; Vigenère, p. 14. Nicolay writes that the crystal pavilion was built by Bayezid II, although Menavino's original passage does not specify the builder.

23 Raby speculates that Mehmed II's invitation to a "christallini" maker from Venice in 1477 might have been related to the construction of the crystal pavilion, Raby, "El Gran Turco," p. 297. For the sultan's invitation, see Suriano, p. 94: "Quando la Signoria fece pace con lui del mille quatrocento settanta sette, prègolla che li mandasse uno, che li facesse christallini, un'altro che li facesse horioli da sonare, e uno buono dipintore." Kurz hypothesizes that the *christallini* maker must have been an expert craftsman, able to grind spectacles, Kurz, pp. 20–21.

24 "In der höhe rundlecht gebawet / und von schönem Chris-

tallinen Gläsern ganss durchsichtig," Heberer, p. 378. Also see Lubenau, 1:160.

25 "In mezzo di detti giardini vi sono molte stanze ben lavorate: ma una in particolare di sei facciate sopra sei grosse colonne, dove trà l'una colonna, e l'altra ci sono tavole di Christallo di montagna: tanto bene incastrate una con l'altra, che alla vista pare tutto un pezzo, & di sopra ha la cupola, con lanterna coperta di piombo, & di sotto è tutta lastricata d'argento indorato lavorato alla zemina, e la lanterna ha le colonne pur di christallo di montagna lavorato, & il resto del coperto di essa stanza è fatto di pezzi di corallo maravigliosamente congiunti, che allo splendor del Sole traspare in modo che, abaglia la vista," Hierosolimitano, *Vera relatione,* pp. 35–36.

26 "Il y a en a un entre les autres qui est basty sur le bord d'un petit estang, l'etage d'en-bas est tout voûté, & enrichi d'incrustations de marbre de plusieurs couleurs. Au dessus il y a une salle dont le haut est soustenu sur huict colomnes de marbre; le reste est tout à iour, n'estant fermé que par des vitres de christal tres-fin. A l'entour de la salle, il y a un grand Coridor de cinq pieds en saillie, garny de balustrades de marbre, duquel l'on voit sortir trente-deux iets d'eau claire, qui tombans dans cet estang rendent un agreable murmure. Le plancher de cette salle, est enrichy de nacques de perle, & de pierres fines, à compartimens: le haut est revestu de lames d'argent doré, & tellement remply de turquoises, de rubis, & d'autres pierres precieuses, qu'il ne se peut rien voir le plus esclatant." It was here that the sultan entertained himself with women; nearby was an even more lavish kiosk, (possibly the Baghdad Kiosk's predecessor): "C'est en ce lieu, où le grand Seigneur se divertit souvent en Esté avec ses femmes, & d'où il prend plaisir à les voir baigner dans cet estang. De cette salle, l'on entre dans une chambre encore plus richement parée, où l'on voit une grande quantité de perles, & de diamans, qu'il semble que l'on y ait amassé les dépoüilles de toutes les Provinces que les Othomans ont subiugées," Courmenin, p. 163.

27 Bon (pp. 63–64) describes the pool as a square lake surrounded by a marble-paved border, with thirty jets of water; see note 168, chapter 7.

28 For the sultan's siestas, see Menavino, p. 91. Angiolello, *Inedito manoscritto,* pp. 23–24: "Il Palazo, dove stanzia il Gran Turco [i.e., the Privy Chamber], il qual Palazo la maggior parte è lavorato in volto, et ha molte camere, et stanze de estate, et da inverno."

29 "Dans le jardin est un vivier et une chambrette faite en forme de lanterne, toute en verre; quand la sultane s'y tient, elle voit par tout le jardin sans être vue de personne," Fresne-Canaye, p. 90.

30 "Emr ḳıldı yapıla bir ḳaṣr-i ʿālī ve bülend / Tāze bir ṭarz-i muferriḥ olmaya resm-i ḳadīm," (He ordered the making of a lofty and tall pavilion / In a rejoicing new style that should not be in the old mode), cited in Şeref, pp. 415–16. For the poems and chronograms, see Cevri, pp. 290–91, 293–96; cited in Evliya, 1:268.

31 Eldem, *Köşkler,* 1:319–28.

32 The two dependent chambers are identified in repair documents as the "bath of the Circumcision Room" *(sünnet odası ḥammāmı* or *ḫitān oṭası ḥammāmı),* and the "toilet of the Circumcision Room" *(ḫitān oṭası ḥelāsı),* TSA, D 9916, no. 6, fol. 2v; E 12359, no. 2, fol. 20r; D 9916, no. 46, fol. 2r; D 9916, no. 50, fol. 4v; D 9916, no. 54, fol. 6r. According to later royal journals, sultans performed ritual ablutions and were shaved at the small bath of the Circumcision Room, TSA, D 10749, fols. 8v, 31v; E 12359, no. 2, fol. 20r; E 12359, no. 4, fol. 35r; D 10749, fols. 8v, 16r, 32v; Salahi, fol. 13v.

33 For the dating of Selim's mosque to 927–33 (1521–27), see Bostan, fols. 13v, 99v; Mehmed Aşık, fol. 365r.

34 For the seventeenth-century rebuilding of the marble terrace, see Eldem and Akozan, pp. 78, 77–79, 85–86. For the tower replaced by Abdülhamid I's pavilion, see ibid., p. 81.

35 Dallam, pp. 62–63.

36 Published in Rosedale, p. 27.

37 Denny, *Ceramics of the Mosque of Rüstem Pasha,* pp. 112–28. For the *Sünnet Odası* (Circumcision Room) tiles, see Erdmann, pp. 144–53.

38 Eldem and Akozan, pp. 67, 78.

39 Mahir, pp. 113–31. For these tiles see Necipoğlu-Kafadar, "From International Timurid to Ottoman." Denny believes that the *ch'i-lin* tiles were originally created for Süleyman I's Chamber of Petitions in the 1550s or 1560s, but as we have already seen, tiles for that building were produced in 1527–28, Denny, *Ceramics of the Mosque of Rüstem Pasha,* pp. 122, 125, 139–42.

40 BA, KK 7097, fol. 33. The ceramicist Usta Ali appears in two wage registers of 932 (1525–26) as the highest paid assistant of the chief ceramicist, Habib, from Tabriz, whose lesser assistants were recruits from Bosnia, Trebizond, Skoplje, Presba, Nevrekop, and Varna, TSA, D 9706, no. 2, D 9706, no. 5. For sources on Persian artists brought by Selim I to Istanbul, and a German translation of one of these wage registers, see R. Anhegger, pp. 180–85. Süleyman I's account books of 1527–28 cite the repairs to a ceramics atelier located in Istanbul, where tiles were made for the palace and other buildings, BA, MM 17884, fols. 61, 70; KK 7097, fol. 58. An inventory of Istanbul's water channels, prepared in 976 (1568–69), shows that the "ceramics atelier" *(kāşīḫāne)* was at Tekfursaray, see Çeçen, p. 104. For tiles produced in this atelier, see Necipoğlu-Kafadar, "From International Timurid to Ottoman."

41 Contemporary buildings where *cuerda seca* tiles appear are Selim I's royal mosque and mausoleum in Istanbul (1521–27), the Kasım Pasha Mosque in Bozüyük (1528–29), and scattered examples at the Circumcision Room, the Chamber of Petitions, and the Baghdad and Revan kiosks, which date from Süleyman I's restorations between 1526 and 1528. Underglaze-painted blue, white, and

turquoise tiles similar to those assembled on the facades of the Privy Chamber and the Circumcision Room are seen in the mausoleum of Süleyman I's vizier, Çoban Mustafa Pasha, at Gebze (d. ca. 1528–29). For a more detailed discussion of these tiles, attributable to Süleyman's royal ceramics atelier in Istanbul, see Necipoğlu-Kafadar, "From International Timurid to Ottoman."

42 For the inscription, see Şeref, p. 419; Davis, pp. 177–79.

43 For this building, see Eldem, *Köşkler,* 1:88–89, 92. It may have been the "tent pavilion," *(çadır köşki, çadır ḳaṣrı, ḳaṣr-i ḫayme)* mentioned in the sources, BA, MM 17887, fol. 5v; TSA, Arşivi, E 12359, no. 1, fol. 2r, 6v; D 2233, fol. 11r; D 9916, no. 42, fol. 4v; D 9916, no. 45, fol. 3v; D 10749, fol. 37r; D 2157, fol. 4r; Bostanzade, fols. 25v–26r. Murad IV's extensive repairs in 1048 (1638–39) at the *ḳaṣr-i çādır, ḳaṣr-i ḫayme* are recorded in BA, KK 7104, fols. 20r–21v. Atâ attributes the kiosk to Mehmed IV (1648–87), Atâ 1:314. The domed seventeenth-century pavilion is seen just in front of the Treasury-Bath complex in Scarella's drawing of 1686 (Pl. 31b); see also Figs. 114a,b for the cross-shaped pavilion at the corner of the terrace.

44 Atâ, 1:313, 298–99; Flachat, pp. 182–83. For the corps of gardeners, see also T. Öz, *Guide to the Museum,* pp. 119–20.

45 TSA, D 9636, fol. 1v.

46 "Nev-sāḫten-i çārṭāḳhā-i bahār-i yāsemenlik der nezd-i ṣoffa-i dārü's-saʿāde der bāġçe-i ḫāṣṣa," BA, MM 511, fols. 3, 26.

47 "Puşīden-i şecere-i turunc ve limon der bāġçe-i ḫāṣṣa ve der pīş-i oda-i ḫāṣṣa," BA, MM 672, fol. 71. For oranges, see also MM 511, fols. 5, 20, 52.

48 "Çārṭāḳhā-i aṣmahā" or "çarṭāḳhā-i bāġ-i engür," BA, MM 383, fol. 73; MM 945, fol. 36; MM 443, fol. 44; MM 424, fol. 39; MM 2126, fol. 105.

49 Dallam, p. 62.

50 Flachat, pp. 183–84.

51 Flachat, pp. 182–83.

52 Tavernier, p. 57.

53 Şeref, p. 285.

54 For the cannons, see Angiolello, *Inedito manoscritto,* p. 29. According to the chronicle of Malipiero, in 1473 a wall twenty paces long was erected and furnished with fourteen bombards at Seraglio Point (then called St. Dimitri), in anticipation of a sea attack from Venice, while Mehmed II was fighting in the East; see Malipiero, p. 87; cited in Babinger, *Mehmed,* pp. 317–18.

55 Menavino, pp. 91–92.

56 Bidlisi, *Tercüme-i Heşt Bihişt,* fol. 53v.

57 Cafer Çelebi, p. 75; Bidlisi, *Tercüme-i Heşt Bihişt,* fol. 53v.

58 Bidlisi, *Tercüme-i Heşt Bihişt,* fols. 52v–53v.

59 Tursun, text fols. 58b–59a.

60 Kemalpaşazade, 1:103, 2:104; Cafer Çelebi, p. 75; Hamidi, p. 130. For similar paradisal imagery, see Kabuli, pp. 51–55.

61 Kritovoulos, p. 208.

62 Angiolello, *Inedito manoscritto,* pp. 24–25.

63 Harff, *Pilgerfahrt,* p. 241; Harff, *Pilgrimage,* p. 206.

64 Menavino, pp. 97–98. For the nine groups of gardeners, see La Croix, *Mémoires,* p. 146; Hezarfen, *Telhis,* fol. 25r. Besides the main dormitory of gardeners, attached to the chief gardener's residence, were numerous smaller ones along the walls; "Le stanze, li bagni, e le cucine loro, sono intorno le mura del serraglio compartite a camerate," Bon, 79.

65 BA, MM 17884, fol. 38; KK 7097, fol. 38.

66 Lokman, *Hünername,* 2:fols. 149v–50r.

67 BA, MD 30, no. 52.

68 BA, MD 28, no. 1028.

69 Published in A. Refik, *Hicrî On Birinci Asırda İstanbul Hayatı,* p. 9, no. 17.

70 BA, MD 36, no. 355, no. 356. The second document is published in A. Refik, *Hicrî On Birinci Asırda İstanbul Hayatı,* p. 6, no. 14.

71 BA, MD 69, no. 177; published in A. Refik, *Hicrî On Birinci Asırda İstanbul Hayatı,* p. 3, no. 6.

72 La Croix, *Mémoires,* p. 146. For the periodic renewal of the red paint on the railings and pergolas, see BA, MM 753, fol. 12; KK 7104, fol. 21r; KK 7097, fol. 24; MM 511, fol. 29; MM 3780, fols. 100, 103, 125, 147; MM 403, fols. 58, 61; MM 1250, fol. 16; MM 424, fol. 40.

73 Fresne-Canaye, pp. 87–88.

74 Wratislaw, pp. 74–75.

75 Sandys, p. 113.

76 Tavernier (pp. 263–67) notes that besides "petits jardins à fleurs en divers appartemens," the rest of the garden was planted with vegetable plots. See also Courmenin, p. 167.

77 Menavino, p. 98. For the inventory of 910 (1505), see T. Öz, *Topkapı Sarayı Müzesi Arşivi Kılavuzu,* facsimile, no. 21, fol. 16.

78 For the animal keeps, see Angiolello, *Inedito manoscritto,* pp. 24–25.

79 TSA, D 9636. Also mentioned in BA, MM 424, fol. 41; MM 699, fol. 15; MM 2126, fols. 105, 110; KK 7104, fol. 23r; MM 403, fol. 121; KK 7097, fols. 34, 100; MM 17884, fols. 54, 56.

80 For the Tokat Garden along the Bosphorus, see Evliya, 1:464; Eremya, p. 51. The hunting grounds of the Old Palace are mentioned in Angiolello, *Inedito manoscritto,* p. 25.

81 BA, MM 672, fol. 72; MM 424, fol. 41.

82 Lokman, *Hünername,* 1:fols. 188v–89r.

83 Bernardo, p. 352.

84 Courmenin, p. 175.

85 Şeref, p. 291; Atâ, 1:303.

86 The aviary is mentioned in the sources as *(kuşḫāne, kuşḫāne-i mīrī, kuşḫāne der bāġçe-i ḫāṣṣa, murġḫāne, murġḫāne-i mīrī, murġḫāne der bāġçe-i ḫāṣṣa),* see TSA, D 9636; D 9916, no. 46, fol. 3v; D 9916, no. 53, fol. 1v; BA, MM 511, fols. 4–5, 21, 34, 47; MM 487, fol. 63; KK 7097, fol. 100; MM 17884, fol. 55; MM 5549, fol. 9; MM 1947, fol. 27; Üsküdari, 2:fol. 123r.

87 Atâ, 1:304–5.

88 Angiolello, *Inedito manoscritto,* p. 21.
89 Eremya, p. 5. For the destroyed Church of St. Menas, located near the Byzantine acropolis, see Müller-Wiener, p. 495.
90 İnciciyan, p. 58.
91 Chishull, p. 46.
92 "Pools of the aviary," (*ḥavżhā-yi kuşḫāne),* BA, MM 5549, fol. 9; MM 1947, fol. 27. Angiolello, *Inedito manoscritto,* pp. 24–25.
93 Gyllius, p. 40.
94 "Meremmet-kerden-i balıkḫāne-i ṭalyān-i mīrī ve nevsāḫten-i nerdüban-i ḳulle-i mezbūre ve iskele-i pādişāh," BA, MM 511, fols. 4, 40. See also MM 17884, fol. 55; Üsküdari, 2:fol. 123r.
95 It is referred to as the "new pavilion near the fishgarth of the imperial garden" (*ḳaṣr-i cedīd der nezd-i ṭalyān-i bāġçe-i ḫāṣṣa),* BA, MM 397, fol. 42.
96 Eremya, p. 5.
97 BA, MM 5549, fols. 7–8; MM 1947, fol. 27; Cevdet 2351, Cevdet 2636; TSA, D 5400; E 12359, no. 1, fol. 7v; D 9916, no. 16, fol. 3r; D 9916, no. 43, fol. 2v; Salahi, fol. 115v; Atâ, 1:314.
98 Şeref, p. 297. Flachat (p. 171) writes: "On apperçoit un peu plus bas, dans la même prairie, la porte qui conduit à une tour de bois bâtie dans la mer. C'est-là qu'on enferme les visirs lorsqu'on les dépose, jusqu'au moment qu'ils partent pour se rendre au lieu de leur exil."
99 "Sedd üzri taḫt-i hümāyūn," "abdest odası," "ḳaṣra muṭṭaṣıl saġīr ṣoffa," "balıkḫānede vāḳiʿ paşa odası," TSA, D 5400.
100 Atâ, 1:305.
101 Lokman, *Hünername,* 1:fol. 230v; Selaniki, *Tarih,* pp. 289, 291.
102 The inscription is recorded in Şeref, p. 296. For this area, see Demangel and Mamboury; Atâ, 1:314; Şeref, pp. 291–99.
103 BA, MM 373, fol. 53.
104 BA, MM 424, fol. 40; MM 699, fol. 15.
105 Tavernier, p. 69.
106 For kiosks in this area, see Şeref, p. 291; Atâ, 1:303. A kiosk built for Murad IV is mentioned in an account book of 1050 (1640–41) as the "new kiosk at the cavalry maidan" (*ḳaṣr-i cedīd der meydān-i cündiyān).* Another one, known as the "Gülḫāne Ḳaṣrı" (Rosegarden Kiosk), is frequently cited in eighteenth- and nineteenth-century sources. An account book of 1215 (1800) lists the following kiosks near the maidan: Gülḫāne, Murādiyye, İncüli, or Pearl Kiosk, and İsḥāḳiyye, BA, MM 373, fol. 53; TSA, D 1098, fols. 50v–51r; D 10749, fol. 14v; D 9916, no. 4, fol. 2v; D 5400; D 9916, no. 4; D 9916, no. 16.
107 Lokman, *Hünername,* 1:fol. 230v.
108 For polo games, see Flachat, 1:210–12. For various activities, see Ömer Efendi, fols. 2r, 4v, 5v, 6r, 7r, 7v, 9v, 10v, 11r, 11v, 12v, 13v, 15r; Salahi, fols. 15r, 22r, 34v, 43v, 53v, 67r.
109 For the term "Sand Maidan," see TSA, D 9916, no. 4, fol. 2r. Sources list expenses for sand to be laid over garden paths and the two maidans amounting to 995 to 1200 boatloads, BA, Cevdet 3323, 4175, 4193, 7473, 7885.
110 For the term "meadow," see BA, MM 511, fols. 4, 43. This area is described as "vastes prairies, & des jardins immenses remplis d'arbres & de fleurs" in Flachat, pp. 170–71. For the gardeners serving this area, see Atâ, 1:302–5. Atâ writes that the Okra and Cabbage groups were instituted after Timur's defeat of the Ottomans, on the model of the blue and green factions of Byzantium; ibid., 1:31, 304.
111 An account book of 988 (1580) mentions "the imperial copper depot in the royal garden" (*baḳırḫāne-i mīrī der bāġçe-i ḫāṣṣa).* A repair document of 1095 (1683–84) indicates that this copper cistern was located along the path that descends from the first court to the Marmara shore, BA, MM 511, fols. 4, 38; MM 699, fol. 15. Üsküdari writes that this depot's copper, which came from Kastamonu, was used for casting cannons and minting coins. He describes the location of this "copper cistern built in the ancient days" (*ḳadīmü'l-eyyāmda binā' olunmış bakır maḫzeni)* as past the Pearl Kiosk, near the aviary (*ḳuşḫāne)* and fishgarth (*ṭalyān-i māhi-yi ḫāṣṣa ḳurbinde),* Üsküdari, 2:fols. 123r–v. For the tinning ateliers near the bakery and palace waterworks, at the east side of the first court, see Tezcan and Şeker. For the Ice Corps located near the bakery, see Eremya, p. 14; BA, Cevdet, 2026. For the cellars of the imperial kitchen and commisary, built by Sinan, see Sa'i, *Mimar Sinan,* pp. 48, 123.
112 Eremya, pp. 7–8. The tower is mentioned as *"ḳulle-i mezbeleciyān," "ḳulle-i mezbelekeşān,"* BA, MM 403, fol. 105. See also Atâ, 1:303; Şeref, p. 293.
113 Evliya, 1:514. Flachat (p. 172) writes: "C'est à peu près dans le même endroit [i.e., the fishing station] qu'est l'egoût d'où l'on jette dans la mer toutes les balayures du serrail. On ne s'attendroit pas que ce lieu fût affermé; il rend néanmoins 700 écus. Les immondices glissent rapidement sur de longs plateaux de bois biens unis, sans qu'il soit possible qu'elles puissent se disperser. De pêcheurs se mettent tous les jours dans l'eau; ils remplissent de ces immondices des especes de bassins de bois assez grands & profonds: à force de les mouvoir, il n'y reste plus que les choses de poids. Il leur arrive souvent d'y trouver des pierreries, des perles, de l'or & de l'argent, & mille petites bijouteries précieuses. Plusieurs de ces pêcheurs se sont promptement enrichis à ce métier pénible & difficile en hiver. Les Bostanchis les méprisent, & se contentent de l'affermer."
114 For these structures, see Atâ, 1:62; Şeref, p. 293; Demangel and Mamboury, pp. 8–10. The gardeners' hospital is mentioned in an account book of 988 (1580) as the "hospital of gardeners" (*bīmārḫāne-i ġılmānān-i bostānīyān, bīmārḫāne-i bostānīyān),* BA, MM 511, fols. 3, 30. İnciciyan refers to the gate of the sea wall in front of

this hospital as the "Gate of the Invalids" *(Hastalar Kapısı)*, İnciciyan, p. 27. Sixteenth-century account books also refer to a "bath at the gardeners' hospital" *(ḥammām-i bostānīyān-i bīmārḫāne, ḥammām-i bīmārḫāne-i bostānīyān)*, BA, MM 511, fols. 4, 42. An eighteenth-century repair document reveals that the hospital contained various rooms, a bath, a kitchen, and a laundry. The neighboring Corps of the Windmill featured a large dormitory, a room for the miller, a windmill, flour and wheat depots, a kitchen, and stables, TSA, E 385, no. 7; D 9916, no. 22; D 2956; BA, Cevdet 648. For the "rosewater distillery" *(gülābḫāne, gülābḫāne-i ḫāṣṣa, gülābḫāne-i mīrī,)* and the "bakery of the rosewater distillery" *(furun-i gülḫāne* or *furun-i gülābḫāne,)* see TSA, D 9636; BA, KK 7100, fol. 18r; MM 511, fols. 4, 21, 33.

115 Ayvansarayi, 1:242; see also Atâ, 1:314.

116 He refers to the building as the "green-tiled masjid near the Corps of Gardeners" *(yeşil kiremidli mescīd der ḳurb-i ocāḳ-i bostānīyān)*, Ayvansarayi, 1:241. For this mosque, frequently mentioned in later sources as *yeşil kiremidli mescīd* or *yeşil kiremidli cāmiʿ-i şerīf*, see Tezcan, "Sur-u Sultanî," p. 395; T Öz, "Topkapı Sarayı Müzesi Onarımları," p. 61; T. Öz, *Istanbul Camileri*, 1:156; Atâ, 1:125; TSA, D 9916, no. 16, fol. 2v.

117 For the dormitory, referred to as the "rooms of gardeners" *(bostāncılar odaları, odahā-i bostānīyān, odahā-i ġılmān-i bostān)*, see Lokman, *Hünername*, 1:fol. 230v; TSA, D 9636; MM 511, fol. 3; BA, KK 7097, fol. 100. Attached to it was the "room of the chief gardener" *(oda-i ser bostān, bostāncıbaşı ḥażretleriyle bostān oğlanlarınuñ odaları)*, BA, KK 7097, fol. 100. Its bath is frequently mentioned as the "bath of gardeners" *(bostāncılar ḥammāmı, ḥammām-i bostāncıyān, ḥammām-i odahā-i bostānīyān-i ḫāṣṣa)*, Atâ, 1:61, 293–94, 314; TSA, D 9636; BA, MM 5633, fol. 79; MM 648, fol. 87; MM 511, fols. 4, 40; MM 487, fol. 63. Sources also refer to "the kitchen of gardeners" *(maṭbāḫ-i bostānīyān)* and the "bakery of gardeners" *(furun-i bostāncıyān* or *furun-i bostānīyān-i ḫāṣṣa)*, BA, MM 648, fol. 88; MM 511, fols. 4, 32; BA, MM 858, fol. 74. For the prison see Flachat, pp. 209, 211. According to Ohsson this prison near the bakery of gardeners was called the "bakery" *(fouroun)*, Ohsson, 7:15–16. Eremya Çelebi and Abdi Pasha write that a vizier was imprisoned in the "chief gardener's gazebo" *(bostāncıbaşı çārdāġı)*. An account book of 1034–35 (1624–25) similarly refers to the prison as "chief gardener's gazebo" *(çārṭāḳ-i aġa-i bostānīyān)*, Eremya, pp. 12, 56; Abdi Pasha, fol. 7v; BA, MM 648, fol. 88.

118 For the chief gardener and gardeners in the fifteenth century see Leysizade, p. 43; Menavino, pp. 97–98.

119 "Vi si osserva di più una quasi diroccata fabrica di Chiesa, ne' volti della quale vi si vede ancora del Musaico, e serve al presente per habitatione de'sudetti Bustangi," Donato, 2:94.

120 "De là [i.e., the harem gate] on va par différentes alées aux appartements du Bostanchi Bachi ... à la Casoda [i.e., Privy Chamber], au vieux serrail, qui est décoré d'une belle collonade & d'une mosaique. Les uns prétendent que c'étoit le palais de Constantin; d'autres assurent avec assez de vraisemblance, que c'étoit un college fameux que les Empereurs honoroient d'une protection spéciale," Flachat, p. 210. For the church and convent of St. Demetrius, see Millingen, p. 249; Müller-Wiener, pp. 40, 495.

121 Leysizade, p. 43. For oarsmen, see also Atâ, 1:308; Hezarfen, *Telhis*, fols. 24v–25r.

122 TSA, D 9636; BA, MM 17884, fol. 56. In a letter dated June 1525, the Venetian bailo Pietro Bragadino writes that a beautiful galley was being built there for Süleyman I, Bragadino, "Sommario," in Sanuto, p. 268. Selaniki confirms that Süleyman I had a red galley made in a boathouse along the seashore of his palace and that his example was followed by Selim II and Murad III; Selaniki, *Tarih*, pp. 210–11.

123 For Melchior Lorichs, see Oberhummer, tafel 4. For the boathouse see also Geuffroy, p. 231; Gyllius, p. 40.

124 Şeref, p. 286. He records a now lost inscription that commemorated the repairs made by Selim III's mother to the Corps of the Boathouse, its bath, its kitchen, and gate.

125 BA, MM 17884, fol. 31. For Sinan's "imperial warehouse cellar, built at the royal garden's shore" *(ḫāṣṣ bāġçede yāluda binā' olan anbār-i ʿāmire maḫzeni, ḫāṣṣ bāġçe yālusında anbār-i ʿāmire)*, see Sa'i, *Mimar Sinan*, pp. 48, 122; Sa'i, *Tezkiretü'l-bünyan*, p. 43.

126 "Sarāy-i cedīd-i ʿāmirede deryā kenarında vāḳiʿ ḳayıḳḫāneler ḳurbinde bıçḳıḫāne ve meremmātçılar ve naḳḳāşlar ve zevraḳçılar kārḫāneleri," BA, MM 1947, fol. 44. Ayvansarayi (1:242) says that these ateliers were located just below the Green-Tiled Masjid, along the shore.

127 Eremya, p. 12. Atâ writes that the "Group of the Repair Warehouse" *(taʿmīrāt anbārı ṭaḳımı)* used to meet at the Shore Kiosk and the Kiosk of Basketmakers, both of which were located near their workshops. Among members of this group, constituting the Corps of Royal Architects, he counts the city commissioner *(şehr emīni)*, the chief architect *(miʿmār aġa)*, the superintendent of waterworks *(ṣu nāẓırı)*, the agha of Istanbul *(İstanbul aġası)*, the chief limeburner *(kireççibaşı)*, the warehouse director *(anbār müdīri)*, the first secretary of the warehouse *(anbār birinci kātibi)*, the chief architect *(sermiʿmār)*, the second architect *(miʿmār-i s̱ānī)*, and the director of repairs *(taʿmīrāt müdīri)*, Atâ, 1:290. For the Corps of Royal Architects, see Turan, pp. 157–202.

128 For the imperial warehouse of the first court, see chapter 2.

129 Fresne-Canaye, p. 129.

130 Eremya, pp. 8–9; Atâ, 1:304; Hierosolimitano, *Vera relatione*, p. 48.

131 Eremya, p. 9. See also İnciciyan, p. 28.

132 Maurand, p. 249.

133 Kemalpaşazade (1:475, 2:430–31) praises the fountains

and round pools *(müdevver ḥavżlar),* carved from single pieces of marble, that decorated the gardens here and there. For extant fountains in the palace garden dating back to Mehmed II's time, see Bilge, pp. 218–22. The fifteenth-century historian Kıvami mentions sarcophagi *(ṭabutlar)* made into fountains *(çeşme),* Kıvami, p. 23. For the Goth's Column, see Müller-Wiener, p. 53. Another column, that of Theodosius I, was preserved by Mehmed II in the garden of the Old Palace; it is shown on the Vavassore map and described by Angiolello, see Angiolello, *Inedito manoscritto,* p. 25. For this column see also Becatti, pp. 83–150, and Fig. 4.

134 La Croix, *Serrail,* fol. 37; Donato, 2:95: "In uno stradone subito sopra la colonna trovasi una cassa grande di pietra, che mostra esser servita per gorna d'acque, in cui è scolpito un segno circolare, con tre segni incrociati nel mezzo, che formano come i razzi di una ruota dentro al vacuo, in cima biforcati, e un'Angelo da una parte, che lo sostiene, non potendosi però sapere di chi fosse memoria."

Chapter 10

1 "Et attorno il detto Palazo vi è un giardino, il quale vien abrasciar tutti tre li cortivi sopradetti da una parte et dall'altra tanto quanto tien lo predetto castello. In Questo giardino vi sono alcune Chiesiole fatte in volto, et lo Gran Turco ne fece racconsciar una, la quale è lavorata di musaico, et in questo giardino vi sono tre Palazzi lontani un dall'altro circa un trar di mano, et sono fatti in diversi modi. Uno è fatto alla Persiana, lavorato al modo del paese Caraman, et è coperto di batudo; il secondo è fatto alla Turchesca; il terzo alla Greca, coperto di piombo," Angiolello, *Inedito manoscritto,* p. 24.

2 Tursun, text fols. 59a–b. These pavilions were located "between the fortress wall and the palace wall ... in the garden" *(ḳalʿanuñ sūrı ile sarāy dīvārınuñ arası ... bu bāġçe içinde),* that is, in the outer garden. Ayverdi and Akdağ identify the Ottoman pavilion as the Inner Treasury, while Örs and Ayverdi think it is the Privy Chamber, see Ayverdi, *Fatih Devri Mimarisi,* p. 324; Ayverdi, *Osmanlı Mimarisinde Fatih Devri,* pp. 715–16; Akdağ, p. 134; Örs, "History of the Topkapı Palace," p. 7; Eldem and Akozan, p. 74. Tursun's passage, however, makes it clear that it was located in the outer garden, and not in the third court.

3 For Mehmed's portraits and medals, see Thuasne, pp. 46, 52, 57–59; Karabacek, pp. 1–64; Andaloro, pp. 185–212; Raby, "Sultan of Paradox," pp. 4–5; Raby, "Pride and Prejudice," passim.

4 Raby, "El Gran Turco," p. 298; Raby, "Sultan of Paradox," pp. 4–5. For the invitations, see Babinger, *Mehmed,* pp. 386–87; Dei, p. 176.

5 For Bellini's alleged role in painting some rooms, see chapters 1 and 7. For the invasion of Otranto, see Babinger, *Mehmed,* pp. 390–92, 394–95.

6 For discussions of the Çinili Köşk, see Eldem, *Köşkler,* 1:61–79; Goodwin, pp. 137–38; Ayverdi, *Osmanlı Mimarisinde Fatih Devri,* pp. 736–55; Akdağ, pp. 56–63.

7 For the sultan's admiration of the Acropolis in Athens, see Kritovoulos, pp. 136–37; Chalkokondyles, p. 632, cited in chapter 1.

8 For the gardeners' dormitory, see chapter 9, Menavino, pp. 90–91; Angiolello, *Inedito manoscritto,* p. 24. Some scholars have wrongly argued that the cloister mentioned by Menavino was converted into a stable by the sixteenth century, Miller, *Beyond the Sublime Porte,* pp. 40–42, 201; Raby, "El Gran Turco," p. 297. D'Aramon, the French ambassador to the Ottoman court from 1547 to 1553, does mention a stable that occupied one of the former dependencies of Hagia Sophia, but it was located in a cloister outside the palace walls: "D'une partie des despendances de cet ediffice, le Grand Seigneur a fait estables pour ses escuries, pour ce qu'il est fort voisin et prèz de son serail, et de ladicte eglise," Chesneau, p. 27. That stable is seen in the *Nuremberg Chronicle* woodcut (Pl. 24), across from the Gate of Stables; the cloister mentioned by Menavino was located near Seraglio Point. For the church and convent of St. Demetrius, see Müller-Wiener, pp. 40, 495.

9 Angiolello, *Inedito manoscritto,* p. 24; Tursun, text fols. 58a, 59a–b; Menavino, p. 90.

10 For the fountain inscription, see Şeref, p. 284. Some repair documents refer to the kiosk as *ṣırça sarāy,* BA, MM 5633, fol. 79; Cevdet 7105, fol. 1v; TSA, D 8583, no. 1, fol. 1v. It is also called *sarāy-i ṣırça,* in BA, MM 6019, fol. 100; MM 858, fol. 72; or *ḳaṣr-i ṣırça,* BA, MM 3780, fol. 189.

11 Babinger, *Mehmed,* pp. 246, 467. On the resettlement of Karamanian artists from Konya and Laranda, see Saded-din, 1:512. Eldem writes that not only a foreign architect, but a whole group of foreign artisans, was responsible for the construction and decoration of this kiosk, Eldem, *Köşkler,* 1:69. The lost inscription is cited in Miller, *Beyond the Sublime Porte,* p. 33. For the extant foundation inscription in Persian that provides the date of completion, see Ayverdi, *Fatih Devri Mimarisi,* pp. 362–64. The chronograms composed for the inauguration of the pavilion are discussed in chapter 1.

12 Angiolello, *Inedito manoscritto,* p. 24. For Angiolello's years in the Karaman region, see Angiolello, *Historia Turchesca,* pp. 40, 42, 62–66; Olivato, p. 144; Babinger, *Mehmed,* pp. 329–31.

13 Şikari, pp. 197–98.

14 For descriptions of Uzun Hasan's pavilion by Josafa Barbaro (1474), see G. Barbaro and A. Contarini, pp. 52–55; and by an anonymous merchant in 1507, see C. Grey, *Travels,* pp. 173–77. Since some sources attribute the Hasht Behisht palace complex to Uzun Hasan's son Ya'qub, he may have completed its construction.

15 Tursun, text fol. 58a.

16 This document from the Topkapı Palace archives (E 3152) is published in Kırımlı, pp. 96–97, 106. Meinecke argues

that the tiles, which differ from Anatolian Seljuk examples, must have been produced by an atelier of wandering craftsmen from Turkestan or Tabriz, see Meinecke, *Fayencedekorationen,* 1:114–20. Eldem notes that the kiosk's architecture has little in common with the Anatolian Seljuk school and suggests that the influence was Central Asian, Eldem, *Köşkler,* 1:62, 68–69. Goodwin also sees a Timurid influence from Central Asia, Goodwin, pp. 137–38. On the basis of the Karaman connection, Raby argues that the origins of the kiosk may lie in the Anatolian Seljuk school, rather than in Timurid Central Asia (Raby, "El Gran Turco," p. 299), but the architecture of fifteenth-century Karaman was closely related to the international Timurid style.

17 For Kuşcı, see Babinger, *Mehmed,* pp. 491–92.

18 For Mehmed II's invitation to Jami, see Babinger, *Mehmed,* pp. 471–72. For the Turanian embassy, see Lokman, *Hünername,* 1:fols. 14v–15r.

19 For the inscription, see Şeref, p. 284. For the pool, see BA, MM 511, fols. 4, 5, 36, 48; MM 424, fol. 43. An account book of 1008–9 (1600–1601) records an extensive renovation in which the fireplace, wall paintings, brick pavements, water installations, and fountains of the *sırça sarāy* were restored, BA, MM 5633, fol. 79.

20 The fire on 26 Receb 1150 (20 November 1737) at the *sırça sarāy* is recorded in Salahi, fol. 157r.

21 For a comparison of their plans, see Eldem, *Köşkler,* 1:68–70.

22 For the original roof, see Eldem, *Köşkler,* 1:74, 79. The substance covering the roof is called "wattle and daub," *batudo,* by Angiolello, *Inedito manoscritto,* p. 24.

23 For the fire, see Salahi, fol. 157r. The repair document from 1739 (BA, Cevdet 7105) mentions the rebuilding of the roof of *sırça sarāy:* "rebuilt according to its old form" *(vaẓ'-i ḳadīmi üzre saḳfı müceddeden binā').*

24 For the inscription, see Ayverdi, *Fatih Devri Mimarisi,* pp. 362–64.

25 Ahmed Pasha, pp. 23–32. For other poems, see Kabuli, pp. 51–54; Hamidi, pp. 247–49 (cited in Atâ, 5:188–89); Hamidi, p. 130; Tacizade, p. 58.

26 "*Ṣadrda şāhāne bir taḫt*"; Cafer Çelebi, p. 76; see also BA, MM 3780, fol. 189, "noble throne of the tile palace," *(taḫt-i şerīf der ḳaṣr-i sırça).*

27 Cafer Çelebi, p. 76.

28 For the tradition of mural painting in Iran and Turan, see Babur, 1:48; B. Gray, "Tradition of Wall Painting," pp. 313–29. The paintings of Uzun Hasan's pavilion in Tabriz are described by an anonymous merchant in a 1507 text, see C. Grey, *Travels,* pp. 174–75. For Ambrogio Contarini's description of Uğurlu Mehmed's palace in Isfahan, see G. Barbaro and A. Contarini, p. 131.

29 Ahmed Pasha, p. 25; Kabuli, p. 52; Hamidi, pp. 131, 247–48.

30 Some scholars write that it was built for Bayezid II during İshak Pasha's second grand vizierate; Atâ, 1:303; Pakalın, *Osmanlı tarih deyimleri,* 2:83; Şeref, pp. 291, 294–95. But İshak Pasha's second term as grand vizier, 875–77 (1470–72), falls into Mehmed II's reign. According to Eldem, this kiosk was known both as the "Sultan Mehmed Köşkü" and the "İshakiye Köşkü," Eldem, *Köşkler,* 2:226.

31 "Ebü'l-Feth Mehmed Ḫān ḥażretleri ḳaṣrı ... çayır ḳaṣrı hümāyūnı ḳurbinde," BA, MM 1947, fols. 26–27.

32 TSA, D 9916, no. 16, fol. 2v.

33 BA, Cevdet Saray 2184, fol. 1v. This document confirms that the "Sulṭān Meḥmed ḳaṣrı" was located near the Pearl Kiosk ("incüli ḳaṣr").

34 The pavilion is mentioned as "Ebü'l-Feth Sulṭān Meḥmed ḳaṣrı," BA, KK 7125, fol. 8.

35 For the demolition of these kiosks, see Atâ, 1:303; Şeref, p. 291.

36 Hierosolimitano, *Vera relatione,* p. 41.

37 "Quand on sçait que le G.S. doit venir se promener, un grand nombre de Bostangis nettoyent promptement les allés où il passe d'ordinaire ... Toutes les fontaines des jardins ont leurs bassins de marbre de differentes couleurs. Proche de chacune il y a un petit échauffaut environné de balustres que l'on couvre de riches tapis & de carreaux de brocard quand le Sultan s'y vient promener, & ce n'est qu'alors qu'on on fait joüer les eaux dont il donne souvent le plaisir aux Princesses qui luy tiennent compagnie," Tavernier, pp. 263–67.

38 "Quando la Maestà Sua vuol star nelli giardini con le donne, per piacere, escono fuori delle porte del serraglio a marina dove vi sono alcuni andj e spazj di terreno, come una fondamenta larga sopra il mare; nè entrano, fino che non sia partita, perchè con le donne mai vi stanno altri uomini, che la persona reale e gli eunuchi negri: anzi, che se per qualche verso alcuno del serraglio facesse qualche prova in alcuna parte per voler veder le donne e che fosse scoperto o accusato, immediate sarebbe forse fatto morire: però quando si sà che il re sta con le donne nelli giardini, ogn'uno fugge più lontano che può, per stare in sicuro da ogni sospetto," Bon, pp. 79–80.

39 La Croix, *Serrail,* fols. 184–87.

40 Angiolello, *Inedito manoscritto,* p. 24; Hierosolimitano, *Vera relatione,* p. 41.

41 Lokman, *Hünername,* 1:fol. 219r.

42 Cited in Hammer *Geschichte,* 2:531–32; Gurlitt, *Baukunst,* 1:45. A waqfiyya of 1517 refers to Abdüsselam Beg as "superintendent of royal expenditures in Istanbul" *(emīn-i iḫrācāt-i sulṭāniyye be-Ḳostantiniyye),* Pakalın, *Maliye Teşkilatı Tarihi,* 1:139.

43 Lutfi, *Tarih,* p. 284.

44 Mottraye, 1:168; Saumery, 1:92. According to Mottraye it was built by a Genoese renegade for Süleyman I: "The Emperor who order'd it to be built, and who (if I mistake not) was *Soliman the Magnificent,* said to the *Renegado* after it was finished, this Roof resembles your Father's Hat, but I'm satisfied with it."

45 Lokman, *Hünername,* 1:fol. 216r.

46 "Sulṭān Selīm ḫān köşki," TSA, D 9636; Selaniki, *Tarih,* p.

299; "ḳaṣr-i Sulṭān Selīm ḫān der ḳurb-i bāb-i ṭob," BA, KK 7104, fols. 15r, 19r, 37v; MM 316, fol. 19; MM 7370, fol. 18; "ḳaṣr-i Sulṭān Selīm ‹an bīrūn-i bāb-i ṭob," BA, MM 1947, fol. 13; MM 7370, fol. 18; MM 316; fol. 19.

47 Clarke, p. 14. For the twelve columns, also see Du Loir (Italian trans.), p. 37; Tournefort, 2:214. Two drawings by Choiseul-Gouffier show the columns reused in the two-story structure, see Eldem, *Köşkler,* 1:figs. 61, 62, pp. 96–97.

48 For a hypothetical reconstruction of this building, see Eldem, *Köşkler,* 1:93–98.

49 "Döşeme-i mermer-i ṣomākī der dīvār-i ḳaṣr-i mezbūr," "meremmāt-i sıva der eṭrāf-i mermerhā der ḳaṣr-i mezbūr," "tebdīl-i ḳurşun der fevḳ-i ḳaṣr-i mezbūr," "tecdīd-i başlıḳ-i ḳorḳuluḳ-i mermer der mābeyn-i sütun-i ḳaṣr-i mezbūr," "meremmāt-i ḳol-i iskemle-i ḥażret-i hüdāvendigār," BA, MM 1947, fol. 13.

50 "Repairing the noble throne inside the pavilion of Sultan Selim outside the Cannon Gate" *(meremmet-kerden-i taht-i şerīf der enderūn-i ḳaṣr-i Sulṭān Selīm ‹an bīrūn-i bāb-i ṭob),"* BA, KK 7104, fol. 15v; MM 7370, fol. 18.

51 BA, MM 17884, fol. 69; MM 3780, fols. 53, 150; MM 403, fol. 64; KK 7100, fol. 18r; KK 7104, fol. 19v.

52 F. Della Valle, p. 17.

53 Anonymous, "Relazione anonima," p. 467. Also described in Badoaro, p. 352.

54 Gyllius, pp. 39–41.

55 Gainsford, p. 36.

56 For the conspicuous consumption of gold and jewels in the early part of Süleyman's reign, see Necipoğlu-Kafadar, "Süleyman the Magnificent," pp. 401–27. For the austere taste that developed in the 1550s, in a context of growing religious orthodoxy, see Necipoğlu-Kafadar, "Süleymaniye Complex in Istanbul," pp. 92–118.

57 Du Loir, cited in Eldem, *Köşkler,* 1:94; Du Loir (Italian trans.) p. 37; Motraye, 1:168.

58 My translation, cited in Karabacek, p. 62; Hammer, *Geschichte,* 2:531; Gurlitt, *Baukunst,* 1:45.

59 Cited in Sarre, "Michelangelo," pp. 61–66.

60 Busbecq, 1:129; Lubenau, 2:3, 8.

61 Schweigger, pp. 126–27. For the Karabali Garden, also see Ayvansarayi, 2:89.

62 Şükrü Bidlisi, fol. 143r. For artists brought to Istanbul from Tabriz, see R. Anhegger, pp. 180–84.

63 The partially effaced legends of Lorichs's panorama (Melchior Lorichs, pl. 1, in Oberhummer) are repeated verbatim in Dilich, pp. 16–17. In Dilich's panorama the kiosk is identified as "Marmorn gebew am thor des Keisers sich darvon aufs Meer umzusehen."

64 Lokman, *Hünername,* 1:fols. 216r–17v.

65 "Ṭop ḳapusında olan ‹adl köşki," TSA, E 8731.

66 Eremya, p. 9.

67 Galland, 1:60–61.

68 For this shore palace, see Şeref, p. 266; Atâ, 1:59; Flachat, pp. 204–5; İnciciyan, p. 31; Clarke, pp. 7–15.

69 Eldem, *Köşkler,* 1:143–47. Eremya, p. 5; İnciciyan, p. 27.

70 TSA, D 1098, fol. 59r; D 5400; Atâ, 1:302, 169; BA, Cevdet 2184, fol. 1v.

71 For the pendants, see Eremya, p. 5. For the importation of pearls, see BA, MD 52, no. 550, no. 1001; MD 68, no. 400.

72 Karaçelebizade, p. 471.

73 Atâ, 1:304; Şeref, p. 293.

74 BA, KK 7125, fol. 4; KK 7104, fol. 22r; MM 373, fol. 44; MM 1947, fols. 16, 24–26; MM 699, fol. 15; MM 753, fol. 12; MM 2126, fol. 105; MM 424, fol. 40; Abdi Pasha, fols. 42v, 194r.

75 Şeref, p. 293.

76 "Sarāy-i ‹āmiremde müceddeden binā' olınan ḳaṣr içün kāşī lāzım olmağın," BA, MD 66, no. 152, published in A. Refik, "İznik Çinileri," p. 40, no. 10. Also published with the false date of Cumada II 997 in A. Refik, *On Altıncı Asırda,* p. 13, no. 32; R. Anhegger, no. 11.

77 "The tiles to be produced in İznik for the buildings made anew in my Imperial Palace," *(sarāy-i ‹āmiremde müceddeden olan binā'lar içün nefs-i iznikde işlenicek kāşīler),* A. Refik, "İznik Çinileri," p. 40, no. 9; R. Anhegger, no. 12.

78 Lokman, *Şehname,* fols. 174v–77v.

79 Selaniki, *Tarih,* pp. 289–91; cited in Eldem, *Köşkler,* 1:145.

80 "Vasaṭ-i ḳubbe-i felek-üslūbda ta‹līḳ olınan mücevher ü muraṣṣa‹ ṭop-i gerdūn-maşḫūb avīzeleri cümle lü'lü'-i şehvār ile riştelere manẓūm," Hasanbeyzade, pp. 136–37. See also Karaçelebizade, pp. 470–71.

81 Selaniki, *Tarih,* pp. 289–91.

82 He refers to the pavilion as "koca Sinan Pasha Kiosk," *(Ḳoca Sinān Paşa ḳaṣrı),* and to its superstructure as "çār külāh ḳurşun örtüli ḳaṣr), Üsküdari, 2:fol. 123r.

83 "Çayır ḳaṣrı fevḳinde olan külāh," "külāh-i mezbūruñ eṭrāf saçaḳları," "ḳāṣr-i mezbūruñ külāhı hedm olınub cedīd tekne ḳubbe olub, ve eṭrāf saçaḳlarında olan ‹atīk ḳurşunları bi'l-külliye tebdīl olındığı," BA, MM 1947, fol. 25. The domical vault that replaced the original cover is mentioned as "una cupola di figura tetragona," in Carbognano, p. 25.

84 Dallam, pp. 78–79.

85 See Demangel and Mamboury; Eldem, *Köşkler,* 1:153–68.

86 "Il est bâti sur des arcades qui soutiennent trois salons terminez par des domes dorez," Tournefort, 2:114.

87 Hasanbeyzade, pp. 136–37; Eldem, *Köşkler,* 1:163.

88 İnciciyan, p. 31.

89 "Ḳaṣr-i mezbūrun ṭaşrasında deryāya nāẓır taḫt-i hümāyūn," see these eighteenth-century furnishing inventories: TSA, D 1098, fol. 59r; D 5400; BA, KK 7125, fols. 5–7. Eldem has published another inventory from 1710, Eldem, *Köşkler,* 1:161–64.

90 "Çayıra nāẓır ayaḳlı taḫt-i hümāyūn," TSA, D 1098, fol. 59r; D 5400.

91 "Ṭaşra meydān ṭarafında olan sīm taḫt-i hümāyūn," TSA, E 12359, no. 4, fol. 35r. According to Hammer, this silver throne was installed in 1160 (1747), cited in Miller, *Beyond the Sublime Porte,* p. 149.

92 BA, KK 7125, fol. 5.

93 BA, KK 7125, fol. 5. The "noble mosque" *(cāmi‹-i şerīf)* and the "mihrab of the meadow kiosk" *(çayır ḳaṣrında mihrāb)* are also cited in BA, MM 2126, fol. 110; Atâ, 1:169.

94 "Maḥall-i ibādet ve menzīl-i ḫilāfetde durmak cā'iz olmaz," Safi, 1:fol. 39r.

95 Rosedale, pp. 8–9.

96 Dallam, pp. 58–60.

97 Ibid., pp. 79–80.

98 Salahi, fols. 3v–4v, 16v, 39r, 42v, 57r, 81r; Ömer Efendi, fols. 4v, 5r; Flachat, p. 170.

99 TSA, E 12359, no. 4.

100 Arvieux, 4:474. See also Thévenot, p. 65; Tournefort, 2:215; Flachat, p. 170; Donato, 2:79–80. Before the Pearl Kiosk was built Gyllius (p. 40) wrote: "The fourth Gate stands South-east near the Ruins of a *Christian* Church, some Tokens of which are still remaining in a Wall, to which *Greeks* to this Day, by their frequent Visits, continue to pay a kind of devotional Reverence."

101 Eremya, pp. 5–6.

102 Abdi Pasha, fols. 42v, 194r.

103 Âli, *Künh* (MS. Nuruosmaniye 3409), fols. 418v–19r. Because of this unfortunate incident, Âli refers to the Pearl Kiosk as "the ill-omened pavilion created by Sinan Pasha" *(Sinān paşa iḥdāṣ itdügi ḳaṣr-i şom)*.

104 "The Kiosk of Sultan Bayezid *(Sulṭān Bāyezīd köşki)*, which had been renovated from its foundations up *(esāsından tecdīd)* by the admiral, was found to be unimpressive *(muḥaḳḳar)* and ordered to be rebuilt *(müceddeden ebnā')*," Karaçelebizade, fol. 252v.

105 Selaniki, *Tarih*, pp. 291–92.

106 TSA, D 9636; D 34, fol. 33r; BA, KK 7100, fol. 18r; MM 511, fols. 3, 6, 29.

107 Melchior Lorichs, pl. 3, in Oberhummer.

108 BA, KK 7100, fol. 18r.

109 Karaçelebizade, fol. 252v; Selaniki, *Tarih*, pp. 291–92. Among the events of 16–25 November 1583, Lokman writes: "Renovating the Kiosk of Bayezid Khan—may he rest in peace—located along the seashore was ordered to the admiral and he proceeded," Lokman, *Silsilename*, fols. 112v–13r.

110 Evliya (1:67–68) writes that the wharf was paved with antique columns from "Selim I's kiosk at Seraglio Point" *(sarāy burnında Selimiye köşki)*, up to the "Kiosk of Sinan Pasha" *(Sinān Paşa ḳaṣrı)* [i.e., Shore Kiosk].

111 He refers to the pavilion as "the lofty pavilion ordered to be built anew on the site of Sultan Bayezid Khan's kiosk" *(sulṭān Bāyezīd ḫān köşki maḥalline müceddeden binā' sı fermān olınan ḳaṣr-i ‹ālī)*, Selaniki, *Tarih*. MS. Gökbilgin, fol. 8v. The same information is provided in Karaçelebizade, p. 473.

112 A book of royal donations gives the date 18 Şevval 1001 for the distribution of rewards when "the kiosk of Sultan Bayezid was rebuilt" *(sulṭān Bāyezīd köşki yeñiden binā' olundıḳda)*, TSA D 34, fol. 172r.

113 BA, MM 750. Excerpts published in Barkan, *Süleymaniye*, 2:266–75; Eldem, *Köşkler*, 1:183–203.

114 BA, MM 750, fols. 130–36.

115 "Ḳaṣr-i ‹ālī," "ḳaṣr-i cedīd ‹an bāb-i yālī," "yālī ḳapusında vāḳi‹ olan ḳaṣr-i hümāyūn," ibid., fols. 1–7, 18, 32, 88, 101, 112, 133–36, 148–56, 182, 194.

116 Ibid. References to these materials and their sources are, respectively: fols. 2, 112; fols. 5, 100, 134; fols. 100, 110, 112–13, 138, 182; fols. 2, 112–13, 182.

117 The lead was for the "new kiosk ordered to be built" *(binā'sı fermān olınan kösk içün)*, BA, MD 67, no. 359.

118 BA, MD 69, no. 332; published in A. Refik, *Hicrî On Birinci Asırda İstanbul Hayatı*, p. 5, no. 9, where the wrong date of 1001 is given.

119 "Ḥāliyā binā' olınan ḳaṣr-i hümāyūnım," MD 69, no. 360; published in A. Refik, *Hicrî On Birinci Asırda İstanbul Hayatı*, pp. 5–6, no. 10, where the wrong date of 1001 is given.

120 "Yālīda müceddeden binā'sı fermān olınan ḳaṣr-i hümāyūn," ibid., MD 69, no. 69; published in A. Refik, *Hicrî On Birinci Asırda İstanbul Hayatı*, p. 2, no. 3, where the wrong date of 1001 is given.

121 TSA, SP 77.

122 Eldem, *Köşkler*, 1:173–207; BA, MM 750, fols. 5, 7, 88–89, 91–95.

123 BA, MM 750, fols. 93–96, 196.

124 Ibid., fols. 96, 196–97.

125 The fountained windows are referred to as "white marble *muqarnas*ed windows with fountains" *(pencere-i mermer-i beyāż-i muḳarnes ve çeşmelü)*, the cupboard as "the large cupboard of white marble at the west side of the interior" *(ṭolāb-i kebīr ‹an mermer-i beyāż ‹an cānīb-i ġarb der enderūn)*, the doors as "large doors of white marble" *(bāb-i kebīr-i mermer-i beyāż)*, and the steps as "large steps of white marble" *(derece-i kebīr-i mermer-i beyāż)*, ibid., fols. 96, 196.

126 For the tiles, see BA, MM 750, fols. 3, 113, 138, 182; some parts published in Barkan, *Süleymanıye*, 2:275. For the terminology of the tile shapes and patterns, see Necipoğlu-Kafadar, "From International Timurid to Ottoman."

127 TSA, SP 77, fols. 2v, 12r–13v, 18v–19r.

128 The globe of the dome is referred to as "the large gilded globe with six compartments produced for the imperial kiosk's middle dome" *(ḳaṣr-i hümāyūnıñ orta ḳubbesine işlenen şeşḫāne müẕehheb ṭop-i kebīre)* and the "smaller globe" as *(küçük ṭop)*, ibid., fols. 18v–19r, attached paper, no. 1a.

129 It is referred to as "the kitchen of the lofty pavilion" *(maṭbāḫ-i ḳaṣr-i ‹ālī)*, ibid., fol. 19r. For this Corps of Gardeners, see Atâ, 1:303–4.

130 For the expenses of the "workshop of painter-designers" *(naḳḳāşḫāne)*, see TSA, SP 77, fols. 3r–v.

131 The designs included calligraphy for the "inscription tiles" *(kāşī-yi muḫaṭṭāṭ)*, ibid., fols. 17r–18v, 19r, 50v.

132 TSA, SP 77, fols. 48v–50v. The terminology used in this

document for different types of tiles is compiled in Necipoğlu-Kafadar, "From International Timurid to Ottoman."

133 *"Ḫārīc kāşīler,"* TSA, E 105, no. 16. The mid-seventeenth-century traveler Michele Benvenga saw the tiles with grapevine motifs: "... hà molti Chiostri [i.e., kiosks] ... una dei quali pompeggia fuori del recinto superbamente, e per li marmi esteriori, e per le loggie attorno constrati di Persia, e per le miniature di Turchino, che sortiscono dalle maioliche del muro in viti, vue, & altri capricci. Nemen ricca de'fregi è la vaghezza di dentro. Ai colori sudetti s'aggiunge l'adulatione dell'acque, che vi garriscono da leggiadrissimi fonti. Apre sopra la riva uno sfondo, ch'è tutto magnificenza, quando particolarmente tra cuscini di broccato, e di gemme vi scerne il Soldano," Benvenga, pp. 120–21.

134 Galland, 1:186–88. For the kiosk, see also Chishull, p. 45.

135 Grelot, p. 87. The kiosk is described by Donato as a: "loggia fabricata in spiaggia del gran Serraglio di Costantinopoli, che riguarda su'l Porto. Dietro questo si passa per un eminente porta in un magnifico Camerone, ò Sala all'uso turchesco costrutta, ove è situato il gran Sophà, il qual con alcuni finestroni domina il Porto, e la spiaggia, e sopra di essi una maestosa Cupola tutta dorata con lavorio Arabo, & alla minutissima Zemina. Corrispondono su lo stesso Sophà alcune cadutine d'Acqua, che scendono sopra un marmo, attacati a lastre nel muro, indi grondando per scaglie di Pesce poste al roverscio, fanno dolcissimo fragore, e con galantissima spruzzaglia somministrano il lavacro per l'ablutione," Donato, pp. 71–72.

136 TSA, E 105, no. 16; BA, KK 7125, fols. 1–4; TSA, D 1098, fol. 53r; see also D 5400, and Eldem, *Köşkler,* 1:204–5.

137 "Ḳaṣr-i mezbūrun bīrūnında deryāya nāẓır ayaḳlı taḫt-i hümāyūn" and "ḳaṣr-i mezbūrun bīrūnında iki taş taḫt-i hümāyūn," Eldem, *Köşkler,* 1:204; BA, KK 7125, fol. 3.

138 The kiosk was extensively renovated in 1747 by Mahmud I, Eldem, *Köşkler,* 1:179.

139 Ohsson, 7:426; Uzunçarşılı, *Merkez ve Bahriye Teşkilatı* p. 437; Donato, 2:73; Charrière, p. 739; Flachat, p. 209; La Croix, *Serrail,* fols. 20–21; Benvenga, p. 120; Naili, fols. 55r–56v; Esad, pp. 97–110; Ömer Efendi, fol. 5r.

140 İnciciyan, p. 31; Safi, 1:fol. 138r. See also Hezarfen, *Telhis,* fol. 32v; Atâ, 1:231.

141 Naima, 3:445; Selaniki (İpşirli, ed.), p. 165; Ömer Efendi, fols. 9v, 14r; Salahi, fols 49r, 63v; TSA, E 12358, fol. 3r; D 10749, fol. 6r.

142 Clarke, p. 19. The silver throne mentioned in the early seventeenth century by Safi was restored in 1162 (1749); the cost of a new "silver throne" *(gümiş taḫt)* made for the Shore Kiosk *(yālī köşki)* is given in BA, Cevdet 6336.

143 Lokman, *Hünername,* 1:fols. 190v–91v.

144 Selaniki, *Tarih,* p. 282.

145 Ibid., pp. 112–14.

146 Orhonlu, pp. 10–12, no. 11; Lokman, *Shahanshāhnāma* 1, fols. 149r, 156v.

147 Selaniki (İpşirli, ed.), pp. 239, 252, 376.

148 Orhonlu, pp. 101, nos. 107, 117, 128, 147.

149 Thévenot, pp. 226, 232; Donato, 2:76–78.

150 Abdi Pasha, fols. 32r, 189v, 198r; Naima, 5:215.

151 Lokman, *Shahanshāhnāma,* 1, fols. 149r, 156v. Thévenot writes: "Le Grand Seigneur vient souvent prendre l'air, il s'embarque en cet endroit dans sa galiote lorsqu'il veut promener sur la mer," Thévenot, p. 65. Sandys (p. 114) refers to the kiosk as the "Sultan's Cabinet, in the forme of a sumptuous Sommer House ... where he solaceth himselfe, with the various objects of the Haven, and from thence takes Barge to passe unto the delightful places of the adjoyning Asia."

152 "Ḳaṣr-i cedīd-i fevḳ-i ḳulle-i ḥisār," "ḳaṣr-i cedīd-i ‹ālī der ḳulle," "ḳaṣr-i ḳulle," BA, MM 750, fols. 7, 100–101, 130–36, 191, 197.

153 "Sāḥil-i baḥrda Sinān Paşa ḳaṣrına havāle bir burc üzrine sepet köşki dimekle ma‹rūf ḳaṣr-i ṣaġīr," Naima, 4:35. Naima says the small kiosk was ordered "enlarged and rebuilt from its foundation" *(esāsından tevsī' ve binā' olınmak)* in Şa'ban 1053 (October–November 1643). See also Karaçelebizade, p. 616. The extant foundation inscription on the second Basketmakers' Kiosk shows that it was built for İbrahim I in 1053 (1643).

154 BA, MM 1756, fol. 81.

155 Bayezid II's hypothetical tower kiosk is mentioned in Akdağ, p. 218; T. Öz, "Topkapı Sarayı Müzesi Onarımları," pp. 7–8; Emler, "Topkapı Sarayı," p. 211. It is included in Akdağ's hypothetical reconstruction of the fifteenth-century palace, which is reproduced in Tansuğ, p. 162.

156 For this corps, see Atâ, 1:303.

157 A decree of Murad III dated 991 (1583) orders the chief gardener of the Edirne Palace to send "willow branches" *(sögüd çıbuḳları)* required for weaving "baskets" *(sepetler)* around the fruit trees of the palace garden, see BA, MD 49, no. 393. Another group of gardeners of the same name was stationed near the Maidan of the Gourd, but the latter came to be known as the "Old Basketmakers" *(sepetçiler-i ‹atīḳ* or *eski sepetçiler),* BA, MM 2126, fol. 105; TSA, D 9916, no. 26, fol. 4r; E 385, no. 20, fol. 3r; D 1098, fols 51r–v; E 12359, no. 1, fols. 7r–v; E 12359, no. 2, fol. 11r.

158 An eighteenth-century writer who identifies the Basketmakers' Kiosk as "Sinan Kioskiu" describes it as: "A rincontro di Galata, fabbricato sopra otto archi, e guarnito d'una cupola; è riconosce per fondare *Sinan-Pascia,* da cui ne trae il nome," Carbognano, p. 25. Grelot's seventeenth-century panorama identifies the enlarged Basketmakers' Kiosk as "Sinan Kiosc." Also see İnciciyan, who refers to this kiosk, raised on a foundation of eight arches, as "Sinan Paşa Köşkü," İnciciyan, p. 31. Eremya refers to the two neighboring pavilions as "Sinan Paşa Kâhı" and "Yalı Köşkü," Eremya, p. 12.

159 "The new construction of the staircase inside the tower

pavilion," *(binā'i cedīd-i nerdübān-i ḳaṣr-i ḳulle der enderūn),* BA, MM 750, fols. 197, 101.

160 "Naḳş-kerden be-ḳaṣr-i cedīd-i fevḳ-i ḳulle-i ḥisār," ibid., fols. 3, 7, 100, 116, 194. The painting expenses are published without identifying the building in Barkan, *Süleymaniye,* 2:270, 274.

161 Grelot (p. 86–87) writes that the rebuilt pavilion was used by women to watch the ceremonies connected to the departure and arrival of the Ottoman navy. For later sultans watching ships from the Basketmakers' Kiosk, see Ömer Efendi, fols. 4r–5v, 7v–8v, 11r–v, 12r–15v.

162 For the extant Basketmakers' Kiosk, see Eldem, *Köşkler,* 1:335–57.

Chapter 11

1 Promontorio, pp. 45–48. Similarly, Spandugino, *Petit Traicté,* pp. 156–57; Mihailović, p. 157. For the identical layout of the military encampment and the palace, with the treasury tent placed next to the public audience tent, see also Lutfi, *Asafname,* pp. 26, 31 and chapters 2–4. For the quotation, see Anonymous, *Risale,* fol. 39b.

2 Richards, fol. 56v; Wheeler, p. 180.

3 Clarke, p. 6.

4 See Mango, *Byzantine Architecture,* p. 28.

5 Bidlisi likens the construction of the New Palace to the erection of royal tents, Bidlisi, *Tercüme-i Heşt Bihişt,* fol. 53r. Ahmed Pasha compares the Tiled Kiosk to a "high tent" *(ḫayme-i vālā),* Ahmed Pasha, p. 27. Mehmed II ordered the ropes of his grand vizier Mahmud Pasha's tent to be cut; the tent suddenly collapsing over his head signified banishment in disgrace, see Babinger, *Mehmed,* p. 272. When Selim I died on his journey from Istanbul to Edirne, his soldiers mourned by cutting the ropes of his imperial tent, Celalzade, *Selimname,* fol. 169b. According to old Turco-Mongol traditions it was considered a bad omen for the ruler's tent to collapse, Taneri, pp. 6, 104, 110, 217. For captured tents exhibited as trophies at İbrahim Pasha's wedding, see Sanuto, 36:445–46, 505; and Hasanbeyzade, p. 10. For tents exhibited in the circumcision festivities of 1530, see Sanuto, 53:447.

6 Suetonius is cited in MacDonald, p. 31. In 1049 Naser-i Khusraw visited the Cairene pavilions, which he described as each measuring one hundred square cubits, "twelve square structures, built one next to the other, each more dazzling than the last," Naser-i Khusraw, pp. 56–57. The Sultaniya palace is described thus: "L'habitation royale se composait d'un pavillon isolé entouré, à une certaine distance, de douze plus petits, ayant chacun une fenêtre sur la cour qui était pavée de marbre, d'une chancellerie assez vaste pour contenir deux mille personnes, et de plusieurs bâtiments," in Hafız-i Abru, 2:7.

7 Hamidi's poem is cited in Atâ, 5:194; Örs, "History of the Topkapı Palace," p. 6; Raby, "Sultan of Paradox," p. 8. For the poem of the Seven Beauties, see Nizami. Babur's palace in Delhi is described in Khwandamir, pp. 28–32, 51, 62.

8 Firdausi, 2:101–2; 6:166. For the crystal pavilions in Spain, see Rubiera, pp. 88–90; sources describing Solomon's crystal pavilion are cited in idem, pp. 49–52.

9 Bidlisi, *Hasht Behisht,* fol. 72r.

10 Tursun, text fol. 59b. Solomon's pavilion is mentioned in Yerasimos, pp. 225–26. For Solomonic allusions within the Alhambra Palace, see Grabar, *Alhambra,* p. 128. Textual references to the palace of Solomon are discussed in Rubiera, pp. 49–52.

11 Grabar, *Alhambra,* pp. 103, 199. For early Islamic palaces, see Grabar, *Formation of Islamic Art,* pp. 139–79.

12 Grabar, *Alhambra,* pp. 181–82.

13 The Takht-i Sulayman is described in Kleiss, pp. 665–70; and Naumann, pp. 35–65. For the garden in Ujan, see Golombek and Wilber, pp. 181–82; the palace in Shangdu is described in Steinhardt, pp. 150–54.

14 For Dadu, see Steinhardt, pp. 154–60. Clavijo is cited in Wilber, *Persian Gardens,* p. 28. For written sources on Timurid palaces, see ibid., pp. 23–37; Golombek and Wilber, pp. 174–83. For the Timurid gardens of Herat, see Allen, *Catalogue* and *Timurid Herat.* For a description of the Hasht Behisht Palace in Tabriz, which consisted of successive courts preceded by a forecourt for retinues and the horses of dignitaries, see C. Grey, *Travels,* pp. 174–75.

15 Bessarion, pp. 252–53; Kritovoulos, p. 207.

16 Kritovoulos, pp. 147, 149.

17 Ibid., pp. 207–8.

18 For the bibliography on the Great Palace, see Eyice, pp. 3–36; Müller-Wiener, pp. 225–37.

19 For the Moukhroutas in the Byzantine Great Palace, see Hunt, chapter 8; the Capella Palatina is discussed in Ćurčić, pp. 125–44.

20 The suburbs of Samarkand are described in Ibn 'Arabshah, pp. 309–10; Lentz and Lowry, p. 42. The Persian source describing Timur's palace in Samarkand is translated to English in Thackston, p. 90. The palaces of Karakorum are described in Juwayni, 1:236–39; Steinhardt, pp. 148–50.

21 Kritovoulos, p. 105, see also pp. 119, 139, 140, 148; Angiolello, *Inedito manoscritto,* pp. 18, 28. For Mehmed II's repopulation of Istanbul, see İnalcık, "Policy of Mehmet II," pp. 231–49; Babinger, *Mehmed,* pp. 103–4, 354.

22 Cited in Babinger, *Mehmed,* p. 472.

23 Hodgson, 3:99–100.

24 Fresne-Canaye, pp. 130–31. For a discussion of the sources of Ottoman ceremonial, see Dilger; Köprülü, pp. 165–313. For Abbasid ceremonial, see Sourdel, "Questions de cérémonial," pp. 121–48; and Hilāl al-Sābi'. For Byzantine ceremonial, see Porphyrogénète, Kodinos, and Cameron; pp. 101–18. Fatimid and Byzantine ceremonial are compared in Canard, pp. 355–420.

25 Hilāl al-Sābi', p. 65.

26 For a Turkish translation of Ivan Peresvetov's text, see

Aykut, pp. 861–82. The dating of this text remains controversial; some scholars believe that it was written sometime in the seventeenth century by a pseudo-Peresvetov for another Russian ruler. For the Bahçe Saray, see Aslanapa, *Kırım ve Kuzey,* pp. 25–33.

27 For the decline of Mediterranean city-states and the rise of empires in the sixteenth century, see Braudel, 1:312–52, 2:657–81.

28 Âli, *Counsel,* p. 38; Âli, *Mevaid,* pp. 136–39. I would like to thank Peter Brown for bringing to my attention Shelly Errington's recent anthropological work, *Meaning and Power in a Southeast Asian Realm,* which shows that the kingdom of Luwu in South Sulawesi developed a similar ceremonial, in which the ruler sat silent and motionless at the symbolic navel of the universe, see Errington.

29 ASV, Busta 5, no. 13, fol. 7r; Busta no. 15, fol. 22r.

30 Iskandar Munshi, 1:168–69.

31 Machiavelli, pp. 10–11. For Soranzo's report, see ASV Busta 5, no. 13, fol. 7r; Busta no. 15, fol. 22r.

32 For Ibrahim's exclusive privilege to eat and sleep in the sultan's private quarters, see Sanuto, 34:359; 35:259; 41:526–27, 535. Navagero reports that unlike İbrahim, Rüstem was not allowed to enter the private palace, Navagero, p. 89. The same information is provided in A. Barbarigo, p. 156.

33 Gyllius, p. 41. "La politique de nos Rois est bien différente de celle des Sultans. Nous entrons dans le château de Versailles avec ce respect tendre qu'inspirent à leurs sujets des Princes qui veulent être aimés, & que l'on aime. On n'ose approcher du serrail qu'avec le saisissement que produit dans tous les coeurs un maître que l'on redoute, & qui se plait à voir tout le monde s'anéantir en sa présence. Nos Rois se montrent avec plaisir à leur sujets: il semble meme qu'ils gémissent de la pompe majesteuse qui les accompagne. Les Sultans seroient volontiers invisibles, s'il étoit possible de l'être & de régner," Flachat, p. 177.

34 Naima, 1:54–55.

35 For the extensive remodeling of the Topkapı Palace in the first half of the eighteenth century, see BA, BNE 15900, 15901, 15899; and TSA, D 2001, 2002, 8583, nos. 1–2, 4462.

36 For this citation (here, my translation) and a detailed study of the eighteenth-century shore palaces, see Artan, p. 45.

37 Pardoe, pp. 18–19.

38 Tavernier, p. 60; Benvenga, p. 120. For a Lacanian analysis of European interpretations of the palace as the heart of despotic rule, see Grosrichard.

Anonymous. *Risāle der beyān-i temeddün ve ‹imāret.* MS. TSK, R 2044.

Anonymous. "Testament de Amyra Sultan Nichemedy," in Süheyl Ünver, *Fatih Sultan Mehmed'in Ölümü ve Hadiseleri Üzerine Bir Vesika.* Istanbul, 1952.

Arvieux, Laurent, Chevalier d'. *Mémoires du chevalier d'Arvieux, envoyé extraordinaire du Roi à la Porte.* Edited by P. Labat. 6 vols. Paris, 1735.

‹Āşıḳpaşazāde, Derviş Aḥmed. *Die altosmanische Chronik des ‹Āşıḳpaşazāde.* Edited by Friedrich Giese. Leipzig, 1929.

‹Aṭā', Aḥmed Ṭayyārzāde. *Tārīḫ-i ‹Aṭā.* 5 vols. Istanbul, 1292–93 (1875–76).

‹Ayn-i ‹Alī Efendi. *Ḳavānīn-i ‹āl-i ‹Os̱mān der Ḫülāṣa-i Meżāmīn-i Defter-i Dīvān.* Edited by Tayyib Gökbilgin. Istanbul, 1979.

Ayvansarāyī, Ḥāfıẓ Ḥüseyin. *Ḥadīḳatü'l-cevāmi‹.* 2 vols. Istanbul, 1865.

Babur, Ẓāhir al-Dīn Muḥammad. *Vekāyi. Babur'un Hātıratı.* Translated by R. R. Arat. 2 vols. Ankara, 1943, 1946.

Badoaro, Andrea. "Relazione [1573]," in Albèri, vol. 1, pp. 347–68.

Barbarigo, Antonio. "Sommario della relazione [1558]," in Albèri, vol. 3, pp. 145–60.

Barbarigo, Daniele. "Relazione [1564]," in Albèri, vol. 2, pp. 1–59.

Barbaro, G., Contarini, A., et al. *Travels to Tana and Persia by Josafa Barbaro and Ambrogio Contarini.* Edited by Lord Stanley of Alderley. Translated by W. Thomas and S. A. Roy. London, 1873.

Barbaro, Marcantonio. "Relazione [1573]," in Albèri, vol. 1, pp. 299–346.

Barbaro, Marcantonio, and Tiepolo, Antonio. *Dell'audientia data da Selim Imp^e de Turchi all'Amb^re et Baili de Venetiani in Costantinopoli* (1573). MS. Venice, Museo Correr, Cod. Cicogna 3723 (no. 6), pp. 33–35.

Barkan, Ömer Lutfi, ed. "İstanbul saraylarına ait Muhasebe Defterleri," *Belgeler* 9, no. 13 (1979):1–380.

—— *Süleymaniye Cami ve İmareti İnşaatı (1550–1557).* 2 vols. Ankara, 1972–79.

Barozzi, Nicolò, and Berchet, Guglielmo, eds. *Le Relazioni degli Stati Europei lette al senato degli ambasciatori Veneziani nel secolo decimosettimo, Turchia.* Venice, 1871.

Bassano da Zara, Luigi. *I Costumi et i modi particolari della vita de' Turchi.* Edited by Franz Babinger, with a facsimile of the Rome 1545 edition. Munich, 1963.

Baudier, Michel. *Histoire générale du Serrail, et de la Cour du Grand Seigneur, Empereur des Turcs, ou se voit l'image de la grandeur Othomane, le Tableau des passions Humaines, et les exemples des inconstances prosperitez de la Cour.* Paris, 1624.

Beauvau, Henry de. *Relation journalière du Voyage du Levant.* Lyons, 1609.

Becagut, Alexis. *Doe littere di mx Alexio Ambassator del Illmo s.nro al Gran s.^re di Turchi scritte al p.^to s.^re del anno M.C.C.C.C.L.X.X.X.X.ij ...* MS. London, British Museum, Harley 3462, fols. 14r–19v.

Beldiceanu, Nicoara, ed. *Code de lois coutumière de Mehmed II.* Wiesbaden, 1967.

Bembo, Lunardo. "Relazione [1520]," in Sanuto, vol. 28, pp. 162ff.

Ben Meir, Joseph ben Joshua. *The Chronicles of Rabbi Joseph Ben Meir, the Sphardi.* Translated from Hebrew by C. H. F. Bialloblotzky. 2 vols. London, 1835–36.

Bent, James Theodore, ed. *Early Voyages and Travels in the Levant.* London, 1893.

Benvenga, Michele. *Viaggio di Levante, con la descrittione di Costantinopoli, e d'ogni altro accidente.* Bologna, 1688.

Bernardo, Lorenzo. "Relazione [1592]," in Albèri, vol. 2, pp. 321–426.

Beşir Çelebi. "Tārih-i Edirne, Hikāyet-i Beşir Çelebi," in *Türk Edebiyatı Örnekleri* III. Edited by İ. H. Ertaylan. Istanbul, 1946.

Bessarion [Cardinal]. "Encomium of Trebizond," in Cyril Mango, *The Art of the Byzantine Empire, 312–1453.* Sources and Documents in the History of Art Series. Edited by H. W. Janson. Englewood Cliffs, N.J., 1972, pp. 252–53.

Betzek, Jacob von. *Gesandtschaftsreise nach Ungarn und in die Türkei in Jahre 1564–65.* Veröffentlichungen und Finnisch Ungarischen Seminars Universität München, no. 10. Edited by K. Nehring. Munich, 1979.

Bidlīsī, İdrīs. *Hasht Behisht.* MS. Istanbul, Süleymaniye Kütüphanesí, Esad Efendi 2198.

—— *Tercüme-i Heşt Bihişt.* MS. TSK, B 196. An eighteenth-century Ottoman translation, dedicated to Mahmud I, based on a Persian manuscript, which is a slightly abbreviated version of MS. Istanbul, Süleymaniye Kütüphanesi, Esad Efendi 2198.

Bihiştī Sinān Çelebi. *Die Chronik des Ahmed Sinān Çelebi Gennant Bihişti; Eine Quelle zur Geschichte des Osmanischen Reiches unter Sultan Bāyezid II.* Edited by Brigitte Moser. Munich, 1980.

Bobovi, Albert. *Description du Serail du Grand Seigneur par M. Girardin, ambassadeur de France à la Porte.* Paris, Bibliothèque Nationale, MS. Français Nouvelle Acquisition 4997. French translation of Bobovi's *Serai Enderum* with some additional explanatory comments by the French ambassador (1644–89) Pierre Girardin.

—— *Mémoires sur les Turcs.* Dated 10 November 1666. MS. Cambridge, Mass., Harvard University, Houghton Library. Count Paul Riant Collection, French 103. The manuscript, which is a copy of the Paris Bibliothèque National manuscript, carries the arms of Pierre Girardin.

—— *Serai Enderum, cioè, Penetrale del Seraglio detto nuovo dei Gran Sgri e Re Ottomani, la descrittione del loro vivere e costumi, et altri essercitii, da me Alberto Bobovio, Sequolitano Pollacho, fatta al qual tempo di Sultan Ibrahim strangolato, et nel'tempo del presente G.S. Sultan Memetto, Figliolo del predetto Sultan Ibrahim, ha qui con ufficio di Paggi di musica parecchi anni habitato.* Dated Pera, 20 May 1665. MS. London, British Museum, Harley 3409.

—— *Serai enderum ... von Alberto Bobovio.* Translated by Nicholas Brenner. Vienna, 1667.

Bon, Ottaviano. "Descrizione del Serraglio del Gransignore fatta dal Bailo Ottaviano Bon [1608]," in Niccolò Barozzi and Guglielmo Berchet, pp. 59–115.

Borderie, Bertrandon de la. *Le Discours du voyage de Constantinople, envoyé dudict lieu à une Damoyselle.* Paris, 1546.

Bostān [Ferdī]. *Süleymānnāme.* MS. Istanbul, Süleymaniye Kütüphanesi, Ayasofya 3317.

Bostānzāde Yahyā bin Meḥmed. *Vaḳʿa-i ʿO̱smāniyye.* MS. TSK, R 1305.

Bragadino, Pietro. "Sommario della relazione [1526]," in Albèri, vol. 3, pp. 99–112.

—— "Sommario della relazione [1526]," in Sanuto, vol. 41, pp. 525ff.

Breuning, Hanß Jacob. *Orientalische Reyß Deß Edlen und Besten.* Strasbourg, 1612.

Brocquière, Bertrandon de la. *Le voyage d'Outremer de Bertrandon de la Brocquière* (1432). Edited by Charles Schefer. Paris, 1892.

Busbecq, Ogier Ghiselin de. *The Life and Letters of Ogier Ghiselin de Busbecq.* Edited by C. T. Forster and J. B. Daniell. 2 vols. London, 1881.

Caʿfer Çelebi, Tācīzāde. "Hevesnāme," in A. S. Levend, *Türk Edebiyatında Şehr-engizler ve Şehr-engizlerde İstanbul.* Istanbul, 1957, pp. 68–95.

Caʿfer Efendi. *Risāle-i miʿmāriyye: An Early Seventeenth-Century Ottoman Treatise on Architecture.* Facsimile, with translation and notes by Howard Crane. Leiden and New York, 1987.

Cantemir, Demetrius. *The History of the Growth and Decay of the Othman Empire.* Translated by R. Tindal. 2 vols. London, 1734–35.

Caoursin, Guglielmo. *Opere storiche di Guglielmo Caoursin.* Edited by E. Acinelli, S. Casali, and F. Rappini. Genoa, 1988.

Carbognano, Comidas de. *Descrizione topografica dello stato presente di Constantinopoli.* Bassano, 1794.

Carlier de Pinon. "Relation du voyage en Orient de Carlier de Pinon (1579)." Edited by E. Blochet. *Revue de l'Orient Latin* 12 (1909–11):112–421.

Castiglione, Baldesar. *The Book of the Courtier.* Translated by G. Bull. Harmondsworth, England, 1967.

Cavalli, Marino. "Relazione [1560]," in Albèri, vol. 1, pp. 271–97.

—— *Geschichte Sultan Süleyman Ḳānūnīs von 1520 bis 1557, oder Ṭabaḳāt ül-Memālik ve Derecāt ül-Mesālik.* Edited by Petra Kappert. Wiesbaden, 1981.

Celālzāde Muṣṭafā [Ḳoca Nişāncı]. *Selīmnāme.* MS. TSK, R 1274.

Cevrī, İbrāhīm Çelebi. *Cevrî, Hayatı, Edebî Kişiliği, Eserleri ve Divanının Tenkidli Metni.* Edited by H. Ayan. Erzurum, 1981.

Chalkokondylas, Laonikos. *L'Histoire de la decadence de l'empire Grec et éstablissement de celuy des Turcs; comprise en dix livres par Nicolas Chalcondyle Athenien.* Translated from Greek by Blaise de Vigenère. Paris, 1577.

Charrière, Ernest. *Négociations de la France dans le Levant.* 4 vols. Paris, 1848.

Chesneau d'Aramon, Jean. *Le voyage de Monsieur d'Aramon, ambassadeur pour le Roy au Levant (1547)*. Edited by Charles Schefer. Paris, 1887.

Chishull, Edmund. *Travels in Turkey and Back to England*. London, 1747.

Choiseul-Gouffier, Comte de. *Voyage pittoresque de la Grèce*. 3 vols. Paris, 1782–1822.

Clarke, Edward Daniel. *Travels in Various Countries of Europe, Asia, and Africa*. Vol. 11. London, 1812.

Clavijo, Ruy Gonzales de. *Embassy to Tamerlane (1403–1406)*. Translated from Spanish by Guy Le Strange. London, 1928.

Codinos [Pseud.]. "Sur les dignitaires du palais et sur les dignités de la Grande Eglise," in R. Guilland, *Recherches sur les institutions byzantines*, Vol. 2, pp. 233–86. Berlin and Amsterdam, 1967.

Coeck van Aelst, Peter. *The Turks in* MDXXXIII: *A series of Drawings made in that year at Constantinople by Peter Coeck of Aelst*. Facsimile published by William Stirling-Maxwell. London and Edinburgh, 1873.

Commynes, Philippe de. *The Memoirs of Philippe de Commynes (1445–1509)*. Edited by Samuel Kinser, translated by Isabelle Cazeaux. 2 vols. Columbia, S.C., 1969, 1973.

Constantios, [Patriarch]. *Constantiniade*. Constantinople, 1846.

Contarini, Bartolomeo. "Sommario della relazione [1519]," in Albèri, vol. 3, pp. 56–68.

Contarini, Iacomo. "Relazione [1507]," in Sanuto, vol. 7, pp. 7ff.

Contarini, Paolo. "Relazione [1583]," in Albèri, vol. 3, pp. 209–50.

Contarini, Tommaso. "Relazione [1528]," in Sanuto, vol. 48, pp. 378ff.

Courmenin, Louis Deshayes de. *Voiage de Levant fait par le Commandement du Roy en l'année 1621*. Paris, 1632.

Courthop, George. "Memoirs of Sir George Courthop (1616–1685)," in *The Camden Miscellany*. Edited by S.C. Lomas. London, 1907.

Curipeschitz, Benedict. "Wegraysz Keyserlicher Maiestat Legation im 32. Jar zu dem Türcken geschickt ... " Appendix to pt. 5, in Gévay, vol. 1.

—— *Yolculuk Günlüğü (1530)*. Translation of *Itinerarium Wegrayss Kün. May.potschafft gen Constantinopel zodem Turkischen Keiser Soleyman. Anno XXX., 1531*. Translated by Ö. Nutku, Ankara, 1977.

Cyriacus of Ancona (Ciriaco d'Ancona). "Letters (1444–1446)," in F. Pall, "Ciriaco d'Ancona e la crociata contro i Turchi," *Bulletin de la section historique de l'Académie Roumaine* 20 (1938): 9–68.

Dallam, Thomas. "The Diary of Master Thomas Dallam 1559–1600," in J. T. Bent, *Early Voyages and Travels in the Levant*. London, 1893, pp. 1–98.

Deffens, Jacques Gassot de. *Le Discours du Voyage de Venise à Constantinople*. Paris, 1550.

Dei, Benedetto. *La Cronica dall'anno 1400 all'anno 1500*. Edited by Roberto Barducci. Florence, 1985.

Dernschwam, Hans. *Hans Dernschwam's Tagebuch einer Reise nach Konstantinopel und Kleinasien (1553–55)*. Edited by Franz Babinger. Munich and Leipzig, 1923.

Dervīş ‹Abdullāh. *Risāle-i Teberdāriye fī Aḥvāl-i Aġa-yi Dārü's-sa‹āde*. MS. Istanbul, Köprülü Kütüphanesi, Yazmalar, 2:233.

Dilich, Wilhelm. *Eigentliche kurtze beschreibung und Abrisz dero weitt berümter Keyserlichen stadt Constantinopel nach itziger ihrer gelegenheit deren gleich vormahls in druck nie ausgangen nunmehr aber verfertigt durch Wilhelm Dilich*. Kassel, 1606.

Donà, Leonardo. "Relazione [1596]," in Federico Seneca, *Il Doge Leonardo Donà, la sua vita, e la sua preparazione politica prima del Dogado*. Padua, 1959, pp. 263–321.

Donato, Giovanni Battista. *Viaggio a Costantinopoli di Gio: Battista Donado, Senator Veneto spedito Bailo alla Porta Ottomana l'Anno 1680–84, Osservati colla raccolta delle più curiose Notitie dal fù Dottor Antonio Benetti*. Edited by A. Benedetti and F. M. Pazzaglia. 4 vols. Venice, 1688.

Donini, Marcantonio. "Relazione [1562]," in Albèri, vol. 3, pp. 173–209.

Doukas. *Decline and Fall of Byzantium to the Ottoman Turks by Doukas: An Annotated Translation of "Historia Turco-Byzantina."* Edited by Harry J. Magoulias. Detroit, 1975.

Du Loir, Sieur. *Les Voyages du Sieur Du Loir*. Paris, 1659. Translated, as *Viaggio di Levante Del Signor di Loir*, by F.F. Secretario. Venice, 1671.

Enverī. *Düsturnāme.* Edited by M. Halil Yınanç. Türk Tarih Encümeni Külliyatı no. 15. Istanbul, 1928.

Eremya Çelebi Kömürcüyan. *İstanbul Tarihi XVII. asırda İstanbul.* Translated from Armenian by H. O. Andreasyan. Istanbul, 1952.

Esʿad Meḥmed Efendi. *Teşrīfāt-i Ḳadīme.* 1287 (1870). Reprint, Istanbul, 1979.

Evliyā Çelebi. *Seyāḥatnāme.* Vol. 1. Istanbul, 1314 (1896–97).

Fauvel, Robert. *Le voyage d'Italie et du Levant, de Messieurs Fermanel, Fauvel, Baudouin de Launay, et de Stochove (1630).* Rouen, 1664.

Ferīdūn Aḥmed Beg. *Nüzhet el-esrār der sefer-i Zigetvār.* MS. TSK, H 1339.

Figānī, *Kanuni Sultan Süleyman şairlerinden Figani ve Divançesi.* Edited by A. Karahan. Istanbul, 1966.

Filarete, Antonio Averlino, called. *Trattato di architettura.* Edited by A. M. Finoli and L. Grassi. 2 vols. Milan, 1972.

Filelfo, G. M. *Amyris.* Edited by A. Manetti. Bologna, 1978.

Firdausī. *The Shāhnāma of Firdausi.* Translated by A. G. Warner and E. Warner. 9 vols. London, 1906.

Flachat, Jean-Claude. *Observations sur le commerce et sur les arts d'une partie de l'Europe, de l'Asie, de l'Afrique, et même des Indes Orientales (1740–1758).* 2 vols. Lyons, 1766, 1767. Vol. 2, pp. 162–235.

Fossati, Caspare. *Aya Sofia, Constantinople as Recently Restored by the Order of H. M. the Sultan Abdul Medjid.* London, 1852.

Fresne-Canaye, Philippe du. *Le voyage du Levant de Philippe du Fresne-Canaye (1573).* Edited by M. H. Hauser. Paris, 1897.

Gainsford, Thomas. *The Glory of England; or, a True Description of many excellent prerogatives and remarkeable blessings, whereby She Triumpheth over all the Nations of the World* ... London, 1618.

Galland, Antoine. *Journal d'Antoine Galland pendant son séjour à Constantinople (1672–1673).* Edited by Charles Schefer. 2 vols. Paris, 1881.

Garzoni, Costantino. "Relazione del impero ottomano [1573]," in Albèri, vol. 1, pp. 369–436.

George of Trebizond. *Collectanea Trapezuntiana: Texts, Documents, and Bibliographies of George of Trebizond.* Edited by J. Monfasani. Binghamton, N.Y., 1984.

Georgius de Hungaria. *Chronica unnd Beschreibung der Türckey mit eyner Vorrhed D. Martini Lutheri. Unveranderter Nachdruck der Ausgabe Nürnberg 1530 sowie fünf weiterer "Türkendrucke" des 15. und 16. Jahrhunderts.* Edited by Carl Göllner. Vienna and Cologne, 1983.

Gerlach, Stefan. *Stephan Gerlachs des Aeltern Tagebuch der von zween glorwurdigsten Römischen Käysern Maximiliano und Rudolpho beyderseits den Andern dieses Nahmens ... an die ottomanische Pforte zu Constantinopel abgefertigten und durch den wohlgebohrenen Herrn David Ungnad ... Gesandtschaft ... (1573–1578) herfür gegeben durch Samuel Gerlach.* Frankfurt, 1674.

Geuffroy, Antoine F. "Briesve description de la court du grant Turc et ung sommaire du regne des Othmans [1542], "in Charles Schefer, *Voyage de Monsieur d'Aramon, ambassadeur pour le Roy au Levant.* Paris, 1887.

Gévay, Anton von. *Urkunden und Actenstücke zur Geschichte der Verhältnisse zwischen Österreich, Ungern und der Pforte im 16. und 17. Jahrhunderte.* 2 vols. Vienna, 1840–42.

Giovio, Paolo. *Gli elogi vite brevemente scritte d'huomini illustri di guerra, antichi et moderni.* Florence, 1554.

Giustinian, Antonio. "Sommario della relazione [1514]," in Albèri, vol. 3, pp. 45–50.

Gontaut-Biron, Jean de [Baron de Salignac]. *Ambassade en Turquie de Jean de Gontaut-Biron, baron de Salignac, (1605 à 1610).* Edited by Comte Théodore de Gontaut. 2 vols. Paris, 1888–89.

Greaves, John. "A Description of the Grand Signor's Seraglio," London, 1653. Reprinted in *Miscellaneous Works of John Greaves.* 2 vols. London, 1737, vol. 2, pp. 585ff. English translation of Ottaviano Bon's account, published without acknowledging the author.

Grelot, Guillaume-Joseph. *Relation nouvelle d'un voyage de Constantinople.* Paris, 1680.

Grey, Charles, ed. and trans. *A Narrative of Italian Travels in Persia in the Fifteenth and Sixteenth Centuries.* London, 1873.

Gritti, Andrea. "Relazione [1503]," in Albèri, vol. 3, pp. 9–43.

——— "Relazione fatta in Pregadi per sier Andrea Gritti ritornato orator dil Signor turcho [1503]," signed by

Gritti's secretary, Gian Giacomo Caroldo. In Sanuto, vol. 5, pp. 449–68.
Gudenus, Philipp Franz [Baron]. "Türkische Reise 1740–42," selections published in Gerhard Fritsch, *Pachas und Pest: Gesandtschaft am Bosporus.* Graz and Vienna, 1962.
Gyllius, Petrus [Gilles, Pierre]. *The Antiquities of Constantinople.* Translated from Latin by John Ball. London, 1729.

Ḥāfız-i Abrū, *Chronique des rois Mongols en Iran.* Translated by K. Bayani, vol. 2. Paris, 1936.
Ḥāmidī. *Külliyāt-i Dīvān-i Mevlānā Ḥāmidī.* Edited by İ. H. Ertaylan. Istanbul, 1949.
Harff, Arnold von. *Die Pilgerfahrt des Ritters Arnold von Harff von Coln (1496–99).* Edited by Eberhard von Groote. Cologne, 1860.
—— *The Pilgrimage of Arnold von Harff.* Translated by Malcolm Letts. London, 1946.
Ḥasanbeyzāde. *Ḥasanbeyzāde Tarihi.* Edited by Nezihi Aykut. Ph.D. diss. İstanbul Üniversitesi Edebiyat Fakültesi, no. 1256, 1980.
Ḥayālī. *Hayālī Bey Divanı.* Edited by A. N. Tarlan. Istanbul, 1945.
Ḥaydar, Çelebi. *Rūznāme.* MS. TSK, R 1955.
Heberer von Bretten, Michael. *Aegyptiaca Servitus.* 1610. Reprint, with an introduction by Karl Teply. Graz, 1967.
Helākī, *Helâkî Dîvanı.* Edited by Mehmed Çavuşoğlu. Istanbul, 1982.
Herberstein, Adam von. *Adam Freihernn zu Herbersteins Gesandtschaftsreise nach Konstantinopel: Ein Beitrag zum Frieden von Zsitvatorok.* Edited by K. Nehring. Munich, 1983.
Hezārfenn, Ḥüseyin. *Telḫīṣü'l-beyān fī ḳavānīn-i āl-i ‹os̱mān.* MS. Paris, Bibliothèque Nationale, Ancien Fonds Turc 40.
—— *Tenḳīh-i tevārīḫ-i mülūk.* MS. TSK, R 1180.
Hierosolimitano, Domenico. *Relatione della Gran Città di Costantinopoli.* MS. London, British Museum, Harley 3408, fols. 83–141.
Hierosolimitano, Domenico [Chierici, Alfonso]. *Vera relatione della gran città di Costantinopoli et in particolare del Serraglio del Gran Turco.* Bracciano, 1621. A plagiarized longer version of Hierosolimitano's British Museum manuscript, in which Chierici claims to be the author.
Ḥilāl al-Ṣābi'. *Rusūm Dār al-Khilāfah: The Rules and Regulations of the ‹Abbāsid Court.* Translated by Elie A. Ṣalem. Beirut, 1977.
Ḫızır İlyās, Ḥāfız. *Leṭā'if-i Enderūn.* Istanbul, 1276 (1859–60).
Hoberdanacz, Iohann. "Bericht Iohann Hoberdanacz's an König Ferdinand I, Innsbruck, 19 Februar 1529," in Gévay, vol. 1, pp. 3–28.

Ibn ‹Arabshāh, Aḥmad. *Tamerlane, or Timur, the Great Amir, from the Arabic Life by Ahmed ibn Arabshah.* Translated by J. H. Sanders. London, 1936.
Ibn Iyās. *Journal d'un bourgeois du Caire: Chronique d'Ibn Iyās.* Translated by Gaston Wiet. 2 vols. Paris, 1955–60.
İnciciyan, G. *XVIII. Asırda İstanbul.* Translated from Armenian by H. D. Andreasyan. Istanbul, 1976.
Iskandar Munshī. *Tārīkh-i ‹ālam-ārā-yi ‹Abbāsī.* Translated, as *The History of Shah ‹Abbas the Great,* by R. M. Savory. 2 vols. Boulder, Col., 1978.

al-Jāḥiz [attributed to]. *Le Livre de la Couronne: Kitāb at-Tāj fī Aḫlāq ul-Mulūk.* Translated by Charles Pellat. Paris, 1954.
Junis Beg [Iounus Bei] and Gritti, Alvise. *Opera nova la quale dechiara tutto il governo del gran turcho ...* Venice, 1537.
Jurischitsch, Nikolaus, and Lamberg, Joseph von. "Bericht Josephs von Lamberg und Nikolaus Jurischitsch's an König Ferdinand I, überreicht in Linz, 23 Februar 1531," in Gévay, vol. I, pt. 4, pp. 25–49.
Juwaynī, ‹Alā' al-Dīn. *The History of the World Conqueror.* Translated by J. A. Boyle. 2 vols. Manchester, England, 1958.

Ḳabulī. *Külliyât-i Dîvân-i Kabulî.* Edited by İ. H. Ertaylan. Istanbul, 1948.
Ḳaraçelebizāde, ‹Abdü'l-‹azīz. *Ravżatü'l-ebrār.* MS. TSK, EH 1375.
Ḳaramānī [Ḳaramanlı], Nişancı Meḥmed Paşa. "Osmanlı Sultanları Tarihi." Translated from Arabic by Nihal Atsız, in *Osmanlı Tarihleri I.* Istanbul, 1925–49, pp. 321–65.
Kātib Çelebi. *Cihānnümā.* MS. TSK, R 1622.
Kemālpaşazāde [İbn Kemāl]. *Tevārīḫ-i āl-i ‹os̱mān.*

Edited by Şerafettin Turan. 2 vols. Ankara, 1954–57.

Khwāndamīr. *Qānūn-i Humāyūnī: Also Known as Humāyūn-nāma.* Translated by Bani Prasad, with the Persian text edited by M. Hidayat Hosain. Calcutta, 1940.

Ḳıvāmī. *Fetḥnāme-i Sulṭān Meḥmed.* Edited by Franz Babinger. Istanbul, 1955.

Knolles, Richard. *The General Historie of the Turkes.* London, 1638.

Ḳoçi Beg, Muṣṭafā. *Risāle-i Ḳoçi Beg.* 1041 (1631–32). Istanbul, 1277 (1861).

Koran. *The Glorious Qur'ān.* Text and explanatory translation by Muhammad Marmaduke Pickthall. New York, 1977.

Kritovoulos of Imbros, *History of Mehmed the Conqueror by Kritovoulos (1451–1467).* Translated from Greek by Charles Riggs. Princeton, 1954.

Küçükçelebizāde, ‹Āṣım Efendi. *Tārīḫ.* Published as vol. 6 of *Tārīḫ-i Rāşid.* 6 vols. Istanbul, 1282 (1865–66).

Kürkçüoğlu, Kemal Edib, ed. *Süleymaniye Vakfiyesi.* Ankara, 1962.

La Croix, François de. *Le Serrail des Empereurs Turcs ou Othomans.* MS. Paris, Bibliothèque National, Fr. 6123.

—— *Mémoires du Sieur de La Croix, cy devant secrétaire de l'ambassade de Constantinople, contenans diverses relations très curieuses de l'Empire othoman.* 2 vols. Paris, 1684.

Laguna, Andres. *Avventure di uno Schiavo dei Turchi.* Edited by C. Acutis. Milan, 1983.

Lamberg, Joseph von, and Jurischitsch, Nikolaus. "Bericht Josephs von Lamberg und Nikolaus Jurischitsch's an König Ferdinand I, überreicht in Linz, 23 Februar 1531," in Gévay, vol. 1, pt. 4, pp. 25–49.

Lamberg, Joseph von, and Nogarola, Leonhard, Graf von. "Bericht Leonhards Grafen von Nogarola und Josephs von Lamberg an König Ferdinand I, überreicht in Linz 11–21 September 1532," in Gévay, vol. 1, pt. 5, pp. 25–42.

Languschi, Giacomo. "Excidio e presa di Costantinopoli nell'anno 1453 (dalla Cronica di Zorzi Dolfin)," in Agostino Pertusi, *Testi inediti e poco noti sulla caduta di Costantinopoli.* Edited posthumously by Antonio Carile. Bologna, 1983, pp. 167–80.

Lāṭīfī. *Evsâf-i İstanbul.* Edited by N. Suner-Pekin. Istanbul, 1977.

Lenoir, Sieur de [pseud.]. *Nouvelle description de la ville de Constantinople.* Paris, 1721. Unacknowledged translation of Hierosolimitano's text.

Lewenklau [Löwenklau, or Loewenklau], Johannes [Hans]. *Neuwe Chronica Türkischer nation von Türken selbs beschrieben.* Frankfurt, 1590.

Leys̲īzāde Meḥmed Efendi. *Ḳānūnnāme-i āl-i ‹os̲mān,* in Abdülkadir Üzcan, "Fatih'in Teşkilat Kanunna mesi ve Nizam-ı Alem için Kardeş Katli Meselesi," *Tarih Dergisi* 33 (1982):7–56. A critical edition of the two extant sixteenth-century copies of Mehmed II's *kanunname;* the Vienna manuscript is published, as *Ḳānūnnāme-i āl-i ‹os̲mān* by Mehmed ‹Ârif in *Tārīḫ-i ‹Os̲mānī Encümeni Mecmū‹ası* [TOEM], nos. 13–19, 1330 (1912); the Leningrad manuscript is published in Bosnalı Ḥüseyin Efendi, *Badā'i‹ al-Waḳā'i‹.* Edited by A. S. Tveritonova. 2 vols. Moscow, 1961, vol. 2, fols. 277v–83v.

Loḳmān bin Seyyid Ḥüseyin. *Hünernāme.* 2 vols. Ca. 1584–85, ca. 1587–88. MSS. TSK, H 1523–24.

—— *Mücmelü't-ṭomār (Ṭomār-i nesebnāme-i ‹āliyye).* 992 (1584). MS. London, British Library, Or. 1135.

—— *Şehnāme-i āl-i ‹os̲mān.* 999 (1590–91), MS. London, British Library, Add. 7931.

—— *Shahanshāhnāma.* 2 vols. 991 (1581–82), 1001 (1592). MSS. İÜ, F 1404 (vol. 1); TSK, B 200 (vol. 2).

—— *Shāhnāma-i Salīm Khān.* Ca. 1581. TSK, A 3595, R 1537.

—— *Silsilenāme.* 994 (1586). MS. TSK, H 1321.

Lubenau, Reinhold. *Beschreibung der Reisen des Reinhold Lubenau.* Edited by W. Sahm. 2 vols. Königsberg, 1912–20.

Ludovisi, Daniello de'. "Relazione" (1534), in Albèri, vol. 1, pp. 1–32.

Luṭfī Paşa. *Das Âṣafnāme des Lutfī Pascha nach den Handschriften zu Wien, Dresden und Konstantinopel.* Edited and translated by Rudolf Tschudi. Leipzig, 1910.

—— *Tārīḫ-i āl-i ‹os̲mān.* Istanbul, 1341 (1922–23).

Machiavelli, Niccolò. *The Prince.* Translated by T. G. Bergin. Northbrook, Ill., 1947.

Magni, Cornelio. *Quanto di più curioso e vago ha potuto raccogliere nel primo biennio da esso consumato viaggi e dimore per la Turchia.* 2 vols. Parma, 1673–

74. An abbreviated version of Albert Bobovi's text is in vol. 1, pp. 502–604.

Majeska, George P., ed. *Russian Travelers to Constantinople in the Fourteenth and Fifteenth Centuries.* Washington, 1984.

Malipiero, Domenico. "Annali Veneti dall'anno 1457 al 1500 del Senatore Domenico Malipiero, Parte prima e seconda degli annali," *Archivio Storico Italiano* 7, no. 1 (1843), 7, no. 2 (1844).

al-Maqrīzi. *Description historique et topographique de l'Égypte.* Translated by P. Casanova, in *Mémoires de l'Institut français d'Archéologie Orientale du Caire,* 3 (1906).

al-Mascūdī. *Les prairies d'or.* Edited and translated by C. Barbier de Maynard and Pavet de Courteille. 9 vols. Paris, 1861–77.

Maurand, Jérôme. *Itinéraire d'Antibes à Constantinople (1544).* Edited and translated by L. Dorez. Paris, 1901. Italian and French texts.

Meḥmed bin cÖmer bin Bāyezīd al-cĀşıḳ. *Menāẓırü'l-avālīm.* 1006 (1597–98). MS. TSK, R 1667.

Meḥmed Ḫalīfe. *Tārīḫ-i Gılmānī.* Edited by A. Refik Altınay, in *Türk Tārīḫ Encümeni Mecmūcası.* Supplement to no. 78 (1924).

Melling, Antoine Ignace. *Voyage pittoresque de Constantinople et des rives du Bosphore.* 2 vols. Paris, 1807–24.

Menavino, Giovantonio. *I cinque libri della legge, religione, et vita de' Turchi et della corte, & d'alcune guerre del Gran Turco.* Florence, 1548.

Mihailović, Konstantin. *Memoirs of a Janissary.* Translated by B. Stolz, with a historical commentary by S. Soucek. Ann Arbor, 1975.

Minio, Marco. "Copia di una lettera da Costantinopoli di sier Marco Minio [1527]," in Sanuto, vol. 45, pp. 288–91.

—— "Relazione di Costantinopoli di Messer Marco Minio [1521]," Edited by G. Perusini. Venice, 1845.

—— "Relazione [1522]," in Albèri, vol. 3, pp. 69–91 (also in Sanuto, vol. 32, pp. 255–56).

—— "Relazione [1527]," in Albèri, vol. 3, pp. 113–18 (also in Sanuto, vol. 46, pp. 175–77).

Minorsky, Vladimir, ed. and trans. *Tadhkirat al-Mulūk: A Manual of Safavid Administration (ca. 1137/1725). Persian text in facsimile (B.M. Or. 9496).* 1943. Reprint, Cambridge, England, 1980.

Mocenigo, Alvise. "Relazione [1518]," in Albèri, vol. 3, pp. 53–55.

Moro, Giovanni. "Relazione [1590]," in Albèri, vol. 3, pp. 323–80.

Morosini, Gianfrancesco. "Relazione [1585]," in Albèri, vol. 3, pp. 251–322.

Moryson, Fynes. *An Itinerary Containing his ten yeeres Travell through the Twelve Dominions of Germany, Bohmerland, Sweitzerland, Netherland, Denmarke, Poland, Italy, Turkey, France, England, Scotland & Ireland.* Vol. 2. Glasgow, 1907.

Motraye, Aubrey de la. *Travels through Europe, Asia, and into Part of Africa.* 2 vols. London, 1723.

Müller, Giuseppe. *Documenti sulle relazioni delle città Toscane coll'oriente christiano e coi Turchi.* Florence, 1879.

Mussi, Nicolò. *Relatione della Città di Costantinopoli e Serraglio con i riti dei Turchi, et grandezza dell'Ottomano Impero.* Bologna and Bassano, 1675. An adaptation of Hierosolimitano's text, without acknowledging the author.

Nādirī, Meḥmed. *Şehnāme.* Ca. 1622. MS. TSK, H 1124.

—— *Dīvān-i Nādirī.* 1572–73. MS. TSK, H 899.

Nā'ilī, cAbdullāh Paşa. *Defter-i Teşrīfāt.* MS. TSK. YY 612. Extracts published as "Dīvān-i Hümāyūna cā'id Teşrīfāt," in *Türk Tārīḫ Encümeni Mecmūcası* 16 (1926):249–60.

Nacīmā, Muṣṭafā. *Tārīḫ-i Nacīmā.* 6 vols. Istanbul, 1281–83 (1864–87).

Nāṣer-i Khosraw. *Book of Travels (Safarnāma).* Translated by W. M. Thackston, Jr. New York, 1986.

Navagero, Bernardo. "Relazione [1553]," in Albèri, vol. 1, pp. 33–110.

Neşrī, Meḥmed. *Kitâb-ı Cihân-nümâ: Neşrî Tarihi.* Edited by F. R. Unat and M. A. Köymen. 2 vols. Ankara, 1949–57.

Nicolay, Nicolas de. *Les quatre premiers livres de Navigations et Peregrinations Orientales.* Lyons, 1568.

Nişāncı Meḥmed Paşa, Ramazānzāde. *Tārīḫ-i Nişāncı Meḥmed Paşa.* Istanbul, 1279 (1862).

Nizāmī of Ganja. *The Haft Paikar (The Seven Beauties), Containing the Life and Adventures of King Bahrām Gūr, and the Seven Stories told him by his Seven Queens.* Translated from Persian with a commentary by C. E. Wilson. 2 vols. London, 1924.

Nogarola, Leonhard, Graf von, and Lamberg, Joseph von. "Bericht Leonhards Grafen von Nogarola und Josephs von Lamberg an König Ferdinand I, überreicht in Linz, 11–21 September 1532," in Gévay, vol. 1, pt. 5, pp. 25–42.

Ohsson, Muradgea Ignace d'. *Tableau général de l'Empire othoman*. 7 vols. Paris, 1787–1824.

ʿÖmer Efendi. *Rūznāme*. 1740–50. MS. Istanbul, Fatih Millet Kütüphanesi, Tarih 423.

Omichius, Franciscus. *Beschreibung einer Legation und Reise von Wien aus Österreich auff Constantinopel durch den wolgebornen Herrn David Ungnad, Freyherrn zu Sonneck und Pfandsherrn auff Bleyburgk, aus Romischer Keyserlichen Maiestat befehlig und abforderung an den Türkischen Keyser, Anno 72. verrichtet*. 1582.

Orhonlu, Cengiz, ed. *Osmanlı Tarihine Âid Belgeler: Telhisler (1597–1607)*. Istanbul, 1970.

Oruç. *Der Fromme Sultan Bayezid: Die Geschichte seiner Herrschaft (1481–1512) nach den altosmanischen Chroniken des Oruç und der Anonymous Hanivaldanus*. Edited and translated by Richard F. Kreutel. Vienna and Cologne, 1978.

—— *Die Frühosmanischen Jahrbücher des Urudsch nach den Handschriften zu Oxford und Cambridge erstmals herausgegeben und eingeleitet*. Edited by Franz Babinger. Hanover, 1925.

Palerne, Jean. *Peregrinations du S. Jean Palerne Foresien*. Lyons, 1606.

Pardoe, Julia, and Bartlett, N. H. *Beauties of the Bosphorus*. London, 1840.

Peçevī, İbrāhīm. *Tārīḫ*. 2 vols. Istanbul, 1281–83 (1864–67).

Pertusi, Agostino, ed. *La Caduta di Costantinopoli*. 2 vols. Vol. 1, *Le testimonianze dei contemporenei*, vol. 2, *L'eco nel mondo*. Verona, 1976.

—— *Testi inediti e poco noti sulla caduta di Costantinopoli*. Edited posthumously by Antonio Carile. Bologna, 1983.

Piccolomini, Aeneas Silvius. *Epistola Ad Mahometam II (Epistle to Mohammad II)*. Edited and translated by Albert R. Bocca. New York, Bern, Frankfurt, Paris. 1990.

Pigafetta, Marc'Antonio. "Itinerario di Marc'Antonio Pigafetta," in P. Matković, *Putavanja po Balkanskom Poluotoku XVI. Vieka: X. Putopis Marka Antuna Pigefette, ili drugo putovanje Antuna Vrancica u Carigrad 1567. godine*. Zagreb, 1890, pp. 108–231.

Porphyrogénète, Constantin VII. *Le Livre des cérémonies*. Edited and translated from Greek by A. Vogt. 2 vols. Paris, 1935–40.

Postel, Guillaume. I. *De la Republique des Turcs; & là où l'occasion s'offrera, des moeurs & loy de tous Muhammedistes ... II. Histoire et consideration de l'origine, loy et coustume des Tartares ... Turcs III. La tierce partie des orientales histoires*. Poitiers, 1560.

Promontorio, Iacopo de Campis. "Die Aufzeichnungen des Genuesen Iacopo de Promontorio de Campis über den Osmanenstaat um 1475." [*Governo et Entrate del Gran Turco 1475. Stato del Gran Turco.*] Edited by Franz Babinger. *Sitzungsberichte, Jahrgang 1956, Heft 8, Bayerische Akademie der Wissenschaften Philosophisch-Historische Klasse*. Munich, 1957.

Ralamb, Claes, N. *Diarium eller resebok ... (1657–1658)*. Stockholm, 1688.

Ramberti, Benedetto. *Libri tre delle cose de Turchi, Nel primo si descrive il viaggio da Venetia à Constantinopoli, con gli nomi de' luoghi antichi moderni; Nel seconda la Porta, cioè la corte de Soltan Soleymano, Signor de' Turchi; Nel terzo il modo del reggere il stato & imperio suo*. Venice, 1539. Reprinted in A. H. Lybyer, *The Government of the Ottoman Empire in the time of Suleiman the Magnificent*. Cambridge, Mass., 1913, appendix, pp. 239–61.

Refik, Ahmet. "Fātīḥ Devrine ʿÂ'id Vesīkalar," *Tārīḫ-i ʿOsmānī Encümeni Mecmūʿası* 49–62 (1335–37/1916–19):1–58.

—— *Hicrî On Birinci Asırda İstanbul Hayatı (1000–1100)*. Istanbul, 1931.

—— "İznik Çinileri," *Darülfünun Edebiyat Fakültesi Mecmuası* 8, no. 4 (1932):36–53.

—— *On Altıncı Asırda İstanbul Hayatı (1553–1591)*. Istanbul, 1935.

Richards, John. *Diary on a journey from Naples to Constantinople, and thence to Vienna, on his discharge from the Venetian service, 15 July, 1699–21 September, 1700*. MS. London, British Museum, Stowe 462.

Rosedale, H. G., ed. *Queen Elizabeth and the Levant*

Company. A Diplomatic and Literary Episode of the Establishment of our Trade with Turkey. London, 1904.

Rūḥī-i Edrenevī. "Edirne'li Rûhî' ye Atfedilen Osmanlı Tarihinden İki Parça." Selections edited by V. L. Ménage in *İsmail Hakkı Uzunçarşılı'ya Armağan*. Ankara, 1976, pp. 311–33.

—— *Tārīḫ-i āl-i ‹osmān*. MS. Berlin, Staatsbibliothek, Or. Quart. 821.

Rüstem Paşa, *Die osmanische Chronik des Rustem Pascha*. Edited by Ludwig Forrer. Leipzig, 1923.

Rycaut, Paul. *The History of the Turkish Empire from the year 1623 to the year 1677*. London, 1680.

Sa‹deddīn, Ḫoca Efendi. *Tācü't-tevārīḫ*. 2 vols. Istanbul, 1279–80 (1862–63).

Ṣāfī, Muṣṭafā bin İbrāhīm. *Zübdetü't-tevārīḫ*. 2 vols. MS. TSK, R 1304.

Sagundino, Alvise. "Relazione [1496]," in Sanuto, vol. 1, p. 323; "Relazione [1499]," in Sanuto, vol. 2, p. 600.

Sā‹ī, Muṣṭafā. *Mimar Sinan, Hayatı, Eseri I: Mimar Sinan'ın Hayatına, Eserlerine Dair Metinler*. Edited by Rıfkı Melul Meriç. Ankara, 1965.

—— *Tezkiretü'l-bünyān*. Istanbul, 1315 (1897–98).

Saint-Blancard, Baron de. "Journal de la croisière du Baron de Saint Blancard" (1537–38) in E. Charrière, vol. 1, pp. 371–83.

Ṣalāḥī Efendi. *Żabṭ-i veḳāyi‹-i şehriyārī*. 1735–38. MS. İÜ, Halis Efendi, T 2518.

Salomone, Cormano. "A narrative of the events which occurred in Constantinople on the death of Sultan Murat and the accession of the new Sultan Mehemet by Salomone the Jewish man," February 1595. Translated from Italian, with a facsimile of the original, in H. G. Rosedale, pp. 19–33.

Sancy, Achille de Harlay [Baron de Mole]. *Description du Serail*. MS. Paris, Bibliothèque Nationale, Fonds Fr. 19029. Translation of Ottaviano Bon's account, without acknowledging the author.

Sanderson, John. *The Travels of John Sanderson in the Levant, 1584–1602*. Edited by Sir William Foster. London, 1931.

Sandys, George. *A Relation of a Journey begun An. Dom: 1610*, in Samuel Purchas, *Purchas His Pilgrimes*. Vol. 8. Glasgow, 1905, pp. 110–71.

Sansovino, Francesco. *Dell'Historia universale dell' origine et imperio de Turchi*. Venice, 1560.

Sanuto, Marino. *I Diarii di Marino Sanuto (1496–1533)*. 58 vols. Venice, 1879–1903.

Ṣarı Meḥmed Paşa, Defterdār. *Ottoman Statecraft: The Book of Counsel for Vezirs and Governors [Naṣā'iḥül-vüzerā ve'l ümerā]*. Translated by Walter Livingston Wright, Jr. Princeton, 1935.

Saumery, Pierre Lambert de. *Mémoires et aventures secrètes et curieuses d'un voyage du Levant*. 3 vols. Liège, 1731.

Scarella, Francesco. *Dissegni della città di Costantinopoli, delle sette torri, serraglio, e delle otto sue reali moschee*. December 1686. MS. Vienna, Nationalbibliothek, Cod. 8627.

Schedel, Hartmann. *Liber Chronicarum [Nuremberg Chronicle]*. Nuremberg, 1493.

Schepper, Corneille Duplicius de [Scepperus]. "Missions diplomatiques de Corneille Duplicius de Schepper (1533–34)." Edited by Baron de Saint-Genois, and G. A. Yssel de Schepper, in *Mémoires de l'Académie Royale de Belgique* 30 (1857):21–224.

Schweigger, Salomon. *Ein newe Reyssbeschreibung auss Teutschland nach Constantinopel und Jerusalem*. Nuremberg, 1608. Reprinted with an introduction by Rudolf Neck. Graz, 1964.

Sehī Beg. *Heşt Bihişt: The Tezkire by Sehī Beg, An Analysis of the First Biographical Work on Ottoman Poets, with a Critical Edition, Based on Süleymaniye Library, Ayasofya O. 3544*. Edited by Günay Kut. Cambridge, Mass., 1978.

Seidel, Friedrich [aus Oppau]. *Denckwürdige Gesandschafft an die ottomanische Pforte welche ehemals auf Röm. Kays. Maj. Rudolphi II Hohen Befehl Herr Friedrich von Kreckwitz* ... 1591. Görlitz, 1721.

Selānikī, Muṣṭafā. *Muṣṭafā Selānikī's History of the Ottomans*. Edited by Mehmet İpşirli. Ph.D. diss., University of Edinburgh, 1976.

—— *Tārīḫ*. MS. Gökbilgin private collection. Contains references to events after 1000 (1591–92), which are omitted in the published edition.

—— *Tārīḫ-i Selānikī*. Istanbul, 1281 (1864–65).

Şemsü'd-dīn Ḳaramānī, Dervīş. *Tercüme-i tārīḫ-i cāmi‹-i Ayaṣofya*. MS. İÜ, T 259.

Seydlitz, Melchior von. *Gründtliche Beschreibung: Der Wallfart nach dem heyligen Lande neben vermeldung der jemmerlichen und lang wirigen Gefengnuß derselben Gesellschaft*. Görlitz, 1580.

Şikārī. *Şikāri'nin Karaman Oğulları Tarihi*. Edited by M. Mesud Koman. Konya, 1946.

Ṣilāḥdār, Fındıḳlılı Meḥmed Ağa. *Ṣilāḥdār Ṭārīḫi*. 2 vols. Istanbul, 1928.

Simeon of Zamosc, *Polonyalı Simeon'un Seyahatnamesi (1608-1619)*. Translated from Armenian by Hrand D. Andreasyan. Istanbul, 1964.

Ṣolaḳzāde, Meḥmed. *Tārīḫ-i āl-i ‹os̱mān*. Istanbul, 1298 (1879).

Sorio, Giuseppe. *Descrizione di Costantinopoli: Lettera di Giuseppe Sorio, Viaggiatore Vicentino*. (1706-7). Vicenza, 1854.

Spandugino, Teodoro. "De la Origine delli imperatori ottomani, ordini de la corte, forma del guerreggiare loro, religione, rito et costumi de la natione," in C. Sathas, *Documents inédits relatifs à l'histoire de la Grèce*. 9 vols. Paris, 1880-90. Vol. 9, pp. 138-261.

—— *Petit Traicté de l'origine des Turcqs par Théodore Spandouyn Cantacasin*. Edited by Charles Schefer. Paris, 1896.

Sphrantzes, George. *The Fall of the Byzantine Empire: A Chronicle by George Sphrantzes (1401-1477)*. Translated by M. Philippides. Amherst, 1980.

Stirling-Maxwell, William. *Soliman the Magnificent Going to Mosque. From a series of engravings on wood published by Domenico de'Franceschi at Venice in MDLXII*. Florence and Edinburgh, 1877.

Şükrü Bidlīsī. *Selīmnāme*. 2 vols. MSS. TSK, H 1597-98.

Şükrullāh. *Behcetü't-tevārīḫ*. Translated from Persian by Nihal Atsız, in *Osmanlı Tarihleri* I. Istanbul, 1925-47, pp. 37-76.

Suriano, Francesco [Fra]. *Il Trattato di Terra Santa e dell'Oriente*. Edited by G. Golubovich. Milan, 1900.

Tācīzāde, Sa‹dī Çelebi. *Münşeāt*. Edited by Necati Lugal and Adnan Erzi. Istanbul, 1956.

Tafur, Pero. *Travels and Adventures (1435-1439)*. Edited and translated by Malcolm Letts. London, 1926.

Ta‹līḳīzāde. *Ta‹līḳī-zāde's Şehnāme-i hümāyūn: A History of the Ottoman Campaign into Hungary, 1593-94*. Edited by Christine Woodhead. Berlin, 1983.

al-Tamgrūtī, Abu'l-Ḥasan ‹Alī bin Muḥammed. *En Nafhat el-Miskiya fi-s-sifarat et-Tourkiya: Relation d'une ambassade marocaine en Turquie, 1589-1591*. Translated by H. de Castries. Paris, 1929.

Ṭāşköprīzāde, Kemāl. *Tārīḫ-i ṣāf*. 2 vols. Istanbul, 1287 (1870-71).

Tavernier, Jean-Baptiste. *Nouvelle Relation de l'Intérieur du Serrail du Grand Seigneur*. Paris, 1675.

Teşrīfātīzāde, Meḥmed. *Defter-i Teşrīfāt*. MS. Istanbul, Süleymaniye Kütüphanesi, Esad Efendi 2150. A late-seventeenth-century *Book of Ceremonies*.

Tevḳī‹ī, ‹Abdü'r-Raḥmān Paşa. *Ḳānūnnāme*. 1087 (1676). In "‹Os̱mānlı ḳānūnnāmeleri," *Millî Tetebbu‹lar Mecmū‹ası* 3 (1331/1912-13):497-544.

Thackston, W. M., comp. and trans. *A Century of Princes: Sources on Timurid Art*. Cambridge, Mass., 1989.

Thévenot, Jean de. *L'Empire du Grand Turc vu par un sujet de Louis XIV (1655)*. Edited by F. Billacois. Paris, 1965.

Ṭopçular Kātibi ‹Abdü'l-ḳādir. *Tevārīḫ-i āl-i ‹os̱mān*. MS. Istanbul, Süleymaniye Kütüphanesi, Esad Efendi 2151.

Tournefort, Joseph Pitton de. *Relation d'un voyage du Levant, fait par ordre du Roy*. 3 vols. Lyons, 1717.

Trevisano, Domenico. "Relazioni dell'Impero Ottomano [1554]," in Albèri vol. 1, pp. 111-92.

Tursun Beg. *The History of Mehmed the Conqueror by Tursun Beg*. Facsimile with commentary by Halil İnalcık and Rhoads Murphey. Minneapolis and Chicago, 1978.

Uğur, Ahmed. *The Reign of Sultan Selīm I in the Light of Selīm-nāme Literature*. Berlin, 1985.

Üsküdārī, ‹Abdullāh bin İbrāhīm. *Vaḳa‹āt-i Sulṭān Süleymān-i S̱ānī*. 3 vols. MSS. TSK, R 1223-25.

Valle, Francesco della. "Narrazione di Francesco dalla Valle Padovano, della grandezza, virtu, valore, ed infelice morte dell Illustrissimo Signor Conte Aloise Gritti," *Magyar Történelmi Tar* 3 (1857):9-60.

Valle, Pietro della. *Il Pellegrino ..., scritte dell'anno 1614 sin al 1626*. Rome, 1650. Translated into French as *Les Fameux Voyages de Pietro della Valle, gentilhomme romain, dans la Turquie, la Palestine, l'Égypte, la Perse, les Indes orientales et autres lieux*. 4 vols. Paris, 1661-64. Vol. 1.

Venier, Maffeo. *Descrittione dell'Imperio Turchesco*. 1582. MS. Venice, Biblioteca Patriarchalis, Sala Monico Cod. 34; and Biblioteca Marciana, Classe VI, Cod. DCCCLXXXII (8505).

Vigenère, Blaise de. *Histoire générale des Turcs, contenant l'histoire de Chalcondyle, traduite par Blaise de Vigenaire avec les illustrations du mesme Autheur et continuée iusques en l'an 1612 par Thomas Artus, en cette edition par le Sieur de Mezeray iusques en l'année 1661*. Paris, 1662.

Wenner, Adam. *Ein gantz new Reysebuch von Prag auß bis gen Constantinopel ... so Anno 1616 angefangen und Anno 1618 glücklich verricht*. Nuremberg, 1622.

Wheeler, George. *A Journey into Greece by George Wheeler Esq. in company of Dr. Spon of Lyons*. London, 1682.

Withers, Robert. "The Grand Signior's Seraglio," in Samuel Purchas, *Purchas His Pilgrimes*. Vol. 9. Glasgow, 1905, pp. 322–406. Translation of Ottaviano Bon's account, without acknowledging the author.

Wratislaw, Wenceslas [Baron]. *Adventures of Baron Wenceslas Wratislaw of Mitrowitz*. Translated from Bohemian by A. H. Wratislaw. London, 1862.

Wyts, Lambert. *Voyages de Lambert Wyts en Turquie, 1574*. MS. Vienna, Nationalbibliothek, Cod. Vindob. 3325*.

Zancani, Andrea. "Relazione [1499]," in Sanuto, vol. 2, pp. 598–600.

Zeno, Caterino. "Descrizione del viazo di Costantinopoli 1550 de ser Catharin Zen, ambassador straordinario a sultan Soliman, e suo ritorno." In P. Matković, ed., *Dva Talijanska Putopisa Po Balkanskom Poluotoku iz XVI. Vieka*. Zagreb, 1878, pp. 3–56.

Zeno, Pietro. "Sommario della Relazione [1523]," in Sanuto, vol. 37, pp. 104–5.

—— "Sommario della Relazione [1524]," in Albèri, vol. 3, pp. 93–97.

—— "Sommario della Relazione [1530]," in Albèri, vol. 3, pp. 119–22.

SELECTED SECONDARY SOURCES

Ackerman, James S. "Sources of the Renaissance Villa," in *Studies in Western Art: Acts of the XXth International Congress of the History of Art*. Vol. 2. Princeton, 1963, pp. 6–18.

—— *The Villa: Form and Ideology of Country Houses*. Princeton, 1990.

Ahat, Bikkul, U. "Topkapı Sarayında Has Ahır." *Güzel Sanatlar* 6 (1949):118–28.

Ahsan, M. M. *Social Life under the Abbasids*. London and New York, 1979.

Akalın, Şehabettin. "Mi'mar Dalgıç Ahmed Paşa." *Tarih Dergisi* 9, no. 13 (1958):71–80.

Akdağ, İffet. "Topkapı Sarayı Manzumesinin İlk Nüvesinin Geçirdiği İnkişafın Kuruluş Prensiplerinin İncelenmesi ve Tesbiti Hakkında bir Deneme." Ph.D. diss., Devlet Güzel Sanatlar Akademisi, Istanbul, 1959.

Akurgal, Ekrem, ed. *The Art and Architecture of Turkey*. New York, 1980.

Alderson, Anthony D. *The Structure of the Ottoman Dynasty*. Oxford, 1956.

Alföldi, A. *Die Ausgestaltung des monarchischen Zeremoniells am römischen Kaiserhofe*. Rome, 1934.

—— *Die monarchische Repraesentation im römischen Kaiserreiche*. Darmstadt, 1970.

Allen, Terry. *A Catalogue of the Toponyms and Monuments of Timurid Herat*. Cambridge, Mass., 1981.

—— *Timurid Herat*. Beihefte zum Tübinger Atlas des Vorderen Orients. Reihe B, nr. 56. Wiesbaden, 1983.

Alpay, Evin, and Schneider, Marcel. *Le Harem impérial de Topkapı*. Paris, 1977.

Altındağ, Ülkü. "Has Oda Teşkilatı." *Türk Etnoğrafya Dergisi* 14 (1974):97–113.

Anafarta, Nigar. *Hünername Minyatürleri ve Sanatçıları*. Istanbul, 1969.

Andaloro, M. "Costanzo da Ferrara: Gli anni a Costantinopoli alla corte di Maometto II." *Storia dell'Arte*

38/40 (1980): 185–212.

Andrews, Walter G. *Poetry's Voice, Society's Song*. Seattle and London, 1985.

Anhegger, Robert. "Quellen zur osmanischen Keramik," in K. Otto-Dorn, *Das islamische Iznik*. Berlin, 1941, pp. 165–95.

Anhegger-Eyüboğlu, Mualla. "Fatih Devrinde Yeni Sarayda da Harem Dairesi (Padişahın Evi) Var Mıydı?" *Sanat Tarihi Yıllığı* 8 (1979):23–36.

—— *Topkapı Sarayı'nda Padişah Evi (Harem)*. Istanbul, 1986.

Arel, Ayda. *Osmanlı Konut Geleneğinde Tarihsel Sorunlar*. Izmir, 1982.

Artan, Tülay. "Architecture as a Theater of Life: Profile of the Eighteenth Century Bosphorus." Ph.D. diss., Massachusetts Institute of Technology, Boston, 1989.

Aslanapa, Oktay. *Edirne'de Osmanlı Devri Abideleri*. Istanbul, 1949.

—— *Kırım ve Kuzey Azerbeycan'da Türk Eserleri*. Istanbul, 1979.

—— *Osmanlı Devri Mimarisi*. Istanbul, 1986.

—— *Turkish Art and Architecture*. London, 1971.

Atasoy, Nurhan. *İbrahim Paşa Sarayı*. Istanbul, 1972.

—— "Matrakçı's Representation of the Seven-Towered Topkapı Palace," in *Fifth International Congress of Turkish Art*. Budapest, 1978, pp. 93–101.

—— "Topkapı Sarayı Zülüflü Baltacılar Koğuşu," *I. Milletlerarası Türkoloji Kongresi (İstanbul, 1973). Türk Sanat Tarihi*. Pt. 3. Istanbul, 1979, pp. 627–32.

Atasoy, Nurhan, and Çağman, Filiz. *Turkish Miniature Painting*. Istanbul, 1974.

Atıl, Esin. *The Age of Sultan Süleyman the Magnificent*. Exh. cat. New York and Washington, 1986.

—— "Ottoman Miniature Painting Under Sultan Mehmed II." *Ars Orientalis* 9 (1973):103–20.

—— *Süleymanname: The Illustrated History of Süleyman the Magnificent*. New York and Washington, 1986.

—— ed. *Turkish Art*. New York and Washington, 1980.

Aykut, Altan. "İvan Peresvetov ve Sultan Mehmet Menkıbesi." *Belleten* 46, nos. 183–84 (1982):861–82.

Ayverdi, Ekrem Hakkı. *Fatih Devri Mimarisi*. Istanbul, 1953.

—— *Osmanlı Mimarisinde Fatih Devri 855–886 (1451–1485)*. Rev. ed. Istanbul, 1974, pp. 682–755.

Babinger, Franz. *Aufsätze und Abhandlungen zur Geschichte Südosteuropas und der Levante*. 3 vols. Munich, 1962–76.

—— "Drei Stadtansichten von Konstantinopel, Galata ("Pera") und Skutari aus dem ende des 16. Jahrhunderts." *Österreichische Akademie der Wissenschaften Philologisch-Historische Klasse. Denkschriften,* 77. Band, 3. *Abhandlung*. Vienna, 1959.

—— *Die Geschichtschreiber der Osmanen und ihre Werke*. Leipzig, 1927.

—— *Mehmed the Conqueror and His Time*. Edited by W. C. Hickman, translated by R. Manheim. Princeton, 1978.

—— "Sultanischer Reliquienschacher im Frankenland," in *Spätmittelalterliche Fränkische Briefschaften aus dem Grossherrlichen Seraj zu Stambul*. Munich and Oldenburg, 1963, pp. 96–119.

—— "Zwei Stambuler Gesamtansichten aus den Jahren 1616 und 1642." *Bayerische Akademie der Wissenschaften Philologisch-Historische Klasse. Abhandlungen,* N. F. Heft 50. Munich, 1960, pp. 1–16.

Baykal, İsmail, H. *Enderun Mektebi Tarihi*. Istanbul, 1953.

Becatti, G. *La Colonna coclide istoriata*. Rome, 1960.

Behrens-Abouseif, Doris. "The Citadel of Cairo: Stage for Mamluk Ceremonial." *Annales Islamologiques* 24 (1988):25–79.

Bentmann, R., and Müller, M. *Die Villa als Herrschaftsarchitektur: Versuch einer kunst- und sozialgeschichtlichen Analyse*. Frankfurt, 1970.

Bernus-Taylor, Marthe, et al. *Soliman le Magnifique*. Exh. cat. Paris, Galeries Nationales du Grand Palais, 1990.

Bertelè, Tommaso. *Il Palazzo degli Ambasciatori di Venezia a Costantinopoli e le sue antiche memorie*. Bologna, 1932.

Białostocki, Jan. *The Art of the Renaissance in Eastern Europe*. Ithaca, N.Y., 1976.

Bilge, Aygen. "Fatih Zamanında Topkapı Sarayı Suyu." *Türk Sanatı Tarihi Araştırma ve İncelemeleri* 2 (1969):214–22.

Binney, Edwin 3d. *Turkish Treasures from the Collection of Edwin Binney, 3rd*. Exhibition at the Portland Art Museum, Portland Or., 1979.

Bombaci, Alesio. "Qutlug Bolzun! A Contribution to the

History of the Concept of Fortune among the Turks, Part One." *Ural-Altaische Jahrbücher* 36 (1964):284–91.

—— "Qutlug Bolsun! ... Part Two." *Ural-Altaische Jahrbücher* 38 (1966):13–43.

Braudel, Fernand. *The Mediterranean and the Mediterranean World in the Age of Philip* II. 2 vols. New York and London, 1976.

Brett, G., Martiny, G., and Stevenson, R. *The Great Palace of the Byzantine Emperors.* Oxford, 1947.

Brown, Patricia Fortini. *Venetian Narrative Painting in the Age of Carpaccio.* New Haven and London, 1988.

Brown, Percy. *Indian Architecture (The Islamic Period).* Bombay, 1949.

Brown, Peter. *The World of Late Antiquity* AD *150–750.* London, 1971.

Bryer, Anthony, and Lowry, Heath, eds. *Continuity and Change in Late Byzantine and Early Ottoman Society.* Birmingham, England, and Washington, D.C., 1986.

Çağman, Filiz. "Altın Hazine Matarası." *Topkapı Sarayı Müzesi Yıllık* 2 (1987):85–123.

—— "Osmanlı Sanatı," in *Anadolu Medeniyetleri.* Exh. cat., vol. 3. Istanbul, 1983, pp. 97–105.

—— "Şahname-i Selim Han ve Minyatürleri." *Sanat Tarihi Yıllığı* 5 (1973):411–42.

—— "Serzergerân Mehmed Usta ve Eserleri," in *Kemal Çığ'a Armağan.* Istanbul, 1984, pp. 51–89.

Cahen, Claude. *Pre-Ottoman Turkey.* Translated by J. Jones-Williams. New York, 1968.

Cameron, Averil. "The Construction of Court Ritual: the Byzantine *Book of Ceremonies,*" in Cannadine and Price, pp. 106–37.

Canard, Maurice. "Le Cérémonial fatimite et cérémonial byzantin: Essai de comparaison." *Byzantion* 21 (1951):355–420.

Cannadine, David, and Price, Simon, eds. *Rituals of Royalty: Power and Ceremonial in Traditional Societies.* New York and London, 1987.

Çeçen, Kazım. *İstanbulda Osmanlı Devrindeki Su Tesisleri.* Istanbul, 1984.

Çığ, Kemal. "The Decoration on the Ceiling of the Throne which Belongs to Mehmed III in the Reception Room of the Topkapı Palace." *Quatrième Congrès International d'Art Turc.* Aix-en-Provence, 1976, pp. 47–48.

—— "Fatih Topkapı Sarayını Niçin Yaptırdı?" in *Kemal Çığ'a Armağan.* Istanbul, 1984, pp. 17–35.

—— "1960–1969 Seneleri Arasında Topkapı Sarayında Yapılan Restorasyonlar Esnasındaki Buluntular." VII. *Türk Tarih Kongresi, Kongreye Sunulan Bildiriler.* II. Ankara, 1973, pp. 693–97.

—— "A Unique Ceiling-Style Newly-Discovered in the Harem of the Topkapı Palace." *Atti del Secondo Congresso Internazionale di Arte Turca.* Naples, 1965, pp. 57–60.

Creswell, K. A. C. *Early Muslim Architecture.* 2 vols. Oxford, 1932, 1940.

Ćurčić, Slobodan. "Some Palatine Aspects of the Capella Palatina in Palermo," in *Studies in Art and Architecture in Honor of Ernst Kitzinger on His Seventy-fifth Birthday.* Edited by W. Tronzo and I. Lavin. Washington, D.C., 1987, pp. 125–44.

Dagron, Gilbert. *Constantinople imaginaire.* Paris, 1984.

Davis, Fanny. *The Palace of Topkapı in Istanbul.* New York, 1970.

Demangel, R., and Mamboury, E. *Le Quartier des Manganes et la première région de Constantinople.* Paris, 1939.

Denny, Walter. *The Ceramics of the Mosque of Rüstem Pasha and the Environment of Change.* New York, 1977.

—— "A Sixteenth-Century Architectural Plan of Istanbul." *Ars Orientalis 8* (1970):49–63.

Dickie, James. "The Hispano-Arab Garden, Its Philosophy and Function." *Bulletin of the School of Oriental and African Studies* 31 (1986):237–48.

Dieterich, Karl. *Christlich-orientalisches Kulturgut des Türken.* Leipzig, 1917.

—— *Hofleben in Byzans.* Voigtländers Quellenbücher, no. 19. Leipzig, 1912.

—— "Türkentum und Byzantinertum." *Beilage der Münchner Neusten Nachrichten* 127/128 (1908).

Dilger, Konrad. *Untersuchungen zur Geschichte des osmanischen Hofzeremoniells im 15. und 16. Jahrhundert.* Beiträge zur Kenntnis Südosteuropas und des Nahen Orients, Band IV. Munich, 1967.

Durukan, Zeynep M. *The Harem of the Topkapı Palace.* Istanbul, 1973.

Ebersolt, J. *Le Grand palais de Constantinople et le livre des cérémonies.* Paris, 1910.

Ehalt, H. Ch. "Schloss und Palastarchitektur im Absolutismus," in H. Stekl, ed., *Architektur und Gesellschaft.* Salzburg, 1980, pp. 161–249.

Eldem, Sedad Hakkı. *Köşkler ve Kasırlar: A Survey of Turkish Kiosks and Pavilions.* 2 vols. Istanbul, 1969–73.

—— *Türk Bahçeleri.* Istanbul, 1976.

—— *Türk Evi: Turkish Houses.* 3 vols. Istanbul, 1984–87.

Eldem, Sedad Hakkı, and Akozan, Feridun. *Topkapı Sarayı: Bir Mimari Araştırma.* Istanbul, 1982.

Elias, Norbert. *The Court Society.* Translated by Edmund Jephcott. New York, 1983.

Emler, Selma. "Le Palais royal de Topkapı et ses restaurations," in *Atti del Secondo Congresso Internazionale di Arte Turca,* Naples, 1965, pp. 65–72.

—— "Topkapı Sarayı Restorasyon ve Çalışmaları." *Türk Sanatı Tarihi Araştırma ve İncelemeleri* 1 (1963):211–312.

Encyclopedia of Islam. 10 vols. 1st ed., Leiden, 1913–42; 2d ed., 1956–.

Erdmann, Kurt. "Die Fliesen am Sünnet odası des Top Kapı Saray in Istanbul," in *Aus der Welt der islamischen Kunst—Festschrift für Ernst Kühnel.* Edited by R. Ettinghausen. Berlin, 1959, pp. 144–53.

Erdoğan, M. "Mimar Davut Ağa'nın Hayatı ve Eserleri." *Türkiyat Mecmuası* 12 (1955):179–204.

Erkins, Ziya. "Osmanlı haremi ne zaman kuruldu?" *Tarih Dünyası* 15 (1950):362–65.

—— *Topkapı Sarayı Müzesi.* Istanbul, 1965.

Errington, Shelly. *Meaning and Power in a Southeast Asian Realm.* Princeton, 1989.

Ettinghausen, Richard. *From Byzantium to Sasanian Iran and the Islamic World.* Leiden, 1972.

—— *Islamic Art and Archaeology.* Berlin, 1985.

Ettinghausen, Richard, and Grabar, Oleg. *The Art and Architecture of Islam, 650–1250.* New York, 1987.

Eyice, Semavi, "İstanbul'da Bizans İmparatorlarının Sarayı Büyük Saray." *Sanat Tarihi Araştırmaları Dergisi* 1, no. 3 (September 1988):3–36.

Fisher, C. G., and Fisher, A. W. "Topkapı Sarayı in the Mid-Seventeenth Century: Bobovi's Description." *Archivium Ottomanicum* 10 (1985 [1987]):5–81.

Fleischer, H. Cornell. *Bureaucrat and Intellectual in the Ottoman Empire: The Historian Mustafa Âli (1541–1600).* Princeton, 1986.

Fletcher, Joseph, Jr. "Turco-Mongolian Monarchic Tradition in the Ottoman Empire." *Harvard Ukrainian Studies* 3–4 (1979–80):236–51.

Gabriel, Albert. *Châteaux turcs du Bosphore.* Paris, 1943.

Geertz, Clifford. *The Interpretation of Cultures.* New York, 1973.

Gibb, H. A. R., and Bowen, Harold. *Islamic Society and the West.* 2 vols. London and New York, 1950, 1957.

Giz, Adnan. "17. Yüzyılda Osmanlı Padişahlarının Günlük Yemek Masrafları." *Belgelerle Türk Tarihi Dergisi* 6 (1968):76–78.

Göllner, Carl. *Turcica: Die europäischen Türkendrucke des* XVI. Jahrhunderts. 2 vols. Bucharest and Berlin, 1961–68.

Golombek, Lisa, and Wilber, Donald. *The Timurid Architecture of Iran and Turan.* 2 vols. Princeton, 1988.

Golvin, Lucien. *Palais et demeures d'Alger à la période ottomane.* Aix-en-Provence, 1988.

Goodwin, Godfrey. *A History of Ottoman Architecture.* Baltimore, 1971.

Grabar, Oleg. *The Alhambra.* Cambridge, Mass., 1978.

—— "Ceremonial and Art at the Umayyad Court." Ph.D. diss., Princeton University, 1955.

—— *The Formation of Islamic Art.* New Haven and London, 1973.

Gray, Basil. "The Tradition of Wall Painting in Iran," in *Highlights of Persian Art.* Edited by Richard E. Ettinghausen and Ehsan Yarshater. Boulder, Col., 1979.

Grosrichard, Alain. *Structure du sérail: La fiction du despotisme asiatique dans l'Occident classique.* Paris, 1979.

Guilland, R. *Études de topographie de Constantinople byzantine.* 2 vols. Berlin and Amsterdam, 1969.

Günay, Reha. "Süleymanname Minyatürlerinde Mekan ve Anlatım Teknikleri." Postdoctoral thesis, Yıldız University, Istanbul, 1987.

Gurlitt, Cornelius. *Die Baukunst Konstantinopels.* 4 portfolios. Berlin, 1907–12.

—— "Der Serai in Konstantinopel, nach europäischen Quellen." *Beiträge zur Kenntnis des Orients* 12 (1915):31–63.

Hale, J. R. "The development of the bastion: an Italian Chronology," in *Europe in the Late Middle Ages.* Edited by J. R. Hale, R. Highfield, and B. Smalley. London, 1965.

—— *Renaissance Fortification: Art or Engineering?.* London, 1977.

Halil, Ethem. *Topkapı Sarayı.* Istanbul, 1931.

Hammer-Purgstall, Joseph von. *Constantinopolis und der Bosporus.* 2 vols. Pest, 1822.

—— *Des osmanischen Reiches Staatsverfassung und Staatsverwaltung.* 2 vols. Vienna, 1815.

—— *Geschichte des osmanischen Reiches.* 10 vols. Pest, 1827–35.

Hersey, G. L. *Pythagorean Palaces: Magic and Architecture in the Italian Renaissance.* Ithaca and London, 1976.

Herzfeld, E. *Geschichte der Stadt Samarra.* Berlin, 1923.

Heyd, Uriel. "Bāb-i Hümāyūn." *Encyclopedia of Islam.* 2d. ed., p. 860.

Heydenreich, Ludwig H. "Federico da Montefeltro as a Building Patron: Some Remarks on the Ducal Palace of Urbino," in *Studies in Renaissance and Baroque Art presented to Anthony Blunt.* London and New York, 1967, pp. 1–6.

Heywood, Colin. "The Activities of the State Cannon-Foundry (*ṭopḫāne-i ʿāmire*) at Istanbul in the early Sixteenth Century, According to an Unpublished Turkish Source," in *Revue de Philologie Orientale* III. *Symposium international d'études pre-ottomans et ottomanes (Sarajevo 1978).* Sarajevo, 1980, pp. 209–17.

Hobsbawm, E., and Ranger, T. eds. *The Invention of Tradition.* Cambridge, England, 1983.

Hodgson, Marshall G.S. *The Venture of Islam.* 3 vols. Chicago, 1974.

Hollingsworth, Mary. "The Architect in Fifteenth-Century Florence." *Art History* 7, no. 4 (1984):385–410.

Huizinga, Johan. *Homo Ludens.* Boston, 1955.

Hunt, Lucy-Anne. "Comnenian Aristocratic Palace Decoration: Descriptions and Islamic Connections," in *The Byzantine Aristocracy,* IX *to* XIII *Centuries.* Edited by M. Angold. London, 1984.

Imber, Colin. *The Ottoman Empire 1300–1481.* Istanbul, 1990.

İnalcık, Halil. *Fatih Devri Üzerinde Tetkikler ve Vesikalar.* Ankara, 1954.

—— "Istanbul." *Encyclopedia of Islam.* 2d. ed., pp. 224–48.

—— "Ḳānūn." *Encyclopedia of Islam.* 2d. ed., pp. 558–62.

—— "Ḳānūnnāme." *Encyclopedia of Islam.* 2d. ed., pp. 562–66.

—— "Osmanlı Hukukuna Giriş." *Ankara Üniversitesi Siyasal Bilgiler Fakültesi Dergisi* 13, no. 2 (1958):102–26.

—— *The Ottoman Empire: The Classical Age, 1300–1600.* Translated by N. Itzkowitz and C. Imber. New York, 1973.

—— "The Policy of Mehmet II toward the Greek Population of Istanbul and the Byzantine Buildings of the City." *Dumbarton Oaks Papers* 23/24 (1969–70): 231–49.

—— "The Rise of the Ottoman Empire," in *A History of the Ottoman Empire to 1730.* Edited by M. A. Cook. Cambridge, England, and New York, 1976, pp. 10–53.

Itzkowitz, Norman. *Ottoman Empire and Islamic Tradition.* New York, 1972.

Jackson, Peter, and Lockhart, Laurence, eds. *The Cambridge History of Iran.* Vol. 6, *The Timurid and Safavid Periods.* London and New York, 1986.

Jacobs, Emil. "Untersuchungen zur Geschichte der Bibliothek im Serai von Konstantinopel." *Sitzungsberichte der Heidelberger Akademie der Wissenschaften Philologisch-Historische Klasse. Abhandlung 24.* Heidelberg, 1919.

Janin, R. *Constantinople byzantine.* 2d. ed. Paris, 1964.

Kamil, Ekrem. "Hicri Onuncu Miladi onaltıncı asırda yurdumuzu dolaşan Arab seyyahlarından Gazzî—Mekkî Seyahatnamesi." *Edebiyat Fakültesi Tarih Semineri Dergisi* 1/2 (1937). Extracts from the Arabic travelogues of Gazzi, 936–37 (1529–30) and Mekkî, 968 (1557).

Kantorowicz, H. Ernst. *The King's Two Bodies: A Study in Medieval Political Theology.* Princeton, 1957.

Kappert, Petra. *Die osmanischen Prinzen und ihre Residenz Amasya im 15. und 16. Jahrhundert.* London, 1976.

Karabacek, Joseph von. "Abendländische Künstler zu Konstantinopel im XV. und XVI. Jahrhunderts." *Kaiserliche Akademie der Wissenschaften in Wien Philologisch-Historische Klasse. Denkschriften* 62. Band 1. Vienna, 1916.

Karpat, Kemal, ed. *The Ottoman State and Its Place in World History*. Leiden, 1974.

Kırımlı, Faik. "İstanbul Çiniciliği." *Sanat Tarihi Yıllığı* 11 (1981):95–111.

Kissling, Hans Joachim. *Sultan Bājezīd's II. Beziehungen zu Markgraf Francesco II von Gonzaga*. Munich, 1965.

Kleiss, Wolfram. "Der Mongolische Palast." *Archäologischer Anzeiger* 4 (1962): 665–70.

Koçu, Reşat Ekrem. *A Guide to the Topkapı Palace Museum*. Istanbul, 1968.

Konyalı, İ. Hakkı. *Fatihin Mimarlarından Azadlı Sinan*. Istanbul, 1953.

—— *İstanbul Abidelerinden İstanbul Sarayları*. Istanbul, 1942.

Köprülü, Mehmet Fuat. "Bizans Müesseselerinin Osmanlı Müesseselerine Tesiri hakkında bazı mülâhazalar," in *Türk Hukuk ve İktisat Tarihi Mecmuası*. Istanbul, 1931, pp. 165–313.

Köseoğlu, Cengiz. *Harem*. Istanbul, 1979.

Kostof, Spiro. *A History of Architecture: Settings and Rituals*. New York and Oxford, 1985.

Kreiser, Klaus. "Archivalisch überlieferte Inschriften aus Istanbul." *Istanbuler Mitteilungen* 32 (1982):258–78.

—— "Zwei unbekannte Beschreibungen des Serails von Edirne aus den Jahren 1740/1." *Osmanlı Araştırmaları* 3 (1982):119–42.

Kuban, Doğan. "Architecture of the Ottoman Period." *The Art and Architecture of Turkey*, ed. E. Akurgal. New York, 1980, pp. 137–69.

Kumbaracı, İzzet. *Hekim-başı Odası, ilk Eczane, Baş-Lala Kulesi*. Istanbul, 1933.

Kunt, Metin. *The Sultan's Servants: The Transformation of Ottoman Provincial Government, 1550–1650*. New York, 1983.

Kuran, Aptullah. *The Mosque in Early Ottoman Architecture*. Chicago, 1968.

—— "The Palace of the Sultans: The Grand Seraglio." *Turkish Review Quarterly Digest* 1, no. 4 (1986):107–19.

—— *Sinan: The Grand Old Man of Ottoman Architecture*. Istanbul, 1987.

Kurz, Otto. *European Clocks and Watches in the Near East*. Leiden, 1975.

Labarte, J. *Le Palais impérial de Constantinople et ses abords*. Paris, 1861.

Lampe, Melek Celal. *Le Vieux Serail des Sultans*. Istanbul, 1959.

Lane, A. "The Ottoman Pottery of İznik." *Ars Orientalis* 2 (1957):241–81.

Lassner, J. *The Topography of Baghdad in the Early Middle Ages*. Detroit, 1970.

Lentz, Thomas W., and Lowry, Glenn D. *Timur and the Princely Vision: Persian Art and Culture in the Fifteenth Century*. Exh. cat. Los Angeles County Museum of Art and Arthur M. Sackler Gallery, Los Angeles, 1989.

Lewis, Bernard. *Istanbul and the Civilization of the Ottoman Empire*. Norman, Ok., 1963.

Lindner, Rudi Paul. *Nomads and Ottomans in Medieval Anatolia*. Bloomington, Ind., 1983.

L'Orange, H. *Studies on the Iconography of Cosmic Kingship*. Oslo, 1953.

Lybyer, A. H. *The Government of the Ottoman Empire in the Time of Suleiman the Magnificent*. Cambridge, Mass., 1913.

MacDonald, William, L. *The Architecture of the Roman Empire*. Vol. 1, *An Introductory Study*. Vol. 2, *An Urban Appraisal*. New Haven and London, 1982, 1988.

MacDougall, E., and Ettinghausen, Richard, eds. *The Islamic Garden*. Dumbarton Oaks Colloquium on the History of Landscape Architecture. Vol. 4. Washington, D.C., 1976.

Mahir, Banu. "Saray Nakkaşhanesinin Ünlü Ressamı Şah Kulu ve Eserleri." *Topkapı Sarayı Müzesi Yıllık* 1 (1986):113–31.

Mamboury, Ernest, and Wiegand, T. *Die Kaiserpaläste von Konstantinopel*. Berlin, 1934.

Mango, Cyril. *The Brazen House: A Study of the Vestibule of the Imperial Palace of Constantinople*. Copenhagen, 1954.

—— *Byzantine Architecture*. New York, 1985.

—— *Le Développement urbain de Constantinople (IVe–VIIe siècles)*. Paris, 1985.

Mansel, Philip. *An Outline of the Political and Social*

History of Royal Guards, 1400–1984: Pillars of Monarchy. London and New York, 1984.

Mantran, Robert. *Istanbul dans la seconde moitié du XVIIe siècle.* Paris, 1962.

—— *La vie quotidienne à Constantinople du temps de Soliman le Magnifique et ses successeurs, XVIe et XVIIe siècles.* Paris, 1965.

Maury, B. *Palais et maisons du Caire (XIVe–XVIIIe s.).* Vol. 4. Cairo, 1983.

Maury, B., Raymond, A., Revault, J, and Zakariya, M. *Palais et maisons du Caire.* Vol. 2, *Epoque ottomane (XVIe–XVIIe s.).* Paris, 1983.

Mayes, Stanley. *An Organ for the Sultan.* London, 1956.

McCormick, Michael. "Analyzing Imperial Ceremonies." *Jahrbuch der Österreichischen Byzantinistik* 35 (1985):1–20.

McNeill, William H. *Europe's Steppe Frontier, 1500–1800.* Chicago, 1964.

Meinecke, Michael. *Fayencedekorationen seldschukischer Sakralbauten in Kleinasien.* 2 vols. Tübingen, 1976.

—— "Mamlukische Marmordekorationen in der osmanischen Türkei." *Mitteilungen des Deutschen Archäologischen Instituts, Abteilung Kairo* 27, no. 2 (1971):207–20.

Meriç, Rıfkı Melul. *Beyazıd Cāmii Mimarı.* Ankara, 1958.

Meyer zur Capellen, Jürg. *Gentile Bellini.* Stuttgart, 1985.

Michell, George, ed. *Architecture of the Islamic World.* London, 1978.

Miller, Barnette. *Beyond the Sublime Porte: The Grand Seraglio of Stambul.* 1913. Reprint, New York, 1970.

—— *The Palace School of Muhammad the Conqueror.* Cambridge, Mass., 1941.

Millingen, A. van. *Byzantine Constantinople: The Walls of the City and Adjoining Historical Sites.* London, 1899.

Moore, Sally F., and Myerhoff, Barbara G. *Secular Ritual.* Assen, 1977.

Moos, Stanislaus von. *Turm und Bollwerk: Beiträge zu einer politischen Ikonographie der italienischen Renaissance architektur.* Zurich and Freiburg, 1974.

Muir, Edward. *Civic Rituals in Venice.* Princeton, 1980.

Müller-Wiener, Wolfgang. *Bildlexikon zur Topographie Istanbul's: Byzantion, Konstantinopolis, Istanbul bis zum Beginn des 17. Jahrhundert.* Tübingen, 1977.

Mumcu, Ahmet. *Hukuksal ve Siyasal Karar Organı Olarak Divan-ı Hümayun.* Ankara, 1976.

Murphey, Rhoads. "The Veliyüddin Telhis: Notes on the Sources and Interrelations between Koçi Bey and Contemporary Writers of Advice to Kings." *Belleten* 43 (1979):547–71.

Naumann, Elisabeth and Rudolf. "Ein Köşk im Sommerpalast des Abaqa Khan auf dem Tacht-i Sulaiman und seine Dekoration," *Forschungen zur Kunst Asiens: Im Memoriam Kurt Erdmann,* ed. O. Aslanapa and R. Naumann, Istanbul, 1969, pp. 35–65.

Necipoğlu, Gülru. "From International Timurid to Ottoman: A Change of Taste in Sixteenth-Century Ceramic Tiles," in *Muqarnas* 7 (1990):136–70.

—— "Süleyman the Magnificent and the Representation of Power in a Context of Ottoman-Hapsburg-Papal Rivalry." *Art Bulletin* 71 (September 1989):401–27.

Necipoğlu-Kafadar, Gülru. "The Account Book of a Fifteenth-Century Ottoman Royal Kiosk," in *Raiyyet Rüsumu: Essays Presented to Halil İnalcık on His Seventieth Birthday, Journal of Turkish Studies* 11 (1987):31–45.

—— "Plans and Models in 15th- and 16th-Century Ottoman Architectural Practice." *Journal of the Society of Architectural Historians* 45 (September 1986):224–43.

—— "The Süleymaniye Complex in Istanbul: An Interpretation." *Muqarnas* 3 (1985):92–118.

Nirven, Saadi Nazım. *İstanbul Suları.* Istanbul, 1946.

Oberhummer, Eugen. *Konstantinopel unter Sultan Suleiman dem Grossen: aufgenommen im Jahre 1559 durch Melchior Lorichs.* Munich, 1902.

Ödekan, Ayla. *Arkeoloji Sanat Tarihi ve Mimarlık Tarihi ile İlgili Yayınlar Bibliografyası (1923–1973).* Istanbul, 1974.

O'Kane, Bernard. *Timurid Architecture in Khurasan.* Costa Mesa, Calif., 1987.

Olivato, Loredana. "Giovan Maria Angiolello: Un Vicentino tra i Turchi nel Rinascimento." *Il Veltro* 23, nos. 2–4 (1979):143–49.

Önge, Y. "Topkapı Sarayında Hırka-i Saadet Dairesi," *Önasya* 3, no. 31 (1968):12–24.

Orgun, Zarif. "Alay Köşkü." *Arkitekt* 309 (1962):153–61.

—— "Çinili Köşk," *Arkitekt* 11/12 (1941–42):252–59.

—— "Kubbealtı ve yapılan merasim," *Güzel Sanatlar* 6 (1949):91–108.

Örs, Hayrullah. "Haremin Muamması." *Türkiyemiz* 2 (1970):2–12.

—— "The History of the Topkapı Palace." *Apollo* 92, no. 101 (1970):6–17.

Osman, Rıfat. *Edirne Sarayı*. Edited by S. Ünver. Ankara, 1957.

Öz, İlban. "Topkapı Sarayının İlk Hünkâr Hamamı," in *Kemal Çığ'a Armağan*. Istanbul, 1984, pp. 157–65.

Öz, Tahsin. *Guide to the Museum of Topkapu Saray*. Translation by S. S. Moralı, Istanbul, 1936.

—— *Hırka-i Saadet dairesi ve Emanat-i Mukaddese*. Istanbul, 1953.

—— *İstanbul Camileri*. 2 vols. Ankara, 1962–65.

—— *Topkapı Sarayı Müzesi Arşivi Kılavuzu* II. Istanbul, 1938.

—— "Topkapı Sarayı Müzesi Arşivinde Fatih II. Sultan Mehmed'e Aid Belgeler." *Belleten* 14, no. 53 (1950).

—— "Topkapı Sarayı Müzesi Onarımları," *Güzel Sanatlar* 6 (1949):6–74.

Pakalın, Mehmed Zeki. *Maliye Teşkilatı Tarihi*. 4 vols. Ankara, 1977.

—— *Osmanlı tarih deyimleri ve terimleri sözlüğü*. 3 vols. Istanbul, 1951.

Penzer, N. M. *The Harem: An Account of the Institution as It Existed in the Palace of the Turkish Sultans with a History of the Grand Seraglio from Its Foundation to the Present Time*. London, 1936.

Petry, Carl F. *The Civilian Elite of Cairo in the Later Middle Ages*. Princeton, 1981.

Petsopoulos, Yani, ed. *Tulips, Arabesques and Turbans: Decorative Arts from the Ottoman Empire*. New York, 1982.

Pitcher, Donald Edgar. *An Historical Geography of the Ottoman Empire*. Leiden, 1972.

Preto, Paolo. *Venezia e i Turchi*. Florence, 1975.

Raby, Julian. "El Gran Turco: Mehmed the Conqueror as a Patron of the Arts of Christendom." Ph.D. diss., Oxford University, 1980.

—— "Mehmed the Conqueror's Greek Scriptorium." *Dumbarton Oaks Papers* 37 (1983):15–34.

—— "Pride and Prejudice: Mehmed the Conqueror and the Portrait Medal," in *Italian Medals*. Edited by J. G. Pollard. Washington, D.C., 1987, pp. 171–94.

—— "A Sultan of Paradox: Mehmed the Conqueror as a Patron of the Arts," *Oxford Art Journal*, no. 1 (1982):3–8.

Raby, Julian, and Yücel, Önsal. "Chinese Porcelain at the Ottoman Court" and "The Archival Documentation," in *Chinese Ceramics in the Topkapı Saray Museum Istanbul*. Edited by J. Ayers. Vol. 1. London, 1986, pp. 27–55, 65–86.

Refik, Mehmed. "Enderūn-i Hümāyūn devā'īr-i ‹ālīyyesinden ‹Arżoṭası." *Tārīḫ-i ‹Os̱mānī Encümeni Mecmū‹ası* 38 (1332/1914):110–16.

Repp, R. C. *The Müfti of Istanbul*. London, 1986.

Restle, Marcell. "Bauplanung und Baugesinnung unter Mehmed II Fātih." *Pantheon* 39 (1981):361–67.

Reuther, Oskar. *Indische Paläste und Wohnhauser*. Berlin, 1925.

Revault, J., and Maury, B. *Palais et maisons du Caire (XIVe–XVIIIe s.)*. 3 vols. Cairo, 1975, 1977, 1979.

Reyhanlı, Tülay. *İngiliz Gezginlerine Göre XVI. Yüzyılda İstanbul'da Hayat (1582–1599)*. Ankara, 1983.

Rogers, J. Michael. "An Ottoman palace inventory of the reign of Bayczid II," CIEPO Proceedings, ed. J.-L. Bacqué-Grammont and E. van Donzel. Istanbul, 1987, pp. 40–53.

—— *The Spread of Islam*. Oxford, 1976.

—— *The Topkapı Saray Museum: Architecture, The Harem and Other Buildings*. Edited and translated from Turkish texts by K. Çığ, S. Batur, and C. Köseoğlu. Boston, 1988.

Rogers, J. M. and Ward, R. M., *Süleyman the Magnificent*, Exh. Cat. London, 1988.

Rouillard, C. D. *The Turk in French History, Thought, and Literature (1520–1660)*. Paris, 1938.

Rubiera, Jesús María. *La Arquitectura en la literatura arabe datos para una estética del placer*. Madrid, 1981.

Sahillioğlu, Halil. "Osmanlı Para Tarihinde Dünya Para ve Maden Hareketlerinin Yeri (1300–1750)." *Ortadoğu Teknik Üniversitesi Gelişme Dergisi, Special Issue, 1978: Türkiye İktisat Tarihi Üzerine Araştırmalar*, pp. 1–38.

Said, Edward. *Orientalism*. New York, 1979.

Sakisian, A. "Les Faiances du bain de Selim II au Harem du Vieux Serail," in *Mélanges syriens offerts à R. Dussaud*. Paris, 1939, pp. 959–63.

Sarre, Friedrich. *Der Kiosk von Konia*. Berlin, 1936.
—— "Michelangelo und der Türkische Hof." *Repertorium für Kunstwissenschaft* 33 (1909), pp. 61–66.
Schneider, Marcel, and Evin, Alpay. *Le Harem impérial de Topkapı*. Paris, 1977.
Schramm, Percy Ernst. *Herrschaftzeichen und Staatsymbolik*. 3 vols. Stuttgart, 1954–56.
—— *Sphaira, Globus, Reichsapfel: Wanderung und Wandlung eines Herrshaftszeichens von Caesar bis zu Elisabeth II, Ein Beitrag zum "Nachleben" der Antike*. Stuttgart, 1958.
Schwoebel, Robert S. *The Shadow of the Crescent: The Renaissance Image of the Turk, 1453–1517*. Nieuwkoop, 1967.
Şehsuvaroğlu, B. N. *İstanbul Sarayları*. Istanbul, 1954.
Şeref, ‹Abdurraḥmān. "Topḳapu Sarāy-i Hümāyūnı." *Tārīḫ-i ‹Os̱mānī Encümeni Mecmū‹ası* 5–12 (1326–27/1910–11).
Sertoğlu, Midhat. *Topkapı Sarayında Gündelik Hayat*. Istanbul, 1974.
Shaw, Stanford, and Kural-Shaw, Ezel. *History of the Ottoman Empire and Modern Turkey*. 2 vols. London and New York, 1976–77.
Skilliter, Susan. "The Letters of the Venetian 'Sultana' Nūr Bānu and Her Kira to Venice," in *Studia turcologica memoriae Alexii Bombaci dicata*. Istituto Universitario Orientale. Naples, 1982, pp. 515–36.
Smith, Earl Baldwin. *Architectural Symbolism of Imperial Rome and the Middle Ages*. New York, 1978.
—— *The Dome: A Study in the History of Ideas*. Princeton, 1971.
Sourdel, Dominique. "Questions de cérémonial abbaside." *Revue des Études Islamiques* (1960):121–48.
Sourdel, Dominique, and Sourdel, Janine. *La Civilization de l'Islam classique*. Paris, 1968.
Sözen, Metin. *Türk Mimarisinin Gelişimi ve Mimar Sinan*. Istanbul, 1975.
Stanley, David James. *The Origin and Development of the Renaissance Belvedere in Central Italy*. Philadelphia, 1978.
Steinhardt, Nancy Shatzman. *Chinese Imperial City Planning*. Honolulu, 1990.
Stowasser, Karl. "Manners and Customs at the Mamluk Court." *Muqarnas* 2 (1984):13–21.
Summerson, John. *Heavenly Mansions and Other Essays on Architecture*. New York, 1963.
Swoboda, M. Karl. "The Problem of Iconography of Late Antique and Early Mediaeval Palaces," *Journal of the Society of Architectural Historians* 20, no. 2 (1961): 78–89.
—— *Romische und romanische Paläste*. Vienna, 1919.

Taneri, Aydın. *Osmanlı Devletinin Kuruluş Döneminde Hükümdarlık Kurumunun Gelişmesi ve Saray Hayatı Teşkilatı*. Ankara, 1978.
Tansuğ, Sezer. "Topkapı Saray bütününün niteliği üzerine bir deneme," in *Karşıtı Aramak, Sanat Tarihi Yazıları*. Istanbul, 1983, pp. 135–68.
Tauer, Felix. "Notice sur les versions persanes de la légende de l'edification d'Ayasofya," in *Fuat Köprülü Armağanı*. Istanbul, 1953, pp. 487–94.
—— "Les versions persannes de la légende de la construction d'Aya Sofya." *Byzantinoslavica* 15 (1954):1–20.
Teply, Karl. *Die kaiserliche Großbotschaft an Sultan Murad IV (1628): Des Freiherrn Hans Ludwig von Kuefsteins Fahrt zur Hohen Pforte*. Vienna, 1976.
—— "Kızıl Elma: Die große türkische Geschichtssage im Licht der Geschichte und der Volkskunde." *Südost-Forschungen* 36 (1977):78–108.
—— *Türkische Sagen und Legenden um die Kaiserstadt Wien*. Vienna, Cologne, and Graz, 1980.
Terzioğlu, Arslan. "Alberto Bobovio'nun Tarifine Göre Topkapı Sarayındaki Enderun Hastanesi'nin 17. Yüzyıldaki Teşkilatı," *I. Milletlerarası Türkoloji Kongresi (İstanbul, 1973). Türk Sanat Tarihi*. Pt. 3. Istanbul, 1979, pp. 874–89.
—— *Die Hofspitäler und andere Gesundheitsein richtiger der osmanischen Palastbauten*. Beiträge zur Kentniss Südosteuropas. Munich, 1979.
Tezcan, Hülya. *Köşkler*. Istanbul, 1978.
—— "Sur-u Sultanî Içinin Bizans Devri Arkeolojisi." Ph.D. diss., Istanbul Üniversitesi Edebiyat Fakültesi Arkeoloji ve Sanat Tarihi Bölümü, 1983.
Tezcan, Hülya, and Şeker, T. "Topkapı Sarayı Müzesi Kurşunluk Hafriyatı," in *Kemal Çığ'a Armağan*. Istanbul, 1984, pp. 203–23.
Thuasne, Louis. *Gentile Bellini et Sultan Mohammed II: Notes sur le séjour du peintre Vénitien à Constantinople (1479–80)*. Paris, 1888.
Tietze, Andreas. "Muṣṭafā ‹Ālī on Luxury and the Status Symbols of Ottoman Gentlemen." *Studia*

turcologica memoriae Alexii Bombaci dicata. Istituto Universitario Orientale. Naples, 1982, pp. 577–90.

Treitinger, Otto. *Die oströmischer Kaiser—und Reichsidee nach ihrer Gestaltung im höfischen Zeremoniell.* Jena, 1938.

Trexler, Richard C. *Public Life in Renaissance Florence.* New York, 1980.

Turan, Osman. "The Ideal of World Domination among the Medieval Turks." *Studia Islamica* 4 (1955):82ff.

Turan, Şerafettin. "Osmanlı Teşkilatında Hassa Mimarları." *Tarih Araştırmaları Dergisi* 1, no. 1 (1963):157–202.

Uluçay, Çağatay. *Harem II.* Ankara, 1971.

—— *Haremden Mektuplar.* Istanbul, 1956.

—— *Padişahların Kadınları ve Kızları.* Ankara, 1985.

Ünsal, Behçet. *Turkish Islamic Architecture in Seljuk and Ottoman Times, 1071–1923.* London, 1959.

Ünver, Süheyl. *Fatih Devri Saray Nakışhanesi ve Baba Nakkaş Çalışmaları.* Istanbul, 1958.

—— *İstanbul Fethiyle Kalelerin Manzum ve Mensur Tarih İbareleri.* Istanbul, 1953.

—— "Süsleme Sanatı Bakımından Topkapı Sarayı Müzesi." *Güzel Sanatlar* 6 (1949):109–15.

Uzunçarşılı, İsmail Hakkı. *Osmanlı Devleti Teşkilatına Medhal.* Ankara, 1941.

—— *Osmanlı Devletinin Merkez ve Bahriye Teşkilatı.* Ankara, 1948.

—— *Osmanlı Devletinin Saray Teşkilatı.* 1945. Reprint. Istanbul, 1984.

—— *Osmanlı Tarihi.* 1947–56. 4 vols. Reprint. Ankara, 1975–83.

Valensi, Lucette. *Venise et la Sublime Porte: La naissance du despote.* Paris, 1987.

Villain-Gandossi, Christiane. "La Cronaca italiana di Teodoro Spandugino." *Il Veltro* 23, nos. 2–4 (1979):151–71.

Vryonis, Speros, Jr. *The Decline of Medieval Hellenism in Asia Minor and the Process of Islamization from the Eleventh through the Fifteenth Century.* 1971. Reprint. Berkeley, Los Angeles, and London, 1986.

Werner, Ernst. *Die Geburt einer Grossmacht—Die Osmanen (1300–1481), ein Beitrag zur Genesis des türkischen Feudalismus.* Berlin, 1966.

—— *Sultan Mehmed der Eroberer und die Epochenwende im 15. Jahrhundert. Sitzungsberichte der Sächsischen Akademie der Wissenschaften zu Leipzig Philologish-Historiche Klasse.* Band 123, Heft 2. Berlin, 1982.

Wilber, Donald N. *The Architecture of Islamic Iran: The Il Khanid Period.* Princeton, 1955.

—— *Persian Gardens and Garden Pavilions.* Washington D.C., 1979.

Wittek, Paul. "Miscellanea ... " *Türkiyat Mecmuası* 14 (1964):266–70.

Woods, John E. *The Aqqoyunlu: Clan, Confederation, Empire.* Minneapolis and Chicago, 1976.

Yerasimos, Stephane. *Légendes d'empire: La fondation de Constantinople et de Sainte-Sophie dans les traditions turques.* Paris, 1990.

Yücel, Erdem. *Topkapı Sarayı Müzesi: Hırka-i Saadet.* Istanbul, 1982.

Yurdaydın, Hüseyin G. "Bostan'ın Süleymannāmesi (Ferdī'ye Atfedilen Eser)." *Belleten* 19, no. 74 (1955):137–202.

Zinkeisen, J. W. *Geschichte des Osmanischen Reiches in Europa.* 7 vols. Hamburg, 1840–63.

Index

Figure and plate references appear in italics following page numbers.